R. Gupta's®

POPULAR MASTER GUIDE

KVS–PGT

Kendriya Vidyalaya Sangathan – Post Graduate Teachers

SUBJECT

CHEMISTRY

Recruitment Exam

by

RPH Editorial Board

AF521453

2026
EDITION

RAMESH PUBLISHING HOUSE, NEW DELHI

Published by
O.P. Gupta *for* Ramesh Publishing House

Admin. Office
12-H, New Daryaganj Road, Opp. Officers' Mess,
New Delhi-110002 ✆ 23275224, 23245124

E-mail: info@rameshpublishinghouse.com
For Online Shopping: www.rameshpublishinghouse.com

Showroom
• Balaji Market, Nai Sarak, Delhi-6 ✆ 23253720, 23282525
• 4457, Nai Sarak, Delhi-6, ✆ 23918938

Book Code: R-1147

ISBN: 978-81-7812-878-8

Price: ₹ 340

Printed at: Deepak Offset, Delhi

CONTENTS

Previous Years' Paper, 2023 1-44

Previous Years' Paper, 2018 1-20

Previous Years' Paper, 2017 1-12

1. Some Basic Concepts of Chemistry 3
2. States of Matter 16
3. Structure of Atom 33
4. Equilibrium 48
5. Surface Chemistry 64
6. Chemical Kinetics 74
7. Redox Reaction and Electrochemistry 86
8. Solutions 103
9. Chemical Bonding and Molecular Structure 118
10. Thermodynamics 136
11. Classification of Elements and Periodicity in Properties 147
12. Inorganic Chemistry 157
13. Co-Ordination Compounds and Organometallics 199
14. Hydrocarbons: Alkanes, Alkenes and Alkynes, Aromatic Hydrocarbons 211
15. Environmental Chemistry 245
16. Haloalkanes and Haloarenes; Alcohols & Phenols 251
17. Aldehydes, Ketones and Carboxylic Acids 270
18. Amines (Organic Compounds Containing Nitrogen) 290
19. Polymers 300
20. Biomolecules (Biochemistry): Carbohydrates, Proteins and Nucleic Acids 303
21. Chemistry in Everyday Life: Drugs and Medicines 308

❑❑❑

Scheme of Written Examination

Test Duration	180 Minutes	
Total Questions	180 Objective Type Multiple Choice Questions	
Total Marks	180 Marks	
Section Name	**Marks per Question**	**No. of Questions**
Part-I : Proficiency in Languages (20 marks)		
1. General English	01 mark per question	10
2. General Hindi		10
Part-II : General Awareness, Reasoning & Proficiency in Computers (20 marks)		
1. General Awareness & Current Affairs	01 mark per question	10
2. Reasoning Ability		5
3. Computer Literacy		5
Part-III : Perspectives on Education and Leadership (40 questions & 40 marks)		
Part-IV : Subject-Specific (Chemistry) (100 questions & 100 marks)		
PROFESSIONAL COMPETENCY TEST: 60 MARKS (Demo Teaching-30 marks and Interview-30 marks)		

Previous Years' Paper

KVS-PGT CHEMISTRY TEACHER

Recruitment Exam–2023

(Exam held on 18-02-2023)

SUBJECT : CHEMISTRY

1. Arsenic (III) sulphide reacts with oxygen to form arsenic (III) oxide and sulphur (IV) oxide:

$$\_As_2S_3 + \_O_2 \rightarrow \_As_2O_3 + \_SO_2$$

What is the coefficient for O_2 when the equation is balanced using whole number coefficients?

A. 5 B. 7
C. 9 D. 11

2. When $FeCl_3$ is ignited in an atmosphere of pure oxygen, the reaction that takes place is:

$$4FeCl_3(s) + 3O_2(g) \rightarrow 2Fe_2O_3(s) + 6Cl_2(g)$$

If 3.0 Mol of $FeCl_3$ are ignited in the presence of 2.0 Mol of O_2 gas, how much of which reagent is present of 2.0 Mol of O_2 gas, how much of which reagent is present in excess and therefore remains unreacted?

A. 0.33 Mol $FeCl_3$
B. 0.67 Mol $FeCl_3$
C. 0.25 Mol O_2
D. 0.50 Mol O_2

3. Magnetite Fe_3O_4, is a mixture of iron (II) oxide and iron (III) oxide. What is the most likely ratio of iron (II) oxide to iron (III) oxide in magnetite?

A. 1 : 1 B. 1 : 2
C. 2 : 3 D. 3 : 2

4. Calculate the volume of 0.110 M Copper (II) nitrate solution that can be prepared by dissolving 33.29 g of Copper (II) nitrate trihydrate in sufficient distilled water.

The Molar mass of $Cu(NO_3)_2 \cdot 3H_2O$ is 241.6 g mol^{-1}

A. 0.50 L B. 1.25 L
C. 2.50 L D. 3.75 L

5. The formula of sodium tungstate is Na_2WO_4 and that of lead phosphate is $Pb_3(PO_4)_2$. What is the formula for lead tungstate?

A. $PbWO_4$
B. $Pb(WO_4)_3$
C. $Pb_3(WO_4)_2$
D. $Pb_3(WO_4)_4$

6. An electron can move from one orbital of a hydrogen atom to another. In which transition will the photon of highest energy be emitted?

A. $2p \rightarrow 1s$ B. $1s \rightarrow 2p$
C. $3s \rightarrow 2s$ D. $2s \rightarrow 3s$

1. C	2. A	3. A	4. B	5. A	6. A

7. Which electron configuration represents a violation of Hund's rules?

A. [↑↓] [↑↓] [↑ | ↑ | ↑]

B. [↑↓] [↑↓] [↑↓ | ↑ | ↑]

C. [↑↓] [↑↓] [↑↓ | ↑↓ | ↑]

D. [↑↓] [↑↓] [↑↓ | ↑ |]

8. Consider the species $^{72}_{30}Zn$, $^{75}_{33}As$ and $^{74}_{32}Ge$. These species have the same number of:

A. Electrons

B. Protons

C. Neutrons

D. Protons and neutrons

9. What is the atomic weight of a hypothetical element consisting of two isotopes one with mass 64.2 u (25%) and the other with mass 65.3 u?

A. 65.3 u B. 64.4 u

C. 64.9 u D. 65.0 u

10. What is the frequency of light having a wavelength of 4.50×10^{-8} m? (Given : c = 3×10^8 ms^{-1}):

A. 2.84×10^{-12} s^{-1}

B. 2.10×10^4 s^{-1}

C. 4.29×10^{14} s^{-1}

D. 6.67×10^{15} s^{-1}

11. When the acids H_2Se, HBr and HI are arranged in order of increasing acid strength, which is the correct order?

A. H_2Se < HBr < HI

B. HBr < HI < H_2Se

C. HBr < H_2Se < HI

D. HI < H_2Se < HBr

12. Which metal requires the least energy to exhibit the photoelectric effect?

A. Cs B. Ca

C. Cu D. Hg

13. Which group of elements is listed in the order of increasing boiling point?

A. Lithium, sodium, potassium

B. Chlorine, bromine, iodine

C. Sulphur, chlorine, argon

D. Zinc, cadmium, mercury

14. Which pair of atoms should form the most polar bond?

A. B and F

B. C and O

C. O and F

D. F and N

15. The first five ionization energies, in kJ mol^{-1}, for a particular element, are shown in the table below:

First	Second	Third	Fourth	Fifth
580	1,815	2,740	11,600	18,500

The element is likely to form ionic compounds in which its charge is:

A. 1+ B. 2+

C. 3+ D. 4+

16. The arrangement of the atoms in the ammonia molecule at its lowest energy is described as:

A. Trigonal pyramidal

B. Trigonal palnar

C. Trigonal bipyramidar

D. Square planar

17. In which of the following compounds would the molecules be expected to be linear?

A. O_3

B. SO_2

C. H_2O

D. CO_2

18. What is the hybridization of the S atom in SF_4?

A. sp^2 B. sp^3

C. sp^3d D. sp^3d^2

7. D	**8.** C	**9.** D	**10.** D	**11.** A	**12.** A
13. B	**14.** A	**15.** C	**16.** A	**17.** D	**18.** C

19. One way of writing the Lewis structure of the cyanate ion OCN^- is $[O = C = N]^-$. What are the formal charges on the O, C and N atoms respectively, for the structure?
A. 0, 0, –1 B. 1, 0, 0
C. –1, +1, –1 D. –2, 1, 0

20. Which one of the following violates the octet rule?
A. PCl_3 B. CBr_4
C. OF_2 D. AsF_5

21. All are state functions except:
A. Pressure B. Heat
C. Free energy D. Enthalpy

22. Calculate the bond energy of the B-F bond in BF_3 (boron trifluoride) gas:
ΔH_f^0 of atomic B = 134.5 kcal/mol
ΔH_f^0 of atomic F = 18.86 kcal/mol
ΔH_f^0 of BF_3 = –271.75 kcal/mol
A. 97.7 kcal/mol B. 116.6 kcal/mol
C. 135.4 kcal/mol D. 154.3 kcal/mol

23. Given the following standard enthalpies of formation : $CO_2(g)$, –394 kJ/mol; $H_2O(l)$, –286 kJ/mol; $C_4H_3(g)$, 16.0 kJ/mol, calculate the heat of combustion of one mole of C_4H_3 if the equation describing the process is:
$C_4H_3(g) + 6O_2(g) \rightarrow 4CO_2(g) + 4H_2O(l)$
A. –2736 kJ/mol
B. –696 kJ/mol
C. 696 kJ/mol
D. 2736 kJ/mol

24. Determine the value of $\Delta G°$ (in kJ) for the following reaction using data from the table below:
$2H_2O(g) + O_2(g) \rightarrow 2H_2O_2(g)$

Substance	**$\Delta G°$(kJ/mol)**
$H_2O(g)$	–228
$H_2O_2(g)$	–105

A. –246 B. 666
C. 246 D. –666

25. How many kJ of heat are liberated when 50.0 g of Mn(s) is burnt to form $Mn_3O_4(s)$ under standard states?
$3Mn(s) + 2O_2(g) \rightarrow Mn_3O_4(s)$
(Atomic mass (Mn) = 55; ΔH_f^0 ($Mn_3O_4(s)$) = –1388 kJ mol^{-1})
A. 421 B. 946
C. 1388 D. 2838

26. A saturated solution of MgF_2 contains 1.16×10^{-3} mol of MgF_2 per litre. What is the K_{sp} of MgF_2?
A. 2.7×10^{-6} B. 1.6×10^{-9}
C. 3.1×10^{-9} D. 6.2×10^{-9}

27. Which will be the same for solutions of 0.50 M NH_3 and 0.50 M NaOH?
1. Concentration of OH^- ions
2. Volume of 0.20 M HCl required for neutralization.

A. 1 only B. Both 1 and 2
C. 2 only D. Neither 1 nor 2

28. For the reaction
$2NO(g) + O_2(g) \rightleftharpoons 2NO_2(g)$
the equilibrium concetrations at a certain temperature are found to be [NO] = 0.10 M, $[O_2]$ = 0.20 M, $[NO_2]$ = 0.30 M. The value of the equilibrum constant for the reaction at this temperature is:
A. 1.5 B. 15
C. 45 D. 150

29. An aqueous solution of which salt would be expected to have the most basic pH?
A. Na_2CO_3
B. $NaC_2H_3O_2$
C. NaCl
D. NH_4Cl

19. A	**20.** D	**21.** B	**22.** D	**23.** A	**24.** C
25. A	**26.** D	**27.** C	**28.** C	**29.** A	

30. If 40.0 mL of 0.20 M CH_3COOH are titrated with 0.20 M NaOH, how many mL of base must be added to form a buffer solution with the greatest buffering capacity?

A. 5.0 B. 10.0
C. 20.0 D. 40.0

31. In which pair does the named substance have the same oxidation number?

A. Sulphur in $H_2S_2O_7$ and H_2SO_4
B. Mercury in Hg^{2+} and Hg_2^{2+}
C. Cobalt in $Co(NH_3)_6^{3+}$ and $Co(NO_3)_2$
D. Oxygen in Na_2O_2 and H_2O.

32. What is the oxidation number for carbon in CaC_2O_4?

A. 0 B. +2
C. +3 D. +4

33. Which of the following is a correct statement?

A. Oxidation is caused by a reducing agent.
B. The oxidation reaction is a redox reaction.
C. Addition of an electropositive element is a type of oxidation.
D. Reduction is the addition of hydrogen.

34. What is the coefficient for Fe^{2+} when the redox equation

$Fe^{2+} + MnO_4^- + H^+ \rightarrow Fe^{3+} + Mn^{2+} + H_2O$

is balanced using the smallest whole number coefficients?

A. 2 B. 3
C. 4 D. 5

35. Which one of the following statements is NOT correct for the given reaction?

$Fe(s) + CuSO_4(aq) \rightarrow FeSO_4(aq) + Cu(s)$

A. Iron is the reducing agent.
B. The solution turns green in colour after the reaction.
C. Copper is a more reactive metal than iron.
D. The reaction is an example of a redox reaction.

36. An aquous solution is 1.00 Molal in KI. Which change will cause the vapour pressure of the solution to increase?

A. Addition of water.
B. Addition of NaCl.
C. Addition of Na_2SO_4.
D. Addition of 1.0 Molal KI.

37. What is the molality of the Li+ ion in a solution prepared by dissolving 2.20 g of Li_2SO_4 (MM = 110.0 g/mol) in enough H_2O to make 50.0 mL of solution?

A. 2.00×10^{-2} M
B. 4.00×10^{-2} M
C. 0.400 M
D. 0.800 M

38. Calculate the Molality of a solution that contains 51.2 g of naphthalene, $C_{10}H_8$, in 500 mL of carbon tetrachloride. The density of CCl_4 is 1.60g/mL:

A. 0.250 M B. 0.500 M
C. 0.750 M D. 0.840 M

39. The vapour pressure of pure water at 85°C is 57.9 kPa. What is the vapour pressure at 85°C of a solution prepared from 100 mL of water (density 1.00 g/mL) and 150g of diglycine, $C_4H_8N_2O_3$, a non-volatile substance?

A. 48.1 kPa B. 52.0 kPa
C. 56.7 kPa D. 51.7 kPa

40. If 45 g of glucose, $C_6H_{12}O_6$, are dissolved in 300 mL of water, what will be the boiling point of the resulting solution? (K_b for water = 0.512°C/m).

A. 101.64°C B. 100.78°C
C. 100.43°C D. 99.626°C

30. C	**31.** A	**32.** C	**33.** D	**34.** D	**35.** C
36. A	**37.** C	**38.** B	**39.** A	**40.** C	

41. The standard reduction potentials for Al^{3+} and Zn^{2+} are −1.66 V and −0.76 V, respectively.
Calculate the Gibbs free energy change for the balanced reaction.

$$2Al(s) + 3Zn^{2+}(aq) \rightarrow 2Al^{3+}(aq) + 3Zn(s) \quad (1F = 96,500\ C)$$

A. -5.2×10^5 J B. -6.0×10^5 J
C. $+9.0 \times 10^5$ J D. $+1.4 \times 10^5$ J

42. Which of the following statements about electrochemical cells is true?
A. Reduction occurs at the anode.
B. An element with a high affinity for electrons is likely to be easily oxidized.
C. Oxidation occurs at the anode.
D. Only oxidation half reactions are important.

43. What is E° for the following balanced reaction?
$Zn(s) + Pb^{2+}(aq) \rightarrow Zn^{2+}(aq) + Pb(s)$

Half-reaction	**Standard Reduction Potential**
$Zn^{2+}(aq) + 2e^- \rightarrow Zn(s)$	−0.763 V
$Pb^{2+}(aq) + 2e^- \rightarrow Pb(s)$	−0.126 V

A. + 0.637 V B. − 0.637 V
C. − 0.889 V D. + 0.889 V

44. Identify the strongest reducing agent based on the following half-reactions:

Half-reaction	**Standard Reduction Potential**
$MnO_2(s) + 4H^+(aq) + 2e^- \rightarrow Mn^{2+}(aq) + 2H_2O(l)$	+1.22 V
$Hg_2SO_4(s) + 2e^- \rightarrow 2Hg(l) + SO_4^{2-}(aq)$	+0.61 V
$SnO_2(s) + 2H_2O(l) + 4e^- \rightarrow Sn(s) + 4OH^-(aq)$	−0.95 V
$Cr(OH)_3(s) + 3e^- \rightarrow Cr(s) + 3OH^-(aq)$	−1.48 V

A. Cr B. MnO_2
C. Sn D. Hg

45. What mass of nickel (atomic mass 58.7u) could be electroplated from a solution of nickel (II) chloride by a current of 0.25 amperes flowing for 10 hours? (1F = 96,500 C)
A. 12 g B. 5.5 g
C. 0.046 g D. 2.7 g

46. The first order reaction
$2N_2O(g) \rightarrow 2N_2(g) + O_2(g)$
has a rate constant of $1.3 \times 10^{-11}\ s^{-1}$ at 227°C and $6.5 \times 10^{-10}\ s^{-1}$ at 327°C. What is the activation energy for the reaction? ($R = 8.3\ JK^{-1}\ mol^{-1}$, $\log_{10}2 = 0.30$)
A. 15 kJ/mol B. 30 kJ/mol
C. 68 kJ/mol D. 97 kJ/mol

47. The rate of the reaction $2NO + Cl_2 \rightarrow 2NOCl$ is given by the rate equation rate $= k[ON]^2\ [Cl_2]$. The value of the rate constant can be increased by:
A. Increasing the concentration of NO.
B. Increasing the concentration of Cl_2.
C. Increasing the temperature.
D. Doing all of these.

48. The ionic reaction $3I^- + S_2O_8^{2-} \rightarrow 2SO_4^{2-} + I_3^-$ is found to be described by the experimental rate equation.
Rate $= k[I^-]\ S_2O_8^{2-}]$
This suggests that:
A. The reaction occurs when three iodide ions collide simultaneously with one $S_2O_8^{2-}$ ion.
B. There must be only one step in the overall reaction since the rate is first order in both reactants.
C. The rate of reaction is inhibited by the presence of I_3^-.
D. A slow step in the overall reaction sequence may involve the collision of a single I^- ion with a single $S_2O_8^{2-}$ ion.

41. A	42. C	43. A	44. A	45. D	46. D	47. C	48. D

49. The rate equation of a reaction is given by Rate = $k[A]^2$
The units of k are:
A. mol dm^{-3} s^{-1} B. dm^3 mol^{-1}
C. s^{-1} D. mol^{-1} dm^3 s^{-1}.

50. Which of the following equations is not correct?
A. $k = A \exp (E_a/RT)$
B. $\Delta G = \Delta H - T\Delta S$
C. $\Delta G_f^o = -RT\ln K_p$
D. $T = pV/nR$

51. Which of the following electron configuration is correct for Nickel?
A. [Xe] $4s^1$ $3d^8$ B. [Kr] $4s^1$ $3d^8$
C. [Kr] $4s^2$ $3d^8$ D. [Ar] $4s^2$ $3d^8$

52. The atomic radii of Zr (145 pm) and Hf (144 pm) are almost equal because of :
A. Their being isoelectronic
B. Their being isotonic.
C. Lanthanoid contraction.
D. Higher atomic number of Zr as compared to Hf.

53. Choose the correct option for Mn_2O_7, CrO_5, and V_2O_5 from the following:
A. Mn_2O_7, CrO_3 and V_2O_5 are acidic.
B. CrO_3 is acidic while Mn_2O_7 and V_2O_5 are basic.
C. V_2O_5 is acidic while CrO_3 and Mn_2O_7 are basic.
D. Mn_2O_7, CrO_3 and V_2O_5 are all basic.

54. The formula of the deep red liquid formed on heating potassium dichromatie with KCl in concentrated sulphuric acid is:
A. $CrCl_3$ B. CrO_2Cl_2
C. CrO_3 D. $CrSO_4$

55. The magnetic moment of Cr^{2+} is:
A. 2.85 BM B. 4.40 BM
C. 5.92 BM D. 3.87 BM

56. Which of the following is a coordination compound?
A. KCl $MgCl_2 \cdot 6H_2O$
B. Fe $SO_4(NH_4)_2$ $SO_4 \cdot 6H_2O$
C. KAl $(SO_4)_2 \cdot 12H_2O$
D. K_3 $[Al$ $(C_2O_4)_3]$

57. The coordination number of cobalt in the complex $[Co(en)_2Br_2]Cl_2$ is:
(en = $NH_2CH_2CH_2NH_2$)
A. 4 B. 6
C. 5 D. 2

58. Which of the following is a hexadentate ligand?
A. Ox(oxalate ion, $C_2O_4^{2-}$)
B. CN^-
C. en(ethylenediamine), $NH_2CH_2CH_2NH_2$
D. EDTA

59. The oxidation state of the central metal atom in the coordination compound $[Pt (NH_3)_3Cl]$ Cl is:
A. +2 B. +1
C. 0 D. −1

60. Given the list of ligands and their corresponding names, choose the pair that does not match.

	Ligand	Name
A.	OH^-	Hydroxo
B.	CN^-	Cyanide
C.	Cl^-	Chloro
D.	H_2O	Aqua

61. The IUPAC name of

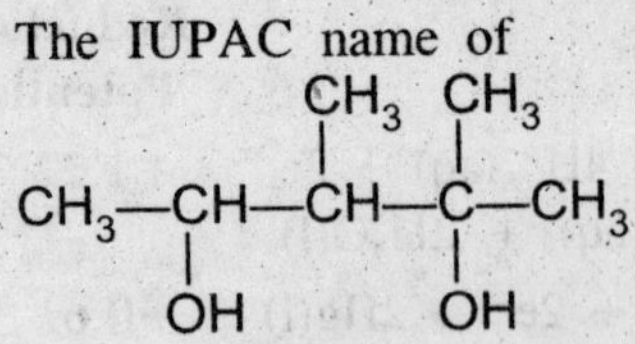

is:
A. 1, 2, 3, 4-tetramethyl-1, 3-propandiol.
B. 1, 1, 2-trimethyl butan-1, 3-diol.
C. 1, 2-dimethyl pentan-2, 4-diol.
D. 2, 3-dimethyl pentan-2, 4-diol.

49. D	50. A	51. D	52. C	53. A	54. B	55. B
56. D	57. B	58. D	59. A	60. B	61. D	

62. Consider the following sequence of reactions:

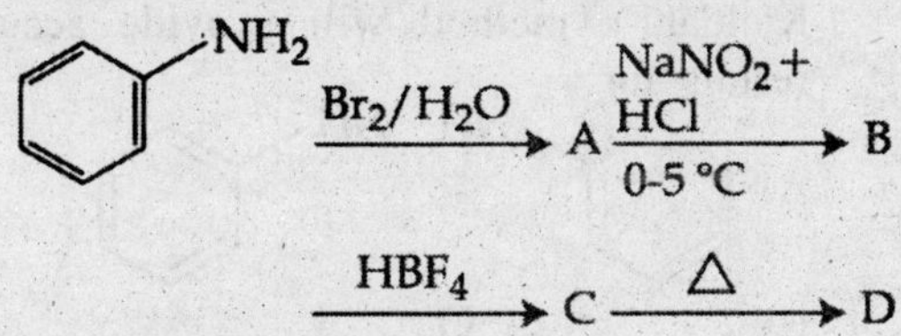

The product 'D' is:

A. 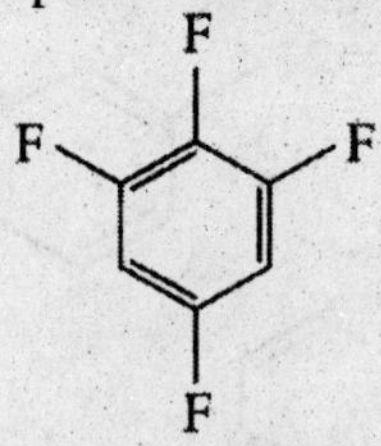
B. 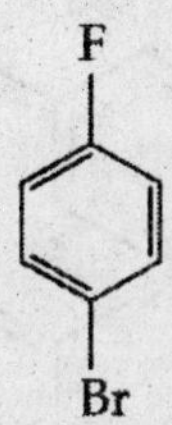
C. 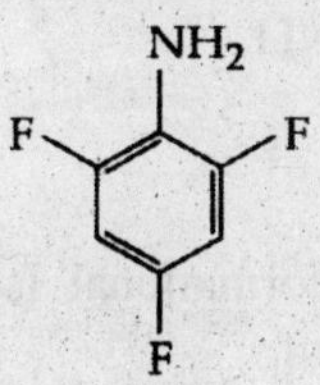
D. 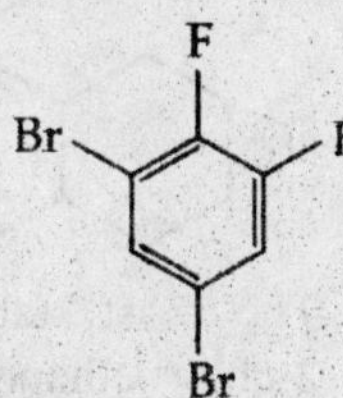

63. Which of the these species is aromatic?

A. 
B. 
C. 
D. 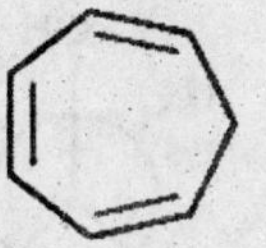

64. In the given molecule:

$CH_2=C=CH_2$

I II III

A. All three carbons are *sp* hybridized.
B. C-I and C-III are sp^2 hybridized and C-II is *sp* hybridized.
C. Both C-I and C-III are *sp* hybridized and C-II sp^2 hybridized.
D. All three carbons are sp^2 hybridized.

65. In pyridine 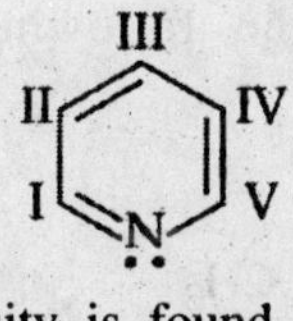, the maximum electron density is found at position:

A. III only
B. II and IV only
C. I and V only
D. I, II, IV and V only

66. The C—Cl bond distance is shortest in:

A. 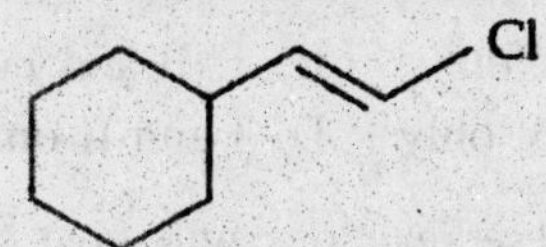
B. 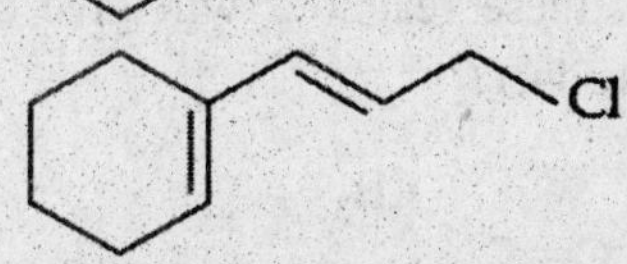
C. 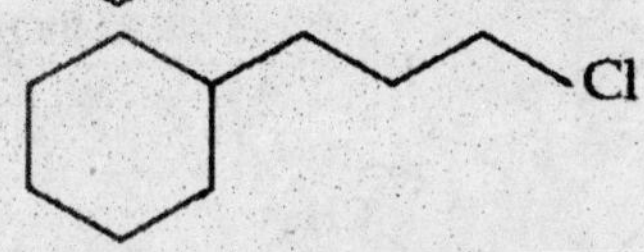
D. 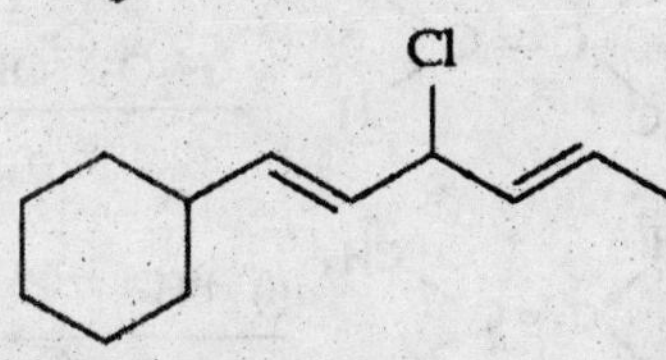

67. Which of these species will produce a precipitate of AgBr most readily when treated with $AgNO_3$.

A. 
B. 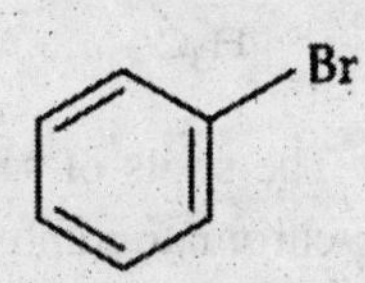
C. 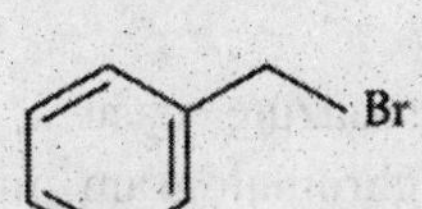
D. 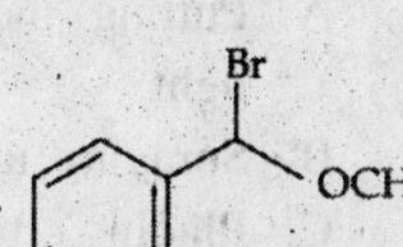

62. D	63. A	64. B	65. B	66. A	67. D

68. Which of the following are structural isomers?

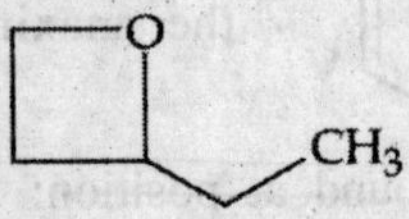

I

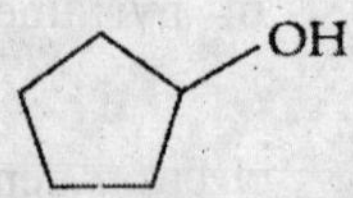

II

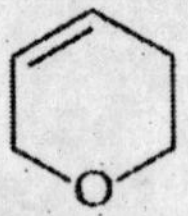

III

$CH_3CH=CH-CH_2-CH_3$

IV

A. II and IV only
B. I, II and IV only
C. III and IV only
D. I and II only

69. Which of these reactions will give cis-diols as the product?

A. 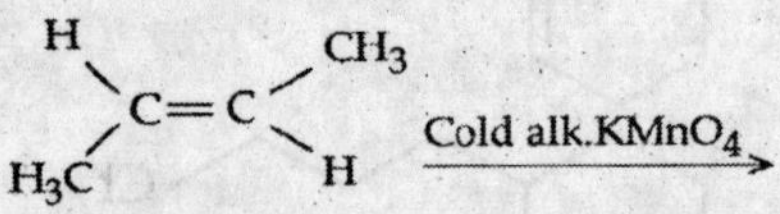

B. 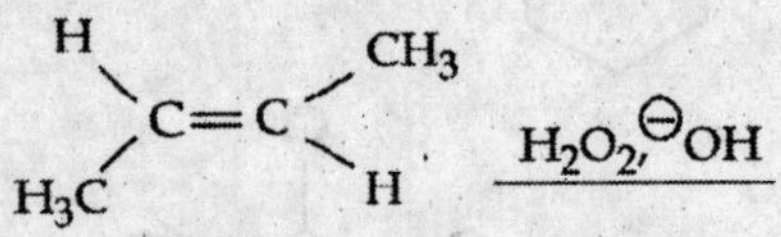

C. 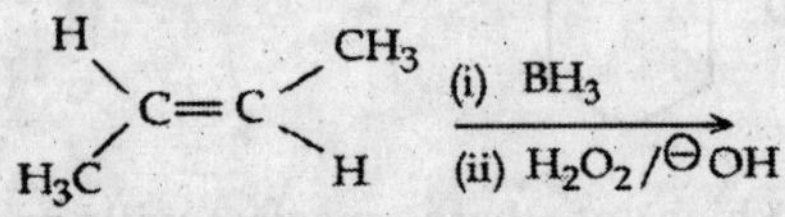

D. 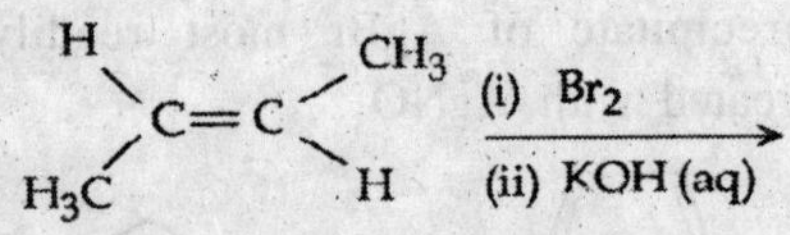

70. The spots of separated components in paper chromatography can be made visible by:

A. Putting the chromatogram under UV light.
B. Spraying a visualizing agent.
C. Placing the chromatogram in a jar containing a few crystals of iodine.
D. By complexing with heavy metal ions.

71. The quantitative estimation of nitrogen by Kjeldahl's method will provide accurate results for:

A. 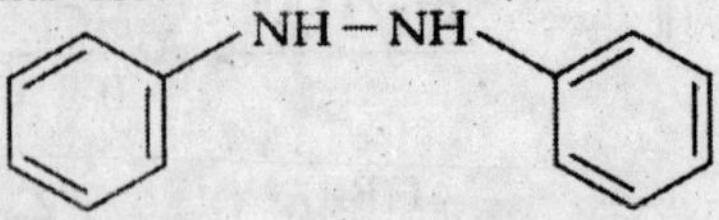

B. 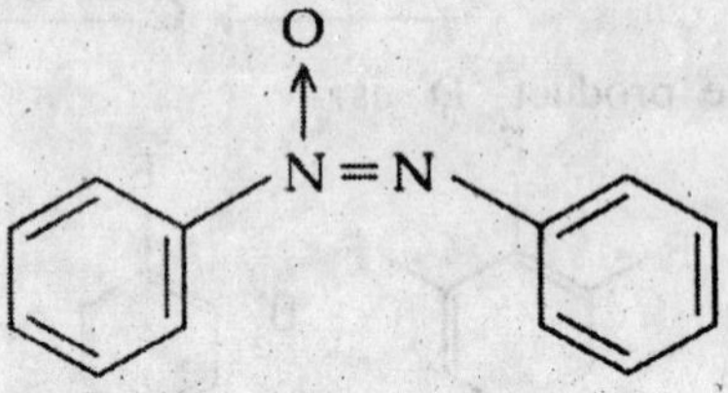

C. 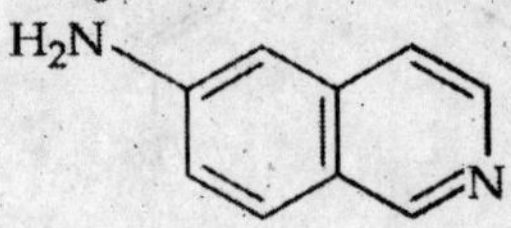

D. 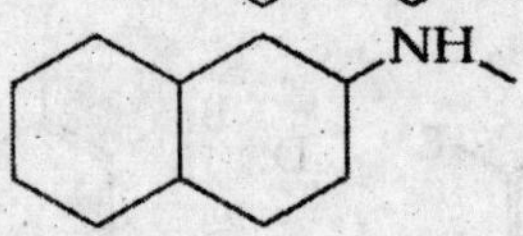

72. The most stable conformational isomer of 2-chloroethanol is:

A. 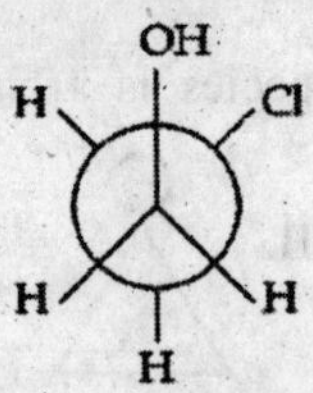

B. 

C. 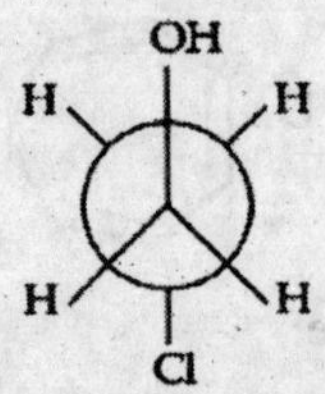

D. 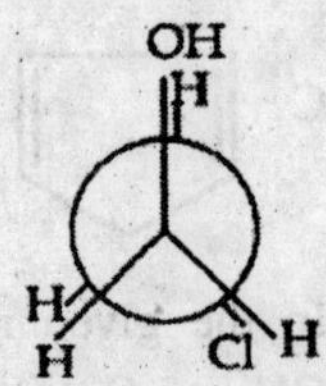

73. Which of these statements is NOT true about the S_N2 reaction?

A. Order of reactivity of alkyl halides is 1° > 2° > 3°.
B. Reaction rate is dependent on the concentration of the nucleophile.
C. Protic solvents facilitate the S_N2 reaction.
D. Order of reactivity with different halides is RI > RBr > RCl.

68. B	69. A	70. D	71. D	72. A	73. C

74. Consider the following sequence of reactions:

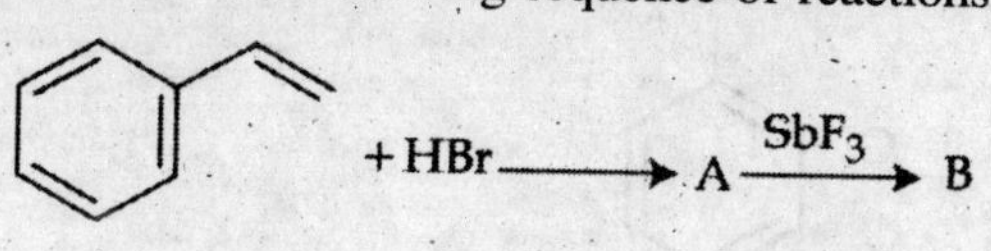

'B' is:

A. 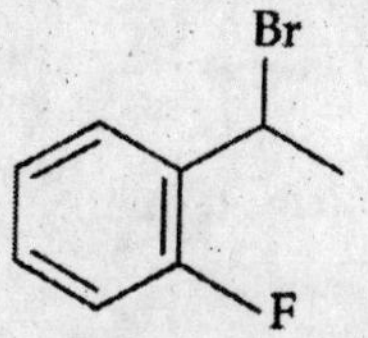

B. 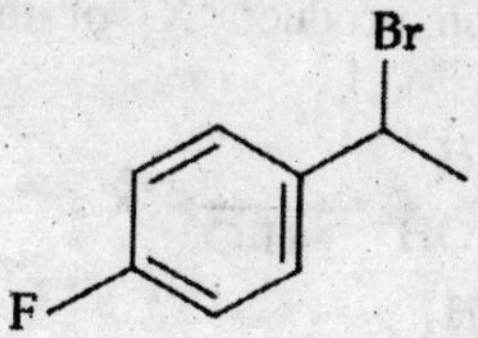

C. 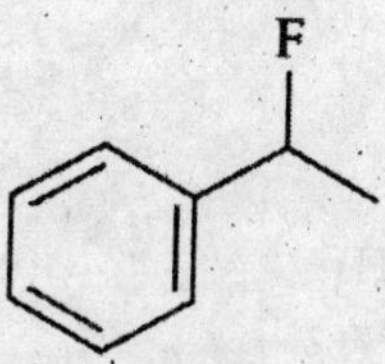

D. 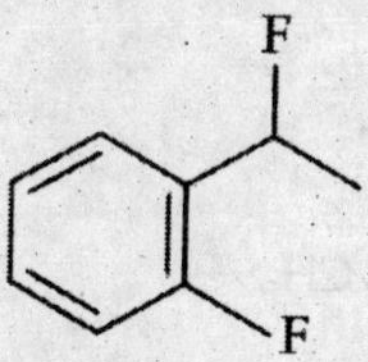

75. In the sequence of reactions given below:

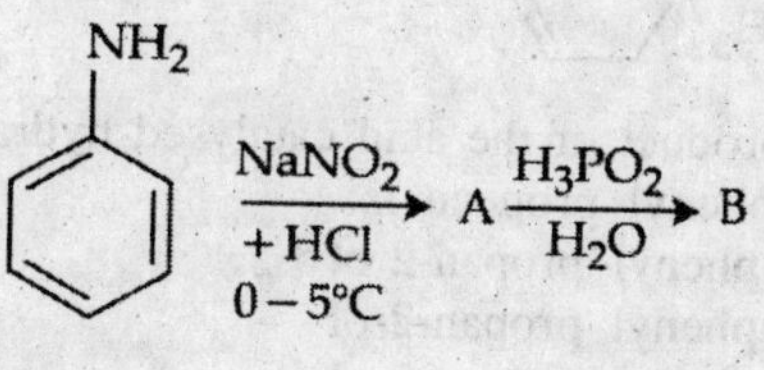

'B' is:

A. 

B. 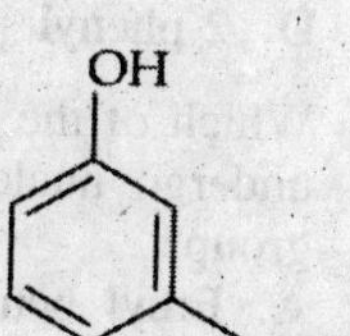

C. 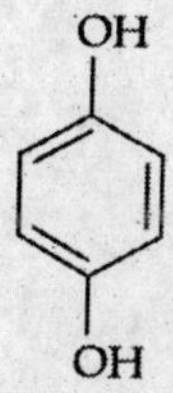

D. 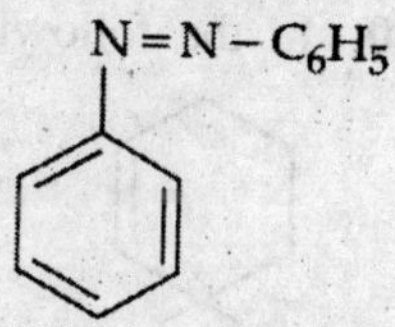

76. The preparation of phenol from chlorobenzene is a/an:

A. Electrophilic addition reaction.

B. Electrophilic substitution reaction.

C. Nucleophilic addition reaction.

D. Nucleophilic substitution reaction.

77. Freons are manufactured using:

A. Sandmeyer's reaction.

B. Swartz reaction.

C. Finkelstein reaction.

D. Gatterman reaction.

78. The enol form of acetylacetone has:

A. 9σ bonds, 4π bonds, 2 lone pairs.

B. 12σ bonds, 2π bonds, 4 lone pairs.

C. 14σ bonds, 2π bonds, 4 lone pairs.

D. 14σ bonds, 4π bonds, 2 lone pairs.

79. Which of these alkyl halides will undergo S_N1 reactions most readily?

A. $C_6H_5-CH_2-I$

B. $C_6H_5-CH_2-O-\overset{O}{\overset{\|}{C}}-CH_3$

C. 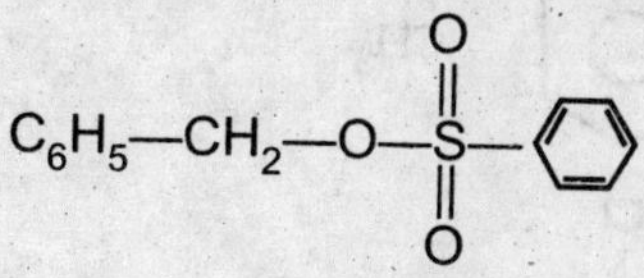

D. 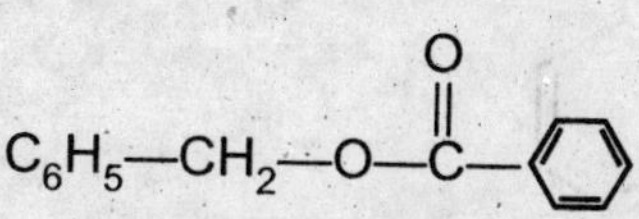

74. C	**75.** A	**76.** D	**77.** B	**78.** C	**79.** C

80. In the following reaction:

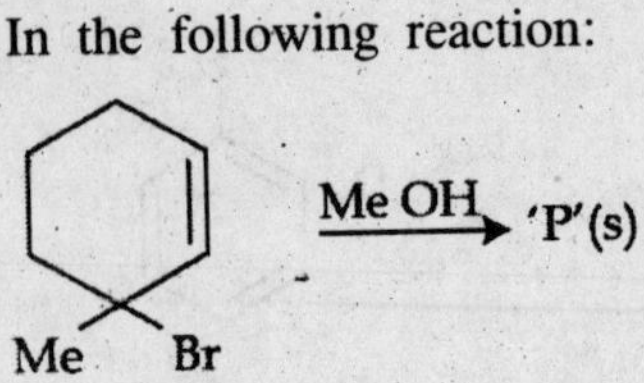

'P' could be:

A. 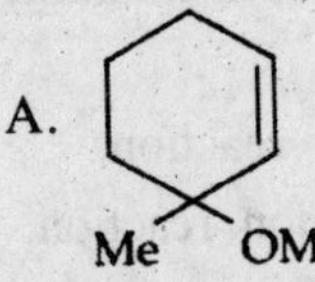 only

B. 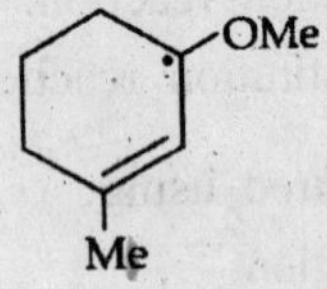 only

C. 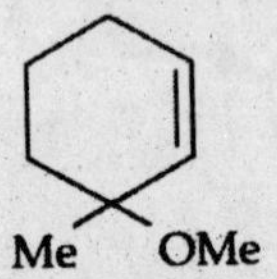 and 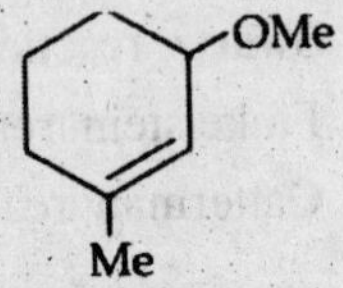 both

D. 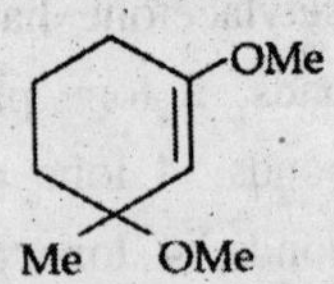 only

81. Which of these compounds is least acidic?
A. Carbolic acid B. Oxalic acid
C. Phthalic acid D. Picric acid

82. Which of these has the shortest C—Cl bond length?

A. 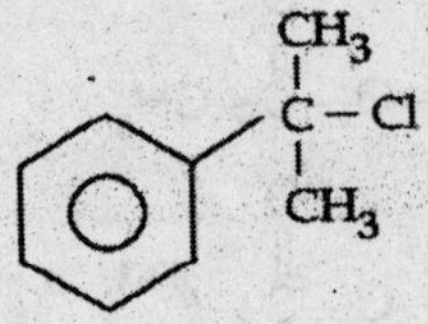

B. 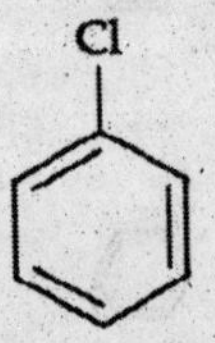

C. 

D. 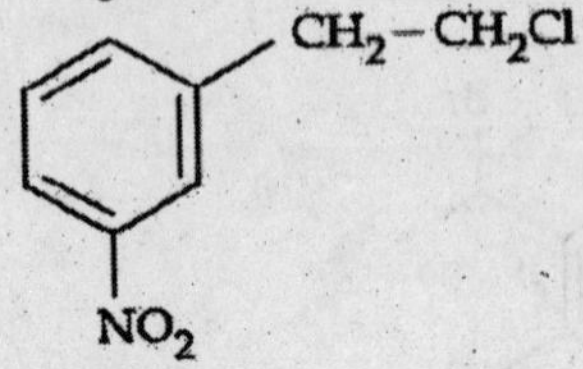

83. The dehydration product 'X' of the given compound

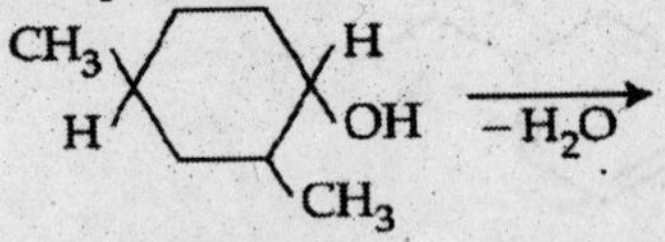

is:

A. 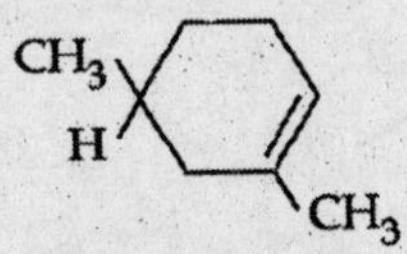

B. 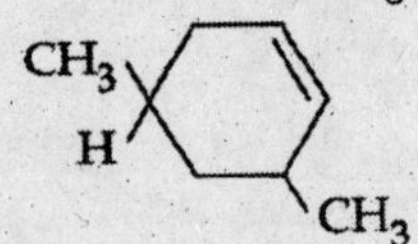

C. 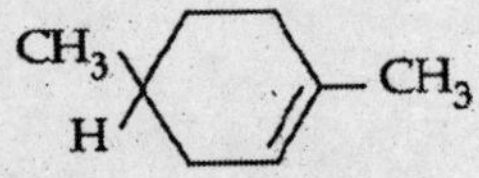

D. 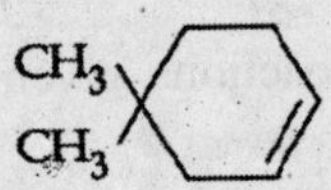

84. The product of the acid catalysed hydration of 2-phenyl propene is:
A. 3-phenyl propan-2-ol
B. 2-phenyl propan-2-ol
C. 1-phenyl propan-2-ol
D. 2-phenyl propan-1-ol

85. Which of the following compounds will not undergo nucleophilic attack by a hydroxyl group?
A. Ethyl benzoate B. Diethyl ether
C. Acetonitrile D. Benzamide

80. C	81. A	82. B	83. A	84. B	85. B

86. Which of the following is the strongest base?

A. 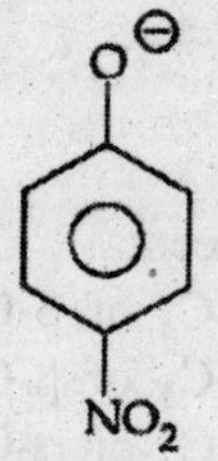

B. 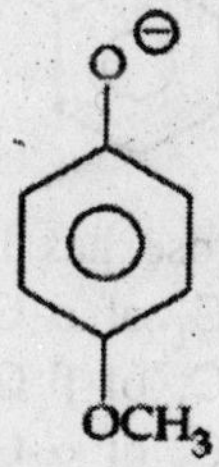

C. 

D. 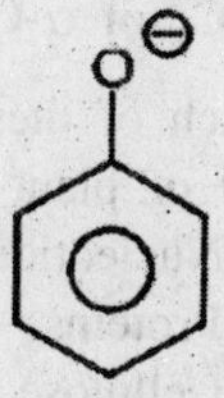

87. Which of these reactions is used to step up the number of carbons in the chain?

A. Hofmann-Bromamide reaction.
B. Hydroboration-oxidation.
C. Stephen reaction.
D. Gatterman-Koch reaction.

88. Consider the following reactions:

$$CH_3-\overset{\overset{\large O}{\|}}{C}-Cl \xrightarrow[\text{Pd-BaSO}_4]{H_2} \text{'P'}$$

'P' is:

A. CH_3CH_3 B. CH_3CH_2OH
C. CH_3CHO D. CH_3CH_2Cl

89. The reaction of benzaldehyde with semicarbazide hydrochloride is an example of :

A. Nucleophilic substitution reaction.
B. Nucleophilic addition reaction.
C. Elimination reaction.
D. Electrophilic addition followed by elimination.

90. In the given sequence of reactions:

$$C_2H_5Br \xrightarrow{\text{Mg/Ether}} A \xrightarrow{CH_3-\overset{\overset{O}{\|}}{C}-OCH_2CH_3} B$$

'B' is:

A. $CH_3-\underset{\underset{CH_2CH_3}{|}}{\overset{\overset{OH}{|}}{C}}-CH_2CH_3$

B. $CH_3CH_2-\underset{\underset{CH_2CH_3}{|}}{\overset{\overset{OH}{|}}{C}}-CH_2CH_3$

C. $CH_3-\underset{\underset{CH_2CH_3}{|}}{\overset{\overset{OH}{|}}{C}}-CH_3$

D. $CH_3-\underset{\underset{CH_2CH_3}{|}}{\overset{\overset{OH}{|}}{C}}-OCH_2CH_3$

91. Assertion (A): Aromatic aldehydes do not respond to Fehling's reagent test.

Reason (R): Aromatic aldehydes are not easily oxidized.

A. (A) and (R) both are correct and (R) is the correct explanation of (A).
B. (A) and (R) both are correct but (R) is not the correct explanation of (A).
C. (A) is correct but (R) is wrong.
D. (A) is wrong but (R) is correct.

92. The number of ether isomers possible for a compound with molecular formula $C_4H_{10}O$ would be:

A. 2 B. 3
C. 4 D. 5

86. B	**87.** D	**88.** C	**89.** B	**90.** A	**91.** A	**92.** B

93. An organic compound has the molecular formula $C_4H_{11}N$. The number of isomers which will give a positive carbylamine test would be:

A. 2 B. 3
C. 4 D. 5

94. Consider the following reaction:

A+ 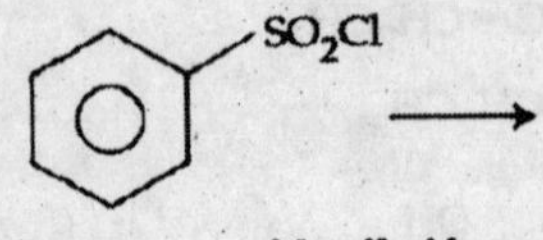

N - alkyl benzene sulphonamide

'A' could be:

A. Aniline
B. N.N-diethyl amine
C. N-Methyl methanamine
D. Methanamine

95. Which of these amines can be prepared by Gabriel phthalimide synthesis?

A. 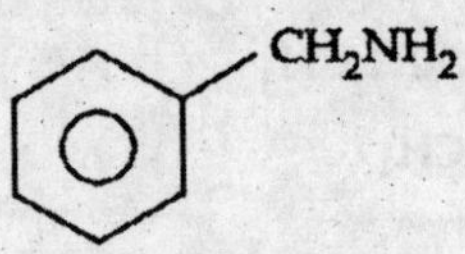

B. 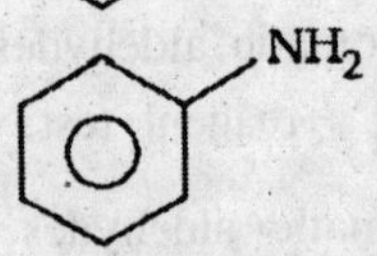

C. 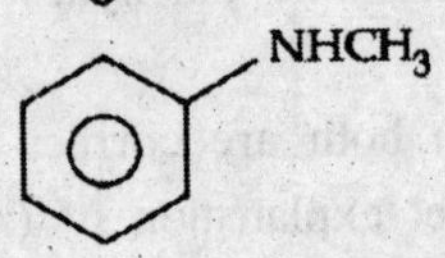

D. 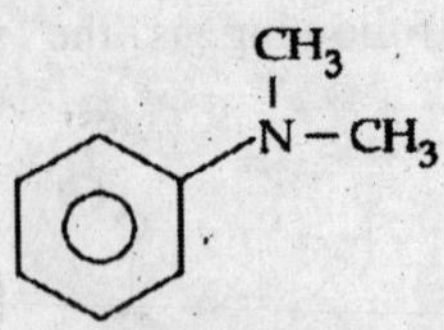

96. Maltose has linkage between:

A. C_1 of α-Glucose and C_4 of β-Glucose.
B. C_1 of β-Glucose and C_4 of β-Glucose.
C. C_1 of α-Glucose and C_4 of α-Glucose.
D. C_1 of α-Glucose and C_2 of β-Glucose.

97. Which of these is a constituent of the cell wall of plant cells?

A. Nucleotides
B. Proteins
C. Cellulose
D. Starch

98. Which of these amino acids does not have any chiral centres?

A. Lysine
B. Cysteine
C. Glycine
D. Tyrosine

99. Which is NOT an essential amino acid?

A. Aspartic acid B. Lysine
C. Arginine D. Methionine

100. RNA does not contain:

A. Adenine B. Guanine
C. Uracil D. Thymine

EXPLANATORY ANSWERS

1. (C): To find the correct coefficient for O_2 in the given reaction: $\_As_2S_3 + \_O_2 \rightarrow \_As_2O_3 + \_SO_2$, we must first balance the equation using whole number coefficients. Count the atoms of each element on both sides of the equation:

- Arsenic (As): 2 on both sides.
- Sulphur (S): 3 on the left, 1 on the right in SO_2, and no sulphur in As_2O_3.
- Oxygen (O): 3 in As_2O_3 and 2 in SO_2.

Adjust the coefficients to balance the sulphur and oxygen:

Place a coefficient of 3 before to balance the sulphur: $As_2S_3 + O_2 \rightarrow AS_2O_3 + 3SO_2$.

93. C	94. D	95. A	96. C	97. C	98. C	99. A	100. D

- Now, there are 3 sulphur atoms on both sides.
- Oxygen now has 9 atoms on the right (3 from As_2O_3 and 6 from 3 SO_2).

Adjust the coefficient of As_2O_3 to balance oxygen atoms:

- Place a coefficient of 1 before As_2O_3 as it already contributes 3 oxygen atoms, and adjust O_2 accordingly.

To balance the oxygen:

- Total oxygen needed on the right is 9 atoms (from step above).
- Since each O_2 molecule contributes 2 oxygen atoms, divide the total needed oxygen atoms by 2 to find the coefficient for O_2:

  $9 \div 2 = 4.5$, but since we need whole numbers, adjust other coefficients to make it a whole number.
- Adjust to use only whole number coefficients:

  Use a coefficient of 9 for O_2 to provide 18 oxygen atoms in total, which then balances with a coefficient of 5 for As_2O_3 and 4 for SO_2 (providing 15 and 8 oxygen atoms respectively).
- The final balanced equation is:

  $As_2S_3 + 9O_2 \rightarrow 5As_2O_3 + 4SO_2$.

Thus, the coefficient for O_2 when the equation is balanced using whole number coefficients is 9.

2. (A): To determine which reagent remains unreacted and its quantity, we can start by understanding the stoichiometry of the given reaction:

$4FeCl_3(s) + 3O_2(g) \rightarrow 2Fe_2O_3(s) + 6Cl_2(g)$

Given:

3.0 mol of $FeCl_3$

2.0 mol of O_2

According to the reaction, 4 moles of $FeCl_3$ require 3 moles of O_2. We need to check if the given amounts of $FeCl_3$ and O_2 are in the correct stoichiometric ratio.

Calculate the required O_2 for the given $FeCl_3$:

$$\text{Required } O_2 = \left(\frac{3 \text{ mol } O_2}{4 \text{ mol } FeCl_3}\right) \times 3.0 \text{ mol}$$

$$FeCl_3 = 2.25 \text{ mol } O_2$$

Compare the required O_2 to the available O_2:

- Required: 2.23 mol O_2
- Available: 2.0 mol O_2

Since the available O_2 (2.0 mol) is less than the required (2.25 mol), O_2 is the limiting reagent. We must adjust the calculation to reflect this:

Calculate how much $FeCl_3$ reacts with 2.0 mol of O_2:

$$FeCl_3 \text{ that reacts} = \left(\frac{4 \text{ mol } FeCl_3}{3 \text{ mol } O_2}\right) \times 2.0$$

$$\text{mol } O_2 = \frac{8}{3} \text{ mol } FeCl_3 \approx 2.67 \text{ mol } FeCl_3$$

Calculate the remaining $FeCl_3$:

$$\text{Remaining } FeCl_3 = 3.0 \text{ mol } FeCl_3 - 2.67 \text{ mol } FeCl_3 = 0.33 \text{ mol } FeCl_3$$

Thus, 0.33 mol of $FeCl_3$ remains unreacted, confirming option A is correct.

3. (A): Magnetite (Fe_3O_4) is composed of both iron(II) oxide (FeO) and iron (III) oxide (Fe_2O_3). The formula Fe_3O_4 can be viewed as a combination of one formula unit of FeO and one formula unit of Fe_2O_3:

$FeO + Fe_2O_3 \rightarrow Fe_3O_4$

This results in a 1 : 1 ratio of FeO to Fe_2O_3, making the correct answer A.

4. (B): To find the volume of a 0.110 M solution of Copper (II) nitrate trihydrate ($(Cu(NO_3))_2.3H_2O$) that can be prepared from 33.29 g:

First, calculate the number of moles of Copper (II) nitrate trihydrate:

$$\text{Number of Moles} = \frac{\text{Mass}}{\text{Molar mass}}$$

$$= \frac{33.29 \text{ g}}{241.6 \text{ g/mol}}$$

$$\approx 0.1378 \text{ mol}$$

Next, calculate the volume of solution that contains this amount of solute at a concentration of 0.110 M.

$$\text{Volume} = \frac{\text{Number of moles}}{\text{Concentration}}$$

$$= \frac{0.1378 \text{ mol}}{0.110 \text{ M}}$$

$$\approx 1.25 \text{ L.}$$

5. **(A):** The formula for lead tungstate can be derived by applying the valency rules used for forming compounds. Sodium tungstate (Na_2WO_4) and lead phosphate ($Pb_3(PO_4)_2$) provide clues:

Sodium tungstate shows that the tungstate (WO_4^{2-}) ion has a charge of –2.

Lead commonly forms a +2 charge in compounds such as lead(II) oxide (PbO).

Using these charges, the formula for lead tungstate where lead has a +2 charge and tungstate has a –2 charge would be $PbWO_4$, where each ion's charge is balanced.

Thus, option A, $PbWO_4$, is the correct formula for lead tungstate.

6. **(A):** To determine which electronic transition in a hydrogen atom results in the emission of the highest energy photon, we must understand how the energy levels of hydrogen are structured and calculate the energy change associated with transitions between these levels.

The energy levels in a hydrogen atom are quantified by:

$$E_n = -\frac{13.6 \text{ eV}}{n^2}$$

where n is the principal quantum number.

The energy emitted when an electron transitions from a higher energy level (n_1) to a lower energy level (n_2) is given by:

$$\Delta E = E_{n_2} - E_{n_1}$$

$$= -13.6 \text{ eV}\left(\frac{1}{n_2^2} - \frac{1}{n_1^2}\right)$$

Here, the change in energy (ΔE) will be positive, indicating energy release, and larger differences in n values yield higher energy releases.

Evaluating the options:

A. 2p → 1s: Transition from $n = 2$ to $n = 1$.

$$\Delta E_A = -13.6 \text{ eV}\left(\frac{1}{1^2} - \frac{1}{2^2}\right) = 10.2 \text{ eV}$$

B. 1s → 2p: This is an absorption process, not emission.

C. 3s → 2s: Transition from $n = 3$ to $n = 2$.

$$\Delta E_C = -13.6 \text{ eV}\left(\frac{1}{2^2} - \frac{1}{3^2}\right) = 1.89 \text{ eV}$$

D. 2s → 3s: Another absorption process.

The largest energy change, and therefore the highest energy photon emitted, is in option A, where the electron transitions from the 2p to the 1s orbital. This transition involves the greatest change in principal quantum number over the shortest distance, resulting in the most significant energy release. Thus, the correct answer is (A).

7. **(D):** Hund's rule states that every orbital in a subshell is singly occupied with one electron before any one orbital is doubly occupied, and all electrons in singly occupied orbitals have the same spin direction. This rule helps to minimize the electron-electron repulsions within an atom and maximize the overall stability of the atom.

Evaluating the electron configurations provided in each option:

A. Shows each orbital in the p-subshell singly occupied before any are doubly occupied. This obeys Hund's rule.

B. Also shows each orbital in the p-subshell singly occupied before any are doubly occupied. This configuration is in compliance with Hund's rule.

C. All orbitals in the p-subshell are singly occupied, following Hund's rule.

D. Shows two electrons in one p-orbital while another p-orbital is singly occupied. This configuration violates Hund's rule because it starts to doubly occupy an orbital before all orbitals in the subshell are singly occupied.

Therefore, the correct answer is (D), as it represents a violation of Hund's rules by not filling all the orbitals singly before any are doubly occupied.

8. (C): To determine which aspect is the same among the isotopes $^{72}_{30}Zn$, $^{75}_{33}As$ and $^{74}_{32}Ge$, we calculate the number of neutrons for each:

For Zinc ($^{72}_{30}Zn$):

Neutrons = 72 – 30 = 42

For Arsenic ($^{75}_{33}As$):

Neutrons = 75 – 33 = 42

For Germanium ($^{74}_{32}Ge$):

Neutrons = 74 – 32 = 42

All three isotopes have 42 neutrons, confirming option (C) as correct.

9. (D): To find the atomic weight of a hypothetical element with two isotopes:

Isotope 1: Mass = 64.2 u, Abundance = 25% of 0.25

Isotope 2: Mass = 65.3 u, Abundance = 75% or 0.75

The average atomic mass is calculated using the formula:

Average atomic mass

$$= (m_1 \times a_1) + (m_2 \times a_2)$$

Substituting the values:

Average atomic mass

$$= (64.2 \times 0.25) + (65.3 \times 0.75)$$

$$= 16.05 + 48.975$$

$$= 65.025\text{u}$$

Rounded to one decimal place, the atomic weight is approximately 65.0 u, which aligns with option (D).

10. (D): To calculate the frequency of light when given its wavelength and the speed of light, you can use the fundamental relationship in wave mechanics that relates frequency (*f*), wavelength (λ), and the speed of light (*c*):

$$f = \frac{c}{\lambda}$$

Where:

c is the speed of light, approximately 3×10^8 meters per second (m/s).

λ is the wavelength, given as 4.50×10^{-8} meters (m).

Plugging the given values into the formula:

$$f = \frac{3 \times 10^8 \text{ m/s}}{4.50 \times 10^{-8} \text{ m}}$$

Performing the division:

$$f = \frac{3 \times 10^8}{4.50 \times 10^{-8}}$$

$$f = \frac{3}{4.50} \times \frac{10^8}{10^{-8}}$$

$$f = 0.6667 \times 10^{16}$$

$$f = 6.67 \times 10^{15}\ \text{s}^{-1}$$

Therefore, the frequency of the light with a wavelength of 4.50×10^{-8} m is 6.67×10^{15} s^{-1}, which corresponds to option (D). This frequency corresponds to extremely high-energy ultraviolet light, bordering on X-rays, reflecting the very short wavelenght given.

11. (A): The acid strength of H_2Se, HBr and HI primarily depends on their bond strengths and the stability of their conjugate bases. Typically, the strength of a hydrogen halide acid increases down the halogen group due to the increase in size and corresponding decrease in bond enthalpy:

H_2Se is a chalcogen hydride and generally less acidic than heavier halogen acids due to weaker bond polarity and different orbital interactions.

HBr and HI are halogen hydrides. As we move down the group from bromine to iodine, the size of the halogen atom increases, which decreases the bond strength (bond enthalpy) between the hydrogen and the halogen. This makes the acid easier to dissociate, thereby increasing its acidity.

Thus, the correct order of increasing acid strength is $H_2Se < HBr < HI$, which aligns with option (A).

12. **(A):** The photoelectric effect refers to the emission of electrons from a material when light is shone upon it. The energy required to exhibit this effect, also known as the work functuion, varies aming different materials: Cesium (Cs) has the lowest work function among common metals. This is due to its large atomic size and the resulting ease with which its outermost electron (which is in 6s orbital) can be removed.

Other metals like calcium (Ca), copper (cu) and mercury (Hg) have higher work functions compared to cesium.

Therefore, cesium requires the least energy to exhibit he photoelectric effect, making option (A) correct.

13. **(B):** Boiling points generally increase with greater molecular mass and stronger intermolecular forces. The elements chlorine (Cl_2), bromine (Br_2) and Iodine (I_2):

Exist as diatomic molecules.

Exhbit increasing molecular weights and stronger London dispersion forces as you move from chlorine to iodine.

As a result, their boiling points increase from chlorine (a gas at room temperature) to bromine (a liquid) to iodine (a solid under standard conditions).

Thus, they are listed in the order of increasing boiling points, correctly matching option (B).

14. **(A):** The polarity of a bond depends on the difference in electronegativity between the two atoms involved. The greater the difference, the more polar the bond is likely to be.

- **Boron (B) and Fluorine (F):** Boron has an electronegativity of approximately 2.04, while fluorine, the most electronegative element, has an electronegativity of approximately 3.98. The different is 1.94.
- **Carbond (C) and Oxygen (O):** Carbon has an electronegativity of about 2.55 and oxygen 3.44, giving a difference of 0.89.
- **Oxygen (O) and Fluorine (F):** The difference in electronegativity is smaller (3.44 for O and 3.98 for F), about 0.54.
- **Nitrogen (N) and Fluorine (F):** Nitrogen has an electronegativity of about 3.04, making the difference with fluorine 0.94.

The pair boron and fluorine (A) shows the largest difference in electronegativity, suggesting that the bond between them will be the most polar, aligning with option (A).

15. **(C):** Analyzing the ionization energies can give insights into how many electrons an element is likely to lose to form stable ionic compounds:

The first three ionization energies (850, 1,815, 2,740 kJ/mol) increase gradually, suggesting that removing the first three electrons is progressively difficult but still feasible.

The large jump to the fourth and fifth ionization energies (11,600 and 18,500 kJ/mol) indicates a significant increase in difficulty when removing more than three electrons. This typically suggests that the element achieves a stable electron configuration after losing three electrons.

The pattern of ionization energies suggests that the element is likely to form 3+ ionic compounds, indicating that its most stable ionic stable is C^{3+}, thus option (C) is correct.

16. (A): The lowest energy arrangement of atoms in the ammonia (NH_3) molecule is trigonal pyramidal:

Ammonia consists of one nitrogen atom surrounded by three hydrogen atoms with a lone pair of electrons on the nitrogen.

The molecular geometry that accommodates these three bonds and one lone pair in the most symmetric arrangement possible while minimizing repulsion between the bonding pairs and the lone pair is trigonal pyramidal.

This geometry is not flat (trigonal planar) nor does it have more than three positions occupied around the central atom (trigonal bipyramidal or square planar).

Thus, option (A) (trigonal pyramidal) is the correct description of the lowest energy arrangement of atoms in an ammonia molecule.

17. (D): To determine if the molecules of the given compounds are linear, we need to consider the molecular geometry, primarily influenced by the arrangement of electron pairs around the central atom according to the VSEPR theory.

- **O_3 (Ozone)** has a bent structure due to the lone pairs on the central oxygen atom.
- **SO_2 (Suphur Dioxide)** also has a bent shape due to the lone pairs on the sulphur atom.
- **H_2O (Water)** is bent, influenced by two lone pairs on the oxygen.
- **CO_2 (Carbon Dioxide)** consists of carbon doubly bonded to two oxygen atoms, with no lone pairs on the carbon.

  The molecular geometry for CO_2 is linear.

Thus, CO_2 is the only molecule among the options that is expected to be linear, making option (D) correct.

18. (C): The hybridization of the sulphur atom is SF_4 can be determined by looking at its steric number, which is the total number of atoms bonded to it plus the number of lone pairs on it.

Sulphur in SF_4 forms four bonds with fluorine atoms and has one lone pair.

The steric number for sulphur is therefore 5 (four bonded atoms + one lone pair).

A steric number of 5 corresponds to sp^3d hybridization.

This places the sulphur atom in an sp^3d hybrid orbital, making option (C) correct.

20. (D): Regarding the octet rule, which states that atoms tend to bond in such a way that they each have eight electrons in their valence shell, the molecules listed are:

- **PCl_3 (Phosphorus Trichloride) and CBr_4 (Carbon Tetrabromide)** generally follow the octet rule.
- **OF_2 (Oxygen Difluoride)** also follows the octet rule as oxygen achieves a full octet through bonding.
- **AsF_5 (Arsenic Pentafluoride)**, however, is an example of a molecule where the central atom, arsenic, exceeds the octet rule by having ten electrons in its valence shell (hypervalency), thus violating the strict traditional interpretation of the octet rule.

Therefore (D) (AsF_5) is the correct answer as it violates the octet rule.

21. (B): State functions are properties that are determined by the state of a system, independent of the path by which the system arrived at that state. Common examples include:

Pressure

Free energy

Enthalpy

Heat, however, is not a state function because the amount of heat absorbed or released can depend on the path of the process, such as whether it occurs at constant pressure or constant volume. Thus, (B) (heat) is the correct answer as it is not a state function.

22. **(D):** To calculate the bond energy of the B-F bond in BF_3, use the given formation enthalpies (ΔH_f^0):

ΔH_f^0 for atomic B = +134.5 kcal/mol (energy required to form one mole of gaseous B atoms)

ΔH_f^0 for atomic F = +18.86 kcal/mol (energy required to form one mole of gaseous F atoms)

ΔH_f^0 for BF_3 = −271.75 kcal/mol

The reaction to form BF_3 from its elements is:

$$B + 3F \rightarrow BF_3$$

Applying Hess's law, the enthalpy change for the reaction is:

$$\Delta H = \Delta H_f^0(BF_3) - [\Delta H_f^0(B) + 3 \times \Delta H_f^0(F)]$$

$$\Delta H = -271.75 - [134.5 + 3 \times 18.86]$$

$$= -271.75 - [134.5 + 56.58]$$

$$= -271.75 - 191.08$$

$$= -462.83$$

This calculation suggests each B-F bond has an energy:

$$\text{Bond energy of B-F} = \frac{-462.83 \text{ kcal/mol}}{3}$$

$$\approx 154.3 \text{ kcal/mol}$$

Thus, Option (D) (154.3 kcal/mol) is the correct answer for the bond energy in BF_3.

23. **(A):** To calculate the heat of combustion of one mole of $C_4H_3(g)$ based on the given reaction and the standard enthalpies of formation, we use Hess's Law. The reaction provided is:

$$C_4H_3(g) + 6O_2(g) \rightarrow 4CO_2(g) + 4H_2O(l)$$

Step 1: Calculate the enthalpy of formation for the products:

For CO_2(g): −394 kJ/mol × 4 = − 1576 kJ

For H_2O(l): − 286 kJ/mol × 4 = −1144 kJ

Total enthalpy of products:

−1576 kJ + (−1144) kJ = −2720 kJ

Step 2: Calculate the enthalpy of formation for the reactants:

For C_4H_3(g): 16.0 kJ/mol

For O_2(g): 0 k/mol (as elemental oxygen is in its standard state)

Total enthalpy of reactants:

16.0 kJ + 0 kJ (6 × O_2) = 16.0 kJ

Step 3: Calculate the heat of reaction (enthalpy change, ΔH_{rxn}) using Hess's Law:

ΔH_{rxn} = Total enthalpy of products − Total enthalpy of reactants

ΔH_{rnx} = −2720 kJ − 16.0 kJ = −2736 kJ

The negative sign indicates that the reaction is exothermic, releasing 2736 kJ of energy per mole of C_4H_3 combusted. Therefore, the correct answer is (A) −2736 kJ/mol. This calculation aligns with the principles of thermochemistry, where the combustion of organic compounds typically releases a large amount of heat.

24. **(C):** To determine the change in Gibbs free energy ($\Delta G°$) for the reaction:

$$2H_2O(g) + O_2(g) \rightarrow 2H_2O_2(g)$$

We utilize the provided standard free energies of formation ($\Delta G_f°$ for each compound:

$\Delta G_f°$ of $H_2O(g)$ = −228 kJ/mol

$\Delta G_f°$ of $O_2(g)$ = 0 kJ/mol (Oxygen in its standard state)

$\Delta G_f°$ of $H_2O_2(g)$ = −105 kJ/mol

Step 1: Calculate $\Delta G°$ for the reactants:

For 2 moles of $H_2O(g)$:

2 × (−228 kJ/mol) = −456 kJ

For 1 mole of $O_2(g)$:

1×0 kJ/mol $= 0$ kJ

Total $\Delta G°$ for reactants:

-456 kJ $+ 0$ kJ $= -456$ kJ

Step 2: Calculate $\Delta G°$ for the products:

For 2 moles of $H_2O_2(g)$:

$2 \times (-105$ kJ/mol$) = -210$ kJ

Total $\Delta G°$ for products:

$= -210$ kJ

Step 3: Calculate the overall $\Delta G°$ for the reaction

$$\Delta G° = (\Delta G° \text{ of products}) - (\Delta G° \text{ of reactants})$$

$$\Delta G° = (-210 \text{ kJ}) - (-456 \text{ kJ})$$

$$\Delta G° = -210 \text{ kJ} + 456 \text{ kJ}$$

$$\Delta G° = 246 \text{ kJ}$$

The reaction has a positive $\Delta G°$ of 246 kJ, indicating that it is not spontaneous under standard conditions. Therefore, option (C) is correct.

25. (A): To calculate how many kilojoules of heat are liberated when 50.0 g of manganese (Mn) is burnt to form manganese (II, III) oxide (Mn_3O_4), follow these steps:

Step 1: Determine moles of Mn.

Atomic mass of Mn $= 55$ g/mol

Mass of Mn $= 50.0$ g

$$\text{Moles of Mn} = \frac{\text{Mass}}{\text{Molar mass}} = \frac{50.0 \text{ g}}{55 \text{ g/mol}} \approx 0.909 \text{ mol}$$

Step 2: Convert moles of Mn to moles of Mn_3O_4.

The balanced chemical equation is

$$3 \text{ Mn} + 2O_2 \rightarrow Mn_3O_4$$

3 moles of Mn yield 1 moles of Mn_3O_4.

$$\text{Moles of } Mn_3O_4 = \frac{0.909 \text{ mol Mn}}{3} \approx 0.303 \text{ mol}$$

Step 3: Calculate the heat released.

$\Delta H°$ of $Mn_3O_4(s) = -1388$ kJ/mol (it is negative, indicating an exothermic reaction).

$$\text{Heat released} = \text{Moles of } Mn_3O_4 \times \Delta H° = 0.303 \text{ mol} \times (-1388) \text{ kJ/mol} \approx -421 \text{ kJ}$$

Thus, approximately 421 kJ of heat are liberated when 50.0 g of Mn is burnt to form Mn_3O_4, making the correct answer (A) 421 kJ. This calculation assumes all of the manganese reacts completely to form manganese (II, III) oxide.

26. (D): To calculate the solubility product (Ksp) of MgF_2, first consider the dissolution of MgF_2 in water:

$MgF_2\ (s) \rightarrow Mg^{2+}\ (aq) + 2F^-\ (aq)$

From the stoichiometry of the reaction, the dissolution of 1 moles of MgF_2 will yield 1 mole of Mg^{2+} ions and 2 moles of F^- ions. If the saturated solution contains 1.16×10^{-3} mol/L of MgF_2, then:

$$[Mg^{2+}] = 1.16 \times 10^{-3} \text{ M}$$

$$[F^-] = 2 \times 1.16 \times 10^{-3} \text{ M} = 2.32 \times 10^{-3} \text{ M}$$

The Ksp can be calculated using the ion concentrations in the solution:

$$Ksp = [Mg^{2+}][F^-]^2$$

$$Ksp = (1.16 \times 10^{-3})(2.32 \times 10^{-3})^2$$

$$Ksp = (1.16 \times 10^{-3})(5.3824 \times 10^{-6})$$

$$Ksp = 6.24339 \times 10^{-9}$$

Rounding to appropriate significant figures, $Ksp \approx 6.2 \times 10^{-9}$.

27. (C): To compare the solutions of 0.50 M NH_3 and 0.50 M NaOH:

- NH_3 is a weak base and partially dissociates in water to form OH^- ions, with its ionization represented as:

  $NH_3 + H_2O \rightleftharpoons NH_4^+ + OH^-$

The concentration of OH^- produced will depend on the Kb of NH_3 and its initial concentration.

- NaOH is a strong base that completely dissociates in water:

$$NaOH \rightarrow Na^+ + OH^-$$

Thus, 0.50 M NaOH produces exactly 0.50 M OH^-.

1. **Concentration of OH^- ions** will be different for NH_3 (due to partial dissociation) and NaOH (complete dissociation). Thus, option 1 is incorrect.
2. **Volume of 0.20 M HCl required for neutralization** for NaOH would be straightforward as it would neutralize the exact amount of OH^- ions present, which is 0.50 M. For NH_3, however, since not all ammonia reacts to form OH^- ions, the actual amount of OH^- available for neutralization is less than 0.50 M. Therefore, less volume of 0.20 M HCl would be needed for NH_3 compared to NaOH. This makes option 2 incorrect as well.

Thus, the answer is (C), only option 2 is the same for both solutions, assuming equimolar neutralization.

28. (C): To calculate the equilibrium constant (K) for the reaction:

$$2NO(g) + O_2(g) \rightleftharpoons 2NO_2(g)$$

The equilibrium expression for this reaction is:

$$K = \frac{[NO_2]^2}{[NO]^2[O_2]}$$

Given the equilibrium concentrations:

$$[NO] = 0.10 \text{ M}$$
$$[O_2] = 0.20 \text{ M}$$
$$[NO_2] = 0.30 \text{ M}$$

Plugging these values into the equilibrium expression, we get:

$$K = \frac{(0.30)^2}{(0.10)^2 \times 0.20}$$

$$K = \frac{0.09}{0.002}$$

$$K = 45$$

Therefore, the value of the equilibrium constant K for this reaction at the given temperature and concentrations is 45, which corresponds to option (C).

29. (A): To determine which salt solution has the most basic pH, evaluate each salt based on the acid and base from which it is derived:

- **Na_2CO_2 (Sodium Carbonate):** Derivd from NaOH (a strong base) and H_2CO_3 (a weak acid). The solution tends to be basic because the weak acid's conjugate base (CO_3^{2-}) hydrolyzes to form OH^-.
- **$NaC_2H_3O_2$ (Sodium Acetate):** Derived from NaOH (a strong base) and CH_3COOH (acetic acid, a weak acid). This solution is also basic but less so than carbonate because acetate is a weaker base than carbonate.
- **NaCl (Sodium Chloride): Derived from** NaOH (a strong acid). The resulting solution is neutral.
- **NH_4Cl (Ammonium Chloride):** Derived from NH_4OH (a weak base) and HCl (a strong acid). The solution is acidic because the weak base's conjugate acid (NH_4^+) hydrolyzes to form H^+.

Comparing these, Na_2CO_3 produces the most basic solution due to the strong hydrolysis of carbonate ions, making it more basic than acetate.

30. (C): The greatest buffering capacity in a CH_3COOH/CH_3COO^- buffer occurs at the point where the concentration of the weak acid (CH_3COOH) equals the concentration of its conjugate base (CH_3COO^-) i.e., at the equivalence point.

Given:

Volume of CH_3COOH = 40.0 mL

Concentration of CH_3COOH = 0.20 M

Concentration of NaOH = 0.20 M

The point of greatest buffering capacity (halfway to the equivalence point):

Moles of CH_3COOH

= Volume × Concentration

= 40.0 mL × 0.20 M

= 8.0 mmol

To reach the point where

$[CH_3COOH] = [CH_3COO^-]$:

Moles of NaOH required

= Moles of CH_3COOH

= 8.0 mmol

$$\text{Volume of NaOH} = \frac{\text{Moles}}{\text{Concentration}}$$

$$= \frac{8.0 \text{ mmol}}{0.20 \text{ M}}$$

= 40.0 mL

For the greatest buffering capacity (half equivalence point), half this volume of NaOH is needed:

$$\text{Volume} = \frac{40.0 \text{ mL}}{2}$$

= 20.0 mL.

31. **(A):** We analyze the oxidation state of sulphur in both $H_2S_2O_7$ (Peroxodisulfuric acid) and H_2SO_4 (Sulphuric acid) to determine consistency in the oxidation numbers:

In H_2SO_4, sulphur is in the +6 oxidation state.

In $H_2S_2O_7$, sulphur's oxidation state can be calculated assuming all oxygens are in the −2 state and hydrogens are +1:

$$2(S) + 2(+1) + 7(-2) = 0$$
$$2S - 12 = 0$$
$$2S = 12$$
$$S = +6$$

Both compounds show sulphur in the +6 oxidation state, confirming option (A) is correct.

32. **(C):** To determine the oxidation number of carbon in CaC_2O_4 (calcium oxalate), we need to consider the overall charge of the compound and the typical charges of the other atoms present:

The formula for calcium oxalate is CaC_2O_4, where Ca typically has a +2 charge.

The compound as a whole is neutral.

Let's assign oxidation numbers:

Calcium (Ca) = +2

Oxygen (O) is usually −2 in compounds except peroxides.

The formula has two carbons and four oxygens. To find the carbon oxidation state:

Total charge = (+2) + 2C + 4(−2) = 0

$$2 + 2C - 8 = 0$$
$$2C - 6 = 0$$
$$2C = 6$$
$$C = +3$$

Thus, the oxidation number for each carbon atom in calcium oxalate is +3, which corresponds to option (C).

33. **(D):** We analyze each statement to identify the correct one:

A. **Oxidation is caused by a reducing agent:** This statement is somewhat misleading. A reducing agent causes reduction in another species while itself being oxidized.

B. **The oxidation reaction is a redox reaction:** This statement is technically correct since oxidation cannot occur without reduction. However, it may not be the answer sought because it does not explicitly cover the full definition of redox, where both oxidation and reduction occur simultaneously.

C. **Addition of an electropositive element is a type of oxidation:** This statement is incorrect as it doesn't correctly represent the meaning of oxidation, which involves loss of electrons, not necessarily the addition of elements.

D. Reduction is the addition of hydrogen: In many chemical contexts, especially in organic chemistry, the addition of hydrogen is indeed a common form of reduction because it typically involves a decrease in the oxidation state (gain of electrons).

Thus, option (D) is the correct statement, aligning well with general chemistry principles. It correctly identifies a common type of reduction reaction.

34. (D): To find the correct coefficients for the redox involving Fe^{2+}, MnO_4^- and H^+, which results in Fe^{3+}, Mn^{2+} and H_2O, we balance the reaction using the method of half-reaction. The half-reactions need to be balanced for both mass and change.

Half-Reactions:

- **Reduction of MnO_4^- to Mn^{2+}:**
  $MnO_4^- + 8H^+ + 5e^- \rightarrow Mn^{2+} + 4H_2O$
- **Oxidation of Fe^{2+} to Fe^{3+}:**
  $Fe^{2+} \rightarrow Fe^{3+} + e^-$

Balancing the Electrons:

The electrons lost in the oxidation half-reaction must equal the electrons gained in the reduction half-reaction. To balance the electrons:

Multiply the oxidation half-reaction by 5 (since 5 electrons are needed for the reduction half-reaction):

$$5(Fe^{2+} \rightarrow Fe^{3+} + e^-) \Rightarrow 5Fe^{2+} \rightarrow 5Fe^{3+} + 5e^-$$

Combining these half-reactions:

Reduction:

$MnO_4^- + 8H^+ + 5e^- \rightarrow Mn^{2+} + 4H_2O$

Oxidation:

$5Fe^{2+} \rightarrow 5Fe^{3+} + 5e^-$

Adding them together and canceling out the electrons:

$$MnO_4^- + 8H^+ + 5Fe^{2+} \rightarrow Mn^{2+} + 4H_2O + 5Fe^{3+}$$

Thus, the coefficient for Fe^{2+} when balancing this redox equation using the smallest whole number coefficients is 5, corresponding to option (D).

35. (C): We are tasked with identifying which statement is not correct for the given reaction:

$Fe(s) + CuSO_4(aq) \rightarrow FeSO_4(aq) + Cu(s)$

Let's examine each statement:

A. Iron is the reducing agent: Correct, In the reaction, iron (Fe) donates electrons to copper (II) ions, reducing them to copper metal. This makes iron the reducing agent as it itself is oxidized from 0 to +2 oxidation state.

B. The solution turns green in colour after the reaction: Correct, The solution initially contains blue copper sulphate. As the reaction proceeds, iron sulphate, which is green, is formed. Thus, the solution would indeed turn green.

C. Copper is a more reactive metal than iron: Not correct, According to the reactivity series of metals, iron is more reactive than copper. This is why iron can displace copper from copper sulfate, indicating iron's higher reactivity.

D. The reaction is an example of a redox reaction: Correct, The reaction involves the transfer of electrons from iron to copper ions, with iron being oxidized and copper being reduced. This is the definition of a redox reaction.

The incorrect statement is (C): "Copper is a more reactive metal than iron". This is false, as iron is indeed more reactive than copper, allowing it to displace copper in the reaction.

36. (A): The vapour pressure of a solution is affected by the concentration of solute particles. According to Raoult's law, the vapour pressure of the solvent decreases when a non-volatile solute is added. In this case, an aqueous solution is 1.00 molal in KI. Consider the options:

A. **Addition of water:** Adding water to the solution dilutes the solute, thereby reducing the concentration of solute particles. This increases the vapour pressure as the relative amount of solvent increases.

B. **Addition of NaCl:** Adding NaCl will increase the number of solute particles in the solution, further lowering the vapour pressure.

C. **Addition of Na_2SO_4:** Similar to NaCl, adding Na_2SO_4 will increase the solute concentration, reducing the vapour pressure.

D. **Addition of 1.0 Molal KI:** Adding more KI increases the concentration of solute particles, which decreases the vapour pressure.

Therefore, the correct option is (A) Addition of water.

38. (B): To calculate the molality of a solution containing 51.2 g of naphthalene ($C_{10}H_8$) in 500 mL of carbon tetrachloride (CCl_4):

Molar mass of $C_{10}H_8$ = 128.2 g/mol

$$\text{Moles of } C_0H_8 = \frac{51.2 \text{ g}}{128.2 \text{ g/mol}} = 0.4 \text{ mol}$$

The density of CCl_4 is 1.60 g/mL:

Volume of CCl_4 = 500 mL

Mass of CCl_4 = 500 mL × 1.60 g/mL = 800 g = 0.800 kg

$$\text{Molality (m)} = \frac{\text{moles of solute}}{\text{kg of solvent}} = \frac{0.4 \text{ mol}}{0.800 \text{ kg}} = 0.5 \text{ mol/kg}$$

Therefore, the correct option is (B) 0.500 M.

39. (A): To determine the vapour pressure of the solution, we use Raoult's Law. Raoult's Law states:

$$P_{solution} = P_{solvent} \times X_{solvent}$$

Where $P_{solution}$ is the vapour pressure of the solution, $P_{solvent}$ is the vapour pressure of the pure solvent, and $X_{solvent}$ is the mole fraction of the solvent.

Calculate moles of water:

Volume of water = 100 mL

Density of water = 1.00 g/mL

Mass of water = 100 g

Molar mass of water (H_2O) = 18.015 g/mol

$$\text{Moles of water} = \frac{100 \text{ g}}{18.015 \text{ g/mol}} = 5.55 \text{ mol}$$

Calculate moles of diglycine (non-volatile solute):

Mass of diglycine = 150 g

Molar mass of diglycine ($C_4H_8N_2O_3$) = 132.12g/mol

$$\text{Moles of diglycine} = \frac{150 \text{ g}}{132.12 \text{ g/mol}} = 1.135 \text{ mol}$$

Calculate mole freaction of water:

$$X_{water} = \frac{\text{moles of water}}{\text{moles of water + moles of diglycine}}$$

$$X_{water} = \frac{5.55}{5.55+1.135} = \frac{5.55}{6.685} = 0.830$$

Calculate vapour pressure of the solution:

$$P_{solution} = P_{solvent} \times X_{solvent}$$

$$P_{solution} = 57.9 \text{ kPa} \times 0.830 = 48.057 \text{ kPa} \approx 48.1 \text{ kPa}$$

Therefore, the correct option is (A) 48.1 kPa.

40. **(C):** To find the boiling point elevation, we use the formula:

$$\Delta T_b = K_b \times m$$

Where ΔT_b is the boiling point elevation, K_b is the ebullioscopic constant, and m is the molality of the solution.

Calculate moles of glucose:

Mass of glucose = 45 g

Molar mass of glucose ($C_6H_{12}O_6$) = 180.16 g/mol

$$\text{Moles of glucose} = \frac{45 \text{ g}}{180.16 \text{ g/mol}} = 0.25 \text{ mol}$$

Calculate mass of water (solvent):

Volume of water = 300 mL

Density of water = 1.00 g/mL

Mass of water = 300 g = 0.300 kg

Calculate molality (m):

$$m = \frac{\text{moles of solute}}{\text{mass of solvent in kg}}$$

$$m = \frac{0.25 \text{ mol}}{0.300 \text{ kg}} = 0.833 \text{ mol/kg}$$

Calculate boiling point elevation:

$$\Delta T_b = K_b \times m$$

$$\Delta T_b = 0.512 \text{ °C/m} \times 0.833 \text{ mol/kg} = 0.426 \text{ °C}$$

Calculate new boiling point:

$$T_b = 100.00 \text{ °C} + 0.426 \text{ °C} = 100.426 \text{ °C} \approx 100.43 \text{ °C}$$

Therefore, the correct option is (C) 100.43°C.

41. **(A):** To find the Gibbs free energy change (ΔG) for the reaction, use the formula:

$$\Delta G = -nFE_{cell}$$

Where n is the number of moles of electrons transferred, F is the Faraday constant (96,500 C/mol), and E_{cell} is the cell potential.

Calculate the cell potential (E_{cell}):

$$E_{cell} = E_{cathode} - E_{anode}$$

$$E_{cathode} = E^\circ_{Zn^{2+}/Zn} = -0.76 \text{ V}$$

$$E_{anode} = E^\circ_{Al^{3+}/Al} = -1.66 \text{ V}$$

$$E_{cell} = -0.76 \text{ V} - (-1.66 \text{ V}) = 0.90 \text{ V}$$

Determine the number of moles of electrons transferred (n):

The balanced reaction is

$$2Al(s) + 3Zn^{2+}(aq) \rightarrow 2Al^{3+}(aq) + 3Zn(s)$$

For each 2 Al atoms, 6 electrons are transferred:

$$n = 6$$

Calculate Gibbs free energy change (ΔG)

$$\Delta G = -nF\,E_{cell}$$

$$\Delta G = -6 \times 96{,}500 \text{ C/mol} \times 0.90\text{V}$$

$$\Delta G = -520{,}000 \text{ J} \approx -5.2 \times 10^5 \text{ J}$$

Therefore, the correct option is (A).

42. **(C):** To determine which statement about electrochemical cells is true, let's examine each statement:

- **A. Reduction occurs at the anode:** Incorrect, Reduction occurs at the cathode, not the anode. The cathode is where the reduction half-reaction takes place.
- **B. An element with a high affinity for electrons is likely to be easily oxidized:** Incorrect, An element with a high affinity for electrons is less likely to be oxidized; it is more likely to gain electrons and be reduced.
- **C. Oxidation occurs at the anode:** Correct, In electrochemical cells, oxidation always occurs at the anode. This is where electrons are lost by a species.
- **D. Only oxidation half-reactions are important:** Incorrect, Both oxidation

and reduction half-reactions are equally important in an electrochemical cell. They occur simultaneously and are necessary for the completion of the overall redox reaction.

Therefore, the correct option is (C) Oxidation occurs at the anode.

43. (A): To determine the standard cell potential (E°) for the given reaction, we need to use the standard reduction potentials of the half-reactions provided. The overall reaction is:

$Zn(s) + Pb^{2+}(aq) \rightarrow Zn^{2+}(aq) + Pb(s)$

The standard reduction potentials for the half-reactions are:

$Zn^{2+}(aq) + 2e^- \rightarrow Zn(s)$ E° = –0.763 V

$Pb^{2+}(aq) + 2e^- \rightarrow Pb(s)$ E° = –0.126 V

To find the standard cell potential (E°_{cell}), we follow these steps:

Identify the anode and cathode:

- **Anode (Oxidation):** Zn(s) is oxidized to Zn^{2+}(aq). The reverse of the given reduction half-reaction:

  $Zn(s) \rightarrow Zn^{2+}(aq) + 2e^-$

  $E^\circ_{oxidation} = +0.763$ V

  (reverse of the reduction potential)

- **Cathode (Reduction):** Pb^{2+} (aq) is reduced to Pb(s). The given reduction half-reaction:

  $Pb^{2+}(aq) + 2e^- \rightarrow Pb(s)$

  $E^\circ_{reduction} = -0.126$ V

Calculate the standard cell potential (E°_{cell}):

$$E^\circ_{cell} = E^\circ_{cathode} - E^\circ_{anode}$$

$$E^\circ_{cell} = (-0.126 \text{ V}) - (-0.763 \text{ V})$$

$$E^\circ_{cell} = -0.126 \text{ V} + 0.763 \text{ V}$$

$$E^\circ_{cell} = +0.637 \text{ V}$$

Therefore, the correct option is (A) +0.637V.

44. (A): To identify the strongest reducing agent based on the provided half-reactions and their standard reduction potentials, we need to understand that the strongest reducing agent is the one that is most easily oxidized. This corresponds to the substance with the lowest (most negative) standard reduction potential.

Given the half-reactions and their standard reduction potentials:

1. $MnO_2(s) + 4H^+(aq) + 2e^- \rightarrow Mn^{2+}(aq) + 2H_2O(l)$ E° = +1.22 V
2. $Hg_2SO_4(s) + 2e^- \rightarrow 2Hg(l) + SO_4^{2-}(aq)$ E° = +0.61 V
3. $SnO_2(s) + 2H_2O(l) + 4e^- \rightarrow Sn(s) + 4OH^-(aq)$ E° = –0.95 V
4. $Cr(OH)_3(s)\ 3e^- \rightarrow Cr(s) + 3OH^-(aq)$ E° = –1.48 V

To determine the strongest reducing agent:

- A reducing agent gets oxidized and loses electrons.
- The stronger the reducing agent, the easier it is to lose electrons.
- Therefore, the strongest reducing agent will have the most negative standard reduction potential.

Among the given potentials:

- $Cr(OH)_3 \rightarrow Cr$ has the most negative reduction potential of –1.48 V.

Thus, the corresponding reducing agent Cr (Chromium) is the strongest reducing agent.

Therefore, the correct option is (A) Cr.

45. (D): To find the mass of nickel that could be electroplated, we use Faraday's laws of electrolysis. The mass (*m*) of a substance deposited or liberated at an electrode is given by:

$$m = \frac{Q \times M}{n \times F}$$

Where:

- Q is the total charge passed through the solution,
- M is the molar mass of the substance,
- *n* is the number of electrons transferred in the half-reaction,

- F is the Faraday constant (96,500 C/mol).

Calculate the total charge (Q):

$$Q = I \times t$$
$$I = 0.25 \text{ A}$$
$$t = 10 \text{ hours} \times 3600 \text{ seconds/hour} = 36{,}000 \text{ seconds}$$
$$Q = 0.25 \text{ A} \times 36{,}000\text{s} = 9{,}000 \text{ C}$$

Nickel reduction half-reaction:

$$Ni^{2+} (aq) + 2e^- \; Ni\ (s)$$

Here, $n = 2$

Calculate the mass of nickel deposited:

$$M = 58.7 \text{ g/mol}$$
$$m = \frac{9{,}000 \text{ C} \times 58.7 \text{ g/mol}}{2 \times 96{,}500 \text{ C/mol}}$$
$$m = \frac{9{,}000 \times 58.7}{2 \times 96{,}500}$$
$$m = \frac{528{,}300}{193{,}000}$$
$$m \approx 2.7 \text{ g}$$

Therefore, the correct option is (D) 2.7 g.

46. (D): To find the activation energy (E_a) for the reaction, we use the Arrhenius equation and its logarithmic form:

$$k = Ae^{-\frac{E_a}{RT}}$$

Taking the natural logarithm of both sides:

$$\ln k = \ln A - \frac{E_a}{RT}$$

Given two rate constants (k_1 and k_2) at two different temperatures (T_1 and T_2), we can write:

$$\ln\left(\frac{k_2}{k_1}\right) = \frac{E_a}{R}\left(\frac{1}{T_1} - \frac{1}{T_2}\right)$$

Given data:

- $k_1 = 1.3 \times 10^{-11}$ s^{-1} at $T_1 = 227°C = 500$ K
- $k_2 = 6.5 \times 10^{-10}$ s^{-1} at $T_2 = 327°C = 600$ K
- $R = 8.3$ J/K/mol
- $\log_{10} 2 = 0.30$

Convert the natural logarithm to base 10:

$$\ln 10 = 2.303$$
$$\log_{10} k = \frac{\ln k}{2.303}$$

Calculate $\ln\left(\frac{k_2}{k_1}\right)$:

$$\ln\left(\frac{k_2}{k_1}\right) = \ln\left(\frac{6.5 \times 10^{-10}}{1.3 \times 10^{-11}}\right)$$
$$\ln\left(\frac{6.5}{1.3} \times 10\right) = \ln (5 \times 10)$$
$$\ln (50) = \ln (5 \times 10)$$
$$\ln (50) = \ln 5 + \ln 10$$
$$\ln (50) = 1.61 + 2.303 = 3.913$$

Calculate E_a:

$$\ln\left(\frac{k_2}{k_1}\right) = \frac{E_a}{R}\left(\frac{1}{T_1} - \frac{1}{T_2}\right)$$
$$3.913 = \frac{E_a}{8.3}\left(\frac{1}{500} - \frac{1}{600}\right)$$
$$3.913 = \frac{E_a}{8.3}\left(\frac{600 - 500}{500 \times 600}\right)$$
$$3.913 = \frac{E_a}{8.3}\left(\frac{100}{300{,}000}\right)$$
$$3.913 = \frac{E_a}{8.3}\left(\frac{1}{3{,}000}\right)$$
$$3.913 \times 3{,}000 = \frac{E_a}{8.3}$$
$$11{,}739 = \frac{E_a}{8.3}$$
$$E_a = 11{,}739 \times 8.3$$
$$\approx 97{,}434 \text{ J/mol}$$
$$\approx 97 \text{ kJ/ml}$$

Therefore, the correct option is (D) 97 kJ/mol.

47. (C): The rate constant (k) of a reaction can be affected by several factors, but concentration changes do not affect the rate constant itself; they affect the rate of reaction. The rate constant is primarily dependent on temperature. Therefore, the factors mentioned are:

A. Increasing the concentration of NO: This increases the rate of reaction but does not affect the rate constant.

B. Increasing the concentration of Cl_2: This also increases the rate of reaction but does not affect the rate constant.

C. Increasing the temperature: This increases the rate constant (k), as it provides the reactant molecules with more energy to overcome the activation energy barrier.

Therefore, the correct option is (C) Increasing the temperature.

48. (D): To determine the correct interpretation of the rate equation for the reaction $3I^- + S_2O_8^{2-}$ $2SO_4^{2-} + I_3^-$ with the rate equation Rate = $k[I^-][S_2O_8^{2-}]$, let's examine the options:

A. The reaction occurs when three iodide ions collide simultaneously with one $S_2O_8^{2-}$ ion: Incorrect, The rate law indicates a bimolecular reaction involving one iodide ion and one $S_2O_8^{2-}$ ion, not a termolecular collision.

B. There must be only one step in the overall reaction since the rate is first order in both reactants: Incorrect, The rate law does not necessarily indicate a single-step mechanism. It suggests the rate-determining step involves one iodide ion and one $S_2O_8^{2-}$ ion.

C. The rate of reaction is inhibited by the presence of I_3^-: Incorrect, The rate law does not suggest inhibition by I_3^-.

D. A slow step in the overall reaction sequence may involve the collision of a single I^- ion with a single $S_2O_8^{2-}$ ion: Correct, The rate law Rate = $k[I^-]$ $[S_2O_8^{2-}]$ suggests that the rate-determining step involves the collision of one iodide ion with one $S_2O_8^{2-}$ ion.

Therefore, the correct option is (D) A slow step in the overall reaction sequence may involve the collision of a single I^- ion with a single $S_2O_8^{2-}$ ion:

49. (D): To determine the units of the rate constant k for the rate equation Rate = $k[A]^2$:

The rate of a reaction typically has units of concentration per unit time, mol dm^{-3} s^{-1}.

For the rate equation Rate = $k[A]^2$:

$$k = \frac{\text{Rate}}{[A]^2}$$

The units of concentration, [A], are mol dm^{-3}.

So, the units of k are:

$$\text{Units of } k = \frac{\text{mol dm}^{-3}\text{ s}^{-1}}{(\text{mol dm}^{-3})^2}$$

$$= \text{mol}^{-1}\text{ dm}^3\text{ s}^{-1}$$

Therefore, the correct option is (D) mol^{-1} dm^3 s^{-1}.

50. (A): To determine which equation is not correct, let's examine each option:

A. $k = A\exp\left(\frac{E_a}{RT}\right)$

Incorrect, The correct Arrhenius equation is $k = A\exp\left(-\frac{E_a}{RT}\right)$. The negative sign in the exponent is crucial.

B. $\Delta G = \Delta H - T\,\Delta S$

Correct, This is the Gibbs free energy equation.

C. $\Delta G° = -RT \ln K_p$

Correct, This relates the standard Gibbs free energy change to the equilibrium constant.

D. $T = \dfrac{pV}{nR}$

Correct, This is the ideal gas law rearranged to solve for temperature.

Therefore the correct option is (A) $k = A\exp\left(\dfrac{E_a}{RT}\right)$.

51. (D): The electron configuration of nickel, which has an atomic number of 28, can be derived from its position on the periodic table. Nickel is in the fourth period and is a transition metal. The correct configuration involves filling the 4s orbital before the 3d orbital, but for nickel, the 4s orbital is filled after the 3d reaches 8 electrons.

The correct electron configuration is $[Ar]\ 3d^8\ 4s^2$. Upon ionization, nickel loses electrons from the 4s orbital first, which can lead to confusion, but the ground state configuration for neutral nickel is indeed $[Ar]\ 4s^2\ 3d^8$.

52. (C): Zirconium (Zr) and Hafnium (Hf) both belong to group 4 of the periodic table and are located in the 5th and 6th period, respectively. Their nearly identical atomic radii can be attributed to the phenomenon known as the lanthanoid contraction. This contraction is a result of the poor shielding effect of the 4*f* electrons in the lanthanide series, which lies between the two elements in the periodic sequence.

As the 4*f* orbitals do not effectively shield the outer electrons from the nuclear charge, elements following the lanthanides exhibit smaller atomic radii than expected. Both Zr and Hf have similar electronic environments and charge densities due to this contraction, explaining their similar atomic sizes despite being in different periods.

53. (A): Mn_2O_7, CrO_3 and V_2O_5 are all compounds of transition metals combined with oxygen, where the metals exhibit high oxidation states. Compounds with metals in high oxidation states generally form acidic oxides due to their strong oxidizing nature and the tendency to accept electrons, thereby generating acidic solutions:

- Mn_2O_7 (manganese heptoxide) is a strong oxidizer and is highly acidic.
- CrO_3 (chromium trioxide) is also known as chromic acid when dissolved in water, indicative of its strong aciditiy.
- V_2O_5 (vanadium pentoxide) reacts with strong bases to form vanadates, which implies that it behaves as an acid in chemical reactions.

54. (B): When potassium dichromate ($K_2Cr_2O_7$) is heated with potassium chloride (KCl) and concentrated sulphuric acid (H_2SO_4), it undergoes a redox reaction where the dichromate is reduced and chlorine is oxidized. The product of this reaction is chromium oxycloride, CrO_2Cl_2, which is deep red liquid. The formula CrO_2Cl_2 reflects the presence of both oxygen and chlorine atoms bonded to chromium.

55. (B): The magnetic moment of an ion is related to the number of unpaired electrons it has, and it can be calculated using the formula $\mu = \sqrt{n(n+2)}$ Bohr Magneton (BM), where n is the number of unpaired electrons. For Cr^{2+}, which has a $[Ar]_3d_4$ electron configuration, there are four unpaired electrons.

Calculating the magnetic moment

$$\mu = \sqrt{4(4+2)} = 24 \approx 4.90 \text{ BM}.$$

The nearest option provided is 4.40 BM, which is a typical experimental value reflecting slight discrepancies due to factors like pairing energy and the crystal field.

56. (D): Coordination compounds are distinguished by their structure, where central metal atoms are surrounded by a number of ligands that are either charged or neutral molecules or ions. $K_3[Al(C_2O_4)_3]$ is a coordination compounds.

In this forumla, Al is the central metal ion, and C_2O_4 (oxalate) acts as a ligand. This complex is characterized by the coordination of oxalate ions around the aluminum, forming a coordination complex. The square brackets typically denote the presence of a coordination entity.

57. **(B):** The coordination number of a metal in a complex refers to the number of points at which ligands are attached to the metal. In the complex $[Co(en)_2Br_2]$, the ligand "en" (ethylenediamine, $NH_2CH_2CH_2NH_2$) is a bidentate ligand, meaning each molecule of en coordinates at two points.

    Therefore, with two molecules of en, there are 4 points of attachment. Adding the two bromide ions, which each coordinate at one point, the total coordination number of cobalt in this complex is 6. This shows cobalt forming an octahedral geometry in the complex.

58. **(D):** A hexadentate ligand can bind to a central metal ion through six donor atoms. Among the options given:

    - Oxalate (Ox, $C_2O_4^{2-}$) is a bidentate ligand.
    - Cyanide (CN^-) is a monodentate ligand.
    - Ethylenediamine (en, $NH_2CH_2CH_2NH_2$) is a bidentate ligand.
    - EDTA (ethylenediaminetetraacetic acid) is a hexadentate ligand, as it has six donor atoms (two nitrogen and four oxygen atoms) that can coordinate with a central metal ion, forming stable complexes. This makes EDTA an effective chelating agent in various chemical applications.

59. **(A):** To determine the oxidation state of platinum in the coordination compound $[Pt(NH_3)_3Cl]Cl$, consider the overall charge of the complex and the known charges of the ligands and counter ion:

    - Ammonia (NH_3) is a neutral ligand, contributing no charge.
    - Chloride (Cl) inside the complex contributes a –1 charge.
    - The complex has an extra chloride ion (Cl) as a counter ion, also with a –1 charge.
    - The overall charge of the complex ion $[Pt(NH_3)_3Cl]$ must be +1 to balance the extra chloride ion outside the brackets. Therefore, considering the internal chloride (–1) platinum must be in a +2 oxidation state to result in a net charge of +1 for the complex ion.

60. **(B):** The task is to identify the pair where the ligand and its corresponding name do not match:

    - OH^- is correctly named hydroxo.
    - CN^- is incorrectly paired with cyanide as the name in coordination chemistry; it should be cyano.
    - Cl^- is correctly named chloro.
    - H_2O is correctly named aqua.

    Hence, the mismatch is with CN^-, which should be referred to as cyano when discussing its role as a ligand in coordination chemistry.

61. **(D):** To determine the IUPAC name of the given molecule, follow the steps below:

    - **Identify the Longest Carbon Chain:** The main carbon chain must include both hydroxyl groups for correct naming as a diol. Here, the longest chain is a five-carbon including all carbons from the leftmost to the rightmost.
    - **Number the chain:** The chain should be numbered to give the substituents (in this case, the hydroxyl groups and methyl groups) the lowest possible numbers. Numbering from right to left gives the OH groups at carbons 2 and 4, which is lower than any alternative numbering.

- **Identify and Position Substituents:** There are two methyl groups located at carbons 2 and 3. The hydroxyl groups are located at carbons 2 and 4.
- **Assemble the Name:** Combining the information:
  - The base name of a five-carbon alcohol is "pentan".
  - The presence of two hydroxyl groups makes it a diol, named as "pentan-2, 4-diol".
  - The positions and names of the methyl groups are added as prefixes in alphabetical order, resulting in "2, 3-dimethyl".

The correct IUPAC name is "2, 3-dimethyl pentan-2, 4-diol", which matches option (D).

62. (D): The chemical transformation of the starting material, aniline, through the sequence of reactions is detailed as follows:

- **Formation of Diazonium Salt:** Aniline reacts with $NaNO_2$ and HCl at 0-5°C to form benzene diazonium chloride (a stable diazonium salt in cold conditions). This step is typical of diazotization reactions involving primary aromatic amines.
- **Bromination:** The benzene diazonium chloride then reacts with Br_2 in water. Typically, this would lead to the formation of a bromobenzene through a diazonium salt reaction, but the presence of Br_2 and H_2O suggests a potential bromination at the diazonium stage.
- **Fluorination:** Subsequently, the product undergoes a reaction with HBF_4. This reagent is commonly used to replace the diazo group with a fluorine atom, transforming the compound into bromofluorobenzene if the bromination step replaced the diazo group with a bromine.
- **Further Transformation:** The final step involves heating the compound which suggests a possible further substitution or rearrangement involving the bromine and fluorine on the benzene ring.

Considering the options provided and the typical reactions of these reagents:

- Option A shows a compound with three fluorine atoms on the benzene ring, which doesn't correlate with the expected outcomes of the given reactions.
- Option B shows a mono-brominated product without fluorination, which is inconsistent with the use of HBF_4.
- Option C shows an amine group that would have been replaced in the first diazotization step, and additional fluorination not aligned with the described chemistry.
- Option D shows a dibrominated product with one fluorine atom, which aligns with the sequential use of bromine and fluorine sources and suggests a secondary bromination that could occur during the final heating step.

Thus, (D) is the correct option as it fits with the sequence of reagents used and their expected transformations on the benzene ring, assuming additional bromination occurs along with the initial fluorination step from HBF_4.

63. (A): To determine the aromaticity of the compounds shown, we apply Huckel's rule for aromaticity, which states that a molecule is a aromatic if it is cyclic, planar, and contains $4n + 2\pi$-electrons, where n is a non-negative integer.

A. This structure is the cyclopropenyl cation, a three-membered ring with a positive charge. It is cyclic and planar. Crucially, it contains 2π-electrons (the lone pair on one carbon is delocalized to create a conjugated system across the three carbons). This fits the $4n + 2$ rule with $n = 0$ (2 electrons), which makes it aromatic due to its stability despite the unusual small ring size.

B. The cyclopropenyl anion, similar in structure to A but negatively charged, has 4π-electrons. This satisfies the $4n$ rule (with $n = 1$), indicating it is antiaromatic because it leads to instability in the ring system.

C. The cyclopentadienyl ring (as drawn without any charge), under normal conditions, would need to be negatively charged to gain aromatic stability (as cyclopentadienyl anion with 6 π-electron). as drawn, it doesn't meet the criteria for aromaticity if considered in a neutral or cationic state.

D. Benzene is a classic example of an aromatic compound with 6π-electrons, fitting the $4n + 2$ rule with $n = 1$. It is cyclic, planar, and highly stable due to its aromatic nature.

Given this analysis, Option (A), the cyclopropenyl cation, is correctly identified as aromatic according to the $4n + 2$ rule, showing that it is indeed the aromatic species among the options provided. This selection emphasizes its unique aromatic stability as a positively charged three-membered ring.

64. (B): In the molecule $CH_2{=}C{=}CH_2$, known as allene, the hybridization states of the carbons can be determined based on their bonding and molecular geometry:

- **Carbon I and Carbon III:** Both are bonded to two hydrogens and are each double bonded to Carbon II. This arrangement requires three bonding regions around each of these carbons, which aligns with sp^2 hybridization. In sp^2 hybridization, one *s* orbital and two *p* orbitals mix to form three sp^2 hybrid orbitals, leaving one *p* orbital unused for π bonding.
- **Carbon II:** This carbon is double bonded to both Carbon I and Carbon III. The geometry of double bonds (a linear arrangement in this particular case) and the existence of two π bonds (one with each adjacent carbon) suggests *sp* hybridization for Carbon II. In *sp* hybridization, one *s* orbital and one *p* orbital mix to form two *sp* hybrid orbitals, which align in a linear configuration, with the remaining two *p* orbitals on Carbon II each forming a π bond with the adjacent carbons.

Thus, the correct assessment of the hybridization states in the molecule $CH_2{=}C{=}CH_2$ is that Carbons I and III are sp^2 hybridized (each forming three σ bonds and part of a π bond), and Carbon II is sp hybridized (forming two σ bonds and two π bonds). This configuration gives the molecule its distinctive linear shape with perpendicular planes of π bonds. Therefore, the answer is (B).

65. (B): In pyridine, a six-membered ring containing one nitrogen atom, the electronic distribution can be analyzed by understanding the nature of nitrogen in the ring and its influence on the π-electron system.

- **Nitrogen Atom:** In pyridine, the nitrogen atom is sp^2 hybridized, similar to the carbon atoms in the ring. However, nitrogen has one lone pair of electrons which is localized in an orbital that is perpendicular to the plane of the ring and does not participate in the conjugated π-electron system.
- **π-electron System:** Pyridine has a conjugated system consisting of the 2p_z orbitals of carbon and nitrogen (except the lone pair). The π-electron system is delocalized over the ring, but the presence of the electronegative nitrogen atom influences the electron density distribution.

- **Maximum Electron Density:** The positions directly adjacent to the nitrogen atom (positions II and IV) will exhibit increased π-electron density. This is due to the fact that the nitrogen atom, being more electronegative than carbon, will pull electron density towards itself along the plane of the ring. Additionally, the ortho positions relative to nitrogen in aromatic compounds generally experience an increase in electron density through resonance stabilization.

Thus, positions II and IV in pyridine are the positions where the maximum electron density is found due to the influence of the adjacent nitrogen atom and the overall resonance stability of the ring system. This explains why option (B) is correct.

66. (A): The shortest C–Cl bond distance in the given options depends on several factors, including the hybridization of the carbon, steric hindrance, and the electron density around the carbon atom bonded to the chlorine. Let's analyze why the bond length in option A is the shortest:

- **Option A:** The chlorine is bonded to a carbon that is part of a cyclohexyl group. This group provides a unique structural arrangement where the carbon, despite being sp^3 hybridized, may exhibit effective overlap in its bond due to the conformational stability and less steric strain in a cyclic structure. Cyclohexane rings typically adopt a chair conformation, which could position the chlorine atom in an axial position, leading to effective orbital overlap and thus a shorter bond length.
- **Options B and C:** Both involve chlorine atoms bonded to sp^3 hybridized carbons at the end of an alkyl chain. These settings can introduce more flexibility and potentially more steric hindrance compared to a rigid cyclohexyl structure. The bond lengths in these configurations may not be as short due to less effective orbital overlap and increased electron repulsion from neighboring groups.
- **Option D:** While the carbon attached to chlorine is sp^2 hybridized, which normally suggests shorter bonds due to increased s-character, the presence of a double bond adjacent to the chlorine may actually lead to slight elongation of the C—Cl bond. This could be due to electronic effects such as the withdrawal of electron density by the double bond, which could potentially lengthen the C—Cl bond.

Given these considerations, Option A is plausible for having the shortest C—Cl bond length due to the structured and potentially less hindered environment of the cyclohexyl group, which might favor a shorter and more effective overlap of bonding orbitals compared to the more flexible and potentially electronically influenced environments in other options. Thus, the answer is (A).

67. (D): The ability of these compounds to produce a precipitate of AgBr when treated with $AgNO_3$ depends largely on the ease with which the bromide ion can be displaced from the aromatic ring by the silver ion. This nucleophilic aromatic substitution is influenced by the electronic effects of substituents attached to the aromatic ring.

A. The compound has two bromine atoms on adjacent carbons. This dibromobenzene lacks any electron-donating groups that would facilitate the release of a bromide ion.
B. This is monobromobenzene. It lacks substituents that could either donate electrons to facilitate the displacement of bromide or withdraw electrons to hinder it.
C. This compound contains a longer alkyl chain attached to the bromobenzene,

which does not significantly affect the reactivity of the bromine atom towards nucleophilic substitution.

D. This molecule features a bromine atom and a methoxy group (OCH_3) on the aromatic ring. The methoxy group is an electron-donating group via resonance and inductive effects. This increases the electron density on the ring, particularly at the ortho and para positions relative to the methoxy group. In this structure, the bromine is located at the para position relative to the OCH_3 group, making the carbon to which it is attached more electron-rich and thus more susceptible to nucleophilic attack.

The increased electron density around the bromine due to the methoxy group in Option D enhances the leaving ability of the bromide ion when treated with $AgNO_3$, facilitating the formation of AgBr precipitate more readily than in the other options. Therefore, the correct answer is D, as it not only provides an environment where the bromide is more activated but also aligns with the principles of nucleophilic aromatic substitution enhanced by electron-donating groups.

69. (A): The reaction using cold alkaline $KMnO_4$ (potassium permanganate) on alkenes is known for producing cis-diols through a process called syn-dihydroxylation. This reaction specifically adds hydroxyl (OH) groups to each of the carbons originally involved in the double bond of the alkene, and it does so from the same side, resulting in a cis-configuration of the diol.

Here's how it works for each option:

A. Cold alkaline $KMnO_4$ reacts with the double bond in the alkene to add OH groups to both carbons of the double bond from the same side, resulting in a cis-diol. This reaction is typical for synthesizing glycols from alkenes in a stereospecific manner.

B. Hydrogen peroxide (H_2O_2) in the presence of UV light typically leads to radical formations and may add across double bonds, but it does not specifically result in the controlled formation of cis-diols.

C. The hydroboration-oxidation sequence using BH_3 followed by H_2O_2/OH^- typically results in anti-Markovnikov addition of hydroxyl groups across the double bond, producing alcohols rather than diols.

D. The reaction sequence using Br_2 followed by KOH in water typically leads to a bromohydrin formation followed by dehydrohalogenation to yield epoxides or other products, not specifically cis-diols.

Therefore, the correct answer is (A), as cold alkaline $KMnO_4$ is the reagent that reliably produces cisdiols from alkenes through syn-dihydroxylation.

70. (D): In paper chromatography, spots of separated components can indeed be made visible through several methods, each appropriate for different types of compounds. The specified options include:

A. Using UV light is effective for compounds that naturally fluoresce or absorb in the UV range. It's common for aromatic compounds.

B. Spraying a visualizing agent, like ninhydrin or other chemical reagents, is a standard method for detecting specific types of molecules, such as amino acids.

C. Iodine vapors are used to visualize spots due to the formation of a complex with iodine, effective for a wide range of organic compounds.

D. Complexing with heavy metal ions is a specific method used to detect compounds that can form complexes with metals, such as those containing phosphate groups or sulphur.

Although all methods are viable under certain circumstances, option (D) highlights a specific technique that can be crucial for detecting certain biochemicals or environmental samples where heavy metal interaction is significant. This method is not the most universally applicable compared to others like UV light or iodine, but it can be critical for specialized applications involving specific molecular interactions with metals. Thus, given the broad nature of the question, (D) is cited as the correct answer.

71. (D): Kjeldahl's method is used for the quantitative determination of nitrogen in chemical substances, particularly effective for substances containing nitrogen in amine (NH_2) forms. This method involves digesting the sample in sulphuric acid, which converts nitrogen into ammonium sulphate. The ammonia formed is then released by alkalinization and measured.

A. Contains hydrazine (—NH—NH—) groups. Kjeldahl's method might not provide accurate results for hydrazine groups as they can decompose or not fully convert during the acid digestion.

B. Features an azo compound (—N=N—). Nitrogen in azo linkages may not be fully converted to ammonium sulfate due to their stability and resistance to acid hydrolysis.

C. Presents a fused aromatic system with amino groups. Although containing amino groups, the complexity and stability of the aromatic system may interfere with complete nitrogen conversion.

D. Shows a simpler structure with clearly defined amine groups more typical of proteins or amino compounds, which are ideal for Kjeldahl analysis. The amino groups in this structure are likely to be efficiently converted to ammonium sulphate during the digestion phase of the Kjeldahl method.

Thus, the correct answer is (D), as it involves simple amino groups which are effectively converted to measurable forms of nitrogen by the Kjeldahl method, providing accurate results.

72. (A): The most stable conformational isomer of 2-chloroethanol is option A, which features the OH and Cl groups in an anti conformation.

- **Conformation A:** Anti position between OH and Cl. This arrangement is generally more stable because it minimizes repulsive interactions between the electron clouds of the polar groups.
- **Conformation B:** Gauche position between OH and Cl. Although gauche interactions can sometimes be stabilizing due to hyperconjugation or favorable dipole-dipole interactions, in this case, the larger spatial separation in the anti conformation provides greater overall stability.
- **Conformation C:** Similar to A, but with the OH and Cl switched, maintaining an anti relationship.
- **Conformation D:** Gauche position similar to B, but less favorable due to increased steric hindrance and eclipsing interactions.

Option (A) is most favorable because the anti conformation typically provides the least steric hindrance and torsional strain, making it energetically preferred for 2-chloroethanol.

73. (C): The statement that "Protic solvents facilitate the S_N2 reaction" is not true.

- **Protic solvents:** These solvents, which can donate hydrogen bonds (like water and alcohols), tend to stabilize the nucleophile through hydrogen bonding. This decreases the nucleophile's reactivity by making it less available to attack the electrophilic carbon.

- **S_N2 reaction:** This is a bimolecular nucleophilic substitution reaction where the reaction rate depends on both the nucleophile and the substrate. The nucleophile must be strong and freely available to attack the substrate directly in a single step, leading to inversion of configuration.
- **Aprotic solvents:** These are more suitable for S_N2 reactions as they do not stabilize the nucleophile through hydrogen bonding, keeping the nucleophile more reactive.

Thus, statement C is incorrect because protic solvents do not facilitate the S_N2 reaction; rather, they often hinder it by stabilizing the nucleophile, reducing its effectiveness in the bimolecular substitution mechanism.

74. (C): The correct answer for 'B' is option C, based on the reaction sequence provided.

- **First Reaction (+HBr):** This addition targets a double bond in the benzene derivative, incorporating a bromine atom. Given the structure shown, this would place the bromine on the side chain.
- **Second Reaction (SbF_3):** Antimony trifluoride (SbF_3) is used for the Friedel-Crafts alkylation. It acts on alkyl bromides converting them into carbocations which then attach to the benzene ring. The side chain in option C has the necessary setup for this transformation.
- **Outcome:** SbF_3 reacts with the benzyl bromide to form a carbocation, which then rearranges or directly attaches to the benzene ring, forming a more complex aromatic structure.

Option C's structure allows for the necessary transformations and rearrangements, making it the correct choice. The other options do not provide the correct configuration of functional groups to undergo the described transformations.

75. (A): The correct product 'B' for the given reaction sequence is option A.

- **First Reaction ($NaNO_2$ + HCl):** This step involves the diazotization of an aniline (NH_2 group on benzene) using sodium nitrite ($NaNO_2$) and hydrochloric acid (HCl) at a low temperature (0-5°C). The NH_2 group is converted to a diazonium salt.
- **Second Reaction (H_3PO_2, H_2O):** This step involves the reduction of the diazonium salt using hypophosphorous acid (H_3PO_2) in water. This reduction typically results in the replacement of the diazonium group with a hydrogen atom, leading to the formation of a simple benzene ring.

Option (A) is the only structure among the choices that shows a benzene ring without any substituent, which is consistent with the expected outcome of these reaction conditions. The other options include groups that are not formed by the reduction of diazonium salts in this reaction scheme.

76. (D): The preparation of phenol from chlorobenzene is a nucleophilic substitution reaction.

- **Nucleophilic Substitution Reaction:** This reaction type typically involves the displacement of a leaving group by a nucleophile. In the case of converting chlorobenzene to phenol, a hydroxide ion (OH^-) acts as the nucleophile that displaces the chlorine atom.
- **Process:** Chlorobenzene is treated under conditions (typically with NaOH at high temperatures and pressure) that facilitate the replacement of the chlorine by an OH group, forming phenol.

This reaction is characterized by the breaking of the C-Cl bond and the formation of a new C-O bond.

77. (B): Freons are manufactured using the Swartz reaction.

- **Swartz Reaction:** This reaction involves the replacement of an alkyl halide's halogen with a fluorine atom using metal fluoride salts such as silver fluoride (AgF) or antimony trifluoride (SbF_3).
- **Relevance to Freons:** Freons, which are chlorofluorocarbons (CFCs), require the incorporation of fluorine atoms into their structure. The Swartz reaction provides a direct method for introducing fluorine into organic molecules, crucial for Freon synthesis.

78. (C): The enol form of acetylacetone has 14σ bonds, 2π bonds, and 4 lone pairs.

- **Structure of Acetylacetone:** Acetylacetone exists in both keto and enol forms due to tautomerization. In the enol form, it features a central carbon doubly bonded to an oxygen and single-bonded to another oxygen which is part of an OH group, with additional single bonds to other carbon atoms.
- **Bond Counting:** The enol form includes:
  - ❑ 14 single (σ) bonds involving carbon-hydrogen and carbon-carbon connections.
  - ❑ 2 double (π) bonds in the C=O and C=C structures.
  - ❑ 4 lone pairs located on the oxygen atoms.

79. (C): The alkyl halide that will undergo SN_1 reactions most readily is C.

- **SN_1 Mechanism:** This is a two-step process where the first step is the rate-determining step involving the formation of a carbocation by the departure of the leaving group.
- **Structure C:** This compound is a benzyl ether with a good leaving group attached to an oxygen. The crucial aspect here is the stabilization provided by the benzene ring through resonance when the leaving group departs, forming a stable benzyl cation.
- **Role of the Phenyl Sulfone Group:** The oxygen connected to the sulfur of the phenyl sulfone group in option C increases the stability of the developing carbocation through resonance stabilization more effectively than the simpler ester or ketone groups in other options.

The specific structure of option C facilitates a rapid SN_1 reaction due to the increased carbocation stability imparted by the adjacent aromatic ring and the electron-withdrawing effect of the sulfone group. The other options lack either sufficient carbocation stabilization or have a structure less conducive to SN_1 mechanisms.

80. (C): In the reaction with methanol (MeOH), both products shown in option C can be formed.

- **Reaction Overview:** The given reaction involves a bromoalkane reacting with methanol, which is a typical nucleophilic substitution (SN) scenario where methanol acts as the nucleophile.
- **Formation of Products:**
  1. Intramolecular reaction: The methoxy group can attack the carbocation formed from the departure of the bromide on the same carbon (intramolecular SN_2), leading to the formation of the first product in C, where the methoxy group replaces the bromine.
  2. Intermolecular reaction: Alternatively, after the formation of the carbocation, methanol can attack intermolecularly at a different carbon, leading to a ring expansion or rearrangement, resulting in the second product shown in option C.

- **Stereochemistry and Mechanism:**
  - ❑ The bromine's departure creates a carbocation, which is subject to rearrangement or direct attack.
  - ❑ Methanol can act both ways—attacking directly where bromine was attached or involving a shift in the carbocation leading to different structural outcomes.

Thus, both structures depicted in option C are plausible outcomes depending on how the methanol interacts with the intermediate carbocation, making it the correct answer. This answer considers both the intramolecular and intermolecular pathways methanol might take in reacting with the carbocation intermediate.

81. **(A):** Carbolic acid is the least acidic among the options listed.

A. Carbolic Acid: Commonly known as phenol, it has a pKa of approximately 10.0. This indicates moderate acidity, primarily due to the ability of the aromatic ring to stabilize the negative charge on the oxygen in the phenoxide ion via resonance. However, this stabilization is not as effective as the stronger electron-withdrawing effects seen in the other acids listed.

B. Oxalic Acid: A dicarboxylic acid with two carboxyl groups, each contributing to an increased acidity due to the inductive effect and hydrogen bonding potential between the -COOH groups. Its pKa values are around 1.25 and 4.14, showing stronger acidity.

C. Phthalic Acid: Another dicarboxylic acid but with the carboxyl groups attached to a benzene ring. The conjugation with the aromatic system provides effective resonance stabilization of the carboxylate form, leading to pKa values of about 2.89 and 5.51.

D. Picric Acid: Extremely acidic among the aromatic acids due to the presence of three nitro groups which are strong electron-withdrawing groups. These groups enhance the stability of the negative charge on the oxygen when the hydrogen is lost as a proton, leading to a very low pKa of around 0.3.

Therefore, compared to oxalic, phthalic, and especially picric acid, which all have strong electron withdrawing groups or multiple acidic groups enhancing their acidity, carbolic acid (phenol) is the least acidic due to its relatively weaker ability to stabilize the negative charge in its conjugate base.

82. **(B):** The molecule with the shortest C—Cl bond length is option (B).

- **Bond Length Consideration:** Shorter bond lengths generally indicate stronger, more stablebonds, often influenced by the electron density around the bonding atoms.
- **Option B:** Features a chlorobenzene molecule where the chlorine atom is directly bonded to a benzene ring. The aromatic system of benzene, being highly electron-rich due to delocalized pi electrons, contributes to partial double bond character between the carbon and chlorine through resonance. This pi-character in the bond can lead to a shorter and stronger C—Cl bond compared to standard single C—Cl bonds.
- **Other Options:**
  - ❑ A has chlorine attached to a tertiary carbon which does not significantly alter bond length through resonance.
  - ❑ C and D show chlorine attached to aliphatic carbons without the potential for resonance stabilization like in aromatic systems.

The resonance stabilization in option B leads to a degree of double bond character between carbon and chlorine, thereby shortening the bond compared to the more typical single bonds in the other options. Thus, B is identified as having the shortest C—Cl bond.

83. (A): The correct dehydration product 'X' of the given compound is option (A).

- **Dehydration Mechanism:** The dehydration of an alcohol typically involves the removal of a water molecule (H_2O), leading to the formation of a double bond. This reaction is catalyzed by acids and can lead to rearrangements depending on the stability of the resulting carbocations.
- **Given Structure Analysis:** The original molecule shows a secondary alcohol linked to a cyclohexane ring.
- **Product Formation:**
  - ❑ The removal of water from the secondary alcohol initially creates a secondary carbocation.
  - ❑ In the case of the molecule given, this carbocation can undergo a 1,2-hydride shift from a neighboring carbon to form a more stable tertiary carbocation at the junction of the ring structure.
  - ❑ The final product, option A, displays a double bond that results from the elimination of water and the stabilization of the carbocation, involving the tertiary center. This structure is consistent with the typical outcomes of dehydration reactions which favour the formation of more stable carbocations and thus more substituted alkenes.

The choice of A reflects the common outcome in dehydration reactions where the structure rearranges to stabilize the carbocation intermediate, leading to the formation of a double bond in the most substituted position possible.

84. (B): The product of the acid-catalyzed hydration of 2-phenyl propene is 2-phenyl propan-2-ol.

- **Reaction Mechanism:** Acid-catalyzed hydration typically follows Markovnikov's rule, where the hydrogen from the acidic water (H_3O^+) adds to the less substituted carbon of the alkene. This results in the more substituted carbon forming the more stable carbocation intermediate.
- **Formation of Carbocation:** In the case of 2-phenyl propene, the carbocation intermediate would initially form at the more substituted carbon adjacent to the phenyl group.
- **Water Addition and Product Formation:** Water then attacks this carbocation, leading to the formation of an alcohol at the more substituted carbon. The resulting product has the OH group on the same carbon as the phenyl group, which corresponds to option B.

85. (B): Diethyl ether will not undergo nucleophilic attack by a hydroxyl group.

- **Reactivity of Diethyl Ether:** Diethyl ether is a relatively inert compound in the presence of nucleophiles like hydroxyl groups due to the lack of a good leaving group. In ethers, the oxygen is connected to two alkyl groups, which are not prone to leave; hence, the ether linkage does not easily participate in nucleophilic substitution reactions.
- **Comparison with Other Compounds:**
  - ❑ **Ethyl Benzoate:** Contains an ester linkage, which can be attacked by nucleophiles.
  - ❑ **Acetonitrile:** The nitrile group can be subject to nucleophilic attack.
  - ❑ **Benzamide:** Contains an amide bond that can also be attacked by nucleophiles under certain conditions.

Thus, B (Diethyl ether) is identified as the compound least likely to undergo a nucleophilic attack by a hydroxyl group due to its stable ether linkage and lack of a suitable leaving group.

86. **(B):** The strongest base among the given compounds is option (B).

- **Basicity and Electron Donation:** Basicity in aromatic systems is significantly influenced by the ability of substituents to donate electrons to the ring. Electron-donating groups increase electron density at the ring, enhancing the ability of the ring to share electrons and thus increasing its basicity.
- **Analysis of Substituents:**
  - **Option A (NO_2):** The nitro group is a strong electron-withdrawing group. It decreases electron density on the ring, making the anion less stable and thereby decreasing basicity.
  - **Option B (OCH_3):** The methoxy group is a strong electron-donating group through resonance and inductive effects. This increases electron density on the ring, enhancing its ability to act as a base.
  - **Option C (CH_3):** The methyl group is an electron-donating group but weaker than the methoxy group. It increases the electron density on the ring, but not as effectively as the methoxy group.
  - **Option D:** Has no additional groups to alter the electron density significantly.

Conclusion: The presence of the methoxy group in option B makes it the strongest base due to its strong electron-donating effect, which stabilizes the negative charge on the oxygen more effectively than the other substituents, enhancing the overall basicity of the molecule.

87. **(D):** The Gatterman-Koch reaction is used to step up the number of carbons in the chain.

- **Gatterman-Koch Reaction:** This reaction involves the formylation of benzene or its derivatives using carbon monoxide (CO) and hydrogen chloride (HCl) in the presence of a Lewis acid catalyst like $AlCl_3$. The reaction effectively adds a formyl group (–CHO) to the aromatic ring.
- **Mechanism and Result:**
  1. **Activation:** The aromatic ring (like benzene) is activated by the Lewis acid, making it more receptive to electrophilic attack.
  2. **Formation of Formyl Chloride:** CO and HCl react in the presence of the Lewis acid to form a complex that acts as a formylating agent.
  3. **Electrophilic Attack:** The formylating agent attacks the activated benzene ring, adding a single carbon atom (from the formyl group) to the ring.
- **Impact on Carbon Chain:** This reaction increases the complexity of the aromatic compound by introducing an additional carbon atom into the structure, expanding the carbon chain attached to the ring.

This method is distinct from other listed reactions, like the Hofmann-Bromamide, Hydroboration-Oxidation, and Stephen reactions, which do not typically increase the carbon count in the core structure they modify.

88. **(C):** The reaction of acetyl chloride (CH_3COCl) with hydrogen (H_2) over a Pd-$BaSO_4$ catalyst results in the formation of acetaldehyde (CH_3CHO).

- **Reaction Mechanism:**
  1. **Hydrogenation:** The hydrogen gas is activated by the Pd-BaSO4 catalyst, allowing it to interact with the acetyl chloride.

2. **Reductive Dechlorination:** The catalytic process facilitates the replacement of the chlorine atom in the acetyl chloride with a hydrogen atom.
3. **Formation of Acetaldehyde:** The net result is the formation of acetaldehyde, CH_3CHO, where the carbonyl group (C=O) remains intact but the chloride is replaced by hydrogen.

- **Role of Pd-$BaSO_4$ Catalyst:** The catalyst is specifically effective for hydrogenation reactions, promoting the reduction of functional groups by hydrogen. Here, it assists in the selective reduction of the acyl chloride to an aldehyde rather than further reduction to an alcohol or complete hydrolysis.

This specific transformation leverages the catalyst's ability to facilitate hydrogen addition while preserving the carbonyl group, which is characteristic of the conversion of acyl chlorides to aldehydes under reducing conditions.

89. (B): The reaction of benzaldehyde with semicarbazide hydrochloride is an example of a nucleophilic addition reaction.

- **Reaction Process:**
  1. **Nucleophilic Addition:** Semicarbazide acts as a nucleophile, where the nitrogen atom donates a pair of electrons to form a bond with the electrophilic carbonyl carbon of benzaldehyde.
  2. **Formation of Semicarbazone:** The initial addition of the nucleophile to the carbonyl group results in the formation of an intermediate that subsequently undergoes dehydration (loss of water) to form a stable semicarbazone derivative.
- **Key Features:**
  - ❑ The carbonyl group's carbon in benzaldehyde is electrophilic due to the oxygen atom's strong electronegativity, which pulls electron density away from the carbon, making it susceptible to nucleophilic attack.
  - ❑ Semicarbazide hydrochloride provides the nucleophile, which attacks the carbon, adding across the carbon-oxygen double bond.

This reaction is characteristic of aldehydes where the carbonyl carbon is the site for nucleophilic attack, leading to the addition of a nucleophile followed by the elimination of a small molecule such as water, although the main mechanism remains nucleophilic addition.

90. (A): The final product 'B' in the given reaction sequence is option A.

- **Reaction Steps:**
  1. **Grignard Formation:** The first step involves the reaction of ethylmagnesium bromide (EtMgBr) with ether as a solvent, which is a typical setup for forming a Grignard reagent.
  2. **Nucleophilic Attack:** The Grignard reagent then acts as a strong nucleophile. It attacks the electrophilic carbonyl carbon of the ester (CH_3-C-OCH_2CH_3).
  3. **Intermediate Formation:** Initially, this attack converts the ester into a ketone as the Grignard reagent adds to the carbonyl carbon, breaking the C-O bond in the ester and forming an alkoxide.
  4. **Second Addition and Hydrolysis:** Typically, Grignard reagents react with esters to form a tertiary alcohol upon hydrolysis. The Grignard adds twice because the intermediate ketone

is also reactive. After the completion of the reaction and subsequent acidic workup, a tertiary alcohol is formed.

- **Structural Analysis:** Option A correctly shows the structure of the tertiary alcohol resulting from the double addition of the ethyl group to the original carbonyl carbon, forming CH_3-C(OH)$(CH_2CH_3)_2$ after hydrolysis.

This reaction exemplifies the typical behavior of Grignard reagents with esters, leading to the formation of tertiary alcohols through the addition to the ester's carbonyl group followed by ketone intermediate reduction.

91. (A): Assertion (A) that aromatic aldehydes do not respond to Fehling's reagent test is correct.

Reason (R) that aromatic aldehydes are not easily oxidized is also correct and is the correct explanation of (A).

- **Fehling's Reagent Test:** This test is used to detect the presence of aldehyde groups in aliphatic compounds, which readily undergo oxidation. Aromatic aldehydes, like benzaldehyde, typically do not respond to Fehling's test because they are more resistant to oxidation under these conditions.
- **Oxidation Resistance:** Aromatic aldehydes have a conjugated system that stabilizes the aldehyde group, making it less reactive toward oxidation.

92. (B): The number of ether isomers possible for a compound with molecular formula $C_4H_{10}O$ is 3.

- **Ether Isomers:** Ethers with the formula $C_4H_{10}O$ can be either symmetrical or asymmetrical. The possible isomers include:
  1. Methoxypropane (CH_3-O-$CH_2CH_2CH_3$)
  2. Ethoxyethane (CH_3CH_2-O-CH_2CH_3)
  3. Diisopropyl ether ($CH^3CH(CH_3)$-O-$CH(CH_3)CH_3$)
- These isomers cover different arrangements of carbon chains around the oxygen atom, accounting for various branching possibilities within the four-carbon limit.

93. (C): The number of isomers of $C_4H_{11}N$ that will give a positive carbylamine test is 4.

- **Carbylamine Test:** This test is specific for primary amines, which react with chloroform and an alkali to form an isocyanide, which is identified by its very unpleasant smell.
- **Isomers of $C_4H_{11}N$:** The primary amine isomers that can be formed from $C_4H_{11}N$ and will test positive are:
  1. Butylamine ($CH_3CH_2CH_2CH_2NH_2$)
  2. Sec-butylamine ($CH_3CH_2CH(NH_2)CH_3$)
  3. Isobutylamine ($CH_3CH(CH_3)CH_2NH_2$)
  4. Tert-butylamine ($C(CH_3)_3NH_2$)

Each of these explanations aligns with the underlying chemical principles dictating the behavior or structure of the compounds in question.

94. (D): Methanamine is the reactant 'A' that when reacted with benzene sulfonyl chloride (SO_2Cl) leads to the formation of N-alkyl benzene sulphonamide.

- **Reaction Analysis:** Benzene sulfonyl chloride reacts with primary and secondary amines to form sulfonamides. Methanamine, being a primary amine (CH_3NH_2), reacts readily with benzene sulfonyl chloride.
- **Mechanism:**
  1. **Nucleophilic Attack:** The nitrogen atom in methanamine, which is a good nucleophile, attacks the sulfur atom of the benzene sulfonyl chloride.
  2. **Formation of Sulfonamide:** This attack leads to the formation of a bond between the nitrogen of

methanamine and the sulfur of the sulfonyl group, simultaneously displacing the chloride ion.

3. **Product Formation:** The final product is N-methyl benzene sulphonamide, where the methyl group (from methanamine) is the N-alkyl part.

The choice of methanamine in this reaction is critical because its small size and primary amine functionality make it very reactive towards sulfonyl chlorides, effectively forming the N-alkyl benzene sulphonamide structure shown. This reaction does not work as effectively with tertiary amines, which lack the hydrogen necessary to form the N-H bond in the sulfonamide linkage.

95. (A): The amine that can be prepared by Gabriel phthalimide synthesis is option (A).

- **Gabriel Phthalimide Synthesis:** This synthetic method is used for preparing primary amines. It involves the reaction of phthalimide with a base to form phthalimide anion, which then undergoes nucleophilic substitution with an alkyl halide followed by hydrolysis to release the primary amine.
- **Suitability of Option A:**
  - ❑ **Structure:** The amine in option A is a primary amine (NH_2 attached to a carbon on a benzene ring, where the carbon is also attached to an additional methyl group (CH_3)).
  - ❑ **Process:** In the Gabriel synthesis, the phthalimide potassium salt would react with an appropriate alkyl halide (in this case, possibly a benzyl chloride type substrate), leading to a substitution that places the amino group on the benzyl carbon, followed by cleavage of the phthalimide to release the primary amine.
- **Why Other Options Are Not Suitable:**
  - ❑ **B:** While this is also a primary amine, the direct attachment to the benzene ring would require a different synthesis approach, not typically achievable via Gabriel synthesis without breaking aromatic stability.
  - ❑ **C and D:** Both involve nitrogen atoms bonded to more than one alkyl group, categorizing them as secondary or tertiary amines, which are not obtainable through Gabriel synthesis as it specifically yields primary amines.

Option A represents a straightforward target for Gabriel synthesis due to the simplicity and accessibility of modifying the primary amine group without additional substitution that would interfere with the reaction conditions or the mechanism.

96. (C): Maltose has a linkage between C_1 of α-Glucose and C_4 of α-Glucose.

- **Maltose Structure:** Maltose is a disaccharide composed of two glucose molecules. It features a glycosidic bond between the anomeric carbon (C_1) of the first α-glucose unit and the C_4 hydroxyl group of the second α-glucose unit.
- **Type of Bond:** This linkage is known as an $\alpha(1 \rightarrow 4)$ glycosidic bond.

97. (C): Cellulose is a constituent of the cell wall of plant cells.

- **Cell Wall Composition:** The primary component of plant cell walls is cellulose, which is a polysaccharide made up of glucose units linked by $\beta(1 \rightarrow 4)$ glycosidic bonds.
- **Function of Cellulose:** It provides structural support and rigidity to plant cells.

98. (C): Glycine does not have any chiral centres.

Chirality in Amino Acids: Most amino acids have a chiral center at the alpha carbon, where the amino group, carboxyl group, hydrogen, and a distinct side chain (R group) are attached. Glycine's R group is a hydrogen, making it symmetric and thus non-chiral.

Lysine is an α-amino acid that is a precursor to many proteins. It contains an α-amino group (which is in the protonated $-NH^{+3}$ form when dissolved in water), an α carboxylic acid group (which is in the deprotonated $-COO-$ form when dissolved in water), and a side chain lysyl $((CH_2)_4NH_2)$, classifying it as a basic, charged (at physiological pH), aliphatic amino acid. It is encoded by the codons AAA and AAG. Like almost all other amino acids, the α-carbon is chiral and lysine may refer to either enantiomer or a racemic mixture of both.

Cysteine is a non-essential amino acid important for making protein, and for other metabolic functions. It's found in beta-keratin. This is the main protein in nails, skin, and hair. Cysteine is important for making collagen.

Tyrosine is one of the 20 standard amino acids that are used by cells to synthesize proteins. It is a non-essential amino acid with a polar side group. The word "tyrosine" is from the Greek tyrós, meaning cheese, as it was first discovered in 1846 by German chemist Justus von Liebig in the protein casein from cheese. It is called tyrosyl when referred to as a functional group or side chain.

99. (A): Aspartic acid is not an essential amino acid.

Essential Amino acids: Those amino acids that are not synthesized by the body but are extremely essential are called essential amino acids. Therefore these amino acids have to be provided from diet. They are needed for proper growth and maintenance of the human body. Out of 20 known amino acids 10 are regarded as essential amino acids. These include leucine, isoleucine, lysine, methionine, phenylalanine, threonine, tryptophan and valine.

Semi essential amino acids: Two amino acids such as arginine and histidine are synthesized in adults but not by growing children, hence they are considered as semi-essential amino acids.

Non-essential amino acids: The amino acids that are synthesized by the body are called nonessential amino acids. Glycine, alanine, serine, cysteine, aspartic, asparagine, glutamate, glutamine, tyrosine and proline are synthesized within the body to meet the biological needs.

100. (D): RNA does not contain thymine.

Nucleotide Composition in RNA: RNA contains adenine, guanine, cytosine, and uracil. Thymine is found in DNA, not RNA, where it is replaced by uracil.

Previous Paper (Solved)

KVS—PGT Teacher Recruitment Exam, 2018*

Subject : Chemistry

1. Which statement about isotopes of hydrogen is **incorrect**?

A. Enthalpy of vaporization of deuterium is greater than that of hydrogen.

B. Deuterium is less reactive than hydrogen.

C. Denisty of tritium amongst all isotopes of hydrogen is maximum.

D. Deuterium is β particle emitter.

2. Glycerol can be separated from 'spent-lye in soap Industry' by using ____ technique.

A. Distillation under reduced pressure

B. Steam distillation

C. Differential extraction

D. Fractional distillation

3. Which one is **wrongly** named as per I.U.P.A.C nomenclature?

A. $[Pt(NH_3)_2Cl(NO_2)]$ – Diammine chlorido nitrito-N-platinum (II)

B. $K[Cr(C_2O_4)_3]$ – Potassium trioxalato chromium (III)

C. $[CoCl_2(en)_2]Cl$ – Dichloridobis (ethane-1, 2-diamine cobalt (III) chloride

D. $Hg[Co(SCN)_4]$ – Mercury (I) tetrathiocyanate-S-cobaltate (III)

4. Given the following half cell reactions and the corresponding reduction potentials:

(*a*) $A^+ + e^- \rightarrow A$ $E_0 = -0.24$ V

(*b*) $B^- + e^- \rightarrow B^{2-}$ $E_0 = 1.25$ V

(*c*) $C + 2e^- \rightarrow C^{2-}$ $E_0 = -1.25$ V

(*d*) $D + 2e^- \rightarrow D^{2-}$ $E_0 = 0.68$ V

(*e*) $E + 4e^- \rightarrow E^{4-}$ $E_0 = 0.38$ V

The combination of two half-cells that results in a cell with the largest potential is:

A. (*a*) and (*c*) B. (*b*) and (*c*)

C. (*b*) and (*d*) D. (*c*) and (*d*)

5. Phosphorus with outer electronic configuration $3s^2\ 3p^3$ does **not** form PH_5 because:

A. +5 oxidation state of phosphorus is less stable than +3 oxidation state

B. High $\Delta_a H$ value of hydrogen molecule and $\Delta_{eg} H$ of hydrogen do not favour the highest oxidation state of P and consequently PH_5

C. Size of phosphorus is relatively bigger than hydrogen

D. '*d*' orbital of phosphrous is more diffused

6. Consider the following 3-D representation of a molecule:

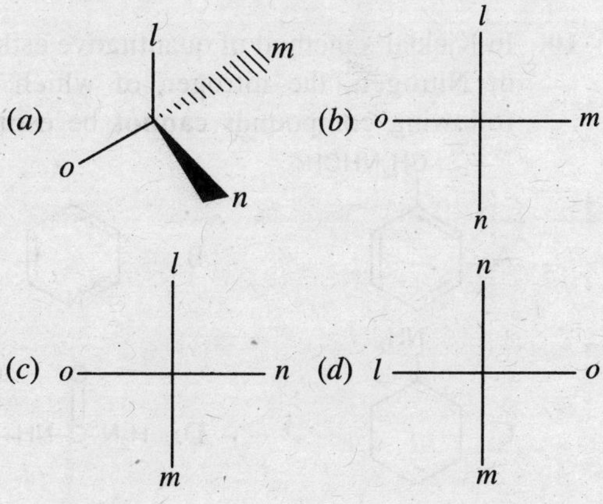

Which of the above structures are identical?

A. (*a*), (*c*) and (*d*)

B. (*a*) and (*b*) ; (*c*) and (*d*) two similar couple

C. (*a*) and (*c*) ; (*b*) and (*d*) two similar couple

D. (*a*) and (*d*) ; (*b*) and (*c*) two similar couple

* *Exam held on 23 Dec. 2018*

7. The General formula for a 3° amine is:
A. $C_nH_{2n+1}N$
B. $C_nH_{2n+2}N$
C. $C_nH_{2n+3}N$
D. $C_nH_{2n}N$

8. The **incorrect** statement among the following is:
A. Physical adsorption is due to van der Waals forces.
B. Physical adsorption decreases at high temperature and low pressure.
C. Physical adsorption is reversible.
D. Adsorption energy for chemical adsorption is generally less than that for physical adsorption.

9. Which of the following polymers is biodegradeable?

A. 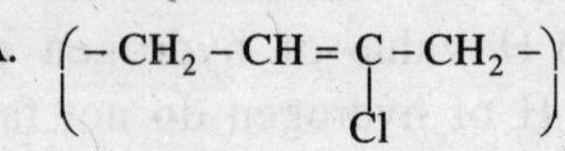

B. 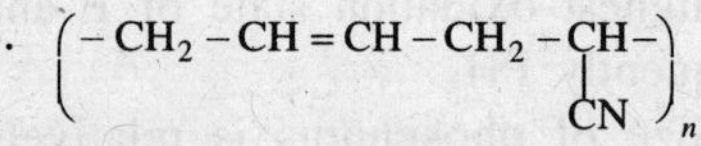

C. 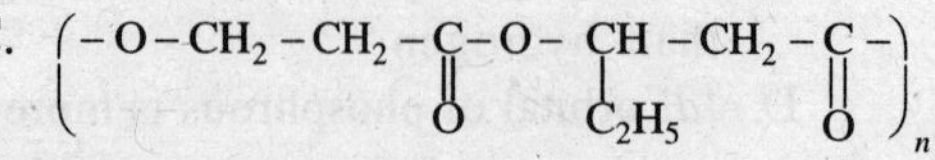

D. 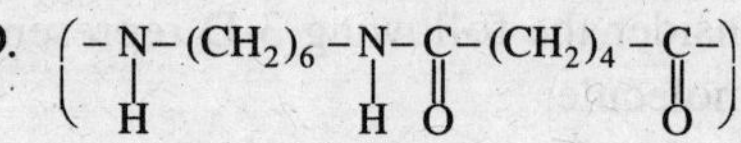

10. In Kjeldal's method of quantitative estimation of Nitrogen, the nitrogen of which of the following compounds **cannot** be estimated?

A. 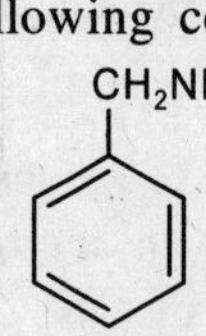

B. 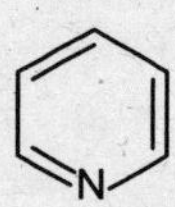

C. 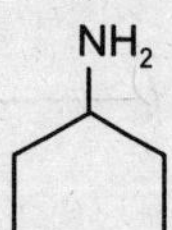

D. 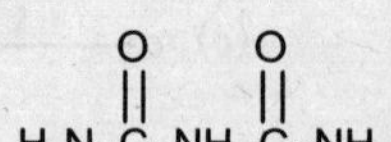

11. Which one has highest value of first ionization enthalpy?
A. N
B. O
C. S
D. P

12. The decomposition of N_2O into N_2 and O in the presence of gaseous argon follows second order kinetics, with

$k = (5.0 \times 10^{11}\ \text{L-mol}^{-1}\ s^{-1})e^{-30000/T}$

Given R = 8.3 $JK^{-1}\ mol^{-1}$, the energy of activation of this reaction is:
A. 249 kJ/mol
B. 300 kJ/mol
C. 500 kJ/mo
D. 830 kJ/mol

13. For the reaction at 298 K.

$2A + B \rightarrow C$

$\Delta H = 400$ kJ and $\Delta S = 0.200$ kJ/K

Assuming ΔH and ΔS to be constant over the temperature range, the temperature at which the reaction will become spontaneous is:
A. 1000 K
B. 2000 K
C. 3000 K
D. 2000 °C

14. The ionization enthalpy of hydrogen atom in its ground state is 13.6 eV. The second ionization enthalpy of helium is closet to:
A. 6.8 eV
B. 13.6 eV
C. 27.2 eV
D. 54.4 eV

15. The temperature at which N_2 molecules have the same average speed as He atoms at 330 K is:
A. 480 K
B. 330 K
C. 1155 K
D. 2310 K

16. Which of the following is **not** a Pyrimidine base?
A. Adenine
B. Cytosine
C. Thymine
D. Uracil

17. Which of the following amines can be synthesised by 'Gabriel Phthalimide Synthesis'?

A. 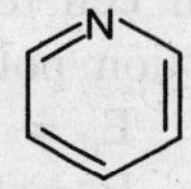

B. 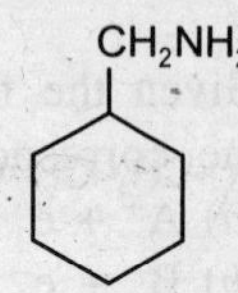

C. 

D. 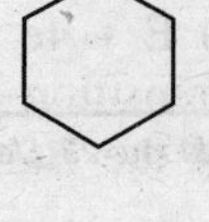

18. In which case on heating, N_2(g) will not be released?

A. NH_4NO_2 B. $(NH_4)_2Cr_2O_7$
C. $Ba(N_3)_2$ D. NH_4NO_3

19. To get *n*-type semiconductor, the impurity to be added to Si should have the following number of valence electrons:

A. 1 B. 2
C. 3 D. 5

20. Which of the following species is **not** an electrophile?

A. $H_3O^{\oplus}$ B. $\overset{\oplus}{N}O_2$
C. $Cl^{\oplus}$ D. SO_3

21. Electronic configurations of four elements (*a*), (*b*), (*c*) and (*d*) are given below:

(*a*) $1s^2\ 2s^2\ 2p^6$ (*b* $1s^2\ 2s^2\ 2p^4$
(*c*) $1s^2\ 2s^2\ 2p^6\ 3s^1$ (*d*) $1s^2\ 2s^2\ 2p^5$

Which of the following is the **correct** order of increasing tendency to gain electron?

A. $(a) < (c) < (b) < (d)$
B. $(a) < (b) < (c) < (d)$
C. $(d) < (b) < (c) < (a)$
D. $(d) < (a) < (b) < (c)$

22. In which of the following polymers, ethylene glycol is one of the monomer units?

A. 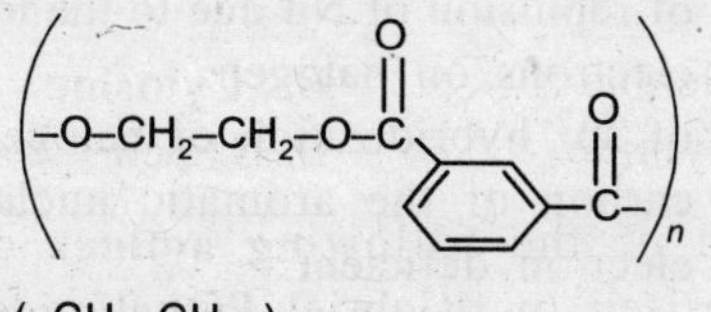

B. $(-CH_2-CH_2-)_n$

C. 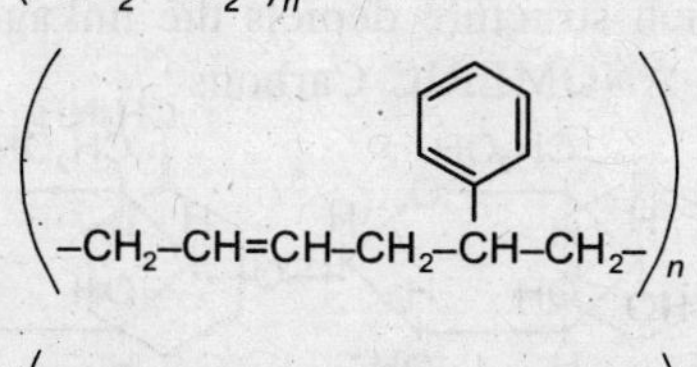

D. 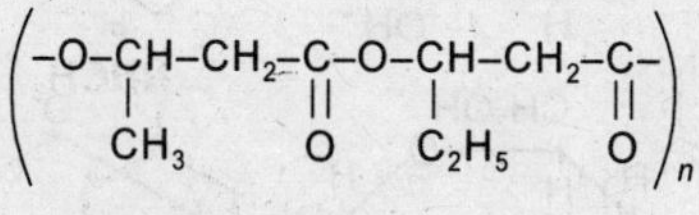

23. The transition that corresponds to the third line of the Balmer series is:

A. 4 → 1 B. 5 → 2
C. 6 → 3 D. 4 → 2

24. Which of the following polymers can be formed using the monomer?

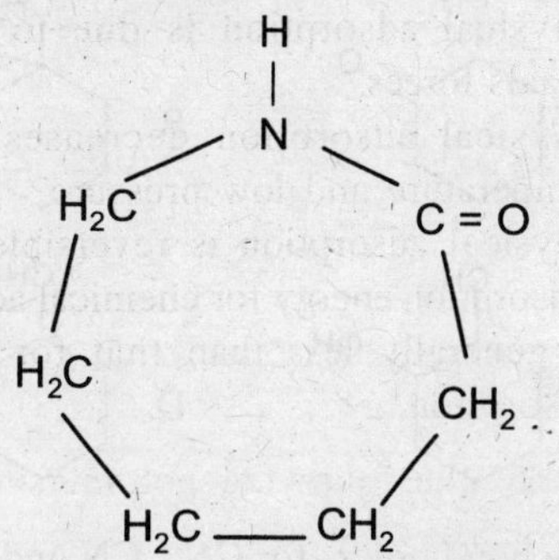

A. Nylon-6, 6 B. Novolac
C. Melamine polymer D. Nylon-6

25. Compound A when heated gave two solids B and C and a gas. Compound A was generated when B was treated with H_2O_2. When C is fused with KOH in the presence of O_2, solid B is formed. Compound A and solid C are formed when B is treated with acid. Identify A, B and C.

A. MnO_2, $KMnO_4$, K_2MnO_4
B. $KMnO_4$, K_2MnO_4, MnO_2
C. $KMnO_4$, MnO_2, K_2MnO_4
D. $KMnO_4$, Mn_2O_3, K_2MnO_4

26. The order of screening effect of electrons of *s*, *p*, *d* and *f* orbitals of a given shell of an atom on its outer shell electrons is:

A. $s > p > d > f$ B. $f > d > p > s$
C. $p < d < s > f$ D. $f > p > s > d$

27. The co-ordination number of copper in $CuSO_4.5H_2O$ is:

A. 5 B. 4
C. 3 D. 2

28. Consider the following sequence of reactions

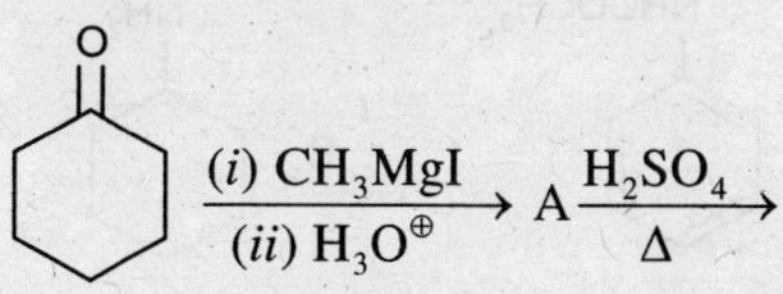

$$B \xrightarrow[(ii)\ H_2O_2/\overset{\ominus}{O}H]{(i)\ BH_3/THF} C \xrightarrow{CrO_3/Py} D$$

The product 'D' is:

A. 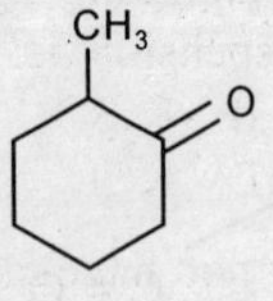

B. 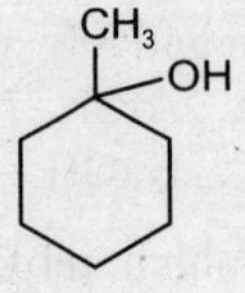

C. 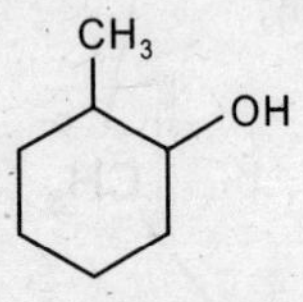

D. 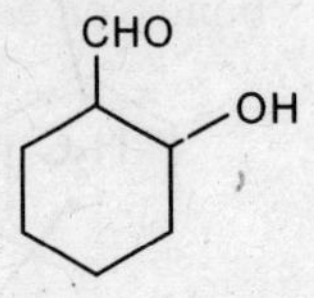

29. The bond orders for CN^-, CN and CN^+ follow the order:

A. $CN^+ > CN > CN^-$ B. $CN^- > CN > CN^+$
C. $CN > CN^+ > CN^-$ D. $CN^+ > CN^- > CN$

30. A sample of concentrated sulphuric acid is 95% H_2SO_4 by weight and its density is 1.80 g/ml. The normality of H_2SO_4 in the sample is:

A. 17.5 B. 18.0
C. 34.9 D. 35.9

31. Which one has the highest melting point?

A. PH_3 B. NH_3
C. AsH_3 D. SbH_3

32. The drug which inhibits the growth or destroys microorganisms is:

A. Salvarsan B. Iproniazid
C. Valium D. Morphine

33. Which of the following has different hybridization about the central atom?

A. BCl_3 B. ClO_3
C. NH_3 D. PCl_3

34. Which of the given amines is the weakest base?

A. 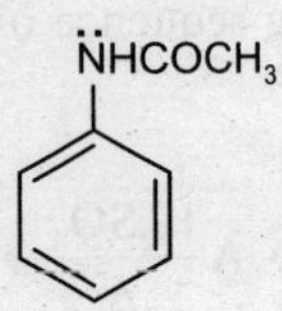

B. 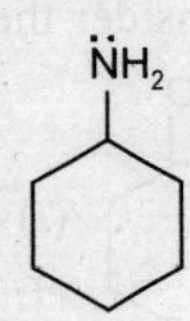

C. 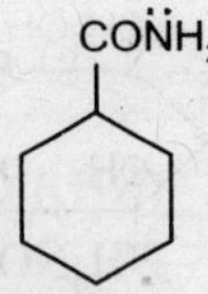

D. 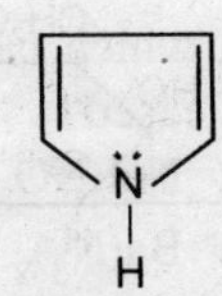

35. Consider the following reaction:

$$CH_3CH = CH - CH_2OH \xrightarrow{\text{Reagent 'R'}} CH_3CH = CH - CHO$$

To carry out the above conversion, the most suitable reagent, in terms of yield obtained, would be:

A. CrO_3
B. Acidic $KMnO_4$
C. Cold alkaline $KMnO_4$
D. Pyridinium Chloro Chromate

36. The dipole moment of HBr is 2.60×10^{-30} Cm, and the interatomic spacing is 140 pm. The per cent ionic character of HBr is:

(Given : $e = 1.60 \times 10^{-19}$ C)

A. 10% B. 11.6%
C. 25% D. 16.2%

37. Identify the **incorrect** reason for the given statement.

Aryl halides are less reactive towards nucleophilic substitution reactions because:

A. of the partial double bond character between halogen and the aromatic nucleus.
B. of repulsion of Nu due to the lone pair of electrons on halogen.
C. of sp^2 hybridization of halogen atom
D. carbon of the aromatic nucleus is not electron deficient.

38. Which structure depicts the linkage between two ANOMERIC Carbons?

A. 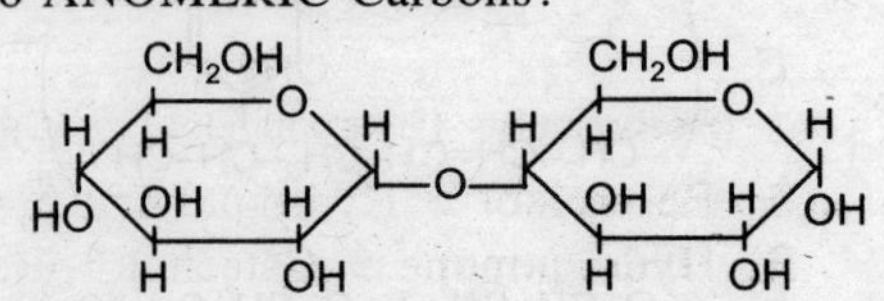

B. 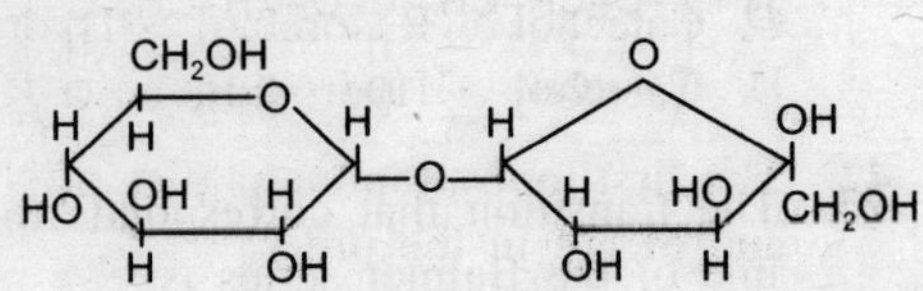

C. 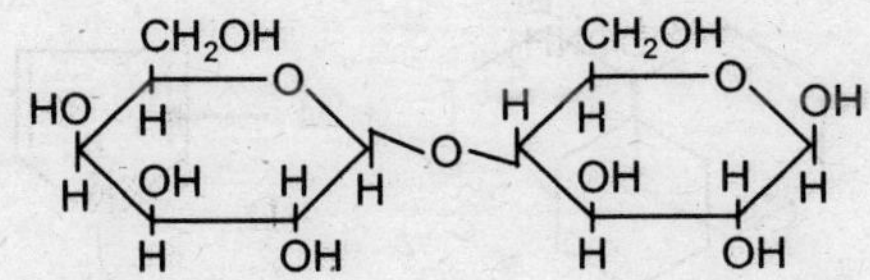

D. 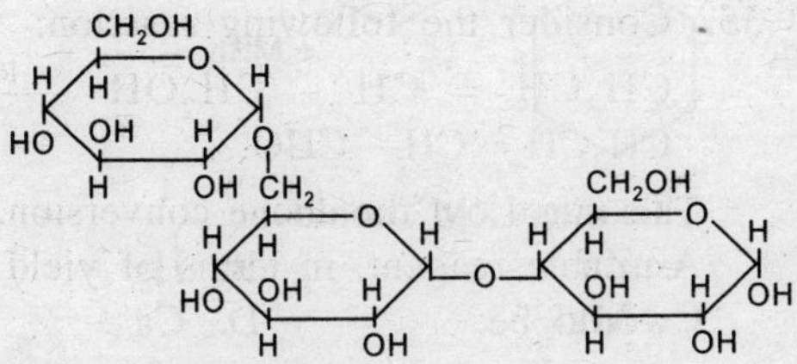

39. State of freezing **does not** involve:
A. Loss of kinetic energy
B. Increased force of attraction
C. Solidification of liquid
D. Melting of solid

40. Use the data below to calculate ΔH for the reaction:

$N_2O_4 + 3CO \rightarrow N_2O + 3CO_2$

Compound	**ΔH_f°, kJ/mol**
CO (g)	−110
CO_2 (g)	−393
N_2O (g)	81
N_2O_4 (g)	9.7

A. −1438 kJ   B. 778 kJ
C. −212 kJ   D. −778 kJ

41. The correct order of decreasing acidity of the phenols is:

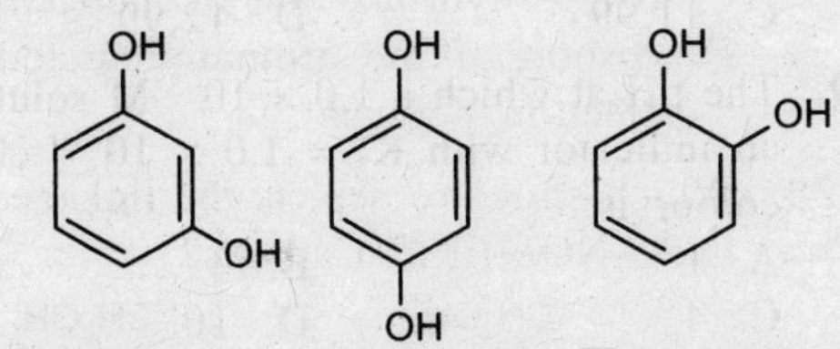

(Resorcinol) (Hydroquinone) (Catechol)

A. Resorcinol > Hydroquinone > Catechol
B. Hydroquinone > Catechol > Resorcinol
C. Catechol > Resorcinol > Hydroquinone
D. Catechol > Hydroquinone > Resorcinol

42. The first ionisation enthalpies of Na, Mg, Al and Si are in the order:
A. Na < Mg > Al < Si
B. Na > Mg > Al > Si
C. Na < Mg < Al < Si
D. Na > Mg > Al < Si

43. The most efficient precipitating agent for a negatively charged suspension is:
A. $AlCl_3$ B. K_2SO_4
C. NaOH + HCl   D. KCl

44. Which molecule does not have the C – C bonds of equal length?

A. 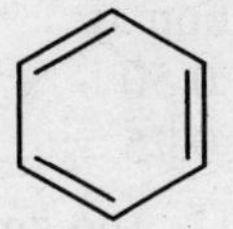 B. 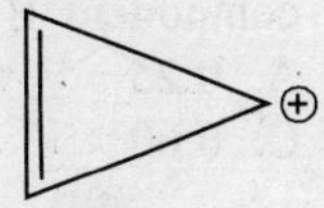

C. 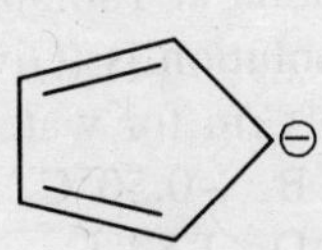 D. 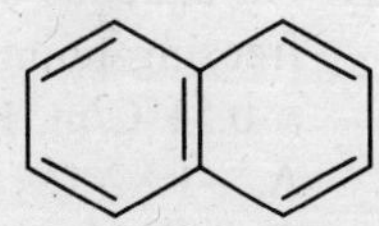

45. Which of the following will shift the equilibrium of the reaction

$$\frac{1}{2} N_2\,(g) + O_2\,(g) \rightleftharpoons NO_2\,(g) + \text{heat}$$

to the right?
A. Decrease in temperature
B. Increase in volume
C. Decrease in O_2 concentration
D. Addition of catalyst

46. The enthalpy of fusion per gram and the corresponding molecular weights are given for several substances:

	Enthalpy of fusion J/g	**Mol. wt. g/mol**
(*a*)	320	18
(*b*)	180	20
(*c*)	360	30
(*d*)	180	60
(*e*)	180	30

The two substances having the same molar enthalpies of fusion are:
A. (*b*) and (*d*)   B. (*b*) and (*e*)
C. (*c*) and (*d*)   D. (*d*) and (*e*)

47. A comound with molecular formula $Co(NH_3)_5Cl_3$ when treated with $AgNO_3$ (aq) yields 2 moles of AgCl(s) per mole of the complex compound. The number of Cl^- ions in the co-ordination sphere is equal to:

A. 1 B. 2
C. 3 D. Zero

48. The vapour pressure of pure liquid solvent A is 0.80 atm. When a non-volatile substance B is added to the solvent, its vapour pressure drops to 0.60 atm. The mole fraction of component B in this solution is:

A. 0.25 B. 0.50
C. 0.60 D. 0.75

49. An aqueous solution boils at 100.50°C. The freezing point of this solution is (Given : K_b = 0.51°C/m, K_f = 1.86°C/m for water):

A. –1.82°C B. –0.50°C
C. 0.50°C D. 1.82°C

50. Which ore **cannot** be concentrated by froth floatation method?

A. Copper Pyrites B. Zinc Blende
C. Cinnabar D. Calamine

51. Which of the following do not cause acid rain?

A. $SO_2(g)$ B. $NO_2(g)$
C. $CH_4(g)$ D. $SO_3(g)$

52. Which one will only act as an oxidising agent?

A. N_2O_5 B. NO_2
C. HNO_2 D. NH_3

53. What is a **wrong** statement about the troposphere?

A. It is a dusty zone containing air, much water vapour and clouds
B. It is lowest region of atmosphere
C. It is a region in which human beings along with other organisms live
D. It has a lot of ozone that cuts off ultraviolet light from the sun to a great extent

54. Vicinal di halides react with metal 'M' to yield alkene

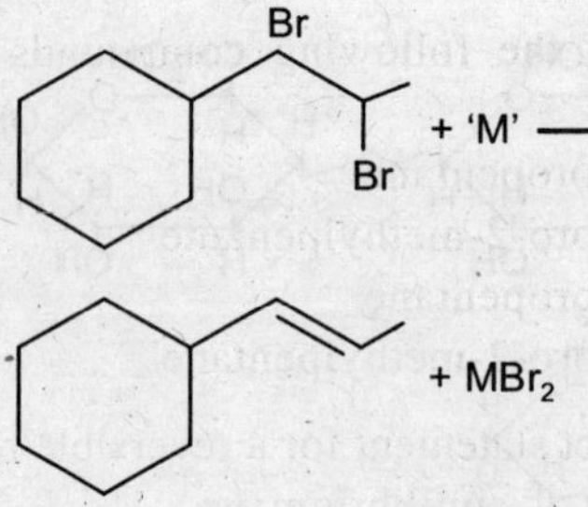

The metal 'M' could be:

A. Zn B. Hg
C. Mg D. Ca

55. Amongst the following the essential amino acid is:

A. Tyrosine B. Lysine
C. Alanine D. Serine

56. Which of the 3 d series transition metal exhibits the largest number of oxidation states?

A. Sc B. Fe
C. Cr D. Mn

57. Which statement is **not** true about sucrose?

A. It is a disaccharide
B. It is a reducing sugar
C. The product of hydrolysis is also known as invert sugar
D. It is a dextrorotatory sugar

58. Carbon occurs in nature as a mixture of atoms of which 98.9% have a mass of 12.00 and the remaining have a mass of 13.00. The atomic weight of carbon is:

A. 12.00 B. 12.01
C. 11.99 D. 12.99

59. The pH at which a 1.0×10^{-3} M solution of an indicator with $K_b = 1.0 \times 10^{-10}$ changes colour is:

A. 1 B. 3
C. 4 D. 10

60. A solid has a structure in which W atoms are located at the cube corners of the unit cell, 0 atoms are located at the cube edge centres, and Na atoms at the cube centres. The formula for this compounds is:

A. Na WO_2 B. Na WO_3
C. Na W_2O D. Na_2 WO

61. Which of the following compounds is **not** chiral?
A. 1-Chloropentane
B. 1-Chloro-2-methylpentane
C. 2-Chloropentane
D. 3-Chloro-2-methylpentane

62. The correct statement for a reversible reaction in a state of equilibrium is:
A. $\Delta G = -2.303\ RT \log K$
B. $\Delta G = 2.303\ RT \log K$
C. $\Delta G^\circ = -2.303\ RT \log K$
D. $\Delta G^\circ = 2.303\ RT \log K$

63. A mixture containing 100 g H_2 and 100 g O_2 is ignited so that water is formed according to the reaction

$$2H_2 + O_2 \rightarrow 2H_2O$$

The amount of water formed is:
A. 100 g B. 113 g
C. 200 g D. 900 g

64. The number of unshared pair of valence electrons in the Lewis electron dot structure of CO is:
A. 0 B. 1
C. 2 D. 3

65. In paper chromatography, the stationary phase is:
A. The glass jar where the paper is hung
B. The cellulose sheet
C. Water trapped in the chromatographic paper
D. Air inside the closed gas jar

66. Which oxide is most acidic?
A. N_2O B. NO
C. N_2O_3 D. NO_2

67. The set of quantum numbers (n, l, m_l, m_s) what represents an impossible arrangement is:
A. $3, 2, -2, \frac{1}{2}$ B. $4, 0, 0, \frac{1}{2}$
C. $3, 2, -3, \frac{1}{2}$ D. $5, 3, 0, -\frac{1}{2}$

68. The combination of solutes that would result in the formation of a buffer solution is:
A. $CH_3COONa + CH_3COOH$
B. HCl + NaCl
C. $HCl + CH_3COOH$
D. NaOH + HCl

69. The enzyme used in conversion of glucose to Ethanol is:
A. Invertase B. Zymase
C. Amylase D. Trypsin

70. A compound 'X' is a potent vasodilator. It is also responsible for the nasal congestion associated with common cold and allergic responses to pollen. 'X' could be:
A. Equanil
B. Codeine
C. Terfenadine
D. Histamine

71. Complexation followed by reduction with Zn is used for the extraction of:
A. Copper
B. Aluminium
C. Silver
D. Iron

72. In the given reaction

$$CH_3COCH_2COOH \xrightarrow{Zn(Hg)\,/\,HCl} \text{'P'}$$

The product 'P' is:
A. $CH_3CH_2CH_2COOH$
B. $CH_3CH_2CH_2CH_2OH$
C. $CH_3CH_2CH_2CH_3$
D. $CH_3CH_2CH_2CHO$

73. The following reaction wave studied at 25°C
$A + B \rightarrow C$
The following sets of data were observed

Initial Concentration (M) (A_0)	(B_0)	(C_0)	Δt/min	Final (C)
0.10	0.05	0.00	25	0.0033
0.10	0.10	0.00	15	0.0039
0.20	0.10	0.00	7.5	0.0077

The rate law is:

A. Rate = k[A] [B] [C]

B. Rate = $k[A]^2$ [B]

C. Rate = k[A] $[B]^2$

D. Rate = k[A] $[B]^3$

74. A current of 2.00 A passing for 5.0 hrs. through a molten tin salt (Sn = 118.7 u) deposits 22.2 g tin. The oxidation state of the tin in the salt is:

A. 1 B. 2

C. 3 D. 4

75. The true statement among the following for the van der Waals constants 'a' and 'b' of H_2O and O_2 is:

A. Both 'a' and 'b' are smaller for H_2O than for O_2.

B. 'a' is smaller but 'b' is larger for H_2O than for O_2.

C. 'a' is larger but 'b' is smaller for H_2O than for O_2.

D. Both 'a' and 'b' are larger for H_2O than for O_2.

76. The initial rate of the reaction

$$A + B \rightarrow C + D$$

is doubled if the initial concentration of A is doubled, but is quadrupled if the initial concentration of B is doubled.

This **cannot** be a:

A. Single-step reaction

B. Two-step reaction

C. Multi-step reaction

D. Complex reaction

77. Which of the following reagents is **not** suitable for the preparation of acid chlorides from a given organic acid?

A. PCl_5

B. PCl_3

C. $SOCl_2$

D. SO_2Cl_2

78. Which of the following Friedel Crafts alkylation reactions would **not** produce the given product in good yield?

A. 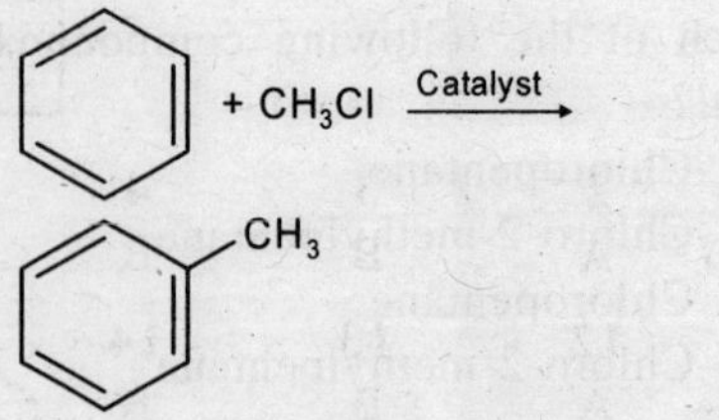

B. 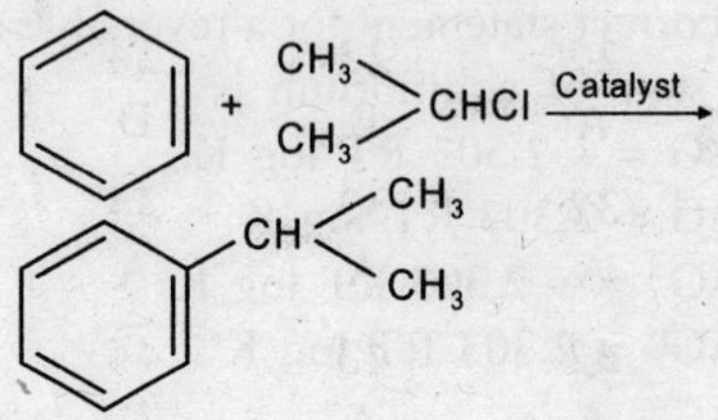

C. 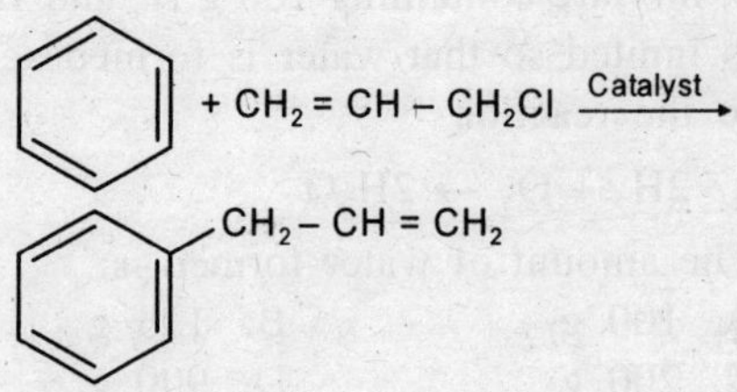

D. 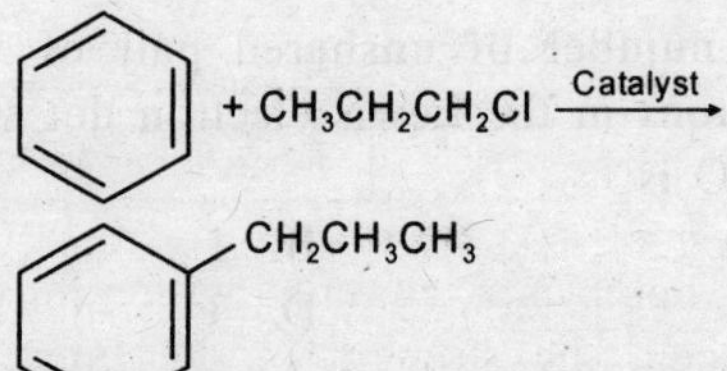

79. At a certain temperature, the value of the equilibrium constant, corresponding to the equation

$$N_2(g) + 2O_2(g) \rightleftharpoons 2\ NO_2(g)$$

is 100. The value of the equilibrium constant for the reaction

$$NO_2(g) \rightleftharpoons \frac{1}{2}N_2(g) + O_2(g) \text{ is:}$$

A. 0.010 B. 0.10

C. 0.020 D. 100

80. Which element **does not** show variable oxidation states?

A. Cr

B. Mn

C. V

D. Sc

ANSWERS

1	2	3	4	5	6	7	8	9	10
D	A	B	B	B	A	C	D	C	B
11	**12**	**13**	**14**	**15**	**16**	**17**	**18**	**19**	**20**
A	A	B	B	D	A	B	D	D	A
21	**22**	**23**	**24**	**25**	**26**	**27**	**28**	**29**	**30**
A	A	B	D	B	A	B	A	B	C
31	**32**	**33**	**34**	**35**	**36**	**37**	**38**	**39**	**40**
B	A	A	A	D	B	C	B	D	D
41	**42**	**43**	**44**	**45**	**46**	**47**	**48**	**49**	**50**
B	A	A	D	A	C	A	A	A	D
51	**52**	**53**	**54**	**55**	**56**	**57**	**58**	**59**	**60**
C	A	D	A	B	D	B	B	C	B
61	**62**	**63**	**64**	**65**	**66**	**67**	**68**	**69**	**70**
A	C	B	D	C	D	C	A	B	D
71	**72**	**73**	**74**	**75**	**76**	**77**	**78**	**79**	**80**
C	A	B	B	C	A	D	D	B	D

EXPLANATORY ANSWERS

1. Since deuterium contains more mass than hydrogen, the strength of the inter atomic forces increases, which makes the enthalpy of vapourisation and fusion greater than hydrogen/protium. Deuterium enters into all chemical reactions characteristic of ordinary hydrogen, forming equivalent compounds. It reacts more slowly than ordinary hydrogen, a criterion that distinguishes the two forms of hydrogen.

When a β particle emitter decays, one of its extra neutrons is converted to a proton, increasing its atomic number by 1 without changing its atomic mass. The breakdown is accompanied by the emission of a negatively charged particle of low mass, called the (beta) particle, and an uncharged particle of low mass, called a neutrino. For example, hydrogen consists of just one proton and one electron. Deuterium (2-H), a component of "heavy water," consists of a proton, an electron, and one neutron, and is a stable isotope. Tritium (3-H) is an unstable isotope of hydrogen, consisting of a proton, an electron, and two neutrons. When an atom of tritium decays, one of the neutrons is converted to a proton, one β-particle and one neutrino are released, and a helium isotope (3-He) remains. Tritium is called a "soft" β emitter, because its β particles have relatively low velocities. A hard β emitter such as 32-P (phosphorous) is more dangerous because its β particles carry more kinetic energy. Hence, correct answer is D.

2. Glycerol with high boiling point (290°C) can be separated from spent lye by distillation under reduced pressure. This process is used to purify liquids having very high boiling points. By this process, the liquid is made to boil at a lower temperature than its boiling point by lowering the pressure on its surface.

3. $K[Cr(C_2O_4)_3]$ is $K_3[Cr(C_2O_4)_3]$ = Potassium tri-oxalato Cromate (III). Hence, it is wrongly named as IUPAC nomenclature.

4. $$E^\circ_{Cell} = E^\circ_{Cathode} - E^\circ_{Anode}$$

$$\therefore \quad E = 1.25 - (-1.25)$$
$$= 1.25 \text{ V} + 1.25 \text{ V}$$

At cathode: $B^{\oplus} + e^- \rightarrow B^{2-}$
and at anode: $C^{2-} \rightarrow C + 2e^{\ominus}$

5. Although phosphorus exhibits +3 and +5 oxidation states. It cannot form PH_5. Besides some other considerations, high $\Delta_a H$ value of dihydrogen and $\Delta_{eg} H$ value of hydrogen do not favour to exhibit the highest oxidation state of P, and consequently the formation of PH_5.

6. A. 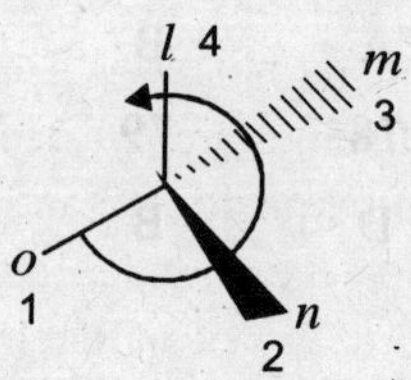

→ R

B. 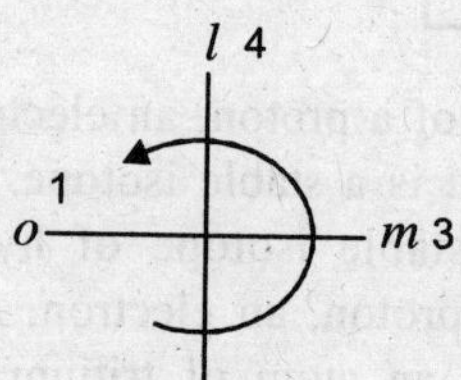

→ S

C. 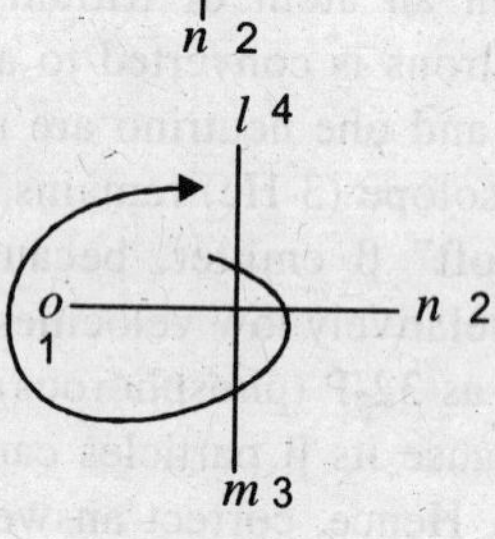

→ R

D. 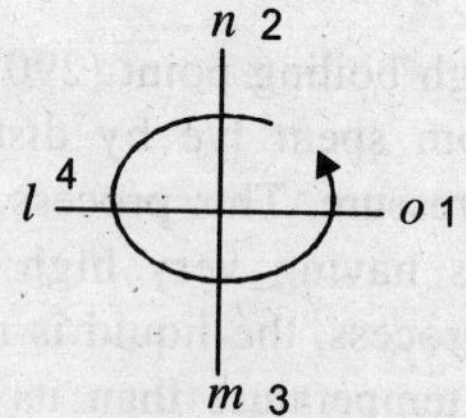

→ R

Hence, A, C and D structures are identical.

7. General formula of 3° amine is C_nH_{2n+3} N.
For example:

(*i*) $(CH_3)N$ or $CH_3 - N - CH_3$ (with CH_3 on N) or C_3H_9O

Trimethyl amine

(*ii*) $(CH_3 - CH_2)_3N$ or $C_6H_{15}N$

or $CH_3 - CH_2 - N - CH_2CH_3$ (with CH_3CH_2 on N)

Trimethylamine

8. Physical adsorption decreases with increase in temperature because less number of molecules get absorbed on the surface with increase in temperature. Adsorption energy for chemical adsorption is generally greater than that of physical adsorption. Physical adsorption is due to van der Waal's forces which are weak forces, hence this type of adsorption is reversible.

9. Poly β-hydroxybutyrate – co-β-hydroxy valerate (PHBV) : It is derived by combining 3-hydroxy butanoic acid and 3-hydroxy pentanoic acid, in which monomers are cross-linked by an ester linkage. It decomposes to form carbon dioxide and water. It is brittle in nature, and it can be used in the production of drugs and the manufacturing of bottles.

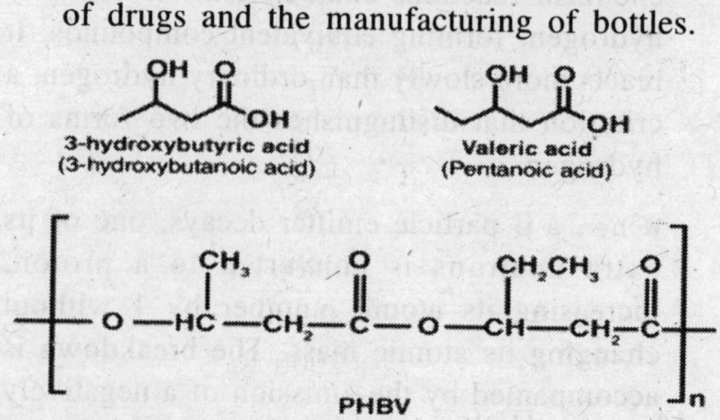

11. Ionization potential → remove the outermost electrons $e^{\ominus}$

First ionization enthalpy to remove first electron.

Size of an atoms, effective nuclear charge, stable electronic configuration etc.

$N \rightarrow 1s^2 2s^2 2p^3 \rightarrow$ symmetric – stable

$O \rightarrow 1s^2 2s^2 2p^4$

$P \rightarrow [Ne]\ 3s^2 3p^3$

$S \rightarrow [Ne]\ 3s^2 3p^4$

Due to stable electronic configuration.

Ionization enthalpy decreases due to increase in atomic size. Hence, N has ionization enthalpy.

$\therefore S < P < O < N$

Hence, N has highest value of first ionization enthalpy.

12. We have,

$$k = (5.0 \times 10^{11}\ \text{L mol}^{-1})e^{-30000/T} \quad ...(i)$$

Since, $$k = Ae^{-E_a/RT} \quad ...(ii)$$

So, we compare both equations

$$\frac{E_a}{RT} = \frac{30000}{T}$$

$$\Rightarrow \quad \frac{E_a}{R} = 30000$$

$$\therefore \quad E_a = 30000 \times R$$
$$= 30000 \times 8.3$$
$$= 249000 \text{ J/mol}$$
$$= 249 \text{ kJ/mol}$$

13. As, $$\Delta S = \frac{\Delta H}{T}$$

$$T = \frac{\Delta H}{\Delta S}$$

$$= \frac{400}{0.200}$$

$$= 2000 \text{ K.}$$

14. H-atom $\rightarrow 1s^1$

He-atom $\rightarrow 1s^2$

$\therefore \quad 1s^1 \rightarrow 13.6$ eV

$\therefore \quad 1s^2 \xrightarrow[-1e^-]{} 1s^1 \rightarrow 13.6$ eV

Hence, the ionisation enthalpy of helium atom is 13.6 eV.

15. Given, $v_{av}(\text{He}) = v_{av}(N_2)$

$$\Rightarrow \quad \sqrt{\frac{T_1}{M_1}} = \sqrt{\frac{T_2}{M_2}}$$

$$\therefore \quad T_2 = \frac{T_1 \times M_2}{M_1}$$

$$= \frac{330 \times 28}{4}$$

$$= 2310 \text{ K}$$

16. Pyrimidine is an aromatic heterocyclic organic compound, similar to pyridine. One of the three diazines (six-membered heterocyclics with two nitrogen atoms in the ring), it has the nitrogen atoms at positions 1 and 3 in the ring. The other diazines are pyrazine (nitrogen atoms at the 1 and 4 positions) and pyridazine (nitrogen atoms at the 1 and 2 positions). In nucleic acids, three types of nucleobases are pyrimidine derivatives: cytosine (C), thymine (T), and uracil (U).

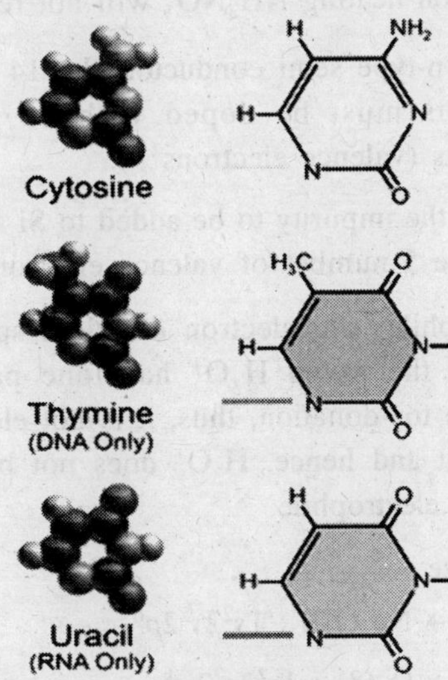

Pyrimidines

Hence, adenine (A) is not a pyrimidine base.

17. Benzylamine by Gabriel Phathalimide synthesis

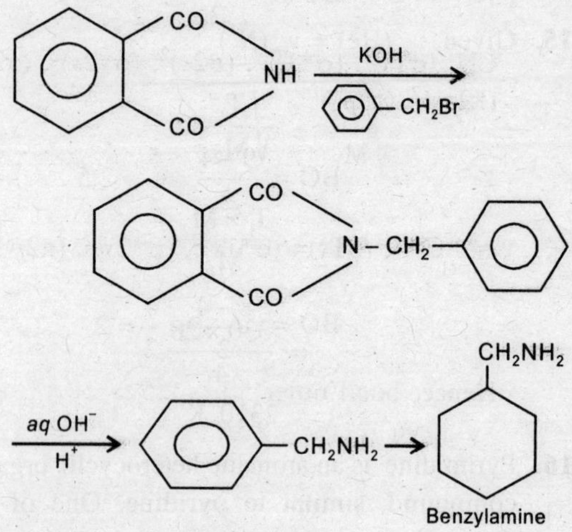

18. We have,

A. $NH_4NO_2 \xrightarrow{\text{Heat}} N_2 + H_2O$

B. $(NH_4)_2Cr_2O_7 \xrightarrow{\text{Heat}} N_2 + Cr_2O_3 + H_2O$

C. $Ba(N_3)_2 \xrightarrow{\text{Heat}} Ba + 3N_2$

D. $NH_4NO_3 \xrightarrow{\text{Heat}} N_2O + 2H_2O$

Hence on heating NH_4NO_3 will not release.

19. To get n-type semi conductor, the 14 group elements must be doped with 15 group elements (valence electrons 5).

Hence, the impurity to be added to Si should have the 5 number of valence electrons.

20. Electrophiles are electron deficient species. Among the given H_3O^+ has lone pair of electron for donation, thus, it is not electron deficient and hence, H_3O^+ does not behave like an electrophile.

21. We Have,

A → Ne (10) : $1s^2 2s^2 2p^6$

B → O (8) : $1s^2 2s^2 2p^4$

C → Na (11) : $1s^2 2s^2 2p^6 3s^1$

D → F (9) : $1s^2 2s^2 2p^5$

The element (A) is noble gas, which is completely filled orbital. Hence, it has no tendency to gain electrons.

Element C(11) prefers to loss electrons ($3s^1$) to attain stable noble gas configuration. Element D(9) has only 1 electron less than stable noble gas configuration. Hence, it has greater tendency to gain electron than element B which has 2 electrons less than the noble gas configuration.

Hence, correct order of increasing tendency to gain electrons

A < C < B < D.

22. Glyptal is synthesised by polymerisation of ethylene (glycol) and phthalic acid.

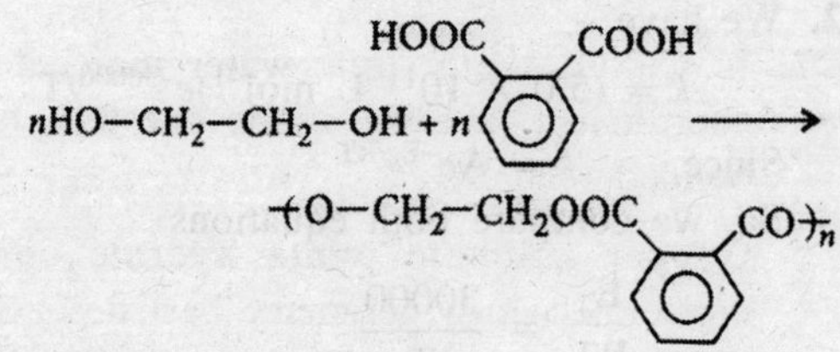

Glyptal

23. When an electron comes down from higher energy level to 2nd energy level the Balmer series of spectrum is obtained.

∴ Wavelength of H-atom is given by

$$\frac{1}{\lambda} = R \times \left|\frac{1}{2^2} - \frac{1}{n_2^2}\right|$$

The 1st line in 3 → 2

2nd line is 4 → 2

3rd line is 5 → 2

∴ In Balmer series of hydrogen atomic spectrum which electronic transition causes third line

O → 2, $n_2 \to 5 \to n_1 = 2$.

24. Nylon-6 is polymer of monomeric unit caprolactum, it is used for the manufacture of tyre cords, fabrics and ropes.

26. The valence electrons experience a shielding or screening effect from the nucleus because of the intervening core electrons, wherein the effective nuclear charge experienced by a valence electron in an atom will be less than the actual charge on the nucleus.

The order of screening effect of electrons of *s, p, d* and *f* orbitals:

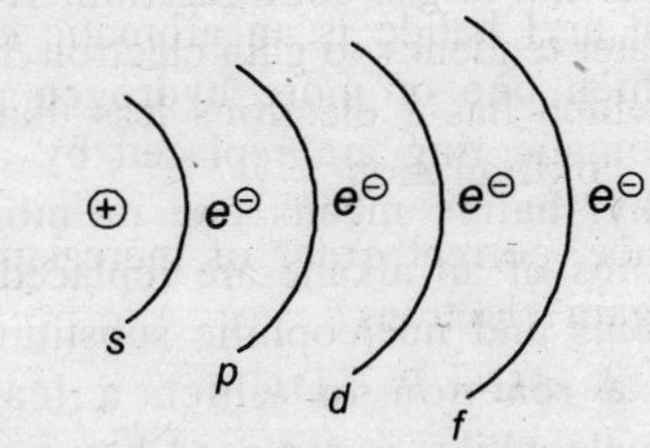

∴ Order of screening effect.

$$s > p > d > f.$$

27. In $CuSO_4.5H_2O$, four water molecules are coordinated to Cu^{+2}, while one is hydrogen bonded with SO_4^{2-}.

Copper sulphate penta hydrate contains copper (II) in a geometry best described as distorted octahedral. The copper (II) is bound to four water molecules in a square-planar geometry and two oxygen atoms from two sulphate ions (one H_2O is H-Bonded here).

This salt dissolves in water to produce the pale-blue $[Cu(H_2O)_6]^{2+}$ ion, in which two of the water molecules are less tightly held and have longer bond distances.

28. 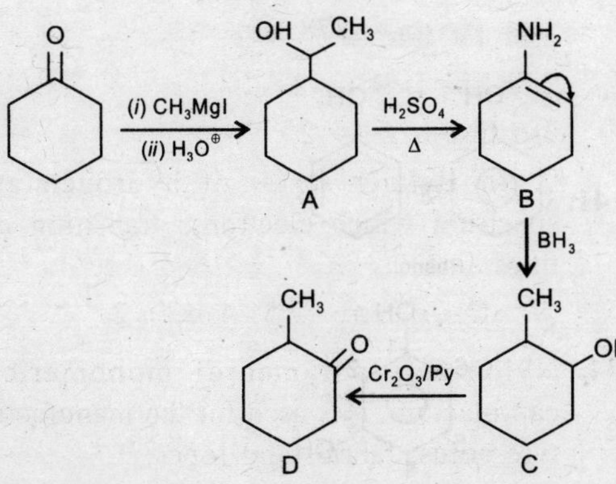

29. We have, CN^-: $(\sigma 1s)^2, (\sigma^* 1s)^2, (\sigma 2s)^2, (\sigma^* 2s)^2, (\pi 2p_x)^2, (\pi 2p_y)^2, (\pi 2p_z)^2$

$$\therefore \quad BO = \frac{10-4}{2} = \frac{6}{2} = 3$$

CN: $(\sigma 1s)^2, (\sigma^* 1s)^2, (\sigma 2s)^2, (\sigma^* 2s)^2, (\pi 2p_x)^2, (\pi 2p_y)^2, (\pi 2p_z)^1$

$$\therefore \quad BO = \frac{9-4}{2} = \frac{5}{2} = 2.5$$

and CN^+: $(\sigma 1s)^2, (\sigma^* 1s)^2, (\sigma^* 2s)^2, (\pi 2p_z)^2$

$$\therefore \quad BO = \frac{8-4}{2} = \frac{4}{2} = 2$$

Hence, bond order : $3 > 2.5 > 2$

i.e., ($CN^- > CN > CN^+$

30. Given, mass = 95%, d = 1.80 g/mL

Molecular weight (Mw) of H_2SO_4 = 98,

Valency of H_2SO_4 = 2

Equivalent weight (Ew)

$$= \frac{\text{Molecular Weight (Mw)}}{\text{Valency}}$$

$$\therefore \text{ Equivalent weight (Ew)} = \frac{98}{2} = 49$$

$$\Rightarrow \quad Ew = 49$$

$$\therefore \quad \text{Normality (N)} = \frac{\text{Mass} \times d \times 100}{100 \times \text{Ew}}$$

$$= \frac{95 \times 1.80 \times 1000}{100 \times 49}$$

$$= 34.9$$

31. The increasing melting point order of the compounds NH_3, PH_3, AsH_3, SbH_3 is given bleow.

$$SbH_3 > AsH_3 > PH_3 > NH_3$$

32. Paul Ehrlich, a German bacteriologist, investigated arsenic based structures in order to produce less toxic substances for the treatment of syphilis. He developed the medicine, arsphenamine, known as salvarsan. Although salvarsan is toxic to human beings, its effect on the bacteria, spirochete, which causes syphilis is much greater than on human beings. Therefore, salvarsan drug which inhibits the growth or destroys microorganisms.

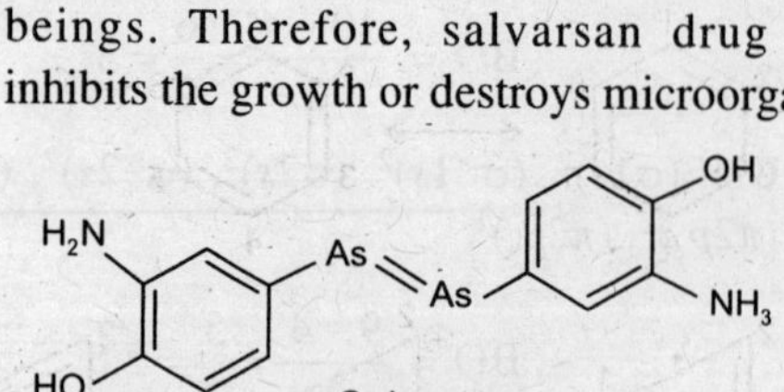

Salvarsan

33. The type of hybridization that occurs in BCl_3 is sp^2 hybridization. In BCl_3 molecule, boron will be the central atom which contains three bonded atoms but no lone pair of electrons.

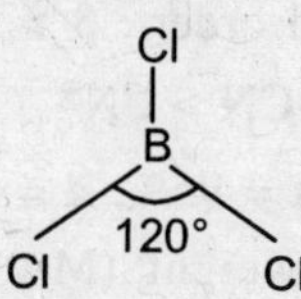

The hybridization of the ClO_3^- is sp^3. Hybridization is important because with its help we can find the most stable structure and geometry of a compound. The atomic orbitals are mixed to form new hybrid orbitals which are different in energy and shape.

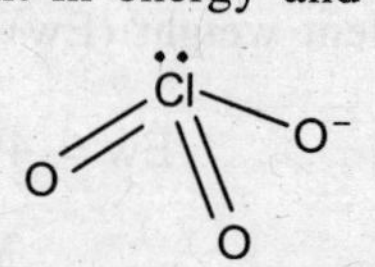

The central atom in the ammonia molecule is sp^3 hybridized.

The hybridization of PCl_3 is sp^3. The hybridization of a molecule generally gives us ideas about the mixing of orbitals in a compound.

36. Given, interatomic spacing

$$d = 140 \text{ pm} = 140 \times 10^{-12} \text{ m}$$

$$e = 1.6 \times 10^{-19} \text{ C}$$

As, $\mu = e \times d$

$$= 1.6 \times 10^{-19} \times 140 \times 10^{-12}$$

$$= 224 \times 10^{-31}$$

Now, the percentage of ionic character of

$$\text{HBr} = \frac{2.60 \times 10^{-30}}{224 \times 10^{-31}} \times 100$$

$$= 11.6\%$$

37. Aryl halides are less reactive towards nucleophilic substitution reaction as compared to alkyl halides is because of resonance stabilization in aryl halide. Due to resonance, C–Cl bond becomes shorter and stronger and cannot be easily replaced by nucleophiles.

An aryl halide is an aromatic compound in which one or more hydrogen atoms of an aromatic ring are replaced by a halide and alkyl halide means one or more hydrogen atoms of an alkane are replaced by halogen atoms and nucleophilic substitution reaction is a reaction in which a leaving group (nucleophile) is replaced by an electron-rich compound (electrophile).

Aryl halides are less reactive towards nucleophilic substitution reactions because:

A. of the partial double bond character between halogen and aromatic nucleus.

B. of repulsion of Nu due to the lone pair of electrons on halogen.

D. carbon of the aromatic nucleus is not electron deficient.

Hence, wrong answer is C.

40. We have,

$$\Delta H = \Delta H_P - \Delta H_R$$

$$= [81 + 3(-393)] - [9.7 + 3(-110)]$$

$$= [81 - 1179] - [9.7 - 330]$$

$$= -1098 + 320.3$$

$$= -777.7 \text{ kJ}$$

$$\simeq -778 \text{ kJ}$$

41. 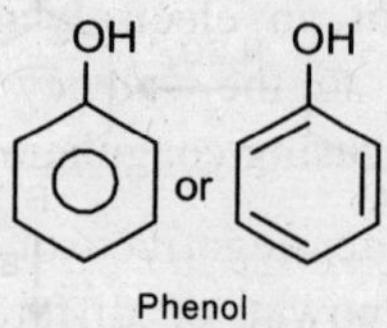

Phenol

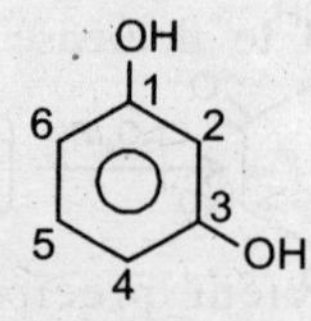

Inductive (–I)

E_w = As ↑ Resorcinol

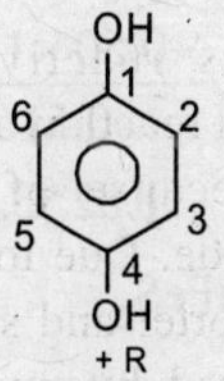

+ R
Hydroquinone

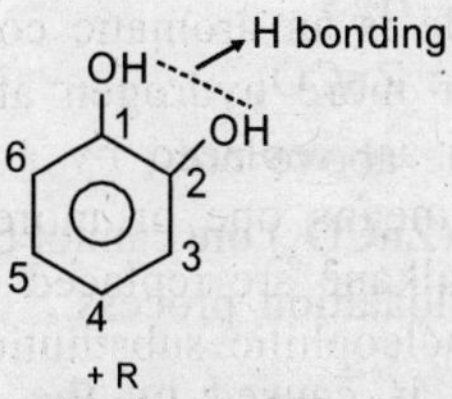

+ R
Catechol

OH = +R effect = –I effect, ED = As↓

hydroquinone > catechol > resorcinol

42. As we move across the period, atomic size decreases hence, ionization enthalpy increases. But for Al($3s^2$ $3p^1$), electron has to be removed from outer 3p orbital whereas in Mg($3s^2$), electron has to be removed from stable fully filled 3s orbital. Thus, I.E. for Mg > Al. So, the correct order of first ionization enthalpies is : Na < Mg > Al < Si.

43. "According to Hardy Schulze rule, greater the valency of the active ion or flocculating ion, greater will be its coagulating power" thus, Hardly Schulze law state:

(*i*) The ions carrying the charge opposite to that of sol particles are effective in causing coagulation of the solution.

(*ii*) Coagulating power of an electrolyte is directly proportional to the valency of the active ions (ions causing coagulation).

For example to coagulate negative sol of As_2S_3, the coagulation power of different cations has been found to decrease in the order as,

$$Al^{3+} > Mg^{2+} > Na^+$$

Hence, the most efficient precipitating agent for a negatively charged suspension is $AlCl_3$.

44. A.

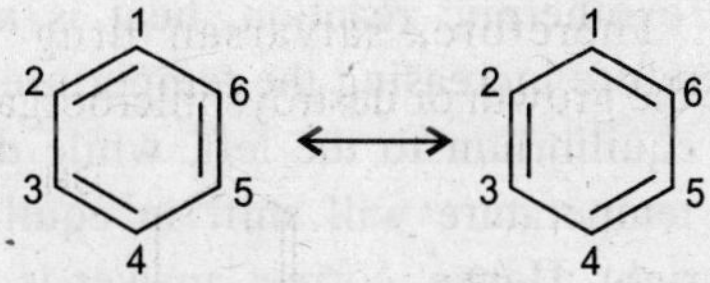

B.

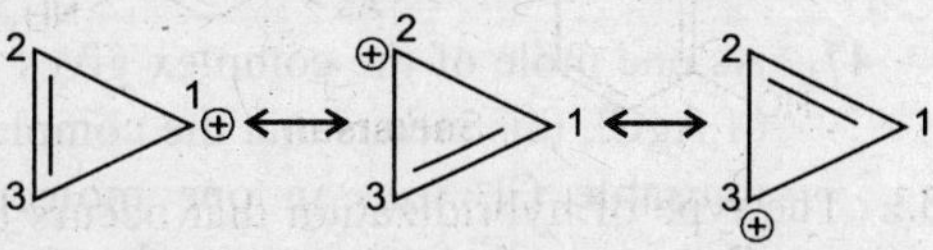

C.

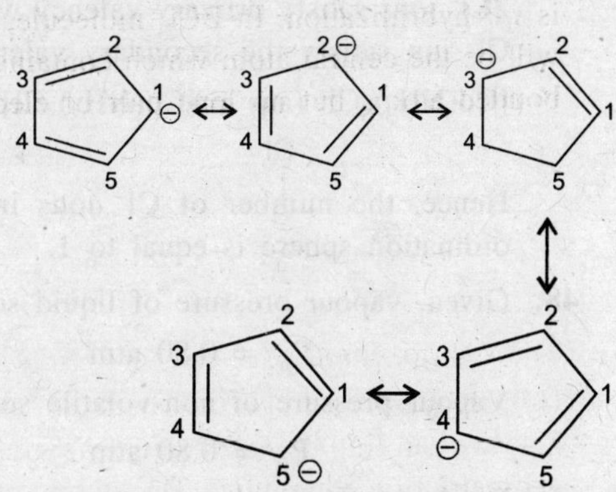

D.

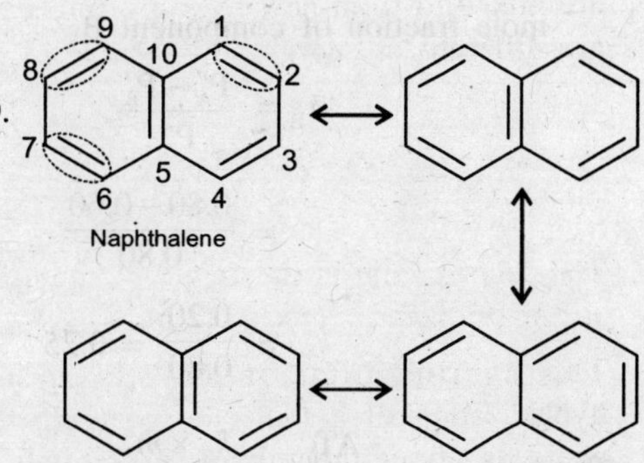

Naphthalene

When benzene rings anneal to form a bicyclic compound an in naphthalene, orbits at the junction rehybridize under steric strain, localizing the bond and electron density. Hence, the bond I and bond II have higher bond order and less antibonding character. Bond 3 not affected by strain and having low bond order and higher bond length. Bond 4 unhindered by bond strain which is having less strain due to unequal bond lengths 1, 2 and 3.

Hence, correct answer is (D).

45. For exothermic reaction, heat is a product. Therefore increasing the temperture will shift the equilibrium to the left, while decreasing the temperature will shift in equilibrium to the right. Hence, correct answer is (A).

47. As one mole of the complex gives two moles of AgCl, this means that the complex has two ionisable Cl^- ions in one molecule. Thus, $2Cl^-$ ions satisfy primary valency while third Cl^- ion satisfy the secondary valency.

$$[Co(NH_3)_5Cl_3\ (aq) \rightleftharpoons [Co(NH_3)_5Cl]^{2+}\ (aq) + 2Cl^-\ (aq)$$

Hence, the number of Cl^- ions in the co-ordination sphere is equal to 1.

48. Given, vapour pressure of liquid solvent A,

$$P_A{}^o = 0.80 \text{ atm}$$

Vapour pressure of non-volatile substance

$$P_B{}^s = 0.80 \text{ atm}$$

We know that,

mole fraction of component B

$$\alpha_B = \frac{P_A^o - P_B^s}{P_A^o}$$

$$= \frac{0.80 - 0.60}{0.80}$$

$$= \frac{0.20}{0.80} = 0.25$$

49. As,

$$\frac{\Delta T_b}{\Delta T_f} = \frac{k_B \times m}{k_f \times m}$$

$$\Rightarrow \quad \frac{\Delta T_b}{\Delta T_f} = \frac{k_B}{k_f}$$

Given, $\Delta T_b = T_i - T_f = 100 - 100.50$

$= -0.50°C$

$k_B = 0.51°C/m$

$k_f = 1.86°C/m$

and $\Delta T_f = T_i - T_f$

$$\therefore \quad \frac{-0.50}{\Delta T_f} = \frac{0.51}{1.86}$$

$$\Rightarrow \quad \Delta T_f = \frac{-0.50 \times 1.86}{0.51}$$

$$= -1.82°C.$$

50. Copper pyrites : $CuFeS_2$

Zinc Blende : ZnS

Cinnabar : HgS

Calamine : $ZnCO_3$

Among the above ores:

Calamine ($ZnCO_3$) ore cannot be concentrated by froth floatation process.

51. Acid rain is caused by the dissolution of oxides into the water molecules of rain in the atmosphere. The oxide dissolves in the water and forms acid. The acid rain is corrosive.

Sulphur dioxide (SO_2) reacting with atmospheric oxygen will result in the formation of sulphur trioxide (SO_3), which would further if come in contact with water forms sulphuric acid (H_2SO_4). So, it would contribute to acid rain.

$$2SO_2 + O_2 \rightarrow 2SO_3$$

$$SO_3 + H_2O \rightarrow H_2SO_4$$

Nitrogen monoxide (NO) reacting with atmospheric oxygen will result in the formation of nitrogen dioxide (NO_2), which would further if come in contact with water forms nitric acid (HNO_3). So, it would contribute to acid rain.

$$NO + O_2 \rightarrow NO_2$$

$$2NO_2 + H_2O \rightarrow HNO_3 + HNO_2$$

CH_4(Methane) does not cause acid rain. It is emitted by natural sources such as wetlands, as well as human activities such as leakage from natural gas systems and the raising of livestock.

52. For N_2O_5, oxidation number of N = + 5

For NO_2, oxidation number of N = + 4

For HNO_2, oxidation number of N = + 3

For NH_3, oxidation number of N = – 3

53. Troposphere contains most of our weather - clouds, rain and snow. In this part of the atmosphere the temperature gets colder as the distance above the earth increases, by about 6.5°C per kilometre. The actual change of temperature with height varies from day to day, depending on the weather.

The troposphere contains about 75% of all of the air in the atmosphere, and almost all of the water vapour (which forms clouds and rain). The decrease in temperature with height is a result of the decreasing pressure. If a parcel of air moves upwards it expands (because of the lower pressure). When air expands it cools. So air higher up is cooler than air lower down. The troposphere is the lowest region of atmosphere. It is the region in which human beings along with other organisms live.

The Stratosphere contains much of the ozone in the atmosphere. The increase in temperature with height occurs because of absorption of ultraviolet (UV) radiation from the sun by this ozone. Temperatures in the stratosphere are highest over the summer pole, and lowest over the winter pole. Hence, correct answer is (D).

55. Lysine is an essential amino acid (a building block of protein). Unlike some other amino acids, the human body cannot make lysine, so it must be eaten in the diet. Sources of lysine include meat, fish, dairy, eggs, and some plants such as soya.

56. Manganese (Mn) exhibits the largest number of oxidation states. It shows the oxidation states +2, +3, +4, +5 ,+6, and + 7. Mn is the highest number of any element in the 3-*d* series. The reason for that is the maximum number of unpaired electrons present in its outermost shell *i.e.*, $3d^5 4s^2$.

57. Sucrose is not a reducing sugar, e.g., it will not reduce Fehling's solution or Tollen's reagent. It does not form an oxime or an osazone, and does not undergo mutarotation. This indicates that hemiacetal group is not present in the rings.

$$\text{Sucrose (Cane sugar)} \xrightarrow{H_3O^{\oplus}} \alpha\text{-glucose} + \beta\text{-fructose}$$

In sucrose, two monosaccharides are joined together by an oxide linkage formed by loss of water molecule. Such linkage through oxygen atom is called glycosidic linkage. In sucrose & fructose are involved in glycosidic bond formation, sucrose is non reducing sugar.

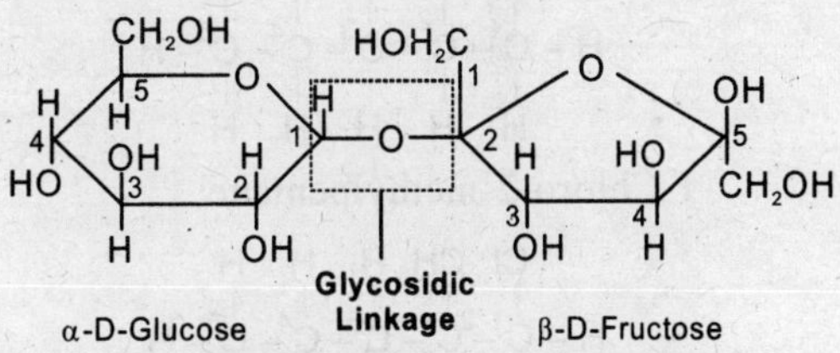

$C_1\alpha$ – D-glucose + $C_2\beta$ – D-fructose

58. Carbon occurs in nature as a mixture of atoms = 98.9%

Remaining mixture = 100 – 98.9% = 1.1%

Mass of Carbon = 12.00

Remaining Mass = 13.00

∴ Atomic weight of Carbon

$$= \frac{98.9}{100} \times 12.00 + \frac{1.1}{100} \times 13.00$$

$$= 11.868 + 0.143$$

$$= 12.011$$

59. Mid-point ⇒ $[In^{\ominus}] = [H\ In]$

$$k_b = \frac{[H\ In]\ [OH^{\ominus}]}{[In\ d^{\ominus}]}$$

$$= [OH^-] = 1 \times 10^{-10}$$

$In\ d^{\ominus} + H_2O \rightarrow H\ In + OH^-$

$$pOH = -\log [OH^-]$$

$$= -\log 10^{-10}$$

$$= 10$$

$$\therefore \quad pH = 14 - 10$$

$$= 4$$

60. W atom per unit cell = $8 \times \frac{1}{8} = 1$ = 1 unit cell

O atom per unit cell = $12 \times \frac{1}{4} = 3$ unit cell

Na atom per unit cell = 1 × 1 = 1 unit cell

∴ Formula of compound = $NaWO_3$.

61. To optically active, compound or structure should possess a chiral or asymmetric carbon atom.

1-Chloropentane:

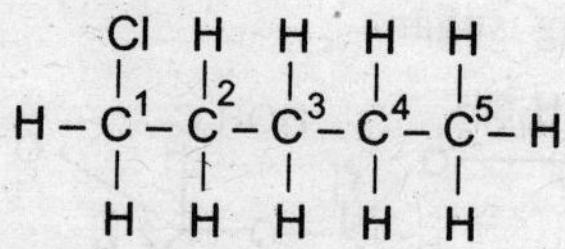

1-Chloro-2-methylpentane

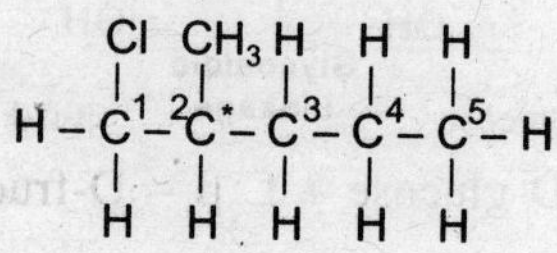

2-Chloropentane

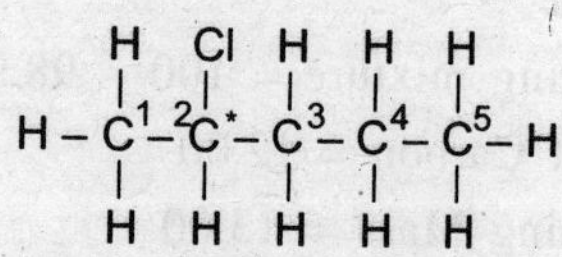

3-Chloro-2-methylpentane

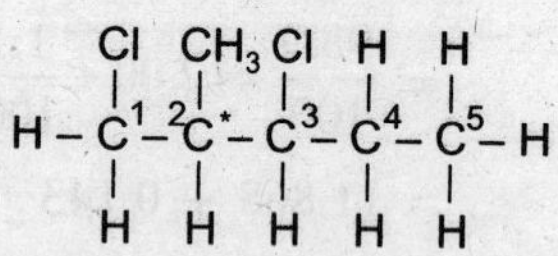

Where, C* → asymmetric atom.

Therefore, 1-chloropentane is not chiral.

62. Mathematical representation of Thermodynamic equilibrium

$$\Delta G = \Delta G° + 2.303 \text{ RT} \log Q$$

At equilibrium, when, $\Delta G = 0$ and $Q = k$

Then, $\Delta G = \Delta G° + 2.303 \text{ RT} \log k = 0$

∴ $\Delta G° = - 2.303 \text{ RT} \log k$

Hence, correct answer is (C).

63. We have, $2H_2 + O_2 \rightarrow 2H_2O$

100 g of $H_2 = \frac{100}{2} = 50$ moles

100 g of $O_2 = \frac{100}{32} = \frac{25}{8} = 3.125$ moles

According to Stiochemistry,

$$2H_2 + O_2 \rightarrow H_2O$$

Since, oxygen is simiting agent

Mole of $H_2O = 3.125 \times 2 = 6.25$

∴ Weight of $H_2O = 6.25 \times 18$

$= 112.5$ g

$\simeq 113$ g

Hence, amount of water formed is 113 g.

64. In CO molecule, the valency of Carbon (C) = 4 and valency of Oxygen (O) = 6

∴ CO = 4 + 6 = 10

Now, Lewis electron dot structure of CO:

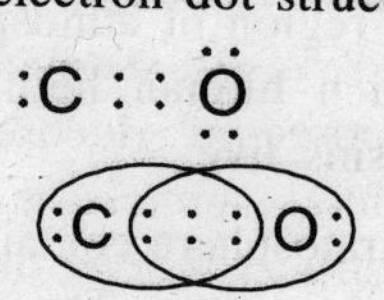

⇒ C ≡ O

Hence, number of unshared pair of valence electrons is 3.

65. Paper Chromatography is a type of partition chromatography. It contains water trapped in it, which acts as the stationary phase. The paper selectively retains different components according to their differing partition in two phases.

66. Nitrous oxide (N_2O) and nitric oxide (NO) are neutral. Dinitrogen trioxide (N_2O_3) and nitrogen dioxide (NO_2) are acidic. Acidic character increases with increase in oxidation number so the order is as follows:

$$N_2O < NO < N_2O_3 < NO_2$$

Hence, NO_2 is most acidic.

67. Here, $n = 3$, $l = 2$, $m = -3$ and $s = \frac{1}{2}$ represent an impossible arrangement.

When, $l = 2$, m cannot be equal to 3. For given values of l, m can have values ..... –1, ... – 0, ... + 1.

68. CH_3COONa (Salt of weak acid, is strong base) $\xrightarrow{\text{Buffer solution}}$ CH_3COOH (Weak acid)

Hence, correct answer is (A).

69. Zymase converts glucose into ethanol through the process of fermentation. It is found naturally in the yeasts and its activity is highly dependent on the type of yeast strains.

Usually, zymase enzymes help in the breakdown of complex sugar moieties in simpler alcohols with release of carbon dioxide. Invertase enzyme causes the alteration of sucrose into simpler fructose and glucose molecules. Amylases are one of the main enzymes used in industry. Such enzymes hydrolyze the starch molecules into polymers composed of glucose units. Amylases have potential application in a wide number of industrial processes such as food, fermentation and pharmaceutical industries. Trypsin is an enzyme that helps us digest protein. In the small intestine, trypsin breaks down proteins, continuing the process of digestion that began in the stomach. It may also be referred to as a proteolytic enzyme, or proteinase. Trypsin is produced by the pancreas in an inactive form called trypsinogen.

70. Histamine - a chemical found in some of the body's cells - causes many of the symptoms of allergies, such as a runny nose or sneezing. When a person is allergic to a particular substance, such as a food or dust, the immune system mistakenly believes that this usually harmless substance is actually harmful to the body. In an attempt to protect the body, the immune system starts a chain reaction that prompts some of the body's cells to release histamine and other chemicals into the bloodstream. The histamine then acts on a person's eyes, nose, throat, lungs, skin, or gastrointestinal tract, causing allergy symptoms.

71. $Ag + CN \longrightarrow [Ag(CN)_2]^-$

$$\downarrow Zn$$

$$[Zn(CN)_4]^{2-} + Ag \text{ (Silver)}$$

74. Given, $I = 2.00$ A

$t = 5 \text{ hrs} = 5 \times 60 \times 60$ sec

$m = 22.2$ g

and atomic mass of Sn = 111.7 U

We know that

$$m = \frac{I\,t\,E}{96500},$$

where E → equivalent mass

$$\Rightarrow \quad E = \frac{m \times 96500}{I\,t}$$

$$= \frac{22.2 \times 96500}{2 \times 5 \times 60 \times 60}$$

$$= 59.5$$

Since, equivalent mass

$$= \frac{\text{Atomic mass (M)}}{\text{Oxidation state } (n)}$$

$$\Rightarrow \quad 59.5 = \frac{118.7}{n}$$

$$\therefore \quad n = \frac{118.7}{59.5}$$

$$= 1.99$$

$$\simeq 2$$

Hence, the oxidation state of tin is 2.

75. vander Waals constants '*a*' and '*b*' of H_2O and O_2 are:

$a = 5.536$ atm L^2 mol^{-2}

and $b = 1.36$ atm L^2 mol^{-2}

Hence, *a* is larger but *b* is smaller for H_2O than for O_2.

76. The rate of proportional to the concentration of A, and so is first order wrt A. It is proportional to the square of the concentration of B and so is second order wrt B. The reaction is third order (1 + 2) overall. The reaction could not be single step reaction, in which the molecularity is equal to the order. For a single step reaction having this equation the rate would be first order wrt each reactant. Hence, this cannot be a single step reaction.

77. SO_2Cl_2 (Sulfuryl chloride) is a colourless liquid with strong irritating odor. It is used in making other chemicals, pharmaceuticals and insecticides and as a solvent, catalyst and disinfectant.

SO_2Cl_2 is not suitable for the preparation of acid chlorides from the given organic acid.

79. The equilibrium constant for the reaction:

$$N_2(g) + 2O_2(g) \rightleftharpoons 2NO_2$$

$$\therefore \quad k_c = \frac{[NO_2]^2}{[N_2][O_2]^2} = 100 \quad ...(i)$$

(*i*) The equilibrium constant equation for the reaction

$$k_1 = \frac{[N_2][O_2]^2}{[NO_2]^2} \quad ...(ii)$$

This equation is reciprocal of equation (*i*),

$$\therefore \quad k_1 = \frac{1}{k_c} = \frac{1}{100} = 1 \times 10^{-2}$$

The equilibrium constant for equation (*i*)

$$k_2 = \frac{[N_2]^{1/2}[O_2]}{[NO_2]} \quad ...(iii)$$

Now comparing equation (*ii*) & (*iii*), we get

$$k_2 = \sqrt{k_1} = \sqrt{10^{-2}}$$

$$= 10^{-1} = 0.10$$

Therefore, the value of the equilibrium constant for the reaction

$NO_2\ (g) \rightleftharpoons \frac{1}{2}N_2(g) + O_2(g)$ is 0.10.

80. All the d-blocks elements exhibit various valencies or have variable oxidation number. But scandium (Sc) does not show because scandium (Sc) has partially filled *d*-orbitals in the ground state. In the case of scandium (Sc), the number of electrons in the 3*d* and 4*s* orbital is 1 and 2. Removing three electrons from its *d* and *s* orbital forms a very stable inert gas configuration. It loses 1 electron from *d* orbital and 2 electrons from *s* orbital to form a Sc^{3+} ion. Thus, scandium –Sc(Z = 21) does not exhibit variable oxidation states.

Previous Paper (Solved)

KVS—PGT Teacher Recruitment Exam 2017*

Subject : Chemistry

1. In $Cu(s)|Cu^{2+}(aq)||Ag^{+}(aq)|Ag(s)$

Which of the following statements is correct?

A. Cell reaction is:
$Cu^{2+}(aq) + 2Ag(s) \rightarrow Cu(s) + 2Ag^{+}(aq)$

B. Silver electrode acts as anode and copper electrode acts as cathode

C. Silver electrode acts as cathode and copper electrode act as anode

D. $E_{cell} = E_{left} - E_{right}$

2. What type of reaction takes place when $(CH_3)_3C - Br$ reacts with aqueous sodium hydroxide?

A. S_N2 reaction

B. Addition reaction

C. Elimination reaction

D. S_N1 reaction

3. In the reaction:

$CO(g) + 2H_2(g) \rightarrow CH_3OH(g)$

How many molecules of H_2 would be needed to consume 2 mol of CO?

A. 2 molecules

B. 1.2×10^{24} molecules

C. 2.4×10^{24} molecules

D. 4 molecules

4. An element is in M^{3+} form, its electronic configuration is $[Ar]3d'$, the ion is:

A. Sc^{3+} B. Ti^{3+}

C. Ti^{4+} D. Ca^{2+}

5. For which one of the following properties of halogens, the sequence F > Cl > Br > I holds good?

A. Boiling point B. Electron affinity

C. Electronegativity D. Atomic radius

6. In $Fe(CO)_5$, the Fe – C bond possesses:

A. σ – character only

B. π – character only

C. Both π and σ characters

D. Ionic character

7. The theoretical molar mass is less than the value as determined from colligative property when *i*(Van't Hoff factor) is:

A. > 2 B. < 1

C. = 1 D. > 1

8. Which of the following oxides of nitrogen is most thermally stable?

A. N_2O_3 B. N_2O_5

C. NO D. N_2O

9. The strongest base in liquid ammonia is:

A. N_2H_4 B. NH_3

C. NH_2^- D. NH_4^+

10. Molecular weight of oxalic acid is 126. The weight of oxalic acid required to neutralise 100 mL of normal solution of NaOH is:

A. 63 g B. 6.3 g

C. 126 g D. 530 g

11. In the reaction with aq. sodium hydroxide, which of the following compounds will undergo inversion and S_N2 mechanism?

A. $CH_3 - CH(Cl) - CH_2 - CH_3$

B. $(C_2H_5)_2CHCl$

C. $(CH_3)_3CCl$

D. $(CH_3)_2CH - CH_2Cl$

* *Exam held on 07/01/2017*

12. Of the following species,
Ti^{3+}, V^{3+}, Sc^{3+}, Fe^{3+}, Co^{3+}, Cu^{+} and Mn^{3+},
which two will not be coloured in aqueous solution?
A. V^{3+} and Co^{3+} B. Ti^{3+} and Sc^{3+}
C. Sc^{3+} and Cu^{+} D. Mn^{3+} and Fe^{3+}

13. Atomic numbers of Cr and Fe are 24 and 26 respectively. Which of the following is paramagnetic with the spin of electrons?
A. $[Cr(CO)_6]$ B. $[Cr(NH_3)_6]^{3+}$
C. $[Fe(CO)_5]$ D. $[Fe(CN)_6]^{4-}$

14. The solubility of Aniline in water is increased by adding:
A. Toluene B. 1 M HCl
C. 1 M NaOH D. Diethyl ether

15. Among the following which one is the most important ore of silver?
A. Horn silver B. Proustite
C. Ruby silver D. Argentite

16. The compound which gives off oxygen on moderate heating is:
A. Aluminum oxide B. Mercuric oxide
C. Cupric oxide D. Zinc oxide

17. 50 mL water is added to a 50 mL solution of $Ba(OH)_2$ of strength 0.01 M. The pH of the resulting solution will be:
A. 12 B. 6
C. 8 D. 10

18. For a reaction A + B → products, rate law expression for rate, $r = K[A][B]^2$.
If the volume of the container is reduced to half of its original volume, the rate of reaction will become:
A. 8 times B. $\frac{1}{4}$ times
C. 2 times D. 4 times

19. Which of the following halogens does not form oxoacid?
A. Iodine B. Fluorine
C. Chlorine D. Bromine

20. Which of the following halides is least stable and has doubtful existence?
A. PbI_4 B. CI_4
C. GeI_4 D. SnI_4

21. Ammonia is a Lewis base. It forms complexes with cations. Which one of the following cations does not form complex with ammonia?
A. Pb^{2+} B. Ag^{+}
C. Cu^{2+} D. Cd^{2+}

22. The rate constant for a first order reaction is $60\ s^{-1}$. How much time will it take to reduce the initial concentration of the rentant to $\frac{1}{16}$ th value?
A. 4.6×10^{-2} seconds
B. 6.9×10^{-2} seconds
C. 3.2×10^{-2} seconds
D. 2.3×10^{-2} seconds

23. The reagent that brings about conversion of Benzyl chloride to phenylmethanamine is:
A. Excess NH_3, pyridine
B. $AgNO_2$
C. Alc. KCN
D. $(n\text{-Bu})_3N$

24. In the free radical halogenation
$$CH_4 + X_2 \xrightarrow{\text{Light}} CH_3X + HX$$
the propagation steps are:
(*a*) $X_2 \xrightarrow{\text{Light}} 2X\bullet$
(*b*) $CH_4 + X\bullet \rightarrow CH_3\bullet + HX$
(*c*) $CH_3\bullet + X\bullet \rightarrow CH_3X$
(*d*) $CH_3\bullet + X_2 \rightarrow CH_3X + X\bullet$
A. (*c*) and (*d*) B. (*a*) and (*b*)
C. (*b*) and (*c*) D. (*b*) and (*d*)

25. With atomic number 25, a divalent ion in aqueous solution has the magnetic moment:
A. 7.18 μ_B B. 3.92 μ_B
C. 5.92 μ_B D. 6.82 μ_B

26. In 1-iodo-2-methyl propane, which of the below given Newman projections is most stable?

A. 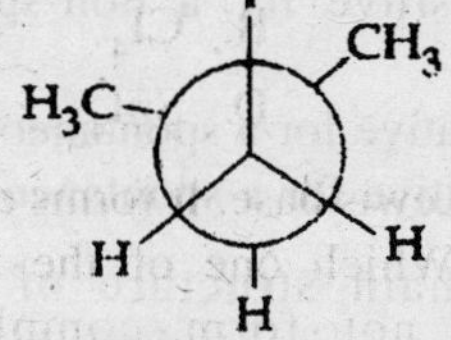

B. 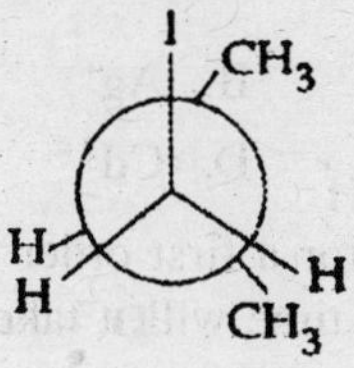

C. 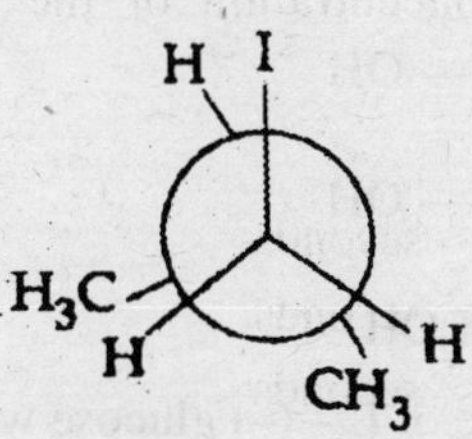

D. 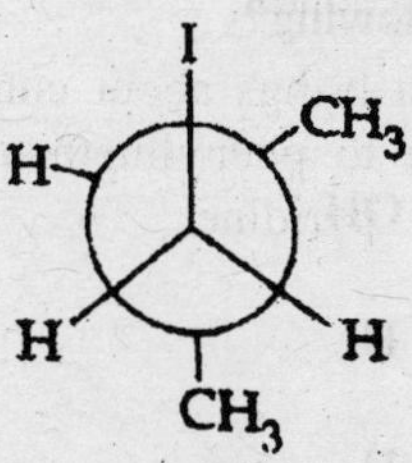

27. Which one of the following is the most easily soluble in water?

A. $BaSO_4$ B. $BeSO_4$

C. $CaSO_4$ D. $SrSO_4$

28. Which of the following sets of ions represents the collection of isoelectronic species?

A. Na^+, Mg^{2+}, Al^{3+}, Cl^-

B. K^+, Cl^-, Mg^{2+}, Sc^{3+}

C. Na^+, Ca^{2+}, Sc^{3+}, F^-

D. K^+, Ca^{2+}, Sc^{3+}, Cl^-

29. How many σ and π bonds are there in the molecule $(CN)_2C = C(CN)_2$?

A. Nine σ and nine π

B. Nine σ and seven π

C. Five σ and nine π

D. Five σ and eight π

30. Which of the following is ***not*** an aromatic species?

A.  B. 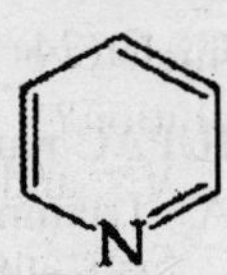

C. 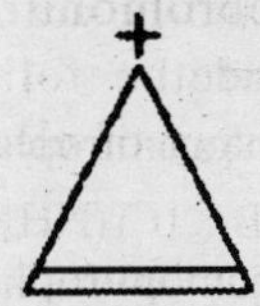 D. 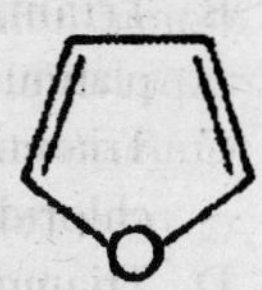

31. Stereo isomers which are not mirror images and are not superimposable to one and another, are called:

A. Tautomers B. Diastereomers

C. Enantiomers D. Mesomers

32. Which of the following statement is ***not*** correct to explain the effect of catalyst on rate of reaction?

A. A catalyst does not change equilibrium constant of a reaction

B. A catalyst reduces the activation energy between reactants and products

C. A catalyst provides an alternate reaction mechanism

D. A catalyst alters the Gibbs energy of a reaction

33. In the reaction

$2H_2(g) + O_2(g) \rightarrow 2H_2O(l)$

The stoichiometry tells that the hydrogen and oxygen react to produce water in the mass ratio of:

A. 4 : 32 B. 2 : 1

C. 4 : 2 D. 4 : 16

34. Which of the following pairs will have effective magnetic moment equal?

A. Ti^{2+} and V^{2+} B. Cr^{3+} and Mn^{2+}

C. Cr^{2+} and Fe^{2+} D. V^{2+} and Sc^{3+}

35. Which one of the following first series of transition elements has 5 unpaired electrons in its +2 oxidation state?

A. Co(27) B. V(23)

C. Cr(24) D. Mn(25)

36. IUPAC name of $[Pt(NH_3)_3Br(NO_2)Cl]Cl$ is:

A. Triamminonitrochlorobromoplatinum (IV) chloride

B. Triamminochlorobromonitro chloro-platinum(IV) chloride

C. Triamminobromochloronitroplatinum (IV) chloride

D. Triamminochlorobromonitroplatinum (IV) chloride

37. Fehling solution A and Fehling solution B are respectively:

A. Aqueous copper sulphate and alkaline sodium potassium tartarate

B. Aqueous copper sulphate and ammoniacal silver nitrate

C. Alkaline sodium potassium tartarate and aqueous copper sulphate

D. Ammoniacal silver nitrate and aqueous copper sulphate

38. In the reaction

$$CH_3CH_2CH_2COOH \xrightarrow[2-H_3O^+]{1-LiAlH_4(\text{excess})}$$

the major organic product formed is:

A. $CH_3CH_2C \equiv CH$

B. $CH_3 - CH_2 - CH_2 - CHO$

C. $CH_3 - CH_2 - CH_2 - CH_2OH$

D. $CH_3CH_2CH_2CH_3$

39. Which one of the following statements is ***not*** correct?

A. The value of Henry's constant K_H is greater for gases with higher solubility

B. The value of molal depression constant depends on the nature of solvent

C. Relative lowering of vapour pressure is a dimensionless quantity

D. The value of Henry's constant, K_H increases with increase in temperature

40. Which one of the following statements is ***not*** correct?

A. ΔG is zero for a reversible reaction

B. ΔG is positive for a non-spontaneous reaction

C. ΔG is negative for a spontaneous reaction

D. ΔG is positive for a spontaneous reaction

41. The open chain structure of naturally occurring glucose, is as given below:

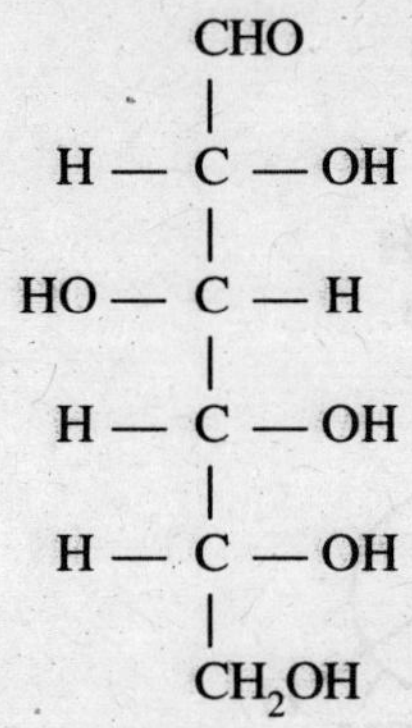

D – (+) – glucose

The structure of L – (–) glucose will be which one of the following?

A.

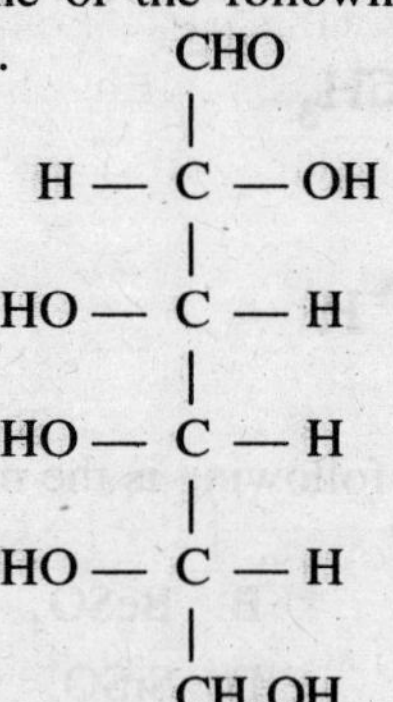

B.

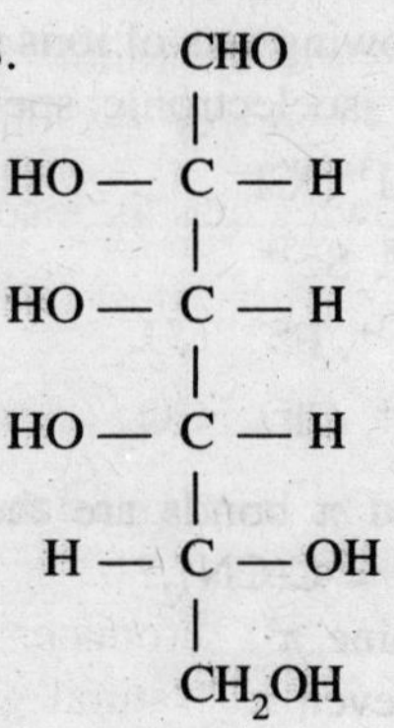

C. 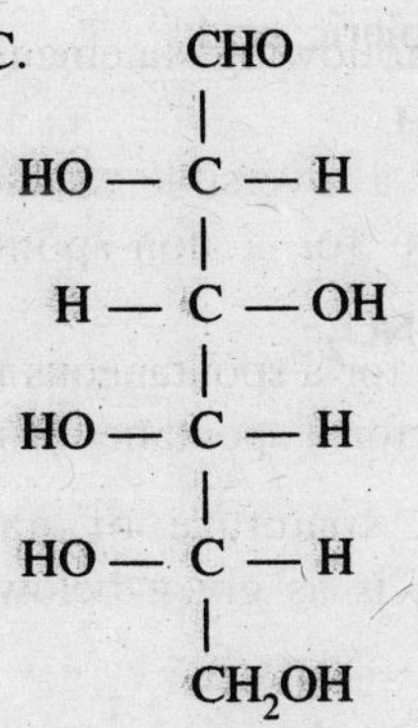

D. 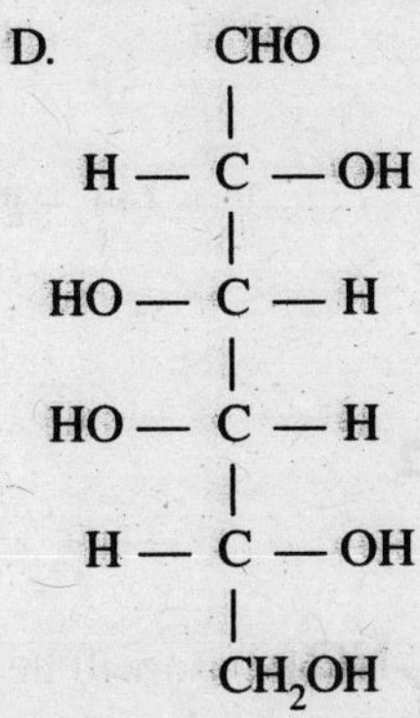

42. In which of the following, concentration value for a solution changes with change in temperature?

A. Molality
B. Mass percentage
C. Molarity
D. Mole fraction

43. The IUPAC name of 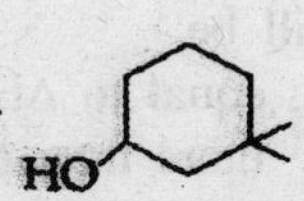 is:

A. 3, 3-Dimethyl-1-hydroxy cyclohexane
B. 3, 3-Dimethyl-cyclohexanol
C. 1, 1-Dimethyl-3-cyclohexanol
D. 1, 1-Dimethyl-3-hydroxy cyclohexane

44. Which of the following gas is insoluble in water?

A. H_2 B. SO_2
C. NH_3 D. CO_2

45. In Bosch's process for production of hydrogen, the gas used is:

A. Water gas B. Producer gas
C. Coal gas D. Natural gas

46. In Lassaigne's test to detect the presence of sulphur in an organic compound, the sodium fusion extract on acidification with acetic acid and lead acetate gives a black precipitate due to:

A. Sodium Sulphide
B. Lead Sulphite
C. Lead Sulphate
D. Lead Sulphide

47. The product of the reaction

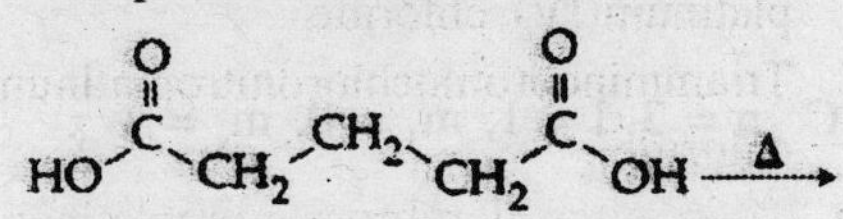

will be:

A. 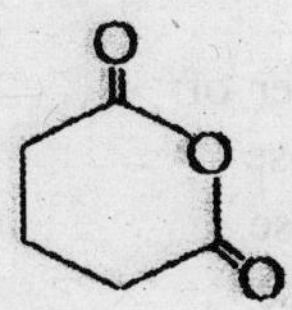

B. 

C. 

D. 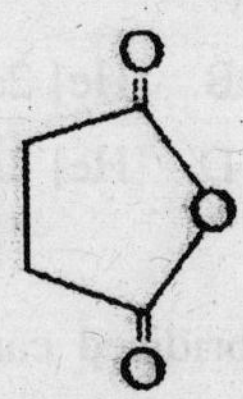

48. Which reagent is used in catalytic amount in an esterification reaction?

(*a*) Aq. NaOH
(*b*) Conc. H_2SO_4

A. Neither (*a*) nor (*b*)
B. (*a*) only
C. (*b*) only
D. Both (*a*) and (*b*)

49. IUPAC name of $CH_2 = CH - CH(CN) - CHO$ is:

A. 3-Cyano-but-1-ene-1-al
B. 2-Formyl-but-3-ene-nitrile

C. 3-Oxo-but-1-ene nitrile
D. 2-Cyano-but-3-ene-1-al

50. Which of the following sets of quantum numbers represent the highest energy of an atom?

A. $n = 4, l = 3, m_l = 2, m_s = +\frac{1}{2}$

B. $n = 3, l = 0, m_l = 0, m_s = +\frac{1}{2}$

C. $n = 3, l = 1, m_l = 0, m_s = +\frac{1}{2}$

D. $n = 3, l = 2, m_l = 1, m_s = +\frac{1}{2}$

51. Amylose is a polymer of:
A. α-D-glucopyranose
B. β-D-glucopyranose
C. β-D-fructofuranose
D. β-D-galactopyranose

52. Which one of the following represents the electronic configuration of the most electropositive element?

A. [Xe] $6s^2$ B. [He] $2s^1$
C. [Xe] $6s^1$ D. [He] $2s^2$

53. 1, 2-Butadiene has:
A. *sp*, sp^2 and sp^3 hybridised carbon atoms
B. Only *sp* hybridised carbon atoms
C. Only sp^2 hybridised carbon atoms
D. sp^2 and sp^3 hybridised carbon atoms

54. Which gas is obtained when urea is heated with HNO_2?
A. NH_3 B. N_2
C. O_2 D. H_2

55. A reaction that converts an amide into an amine is called:
A. Gattermann Koch reaction
B. Carbylamine reaction
C. Gabriel phthalimide reaction
D. Hoffmann bromamide reaction

56. The formula of picric acid:

A. 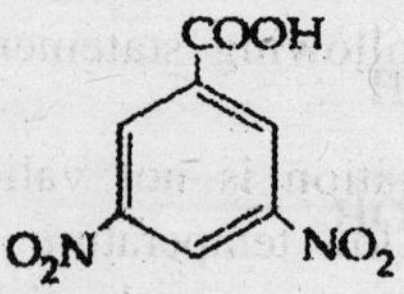

B. 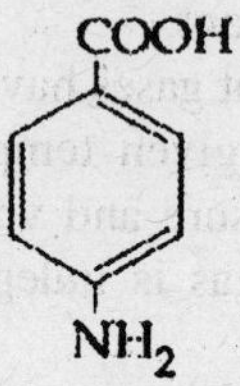

C. 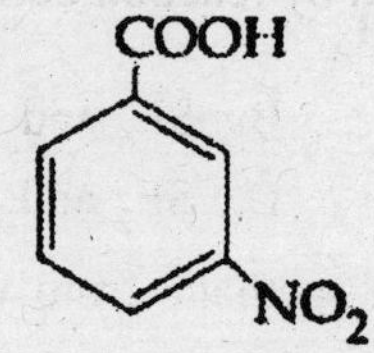

D. 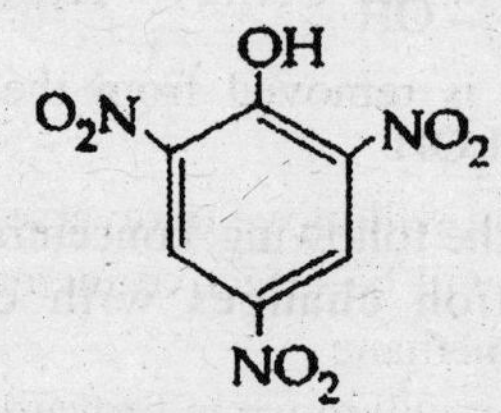

57. For an endothermic reaction, where ΔH represents enthalpy of reaction in kJ mol^{-1}, the minimum value for energy of activation will be:
A. equal to ΔH B. zero
C. more than ΔH D. less than ΔH

58. For the reaction $H_2(g) + I_2(g) \rightleftharpoons 2HI(g)$, the standard free energy is greater than zero ($\Delta G^\circ > 0$). The value of the equilibrium constant will be:
A. $K < 1$ B. $K = 1$
C. $K = 0$ D. $K > 1$

59. By which method is a ketone converted into a hydrocarbon?
A. Wolff-Kishner reduction.
B. Reimer-Tiemann reaction
C. Cannizzaro's reaction
D. Aldol condensation

60. Which of the following statements is ***not*** correct?

A. The gas equation is not valid at high pressure and low temperature

B. The gas constant per molecule is known as Boltzmann constant

C. Molecules of different gases have the same kinetic energy at a given temperature

D. The product of pressure and volume of a fixed amount of a gas is independent of temperature

61. The products formed by reaction between H_2S and fluorine are:

A. SF_4 and HF B. SF_6 and HF

C. SF_6, S and HF D. SF_2 and HF

62. In the formation of methane from water gas

$CO(g) + 3H_2(g) \rightleftharpoons CH_4(g) + H_2O(g)$, if the water vapour is removed from the reaction mixture:

A. the reaction will move in reverse direction and there will be effective increase in the yield of methane

B. the reaction will move in forward direction and there will be effective increase in the yield of methane.

C. the reaction will move in forward direction but there will be effective decrease in the yield of methane.

D. the reaction will move in reverse direction and there will be effective decrease in the yield of methane.

63. You are given standard electrode potential (E°)

$Zn^{2+}/ZN = -0.76$ V, $Na^{+}/Na = -2.71$ V

$Mg^{2+}/Mg = -2.36$ V, $K^{+}/K = -2.93$ V

Which one is the strongest reducing agent?

A. K B. Zn

C. Na D. Mg

64. Phenol is more readily soluble in:

A. Sodium bicarbonate solution

B. Dilute HCl

C. Both NaOH and HCl

D. NaOH solution

65. For the process $H_2O(l$, 1 bar, 373 K) $\rightarrow H_2O$ (g, 1 bar, 373 K), the thermodynamic parameters are:

A. $\Delta G = -ve$, $\Delta S = +ve$

B. $\Delta G = 0$, $\Delta S = +ve$

C. $\Delta G = 0$, $\Delta S = -ve$

D. $\Delta G = +ve$, $\Delta S = 0$

66. Which one of the following arrangements is ***not*** in order of the property indicated against it?

HF	HCl	HBr	HI
(a)	(b)	(c)	(d)

A. Dipole moment — (a) > (b) > (c) > (d)

B. M.P. — (a) < (b) < (c) < (d)

C. B.P. — (a) < (d) < (c) < (b)

D. Bond length — (a) < (b) < (c) < (d)

67. Which one of the following is the strongest acid?

A. 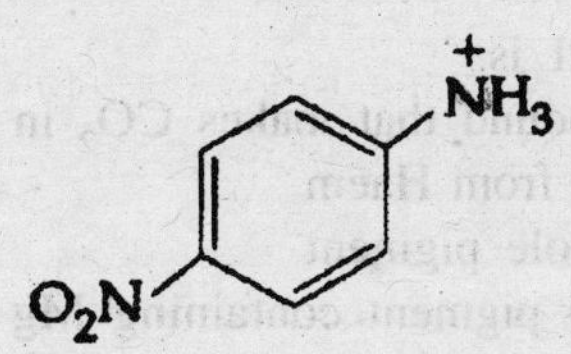

B. 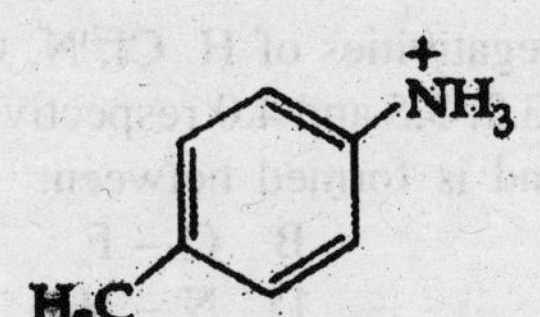

C. 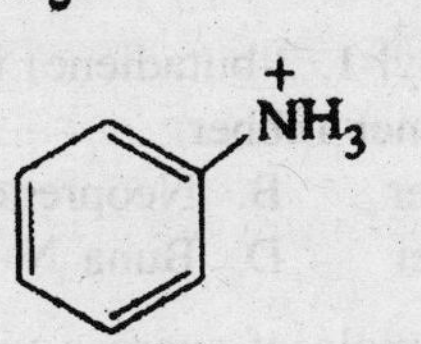

D. 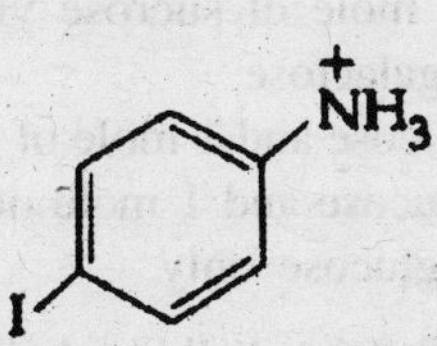

68. Among the following which is the most commonly used reducing agent?

A. $SnCl_2$ B. $BeCl_2$

C. $AlCl_3$ D. $PbCl_2$

69. The compound 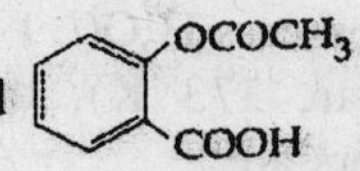

behaves as:

A. analgesic
B. insecticides
C. antacid
D. antihistamine

70. The correct order of reactivity in hydrolysis of the following compounds

CH_3COCl, CH_3CONH_2, CH_3COOCH_3 and $(CH_3CO)_2O$ is:

A. $CH_3COCl > (CH_3CO)_2O > CH_3COOCH_3 > CH_3CONH_2$
B. $CH_3CONH_2 > CH_3COOCH_3 > (CH_3CO)_2O > CH_3COCl$
C. $CH_3COOCH_3 > (CH_3CO)_2O > CH_3CONH_2 > CH_3COCl$
D. $(CH_3CO)_2O > CH_3CONH_2 > CH_3COOCH_3 > CH_3COCl$

71. Chlorophyll is:

A. a compound that makes CO_2 in plants
B. derived from Haem
C. a dipyrole pigment
D. a green pigment containing Mg

72. The electronegativities of H, Cl, N, O and F are 2.1, 3.0, 3.2, 3.5 and 4.0 respectively. The strongest bond is formed between:

A. O – Cl
B. O – F
C. H – O
D. N – H

73. Isoprene (2-methyl-1, 3-butadiene) is a basic unit of the polymer rubber:

A. Buna S rubber
B. Neoprene rubber
C. Natural rubber
D. Buna N rubber

74. Hydrolysis of 1 mole of sucrose yields:

A. 2 moles of galactose
B. 1 mole of glucose and 1 mole of galactose
C. 1 mole of glucose and 1 mole of fructose
D. 2 moles of glucose only

75. Which of the following halides shall produce isobutyl amine in phthalimide reaction?

A. $CH_3 — CH(Br) — CH_2CH_3$
B. $CH_3CH_2CH_2 — CH_2Br$
C. $(CH_3)_3\,C — Br$
D. $CH_3 — CH(CH_3) — CH_2Br$

76. Which of the following ions has largest heat of hydration?

A. Be^{2+}
B. Ba^{2+}
C. K^+
D. Li^+

77. Bond angle is minimum for which of the following?

A. H_2Te
B. H_2O
C. H_2S
D. H_2Se

78. **Assertion:** Orthoboric acid behaves as a Lewis acid.

Reason: It donates an electron pair to OH^- ion and forms a tetrahedral metaborate ion.

A. Assertion is false but Reason is true
B. Both Assertion and Reason are true and Reason is correct explanation for Assertion
C. Both Assertion and Reason are true but Reason is not correct explanation for Assertion
D. Assertion is true but Reason is false

79. Which one of the following outer electron configurations is ***not*** correct?

A. O : $2s^22p^4$
B. Al : $3s^23p^3$
C. B : $2s^22p^1$
D. N : $2s^22p^3$

80. In Rosenmund's reduction, the compound reduced is:

A. amide
B. aldehyde
C. acid chloride
D. alkyl cyanide

81. Which of the following has highest paramagnetic character?

A. Ni(11)
B. Mn(11)
C. Fe(11)
D. Co(11)

82. In the brown ring test in the complex $Fe(H_2O)_5(NO)SO_4$, nitric oxide behaves as:

A. NO^{2-}
B. NO^+

C. NO^-
D. Neutral NO molecule

83. The decomposition of HI into H_2 and I_2 is an example of:
A. second order reaction
B. zero order reaction
C. pseudo first order reaction
D. first order reaction

84. Which reagent brings about the following conversion?

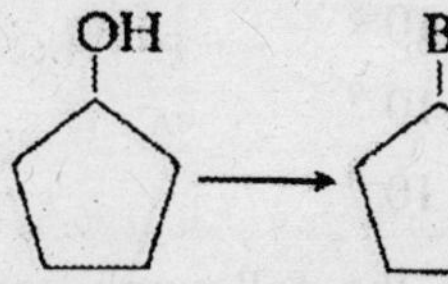

A. Br_2, H_2O B. NaBr
C. PBr_3 D. Br_2, CCl_4

85. The product formed in the reaction sequence

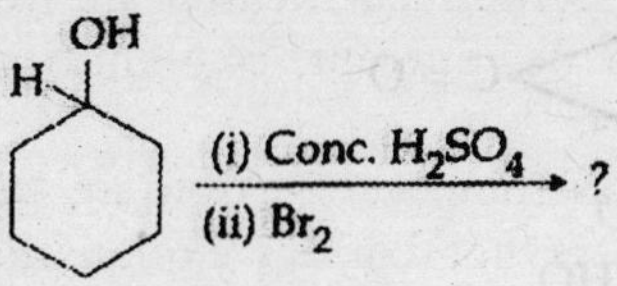

is:

A. 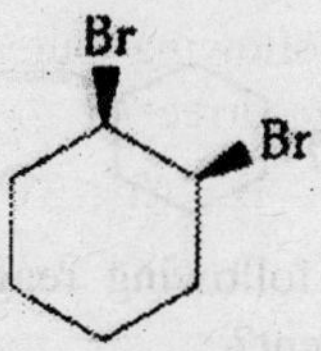 B. 

C. 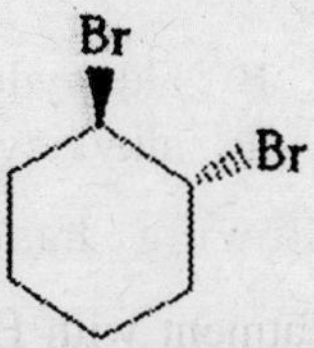 D. 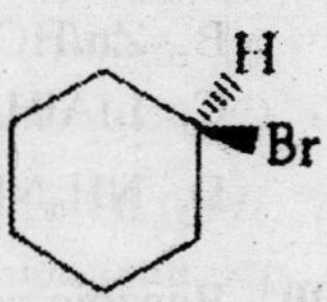

86. The enthalpies of all elements in their standard states are:
A. different for each element
B. zero
C. unity
D. less than zero

87. Which of the following pairs of metals is purified by Van Arkel process?
A. Ag and Au
B. Ni and Fe
C. Ga and In
D. Zn and Ti

88. A piece of wood from an archaeological source shows a ^{14}C activity which is 60% of the activity found in fresh wood today. Calculate the age of the archaeological sample. ($t_{1/2}$ ^{14}C = 5770 years)
A. 4252 years
B. 1920 years
C. 2041 years
D. 3052 years

89. For preparation of α-chloroacetic acid, which reaction is most suitable?
A. Hell-Volhard Zelinsky reaction
B. Wurtz reaction
C. Stephen's reaction
D. Perkin's reaction

90. Reaction of acetic acid with sodium bicarbonate, gives CO_2. The C of CO_2 comes from:
A. H – CH_2 – methylene group
B. $-CH_3$ group of CH_3COOH
C. $-COOH$ group in CH_3COOH
D. $H\bar{C}O_3$ group

91. To determine molar mass of protein, which colligative property can be helpful?
A. Osmotic pressure
B. Depression in freezing point
C. Elevation in boiling point
D. Relative lowering of vapour pressure

92. The chemical reaction

$(CH_3)_3CBr + H_2O \rightarrow (CH_3)_3COH + HBr$ is an example of:
A. Electrophilic substitution
B. Nucleophilic substitution
C. Free-radical substitution
D. Elimination reaction

93. Which of the following reaction shall produce benzoic acid?

A. 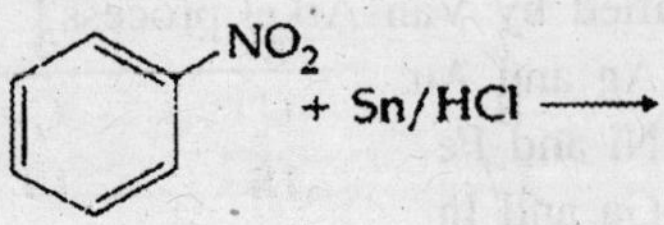

B. 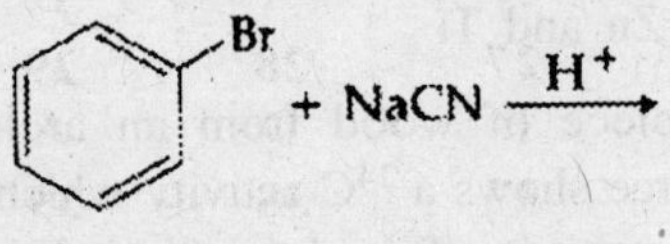

C. 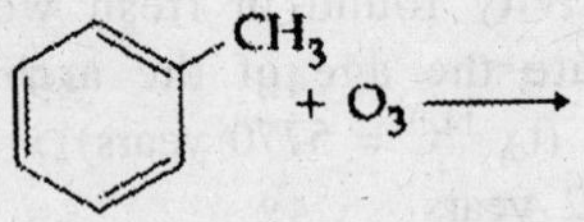

D. 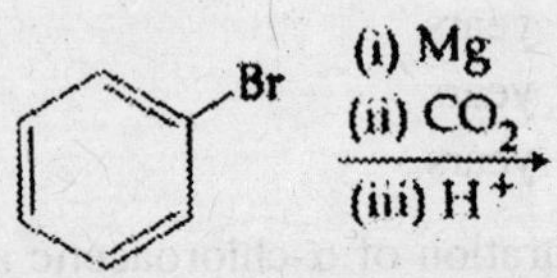

94. Cetyl trimethyl ammonium bromide is a:

A. ester of glycerol
B. anionic detergent
C. cationic detergent
D. soap

95. For the process

$Br_2(l) \rightarrow Br_2(g)$

$\Delta H° = 31 \text{ kJ mol}^{-1}$ and

$\Delta S° = 90 \text{ JK}^{-1} \text{ mol}^{-1}$. The temperature at which gaseous and liquid bromine will coexist in equilibrium will be:

A. 666 K
B. 333 K
C. 300 K
D. 500 K

96. The reaction of bromine with which of the following phenols shall produce tribromo derivative?

A. 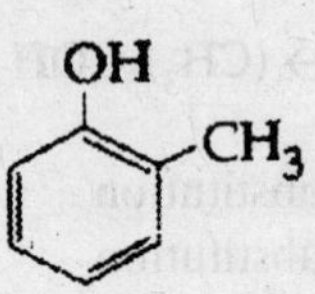

B. 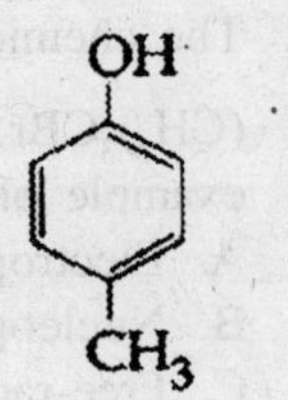

C. 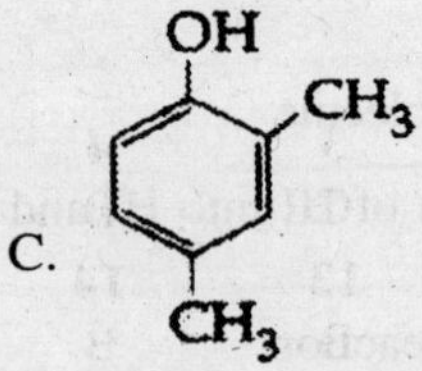

D. 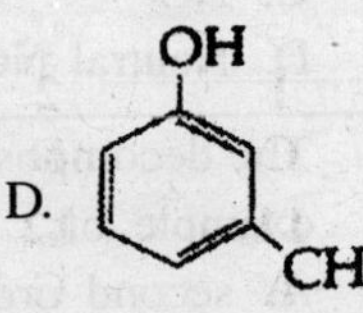

97. Solubility product (K_{sp}) of $BaSO_4$ is 1.1×10^{-10}. What will be molar solubility of barium sulphate in 0.05 M barium chloride solution?

A. 2.8×10^{-9}
B. 2.2×10^{-8}
C. 2.2×10^{-9}
D. 1.2×10^{-8}

98. Which of the following compounds shall produce an ester on treatment with aluminium ethoxide?

A. $C_6H_5 \cdot CHO$
B. $(CH_3)_2C=O$
C. HCHO
D. CH_3CHO

99. In the below given conversion

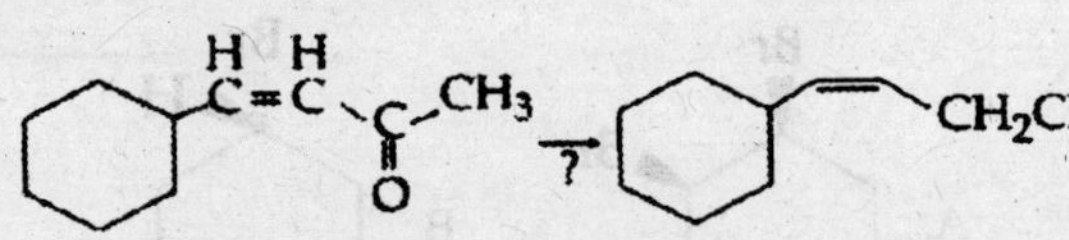

which one of the following reagents is the most suitable reagent?

A. Na/Liquid NH_3
B. Zn/HCl
C. $LiAlH_4$
D. NH_2NH_2; $\bar{O}Et$

100. Benzoic acid on treatment with HNO_3 in the presence of H_2SO_4 gives:

A. Benzene sulphonic acid
B. *m*-nitrobenzoic acid
C. nitrobenzene
D. *o*-nitrobenzoic acid

ANSWERS

1	2	3	4	5	6	7	8	9	10
C	D	C	B	C	C	B	C	C	B
11	12	13	14	15	16	17	18	19	20
A	C	B	B	D	B	A	A	B	B
21	22	23	24	25	26	27	28	29	30
A	A	A	D	C	D	B	D	A	A
31	32	33	34	35	36	37	38	39	40
B	D	A	C	D	C	A	C	A	D
41	42	43	44	45	46	47	48	49	50
C	C	B	A	A	D	A	C	D	A
51	52	53	54	55	56	57	58	59	60
A	C	A	B	D	D	C	A	A	D
61	62	63	64	65	66	67	68	69	70
B	B	A	D	B	C	A	A	A	A
71	72	73	74	75	76	77	78	79	80
D	C	C	C	D	A	A	D	B	C
81	82	83	84	85	86	87	88	89	90
B	B	A	C	C	B	*	A	A	D
91	92	93	94	95	96	97	98	99	100
A	B	D	C	B	D	C	D	D	B

CHEMISTRY

1

SOME BASIC CONCEPTS OF CHEMISTRY

INTRODUCTION

In order to express and to compare the magnitude of any physical quantity, it is necessary to fix some fundamental units. These are the units of length, mass, time and temperature.

Length : The fundamental unit of length is centimetre (cm). From this unit we can derive the unit of area as 1 square centimetre (1 cm^2) and the unit of volume as 1 cubic centimetre (1 cm^3 or 1 c.c.). Another unit of volume, called the *litre* is defined as the volume of 1 kilogram of water at 4°C. Accurate measurements have shown that

$$1 \text{ litre} = 1000.027 \text{ c.c.}$$

or

$$1 \text{ millilitre} = 1.000027 \text{ c.c.}$$

However, for all practical purposes, 1 ml is taken as 1 c.c.

In order to express very small magnitudes of length, it is customary to use the following units:

$$1 \text{ millimetre (mm)} = 10^{-1} \text{ cm}$$
$$1 \text{ micron } (\mu) = 10^{-4} \text{ cm}$$
$$1 \text{ millimicron } (m\mu) = 10^{-7} \text{ cm}$$
$$1 \text{ Angstrom } (\text{Å}) = 10^{-8} \text{ cm}$$

Mass : The fundamental unit of mass is called the gram (g). Some other derived units are the kilogram (kg) = 1000 g and the milligram (mg) = 10^{-3} gm. In chemistry, mass is frequently expressed in terms of *gram atom, gram equivalent* or *gram molecule.*

Gram Atom : It is defined as the atomic weight in grams. For instance, 16 g oxygen means 1 g atom of oxygen.

Gram Equivalent : It is defined as the equivalent weight in grams, for example, 1.008 g (1g atom) of hydrogen constitutes 1 g equivalent of hydrogens. Similarly, 8 g (or half g atom) of oxygen means ½ g equivalent of oxygen.

Gram Molecule (or gram Mole) : It is defined as the molecular weight in grams. For instance, 32 g of oxygen means 1 gm molecule or 1 g mole of oxygen and 98 g of sulphuric acid means 1 g molecule or 1 g mole of sulphuric acid.

The concentrations of aqueous solutions are generally expressed in terms of NORMALITY or MOLARITY.

A NORMAL SOLUTION contains one gram equivalent of a substance dissolved per litre of the solution and a MOLAR SOLUTION contains one gram molecule of the substance dissolved per litre of the solution.

Time : The fundamental unit of time is called the second (s). The derived units include the minute which is equal to 60 seconds and hour, which is equal to 60 minutes.

Temperature : The fundamental unit of temperature is called the degree centigrade (°C). In physical chemistry, temperature is usually expressed in *absolute* or *Kelvin scale.* The zero of this scale is – 273.15 °C.

International System of Units (S.I. Units)

A comprehensive system of units, which are both rational and coherent in nature, was introduced by the General Conference of Weights and Measures in its meeting held in October 1960. These units are called S.I. units and are now being adopted almost universally in scientific field.

Fundamental Units : The seven fundamental units are given below in table:

Quantity	*Unit*	*Symbol*
Mass	kilogram	kg
Length	meter	m
Time	second	s
Temperature	kelvin	K
Current	ampere	A
Amount of Substance	mole	mol
Luminous Intensity	Candela	Cd

Derived Units : The S.I. system has a large number of derived units, the important amongst which have been listed below:

Common Derived S.I. Units

Physical Quantity	*Name of Unit*	*Symbol*
Area	→ square metre	→ m^2
Volume	→ cubic metre	→ m^3
Density	→ kg per cubic metre	→ $kg\ m^{-3}$
Velocity	→ metre per second	→ ms^{-1}
Acceleration	→ metre per square second	→ ms^{-2}
Force	→ newton	→ N ($kgms^{-2}$)
Pressure	→ newton per square metre	→ Nm^{-2}
Work, Energy & → J(Kgm^2s^{-2}) Quantity of heat	joule	→
Power	→ watt	→ W (Js^{-1})
Frequency	→ hertz	→ Hz (s^{-1})
Electric Charge	→ coulomb	→ C (As)
Potential difference	→ volt	→ V
Capacitance	→ farad	→ F

Prefixes: For expressing various magnitudes of quantities in S.I. units are given below:

pico	⇒	p	⇒	10^{-12}
nano	⇒	n	⇒	10^{-9}
micro	⇒	μ	⇒	10^{-6}
milli	⇒	m	⇒	10^{-3}
centi	⇒	c	⇒	10^{-2}
deci	⇒	d	⇒	10^{-1}
kilo	⇒	k	⇒	10^{3}
mega	⇒	M	⇒	10^{6}

Conversion Factors : Some of the important conversion factors required to express physical quantities in S.I. units from those given in C.G.S. units and *vice versa*, are given below:

1 Å	$= 10^{-8}$ cm $= 10^{-10}$ m
1 litre	= 1000 c.c. $= 10^{-3}\ m^3$
1 atm	$= 101{,}325\ N\ m^{-2}$
1 newton (N)	$= 10^5$ dynes
1 cal	$= 4.184\ J = 4.184 \times 10^7$ ergs
1 erg	$= 10^{-7}$ J
1 eV	$= 1.60206 \times 10^{-19}$ J
	$= 1.60206 \times 10^{-12}$ erg
	$= 3.83 \times 10^{-23}$ kcal
1 joule	= 0.2390 cal.

Values of some useful constants and correlations in S.I. as well as in C.G.S. units, are given below:

Constant	*Value in S.I. Units*	*Value in C.G.S. units*
Avogadro's number (N_0)	$6.022 \times 10^{23}\ mol^{-1}$	$6.022 \times 10^{23}\ mol^{-1}$
Planck's Constant (h)	6.626×10^{-34} Js	6.626×10^{-27} erg s
Velocity of Light (c)	$2.997925 \times 10^8\ ms^{-1} = 3 \times 10^8\ ms^{-1}$	$2.997925 \times 10^{10}\ cms^{-1} = 3 \times 10^{10}\ cms^{-1}$
Electron Mass	9.1091×10^{-31} kg	9.1091×10^{-28} g
Proton Mass	1.6725×10^{-27} kg	1.6725×10^{-24} g
Electron Charge (e)	1.60206×10^{-19} C	9.8022×10^{-10} e.s.u.
Newtron Mass	1.6748×10^{-27} kg	1.6748×10^{-24} g
Bohr radius (a_0)	5.29×10^{-11} m = 0.529 Å	5.29×10^{-9} cm = 0.529 Å
Faraday (F)	$96496\ C\ equiv^{-1} \simeq 96500\ C\ equiv^{-1}$	$96496\ C\ equiv^{-1} \simeq 96500\ C\ equiv^{-1}$
Boltzman Constant (k)	$1.3806 \times 10^{-23}\ JK^{-1}$	$1.3806 \times 10^{-16}\ erg\ K^{-1}$
Gas Constant (R)	$0.08206\ 1\ atm\ K^{-1} mol^{-1}$ $= 8.3143\ JK^{-1}\ mol^{-1}$	$0.08206\ 1\ atm\ K^{-1}\ mol^{-1}$ $= 8.3143 \times 10^7\ ergs\ K^{-1}\ mol^{-1}$ $= 1.987\ cal\ K^{-1} mol^{-1}$
Atmospheric pressure (1 atm)	$1\ atm = 101{,}325\ Nm^{-2}$	1 atm = 76 cm of mercury $= 76 \times 13.6 \times 981\ dyn\ cm^{-2}$
Standard molar gas volume	$0.022414\ m^3 \simeq 0.224\ m^3$	22.4 litre = 22.400 c.c.
Permittivity factor, $4\pi \epsilon_0$	$1.11264 \times 10^{-10}\ C^2\ N^{-1} m^{-2}$	

Laws of Chemical Combinations : By studying the results of quantitative measurments of many reactions, it was observed that whenever substances react, they do so according to certain laws. These laws are known as *laws of chemical combination.*

1. Law of Conservation of Mass : The great French chemist, Antoine Laurent Lavoisier (1743-1794) established that *matter can neither be created nor destroyed.* This was verified by *Landolt.* In a chemical reaction total mass of the products is equal to total mass of the reactants. Law of conservation of mass does not hold good for nuclear reaction.

e.g., $2H_2 + O_2 \rightarrow 2H_2O$

$4g + 32g \qquad 36g$

The law of conservation of mass is also known as law of indestructibility of matter.

2. Law of Constant Composition : The law of conservation of mass helped in establishing the law of constant composition. This law was discovered by the French Chemist Joseph Proust (1799) and it is also known as *law of definite* proportions. This law states that a sample of pure compound, whatever its source; always consist of same elements combining in same proportions by mass. Law of definite proportions does not hold good for non-stoichiometric compounds, e.g., Wusitite $Fe_{0.95}O$

e.g., H_2O has H & O in the ratio 2 : 1

3. Law of Multiple Proportions : John Dalton (1803) observed that an element may form more than one compound with another element. He noted that for a given mass of an element, the masses of other element in two or more compounds are in ratio small integers. There observations of Dalton led him to formulate *atomic theory.*

e.g., N & O can combine to form N_2O & NO

In N_2O, 28g of N is combining with 16g of O

In NO, 14g of N is combining with 16g of O

∴ The mass of N that combines with O in both the compounds is in the ratio of 2 : 1.

In NH_3, 14g of N combines with 3 gm of hydrogen and in N_2H_4, 28g of N combines with 4g of hydrogen, i.e., the masses of hydrogen which combines with the fixed mass of nitrogen are in simple ratio of 3 : 2.

4. Law of Reciprocal Proportions : This law was proposed by Richter (1792) which states as "when two elements combine separately with a fixed mass of a third element, then the ratio of their masses in which they do so is either same or some whole number multiple of the ratio in which they combine with each other.

e.g., C & H combine with O to form CO_2 and H_2O repectively.

$$CO_2 = 12g\ C + 32g\ O$$
$$H_2O = 2g\ H + 16g\ O$$

C & H also react to form CH_4

$$CH_4 = 12\ g\ C + 4\ g\ H$$

Thus the C : H ratio combining with O in CO_2 and H_2O is same as in CH_4.

This law was verified by Stas.

Another example is

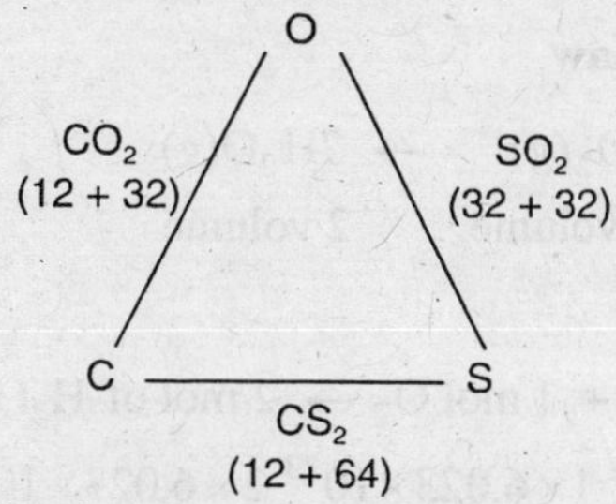

Ratio of masses of C and S which combines with fixed mass (32 parts) of O is

$$12 : 32$$
$$\Rightarrow \quad 3 : 8 \qquad ....(i)$$

Ratio of masses of C & S in CS_2 is

$$12 : 64$$
$$3 : 16 \qquad ....(ii)$$

Two ratios are related as

$$\frac{3}{8} : \frac{3}{16}$$
$$2 : 1$$

The law of reciprocal proportions is also known as *law of equivalent proportions* because the masses of two elements which combine with fixed mass of some third element are known as *equivalent masses.*

5. Law of Combining Volumes : French Chemist Gay-Lussac experimented with reactions of gases and proposed the following law :

When gases react with each other they do so in volumes which bear simple whole number ratio to one another and to the volumes of products. If there are also gases, provided all volumes are measured under similar conditions of temperature and pressure.

Gay-Lussac's discovery of integral ratio in volume relationship is actually the law of definite proportions by volumes'. This was explained properly by the work of Italian physicist and lawyer *Amedeo Avogadro* in 1811. Avogadro's law states that

"The volume of a gas at fixed temperature and pressure is proportional to the number of molecules or moles present.

$V \alpha n$, n = Number of moles.

In simpler way "Equal volumes of all gases contain equal number of molecules under similar conditions of temperature and pressure".

Both Gay-Lussac's and Avogadro's laws can be illustrated as

Gay-Lussac's Law

$$\begin{cases} 2H_2(g) \quad + \quad O_2(g) \quad \rightarrow 2H_2O(g) \\ 2 \text{ volume} \quad 1 \text{ volume} \quad 2 \text{ volume} \end{cases}$$

Avogadro's law

$$\begin{cases} 2 \text{ mol } H_2 \quad + 1 \text{ mol } O_2 \rightarrow 2 \text{ mol of } H_2O \\ 2 \times 6.023 \times 10^{23} \quad 1 \times 6.023 \times 10^{23} \quad 2 \times 6.023 \times 10^{23} \\ \text{molecule} \quad \text{molecule} \quad \text{molecule} \end{cases}$$

Atomic Mass : Atomic mass of an element is the weight of an atom with respect to $\frac{1}{12}$th of the weight of one atom of C^{12}.

Atomic weight can also be defined as the weight of 1 mole (6.023×10^{23} atoms) of an element.

e.g., weight of 1 mole of nitrogen atom = 14g

One *atomic mass unit* (1 a.m.u.) is therefore a mass unit equal to exactly one twelfth (1/12) part of the mass of C^{12} atom.

$$1 \text{ a.m.u.} = \frac{1}{12} \times 1.9926 \times 10^{-23} \text{ gm}$$
$$= 1.6605 \times 10^{-24} \text{ gm}$$

For example,

$$\text{mass of one H atom} = \frac{\text{atomic mass}}{N_0}$$
$$= \frac{1}{6.023 \times 10^{23}}$$
$$= 1.66 \times 10^{-24} \text{ g}$$
$$= 1 \text{ a.m.u.}$$

$$\text{mass of one N atom} = \frac{14}{6.023 \times 10^{23}}$$
$$= 14 \times 1.66 \times 10^{-24} \text{ g}$$
$$= 14 \text{ a.m.u.}$$

Methods of determination of Atomic Weight

(*a*) Dulong & Petit's law:
Atomic weight × Specific heat ≃ 6.4 for metals

(*b*) Victor Meyer Method:
Atomic weight = Equivalent weight × valency

(*c*) Average atomic weight of a mixture of isotopes of an element

$$= \frac{W_1 \times X_1 + W_2 \times X_2}{X_1 + X_2}$$

where W_1 & W_2 are the atomic weights of the two isotopes and X_1 & X_2 are their respective amount present in mixture.

(*d*) Specific Heat Method:
Atomic mass of a gaseous element

$$= \frac{\text{Molecular mass of gas}}{\text{Atomicity of gas}}$$

Atomicity is the number of atoms in a molecule of gas.

(*e*) Isomorphism Method:

$$\frac{\text{wt. of element A that combines with certain wt. of other elements}}{\text{wt. of element B that combines with same wt. of other elements}}$$
$$= \frac{\text{At. mass of A}}{\text{At. mass of B}}$$

Molecular Mass : Molecular mass of a compound is the weight of one molecule of the compound with respect to $\frac{1}{12}$th weight of one atom of C^{12}.

Molecular Mass

$$= \frac{\text{Mass of one molecule of a substance}}{\frac{1}{12} \times \text{Mass of one } C^{12} \text{ atom}}$$

It can also be defined as the weight of 1 mole (6.023×10^{23} molecules) of molecule. e.g.,

Molecular weight of O_2 = 32 grams
= Weight of 1 mole of O_2

Methods of Determination of Molecular Weight

(*a*) Vapour Density Method:
Molecular weight = 2 × Vapour density

(*b*) Cryoscopic Method:

$$M = \frac{1000 \times K_f \times w}{\Delta T_f \times W}$$

(*c*) Ebulloscopic Mothod:

$$M = \frac{1000 \times K_b \times w}{\Delta T_b \times W}$$

(*d*) Lowering of Vapour Pressure Method:

$$\frac{P_o - P_s}{P_o} = \frac{w/m}{W/M}$$

(*e*) Rate of Diffusion Method:

$$\frac{r_1}{r_2} = \sqrt{\frac{M_2}{M_1}}$$

Mole Concept

A mole is defined as the amount of a substance containing as many atoms, molecules, ions, electrons or other elementary entities as present in exactly 12g of C^{12}.

The number of carbon atom is 12g of C^{12} is 6.023×10^{23}. This number is called Avogadro Number and is represented by N. The symbol for mole is *mol.* A mole of a molecule and a mole of atom are termed as gram-molecule and gram atom respectively. For gases, a mole is represented with gram molecular volume, i.e., 22.4 litre at NTP. The number of molcule in $1 cm^3$ of gas at STP is called Loschmidt number. Its value is 2.688×10^{19}. One atomic mass unit (a.m.u.) is equal to 1/12th of the mass of C^{12} ($_6C^{12}$) atom which has been assigned a mass of 12.00 a.m.u.

Some Important Relations

(*i*) For Atomic Substance

$$\text{Gram atom} = \frac{\text{Weight in } g}{\text{Atomic weight}}$$

(*ii*) $\text{Gram molecule} = \frac{\text{Weight in } g}{\text{Molecular weight}}$

(*iii*) Gram molecular volume of gas

$$= \frac{\text{Volume at NTP}}{\text{Standard molar volume}}$$

(*iv*) 1 mole of an element or molecule $= 6.023 \times 10^{23}$ atoms or molecules

(*v*) 1 mole of a gaseous substance $= 6.023 \times 10^{23}$ molecules of the gas.
Volume occupied by 1 mole of a gas at NTP = 22.4 litre.

(*vi*) For a compound A_xB_y, *x* moles of B = *y* moles of A.

Molar Mass : The mass of 1 mole of any substance will be its *molar mass*. Thus 1 mol of sodium means 6.023×10^{23} atoms of sodium weighing 23.0 gm. Hence Molar mass of Na = 23.0 g/mol or 23 g mol^{-1} similarly 1 mol of oxygen molecule (O_2) means 6.023×10^{23} molecules of oxygen weighing 32.0 gm/mol or 32.0 g mol^{-1}.

Determination of Molecular Formula

Molecular formula = *n* × empirical formula

$$n = \frac{\text{Molecular weight of compound}}{\text{Empirical formula weight of compound}}$$

Empirical formula of a compound is determined by using the percentage of elements present in it.

Relative No. of atoms : Divide the perentage of each element present in compound by its atomic weight. This gives the relative number of atomes present in the compound.

Simplest Ratio : Find out lowest value of relative number of atoms and divide each value of relative number of atoms by this value to get simplest ratio of elements.

If the simplest ratio obtained are not complete integers, multiply them by a common factor to get integer values of simplest ratio.

Chemical Equation : It is a brief representation of chemical reactions with the help of symbols and formula of various reactants and products involved. An equation must be balanced with respect to all the atoms and molecules.

Stoichiometry of Chemical Reactions

Stoichiometry involves calculations based on the ratio of the weights of the reactants and products in a chemical equation.

A chemical equation provides information related to the molar ratio, mass ratio and volume ratio (for gaseous species) of the reactants and products.

For the sake of undertanding, stoichiometry can be studied under the following headings

(*i*) Gravimetric analysis (stoichiometry-I)

(*ii*) Volumetric analysis (stoichiometry-II)

Calculations based on stoichiometry can be divided into three types :

(*a*) Mass-Mass relationship

(*b*) Mass-Volume relationship

(*c*) Volume - Volume relationship

(*a*) Mass-Mass Relationships : Involves weights of Reactants & Products

(*i*) Write a balanced chemical equation representing the chemical change.

(*ii*) Write the number of moles and molecular weights of the reactants and products below them.

(*iii*) Apply the unitary method to calculate the unknown factor or factors.

(*b*) Mass-Volume Relationship : Weight of solids can be related to the volume of the gases through the following relation :

1 mole of gas = 22.4 litre or 22400 c.c. at N.T.P.

Instruction

(*i*) Write a balanced chemical equation with the weight of the reactants and products mentioned below:

(*ii*) Volume of the gaseous entities should be mentioned (at N.T.P.)

(*iii*) Volume of a gas at given temperature and pressure can be converted into weight by using the equation

$$PV = \frac{w \times RT}{W}$$

w = Mass or weight of the gas

W = Molecular weight of the gas

(*iv*) Calculate the unknown factor by unitary method.

(*c*) Volume-volume Relationship

(*i*) With the help of a balanced chemical equation; write the volume of each of the reactants and products (are the relation 1 gm mole = 22.4 litre, for gaseous substance)

(*ii*) Convert the volumes given to volume at NTP, using the relation $PV = \frac{w}{M}RT$.

(*iii*) Keep in mind the Avogaro's hypothesis "gases under same conditions of temperature and pressure contain the some number of molecules".

OBJECTIVE QUESTIONS

1. The balancing of a chemical reaction is based upon

A. Law of combining volumes
B. Law of definite proportion
C. Law of conservation of mass
D. All of these

2. The number of moles of CO_2 which contain 8 gm of oxygen is

A. 0.2 mole B. 0.25 mole
C. 0.4 mole D. 0.5 mole

3. The number of atoms present in 0.5 gm atoms of nitrogen is the same as the atoms present in

A. 12 g of carbon
B. 24 g of magnesium
C. 8 g of oxygen
D. 32 g of sulphur

4. 5.6 litre of a gas weighs 8.0 gm at STP. The vapour density (V.D.) of the gas will be

A. 8 B. 16
C. 24 D. 32

5. The density of water at 278 k is 1 gm/cm³. The molar volume of water at this temperature will be

A. 22.4 lit. B. 18.0 lit.
C. 18 cm³ D. None

6. An atom of an element is 12 times heavier than $\frac{1}{12}$th of mass of a C–12 atom. The mass of the atom of the element in a m u will be

A. 1.66×10^{-24} a m u B. 1.2 a m u
C. 12 a m u D. None

7. When N_A is Avogadro's number then the number of oxygen atoms in one gm. equivalent of oxygen is

A. N_A B. $\frac{N_A}{2}$
C. $\frac{N_A}{4}$ D. $2 \times N_A$

8. Which of the following will weigh highest among the following?
A. 3.01×10^{23} atoms of sulphur
B. 0.1 gm alom of silver
C. 5 gm atom of nitrogen
D. 20.0 gm of iron

9. Which of the following is not an element?
A. Diamond B. Ozone
C. Graphite D. Silica

10. 3.0 gm of a metal oxide converted to 5.0 gm of metal chloride. The equivalent weight of the metal is
A. 3.325 B. 66.50
C. 33.25 D. 25.33

11. 7.0 gm of a gas occupy 5.6 litre of volume at STP. The gas is
A. CO_2 B. NO_2
C. CO D. NO

12. The number of water molecules in a drop of water having volume of 0.0018 ml at room temperature will be–
(Density of water = 1 g cm^3)
A. 6.023×10^{23} B. $6.023 \times^{-23}$
C. 6.023×10^{19} D. 2.00×10^{19}

13. The law of mutiple proportions was proposed by
A. Dalton B. Lavoisier
C. Proust D. None

14. Which one of the following properties of an element can never be variable?
A. Valeney B. Atomic weight
C. Equivalent Mass D. None

15. The number of H_2O molecules in 1000 ml of water will be—
A. 18×1000 B. 6.023×10^{23}
C. 18 D. $55.55 \times N_A$

16. The number of valence shell electrons in 4.2 gm of nitride ion will be equal to–
A. $1.6 \times 6.02 \times 10^{23}$ B. $2.4 \times 6.02 \times 10^{23}$
C. $3.2 \times 6.02 \times 10^{23}$ D. None

17. The mass of one molcule of water is
A. 3×10^{-25} kg B. 3×10^{-26} kg
C. 1.5×10^{-26} kg D. 2.5×10^{-26} kg

18. When 0.44 gm of a colourless oxide of nitrogen occupies 224 ml at 1520 mm Hg and 273°C, then the oxide is
A. N_2O_5 B. N_2O_3
C. NO_2 D. N_2O

19. 12 gm of an alkaline earth metal gives 14.8 gm of its nitride. The atomic mass of metal is
A. 12 B. 24
C. 20 D. 40

20. 0.84 gm of a metal hydride contains 0.042 gm of hydrogen. The equivalent mass of metal is
A. 10 B. 20
C. 30 D. 40

21. The isotiopes of chlorine with mass numbers 35 and 37 exist in the ratio of
A. 1 : 1 B. 2 : 1
C. 3 : 1 D. 3 : 2

22. If atomic mass of oxygen is taken as 100, the molecular mass of water would be approximately
A. 6.25 B. 112.5
C. 102 D. 106.25

23. The prefix femto stands for
A. 10^9 m B. 10^{-12} m
C. 10^{-15} m D. 10^5 m

24. Which one of the following statements is incorrect?
A. All elements are homogeneous
B. Compounds made up of a number of elements
C. A mixture is not always heterogeneous
D. Air is a heterogeneous mixture

25. Which one of the following is not a mixture?
A. Iodized table salt
B. Gasoline
C. Liquefied Petroleum Gas (L.P.G.)
D. Distilled water

26. A mixture of $ZnCl_2$ and $PbCl_2$ can be separated by
A. Distillation B. Crystallisation
C. Sublimation D. Adding acetic acid

27. A mixture of red and blue ink can be separated by
A. Distillation B. Crystallisation
C. Chromatography D. Sublimation

28. Two gaseous samples were analysed. One contained 1.2 g of carbon and 3.2 g of oxygen. The other contained 27.3% carbon and 72.7% oxygen. The experimental data are in accordance with
A. Law of conservation of mass
B. Law of definite proportions

C. Law of reciprocal proportions
D. Law of multiple proportions

29. Which one of the following represents Avogadro's hypothesis
A. Equal volumes of all gases under same conditions of temperature and pressure contain equal number of atoms
B. Equal volumes of all gases under same conditions of temperature and pressure contain equal number of molecules.
C. Gases react together in volumes which bear a simple ratio to one another
D. The rates of diffusion of gases are inversely proportional to the square-root of their densities.

30. Choose the correct statement
The use of ^{12}C scale has superseded the older scale of atomic mass based on ^{16}O isotope, one important advantage of the former being
A. The atomic masses on ^{12}C scale became whole numbers.
B. ^{12}C is more abundant in the earth's crust than ^{16}O
C. The difference between the physical and chemical atomic masses got narrowed down significantly
D. ^{12}C is situated midway between metals and non-metals in the periodic table

31. 5.6 litres of a gas at N.T.P. are found to have a mass of 11 g. The molecular mass of the gas is
A. 22 B. 44
C. 88 D. 32

32. Which of the following has the largest number of atoms?
A. 0.5 g atom of Cu B. 0.635 g of Cu
C. 0.25 mole of Cu D. 6.35×10^{20} amu of Cu

33. The number of molecules present in a drop of water weighing 0.06 g is approximately
A. 10^{21} B. 2×10^{21}
C. 3×10^{21} D. 4×10^{21}

34. The mass of one atom of hydrogen is approximately
A. 1 g B. 0.5 g
C. 1.6×10^{-24} g D. 3.2×10^{-24} g

35. A gaseous mixture contains oxygen and nitrogen in the ratio of 1 : 4 by weight. Therefore, the ratio of their number of molecules is
A. 1 : 4 B. 1 : 8
C. 7 : 32 D. 3 : 16

36. Volume at N.T.P. of 0.22 g of CO_2 is same as that of
A. 0.01 g of hydrogen
B. 0.085 g of NH_3
C. 320 mg of gaseous SO_2
D. All of the above

37. 0.6 g of carbon was burnt in the air to form CO_2. The number of molecules of CO_2 introduced into the air will be
A. 6.02×10^{23} B. 3.01×10^{23}
C. 6.02×10^{24} D. 5.4×10^{21}

38. An electric bulb was filled with 100 cc of argon gas (At. mass = 40) at 25°C and 1 atm pressure. The number of atoms of argon present in the bulb is
A. 40000 B. 2.5×10^{21}
C. 3.3×10^{24} D. 5.4×10^{21}

39. The crystalline salt, $Na_2SO_4xH_2O$ on heating loses 55.9% of its weight. The formula of the cystalline salt is
A. $Na_2SO_4.5H_2O$ B. $Na_2SO_4.7H_2O$
C. $Na_2SO_4.10H_2O$ D. None of these

40. At N.T.P., 5.6 litres of a gas weigh 8 gram. The vapour density of the gas is
A. 32 B. 40
C. 16 D. 8

41. Which of the following represents the formula of a substance which contains about 26% nitrogen and 74% oxygen.
A. N_2O B. NO
C. NO_2 D. N_2O_5

42. How many atoms are present in a mole of H_2SO_4?
A. $3 \times 6.02 \times 10^{23}$ B. $5 \times 6.02 \times 10^{23}$
C. $6 \times 6.02 \times 10^{23}$ D. $7 \times 6.02 \times 10^{23}$

43. An oxide of iodine (I = 127) contains 25.4 grams of iodine and 8 grams of oxygen. Its formula could be
A. I_2O_3 B. I_2O
C. I_2O_5 D. I_2O_7

44. One litre of a gas is at a pressure of 10^{-6} mm of Hg at 25°C. How many molecules are present in the vessel?
A. 3.2×10^{6} B. 3.2×10^{13}
C. 3.2×10^{10} D. 3×10^{4}

45. A compound contains 69.5% oxygen and 30.5% nitrogen and its molecular weight is 92. The formula of the compound is
A. N_2O B. NO_2
C. N_2O_4 D. N_2O_5

46. On reduction with hydrogen, 3.6 g of an oxide of metal left 3.2 g of the metal. If the atomic weight of the metal is 64, the simplest formula of the oxide would be
A. M_2O_3 B. M_2O
C. MO D. MO_2

47. 280 ml of sulphur vapour at NTP wigh 3.2 g. The molecular formula of the sulphur vapour is
A. S B. S_2
C. S_4 D. S_8

48. A person adds 1.71 gram of sugar ($C_{12}H_{22}O_{11}$) in order to sweeten his tea. The number of carbon atoms added are (mol. mass of sugar = 342)
A. 3.6×10^{22} B. 7.2×10^{21}
C. 0.05 D. 6.6×10^{22}

49. 0.5 g of a metal on oxidation gave 0.79 g of its oxide. The equivalent weight of the metal is
A. 10 B. 14
C. 20 D. 40

50. Approximate atomic weight of an element is 29.89. If its eq. wt. is 8.9, the exact atomic weight is :
A. 26.89 B. 8.9
C. 17.8 D. 26.7

51. The equivalent weight of iron in Fe_2O_3 would be
A. 18.6 B. 28
C. 56 D. 112.0

52. 20 cc of CO_2 are passed over red hot coke. The volume of CO evolved is
A. 10 cc B. 20 cc
C. 30 cc D. 40 cc

53. 27 g of Al (at mass = 27) will react completely with oxygen equal to
A. 24 g B. 8 g
C. 40 g D. 10 g

54. How many moles of helium gas occupy 22.4 litre at 30°C and 1 atmosphere?
A. 0.11 B. 0.90
C. 1.0 D. 1.11

55. If a compound contains two oxygen atoms, four carbon atoms and number of hydrogen atoms is double of carbon atoms, the density of its vapour shall be
A. 88 B. 44
C. 132 D. 72

56. If oxygen is present in one litre flask at pressure of 7.6×10^{-10} mm Hg, then the number of oxygen molecules in the flask at 0°C will be
A. 27×10^{10} B. 0.27×10^{10}
C. 0.027×10^{10} D. 2.7×10^{10}

57. Which has maximum number of atoms?
A. 24 g of C (12) B. 56 g of Fe (56)
C. 27 g of Al (27) D. 108 g of Ag (108)

58. A mixture of NaI and NaCI on reaction with H_2SO_4 gave Na_2SO_4 equal to the weight of original mixture taken. The percentage of NaI in the mixture is
A. 82.38 B. 26.28
C. 62.38 D. 28.38

59. If LPG cylinder contains a mixture of butane and isobutane, then the amount of oxygen that would be required for combustion of 1 kg of it will be
A. 1.8 kg B. 2.7 kg
C. 4.5 kg D. 3.58 kg

60. The mass of 7% H_2SO_4 required for neutralisation of 1 mole of NaOH is
A. 49 g B. 98 g
C. 70 g D. 34 g

61. In Haber's process, gaseous nitrogen and hydrogen react to form ammonia whose volume as compared to that of reactants (N.T.P.) would be :
A. One fourth B. One half
C. The same D. Three fourth

62. 30g of Magnesium and 30 g of oxygen are reacted, then the residual mixture contains
A. 60 g of Magnesium oxide only
B. 40 g of Magnesium oxide and 20 g of oxygen
C. 45 g of Magnesium oxide and 15 g of oxygen
D. 50 g of Magnesium oxide and 10 g of oxygen

63. What will be the volume of the mixture after the reaction?
$NH_3(g)\ (1\ L) + HCl\ (1.5\ L) \rightarrow NH_4Cl\ (s)$
A. 1.5 L B. 0.5 L
C. 1 L D. 0 L

64. A metallic oxide contains 60% of the metal. The equivalent weight of the metal is
A. 12 B. 24
C. 40 D. 48

65. The specific heat of a metal is 0.11 and its equivalent weight is 18.61. Its exact atomic weight is
A. 58.2 B. 29.1
C. 55.38 D. 27.91

66. In alkaline medium, $KMnO_4$ as reacts follows :
$2 KMnO_4 + 2 KOH \rightarrow 2 K_2MnO_4 + H_2O + O$.
Therefore, the equivalent weight of $KMnO_4$ will be
A. 31.6 B. 52.7
C. 7.0 D. 158.0

67. The percentage of nitrogen in urea is about
A. 46 B. 85
C. 18 D. 28

68. The percentage of P_2O_5 in diammonium hydrogen phosphate, $(NH_4)_2HPO_4$ is
A. 23.48 B. 46.96
C. 53.78 D. 71.00

69. The simplest formula of a compound containing 50% of element X (atomic mass 10) and 50% of element Y (atomic mass 20) is
A. XY B. X_2Y
C. XY_3 D. X_2Y_3

70. In a hydrocarbon, the mas ratio of hydrogen to carbon is 1 : 3 the empirical formula of the hydrocarbon is
A. CH_4 B. CH_2
C. C_2H D. CH_3

71. The modern atomic weight scale is based on :
A. C^{12} B. O^{16}
C. H^1 D. C^{13}

72. Difference in density is the basis of
A. Ultrafiltration
B. Molecular sieving
C. Atomic absorption
D. Molecular attraction

73. Which of the following halogen can be purified by sublimation?
A. F_2 B. Cl_2
C. Br_2 D. I_2

74. How much of NaOH is required to neutralise 1500 cm³ of 0.1 N HCl? (Na = 23)
A. 40 g B. 4 g
C. 6 g D. 60 g

75. Number of grams of oxygen in 32.2 g $Na_2SO_4 10H_2O$ is
A. 20.8 B. 22.4
C. 2.24 D. 2.08

76. The number of water molecules present in a drop of water (volume 0.0018 ml) at room temperature is
A. 6.023×10^{19} B. 1.084×10^{18}
C. 4.84×10^{17} D. 6.023×10^{23}

77. Assuming fully deomposed, the volume of CO_2 released at STP on heating 9.85 g of $BaCO_3$ (Atomic mass, Ba = 137) will be
A. 0.84 L B. 2.24 L
C. 4.06 L D. 1.12 L

78. One mole of calcium phosphide on reaction with excess of water gives
A. One mole of phosphine
B. Two moles of phosphoric acid
C. Two moles of phosphine
D. One mole of phosphorus pentoxide

79. In the reaction
$4NH_3 (g) + 5 O_2 (g) \rightarrow 4 NO (g) + 6 H_2O (l)$, when 1 mole of ammonia and 1 mole of O_2 are made to react to completion
A. 1.0 mole of H_2O is produced
B. 1.0 mole of NO will be produced
C. All the oxygen will be consumed
D. All the ammonia will be consumed

80. 1 amu is equal to
A. $\frac{1}{12}$ part of an atom of C^{12}
B. $\frac{1}{14}$ part of an atom of O^{16}
C. 1 g of H_2
D. 1.66×10^{-23} kg

81. The vapour density of a gas is 11.2. The volume occupied by 11.2 g of the gas at NTP will be
A. 11.2 L B. 22.4 L
C. 1 L D. 44.8 L

82. The number of moles of oxygen in one litre of air containing 21% oxygen by volume, in standard condition is :

A. 0.186 mole B. 0.21 mole
C. 2.10 mole D. 0.0093 mole

83. In the final answer of the expression $\frac{(29.2-20.2)(1.79\times10^5)}{1.37}$ the number of significant figures is :
A. 1 B. 2
C. 3 D. 4

84. 1.12 mL of a gas is produced at S.T.P. by the action of 4.12 mg of alcohol. ROH, with methyl magnesium iodide. The molecular mass of alcohol is
A. 16.0 B. 41.2
C. 82.4 D. 156.0

85. The total number of protons in 10 g of calcium carbonate is ($N_0 = 6.023 \times 10^{23}$)
A. 1.5057×10^{24} B. 2.0478×10^{24}
C. 3.0115×10^{24} D. 4.0956×10^{24}

86. 100 mL of 1.0 M HCl are mixed with 75 ml of 1.0 M Na_2CO_3. The resulting solution will be
A. Acidic B. Basic
C. Neutral D. Amphoteric

87. A 5 molar solution of H_2SO_4 is diluted from 1 litre to a volume of 10 litres, the normality of the solution will be
A. 1 N B. 0.1 N
C. 5 N D. 0.5 N

88. The number of oxygen atoms in 4.4 g of CO_2 is approx.
A. 1.2×10^{23} B. 6×10^{22}
C. 6×10^{23} D. 12×10^{23}

89. The number of gram molecules of oxygen in 6.02×10^{24} CO molecules is
A. 10 gm molecule B. 5 gm molecule
C. 1 gm molecule D. 0.5 gm molecule

90. What is the weight of oxygen required for the complete combustion of 2.8 kg of ethylene?
A. 2.8 kg B. 6.4 kg
C. 9.6 kg D. 96 kg

91. When potassium permanganate is tritrated against ferrous ammonium sulphate, the equivalent weight of potassium permanganate is
A. molecular weight/10
B. molecular weight/5
C. moleculat weight/2
D. molecular weight

92. Avogadro number is
A. Number of atoms in one gram of element
B. Number of millilitres which one mole of a gaseous substance occupies at N.T.P.
C. Number of molecules present in one gram molecular mass of substance
D. All are correct

93. Which one of the following pairs of gases contains the same number of molecules?
A. 16 g of O_2 and 14 g of N_2
B. 8 g of O_2 and 22 g of CO_2
C. 22 g of N_2 and 22 g of CO_2
D. 32 g of O_2 and 32 g of N_2

94. The density of gas A is three times that of gas B. If the molecular weight of A is M, the molecular weight of B is
A. 3 M B. $\sqrt{3M}$
C. M/3 D. $M/\sqrt{3}$

95. If two compounds have the same empirical formula but different molecular formulae, they must have
A. Different percentage composition
B. Different molecular weights
C. Same viscosity
D. Same vapour density

96. A molar solution is one that contains one mole of a solute in
A. 1000 g of the solvent
B. One litre of the solvent
C. One litre of the solution
D. 22.4 litres of the solution

97. Crystals of which pair are isomorphous?
A. $ZnSO_4$, $SnSO_4$ B. $MgSO_4$, $CaSO_4$
C. $ZnSO_4$, $MgSO_4$ D. $PbSO_4$, $NiSO_4$

98. In known elements, the maximum number is of
A. Metals B. Non-metals
C. Metalloids D. None of the above

99. In chlorine gas, ratio of Cl^{35} and Cl^{37} is
A. 1 : 3 B. 3 : 1
C. 1 : 1 D. 1 : 4

100. A gas is found to have the formula $(CO)_x$. Its V.D. is 70. The value of x must be
A. 7 B. 4
C. 5 D.6

101. What is the normality of 1 M solution of H_3PO_4?
A. 0.5 N B. 1 N
C. 2 N D. 3 N

102. If 10^{24} molecules are removed from 200 mg of CO_2, then the number of moles of CO_2 left are
A. 2.88×10^{-3} B. 28.8×10^{-3}
C. 0.288×10^{-3} D. 1.66×10^{-2}

103. The percentage of copper and oxygen in samples of CuO obtained by different methods were found to be the same. This illustrates the law of
A. Constant proportions
B. Conservation of mass
C. Multiple proportions
D. reciprocal proportions

104. When 100 ml of 1 M NaOH solution and 10 ml of 10 N H_2SO_4 solution are mixed together, the resulting solution will be :
A. Alkaline B. Acidic
C. Strongly acidic D. Neutral

105. One gram of hydrogen is found to combine with 80 g of bromine. One gram of calcium (valency = 2) combines with 4 g of bromine. The equivalent weight of calcium is
A. 10 B. 20
C. 40 D. 80

106. Vapour density of a metal chloride is 66. Its oxide contains 53% metal. The atomic weight of the metal is
A. 21 B. 54
C. 27.06 D. 2.086

107. In chemical scale, the relative mass of the isotopic mixture of oxygen atoms (O_{16}, O_{17}, O_{18}) is assumed to be equal to
A. 16.002 B. 16.00
C. 17.00 D. 11.00

108. Which one of the following properties of an element is not variable?
A. Valency
B. Atomic weight
C. Equivalent weight
D. All of te above

109. What quantity of lime stone ($CaCO_3$) on heating will give 56 kg of CaO?
A. 1000 kg B. 56 kg
C. 44 kg D. 100 kg

110. If 0.5 mol of $BaCl_2$ is mixed with 0.2 mol of Na_3PO_4, the maximum number of moles of $Ba_3(PO_4)_2$ that can be formed is
A. 0.7 B. 0.5
C. 0.30 D. 0.10

111. Four one-litre flasks are separately filled with the gases hydrogen, helium, oxygen and ozone at the same room temperature and pressure. The ratio of total number of atoms of these gases present in the different flasks would be
A. 1 : 1 : 1 : 1 B. 1 : 2 : 2 : 3
C. 2 : 1 : 2 : 3 D. 3 : 2 : 2 : 1

112 If $1\frac{1}{2}$ moles of oxygen combine with Al to form Al_2O_3, the weight of Al used in the reaction is ($Al = 27$)
A. 27 g B. 54 g
C. 40.5 g D. 81 g

113. The total number of electrons present in 18 ml of water (density of water is 1 gm^{-1}) is
A. 6.02×10^{23} B. 6.02×10^{22}
C. 6.02×10^{24} D. 6.02×10^{25}

114. The moles of O_2 required for reacting with 6.8 g of ammonia
(.... NH_3 + ... $O_2 \rightarrow$ .... NO + ... H_2O) is
A. 5 B. 2.5
C. 1 D. 0.5

115. The number of moles of $BaCO_3$ which contains 1.5 moles of oxygen atoms is
A. 0.5 B. 1
C. 3 D. 6.02×10^{23}

116. The law of multiple proportions was proposed by
A. Lavoisier
B. Dalton
C. Proust
D. Gay-Lussac

117. A solution containing Na_2CO_3 and NaOH requires 300 mL of 0.1 N HCl using phenolphthalein as an indicator. Methyl orange is then added to above titrated solution when a further 25 mL of 0.2 N HCl is required. The amount of NaOH present in solutions is [NaOH = 40, Na_2CO_3 = 106]

A. 0.8 g B. 1.0 g
C. 1.5 g D. 2.0 g

118. What quantity of ammonium sulphate is necessary for the production of NH_3 gas sufficient to neutralize a solution containing 292 g of HCl? [HCl = 36.5; $(NH_4)_2SO_4$ = 132; NH_3 = 17]

A. 272 g B. 408 g
C. 528 g D. 500 g

ANSWERS

1	2	3	4	5	6	7	8	9	10
C	B	C	B	C	C	B	C	D	B
11	12	13	14	15	16	17	18	19	20
C	C	A	B	D	B	B	D	D	B
21	22	23	24	25	26	27	28	29	30
C	B	C	B	D	B	C	D	B	C
31	32	33	34	35	36	37	38	39	40
B	A	B	C	C	D	D	B	C	C
41	42	43	44	45	46	47	48	49	50
D	D	C	B	C	B	D	A	B	D
51	52	53	54	55	56	57	58	59	60
A	D	A	B	B	C	A	D	D	C
61	62	63	64	65	66	67	68	69	70
B	D	B	A	C	D	A	C	B	A
71	72	73	74	75	76	77	78	79	80
A	C	D	C	B	A	D	C	C	A
81	82	83	84	85	86	87	88	89	90
A	D	B	C	C	B	A	A	B	C
91	92	93	94	95	96	97	98	99	100
B	C	A	C	B	C	C	A	B	C
101	102	103	104	105	106	107	108	109	110
D	A	A	D	B	C	B	B	D	D
111	112	113	114	115	116	117	118		
C	B	C	D	A	B	B	C		

2

STATES OF MATTER

Matter : Solid, liquid and gaseous states represent three different states of aggregation and provide a basis of physical classification of matter. Gaseous state of matter at very high temperature containing gaseous ions and free electrons is known as *plasma state*.

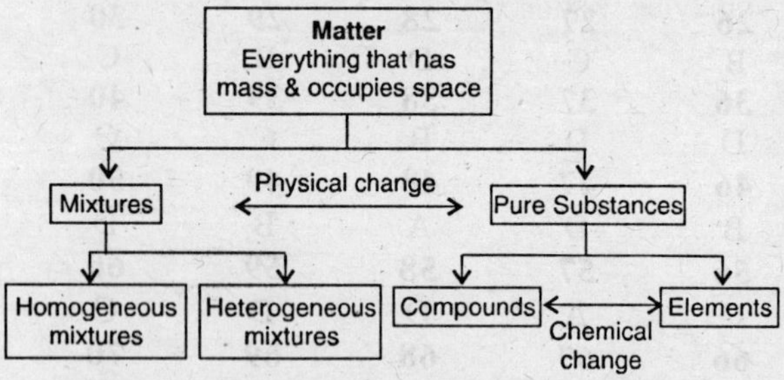

Gases : A form of matter, such as air, in whih the molecules move randomly in otherwise empty space, filling any size or shape of container into which the gas is put. Gases can be liquified by cooling which reduces the speed of the molecules and enables attractive forces between them to bind them together.

Important Characteristics of Gases :

(i) When the forces of attraction between the particles of matter is minimum, the particles exist in a state called gaseous. In this state, the molecules are far apart from one another and their positions are not fixed.

(ii) Gases have neither definite shape nor definite volume.

(iii) Gases even in their mixtures are homogeneous in composition.

(iv) Gases have very low density.

(v) Gases have infinite expansibility and high compressibility.

(vi) Gases exert pressure.

(vii) Gases possess diffusibility.

(viii) Gases can be liquified by cooling under high pressure.

(ix) Gases undergo similar change with the change of temperature and pressure. This behaviour of gases is governed by certain laws known as *gas laws*.

Boyle's Law : The product of pressure and volume of a given mass of a gas is constant at constant temperature.

$V \propto \frac{1}{P}$ (at constant temperature)

$PV = K$ (where K is proportionality constant)

If the volume V_1 and pressure P_1 of a given mass of gas are changed to V_2 and P_2 respectively temperature remaining constant, then

$$P_1 \times V_1 = P_2 \times V_2$$

Charle's Law : At constant pressure, the volume of a given mass of a gas is directly proportional to absolute temperature (Absolute temperature = temperature in °C + 273.15)

$V \propto T$ (P being constant)

or $\frac{V}{T} = \text{constant}.$

If the volume V_1 of a given mass of a gas at temperature T_1 changes to V_2 at temperature T_2, pressure remaining constant, then

$$\frac{V_1}{T_1} = \frac{V_2}{T_2}.$$

The Gas Equation : This equation combines Charle's and Boyle's law :

$V \propto \frac{1}{P}$ at constant T (Boyle's law)

$V \propto T$ at constant P (Charle's law)

Combining two law's $V \propto \frac{1}{P} \times T$

$V \propto \frac{T}{P}$ or $\frac{PV}{T} = \text{constant (R)}$

Nature of R (Gas constant)
For one mole of a gas

$$R = \frac{PV}{T} = \frac{\text{Pressure} \times \text{Volume}}{\text{Temperature}}$$

$$= \frac{\text{Force}}{\text{Area}} \times \frac{\text{Volume}}{\text{Temperature}}$$

Since, Volume = Area × Length

$$R = \frac{\text{Force} \times \text{Length}}{\text{Temperature}} = \frac{\text{Work}}{\text{Temperature}}$$

Thus, the dimensions of R are energy per degree per mole

Numerical Values of

$$\begin{aligned} R &= 0.821 \text{ litre-atm/k/mole} \\ &= 8.314 \times 10^7 \text{ erg/k/mole} \\ &= 8.314 \text{ joules/kelvin/mole} \\ &= 1.99 \text{ calories/kelvin/mole} \\ &= 0.002 \text{ K cal/kelvin/mole} \\ &= 5.28 \times 10^{19} \text{ eV/kelvin/mole} \end{aligned}$$

for '*n*' moles of a gas; the gas equation becomes

$$\boxed{PV = nRT}$$

This is called IDEAL GAS EQUATION

or $PV = \frac{m}{M} RT$

where m = Mass of the gas
and M = Mol. wt. of the gas.

While using gas equation, V should be in litre, P in atmosphere and T in absolute scale.

Initial pressure P_1, volume V_1 and temperature T_1 of a gas may be related with the final pressure P_2, volume V_2 and temperature T_2 as given below :

$$\boxed{\frac{P_1V_1}{T_1} = \frac{P_2V_2}{T_2}}$$

While using the above relation, standard (or normal) conditions are usually given, standard (normal) conditions mean that temperature is 0°C or 273K and pressure is 1 atmosphere or 760 mm. It is because of the fact that the volume of any gas at 0°C and 1 atmospheric pressure is considered as volume at standard (or normal) temperature and pressure, *i.e.* at STP or NTP.

Explanation of Behaviour of Real gases on the basis of Van der Waal's equation

Unlike ideal gas equation, the Van der Waal's equation explains the behaviour of real gases under different conditions of temperature and pressure.

(i) At low pressures : At low pressures, volume V is very large and hence the correction term '*b*' (a constant of small value) can be neglected in comparison to very large value of V. Thus, Van der Waal's equation for 1 mole of a gas, *i.e.*

$$\left(P + \frac{a}{V^2}\right)(V - b) = RT \qquad ...(i)$$

may be written as

$$\left(P + \frac{a}{V^2}\right)V = RT$$

$$\Rightarrow \qquad PV + \frac{a}{V} = RT$$

$$\Rightarrow \qquad PV = RT - \frac{a}{V} \qquad ...(ii)$$

At extremely low pressure: Since V is very large, the value of $\frac{a}{V}$ is very small and hence can be ignored. Consequently, at very low pressures, the Van der Waal's equation is reduced to ideal gas equation, *i.e.*

$$PV = RT$$

This explains why at extremely low pressures, the real gases obey the ideal gas equation.

The equation *(ii)* shows that PV is less than RT by an amount equal to $\frac{a}{V}$. As pressure increases, V decreases, $\frac{a}{V}$ increases and ultimately PV becomes smaller and smaller. This explains the dip in the isotherms of most of the gases (*e.g.* CO and CH_4).

(ii) At high pressures : At high pressures, volume V is quite small and hence the term *b* cannot be neglected in comparison to V. Secondly, under these conditions although the term $\frac{a}{V^2}$ is quite large, it is so small in comparison to high pressure P that it can be neglected. Thus, the Van der Waal's equation is reduced to

$$P(V-b) = RT$$
$$\Rightarrow PV - Pb = RT$$
$$\Rightarrow PV = RT + Pb \quad ...(iii)$$

Thus PV is greater than RT by an amount equal to P*b*. As the pressure increases, the factor P*b* increases and hence PV increases. This explains why the value of PV, *after reaching a minimum, increases with further increase of pressure.*

(iii) At high temperature : At any given pressures, if the temperature is sufficiently high, V is very large and hence the terms $\frac{a}{V^2}$ and '*b*' can be neglected as in case *(i)* and thus the Van der Waal's equation reduces to PV = RT. This explains why the real gases behave like ideal gas at high temperatures.

(iv) At low temperature : At low temperatures both P and V are small, hence both pressure and volume corrections are appreciable, with the result the deviations are more pronounced.

(v) Exceptional behaviour of hydrogen and helium : Since hydrogen and helium have very small masses, the intermolecular forces of attraction are extremely small even at low pressures. In orther words, the factor $\frac{a}{V^2}$ is negligible at all pressures. Hence the Van der Waal's equation is reduced to

$$P(V-b) = RT$$
$$PV = RT + Pb$$

This explains why hydrogen and helium show positive deviations only with increase in the value of P.

Boyle's temperatures : The temperature at which a real gas obeys Boyle's law is known as Boyle's temperature, T_B.

T_B and the two Van der Waal's constants are related as below :

$$T_B = \frac{a}{bR}$$

where *a* and *b* are Van der Waal's constants. Boyle's temperature of a gas is always higher than its critical temperature.

Limitations of van der Waal's Equation : Although van der Waal's equation is much more accurate than the ideal gas equation, appreciable deviations have been observed at too low temperatures or too high pressures. This is due to the fact that the values of Van der Waal's constant *a* and *b* do not remain constant over the entire range of temperatures and pressures and hence the Van der Waal's equation is also valid over specific range of temperature and pressure.

Kinetic Theory of Gases

It is mathematical explanation of the behaviour of gases based on the following postulates:

(i) Gases consist of very large number of minute particles called 'molecules'.

(ii) The molecules of a gas are so small that their actual volume is negligible as compared to the total volume of the gas.

(iii) There is no attractive force between the molecules, as they move independent of each other.

(iv) Molecules are moving very fast in all directions in a straight line until their directions are changed on collision with each other or with the walls of the container.

(v) The molecular collisions are perfectly elastic and there is no loss of kinetic energy due to their collisions. However, there may be redistribution of energy during such collisions.

(vi) The pressure exerted by the gas is the result of collisions of the molecules on the walls of the container.

(vii) Since different molecules in a system move with different velocities, they possess different kinetic energies. However, the average kinetic energy of molecules is directly pro-portional to the absolute temperature of the gas.

The above postulates are applicable only to ideal gases and are approximately valid for real gases.

On the basis of the above postulations, following mathematical expression, commonly known as *kinetic gas equation* is derived.

$$PV = \frac{1}{3} mnu^2$$

where P = Pressure of the gas
V = Volume of the gas
m = Mass of a molecule
u = root mean square velocity (RMS)
n = Number of molecules present in the given amount of gas.

For 1 mole of a gas, since n = N, where N is the Avogadro's number (6.02×10^{23}), the above kinetic gas equation may be written as

$$PV = RT = \frac{1}{3} mNu^2$$

$$\Rightarrow \quad PV = RT = \frac{1}{3} Mu^2$$

($\because$ m × N = M, where M is the molecular weight of the gas)

$$u = \sqrt{\frac{3RT}{M}} = \sqrt{\frac{3PV}{M}} = \sqrt{\frac{3P}{d}}$$

$$\left(\because \frac{M}{V} = d, \text{density}\right)$$

In the above equation, if M is expressed in g/mole and 'u' in cm/sec, then R must be expressed in ergs K^{-1} $mole^{-1}$. The various values of R in different units are as below :

R = 8.314 joules K^{-1} $mole^{-1}$
= 1.99 calories K^{-1} $mole^{-1}$

Ideal and Real Gases

A gas which obeys Boyle's law, Charle's law etc., under all conditions of temperature and pressure is known as an *ideal gas* or a *perfect gas.*

Further, since the gas equation (PV = nRT) is desired by combining Boyle's law and Charle's law, an *ideal gas* may be defined as a gas which obeys the gas equation (PV = nRT) under all conditions of temperature and pressure, and hence the gas equation is also known as "ideal gas equation". However, *no gas is perfect and the concept of perfect gas is only theoretical.* Gases tend to show ideal behaviour more and more as the temperature rises above the boiling points of their liquified forms and the pressure is lowered. Such gases are known as *real gases.* Thus, a real gas may be defined as a gas which obeys the gas laws under low pressure or high temperature.

All gases are real gases. They show more and more deviation from the gas laws (i.e. from ideal behaviour) as the pressure is increased or temperature is decreased.

Dalton's Law of Partial Pressure: The total pressure (P) exerted by a mixture of gases is equal to the sum of partial pressures (p) of the components of the gas mixture. The *partial pressure* is defined as the pressures the gas would exert if it was contained in the same volume as that occupied by the mixture.

SOLIDS

Solids are characterized by incompressibility, rigidity and mechanical strength. This reveals that the molecules, atoms or ions that make up a solid are very closely packed unlike liquid and gases.

The solids are broadly classified into two categories:

(a) Crystalline solids
(b) Amorphous solids

***(a)* Crystalline solids :** A substance whose constituent particles are arranged in an orderly manner giving rise to a definite geometrical form is known as crystalline solid. The regular arrangement of constituents extends over large distance in three dimensional network, that is, they exhibit long range order e.g. sodium chloride, diamond, sugar etc.

***(b)* Amorphous Solids:** A substance whose constituents are not arranged in an orderly manner is called an amorphous solid. They do not have definite geometrical forms. Some amorphous solids may have some orderly arrangement but it does not extend to more than a few angstrom units.

The amorphous solids have only short range order. For example plastics, rubber, glass etc. These crystalline parts of an amorphous solids are called *crystallites.* Amorphous solids are sometimes known as ***super cooled liquids*** because they possess disorderly arrangements like liquids.

The crystalline solids may be further divided into five classes on the basis of nature of constituent particles and the interparticle forces. Some of the important characteristics of these classes have been given below :

Crystal Classification :

(a) Atomic *(b)* Molecular
(c) Ionic *(d)* Covalent
(e) Metallic

(a) Atomic Crystals :

(i) Unit particles-atoms

(ii) Interparticle forces : London dispersion forces.

(iii) Properties : Soft, very low m.p., poor thermal and electrical conductors.

(iv) Example : Noble gases

(b) Molecular Crystals :

(i) Unit particles : Polar or non-polar molecules.

(ii) *Interparticle forces :* Van der Waal's force (London) dispersion, dipole-dipole forces and hydrogen bonds.

(iii) *Properties :* Fairly soft, low to moderately high m.p., poor thermal and electrical conductor.

(iv) *Examples :* Dry ice (solid CO_2), methane (CH_4)

(c) Ionic Crystals :

(i) *Unit particles :* Positive and negative ions.

(ii) *Interparticles forces :* Ionic bonds

(iii) *Properties :* Hard and brittle, high melting points, high heats of fusion, poor thermal and electrical conductors.

(iv) *Examples :* NaCl, ZnS

(d) Covalent Crystals :

(i) *Unit particles :* Atoms that are connected in covalent bond network.

(ii) *Interparticle forces :* Covalent bonds

(iii) *Properties :* Very hard, very high m.p., poor thermal and electrical conductors.

(iv) *Example :* Diamond, quartz, silicon.

(e) Metallic Crystals :

(i) *Unit Particles :* Cations in electric cloud.

(ii) *Interparticle forces :* Metallic bonds

(iii) *Properties :* Soft to very hard, low to very high melting points, excellent thermal and electrical conductors, malleable and ductile.

(iv) *Examples :* All metallic elements as Cu, Zn, Fe.

Principles of Crystal Structures

Unit Cells and Crystal Lattice : All the crystal lattices are built of Unit Cells, the smallest repeating unit that has all of the symmetry characteristics of the way the atoms are arranged. To understand the idea of the unit cell, look at the repeating pattern of circles in the following figure.

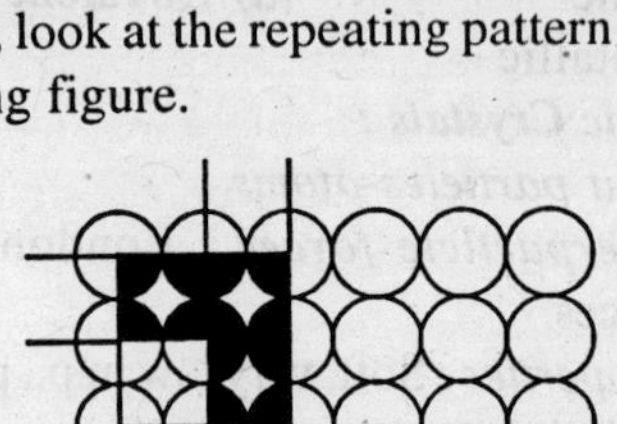

Fig. *Unit cells for a "two dimensional solid"*

A unit cell could be drawn around each atom but this unit cell would not reveal how the circles are arranged with respect to each other, that is, it would not show the symmetry of arrangement of circles.

A way to draw a cell that shows this is to draw lines from the centre of one circle to the centres of neighbouring circles, a square unit cell results. Furthermore, since each of the four circles contribute one quarter of itself to the square's contents, a net of one circle is located within each square. Thus unit cell reveals the pattern of circles and the entire pattern can be built by joining identical square unit cells edge to edge, each cell containing the equivalent of one circle. Solids can be built up by filling up three dimensional unit cells like building blocks.

The corners defining each unit cells in simple solids have identical environment in an ionic solid, in a metallic solid or in a molecular solid, such points are equivalent to each other and collectively they define the Crystal Lattice. Ions, atoms or molecules are centred at these points. Thus, it may be noted that the lattice points do not represent the actual atoms in the crystal rather they reflect their special arrangements in the crystal. The size and shape of the unit cell is determined by the lengths (a, b and c) of the edges of the unit cell and the angles (α, β and γ) at which these edges intersect each other.

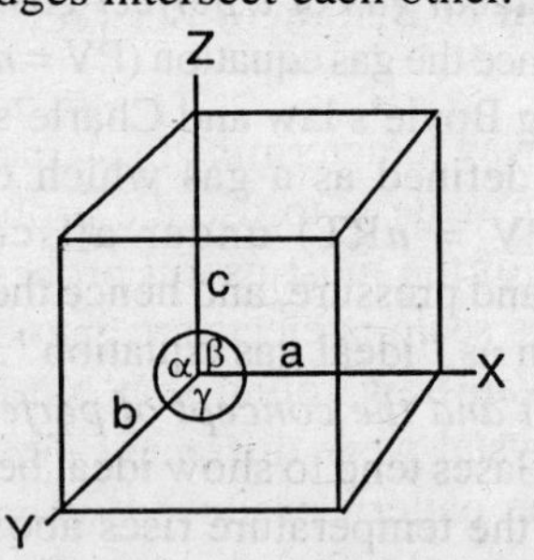

Fig. *Representation of dimensions of a unit cell*

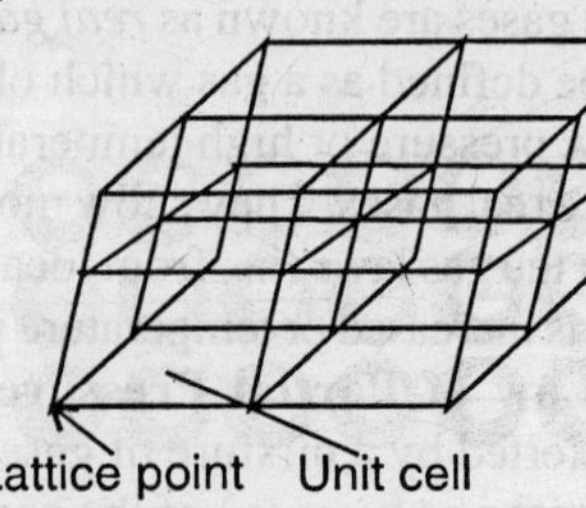

Fig. *Simple crystal lasttice and its associated unit cell*

Each unit cell is defined in terms of Lattice Points, the points in space about which the particles are free to vibrate in a crystal. In 1850, Auguste Bravis showed that crystal could be divided into 14 units cells that meet the following criteria :

(i) The unit cell is the simplest repeating unit in the crystal.

(ii) Opposite faces unit cell are parallel.

(iii) The edge of the unit cell connects equivalent points.

The fourteen Bravis unit cells are shown below. These unit cells fall into seven kinds, which differ in the three unit cell edge lengths (a, b, and c) and the three internal angles (α, β and γ).

The Seven Categories of Bravais Unit Cells

Category	*Edge Lengths*	*Internal Angles*
Cubic	$(a = b = c)$	$(\alpha = \beta = \gamma = 90°)$
Tetragonal	$(a = b \neq c)$	$(\alpha = \beta = \gamma = 90°)$
Monoclinic	$(a \neq b \neq c)$	$(\alpha = \gamma = 90°, \beta \neq 90°)$
Orthorhombic	$(a \neq b \neq c)$	$(\alpha = \beta = \gamma = 90°)$
Rhombohedral	$(a = b = c)$	$(\alpha = \beta = \gamma \neq 90°)$
Hexagonal	$(a = b \neq c)$	$(\alpha = \beta = 90°, \gamma = 120°)$
Triclinic	$(a \neq b \neq c)$	$(\alpha \neq \beta \neq \gamma \neq 90°)$

Measurement of Distances Between Particles in a Unit Cell

The only way to determine the structure of matter on the atomic scale is to use the probe that is even smaller. One of the most useful probes for studying matter on this scale is electromagnetic radiation. In 1912, Max Van Law found that X-rays struck the surface of crystal were diffracted into patterns that resembled the pattern produced when light passes through a narrow slit. Shortly, thereafter, William

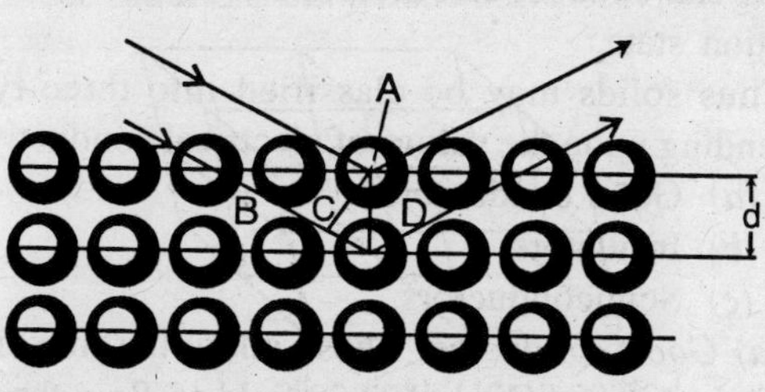

Fig. *The diffraction of X-rays by the first and second planes in a crystal*

Laurence Bragg, who was just completing his undergraduate degree in physics at Cambridge, explained Van Law's results. Bragg argued that X-rays were reflected from the planes of atoms near the surface of crystal.

X-rays that were reflected from different planes of atoms would be no longer in phase and they would tend to cancel each other. They could stay in phase only if the extra distance (BC + CD) the X-ray moved when it struck the second plane of atoms was equal to an integer (*n*) times the wavelength (λ) of the radiation.

$$BC + CD = n\lambda$$

Bragg defined the angle between the beam of X-rays and the plane of crystal as θ. Because the BAC angle is also equal to θ, the BC distance is equal to AB distance times the sine of θ.

$$BC = AB \sin\theta$$

Because the distance AB is equal to the distance between the planes of atoms, *d*. The relationship between BC and AB will be

$$BC = d \sin\theta$$

Because the BC distance is equal to the CD distance, following relationship is arrived at

$$BC + CD = 2d\sin\theta.$$

Substituting the relationship between BC + CD and $n\lambda$ gives a formula known as Bragg Equation which shows us to calculate the distance between planes of atoms in the crystal from the pattern of diffraction of X-rays of known wavelength

$$n\lambda = 2d \sin\theta.$$

The pattern by which X-rays are diffracted by nickel metal suggests that this metal packs in cubic unit cell with a distance (*d*) between planes of atoms of 0.3525 nm. Thus the cell edge length in the crystal must be 0.3524 nm. Knowing that nickel crystallises in a cubic unit cell is not enough. One still has to decide whether it is a simple cube, body centered cubic or face centered cubic unit cell. This can be done by measuring the density of metal.

Lattice Energy

The amount of energy released when cations and anions in their gaseous states are brought from infinity to their respective equilibrium sites in the crystal lattice to form a mole of the *ionic solid,* is known as lattice energy of that solid. Higher the magnitude of lattice energy, the greater is the tendency of formation of ionic solid.

Lattice Energies of Various Alkali Metal Halides ($kJ\ mol^{-1}$)

Halide Ion	Li^+	Na^+	K^+	Rb^+	Cs^+
F^-	– 994.5	– 894.5	– 790.2	– 756.7	– 719.0
Cl^-	– 802.6	– 758.7	– 681.4	– 666.6	– 618.7
Br^-	– 760.8	– 714.8	– 656.3	– 631.3	– 593.6
I^-	– 710.6	– 668.8	– 618.7	– 597.7	– 564.3

It can be concluded that for a given anion, the smaller the radius of the cation the greater is the lattice energy. Similarly, for a given cation, the smaller is the radius of the anion, the greater is the value of lattice energy or greater is the strength of ionic bond.

The most essential feature of crystalline solids is that the constituent molecules, atoms or ions are arranged in a completely regular three dimensional manner. Since the atoms or ions have considerable degree of thermal vibrations, the crystalline state is far from being totally static, and the pattern is seldom perfect. Many of the properties of crystalline solids are related to the thermal vibrations of constituents, the presence of impurities and the existence of defects. Crystalline solids have two kinds of crystal defects :

(1) Stoichiometric Defect
(2) Non-Stoichiometric Defect

(1) Stoichiometric Defect : Stoichiometric compounds are those where the numbers of different types of atoms or ions present are exactly in the ratio indicated by their chemical formula. They obey the law of constant composition. At one time, they were called DALTONIDE compounds, in contrast to BERTHOLLIDE or Non-Stoichiometric compounds where the chemical composition of a compound is variable or not constant.

(2) Non-Stoichiometric Defects : Non-Stoichiometric or Berthollide compounds exist over a range of chemical composition. The ratio of the number of atoms of one kind to the number of atoms of the other kind does not correspond exactly to the ideal whole number ratio implied by the formula. Such compounds do not obey the law of constant composition. There are many examples of these compounds particularly in the oxides and sulphides of the transition elements. Thus in FeO, FeS or CuS, the ratio of Fe : O, Fe : S or Cu : S differs from that indicated by the ideal chemical formula. If the ratio of atoms is not exactly 1 : 1 in the above cases, there must be either an excess of metal ions or a deficiency of metal ions. For example $Fe_{0.84}O - Fe_{0.94}O$, $Fe_{0.9}S$. The electrical neutrality in the crystal is maintained either by having extra electrons in the solid or changing the charge on some of the metal ions. This makes the structure of crystal irregular due to some kind of defects in the crystal. These defects so caused are in addition to the normal thermodynamic defects.

Properties of Solids (Crystals)

The imperfections (defects) developed in crystals gives some characteristic changes in the properties of ionic compound. These properties of solids are directly related to their composition, their lattice structure and the nature of bonds. Some of the properties of solids are

(i) Electrical
(ii) Magnetic
(iii) Dielectric

(i) Electrical : Electrical conductivity of solids may arise through the motion of electrons or positive holes (electronic conductivity) or through the motion of ions (ionic conductivity). Conduction through ions or positive holes is due to electronic imperfection. The conduction through electrons is called *n*-type conduction (*n* for negative) and through positive holes is called *p*-type conduction (*p* for positive).

Pure ionic solids where conduction takes place only through motion of ions are Insulators. Ionic solids can conduct electric current in the molten or solution state.

Thus solids may be classified into three types depending upon the values of electrical conductivity.

(a) Good conductors
(b) Insulators
(c) Semiconductors.

(a) Good conductor: These allow the maximum portion of the applied electric field to flow through them. The electrical conductivity of good conductors is of the order of $10^8\ ohm^{-1}\ cm^{-1}$.

Metals are good examples of good conductors of electricity.

(b) Insulators : They do not practically allow the electric current to flow through them. Electrical conductivity is of the order of 10^{-22} ohm^{-1} cm^{-1}. Most of the organic and inorganic solids (except graphite) are poor conductors of electricity.

(c) Semiconductors : This topic is already covered in the topic Intrinsic semiconduction.

(ii) Magnetic Properties : Solid substances are classified into

(a) Paramagnetic
(b) Diamagnetic
(c) Ferromagnetic substances

(a) Paramagnetic Substances : The substances which are weakly attracted when placed in the external magnetic field are termed as paramagnetic substances. The paramagnetic property of the solids is due to the presence of ions, atoms or molecules containing unpaired electrons. The unpaired electrons have magnetic moment (electron spin) but their random orientation cancel each other's effect. However, in the presence of external magnetic field, these unpaired electrons are aligned and shows the temporary magnetism.

Examples :

Molecules : NO and O_2
Transition metals : Cr, Mn, Al, Pt, etc.
Metal ions : Cu^{2+}, Ni^{2+}, Fe^{3+}, etc.
Metal oxide : VO_2 and CuO

(b) Diamagnetic Substances : These are weakly repelled by the external magnetic field. It is because of the fact that all electrons are paired in ions, atoms or molecules showing diamagnetism. Being paired, the magnetic moment of one electron is compensated by equal and opposite magnetic moment of other electron.

Examples : N_2, NaCl, TiO_2, Zn, Cd, Cu^+, etc.

(1) Ferromagnetic : These substances are strongly attracted by magnetic field. This type of substances have aligment of all the unpaired electrons in the same direction (orientation). These substances are permanently magnetised, i.e., these substances show magnetism even in the absence of magnetic field.

Examples : Ni, Fe, Co and CrO_2.

(2) Antiferromagnetic : When equal number of unpaired electrons are aligned in opposite directions, their magnetic moment (electrons spin) will compensate each other's magnetic moment. Such substances are termed as antiferromagnetic.

Examples : MnO, Mn_2O_3 and MnO_2.

(3) Ferrimagnetic Substances : When unequal number of unpaired electrons are aligned in opposite directions, the net magnetic moment is not zero. Such substances are termed as *Ferrimagnetic* e.g. Ferrite, Fe_2O_3.

It has been observed that the ferro-magnetic, ferrimagnetic and antiferromagnetic substances show paramagnetic nature at higher temperature. This arises due to randomisation of spins at higher temperature e.g. Fe_3O_4 is ferrimagnetic at room temperature but becomes paramagnetic at 850 K.

(iii) Dielectric Properties : A substance through which there is no net flow of electric charge when placed under an applied electrical field is defined as dielectric material. This is due to the fact that the electrons in the dielectric material are tightly held by individual atoms or ions. However, the applied field polarises the dielectric material and thus results in the creation of dipoles. The electrical dipoles are developed in the polar bonds with two equal and opposite charges. Such electrical dipoles interact with the applied external field in the following manners :

→ These dipoles may align themselves in such a manner that the dipole moment cancel each other completely giving no net dipole moment in the crystal.

→ The dipoles are so orderly oriented that these results in a net dipole moment in the crystal.

The crystals of second type, having some net dipole moment show following electrical properties.

(a) Piezoelectricity : When the crystals, in which the dipoles are oriented in an ordered manner, are subjected produces piezoelectricity. Such crystals are termed as Piezoelectric Crystals. In these, electricity is produced due to displacement of ions, from their orderly arrangement by the application of mechanical stress.

Such crystals are used as pick ups in record players where they produce electrical signals by application of pressure.

(b) Pyroelectricity : Upon heating, if the orderly arrangement of ions or atoms in the crystal get displaced and produces electricity, then the property of the crystal is termed as pyroelectricity.

(c) Ferroelectricity : Certain piezoelectric crystals show permanent alignment of dioples even in the absence of electric field. When the electric field is applied on such crystals, then the direction of polarisation of ions is altered. Such solids are called ferroelectric substances, and the phenomenon is termed as ferroelectricity, sodium-potassium tartarte (Rochelle salt), potassium dihydrogen phosphate (KH_2PO_4) and barium titanate ($BiTiO_3$) are examples of ferroelectric solids.

(d) Antiferroelectricity : If the crystal is having the alternate electrical dipoles pointing in opposite directions then it shall not exhibit ferroelectric properties. The net dipole moment in such solids is zero and are termed as antiferroelectric crystals. Lead zirconate ($PbZrO_3$) is a typical antiferroelectric solid.

Amorphous Solids

An amorphous solid is that substance in which the constituent particles are not arranged in an orderly manner. However, these may possess orderly arrangement in small regions. The examples of amorphous solids are glass, plastics, coal and rubber. Amorphous solids have properties entirely different from that of the crystalline solids. The shape of amorphous solids are easily distorted even under mild distortion forces or under its own weight. Thus, these are also termed as Pseudosolids. Glass is a hard, brittle and transparent amorphous solid. It is produced by the fusion of acidic oxides with basic oxides of alkali or alkaline earth metals or lead. The fused material is cooled very slowly and the process is called Annealing.

Itching on the glass is done by HF. Glass has a characteristic property that on heating, it changes to semi-solid and subsequently it flows freely like liquids. Hence, it is also known as *super-cooled liquid.*

OBJECTIVE QUESTIONS

1. A gas behaves like an ideal gas at

A. High pressure and low temperature
B. Low pressure and high temperature
C. High pressure and high temperature
D. Low pressure and low temperature

2. The pressure p of a gas is plotted against its absolute temperature T for two different constant volumes V_1 and V_2. When $V_1 > V_2$, the

A. curves have the same slope and do not interest
B. curves must intersect at some point other than T = 0
C. curve for V_2 has a greater slope than that for V_1
D. curve for V_1 has a greater slope than that for V_2

3. Which of the following quantity is the same for all ideal gases at the same temperature?

A. The kinetic energy of 1 mol
B. The kinetic energy of 1 g
C. The number of molecules in 1 mol
D. The number of molecules in 1 g

4. Which of the following graph represents Boyle's law?

A. 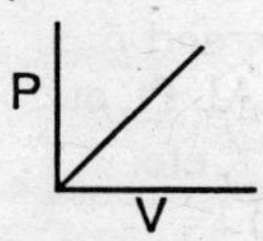

B. 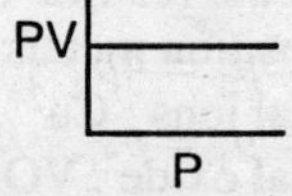

C. 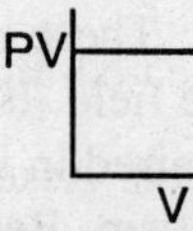

D. 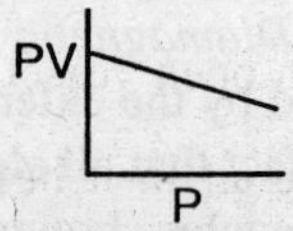

5. Which of the following graphs is not a straight line for an ideal gas?

A. $n \rightarrow T$
B. $T \rightarrow p$
C. $n \rightarrow \frac{1}{T}$
D. $n \rightarrow \frac{1}{p}$

6. Which of the following statements are *correct* on the basis of Charle's law?

A. The volume of an ideal gas can never be zero
B. The pressure of an ideal gas can be zero
C. At zero pressure, all molecular motion ceases in a gas, and it does not exert any pressure on the walls of the container.
D. It is not possible to attain absolute zero.

7. The density of a gas A is twice that of a gas B at the same temperature. The molecular weight of gas B is thrice that of A. The ratio of the pressures acting on A and B will be

A. $\frac{1}{6}$ B. $\frac{7}{8}$

C. $\frac{2}{5}$ D. $\frac{1}{4}$

8. Two closed vessels of equal volume containing air at pressure p_1 and temperature T_1 are connected to each other through a narrow tube. If the temperature in one of the vessels is now maintained at T_1 and that in the other at T_2, what will be the pressure is the vessels?

A. $\frac{2p_1T_1}{T_1+T_2}$ B. $\frac{T_1}{2p_1T_2}$

C. $\frac{2p_1T_2}{T_1+T_2}$ D. $\frac{2p_1}{T_1+T_2}$

9. Two vessels A and B have volumes V and 4V respectively. Both vessels contain some amount of water. The pressure in the space above water is p_1 for vessel A and p_2 for vessel B. What will be the relation between p_1 and p_2?

A. $p_1 = 4p_2$ B. $4p_1 = p_2$

C. $p_1 = p_2$ D. $p_1 = 16p_2$

10. An open vessel at 27°C is heated until $\frac{3}{8}$th of the air in it has been expelled. Assuming that the volume remains constant, calculate the temperature at which the vessel was heated.

A. 307°C B. 107°C

C. 480°C D. 207°C

11. At 100°C and 1 atm if the identity of liquid water is 1.0 g cm^{-3} and that of water vapour is 0.0006 cm^{-3}, then the volume occupied by water molecules in 1 litre of steam at that temperature is

A. 6 cm^3 B. 60 cm^3

C. 0.6 cm^3 D. 0.06 cm^3

12. A preweighed vessel was filled with CO_2 as STP and weighed. It was then evacuated, filled with SO_2 at the same temperature and pressure and again weighed. The weight of the CO_2 will be

A. The same as that of the SO_2

B. Twice of that of the SO_2

C. Half that of the SO_2

D. One-fourth of that of the SO_2

13. A bottle of dry ammonia and one of dry hydrogen chloride are connected through a long tube. The stoppers at both ends of the tube are opened simultaneously. The white ammonium chloride ring first formed will be

A. At the centre of the tube

B. Near the hydrogen chloride bottle

C. Near the ammonia bottle

D. Throughout the length of the tube

14. Which of the following statements are *correct*?

A. Helium diffuses at a rate 8.65 times as much as CO does

B. Helium escapes at a rate 2.65 times as fast as CO does

C. Helium escapes at a rate 4 times as fast as CO_2 does

D. Helium escapes at a rate 4 times as fast as SO_2 does

15. According to the kinetic theory of gases,

A. The pressure exerted by a gas is proportional to the mean square velocity of the molecules.

B. The pressure exerted by the gas is proportional to the root mean square velocity of the molecules.

C. The root mean square velocity is inversely proportional to the temperature

D. The mean translational kinetic energy of the molecule is directly proportional to the absolute temperature.

16. Indicate which of the following statements are *correct*?

A. At constant temperature, the Kinetic Energy (KE) of all gas molecules will be the same

B. At constant temperature, the Kinetic Energy (KE) of different molecules will be different

C. At constant temperature, the Kinetic Energy (KE) will be greater for heavier gas molecules

D. At constant temperature, the Kinetic Energy (KE) will be less for heavier gas molecules.

17. The RMS velocity of N_2 molecules in a gas is *u*. If the temperature is doubled and the nitrogen molecules dissociate into nitrogen atoms, the RMS speed becomes

A. $\frac{u}{2}$ B. $2u$

C. $4u$ D. $14u$

18. The translational kinetic energy of an ideal gas depends only on its

A. Pressure B. Force

C. Temperature D. Molar mass

19. The compressibility of a gas is less than unity at STP. Therefore,

A. $Vm > 22.4$ L B. $Vm < 22.4$ L

C. $Vm = 22.4$ L D. $Vm = 44.8$ L

20. The temperature at which real gases obey the ideal gas laws over a wide range of pressure is called

A. Critical temperature

B. Inversion temperature

C. Boyle's temperature

D. Reduced temperature

21. However large the presssure, a gas cannot be liquefied above its

A. Boyle's temperature

B. Inversion temperature

C. Critical temperature

D. Room temperature

22. Real gases approach ideal gas behaviour at

A. Low temperature and low pressure

B. Low temperature and high pressure

C. High temperature and high pressure

D. High temperature and low pressure

23. Which of the following is *correct* for critical temperature?

A. It is the highest temperature at which liquid and vapour can coexist

B. Beyond the critical temperature, there is no distinction between the two phases and a gas cannot be liquefied by compression

C. At critical temperature (Tc) the surface tension of the system is zero

D. All of the above

24. 500 ml of nitrogen at 27°C is cooled to – 5°C at the same pressure. Calculate the new volume.

A. 500 ml B. 446.66 ml

C. 44.66 ml D. 468 ml

25. A gas cylinder containing cooking gas can withstand a pressure of 14.9 atmosphere. The pressure gauge of the cylinder indicates 12 atmosphere at 27°C. Due to a sudden fire in the building, the temperature starts rising. At what temperature will the cylinder explode?

A. 48°C B. 99.5°C

C. 73°C D. 27°C

26. An iron cylinder contains helium at a pressure of 250 kPa at 300 K. The cylinder can withstand a pressure of 1×10^6 Pa. The room in which cylinder is placed catches fire. Predict whether the cylinder will blow up before it melts or not? (M.P. of the cylinder = 1800 K)

A. Cylinder will not blow up before it melts

B. Cylinder will blow up at m.p. of the cylinder when the pressure becomes 1.5×10^6 Pa

C. Cylinder will blow up at m.p. of the cylinder when the pressure becomes 1.0×10^6 Pa

D. None of these

27. What is volume of 6 g of hydrogen at 1.5 atmosphere and 273°C?

A. 86.9 litres B. 89.6 litres

C. 73.2 litres D. 72.1 litres

28. The pressure exerted by 12g of an ideal gas at temperature t°C in a vessel of volume V litre is one atm. When the temperature is increased by 10°C at the same volume, the pressure increased by 10%, calculate the temperature t and volume V (molecular weight of the gas = 120).

A. temperature (t) = 173°C
Volume (V) = 82 litre

B. t = 173°C
V = 0.82 litre

C. t = 273°C
V = 192 litre

D. None of these

29. Calculate the volume occupied by 7 g of nitrogen at 27°C and 750 mm pressure.

A. 1.2 litre B. 6.232 litre

C. 23.0 litre D. 32 litre

30. Calculate the temperature of 2.0 moles of a gas occupying a volume of 5.0 litres at 2.46 atmospheric pressure.

A. – 173°C B. 198°C

C. – 198°C D. 173°C

31. Calculate the density of NH_3 at 30°C and 5 atmospheric pressure.

A. 1.2 g/litre B. 3.42 g/litre
C. 4.32 g/litre D. 1.14 g/litre

32. An evacuated glass vessel weights 50.0 g when empty, 148.0 when filled with a liquid of density 0.98 ml^{-1} and 50.5 when filled with an ideal gas at 760 mm Hg at 300 K. Determine the molecular weight of the gas

A. 0.082 g mol^{-1} B. 300 g mol^{-1}
C. 123.15 g mol^{-1} D. 148 g mol^{-1}

33. An open vessel at 27°C is heated until three-fifths of the air in it has been expelled. Assuming that the volume of the vessel remains constant, find the temperature to which the vessel has been heated?

A. 47°C B. 477°C
C. 431°C D. 81°C

34. Critical temperature is the temperature above which a gas cannot be liquified,

A. The statement is correct
B. The statement is correct only at low pressure
C. The statement is correct only at high pressure
D. None of the above

35. How many years it would take to spend Avagadro number of rupees at the rate of 10 lakh rupees per second?

A. 1.8 year B. 10 years
C. 95 years D. 1.9×10^{10} years

36. Calculate the total number of electrons present in 1.6 g of methane

A. 10^{23} electrons B. 6.023×10^{23} electrons
C. 100 electrons D. 63 electrons

37. A plant virus is found to consist of uniform cylindrical particles of 150 Å in diameter and 5000 Å long. The specific volume of the virus is 0.75 cm^3/g. If the virus is considered to be a simple particle, find its molecular weight:

A. 10.8×10^6 g/mole
B. 70.8×10^6 g/mole
C. 6.023×10^{23} g/mole
D. 8.83×10^{-17} g/mole

38. Calculate the number of oxalic acid molecules in 100 ml of 0.02 N oxalic acid solution.

A. 10^2 B. 10^{-2}
C. 10^6 D. 10^{-3}

39. Oxygen is present in a litre flask at a pressure of 7.6×10^{-10} mm of Hg. Calculate the number of oxygen molecules in the flask at 0°C.

A. 3.7 molecules
B. 2.7×10^{10} molecules
C. 3.9×10^{10} molecules
D. 2.7×10^6 molecules

40. A balloon of diameter 20 m weighs 100 kg. Calculate its payload if it is filled with He at 1 atm and 27°C. Density of air is 1.2 kg m^{-3} (R = 0.082 dm^3 atm K^{-1} mol^{-1})

A. 4243.6 kg. B. 1243.6 kg
C. 1431.3 kg D. 4444.2 kg

41. Calculate the volume occupied by 5.0 g of acetylene gas at 50°C and 740 mm pressure.

A. 4.23 l B. 5.23 l
C. 3.23 l D. 1.23 l

42. When 2 g of a gas A is introduced into an evacuated flask kept at 25°C, the pressure is found to be one atmosphere. If 3 gm of another gas B is then added to the same flask, the total pressure becomes 1.5 atm. Assuming ideal gas behaviour, calculate the ratio of molecular weights $M_A : M_B$.

A. 1 : 1 B. 3 : 1
C. 1 : 3 D. 1 : 4

43. The weight of 350 ml of a diatomic gas at 0°C and 2 atm pressure is 1 g, calculate the weight in g of one atom at NTP.

A. 3.86 g B. 2.64 g
C. 2.64×10^{-23} g D. 1.13×10^{-23} g

44. A straight glass tube has two inlets X and Y at the two ends. The length of the tube is 200 cm. HCl gas through inlet X and NH_3 gas through inlet Y are allowed to enter the tube at the same time. White fumes first appear at point P inside the tube. Find the distance of P from X.

A. 112 cm B. 13.2 cm
C. 81.12 cm D. 12.81 cm

45. At 27°C, hydrogen is leaked through a tiny hole into a vessel for 20 minutes. Another unknown gas at the same temperature and pressure, as that of H_2, is leaked through same hole for 20 minutes. After the effusion of the gases the mixture exerts a pressure of 6 atmosphere. The hydrogen content of the mixture in 0.7 mole. If the volume of the container is 3 litres, what is the molecular weight of the unknown gas?

A. 1231 B. 1033
C. 1300 D. 1211

46. The composition of the equilibrium mixture ($Cl_2 \rightleftharpoons 2Cl$), which is attained at 1200°C, is determined by measuring the rate of effusion through a pin-hole. It is observed that at 1.80 mm Hg pressure, the mixture effuses 1.16 times as fast as krypton effuses under the same conditions. Calculate the fraction of chlorine molecules dissociated into atoms (atomic weight of Kr = 84)

A. 0.137 B. 137
C. 13.7 D. 137.0

47. At room temperature, ammonia gas at one atmospheric pressure and hydrogen chloride gas at P atm pressure are allowed to effuse through identical pin holes from opposite ends of a glass tube of one metre length and of uniform cross section, NH_4Cl is first formed at a distance of 60 cm from the end through which HCl gas is sent in. What is the value of P?

A. 21 atm B. 29 atm
C. 97 atm D. 2.197 atm

48. A 4 : 1 molar mixture of He and CH_4 is contained in a vessel at 20 bar pressure. Due to a hole in the vessel, the gas mixture leaks out. What is the composition of the mixture effusing out initially?

A. 1 : 8 B. 8 : 1
C. 5 : 1 D. 1 : 2

49. One mole of nitrogen gas at 0.8 atm takes 38 s to diffuse through a pin hole, whereas one mole of an unknown compound of xenon with fluoride at 1.6 atm takes 57 s to diffuse through the same hole. Calculate the molecular formula of the compound.

A. Xenon fluoride is XeF_2
B. Xenon fluoride is XeF_1
C. Xenon fluoride is XeF_6
D. None of these

50. The pressure in a bulb dropped from 2000 to 1500 mm of mercury is 47 minutes when the contained oxygen leaked through a small hole. The bulb was then completely evacuated. A mixture of oxygen and another gas of molecular weight 79 in the molar ratio of 1 : 1 at a total pressure of 4000 mm of mercury was introduced. Find the molar ratio of the two gases remaining in the bulb after a period of 74 minutes.

A. 7.3 : 1 B. 1.24 : 1
C. 8.24 : 3 D. 8 : 1

51. Calculate the average kinetic energy in joules of molecules in 8.0 gm of methane at 27°C

A. 21 joules/molecule
B. 6.21 joules/molecule
C. 10^{-21} joules/molecules
D. 6.21×10^{-21} joules/molecules

52. The molar volume of liquid benzene (density = 0.877 g ml^{-1}) increases by a factor of 2750 as it vaporises at 20°C and that of liquid toluene (density = 0.867 g ml^{-1}) increases by a factor of 7720 at 20°C. A solution of benzene and toluene at 20°C has vapour of 46.0 torr. Find the mole fraction of benzene in the vapour above the solution.

A. 0.24 B. 0.39
C. 0.74 D. 0.91

53. The average velocity at T_1K, and the most probable velocity at T_2K of CO_2 gas is 9.0×10^4 cm sec^{-1} calculate the value of T_1 and T_2.

A. $T_1 = 1152$ K, $T_2 = 1143$ K
B. $T_1 = 1268$ K, $T_2 = 1913$ K
C. $T_1 = 1682.5$ K, $T_2 = 2143.4$ K
D. $T_1 = 1682.5$ K, $T_2 = 1143.4$ K

54. A gas bulb of 1 litre capacity contains 2.0×10^{21} molecules of nitrogen exerting a pressure of 7.57×10^3 N m^{-2}. Calculate the root mean square (r.m.s.) speed and the temperature of the gas molecules. If the ratio of the most probable speed to the root mean square speed is 0.82, calculate the most probable velocity for these molecules at this temperature.

A. rms = 19 m/sec, T = 174 K,
α = 405.2 m/sec.
B. rms = 494.16 m/sec, T = 293 K,
α = 105 m/sec.
C. rms = 194.16 m/sec, T = 274.13 K,
α = 113 m/sec.
D. rms = 494.16 m/sec, T = 274.13 K,
α = 405.2 m/sec.

55. According to kinetic theory of gases, for a diatomic molecule

A. The pressure exerted by the gas is proportional to the mean velocity of the molecule.

B. The pressure exerted by the gas is propotional to the root mean square velocity of the molecules.

C. The root mean square velocity of the molecule is inversely proportional to the temperature.

D. The mean translational kinetic energy of the molecules is proportional to the absolute temperature.

56. Equal weights of methane and oxygen are mixed in an empty container at 25°C. The fraction of the total pressure exerted by oxygen is

A. $\frac{1}{3}$ B. $\frac{1}{2}$

C. $\frac{2}{3}$ D. $\frac{1}{3} \times \frac{273}{298}$

57. Equal weights of ethane and hydrogen are mixed in an empty container at 25°C. The fraction of the total pressure exerted by hydrogen is

A. 1 : 2 B. 1 : 1

C. 1 : 16 D. 15 : 16

58. In a closed room of 1000 m^3, a perfume bottle is opened up. The whole room develops smell. This is due to which property of gases?

A. Viscocity B. Density

C. Diffusion D. None

59. X ml of H_2 gas effuses through a hole in a container in 5 seconds. The time taken for the effusion of the same volume of the gas specified below under identical condition is

A. 10 seconds (He) B. 20 seconds (O_2)

C. 25 seconds (CO) D. 55 seconds (CO_2)

60. The rate of diffusion of methane at a given temperature is twice that of a gas X. The molecular weight of X is

A. 64.0 B. 32.0

C. 4.0 D. 8.0

61. At constant volume, for a fixed number of moles of a gas, the pressure of the gas increases with rise of temperature due to

A. Increase in average molecular speed

B. Increased rate of collisions amongst molecules

C. Increase in molecular attraction

D. Decrease in mean free path

62. The ratio between the root mean square velocity at H_2 at 50 K and that of O_2 at 800 K is

A. 4 B. 2

C. 1 D. $\frac{1}{4}$

63. The ratio of the average kinetic energy of O_3 to that of H_2, both at 300 K, is

A. 1 : 1 B. 3 : 1

C. 3 : 2 D. 24 : 1

64. If a gas expands at constant temperature,

A. The pressure decreases

B. The kinetic energy of the molecules remains same

C. The kinetic energy of the molecules decreases

D. The number of molecules of the gas increases

65. One litre of a gas weighs 2 g at 300 K and 1 atm pressure. If the pressure is made 0.75 atm, at which of the following temperature will 1 litre of the same gas weigh 1 gm?

A. 450 K B. 600 K

C. 800 K D. 900 K

66. The density of a gas at 27°C and 1 atm pressure is *d*. Pressure remaining constant, at which of the following temperatures will its density become 0.75 *d*?

A. 20°C B. 30°C

C. 400 K D. 300 K

67. 50 ml of gas A diffuses through a membrane in the same time as for the diffusion of 40 ml of a gas B under identical pressure-temperature conditions. If the molecular weight of A is 64 that of B would be

A. 100 B. 250

C. 200 D. 80

68. Which is *not* true in case of an ideal gas?

A. It cannot be converted into a liquid

B. There is no interaction between the molecules

C. All molecules of the gas move with the same speed
D. At a given temperature, PV is proportional to the amount of gas

69. The critical temperature of water is higher than that of O_2 because the H_2O molecules has
A. Fewer electrons than O_2
B. Two covalent bonds
C. V-shape
D. Dipole moment

70. The compressibility factor of an ideal gas is
A. 1.5 B. 1.0
C. 2.0 D. ∞

71. When an ideal gas undergoes unrestrained expansion, no cooling occurs because the molecules.
A. Are above the inversion temperature
B. Exert no effective force on each other
C. Do work equal to loss in kinetic energy
D. Collide without loss of energy

72. In the gas equation PV = nRT, the value of universal gas constant depends upon
A. The nature of the gas
B. The pressure of the gas
C. The temperature of the gas
D. The units of measurement

73. Gases deviate from ideal gas behaviour because their molecules
A. Possess negligible volume
B. Have forces of attraction between them
C. Are polyatomic
D. All of these

74. A perfect gas of a given mass is heated first in a small vessel and then in a large vessel, such that their volume remains unchanged. The P – T curves are
A. Parabolic with same curvature
B. Parabolic with different curvature
C. Linear with same slope
D. Linear with different slope

75. Oxygen gas is collected by downward displacement of water in a jar. The level of water inside the jar is adjusted to the height of water outside the jar. When the adjustment is made, the pressure exerted by the oxygen is
A. Equal to the atmospheric pressure
B. Equal to the vapour pressure of oxygen at that temperature
C. Equal to atmospheric pressure plus aqueous tension at that temperature
D. Equal to atmospheric pressure minus aqueous tension at that temperature

76. At STP, the order of rms speed of molecules H_2, N_2, O_2, and HBr is
A. $H_2 > N_2 > O_2 > HBr$
B. $HBr > O_2 > N_2 > H_2$
C. $HBr > H_2 > O_2 > N_2$
D. $N_2 > O_2 > H_2 > HBr$

77. The cooling caused by the adiabatic expansion of a compressed gas below its inversion temperature (T_i) without doing external work is called
A. Joule-Thomson effect
B. Adiabatic diamagnetism
C. Tyndall effect
D. Crompton effect

78. Which gas cannot be kept in a glass bottle because it chemically reacts with glass.
A. F_2 B. Cl_2
C. Br_2 D. SO_2

79. The inversion temperature (T_i) for a gas is given by
A. $\frac{a}{Rb}$ B. $\frac{2a}{Rb}$
C. $\frac{Rb}{a}$ D. $\frac{2Rb}{a}$

80. Equal volumes of two gases are kept in separate containers at the same temperature and pressure. Then,
A. Masses of the two gases are same
B. Molecular structure of two gases would be similar
C. The two gases contain the same number of molecules
D. The two gases, if allowed to diffuse would do so at the same rate.

81. The free path of a gas molecule is the distance
A. Between the two opposite walls of the container
B. Which molecules travel in one second

C. Through which a molecule moves between two successive collisions
D. None of these

82. Consider an ideal gas contained in a vessel. If the intermolecular interactions suddenly begins to act, which of the following will happen
A. The pressure decreases
B. The pressure increases
C. The pressure remains unchanged
D. The gas collapses

83. The compressibility factor of a gas is defined as $Z = \frac{PV}{nRT}$. The compressibility factor of an ideal gas is
A. Zero B. Infinite
C. 1 D. – 1

84. The term that accounts for intermolecular force in Van der Waal's equation for non ideal gas is
A. RT B. $V - b$
C. $\left(P + \frac{a}{V^2}\right)$ D. $[RT]^{-1}$

85. It is easier to liquify oxygen than hydrogen because
A. Oxygen has a higher critical temperature and lower inversion temperature than hydrogen.
B. Oxygen has a lower critical temperature and higher inversion temperature than hydrogen
C. Oxygen has a higher critical temperature and a higher inversion temperature than hydrogen
D. The critical temperature and inversion temperature of oxygen is very low.

86. The value of Vander Waal's constant '*a*' for gases O_2, N_2, NH_3 and CH_4 are 1.360, 1.390, 4.170 and 2.253 litre^2 atm mol^{-1} respectively. The gas which can most easily be liquefied is
A. O_2 B. N_2
C. NH_3 D. CH_4

87. Vapours of a liquid exist only
A. Below boiling point
B. Below critical temperature
C. Below inversion temperature
D. Above critical temperature

88. If a gas is expanded at constant temperature
A. Number of molecules of the gas decreases
B. The kinetic energy of the molecules decreases
C. The kinetic energy of the molecules remains the same
D. The kinetic energy of the molecules increases

89. At constant volume, for a fixed number of mole of a gas, the pressure of the gas increases with rise of temperature due to
A. Increase in average molecular speed
B. Increase in number of mole
C. Increase in molecular attraction
D. Decrease in mean free path

90. Graham's law deals with the relation between
A. Pressure and volume
B. Density and rate of diffusion
C. Rate of diffusion and volume
D. Rate of diffusion and viscocity

91. In a closed flask of 5 litre, 1.0 g of H_2 is heated from 300 to 600 K. Which statement is *not* correct?
A. Pressure of the gas increases
B. The rate of collison increases
C. The number of mole of gas increases
D. The energy of gaseous molecules increases

92. The density of neon will be highest at
A. STP B. 0°C, 2 atm
C. 273°C, 1 atm D. 273°C, 2 atm

93. How many mole of He gas occupy 22.4 litre at 30°C and one atmospheric pressure.
A. 0.90 B. 1.11
C. 0.11 D. 1.00

94. The number of molecules in 4.25 g of ammonia is approximately
A. 0.5×10^{23} B. 1.5×10^{23}
C. 3.5×10^{23} D. 2.5×10^{23}

95. If one mole of a monoatomic gas $\left(r = \frac{5}{3}\right)$ is mixed with one mole of a diatomic gas $\left(r = \frac{7}{5}\right)$, the value of r for the mixture is
A. 1.4 B. 1.5
C. 1.53 D. 3.07

96. A gas is heated from 0°C to 100°C at 1.0 atm pressure. If the initial volume of the gas is 10 litre its final volume would be

A. 7.32 litre B. 10.0 litre
C. 13.66 litre D. 20.0 litre

97. In an experiment during the anlaysis of a carbon compound, 145 ml of H_2 was collected at 760 mm Hg pressure and 27°C. The weight of H_2 is nearly.

A. 10 mg B. 12 mg
C. 6 mg D. 8 g

98. The rms speed of hydrogen is $\sqrt{7}$ times the rms speed of nitrogen. If T is the temperature of the gas time

A. $TH_2 = TN_2$ B. $TH_2 > TN_2$
C. $TH_2 < TN_2$ D. $TH_2 = \sqrt{7}\, TN_2$

99. At 100°C and 1 atm, if the density of liquid water is 1.0 g cm^{-3} and that of water vapour is 0.0006 g cm^{-3}, then the volume occupied by water is one litre of steam at that temperature is

A. 6 cm^3 B. 60 cm^3
C. 0.6 cm^3 D. 0.06 cm^3

100. The rms speed of the molecules of a gas of density 4 kg m^{-3} and pressure 1.2×10^5 Nm^{-2} is

A. 120 ms^{-1} B. 300 ms^{-1}
C. 600 ms^{-1} D. 900 ms^{-1}

ANSWERS

1	**2**	**3**	**4**	**5**	**6**	**7**	**8**	**9**	**10**
B	D	A,C	B,C	D	A,C,D	A	A	D	D
11	**12**	**13**	**14**	**15**	**16**	**17**	**18**	**19**	**20**
C	C	B	B,D	B,C	A	B	C	B	C
21	**22**	**23**	**24**	**25**	**26**	**27**	**28**	**29**	**30**
C	D	D	B	B	B	B	B	B	C
31	**32**	**33**	**34**	**35**	**36**	**37**	**38**	**39**	**40**
B	C	B	A	D	B	B	D	B	A
41 42	**43**	**44**	**45**	**46**	**47**	**48**	**49**	**50**	
B	C	C	C	B	A	D	B	C	B
51	**52**	**53**	**54**	**55**	**56**	**57**	**58**	**59**	**60**
D	C	C	D	D	A	D	C	B	A
61	**62**	**63**	**64**	**65**	**66**	**67**	**68**	**69**	**70**
C	C	A	D	C	C	D	C	D	B
71	**72**	**73**	**74**	**75**	**76**	**77**	**78**	**79**	**80**
A	D	B	D	D	A	A	A	B	C
81	**82**	**83**	**84**	**85**	**86**	**87**	**88**	**89**	**90**
C	A	C	C	C	C	B	C	A	B
91	**92**	**93**	**94**	**95**	**96**	**97**	**98**	**99**	**100**
C	B	A	B	B	C	B	C	C	B

3

STRUCTURE OF ATOM

Dalton's Atomic Theory and Its Failure

John Dalton in 1809, developed his famous theory of the atom. He regarded atom as a hard, dense, and the *smallest indivisible* particle of matter. However, certain experiments on passage of electricity through gases at low pressures, conducted towards the end of the nineteenth century, revealed the presence of negatively and positively charged particles coming out of the gases. The discovery of radioactivity showed the emission of small charged particles from radioactive elements. These and several other observations provided sufficient evidence to convince scientists that atom is not indivisible but consists of much smaller fundamental particles.

Although atom is extremely small, it has a definite complicated structure. Modern atomic structure is based mainly on Rutherford's scattering experiment of atoms.

Bohr's Model of Atom

In order to remove the drawback's of Rutherford's atomic model, Neils Bohr (1913) proposed a new model of atom based upon quantum theory of radiations. The salient points of this model are :

(i) The electron in an atom revolve around the nucleus only in certain circular orbits. These orbits are associated with definite energies and there are called *energy shells* or the *energy levels.*

Orbits are numbered as 1, 2, 3, 4, ... etc. or designated as K, L, M, N, ... etc.

Electrons while revolve around the dense nucleus in circular orbits, they do not emit any energy. This orbital rotation without emitting energy (radiations) follows the Newtonian law, i.e., the force of attraction between the nucleus and an electron is equal to the centrifugal force of the moving electron.

(ii) Of the infinite number of possible circular orbitals around the nucleus, an electron can revolve only in those orbits whose *angular momentum* (*mvr*) is an integral multiple of the factor $\frac{h}{2\pi}$, i.e., Angular momentum of electron

$$mvr = n\frac{h}{2\pi}$$

In other words the angular momentum of an electron in an atom is quantized,

where n = 1, 2, 3
m = mass of electron
v = velocity of electron
r = radius of orbit

Thus angular momentum of electron for single electron species (H, He^+, Li^{+2}, etc.) in various shells will be

$$\text{(K shell)}\ 1 \times \frac{h}{2\pi} = \frac{h}{2\pi}$$

$$\text{(L shell)}\ 2 \times \frac{h}{2\pi} = \frac{h}{\pi}$$

$$\text{(M shell)}\ 3 \times \frac{h}{2\pi} = \frac{3h}{2\pi}$$

(iii) As long as the electron remains in a particular orbit, it does not lose or gain energy. This is the reason that these orbits are called ***Stationary States***. Each stationary state is associated with a definite amount of energy and is, therefore, also known as *energy level.* The greater the distance of the energy level from the nucleus, the more is energy associated with it.

(iv) Ordinarily, an electron continues to move in a particular stationary state without losing energy. Such a state of the atom is called *ground* or *normal state.* This is the most stable state of the atom.

(v) When energy from external source is supplied to the electron, it may jump to some higher energy levels by absorbing energy (equal to the difference in

energy between two energy levels.) When electrons jump back to the lower energy level, it radiates some amount of energy in the form of photons of radiation.

$$\Delta E = E_2 - E_1 = h\nu$$

$$\nu = \frac{E_2 - E_1}{h}$$

The new state of electron is called the *excited state.*

E_1 and E_2 are the energies of electron in the first and second energy levels, and ν is the frequency of radiation absorbed or emitted.

Dual Nature of Particle

Louis de Broglie (1924) propounded that just as radiations have particle nature, the matter particles are also associated with wave nature.

He gave following relation for calculating the wavelength of the wave associated with a particle of mass, m moving with a velocity of ν.

$$\lambda = \frac{h}{m\nu}$$

Derivation of de Broglie relation.

Energy of photon is given by

$E = h\nu$ (Planck's equation)

Also, $E = mc^2$ (Einstein equation), where m is the mass of photon

From two equations mentioned above, we get

$$mc^2 = h\nu$$

$$mc^2 = h.\frac{c}{\lambda} \quad \left(\nu = \frac{c}{\lambda}\right)$$

$$\lambda = \frac{h}{mc}$$

de Broglie pointed out that the same equation might be applied to material particle by using m for mass of particle, instead the mass of photon and replacing c, the velocity by ν the velocity of the particle.

$$\lambda = \frac{h}{m\nu}$$

or $$\lambda = \frac{h}{p} \quad (P = \text{Momentum})$$

This equation is known as *de Broglie equation.*

Heisenberg's Uncertainity Principle

The position and velocity of bodies can be determined precisely at a particular time. Hence, the paths or the *trajectories* of such bodies can be predicted. However, in case of small particles such as electron, it is impossible to determine simultaneously its position and velocity at a given moment with certainty. Hence, it is not possible to talk of trajectory of an electron.

Wernes, Heisenberg (1927) put forth in the form of principle known as *Heisenberg's uncertainty principle*, which may be expressed as

$$\Delta x.\Delta p \geq \frac{h}{4\pi}$$

Δx = Uncertainty in position

Δp = Uncertainty in momentum

h = Planck's constant

The sign $\geq$ means that the product of Δx and Δp can either be greater or equal to $\frac{h}{4\pi}$, since the minimum product of Δx and Δp is constant. It means that

$$\Delta x \propto \frac{1}{\Delta p}$$

If uncertainty Δx is less than unceratinty in Δp will be large and vice versa.

It can be concluded that the position of electron cannot be known exactly at a particular moment, as postulated by Bohr. Instead, it is possible to predict the probable region in a given space, where one can find the electron. Thus, Heisenberg replaced the concept of definite orbits by *concept of probability.*

Quantum Numbers

The planetary electron in an atom or the atoms in a molecule, possess energy due to type, rotation, vibration or spin. According to the quantum theory, the energy possessed by such a particle is quantized i.e. can only have certain definite values. Each such value for a particular form of energy is a multiple which is invariably a small whole number, or sometimes one half of a quantum, which is characteristic of the form of energy under consideration. This multiple, which defines the energy of the particle, is called the quantum number.

Each electron has four characteristic quantum numbers, which are interrelated :

***(a)* Principal quantum number :** It is represented by n and has values 1, 2, 3, ..., this denotes the overall size and energy of the electron.

***(b)* Azimuthal quantum number :** It is represented by l and have values 0, 1, 2, 3, ..., $n-1$. This denotes the angular momentum and thus shape of the most probable electron distribution correspond-ing to the shape of the orbital. Azimuthal quantum numbers with $l = 0, 1, 2$ and 3 are also called *s, p, d* and *f* respectively.

***(c)* Magnetic quantum number :** It is represented by m, and have values $-l, -l+1, ...0.... l-1, l$. This denotes the orientation of the orbital.

(d) A spin quantum number $s = \pm\frac{1}{2}$.

Pauli's Exclusion Principle

In any atom no two electrons can have all four quantum numbers the same e.g. $n = 1, l = 0, m = 0$ $s = +1/2$

$n = 1, l = 0, m = 0$ $s = -1/2$

Hund's Rule

Rules which describe the electronic configuration of degenerate orbitals in the ground state. The electronic configuration will have the maximum number of unpaired electrons, i.e. p^3, $\underline{\uparrow}\,\underline{\uparrow}\,\underline{\uparrow}$ rather than $\underline{\uparrow\downarrow}\,\underline{\uparrow}\,\underline{\ }$

The ground state will have the maximum orbital angular momentum.

Aufbau Principle

In building up the electronic configuration of an atom or a molecule in its ground state, the electrons are placed in order of increasing energy or the orbital with a lower energy is filled up first before the filling of the orbital with a higher energy commences. The sequence is represented as:

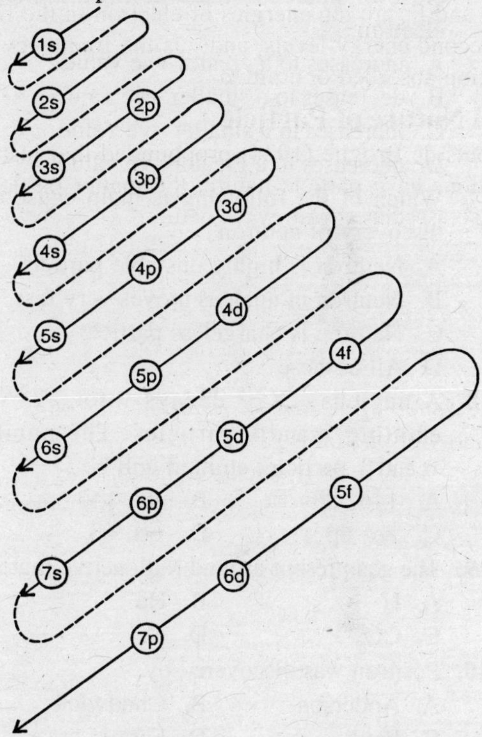

OBJECTIVE QUESTIONS

1. The construction of an electron microscope is based on
   A. de Broglie's principle
   B. Heisenberg's principle
   C. Bohr's theory
   D. Rutherford concept

2. Which of the following units is used to measure the size of a nucleus?
   A. cm B. Å
   C. Fermi D. a.m.u.

3. Which of the following statements does not make a part of Bohr's model of atom?
   A. The electron in the orbit nearest to the nucleus is in the lowest energy.
   B. Energy of an electron in an orbit is quantized.
   C. Electrons revolve around nucleus in orbits of definite energy.
   D. Electron can jump from one orbit to another on its own.

4. The sum of nucleus in an isotope of hydrogen may be
   A. 3 B. 6
   C. 5 D. 4

5. The nature of anode rays depends upon
A. Nature of gas filled in the discharge tube
B. Nature of electrode
C. Nature of discharge tube
D. None of these

6. As an electron is brought from an infinite distance close of nucleus of the atom, the energy of electron
A. increases to a greater +ve value
B. decreases to a smaller +ve value
C. increases to a smaller –ve value
D. decreases to a greater –ve value

7. Which of the following is main cause of late discovery of neutron
A. Neutron is highly unstable particle
B. Neutron in nucleus moves very fast
C. Neutron is chargeless particle
D. All of these

8. A nucleus ${}_{92}X^{225}$ decays into ${}_{90}Y^{203}$ after emitting α and β particles. The number of α and β particles emitted will be
A. 14α, 8β   B. 8α, 14β
C. 8α, 6β   D. 6α, 6β

9. The gas present around radioactive material is
A. H   B. He
C. CO_2 D. Ne

10. Positron was discovered by
A. Anderson   B. Chadwick
C. Pauli   D. Fermi

11. If a radioactive substance is kept in a vessel and is subjected to very high temperature and pressure, its rate of radioactive disintegration will
A. Increase
B. Decrease
C. Remain uncharged
D. Decrease very slightly

12. The half life of a radioactive substance is 10 hours. How long does it take for 93.75 per cent of a sample of this substance to decay?
A. 40 hrs   B. 60 hrs
C. 80 hrs   D. 100 hrs

13. The radioactive elements X and Y have half lives of 5 minutes and 45 minutes respectively. When the activity of each is the same, the ratio of the number of atoms X to the number of atoms Y is
A. 1 : 1   B. 1 : 9
C. 9 : 1   D. 5 : 1

14. The radioactivity of a sample is R, at time t_1 and $\frac{1}{2}$R, at time t_2. The half life of this element is
A. t_1 B. t_2
C. $(t_2 - t_1)$ D. $t_2 + t_1$

15. Which of the following is used in dating archaeological findings?
A. ${}_{92}U^{235}$ B. ${}_{6}C^{14}$
C. ${}_{1}H^{3}$ D. ${}_{26}Fe^{27}$

16. An isolated radioactive atom may decay by emitting
A. α, β and γ - rays   B. α and β - rays
C. β and γ - rays   D. α and X rays

17. β - decay
A. Increases the $\frac{N}{2}$ ratio
B. Decreases the $\frac{N}{2}$ ratio
C. Does not change $\frac{N}{2}$ ratio
D. None of these

18. Radioactive substances do not emit
A. Helium nuclei   B. Electrons
C. Protons   D. Photons

19. Which among the following sets of quantum numbers is not allowed?
A. $n = 1, l = 0, m = 0, s = +\frac{1}{2}$
B. $n = 1, l = 0, m = 0, s = -\frac{1}{2}$
C. $n = 2, l = 1, m = -1, s = +\frac{1}{2}$
D. $n = 2, l = 0, m = 0, s = -\frac{1}{2}$

20. The principal quantum number in an atom represents
A. Shape of an orbital
B. Size of an orbital
C. Orientations of a sub-shell
D. Angular momentum of an electron

21. The magnetic quantum number specifies
A. Shape and size of an orbital
B. Distance of an orbital from nucleus
C. Orientations of a sub-shell in the space
D. Number of electrons in an orbit

22. Which one of the following sets of quantum numbers gives correct information regarding the 21st electron of scandium atom?
A. $n = 2, l = 1, m = 0, s = +\frac{1}{2}$
B. $n = 3, l = 2, m = -2, s = +\frac{1}{2}$
C. $n = 3, l = 2, m = +2, s = -\frac{1}{2}$
D. None of these

23. For 4*p* sub-shell, the quantum number for all electrons should be
A. $n = 4, l = 0, s = \pm\frac{1}{2}$
B. $l = 0, s = +\frac{1}{2}$
C. $l = 1$
D. $s = \pm\frac{1}{2}$

24. The probability of finding an electron in a d_{xy} orbital is maximum
A. Parallel to *x*-axis
B. Parallel to *y*-axis
C. Parallel to *x* and *y*-axis
D. At an angle of 45° from *x* and *y* axis.

25. Visible light photons do not show Compton effect because they
A. Move very slowly
B. Have no momentum
C. Have very less mass
D. Have larger wavelength

26. The '*g*' sub-shell is characterized by
A. $n = 6$ B. $m = 2$
C. $l = 4$ D. $l = 5$

27. For which one of the following sets of four quantum numbers, an electron will have highest energy?
A. $n = 3, l = 2, m = 1, s = +\frac{1}{2}$
B. $n = 4, l = 2, m = -1, s = +\frac{1}{2}$
C. $n = 4, l = 1, m = 0, s = -\frac{1}{2}$
D. $n = 5, l = 0, m = 0, s = -\frac{1}{2}$

28. An expression which represents the orbital angular momentum of electron is
A. $\frac{h}{2\pi}.(l+1)$ B. $\frac{h}{2\pi}.(2l+1)$
C. $\frac{h}{2\pi}.\sqrt{l(l+1)}$ D. $\sqrt{\frac{h}{2\pi}(l+1)}$

29. The splitting of atomic spectral lines in the applied electric field is known as
A. Zeeman effect B. Compton effect
C. Stark effect D. Newman effect

30. When α-particles are sent through a thin metal foil, most of them go straight through the foil because
A. α-particles are less heavier than electrons
B. α-particles are positively charged
C. Most part of atom is empty space
D. α-particles move with high velocity

31. Rutherford's experiment, on scattering of α-particles, showed for the first time that the atom has
A. Electrons B. Protons
C. Nucleus D. Neutrons

32. The heaviest particle is
A. α B. Electron
C. Proton D. Neutron

33. The wavelength of a spectral line for an electronic transition is inversely related to
A. The number of electrons undergoing the transition
B. The nuclear charge of the atom
C. The difference in the energy of the energy levels involved in the transition
D. The velocity of the electron undergoing the transition

34. For a '*d*' electron the orbital angular momentum is
A. $\sqrt{6}\,h$ B. $\sqrt{2}\,h$
C. h D. $2h$

35. The number of electrons in Al^{+3} is

A. 13 B. 16
C. 10 D. 19

36. The decay constant of a radioactive element is defined as the reciprocal of the time interval after which the number of atoms of the radioactive element falls to nearly

A. 50% of its original number
B. 36.8% of its original number
C. 63.2% of its original number
D. 75% of its original number

37. Many elements have non-integral atomic masses because

A. They have isotopes
B. Their isotopes have non-identical masses
C. Their isotopes have same masses
D. The constituents neutrons, protons, electrons combine to give fractional masses

38. Isotone of $_{32}Ge^{76}$ is

A. $_{32}Ge^{77}$ B. $_{33}As^{77}$
C. $_{34}Se^{77}$ D. All of these

39. Nuclides having the same atomic numbers are known as

A. Isomers B. Isotopes
C. Isotones D. Isobars

40. Which of the following nuclei is unstable

A. $_5B^{10}$ B. $_4Be^{10}$
C. $_7N^{14}$ D. $_8O^{16}$

41. The end product formed by the disintegration of $_{88}Ra^{226}$ is

A. $_{81}Tl^{204}$ B. $_{82}Pb^{206}$
C. $_{86}Ra^{222}$ D. $_{83}Pi^{207}$

42. Which of the following does not characterise X-rays?

A. The radiation can ionize gases
B. It causes ZnS to flurescence
C. Deflected by electric and magnetic fields
D. Have wavelengths shorter than UV-rays.

43. Radioactive distintegration differs from a chemical change in being

A. An exothermic change
B. A spontaneous process
C. A numbered process
D. A unimolecular first order reaction

44. The radius of an atomic nucleus is of the order of

A. 10^{-10} cm B. 10^{-13} cm
C. 10^{-15} cm D. 10^{-8} cm

45. The ratio of the energy of a photon of 2000 Å wavelength radiation to that of 4000 Å radiation is

A. $\frac{1}{4}$ B. 4
C. $\frac{1}{2}$ D. 2

46. How many unpaired electrons are there is Ni^{2+} ($z = 28$)?

A. 0 B. 2
C. 4 D. 8

47. Decrease in atomic number is observed during

A. α-emission
B. Positron emission
C. Electron capture
D. All of these

48. An oil drop has 6.39×10^{-19} charge. What will be the number of electrons in this drop?

A. 2 B. 4
C. 8 D. 16

49. A bulb emits light of wavelength 4500 Å. The bulb is rated as 150 watt and 8% of the energy is emitted as light. How many photons are emitted by the bulb per second?

A. 27.2×10^{18} B. 2.72×10^{16}
C. 27.5×10^{4} D. 27.2×10^{8}

50. Calculate the energy emitted when electrons of 1.0 g atom of hydrogen undergo transition giving the spectral line lowest energy in the visible region of its atomic spectrum.

A. 182.5 kJ B. 185.2 kJ
C. 158.2 kJ D. 155.2 kJ

51. In the Balmer series of atomic spectra of hydrogen, there is a line corresponding to wavelength 4344 Å. Calculate the number of higher orbits from which the electron drops to generate other line

A. 1 B. 2
C. 3 D. 5

52. Calculate the loss in mass accompanying combustion of one mole of the given fuel which yields 900 kJ of heat energy.

A. 1×10^{10} kg B. 1×10^{-11} kg
C. 1×10^{11} kg D. 1×10^{-10} kg

53. One of the hazards of explosion is the generation of ^{90}Sr and its subsequent incorporation in bones. This nuclide has a half-life of 28.1 years. Suppose one microgram was absorbed by a new-born child, how much ^{90} Sr will remain in his bones after 20 years?

A. 1 gm B. 1 μg
C. 0.061 μg D. 0.061 mg

54. Calculate the weight of C^{14} (half-life = 5720 years) atoms which gives 3.7×10^7 disintegration per second.

A. 2.345×10^{-3} gram
B. 0.234×10^{-3} gram
C. 3.234×10^3 gram
D. 2.345×10^3 gram

55. A piece of wood was found to have $\frac{C^{14}}{C^{12}}$ ratio 0.7 times than that in a living plant. Calculate the period when the plant died. Half-life of C^{14} = 5760 years.

A. 2790 years B. 2970 years
C. 5760 years D. 5670 years

56. The speed of the electron in the innermost orbit of the hydrogen atom is 2.18×10^8 cm/s. What is the Bohr radius of the orbit (mass of electron = 9.1096×10^{-28}g)

A. 0.531 Å B. 5.310 Å
C. 1.315 Å D. 0.001 Å

57. A neutron breaks into a proton and an electron. Calculate the energy produced in this reaction in MeV. Mass of electron, proton and neutron are 9×10^{-31} kg, 1.6725×10^{-27} kg and 1.6747×10^{-27} kg respectively.

A. 0.43 MeV B. 0.73 MeV
C. 1.73 MeV D. None of these

58. Radium-226 undergoes α-ray change, its half-life being 1620 years. What is the activity (rate of disintegration) of 0.001 g of the sample?

A. 1.672×10^9 atoms/min
B. 2.167×10^9 atoms/min
C. 3.167×10^9 atoms/min
D. 2.167×10^7 atoms/min

59. Which statement is *correct*?

A. Volume of proton is approximately $\left(\frac{4}{3}\pi r^3\right)$ 1.5×10^{-38} cm^3
B. The radius of electron is 42.8×10^{-13} cm
C. The density of nucleus is 10^{14} g/cm^3
D. All of the above

60. The number of electrons in an atom with atomic number 105 having $(n + l) = 8$ are

A. 30 B. 15
C. 17 D. 39

61. The number of electrons in a neutral atom of an element is equal to its

A. atomic weight B. equivalent weight
C. atomic number D. electron affinity

62. The de Broglie wavelength associated with a material particle is

A. Inversely proportional to momentum
B. Inversely proportional to its energy
C. Directly proportional to momentum
D. Directly proportional to its energy

63. In an atom, no two electrons can have the same value for all the quantum numbers. This was proposed by :

A. Hund B. Pauli
C. Dalton D. Avogadro

64. The ratio e/m i.e., specific charge for a cathode ray.

A. has the smallest value when the discharge tube is filled with H_2
B. is constant
C. varies with the atomic number of gas in the discharge tube
D. varies with the atomic number of an element forming the cathode.

65. When greater number of excited hydrogen atoms reach the ground state, then

A. more number of lines are found in Lyman series
B. the intensity of lines in Balmer series increases
C. the intensity of lines in Lyman series increase
D. both the intensity and number of lines in Lyman series increases

66. The maximum sum of the number of neutrons and protons in an isotope of hydrogen is
A. 6 B. 5
C. 4 D. 3

67. Which *d*-orbital has different shape from rest of all *d*-orbitals :
A. $d_{x^2-y^2}$ B. d_{z^2}
C. d_{x^2y} D. d_{yz}

68. Which statement does not form part of Bohr's model of the hydrogen atom
A. Energy of the electrons in the orbit is quantized
B. The electron in the orbit nearest the nucleus is in the lowest energy state
C. Electrons revolve in different orbits around the nucleus
D. The position and velocity of the electrons in the orbit cannot be determined simultaneously

69. Which is not characteristics of Planck's quantum theory of radiation
A. Radiation is associated with energy
B. Energy is not absorbed or emitted in whole number or multiples of quantum
C. The magnitude of energy associated with a quantum is proportional to the frequency
D. Radiation energy is neither emitted nor absorbed continuously but in small packets called quanta

70. Mosley's name is connected with the discovery of
A. Protons B. Neutrons
C. Atomic number D. Atomic weight

71. The value of charge on the oil droplets experimentally observed were -1.6×10^{-19} and -4×10^{-19} coulomb. The value of the electronic charge, indicated by these results is
A. 1.6×10^{-19} B. -2.4×10^{-19}
C. -4×10^{-19} D. -0.8×10^{-19}

72. The amount of energy required to remove the electron from a Li^{+2} ion in its ground state is how many times greater than the amount of energy required to remove the electron from an H atom in its ground state :
A. 9 B. 2
C. 3 D. 5

73. The momentum of a photon is *p*. The corresponding wavelength is
A. $\frac{h}{p}$ B. hp
C. $\frac{p}{h}$ D. $\frac{h}{\sqrt{p}}$

74. Ultraviolet light of 6.2 eV falls on Aluminium surface (work function = 4.2 eV). The kinetic energy (in joule) of the fastest electron emitted is approximately
A. 3×10^{-21} B. 3×10^{-19}
C. 3×10^{-17} D. 3×10^{-15}

75. If S_1 be the specific charge (e/m) of cathode rays and S_2 be that of positive ray then which is true?
A. $S_1 = S_2$ B. $S_1 > S_2$
C. $S_1 < S_2$ D. Either of these

76. The radius of second stationary orbit in Bohr's atom is R. The radius of third orbit will be
A. 3R B. 9R
C. 2 : 25 R D. $\frac{R}{3}$

77. Ionisation potential of Hydrogen atom is 13.6 eV. Hydrogen atom in the ground state are excited by monochromatic light of energy 12.1 eV. The spectral lines emitted by hydrogen according to Bohr's theory will be
A. 1 B. 2
C. 3 D. 4

78. The mass of an electron is *m*, its charge *e* and it is accelerated from rest through a potential difference V. The velocity acquired by the electron will be
A. $\sqrt{\left(\frac{V}{m}\right)}$ B. $\sqrt{\left(\frac{2eV}{m}\right)}$
C. $\sqrt{\left(\frac{eV}{m}\right)}$ D. None

79. Positive rays were discovered by
A. Thomson B. Aston
C. Goldstein D. Bragg

80. Energy levels A, B, C of a certain atoms correspond to increasing values of every level i.e., $E_A < E_B < E_C$. If λ_1, λ_2 and λ_3 are the wavelengths of radiations corresponding to the transitions C to B, B to A and C to A respectively which of the following statement is correct?

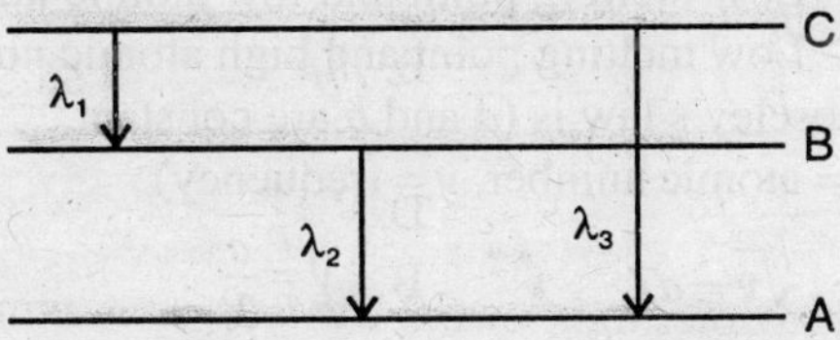

A. $\lambda_3 = \lambda_1 + \lambda_2$ B. $\lambda_3 = \dfrac{\lambda_1\lambda_2}{\lambda_1 + \lambda_2}$

C. $\lambda_1 + \lambda_2 + \lambda_3 = 0$ D. $\lambda_3^2 = \lambda_1^2 + \lambda_2^2$

81. The energy difference between the states $n = 2$ and $n = 3$ is E eV, in Hydrogen atom. The ionisation potential of H atom is

A. 3.2 E B. 7.2 E

C. 5.6 E D. 13.2 E

82. Suppose 10^{-17} J of light energy is needed by the interior of human eye to see an object. The photons of green light ($\lambda = 550$ nm) needed to see the objects are

A. 27 B. 29

C. 28 D. 30

83. The momentum of radiation of wavelength 0.33 nm is .... km sec^{-1}

A. 2×10^{-24} B. 2×10^{-12}

C. 2×10^{-6} D. 2×10^{-48}

84. An oxide of N has vapour density 46. Total number of electrons in its 92 g are

A. 48 N B. 46 N

C. 92 N D. None

85. The de Broglie wavelength of a particle with mass 1 g and velocity 100 m/s is

A. 6.63×10^{-33} m B. 6.63×10^{-35} m

C. 6.63×10^{-34} m D. 6.65×10^{-35} m

86. Electronic configuration of Ni is [Ar] $3d^8, 4s^2$. The electronic configuration of next element will be

A. [Ar] $3d^1, 4s^1$ B. [Ar] $3d^8, 4s^2$

C. [Ar] $3d^8, 4s^2, 4p^1$ D. None

87. E_1 for He^+ is – 54.4 eV. The E_2 for He^+ would be

A. – 6.8 eV B. – 13.6 eV

C. – 27.2 eV D. –108.8 eV

88. The work function of a photoelectric material is 3.3 eV. Its threshold frequency will be

A. 8×10^{14} Hz B. 8×10^{10} Hz

C. 5×10^{33} Hz D. 4×10^{11} Hz

89. We can say that the energy of a photon of frequency ν is given by $E = h\nu$, where h is Planck's constant. The momentum of a photon is $p = \dfrac{h}{\lambda}$, where λ is the wavelength of photon. Then we may conclude that velocity of light is equal to

A. $\left(\dfrac{E}{p}\right)^{1/2}$ B. $\dfrac{E}{p}$

C. Ep D. $\left(\dfrac{E}{p}\right)^2$

90. The uncertainty in the momentum of an electron is 10^{-5} kg ms^{-1}. The uncertainty in its position will be

A. 1.05×10^{-28} m B. 1.05×10^{-26} m

C. 5.27×10^{-30} m D. 5.25×10^{-28} m

91. The wavelength of radiation emitted when electron falls from 4th Bohr's orbit to 2nd in H atom is ($R_H = 1.09678 \times 10^{-7}$ m^{-1})

A. 972 nm B. 486 nm

C. 243 nm D. 182 nm

92. The approximate quantum number of a circular orbit of a diameter, 20.6 nm of the Hydrogen atom according to Bohr's theory is

A. 10 B. 19

C. 12 D. 16

93. Photoelectric effect of the phenomenon in which

A. Photon comes out of a metal when it is hit by a beam of electrons

B. Photons come out of the nucleus of an atom under the action of an electric field

C. Electrons come out of a metal with a constant velocity which depends on the frequency and intensity of incident light wave

D. Electrons come out of a metal with different velocities not greater than a certain value which depends only on the frequency of the incident light wave and not on its intensity

94. In photoelectric effect, the number of photoelectrons emitted is proportional to

A. Intensity of incident beam

B. Frequency of incident beam

C. Velocity of incident beam
D. Work function of photo cathode

95. Einstein's photoelectric equation states that $E_k = h\nu - w$. In this equation, E_k refers to :
A. Kinetic energy of all ejected electrons
B. Maximum kinetic energy of emitted electrons
C. Mean kinetic energy of emitted electrons
D. Minimum kinetic energy of emitted electrons

96. The best metal to be used for photoemission is
A. Potassium B. Sodium
C. Ceasium D. Lithium

97. The photoelectric effect occurs only when the incident light has more frequency than a certain minimum
A. Frequency B. Speed
C. Wavelength D. Charge

98. A surface ejects electrons when hit by green light but not when hit by yellow light. Will electrons be ejected if the surface is hit by red light
A. Yes
B. No
C. Yes, if the red beam is quite intense
D. Yes, if the red beam continues to fall upon the surface for a long time

99. Of the following transitions in Hydrogen atom, the one which gives an absorption line of lowest frequency is
A. $n = 1$ to $n = 2$ B. $n = 3$ to $n = 8$
C. $n = 2$ to $n = 1$ D. $n = 8$ to $n = 3$

100. According to Bohr's model for the Hydrogen atom, the radius of a stationary orbit characterized by the principal quantum number n is proportional to
A. n^{-1} B. n
C. n^{-2} D. n^2

101. The angular momentum of electron in the nth orbit is given by
A. nh B. $\frac{h}{2\pi n}$
C. $\frac{nh}{2\pi}$ D. $\frac{n^2 h}{2\pi}$

102. The target used for production of X-ray beam must have
A. High melting point and high atomic number
B. High melting point and low atomic number
C. Low melting point and low atomic number
D. Low melting point and high atomic number

103. Moseley's law is (a and b are constant, Z = atomic number, ν = frequency)
A. $\sqrt{\nu} = aZ$ B. $\nu = \frac{c}{\lambda}$
C. $2d \sin\theta = nd$ D. $\sqrt{\nu} = a(Z - b)$

104. If λ_1 and λ_2 are the wavelengths of characteristic X-rays and gamma rays respectively, then the relation between them is
A. $\lambda_1 = \frac{1}{\lambda_2}$ B. $\lambda_1 = \lambda_2$
C. $\lambda_1 > \lambda_2$ D. $\lambda_1 < \lambda_2$

105. Wavelength of an electron is equal to distance travelled by it in one second, then correct relation is
A. $\lambda = \frac{h}{p}$ B. $\lambda = \sqrt{\frac{h}{p}}$
C. $\lambda = \frac{h}{m}$ D. $\lambda = \sqrt{\frac{h}{m}}$

106. The orbital angular momentum of an electron in 2s orbital is
A. $\frac{h}{4\pi}$ B. Zero
C. $\frac{h}{2\pi}$ D. $\sqrt{2}.\frac{h}{2\pi}$

107. Which one of the following represents an impossible arrangement

	n	l	m	s
A.	3	2	– 2	1/2
B.	4	0	0	1/2
C.	3	2	– 3	1/2
D.	5	3	0	1/2

108. Which one of the following orbital is dumb-bell shaped
A. s B. $2p_y$
C. $3s$ D. $3d_{z^2}$

109. The orbital diagram in which Aufbau principle is violated in

A. [↓↑] [↓↑ | ↑ |]

B. [↑] [↑↓ | ↑ | ↑]

C. [↑↓] [↑ | ↑ | ↑]

D. [↑↓] [↑↓ | ↑↓ | ↑]

110. Correct set of four quantum number for valeney (outermost) electron of rubidium (Z = 37) is

A. $5, 0, 0, +\frac{1}{2}$ B. $5, 1, 1, +\frac{1}{2}$

C. $5, 1, 0, +\frac{1}{2}$ D. $6, 0, 0, +\frac{1}{2}$

111. In Potassium, the order of energy level for 19th electron is

A. $3s > 3d$ B. $4s < 3d$

C. $4s > 4p$ D. $4s = 3d$

112. The ratio of masses of proton and neutron are

A. > 1 B. $= 1$

C. < 1 D. $> \sqrt{1}$

113. When the speed of electron increases, the specific charge

A. Decreases B. Increases

C. Remains same D. None

114. The $(n + l)$ value for $4f$ electron is

A. 6 B. 4

C. 7 D. 8

115. The electronic configuration for $_{26}Fe$ is

A. $[Ar]\, 3d^6, 4s^2$ B. $[Ar]\, 3d^7, 4s^2$

C. $[Ar]\, 3d^5, 4s^2$ D. $[Ar]\, 3d^7, 4s^1$

116. Predict the total spin in Ni^{2+} ion

A. $\pm\frac{5}{2}$ B. $\pm\frac{3}{2}$

C. $\pm\frac{1}{2}$ D. ± 1

117. Li^{+2} and B^{+3} are

A. Isotopes B. Isomers

C. Isobars D. Isoelectronic

118. The volume of a proton is approximately

A. $1.5 \times 10^{-30}\, cm^3$ B. $1.5 \times 10^{-38}\, cm^3$

C. $1.5 \times 10^{-34}\, cm^3$ D. None of the above

119. Three electrons in p sub-level must have the quantum number

A. $n = 2$ B. $m = 0$

C. $l = 0$ D. $s = -\frac{1}{2}$ or $+\frac{1}{2}$

120. The total number of valency electrons for NH_4^+ is

A. 9 B. 8

C. 6 D. 11

121. A neutral atom always consists of

A. Proton

B. Neutrons + Protons

C. Neutrons + Electrons

D. Neutrons + Protons + Electrons

122. Which of the following has the maximum number of unpaired electrons

A. Mg^{2+} B. V^{3+}

C. Ti^{3+} D. Fe^{2+}

123. The first use of quantum theory to explain the structure of atom was made by

A. Heisenberg B. Bohr

C. Planck D. Einstein

124. The zero probability of finding the electron in p_x orbital is

A. Maximum on two opposite sides of the nucleus along x-axis

B. In the nucleus

C. Some on all the sides around the nucleus

D. None of the above

125. Which element possess non-spherical shells

A. He B. B

C. Be D. Li

126. When a neutral atom is converted into cation, there is

A. Decrease in atomic number

B. An increase in atomic number

C. A decrease in size

D. An increase in size

127. Which transition of electron in the Hydrogen atom emits maximum energy

A. $2 \rightarrow 1$ B. $1 \rightarrow 4$

C. $4 \rightarrow 3$ D. $3 \rightarrow 2$

128. n and l values of an orbital "A" are 3 and 2 and of another orbital "B" are 5 and 0. The energy of

A. B is more than A

B. A is more than B

C. A and B have same energy

D. None

129. Principal, azimuthal and the magnetic quantum numbers are respectively related to
A. Size, shape and orientation
B. Shape, size and orientation
C. Size, orientation and shape
D. None of the above

130. The magnet will cause greatest deflection in
A. α - rays B. β - rays
C. γ - rays D. Neutrons

131. Which electromagnetic radiation has extremely small wavelength
A. Radiowave B. Cosmic rays
C. Infrared rays D. Microwaves

132. Maximum number of electrons in an orbit is given by
A. n^2 B. $2n^2$
C. $\frac{n^2}{2}$ D. None

133. The correct Schrödinger's wave equation for an electron with E as total energy and V as potential energy is

A. $\frac{\partial^2\psi}{\partial x^2}+\frac{\partial^2\psi}{\partial y^2}+\frac{\partial^2\psi}{\partial z^2}+\frac{8\pi^2}{mh^2}(E-V)\psi=0$

B. $\frac{\partial^2\psi}{\partial x^2}+\frac{\partial^2\psi}{\partial y^2}+\frac{\partial^2\psi}{\partial z^2}+\frac{8\pi m}{h^2}(E-V)\psi=0$

C. $\frac{\partial^2\psi}{\partial x^2}+\frac{\partial^2\psi}{\partial y^2}+\frac{\partial^2\psi}{\partial z^2}+\frac{8\pi^2 m}{h^2}(E-V)\psi=0$

D. $\frac{\partial^2\psi}{\partial x^2}+\frac{\partial^2\psi}{\partial y^2}+\frac{\partial^2\psi}{\partial z^2}+\frac{8\pi m^2}{h}(E-V)\psi=0$

134. An electron has principal quantum number 3. The number of its *(i)* sub-shell and *(ii)* orbitals would be respectively
A. 3 and 5 B. 3 and 7
C. 3 and 9 D. 2 and 5

135. The probability of finding an electron residing in a P_x orbital is not zero
A. In the *yz* plane B. In the *xy* plane
C. In the *y* direction D. In the *z* direction

136. Ψ^2(*psi*) the wave function represents the probability of finding electron. Its value depends
A. Inside the nucleus
B. Far from the nucleus
C. Near the nucleus
D. Upon the type of orbital

137. If R_H is the Rydberg constant, then the energy of an electron in the ground state of Hydrogen atom is
A. $\frac{R_H c}{h}$ B. $\frac{1}{R_H ch}$
C. $\frac{hc}{R_H}$ D. $-R_H hc$

138. The configuration $1s^2, 2s^2, 2p^5, 3s^1$ shows
A. Ground state of fluorine
B. Excited state of fluorine
C. Excited state of neon atom
D. Excited state of O_2^- ion

139. Amplification of electromagnetic waves by simulated emission of radiation produces
A. Polarised light B. Neutrons
C. Laser D. γ - rays

140. The radioisotope used in treatment of cancer is
A. C^{12} B. Co^{60}
C. I^{131} D. P^{31}

141. The total energy given out during binding up of nucleons in nucleus is
A. Nuclear energy B. Binding energy
C. Packing fraction D. Fusion energy

142. A device used for the measurement of radioactivity is
A. Mass spectrometer
B. Cyclotron
C. Nuclear reactor
D. G.M. counter

143. In case of radioactive equilibrium the one with higher average life is present in .... amount than other with short average life
A. Lesser B. Greater
C. Equal D. Either

144. Madam Curie was awarded Nobel Prize in Physics. She was again awarded Nobel Prize in 1911 for the discovery of
A. Radioactivity B. Radium
C. Uranium D. Nuclear fission

145. Which of the following statement is *correct*?
A. Isotopes are always radioactive

B. α-rays are always negatively charged
C. β-rays are always negatively charged particles
D. γ-rays can be deflected in a magnetic field

146. The order of penetration of three radioactive rays through metal sheet is
A. $\gamma > \beta > \alpha$ B. $\alpha > \beta > \gamma$
C. $\beta > \alpha > \gamma$ D. None

147. The appreciable radioactivity of Uranium minerals is mainly due to
A. An Uranium isotope of mass number 235
B. A Thorium isotope of mass number 232
C. Actinium
D. Radium

148. $^{60}_{27}Co$ is radioactive because
A. Its atomic number is high
B. It has high $\frac{p}{n}$ ratio
C. It has high $\frac{n}{p}$ ratio
D. None of the above

149. The negative value of packing fraction indicates that the isotope is
A. Unstable B. Artificial
C. Very stable D. Stable

150. A nuclear reactor may be cooled by transferring heat generated from the reactor to a turbine steam boiler by using
A. Iron vapour
B. Radioactive carbon
C. Molten Sodium
D. Compressed Hydrogen

151. Pair of similar radiations is
A. α and γ-rays B. β and X-rays
C. α and β-rays D. γ and X-rays

152. The huge amount of energy, which is released during atomic fission is due to
A. Loss of mass
B. Loss of proton
C. Loss of α-particle
D. Loss of electrons

153. A possible material for use in nuclear reactors as a fuel is
A. Th B. Zr
C. Be D. Pu

154. Which particle is used to bombard $^{27}_{13}Al$ and $^{31}_{15}P$
A. Proton B. Neutron
C. α-particles D. Deutron

155. By measuring the radiations emitted by radioactive substances added to blood, the volume of the latter can be obtained. The added radioactive isotope is
A. Na^{24} B. H^3
C. C^{13} D. U^{238}

156. The decay of radioactive element follows first order kinetics. Hence,
A. Half life period $= \frac{\text{constant}}{\lambda_1}$ where λ is decay constant
B. The rate of decay is independent of temperature
C. The rate can be altered by changing chemical conditions
D. The element will be completly transformed into a new element after expiry of two half-life periods

157. In sun, the source of energy is
A. Fusion of heavy nuclei
B. Fission of heavy nuclei
C. Fusion of Hydrogen atoms
D. Fusion of Uranium atoms

158. Control rods used in nuclear reactors are made up of
A. Graphite B. Aluminium
C. Cadmium D. Sodium

159. In a Hydrogen bomb, Hydrogen is converted into
A. Barium B. U^{235}
C. U^{238} D. Helium

160. In nuclear reactors, control rods are used to
A. Increase the rate of reaction
B. Decrease the rate of reaction
C. Either *a* or *b*
D. Control the temperature

161. Nuclear reactions accompanied with emission of neutron(s) are
A. ${}_{13}Al^{27} + {}_{2}He^{4} \rightarrow {}_{15}P^{30}$
B. ${}_{6}C^{12} + {}_{1}H^{1} \rightarrow {}_{7}N^{13}$

C. $_{15}P^{30} \rightarrow _{14}Si^{30} + _{1}e^{0}$

D. $_{96}Am^{240} + _{2}He^{4} \rightarrow _{97}Bk^{244} + _{1}e^{0}$

162. As an α-particle approaches a $^{14}_{7}N$ nucleus, the potential energy

A. Increases as it approaches the nucleus
B. Attains maximum value as inter-nuclear distance is approached
C. Reaches to a minimum at the time of fusion
D. All of the above

163. Of the three isotopes of Hydrogen $_{1}H^{1}$, $_{1}H^{2}$ and $_{1}H^{3}$

A. All are stable
B. Two are unstable
C. $_{1}H^{3}$ decays to $_{1}H^{1}$
D. $_{1}H^{3}$ decays to $_{2}He^{3}$

164. Microcurie of radioactivity is equal to

A. 1 micro-becquerel
B. 3.7×10^{2} becquerel
C. 3.7×10^{10} becquerel
D. 3.7×10^{4} becquerel

165. Stable nuclides are those whose $\frac{n}{p}$ ratio is

A. $\frac{n}{p} = 1$ B. $\frac{n}{p} > 1$
C. $\frac{n}{p} = 2$ D. $\frac{n}{p} < 1$

166. Reaction

$_{1}D^{2} + _{1}T^{3} \rightarrow _{2}He^{4} + _{0}n^{1} + \text{energy}$

is an example of

A. Nuclear fission
B. Nuclear fusion
C. Artificial radioactivity
D. Radioactive disintegration

167. Which transformation is not reported correctly

A. $_{96}Cm^{242}\ (\alpha, 2n)\ _{97}Bk^{243}$
B. $_{5}B^{10}\ (\alpha, n)\ _{7}N^{13}$
C. $_{7}N^{14}\ (n, p)\ _{6}C^{14}$
D. $_{14}Si^{28}\ (d, p)\ _{15}P^{29}$

168. The radioactivity due to C^{14} isotope ($t_{1/2} = 6000$ year) of a sample of wood from an ancient tomb was found to be nearly half that of fresh wood, the tomb is, therefore, about

A. 3000 year old B. 6000 year old
C. 9000 year old D. 12000 year old

169. 75% of a first order reaction was completed in 32 minute. When will be 50% of the reaction complete

A. 24 minute B. 16 minute
C. 8 minute D. 4 minute

170. Radioactive material is decaying with $t_{1/2} =$ 30 day. On being separated into two fractions one of the fractions, immediately after separation decays with $t_{1/2} = 2$ day. The other fraction, immediately after separation, would show :

A. Constant specific gravity
B. Increasing specific gravity
C. Decay with $t_{1/2} = 30$ days
D. Decay with $t_{1/2} = 28$ days

171. The sample of a radioactive isotope with a half-life of 20 day weighs 1 g. After 40 day, the weight of the remaining element is

A. 0.5 g B. Zero
C. 0.25 g D. $\frac{1}{6}$ g

172. The energy released during the fission of 1 kg of uranium is

A. 9×10^{20} erg B. 9.0×10^{10} erg
C. 9.0×10^{18} erg D. 9.0×10^{8} erg

173. If the amount of radioactive substance is increased three times, the number of atoms disintegrated per unit time would

A. Be double B. Be triple
C. Remain one third D. Not change

174. The nucleus and an atom can be assumed to be spherical. The radius of the nucleus of mass number A is given by $1.25 \times 10^{-13} \times A^{1/3}$ cm. The atomic radius of an atom is 1 Å. If the mass number is 64, the fraction of the atomic volume that is occupied by the nucleus is

A. 1.0×10^{-13} B. 5.0×10^{-5}
C. 2.0×10^{-2} D. 1.25×10^{-13}

ANSWERS

1	2	3	4	5	6	7	8	9	10
A	C	D	A	A	D	C	B	B	A
11	12	13	14	15	16	17	18	19	20
C	A	B	C	B	C	B	C	B	B
21	22	23	24	25	26	27	28	29	30
C	B	C	D	D	C	B	C	C	C
31	32	33	34	35	36	37	38	39	40
C	A	C	A	C	B	A	B	A	B
41	42	43	44	45	46	47	48	49	50
B	C	C	B	D	B	D	B	A	A
51	52	53	54	55	56	57	58	59	60
D	B	C	B	B	A	B	B	D	C
61	62	63	64	65	66	67	68	69	70
B	A	B	B	C	D	B	D	B	C
71	72	73	74	75	76	77	78	79	80
D	A	A	B	C	C	C	C	C	B
81	82	83	84	85	86	87	88	89	90
B	C	A	B	A	A	B	A	B	C
91	92	93	94	95	96	97	98	99	100
B	B	D	A	B	C	A	B	B	D
101	102	103	104	105	106	107	108	109	110
C	A	D	C	D	B	C	B	B	A
111	112	113	114	115	116	117	118	119	120
B	C	A	C	A	D	D	B	C	B
121	122	123	124	125	126	127	128	129	130
A	D	B	B	B	C	A	A	A	B
131	132	133	134	135	136	137	138	139	140
B	B	C	C	B	D	D	C	C	B
141	142	143	144	145	146	147	148	149	150
B	D	B	B	C	A	D	C	D	C
151	152	153	154	155	156	157	158	159	160
D	A	D	C	A	A	C	C	D	B
161	162	163	164	165	166	167	168	169	170
A	D	D	D	A	B	A	B	B	B
171	172	173	174						
C	A	B	D						

4

EQUILIBRIUM

Introduction

The change in concentration of the reactant per unit time (i.e., the amount of substance reacting per unit time) is called the *Rate of Reaction*. As the reaction proceeds, the concentration of the reactant is decreases with time while concentration of product increases with time. In the study of chemical equilibrium, concentration of a reactant a expressed in moles per litre, this is commonly known as ACTIVE MASS. It is usually expressed by placing the concerned reactant(s) within a bracket of the type '[ ]'.

Reactions in which its products can be reconverted back into reactants are known as Reversible Reactions and these are indicated by putting two half arrows ($\rightleftharpoons$) between the reactants and the products because such reactions can proceed in forward as well as backward directions. On the other hand, reactions whose products cannot be converted back to reactants are known as Irreversible Reactions. Such reactions proceed only in one direction.

In irreversible reactions, generally one or more of the products separate out as *insoluble* or *volatile species* (e.g., AgCl and HCl in following reactions.

$$NaCl + AgNO_3 \rightarrow AgCl\downarrow + NaNO_3$$

$$NaCl + H_2SO_4 \rightarrow NaHSO_4 + HCl\uparrow$$

An insoluble or a volatile product serves as so-called sink and make the reaction *unidirectional.*

Free energy change (ΔG) in a reversible reaction is *Zero* and in an irreversible reaction is *Zero.*

Characteristics of Chemical Equilibrium

When a reversible reaction is carried out in a closed vessel, a stage is reached when the forward and the backward reactions proceed with the same speed. This stage is known as *chemical equilibrium.*

(i) It is a dynamic equilibrium, i.e., at this stage, the reaction, although appears to be stopped, actually takes place in both the directions with the same speed, and it is permanent.

(ii) Equilibrium state can be approached from both sides.

(iii) At equilibrium state, composition of the reactants and products remain constant and a reversible reaction never goes to completion unless it is acted upon by some external factors, e.g.; the removal of the products from the reaction system, the effect of pressure etc.

(iv) Equilibrium is not affected by the presence of catalyst, the catalyst only hastes the approach of equilibrium state.

(v) Change in pressure, temperature or concentra-tion favours one of the reactions and thus shifts the equilibrium point in one direction.

(vi) At equilibrium ΔG is zero.

Law of Mass Action

It was first stated by Norwegian Chemist Cato Guldberg and Peter Waage in 1863. "At constant temperature, the rate of a homogeneous reaction at a given instant is usually proportional to some power of the concentration of each reactant at that instant" or in other words, under a given set of conditions, the rate of chemical reaction is directly proportional to the product of concentration (active mass) of the reacting substances.

Active mass (Molar concentration)

$$= \frac{\text{No. of moles}}{\text{Vol. in litres}}$$

Note : Active mass of a gas or liquid means it molar concentration, while active mass of a solid is always taken as unity; irrespective of the quantity.

Law of mass action is applicable only to reversible reactions.

Equilibrium Constant Expression : Let us consider a homogeneous reversible reaction

$$A + B \rightleftharpoons C + D$$

By applying law of mass action in this reversible reaction, we get

$$r_f \alpha \; [A]^1 [B]^1$$

$$r_f = K_1 [A]^1 [B]^1 \qquad ...(i)$$

Similarly, $r_b \alpha \; [C]^1 [D]^1$

$$r_b = K_2 [C]^1 [D]^1 \qquad ...(ii)$$

where K_1 and K_2 are called velocity constants for forward and backward reactions.

Now, at equilibrium

$$r_f = r_b$$

From *(i)* and *(ii)*

$$K_1 [A]^1 [B]^1 = K_2 [C]^1 [D]^1$$

$$\frac{K_1}{K_2} = \frac{[C]^1 [D]^1}{[A]^1 [B]^1}$$

$$K_c = \frac{[C][D]}{[A][B]} = \frac{K_1}{K_2}$$

where K_c is called equilibrium constant :

Illustration-Reactions :

(a) $N_2(g) + 3H_2(g) \rightleftharpoons 2NH_3(g)$

$$K_c = \frac{[NH_3]^2}{[N_2]^1 [H_2]^3}$$

(b) $PCl_3(g) + Cl_2(g) \rightleftharpoons PCl_5(g)$

$$K_c = \frac{[PCl_5]^1}{[PCl_3]^1 [Cl_2]^1}$$

Graphs :

(a) Reaction rate *vs* time

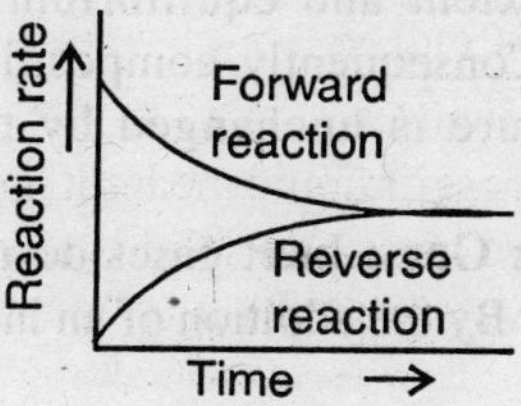

(b) Concentration *vs* time of reactants and products:

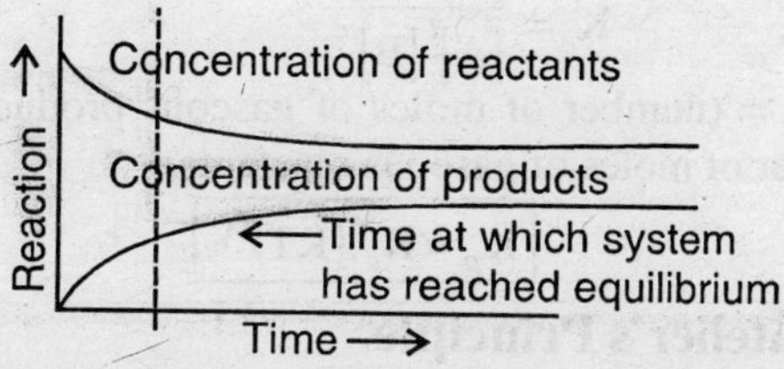

Relationship between K_p and K_c : In case of gaseous relation, the term active mass (mole per litre) is replaced by partial pressure.

Thus, when concentrations of the reaction are expressed in terms of molarity (moles per litre), the equilibrium constant K is represented as K_c while when concentrations are expressed in terms of partial pressures, K is represented as K_p.

K_p and K_c are related as below:

$$K_p = K_c \times (RT)^{\Delta n}$$

where, Δn = No. of moles of products – No. of moles of reactants

R = Gas constant

T = Absolute temperature.

Let us assume a homogeneous reversible gaseous reaction,

$$lA + mB \rightleftharpoons gX + hY$$

$$K_c = \frac{[X]^g [Y]^h}{[A]^l [B]^m} \qquad ...(i)$$

$$K_p = \frac{P_X^g . P_Y^h}{P_A^l . P_B^m} \qquad ...(ii)$$

For gases the partial pressure is related to the molar concentration in a simple way

$$P_A = \frac{nART}{V} = [A]RT$$

where [A] = concentration of A, no. of moles/litre or molal concentration

Similarly, $P_B = [B]RT$

$P_X = [X]RT$

and $P_Y = [Y]RT$

By putting these values in equation *(ii)* for K_p, we get

$$K_p = \frac{\{[X]RT\}^g \{[Y]RT\}^h}{\{[A]RT\}^l \{[B]RT\}^m} = \frac{[X]^g [Y]^h}{[A]^l [B]^m} \times \frac{(RT)^{g+h}}{(RT)^{l+m}}$$

$$K_p = K_c.(RT)^{(g+h)-(l+m)} \Rightarrow K_p = K_c.(RT)^{\Delta n}$$

Since, $K_c = \dfrac{[X]^g[Y]^h}{[A]^l[B]^m}$

so Δn = (number of moles of gaseous products) – (number of moles of gaseous reactants)

$$\therefore \quad \boxed{K_p = K_c.(RT)^{\Delta n}}$$

Le-Chatelier's Principle

It was first of all stated in 1884. The effect of pressures, temperature and concentration on the equilibrium condition of system may be predicted by the application of a general rule known as Le-Chatelier's Principle.

According to this principle "If a system at equilibrium is subjected to a stress by changing pressure, temperature or concentration, the reaction proceeds in such a way as to tend to minimise the effect of that change. The presence of catalyst has no effect on the position of equilibrium."

(A) Effect of Pressure : Change in pressure or volume affect the equilibrium system in which at least one of the components is gas and also in which the no. of moles of gaseous reactants and gaseous products are different.

(i.e. $\Delta n \neq 0$)

(a) If $\Delta n = 0$, there is no effect of pressure e.g.
$H_2(g) + I_2(g) \rightleftharpoons 2HI(g)$

(b) If $\Delta n > 0$, i.e., +ve, low pressure will be favourable e.g.
$PCl_5(g) \rightleftharpoons PCl_3(g) + Cl_2(g)$

(c) If $\Delta n < 0$, i.e., –ve, high pressure will be favourable, e.g.,
$N_2(g) + 3H_2(g) \rightleftharpoons 2NH_3(g)$

(B) Effect of Concentration of One of the Components : The increase in concentrations of one of the substances in the equilibrium mixture displaces the equilibrium in that direction which uses up some of the materials added. Conversely, by decreasing the concentration of a substance causes the production of more of that substance.

Example : $N_2 + 3H_2 \rightleftharpoons 2NH_3$

At equilibrium, if more N_2 is added without changing the volume, the reaction quotient Q is smaller than K, because,

$$Q = \frac{[NH_3]^2}{[N_2][H_2]^3}$$

The numerator must increase to maintain constancy of K, hence $[NH_3]$ must increase.

(C) Effect of Temperature : Increase in temperature causes reaction to occur in that direction which results in the absorption of heat, that is endothermic reactions are favoured at high temperature.

Obviously, exothermic reactions give high yield at low temperature.

Important :

(i) K increases with increase in temperature for an endothermic reaction (ΔH = positive).

(ii) K decreases with increase in temperature for an exothermic reaction (ΔH = negative).

(iii) When $\Delta H = 0$, the temperature change has no effect on the equilibrium composition, because K is independent of temperature for which $\Delta H = 0$.

Cause : The equilibrium constant K, is constant only as long as the temperature does not change since $K = \dfrac{K_1}{K_2}$ and rate constant $Ae^{-E_a/RT}$

At a particular temperature the activation energies for the forward and reverse reaction are different.

The values of K_1 and K_2 change disproportionately, hence, the change in value of K.

The variation of K with temperature is expressed quantitatively as

$$\log \frac{K_2}{K_1} = \frac{\Delta H°}{2.303\,R}\left(\frac{1}{T_1} - \frac{1}{T_2}\right)$$

where $T_2 > T_1$ and $\Delta H°$ = enthalpy reaction assumed to be constant for the given temperature range.

(D) Effect of Catalyst : The addition of a catalyst has no effect on position of equilibrium in a reversible reaction, since it accelerates the forward and reverse reactions to the same extent and equilibrium is achieved more rapidly. Consequently composition of the equilibrium mixture is unchanged by the presence of a catalyst.

(E) Effect of an Inert Gas : Inert gases do not participate in the reaction. By the addition of an inert gas:

(i) When the Volume is constant : The total gas pressure will increase but the concentration (or partial pressure) of all the components will remains constant.

Hence an inert gas has no effect on an equilibrium condition.

(ii) When the Pressure is constant : The reaction volume will increase and the equilibrium condition will shift to the side of the reaction where there is greater number of moles of gas.

Ionic Equilibria in Aqueous Solutions : When certain substances are dissolved in water, they split up into charged particles called ions. The process of splitting or breaking up of a compound in solution into ions is called *ionization*.

But this dissociation into ions seldom occurs to completion due to reversible nature of this process. There is a state of dynamic equilibrium between ionized and unionized molecules and the equilibrium thus established between the two opposing processes is called ionic equilibrium.

$$XY + Water \rightleftharpoons X^+(aq) + Y^-(aq)$$

The substances which conduct electricity in aqueous state and split up into ions are known as *electrolytes*. Substances which when dissolved in water dissociate almost completely into ions are called **strong electrolytes**, e.g., HCl, NaCl, KOH, etc.

Ionisation of Weak Electrolytes : Ostwald's Dilution Law : In an aqueous solution of a weak electrolyte like BA; a fraction of it dissociates into ions and there exists an equilibrium between the free ions B^+ and A^-, and the undissociated electrolyte. Thus,

$$BA \xrightleftharpoons{water} B^+ + A^-$$

As ionization is a reversible process, therefore the rate of formation of ions and their removal by recombination will be governed by the law of mass action.

Suppose that originally C mole of the binary electrolyte BA is dissolved in one litre of solution and that its *degree of dissociation* is α, then the state of affairs at the equilibrium will be

C	0	0	Original
AB ⇌	B^+	A^-	
C(1 – *a*)	Ca	Cu	At equilibrium

and the respective molar concentration at equilibrium will be

$$[BA] = C(1-\alpha)$$
$$[B^+] = C\alpha$$
$$[A^-] = C\alpha$$

According to the law of chemical equilibrium,

$$K = \frac{[B^+][A^-]}{[BA]}$$

where K is a constant, and is known as *dissociation* or *ionization constant.*

$$\therefore \ K = \frac{C\alpha \times C\alpha}{C(1-\alpha)} \text{ or } K = \frac{C\alpha^2}{1-\alpha} = \frac{\alpha^2}{(1-\alpha)V}$$

This mathematical expression is known as *Ostwald's dilution law.*

If degree of dissociation 'α' is very small as is usually the case of weak electrolyte at ordinary concentration, then $(1-\alpha)$ will be approximately equal to unity, so the dilution law becomes

$$C\alpha^2 = K \text{ or } \alpha = \sqrt{\frac{K}{C}}$$

i.e. "the degree of dissociation of weak electrolyte is inversely proportional to the square root of the molar concentration of solution. Thus, it follows that the degree of dissociation would increase with dilution and in case of very dilute solution will be nearly equal to unity." This implies that even weak electrolytes are almost completely ionized in very dilute solutions. Further, since C is reciprocal to V (volume)

$$\therefore \quad \alpha = \sqrt{K \times V}$$

or α is directly proportional to the volume.

Solubility Product : When silver chloride is dissolved in water, an equilibrium exists between the undissolved solid silver chloride and silver ions and chloride ions, i.e., $AgCl(s) \rightleftharpoons Ag^+(aq) + Cl^-(aq)$

Thus equilibrium constant expression for this reaction is :

$$K = \frac{[Ag^+][Cl^-]}{[AgCl]}$$

As the active mass or molar concentrations of a solid is taken to be constant, therefore [AgCl] is constant.

$\therefore$ K × [AgCl] = $[Ag^+][Cl^-]$ or $K_{sp} = [Ag^+]$ $[Cl^-]$

Where K_{sp} is a new constant called 'Solubility Product Constant'. Its value is constant at a given temperature. It is equal to the product of ionic concentrations in a saturated solution. As solubility increases with temperature, K_{sp} also increases. For a sparingly soluble salt that dissolves to give unequal number of cations and anions, the concentration of each ions is raised to a power given by the exponent in the balanced chemical equation. In general, for

$A_xB_y(s) \rightleftharpoons xA^{y+}(aq) + yB^{x-}(aq)$

K_{sp} is given by

$$K_{sp} = \left[A^{y+}\right]^x \left[B^{x-}\right]^y$$

Arrhenius Concept of Acids and Bases

Acid : An acid is a substance which furnishes hydrogen ions in its aqueous solution, e.g., HCl, HNO_3, CH_3COOH, etc., are regarded as acids as they furnish hydrogen ions in their aqueous solutions.

$$\underset{\text{Hydrochloric acid}}{HCl} \xrightleftharpoons{\text{water}} H^+ + Cl^-$$

In fact, the all properties of acids are due to the properties of H^+. Thus,

(i) They turn blue litmus red
(ii) They neutralize base
(iii) They react with active metals to liberate hydrogen gas
(iv) They decompose carbonates and bicarbonate.

Base : A base is a substance which furnishes hydroxyl ions in its aqueous solution, e.g., NaOH, KOH, NH_4OH, etc., are regarded as bases as they furnish hydroxyl ions in their aqueous solution.

$$\underset{\text{Sodium hydroxide}}{NaOH} \xrightleftharpoons{\text{water}} Na^+ + OH^-$$

In fact, all the properties of bases are due to the properties of hydroxyl ion. Thus,

(i) They turn red litmus blue
(ii) They neutralize acids

"The relative strength of weak acids may be compared in terms of their dissociation constants."

For example, the dissociation of a weak acid HA is represented as :

$$HA \rightleftharpoons H^+(aq) + A^-(aq)$$

Applying law of chemical equilibrium to this reversible reaction, we get

$$K_a = \frac{\left[H^+\right]\left[A^-\right]}{[HA]}$$

"The relative strength of weak bases may be compared in terms of their dissociation constants."

For example, the dissociation of a weak base MOH is represented as

$$MOH \rightleftharpoons M^+(aq) + OH^-(aq)$$

Applying law of chemical equilibrium to this reversible reaction.

$$K_b = \frac{\left[M^+\right]\left[OH^-\right]}{[MOH]}$$

where "K_b is known as the dissociation constant of the weak base. From the equation, it is clear that K_b is directly proportional to OH^- ion concentration. Hence, greater the dissociation constant, the stronger would be the base".

The strength of the acids as well as the bases does not depend upon their concentration. Instead, it merely depends upon the extent of ionization on dilution the concentation decrease while strength increases.

A diprotic acid furnishes two H^+ ions per molecule on ionization. It ionizes in two steps and have two ionization constants, one for each step. Sulphuric acid is a diprotic acid and has two ionization constants.

$$H_2SO_4 \rightleftharpoons H^+ + HSO_4^-$$

$$K_{a_1} = \frac{\left[H^+\right]\left[HSO_4^-\right]}{\left[H_2SO_4\right]} = 1 \times 10^2$$

$$H_2PO_4^- \rightleftharpoons H^+ + HPO_4^{2-}$$

$$K_{a_2} = \frac{\left[H^+\right]\left[HPO_4^{2-}\right]}{\left[H_2PO_4^-\right]} = 6.2 \times 10^{-8}$$

$$HPO_4^{2-} \rightleftharpoons H^+ + PO_4^{3-}$$

$$K_{a_3} = \frac{\left[H^+\right]\left[PO_4^{3-}\right]}{\left[HPO_4^{2-}\right]} = 10^{-12}$$

Bronsted-Lowry Concept of Acids and Bases

According to this concept, a substance (molecular or ionic that donates a hydrogen ion (H^+) to another substance is known as an acid whereas a substance (molecular or ionic) which accepts a proton from any other substance is called a base. In other words, an acid is a proton donor while a base is a proton acceptor.

For example, consider the reaction between HCl and H_2O,

$$HCl + H_2O \rightleftharpoons H_3O^{\oplus} + Cl^-$$

As HCl donates a proton to water, hence HCl is an acid. On the other hand, H_2O accepts a proton from HCl, hence H_2O is a base.

All bronsted acids are Arrhenius acids but all Bronsted bases are not Arrhenius bases.

Conjugate Acid-Base Pairs : For example,

$$HCl + H_2O \rightleftharpoons H_3O^+ + Cl^-$$

In this forward reaction, HCl donates a proton and thus behaves as an acid, water accepts a proton and thus behaves as a base. In the reverse reaction, H_3O^+ is an acid while Cl^- is a base. "Such pairs of substances which are formed from one another by gain or loss of a proton are known as conjugate acid-base pair". Thus hydrochloric acid is a conjugate acid of chloride ion while water is a conjugate base of hydronium ion.

Relative Strength of Acids and Bases : According to Bronsted-Lowery concept, the strength of an acid depends upon its tendency to lose protons while the strength of a base depends upon its tendency to gain protons.

(i) Let us consider hydrochloric acid in water.

$$\underset{\text{Strong acid}}{HCl + H_2O} \rightleftharpoons \underset{\text{Weak conjugate base}}{H_3O^+ + Cl^-}$$

HCl being a strong acid is highly ionized acid thus the equilibrium shifts towards right hand side. On the other hand, Cl^- (Conjugate base of HCl) has a less tendency to accept a proton. Thus strong acid has a weak conjugate base.

Strong acid $\rightleftharpoons$ H^+ + Weak conjugate base.

(ii) Now, let us consider acetic acid in water.

$$\underset{\text{Weak acid}}{CH_3COOH + H_2O} \rightleftharpoons \underset{\text{Strong conjugate base}}{H_3O^{\oplus} + CH_3COO^-}$$

CH_3COOH, being a weak acid, is only slightly ionized and thus the equilibrium shifts towards left hand side. On the other hand, CH_3COO^- (conjugate acid of CH_3COOH) has a greater tendency to accept a proton. Thus weak acid has a strong conjugate base.

Weak acid + $H^{\oplus}$ $\rightleftharpoons$ Strong conjugate base.

Lewis Concept of Acids and Bases

An acid is a substance which can accept a pair of electrons to from a coordinate bond and a base is a substance which can donate a pair of electrons to form a coordinate bond. Thus the base is an electron pair donor and acid is an electron pair acceptor.

The molecule of a Lewis acid with a central atom having incomplete octet, and a Lewis base with complete octet and one or more unshared pair of electrons which are available for donation, e.g.

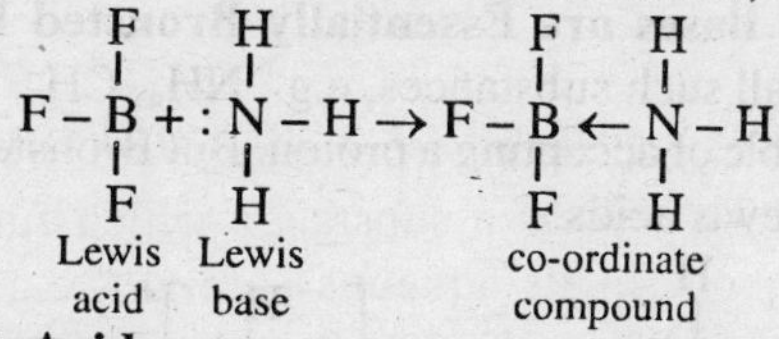

Lewis Acid :

(i) The molecule of a Lewis acid containing multiple bonds, e.g., SO_3 has multiple bonds

$$Ca_2\left[:\ddot{O}:\right]^{2-} + SO_3 \rightarrow \left[SO_4\right]^{2-} Ca^{2+}$$

Lewis base, Lewis acid

In such molecules the Lewis acid character is attributed to the polarization of π -electron cloud on approach of a Lewis base towards carbon or sulphur atom of the multiple bond in which they are bonded with oxygen or nitrogen atoms.

(ii) Simple Cation : Simple cation like Al^{3+}, Ag^+, act as Lewis acids, because they have empty orbitals in their outermost energy levels.

$$\underset{\text{Lewis acid}}{Ag^+} + \underset{\text{Lewis base}}{2NH_3} \rightarrow [H_3N \rightarrow Ag \leftarrow NH_3]^+$$

$$\underset{\text{Lewis acid}}{Al^3} + \underset{\text{Lewis base}}{6H_2O:} \rightarrow \left[Al(H_2O)_6\right]^{3+}$$

(iii) The molecule of a Lewis acid having central atom with incomplete octet like BF_3, $AlCl_3$, $FeCl_3$, BeF_2, etc., and molecules with empty *d*-orbitals. Sn in $SnCl_4$ has empty *d*-orbitals which are used up to make $SnCl_4$, a Lewis acid, the base is negative ion,

$$\underset{\text{Lewis acid}}{SnCl_4} + \underset{\text{Lewis base}}{2Cl^-} \rightarrow SnCl_6^{2-}$$

Lewis Bases : All anions (OH^-, CN^-, CN_2^-, O_2^-, etc) act as Lewis bases. Base strength depends upon its capacity to donate electrons to acid which further depends upon the charge density of the anion.

(i) The greater the charge density on the anion, the stronger is the base.

(ii) Substances having unshared pairs of electrons act as Lewis base. For example, $SH_2\ddot{O}:$, NH_3,

$R_2C = \ddot{O}:$, etc. Lower the electronegativity of the donor atom, greater is its electron donating power and hence stronger is its base strength.

(iii) Substances like CO, alkenes, alkynes, butadiene, benzene, etc. donate electrons from ion pair or through π-electrons donation to form π-complexes with metals in low oxidation states.

Lewis Bases are Essentially Bronsted Bases : Because all such substances, e.g., NH_3, CH^-, etc. are also capable of accepting a proton. But Bronsted acids are not Lewis acids.

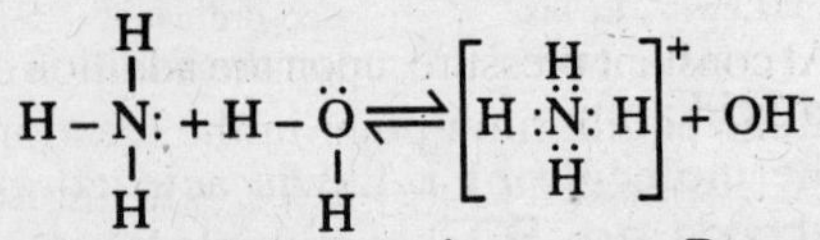

Water in the above reaction acts as Bronsted acid (donates a proton).However, water is not Lewis acid (does not accept electrons pair).

pH and pOH

Water undergoes self ionisation and forms hydronium (H_3O^+) and hydroxide (OH^-) ions in equal amounts.

$$H_2O + H_2O \rightleftharpoons H_3O^+ + OH^-$$
$$K_w = [H_3O^+][OH^-]$$
$$K_w = 1.0 \times 10^{-14} \text{ at } 25°C$$

The degree of ionization increases as the temperature increases. At 100°C, $K_w \approx 10^{-12}$. On adding acid to H_2O, the $[H_3O^+]$ increases and becomes larger than 10^{-7} M, and the $[OH^-]$ becomes less than 10^{-7} M, but never equal to zero. On adding base to H_2O, the $[OH^-]$ becomes greater than 10^{-7} M and $[H_3O^+]$ decreases. However, the product $[H_3O^+]$ $[OH^-]$ is always constant at given temperature.

Most convenient way to represent very small concentrations in solutions is to use a logarithmic scale, such as pH scale.

$pH = -\log [H_3O^+]$ or $[H_3O^+] = 10^{-pH}$

Similarly pOH = $-\log [OH^-]$ or $[OH^-] = 10^{-pOH}$

Also pH, = pOH = pK_w = 14.

Using above equations, one can find out pH if percentage ionisation is known for a weak electrolyte and pH of a solution if concentration of a strong electrolyte is known.

Buffer Solutions

"A buffer solution is a solution which resists any change in its pH value on dilution or on addition of solution of an acid or alkali."

The process by which added H^+ or OH^- ions are removed so that pH remains constant is known as Buffer Action.

Type of Buffers

1. Simple Buffers :

(a) A salt of weak acid and weak base in water, e.g. CH_3COONH_4, NH_4CN

(b) Proteins and amino acids

(c) A mixture of an acid salt and normal of a poly basic acid, e.g. $Na_2HO_4 + Na_3PO_4$.

2. Mixed Buffer : These are commonly encountered and are of two types :

(i) Acid Buffer Solutions

(ii) Basic Buffer Solutions

(i) Acid Buffer Solution : "An acid buffer solution consists of solution of a weak acid and its salt with strong base." The best known example is a mixture of solution of acetic acid and sodium acetate.

$CH_3COOH \rightleftharpoons CH_3COO^- + H^+$ (Weakly ionised)

$CH_3COONa \rightleftharpoons CH_3COO^- + Na^+$ (Highly ionised)

(ii) Basic Buffer Solution : "A basic buffer solution consists of a mixture of a weak base and its salt with strong acid." The best known example is a mixture of ammonium hydroxide and ammonium chloride.

$NH_4OH \rightleftharpoons NH_4^+ + OH^-$ (Weakly ionised)

$NH_4Cl \rightleftharpoons NH_4^+ + Cl^-$ (Highly ionised)

The NH_4^+ ions from completely ionised NH_4Cl suppresses the ionisation of NH_4OH which is already a weak ionisable substance. Thus, the concentration of OH^- ions remains constant.

OBJECTIVE QUESTIONS

1. Pure water is

A. Neutral B. Acidic

C. Basic D. All of these

2. Contribution of H_2O self-ionisation is taken into account when $[H_3O^+]$ is

A. Less than 4.5×10^{-7} M at 25°C

B. More than 4.5×10^{-7} M at 25°C
C. Equal to 4.5×10^{-7} M at 25°C
D. None of the above

3. Product of K_a and K_b is equal to
A. K_w B. $\sqrt{K_w}$
C. K_w^2 D. None of the above

4. At 25°C, pH + pOH is equal to
A. 7 B. 10
C. 14 D. 1

5. Ionisation constant of weak acid, HA, is given as

A. $K_a = \dfrac{[H_3O^+][A^-]}{[HA]}$

B. $K_a = \dfrac{[H_2O][HA]}{[H_3O^+]}$

C. $K_a = \dfrac{[H_3O^+][OH^-]}{[H_2O]}$

D. All of the above

6. The condition for spontaneity in a chemical reaction is
A. $(\Delta G)_{T,P} \leq 0$ B. $(\Delta H)_{S,P} \geq 0$
C. $(\Delta U)_{S,V} \leq 0$ D. $(\Delta S)_{U,V} \geq 0$
E. All of these

7. In which of the following systems will the equilibrium be shifted to the right if the volume is increased at constant temperatures.
A. $A_2(g) + B_2(g) \rightleftharpoons 2AB(g)$
B. $A_2(g) + 3O_2(g) \rightleftharpoons 2AO_3$
C. $A_2(g) \rightleftharpoons 2A(g)$
D. $A_2(g) + 4B_2(g) \rightleftharpoons 2AB_4(g)$

8. For a reaction $AB(g) \rightleftharpoons A(g) + B(g)$. AB is 33% dissociated at a total pressure of p, then
A. $p = K_p$ B. $p = 3K_p$
C. $p = 4K_p$ D. $p = 8K_p$

9. In which of the following reactions is $K_p < K_c$?
A. $CO(g) + Cl_2(g) \rightleftharpoons COCl_2(g)$
B. $CO(g) + 3H_2(g) \rightleftharpoons CH_4(g) + H_2O(g)$
C. $2BrCl(g) \rightleftharpoons Cl_2(g) + Br_2(g)$
D. A and B

10. When pressure is applied to the equilibrium system. $Ice(s) \rightleftharpoons H_2O(l)$, which of the following will happen?
A. More ice will be formed
B. Water will be evaporated
C. More water will be formed
D. Equilibrium will not be reached

11. Which of the following is correct for the equilibrium of the reaction
$C(s) + H_2O(g) \rightleftharpoons CO(g) + H_2(g)$
A. $pH_2 \propto pH_2O$ B. $pH_2 \propto \sqrt{pH_2O}$
C. $pH_2 \propto pH_2O^2$ D. $pH_2 \propto \dfrac{pH_2O^2}{pCO}$

12. At constant pressure, upon the addition of helium at the equilibrium point in the reaction, $PCl_5(g) \rightleftharpoons PCl_3(g) + Cl_2(g)$, the degree of dissociation of
A. PCl_5 will decrease B. PCl_5 will increase
C. PCl_3 will increase D. Cl_2 will increase

13. Which of the following graph represents an exothermic reaction?

A. 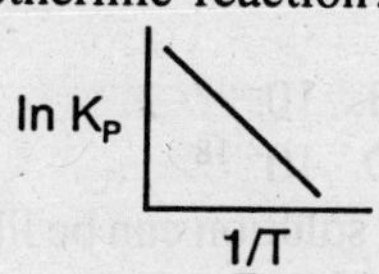

B. 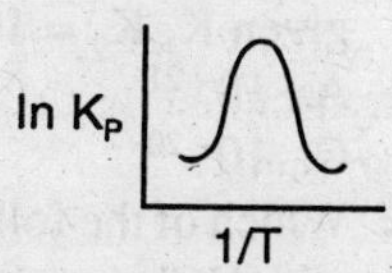

C. 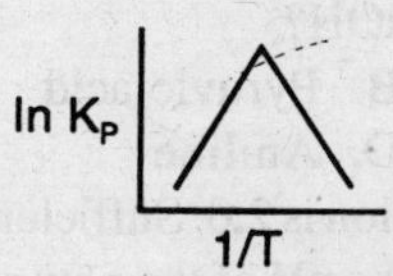

D. 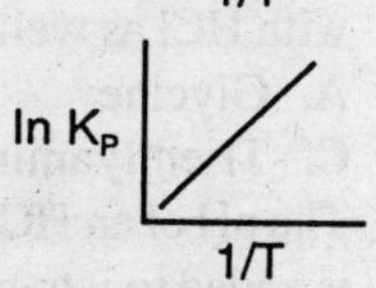

14. $N_2(g) + 3H_2(g) \underset{500°C}{\overset{catalyst}{\rightleftharpoons}} 2NH_3 + Heat$
In the above reaction, the direction of equilibrium will be shifted to the right by
A. Increasing the concentration of nitrogen
B. Compressing the reaction mixture
C. Decreasing the concentration of ammonia
D. All of the above

15. If the H^+ ion concentration of a solution is increased to ten times its initial value, its pH will
A. Increase by one B. Remain unchanged
C. Decrease by one D. Increase by ten

16. Determine the pH of the solution that results from the addition of 20.00 mL of 0.01 M $Ca(OH)_2$ to 30.00 mL of 0.01 M HCl
A. 11.30 B. 10.53
C. 2.70 D. 8.35

17. The pH of milk lies between
A. 6.6 and 6.9 B. 2.60 and 4.40
C. 7.0 and 7.5 D. 7.35 and 7.45

18. Which of the following concentrations has the largest degree of dissociation for a weak acid?
A. 1.0 M B. 0.5 M
C. 0.10 M D. 0.01 M

19. A given weak acid (0.01 M) has $pK_a = 6$. The pH of the solution is
A. 3 B. 4
C. 5 D. 6

20. Two weak solutions are isohydric when their
A. Hydrogen ion concentrations are the same before and after mixing
B. Hydrogen ion concentrations are not the same before and after mixing
C. Degree of dissociation are the same
D. Chemical properties are the same

21. An acidic solution (0.1 M) of salt is saturated with H_2S (0.1 M). The concentration of H_2S is, given $K_1.K_2 = 10^{-21}$
A. 10^{-21} B. 10^{-19}
C. 10^{-20} D. 10^{-18}

22. Which of the following solution can be liberated with HCl as well as NaOH?
A. Glycine B. Pyruvic acid
C. Triethlyamine D. Aniline

23. The pH of an HCl solution is 2.0. Sufficient water is added to it to make the pH of the new solution equal to 5.0. The decrease in the hydrogen ion concentration is
A. 10 times B. 7 times
C. 1000 times D. 100 times

24. Which of the following mixture constitute a buffer?
A. $CH_3COOH + CH_3COONa$
B. $Na_2CO_3 + NaHCO_3$
C. $NaCl + HCl$
D. $NH_4Cl + (NH_4)_2SO_4$
E. A and B

25. An acetic acid and sodium acetate buffer has pH = 5.36. The ratio of concentration $\frac{[OAc^-]}{[HOAc]}$ is
A. 6 : 1 B. 4 : 3
C. 1 : 1 D. 4 : 1

26. In which of the following pairs of solutions there is no effect on the pH upon dilution?
A. 0.1 M NH_3 and 0.1 M $(NH_4)_2SO_4$
B. 0.1 M NaH_2PO_4 and 0.1 M Na_4HPO_4
C. 0.1 M HCl and 0.01 M NaOH
D. 0.1 M KCl and 0.1 M HCl

27. A buffer solution is used in the
A. Preparation of chrome alum
B. Removal of PO_4^{3-} ions in qualitative analysis
C. Precipitation of $Zn(OH)_2$ from $ZnSO_4$
D. Determination of the ionic product of water

28. Fear or excitement generally causes one to breathe rapidly and results in the decrease of CO_2 concentration in one's blood. In what way does this change the pH of blood?
A. pH will increase
B. pH will decrease
C. There will be no change in the pH
D. The pH level will be adjusted at 7.

29. The pK_a of acetyl salicylic acid (aspirin) is 3.5. The pH of gastric juice in the human stomach is about 2-3 and that in the small intestine about 8.0. Aspirin will be
A. Unionized in the small intestine and in the stomach
B. Completely ionized in the small intestine and in the stomach
C. Ionized in the stomach and almost unionized in the small intestine
D. Ionized in the small intestine and almost unionized in the stomach

30. The pH of blood does not appreciably change by a small addition of acid or a base because blood
A. Contains serum protein which acts as buffer
B. Contains iron as a part of the molecule
C. Can be easily coagulated
D. Is a body fluid

31. For the precipitation of cations of groups IV in qualitative analysis, the medium is made alkaline before passing H_2S gas. The medium is made alkaline because this helps
A. Suppress the ionization of H_2S
B. Increase the ionization of H_2S
C. Increase the ionization of metal salts
D. Decrease the ionization of metal salts

32. The solubility of a salt A_2B_3 in 1.0×10^{-3} M. Its solubility products is

A. 1.08×10^{-13} B. 1.08×10^{-15}

C. 1.08×10^{-10} D. 1.08×10^{-17}

33. Why does only As^{3+} get precipitated as As_2S_3 and not Zn^{2+} as ZnS when H_2S is passed through an acidic solution containing Ag^{3+} and Zn^{2+}?

A. The solubility product of As_2S_3 is less than that of ZnS.

B. Enough As^{3+} ions are present in an acidic medium.

C. A zinc salt does not ionize in acidic medium

D. The solubility product changes in the presence of an acid

34. Which of the following will not hydrolyse in an aqueous solution?

A. A salt of strong acid and a strong base

B. A salt of strong acid and a weak base

C. A salt of weak acid and strong base

D. A salt of weak acid and weak base

35. The equilibrium constant for the reaction $PCl_5(g) \rightleftharpoons PCl_3(g) + Cl_2(g)$ is 2.4×10^{-3}. What will be the equilibrium constant for the backward reaction at the same temperature.

A. 4.4×10^2 B. 4.2×10^2

C. 4.4×10^{-2} D. 4.4×10^4

36. For the reaction $[Ag(CN)_2]^- \rightleftharpoons Ag^+ + 2CN^-$, the equilibrium constant at 25°C is 4.0×10^{-19}. Calculate the silver ion concentration in a solution which was originally 0.10 molar in KCN and 0.03 molar in $AgNO_3$.

A. 7.5×10^{18} M B. 7.5×10^{-18} M

C. 7.7×10^{10} M D. 7.7×10^{-10} M

37. Calculate the present dissociation of $H_2S(g)$ if 0.1 mole of H_2S is kept in 0.4 litre vessel at 1,000 K. For the reaction, $2H_2S(g) \rightleftharpoons 2H_2(g) + S_2(g)$ the value of K_c is 1.0×10^{-6}

A. 2% B. 4%

C. 6% D. 8%

38. Some solid NH_4HS is placed in a flask containing 0.5 atm of NH_3. What would be the pressures of NH_3 and H_2S when equilibrium is reached?

A. $pNH_3 = 0.6653$ atm, $pH_2S = 0.2612$ atm

B. $pNH_3 = 0.6653$ atm, $pH_2S = 0.1653$ atm

C. $pNH_3 = 0.5412$ atm, $pH_2S = 0.1653$ atm

D. $pNH_3 = 0.6653$ atm, $pH_2S = 0.1719$ atm

39. Ammonia under a pressure of 15 atm at 27°C is heated to 347°C in a closed vessel in the presence of a catalyst. Under the condition, NH_3 is partially decomposed according to the equation, $2NH_3 \rightleftharpoons N_2 + 3H_2$. The vessel is such that the volume remains effectively constant whereas pressure increases to 50 atm. Calculate the percentage of NH_3 actually decomposed.

A. 81.4% B. 69%

C. 61.3% D. 71.1%

40. At temperature T, composed $AB_2(g)$ dissociates according to the reaction
$2AB_2(g) \rightleftharpoons 2AB(g) + B_2(g)$
with a degree of dissociation, x, which is small compared with unity. Deduce the expression for x in terms of the equilibrium constant, K_p and the total pressure P.

A. $x = \frac{K_p}{P}$ B. $x = \left[\frac{2K_p}{P}\right]^{1/3}$

C. $x = \frac{2K_p}{P}$ D. $x = \sqrt{\frac{2K_p}{P}}$

41. A sample of air consisting of N_2 and O_2 was heated at 2500 K until the equilibrium
$N_2(g) + O_2(g) \rightleftharpoons 2NO(g)$
was established with an equilibrium constant $K_c = 2.1 \times 10^{-3}$. At equilibrium, the mole % of NO was 1.8. Estimate the initial composition of air in mole fraction of N_2 and O_2.

A. $N_2 = 80\%, O_2 = 20\%$

B. $N_2 = 79\%, O_2 = 21\%$

C. $N_2 = 69\%, O_2 = 31\%$

D. $N_2 = 40\%, O_2 = 60\%$

42. One mole of nitrogen is mixed with three moles of hydrogen in a 4 litre container. If 0.0025 mole of nitrogen is converted to ammonia by the following reaction,
$N_2(g) + 3H_2(g) \rightleftharpoons 2NH_3(g)$
Calculate the equilibrium constant (K_c) for the following equilibrium.

$$\frac{1}{2}N_2(g) + \frac{3}{2}H_2(g) \rightleftharpoons NH_3(g)$$

A. 1.48×10^{-5} litre^2 mol^{-2}

B. 3.82×10^{-3} litre mol^{-1}

C. 4.40×10^{-4} litre mol^{-1}

D. 3.82×10^{-5} $litre^2$ mol^{-1}

43. At a certain temperature, equilibrium constant (K_c) is 16 for the reaction
$SO_2(g) + NO_2(g) \rightleftharpoons SO_3(g) + NO(g)$
If we take one mole each of all the four gases in a one litre container, what would be the equilibrium concentration of NO(g) and $NO_2(g)$?

A. NO = 1.2 moles, NO_2 = 0.8 moles

B. NO = 1.3 moles, NO_2 = 0.7 moles

C. NO = 1.6 moles, NO_2 = 0.4 moles

D. NO = 2.0 moles, NO_2 = 0.0 moles

44. The equilibrium constant of the reaction $A_2(g) + B_2(g) \rightleftharpoons 2AB(g)$ at 100°C is 50. If a one litre flask containing one mole of A_2 is connected to a two litre flask containing two moles of B_2, how many moles of AB will be formed at 373°C?

A. 2.021 B. 1.886

C. 1.749 D. 1.012

45. One mole of Cl_2 and 3 moles of PCl_5 are placed in a 100 litre vessel heated to 227°C. The equilibrium pressure is 2.05 atmospheres. Assuming ideal behaviour, calculate the degree of dissociation for PCl_5 and K_p for the reaction.
$PCl_5(g) \rightleftharpoons PCl_3(g) + Cl_2(g)$

A. 0.23 B. 0.41

C. 0.91 D. 2.0

46. For the reaction, $CO(g) + 2H_2(g) \rightleftharpoons CH_3OH(g)$, hydrogen gas is introduced into a five litre flask at 327°C, containing 0.2 mole of CO(g) and a catalyst, until the pressure is 4.92 atm. At this point 0.1 mole of $CH_3OH(g)$ is formed. Calculate the equilibrium constants K_p and K_c.

A. $K_c = 21.2$ $mole^{-2}$ l^{-2}, $K_p = 0.1144$ atm^{-2}

B. $K_c = 21.1$ $mole^{-2}$ l^{-2}, $K_p = 0.1916$ atm^{-2}

C. $K_c = 277.78$ $mole^{-2}$ l^{-2}, $K_p = 0.1144$ atm^{-2}

D. $K_c = 27.1$ $mole^{-2}$ l^{-2}, $K_p = 0.1313$ atm^{-2}

47. At some temperature and under a pressure of 4 atm, PCl_5 is 10% dissociated calculate the pressure at which PCl_5 will be 20% dissociated, temperature remaining same.

A. 0.46 atm B. 0.96 atm

C. 1.46 atm D. 1.96 atm

48. N_2O_4 is 25% dissociated at 37°C and one atmosphere pressure. Calculate K_p and the percentage dissociation at 0.1 atmosphere and 37°C.

A. 0.166 atm and 37% respectively

B. 0.266 atm and 87% respectively

C. 0.316 atm and 47% respectively

D. 0.316 atm and 37% respectively

49. In the reversible reaction of the type $A + B \rightleftharpoons AB$, in general.

A. Neither the reaction will be endothermic

B. Both reactions will be exothermic

C. The combination reaction will be endothermic and the dissociation reaction will be exothermic

D. The combination reaction will be exothermic and the dissociation reaction will be endothermic

50. When $NaNO_3$ is heated in a closed vessel, oxygen is liberated and $NaNO_2$ is left behind. At equilibrium

A. An addition of $NaNO_2$ favours reverse reaction

B. An addition of $NaNO_3$ favours forward reaction

C. Increasing temperature favours forward reaction

D. All of the above

51. Pure ammonia is placed in a vessel at a temperature where its dissociation constant is appreciable. At equilibrium.

A. K_p does not change significantly with pressure

B. α does not change with pressure

C. Concentration of ammonia does not change with pressure

D. Concentration of hydrogen is less than that of nitrogen

52. For the gas phase reaction, $C_2H_4 + H_2 \rightleftharpoons C_2H_6$, ΔH = – 32.7 K cal carried out in a vessel, the equilibrium concentration of C_2H_4 can be increased by

A. Increasing temperature

B. Decreasing pressure

C. Removing some H_2

D. Adding some C_2H_6

E. All of the above

53. For the chemical reaction $3X(g) + Y(g) \rightleftharpoons X_3Y(g)$, the amount of X_3Y at equilibrium is affected by

A. Temperature and pressure
B. Temperature only
C. Pressure only
D. Temprature, pressure and catalyst

54. Calculate the dissociation constant of monobasic acid which is 3.5% dissociated in $\frac{N}{20}$ solution at 20°C.

A. 1.24×10^{-3} B. 6.34×10^{-5}
C. 6.34×10^{-3} D. 7.11×10^{-5}

55. Nicotinic acid ($K_a = 1.4 \times 10^{-5}$) is represented by the formula HNic. Calculate its percent dissociation in a solution which contains 0.10 mol of nicotinic acid per 2.0 litre of solution.

A. 6.66% B. 1.66%
C. 2.14% D. 2.16%

56. Calculate the hydrogen ion concentration in 10 litres of 0.1 N solution, an acid having dissociation constant 4.0×10^{-16}

A. 3.62×10^{-6} g ion litre^{-1}
B. 6.32×10^{-6} g ion litre^{-1}
C. 8.11×10^{-6} g ion litre^{-1}
D. 3.16×10^{-6} g ion litre^{-1}

57. A certain weak acid has $K_a = 1.0 \times 10^{-14}$. Calculate the equilibrium constant for its reaction with strong base

A. 10^6 B. 10^4
C. 10^{10} D. 10^{14}

58. What is the pH of a 0.50 M aqueous NaCN solution? pK_b of CN^- is 4.70

A. pH = 6.5 B. pH = 4.3
C. pH = 13.2 D. pH = 11.5

59. How many moles of calcium hydroxide must be dissolved to produce 250 ml of an aqueous solution of pH 10.65? Assume complete dissociation.

A. 1.6×10^{-4} B. 0.56×10^{-4}
C. 0.31×10^{-3} D. 0.44×10^{-4}

60. The pH of 0.05 M aqueous of diethylamine is 12. Calculate its K_b.

A. 5.2×10^3 B. 2.5×10^{-3}
C. 10^{-2} D. 3.4×10^{-2}

61. What will be the resultant pH when 200 ml of an aqueous solution of HCl (pH = 2.0) is mixed with 300 ml of an aqueous solution of NaOH (pH = 12.0)

A. 1.312 B. 11.3020
C. 13.1121 D. 14.00

62. What is the pH of a 1.0 M solution of acetic acid? To what volume must one litre of thin solution be diluted so that the pH of the resulting solution will be twice the original value? Given $K_a = 1.8 \times 10^{-5}$.

A. pH = 2.3724, V = 2.78×10^4 litres
B. pH = 3.113, V = 1.314×10^5 litres
C. pH = 2.312, V = 2.011×10^6 litres
D. pH = 1.1011, V = 1.2131×10^4 litres

63. For 0.50 M aqueous solution of sodium cyanide, (pK_b of CN^- is 4.70), calculate

(i) hydrolysis constant
(ii) Degree hydrolysis
(iii) pH

A. *(i)* 2×10^{-3} *(ii)* 6.3×10^{-2} *(iii)* 6.5
B. *(i)* 2×10^{-5} *(ii)* 6.3×10^{-3} *(iii)* 11.5
C. *(i)* 3×10^{-5} *(ii)* 3.1×10^{-2} *(iii)* 11.5
D. *(i)* 2×10^{-5} *(ii)* 6.3×10^{-3} *(iii)* 1.15

64. Calculate the pH of an aqueous solution of 1.0 M ammonium formate assuming complete dissociation (pK_a of formic acid = 3.8 and pK_b of ammonia = 4.8)

A. 2.3 B. 6.5
C. 3.1 D. 4.2

65. How many gram mole of HCl will be required to prepare one litre of a buffer solution (containing NaCN and HCN) of pH 8.5 using 0.01 gram formula weight of NaCN?

A. 2.85×10^{-3} M B. 8.85×10^{-3} M
C. 3.14×10^{-3} M D. 6.13×10^{-3} M

66. What is the pH of the solution when 0.20 mole of hydrochloric acid is added to one litre of a solution containing

(i) 1 M each acetic acid and acetate ion?
(ii) 0.1 M each of acetic acid and acetate ion?

The dissociation constant of acetic acid is 1.8×10^{-5}

A. *(i)* 4.5686 *(ii)* 1 B. *(i)* 3.12 *(ii)* 2
C. *(i)* 6.14 *(ii)* 3 D. *(i)* 6.14 *(ii)* 1

67. A sample of hard water contains 0.005 moles of $CaCl_2$ per litre. What is the minimum conc. of Na_2SO_4 which must be added for removing Ca^{2+} ions from the water sample. K_{sp} for $CaSO_4$ is 2.4 × 10^{-5} at 25°C

A. 2.8 × 10^{-5} M B. 4.8 × 10^{-3} M
C. 6.1 × 10^{-3} M D. 4.1 × 10^{-5} M

68. The solubility product (K_{sp}) of $Ca(OH)_2$ at 25°C is 4.42 × 10^{-5}. A 500 ml of saturated solution of $Ca(OH)_2$ is mixed with equal volume of 0.4 M NaOH. How much $Ca(OH)_2$ in milligrams is precipitated?

A. 760 gm B. 743.3 mg
C. 711 gm D. 710 mg

69. A sample of AgCl was treated with 5.00 ml of 1.5 M Na_2CO_3 solution to give Ag_2CO_3. The remaining solution contained 0.0026 g of Cl^- per litre. Calculate the solubility product of AgCl [K_{sp} Ag_2CO_3 = 8.2 × 10^{-12}]

A. 1.1 × 10^{-2} B. 1.71 × 10^{-11}
C. 1.71 × 10^{-10} D. 1.32 × 10^{-9}

70. The solubility of $Pb(OH)_2$ in water is 6.7 × 10^{-6} M. Calculate the solubility of $Pb(OH)_2$ in a buffer solution of pH = 8.

A. 1.0 × 10^{-2} M B. 1.3 × 10^{-5} M
C. 1.2 × 10^{-3} M D. 2.1 × 10^{-3} M

71. The solubility product of $Ag_2C_2O_4$ at 25°C is 1.24 × 10^{-11} $mol^3\ l^{-3}$. A solution of $K_2C_2O_4$ containing 0.1520 moles in 500 ml. Water is shaken at 25°C with excess Ag_2CO_3 till the following equilibrium is reached :

$Ag_2CO_3 + K_2C_2O_4 \rightleftharpoons Ag_2C_2O_4 + K_2CO_3$.

At equilibrium, the solution contains 0.0358 moles of K_2CO_3. Assuming the degree of dissociation of $K_2C_2O_4$ and K_2CO_3 to be equal, calculate the solubility product of Ag_2CO_3.

A. 1.194 × 10^{-10} $mol^2\ l^{-2}$
B. 3.974 × 10^{-12} $mol^2\ l^{-3}$
C. 3.974 × 10^{-12} $mol^2\ l^{-3}$
D. 1.164 × 10^{-10} $mol^2\ l^{-3}$

72. An aqueous solution of a metal bromide MBr_2 (0.05 M) is saturated with H_2S. What is the minimum pH at which MS will precipitate. K_{sp} for MS = 6.0 × 10^{-21}, concentration of saturated H_2S = 0.1 M : $K_1 = 10^{-7}$ and K_2 = 1.3 × 10^{-13} for H_2S

A. pH = 1.6 B. pH = 0.67
C. pH = 0.987 D. pH = 0.771

73. Molten sodium chloride conducts electricity due to the presence of

A. Free electrons
B. Free ions
C. Free molecules
D. Atoms of sodium and chloride

74. The aqueous solution of aluminium chloride is acidic due to

A. Cation hydrolysis
B. Anion hydrolysis
C. Hydrolysis of both anion and cation
D. Dissociation

75. The compound whose 0.1 M solution is basic is

A. Ammonium acetate
B. Ammonium chloride
C. Ammonium sulphate
D. Sodium acetate

76. Addition of solid potassium cyanide to water would cause

A. Increase in pH
B. Decrease in pH
C. No change in pH
D. No change in electrical conductivity

77. An acidic buffer solution can be prepared by mixing solution of

A. Ammonium acetate and acetic acid
B. Ammonium chloride and Aluminium chloride
C. Sulphuric acid and sodium sulphate
D. Sodium chloride and sodium hydroxide

78. A precipitate is formed when

A. The solution becomes saturated
B. The ionic product is less than the solubility product
C. The ionic product is nearly equal to the solubility product
D. The ionic product exceeds the solubility product

79. Solubility of a salt M_2X_3 is x gm mole^{-1}. The solubility product of the salt will be

A. x^2 B. $16x^2$

C. $96\ x^2$ D. $108\ x^5$

80. When common salt is added to the saponified product of oil, the soap is thrown out because

A. Common salt is an ionic compound

B. The concentration of sodium ions is increased

C. The solubility product of common salt decreases in the presence of soap

D. Soap is insoluble in the presence of chloride ions

81. Pure NaCl is prepared by saturating a cold saturated solution of common salt in water HCl gas. The principle used is

A. Le Chatelier principle

B. Displacement law

C. Common ion effect

D. Fractional distillation

82. A certain weak acid has a dissociation constant of 1.0×10^{-4}. The equilibrium constant for its reaction with a strong base is

A. 1.0×10^{-4} B. 1.0×10^{-10}

C. 1.0×10^{10} D. 1.0×10^{14}

83. The concentration of a pure solid or liquid phase is not included in the expression of equilibrium constant because

A. Solid and liquid concentrations are independent of their quantities

B. Solids and liquids react slowly

C. Solids and liquids at equilibrium do not interact with gaseous phase

D. The molecules of solids and liquids cannot migrate to the gaseous phase

84. The vapour density of completely dissociated NH_4Cl would be

A. Slightly less than half of that of ammonium chloride

B. Half of that of ammonium chloride

C. Double of that of ammonium chloride

D. Determined by the amount of solid ammonium chloride used in the experiment

85. A higher value for equilibrium constant, K shows that

A. The reaction has gone to near completion towards right

B. The reaction has not yet started

C. The reaction has gone to near completion towards left

D. None of these

86. When a system is in equilibrium

A. The mass of the product is equal to the mass of the reactant

B. The ratio of the product of the mass of the products and that of the reactants is a constant

C. The ratio of the velocity of the forward reaction and backward reaction is one

D. Number of mole of the product and that of the reactant are the same

87. A chemical system is in equilibrium. Addition of a catalyst would result in

A. Increase in the rate of forward reaction

B. Increase in the rate of reverse reaction

C. A new reaction pathway to reaction

D. Increase the amount of heat evolved in the reaction

88. Dissolution of sugar being an endothermic reaction is favoured by

A. Low T B. High T

C. High P D. Low P

89. When a bottle of cold drink is opened, the gas comes out with a fizz due to

A. Decrease in pressure suddenly which results in a decrease in solubility of CO_2 gas in water

B. Decrease in temperature

C. Increase in pressure

D. None of the above

90. A cylinder fitted with a movable piston contains liquid water in equilibrium with water vapour at 25°C. Which operation results in a decrease in the equilibrium vapour pressure

A. Moving the piston downward a short-distance

B. Removing a small amount of vapour

C. Removing a small amount of liquid water

D. Dissolving salt in the water

91. Just before a reversible reaction attains equilibrium, it is found that

A. The velocity of both forward and backward reaction is also increasing
B. The velocity of the forward reaction is decreasing and that of backward reaction is increasing
C. The velocity of both forward and backward reactions is decreasing
D. All of the above

92. A reaction attains equilibrium when the free energy change accompanying the reaction is
A. Positive and large B. Zero
C. Negative and large D. Negative and small

93. Which of the following is incorrect for a reversible reaction
A. The reaction is never completed
B. The reactants are present in the initial stage but after that reactants and products are always present in the reaction mixture
C. At equilibrium only products are present
D. When the reaction is carried out in closed space, it attains equilibrium state after suitable time

94. A dibasic acid can form
A. Complex salts
B. Normal salts
C. Acidic salts and normal salts
D. Double salts

95. Strong acids are generally used as standard solution in acid-base titration because
A. The pH at equivalence point will be 7
B. They titrate both strong and weak base
C. They form more stable solution than weak acid
D. The salts of strong acids do not hydrolyse

96. Basic soda is a/an
A. Basic salt B. Double salt
C. Complex salt D. Acidic salt

97. The metal that reacts with both acids and alkalies with the liberation of hydrogen is
A. Cu B. Ag
C. Zn D. Pb

98. Conjugate acid of ammonia is
A. H_2SO_4 B. NH_4^+
C. NH_4OH D. H_3O^+

99. The solvent which is neither proton donor nor proton acceptor is called
A. Amphoteric B. Neutral
C. Aprotic D. Protonic

100. Acids are substances which can release hydrogen ions. In a neutral solution,
A. There are no hydroxyl ions
B. Hydrogen and hydroxyl ions are both present in very small but equivalent amounts
C. There are no hydrogen ions
D. Hydrogen and hydroxyl ions are both completely absent

101. The interferring radicals interfere in the test of usual inorganic analysis after II group analysis due to
A. Their solubility in acid medium
B. Their solubility in alkaline medium
C. Their insoluble nature in alkaline medium
D. None

102. Some salts although containing two different metallic elements give test for only one of them in solution. Such salts are
A. Double salts B. Normal salts
C. Complex salts D. None

103. The phenomenon of interaction of anions and cations furnished by a electrolyte with the H^+ and OH^- ions of water to produce acidic nature or alkalinity is known as hydrolysis. In hydrolysis
A. The pH may either increase or decrease
B. All the salts (except those made up with strong acid and base) undergo hydrolysis
C. The variation of pH depends upon the nature of salts as well as on the temperature
D. All of the above

104. The indicator used in the titration of sodium carbonate with sulphuric acid is
A. Potassium ferrocyanide
B. Potassium ferricyanide
C. Methyl orange
D. Phenophthalein

105. The theory of electrolytic dissociation suggests that
A. The electrolyte on dissolution in water split up into two types of charged particles i.e. cations and anions

B. The dissociation being a reversible process in nature

C. The properties of electrolytes in solutions are the properties of ions furnished by them

D. All of the above

106. In a buffer solution consisting of a weak acid and its salt, the ratio of concentration of salt to acid increased ten fold, then the pH of the solution will

A. Increase by one

B. Increase ten folds

C. Decrease by one

D. Decrease ten fold

ANSWERS

1	2	3	4	5	6	7	8	9	10
A	A	A	C	A	E	C	D	E	C
11	**12**	**13**	**14**	**15**	**16**	**17**	**18**	**19**	**20**
B	B	D	D	C	A	A	D	B	A
21	**22**	**23**	**24**	**25**	**26**	**27**	**28**	**29**	**30**
C	A	C	E	D	A	B	C	D	A
31	**32**	**33**	**34**	**35**	**36**	**37**	**38**	**39**	**40**
B	A	A	A	B	B	A	B	C	B
41	**42**	**43**	**44**	**45**	**46**	**47**	**48**	**49**	**50**
B	B	C	B	B	C	B	B	D	D
51	**52**	**53**	**54**	**55**	**56**	**57**	**58**	**59**	**60**
A	E	A	B	B	B	C	D	B	B
61	**62**	**63**	**64**	**65**	**66**	**67**	**68**	**69**	**70**
B	A	B	B	B	A	B	B	C	C
71	**72**	**73**	**74**	**75**	**76**	**77**	**78**	**79**	**80**
C	C	B	A	D	A	A	D	D	D
81	**82**	**83**	**84**	**85**	**86**	**87**	**88**	**89**	**90**
C	B	A	B	A	C	C	B	A	D
91	**92**	**93**	**94**	**95**	**96**	**97**	**98**	**99**	**100**
B	B	C	C	B	D	C	B	C	B
101	**102**	**103**	**104**	**105**	**106**				
C	C	D	C	D	A				

5

SURFACE CHEMISTRY

Surfaces : The uppermost layer of any solid or liquid is its surface. Unbalanced or residual forces act along the surface of a liquid giving rise to surface tension. Such forces also exist on the surface of a solid. As a result of these residual forces, the surface of a solid has a tendency to attract and retain molecules of other species with which it is brought into contact. As there molecules remain only at the surface and do not go deeper into the bulk; their concentration is more at the surface than in the bulk of the solid. A simple picture of a perfect crystal surface is as a tray of oranges in a grocery store. A gas molecule that collides with the surface can be imagined as ping-pong ball bouncing erratically over the oranges. The molecule losses energy as it bounces, but it is likely to escape from the surface before it has lost enough kinetic energy to be trapped. The same is true to some extent of an ionic crystal in contact with a solution. There is little energy advantage for an ion in solution to discard some of its solvating molecules and stick at an exposed position on the surface.

Adsorption : The phenomenon of higher concentration of any molecular species at the surface than in the bulk of a solid (or liquid) is known as *Adsorption*. The forces involved are Van der Waals's forces. The phenomenon, is quite general thus, the attachement of particles to a surface is called *Adsorption*. The substance that adsorbs is the *Adsorbate* and the underlying material that are concerned with is the *Adsorbent*, or *Substrate*.

The reverse of adsorption is *Desorption*. Colloids on account of their extremely small dimensions, possess enormous surface area per unit mass and are therefore, good adsorbents. The examples are Charcoal, Silica gel, Alumina gel, clay, fuller's earth etc. *Adsorption* is to be carefully *dislinguished* from *absorption*. Absorption implies that a substance is uniformly distributed throughout the body of a solid or a liquid. Thus, while water vapours are *absorbed* by anhydrous calcium chloride, there are *adsorbed* by silica gel. Similarly, while ammonia is *absorbed* in water, it is *adsorbed* by charcoal. When a hot crucible is cooled in atmosphere, a film of moisture collects at the surface. This is a care of *adsorption* of water vapour on the material of the crucible. Charcoal, when mixed with a coloured solution of sugar; *adsorbs* the colouring matter and is used as a decolouriser.

McBain suggested the term *Sorption* to describe a process in which both *absorption* and *adsorption* take place simultaneously.

Factors Influencing Adsorption are:

(i) Temperature

(ii) Pressure

(iii) Nature of the gas

(iv) Nature of adsorbent

The decrease of temperature and increase of pressure, both tend to cause increase in the magnitude of adsorption of a gas or a solid.

It has been found that the more readily soluble and easily liquefiable gases such as ammonia, hydrochloric acid, chlorine and sulphur dioxide are adsorbed more than the permanent gases such as hydrogen, nitrogen and oxygen. The reason is that Van der Waal's or molecular forces which are involved in adsorption are more predominant in the former category than in the latter category of gases.

Since adsorption is a surface phenomenon, it is evident that the greater the surface area per unit mass of the adsorbent the greater is its capacity for adsorption under the given conditions of temperature and pressure.

Physical and Chemical Adsorption (Physisorption & Chemisorption)

Physisorption

Molecules and atoms can attach to surfaces in two ways. In physisorption there is a Van der Waals interaction (for example, a dispersion or a dipolar interaction) between the adsorbate and the substrate. Van der Waals interactions have a long range but are weak, and the energy released when a particle is physisorbed in the the same order of magnitude as the enthalpy of condensation. Such small energies can be absorbed as vibrations of the lattice and dissipated as thermal motion; and a molecule bouncing across the surface will gradually lose its energy and finally adsorbs to it in the process called *accommodation.*

The enthalpy of physisorption can be measured by monitoring the rise in temperature of a sample of known heat capacity, and typical values are in the region of 20 kJmol^{-1}. This small enthalpy change is insufficient to lead to bond breaking, so a physisorbed molecule retain its identity, although it might be distorted by the presence of the surface.

Maximum Observed Enthalpies of Physisorption

$\Delta_{ad}H^{\phi}/(kJmol^{-1})$

Adsorbate	
CH_4	– 21
H_2	– 84
H_2O	– 59
N_2	– 21

Chemisorption : In chemisorption, the molecules (or atoms) stick to the surface by forming a chemical (usually covalent) bond, and tend to find sites that maximize their coordination number with the substrate. The enthalpy of chemisorption is very much greater than that of physisorption; and typical values are in the region of 200 kJ mol^{-1}. The distance between the surface and the closest adsorbate atom is also typically shorter for chemisorption than for physisorption. A chemisorbed molecule may be torn apart at the demand of the unsatisfied valancies of the surface atoms, and the existence of molecular fragments on the surface as a result of chemisorption is one reason why solid surfaces catalyse reactions.

Enthalpies of Chemisorption, $\Delta_{ad}H^{\phi}/(kJmol^{-1})$

Adsorbate	*Adsorbent (Substrate)*		
	Cr	Fe	Ni
C_2H_4	– 427	– 285	– 243
CO		– 192	
H_2	– 188	– 134	
NH_3		– 188	– 155

Except in special cases, chemisorption must be *exothermic.* A spontaneous process requires $\Delta G < 0$. Because the translational freedom of the adsorbates reduced when it is adsorbed; ΔS is negative. Therefore, in order for $\Delta G = \Delta H - T\Delta S$ to be negative. ΔH must be negative (that is, the process is exothermic). Exceptions may occur if the adsorbate dissociates and has high translational mobility on the surface. For example; H_2 adsorbs endothermically on glass because there is a large increase of translational entropy accompanying the dissociation of the molecules into atoms that move quite freely over the surface. In its case; the entropy change in the process

$H_2(s) \rightarrow 2H$ (glass) is sufficiently positive to overcome the small possitive enthalpy change.

Other examples of chemisorption are oxygen is chemisorbed by carbon and hydrogen is chemisorbed by nickel under suitable conditions. In each case a stable surface compound, frequently referred to as *surface complex* results.

Applications Of Adsorption

(i) A very good method of creating a high vacuum is to connect a **luck** of charcoal cooled in liquid air to a vessel which has already been exhausted as far as possible by a vaccum pump. Since the magnitude of adsorption at such low temperatures is quite high, the remaining traces of air, in spite of the low pressure, are adsorbed by the charcoal almost completely.

(ii) Activated charcoal is used in gas masks in which all toxic gasses and vapour are adsorbed by the charcoal while pure air passes through its pores practically unchanged.

(iii) Silica and alumina gels are used as adsorbents for removing moisture and for controlling humidities of rooms.

(iv) Animal charcoal is used as a decoloriser in the manufacture of cane-sugar.

(v) Soil contains small amounts of colloidal fractions in the form of very fine particles of clay. It can therefore, always adsorb and retain certain amount of moisture in which nutrients such as compounds of nitrogen, phosphorus and potassium, can dissolve and pass up to the plant through roots.

(vi) Adsorption also plays an important role in heterogeneous catalysis, e.g. the role of finely divided iron in the manufacture of ammonia and that of finely divided nickel in the hydrogenation of oils.

Adsorption Isotherms

The variation of adsorption with pressure at a given constant temperature is generally expressed graphically as in following figure:

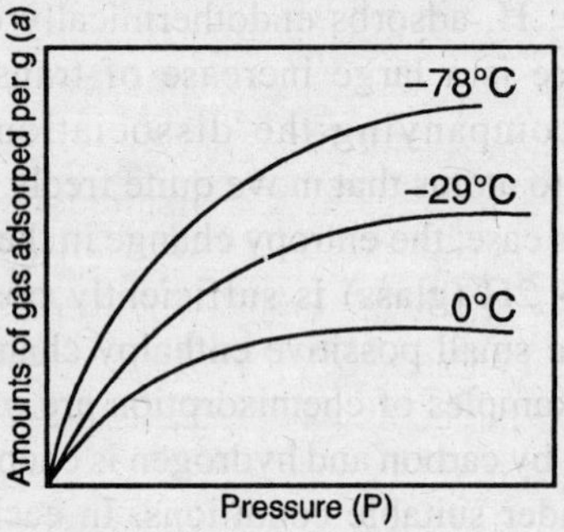

Fig. *Adsorption isotherm.*

Each curve is known as *adsorption isotherm* for the particular temperature.

The relationship between the magnitude of adsorption and pressure can be expressed mathematically by an *empirical equation* commonly known as *Freundlich isotherm,*

$$a = kp^n$$

where a is the amount of the gas adsorbed per unit mass of the adsorbent at pressure p and k and n are constants depending upon the nature of the gas and the nature of the adsorbent. The value of n is less than 1 and therefore a does not increases as rapidly as p, as is evident from the isotherm.

Since adsorption is a surface phenomenon, it is evident that the greater the surface area per unit mass of the adsorbent, the greater is its capacity for adsorption under the given conditions of temperature and pressure.

A. The Langmuir Isotherm: The simplest physically plausible isotherm is based on three assumptions:

(i) Adsorption cannot proceed beyond monolayer coverage.

(ii) All sites are equivalent and the surface is uniform (i.e., the surface is perfectly flat on a microscopic scale).

(iii) The ability of a molecule to adsorb at a given site is independent of the occupation of neigbouring sites.

The third assumption supposes that there are no interactions between adsorbed molecules. The dynamic equilibrium is

$$A_{(g)} + M_{(\text{surface})} \rightleftharpoons AM \text{ (surface)}$$

With rate constants K_a for adsorption and K_d for desorption. The rate of change of surface coverage due to adsorption is proportional to the partial pressrue p of A and the number of vacant sites (N(1 – θ), where N is the total number of sites:

$$\frac{d\theta}{dt} = k_{a}p\text{N}(1-\theta) \ldots \quad (i)$$

The rate of change of θ due to desorption is proportional to the number of adsorbed species, N_θ

$$\frac{d\theta}{dt} = -k_d\text{N}\theta \ldots \quad (ii)$$

At equilibrium there is no net change (that is, the sum of these two rates is zero), and solving for θ gives the *Langmuir isotherm* :

$$\theta = \frac{\text{K}p}{1+\text{K}p}, \text{K} = \frac{\text{K}_a}{\text{K}_d} \ldots \quad (iii)$$

Colloids

Preparation & General Properties.

A *Colloid,* or *disperse phase* is a dispersion of small particles of one material in other. Here 'small' means something less than about 500 mm in diameter (about the wavelength of visible light). In general, colloidal particles are aggregates of numerous atoms or molecules, but are too small to be seen with an ordinary optical microscope. They pass through most filter papers, but can be detected by light scattering and sedimentation.

The name given to colloids depends on the two phases involved. A *sol* is a dispersion of a solid in a liquid (such as clusters of gold atoms in water) or of a solid in a solid (as ruby glass, which is a gold-in-glass sol; and achieves its colour by light scattering).

An *aerosol* is a dispersion of a liquid in a gas (like fog and many spray) or a solid in a gas (such as smoke). The particles are often large enough to be seen with a microscope. An *emulsion* is a dispersion of a liquid in a liquid (such as milk).

A further classification of colloids is *lyophilic*, or solvent-attracting and lyophobic, solvent repelling. If the solvent is water. The terms *hydrophilic* & *hydropholic* respectively are used.

Lyophobic colloids include the metal sols. Lyophilic colloids generally have some chemical similarity to the solvent, such as-OH groups able to form hydrogen bonds. A *gel* is a semirigid mass of lyophilic sol in which all the dispersion medium has penetrated into the sol particles.

Preparation : The preparation of *aerosols* is easy. Materials like quartz may be ground in the presence of the dispersion medium. Passing a heavy electric current through a cell may lead to the sputtering (crumbling) of an electrode into colloidal particles. Arcing between electrodes immersed in the support medium also produces a colloid. Chemical precipitation sometimes results in a colloid. A precipitate, for (example, silver iodide) by the addition of a peptizing agent (for example, potassium iodide). (lays may be peptized by alkalis the OH^- ion being the active agent).

Emulsions are normally prepared by shaking the two components together vigorously although some kind of emulsifying agent usually has to be added to stablize the product. This emulsifying agent may be a soap (the salt of a long-chain carboxylic acid) or other *surfectant* (surface active) species, or a lyophilic sol that forms a protective film around the dispersed phase. In milk, which is an emulsion of fats in water, the emulsifying agent is casein, a protein containing phosphate groups. It is clear from the formation of cream on the surface of milk that casein is not completely successful in stabilizing milk; the dispersed fats coalesce into oily droplets that float to the surface. This coagulation may be prevented by ensuring that the emulsion is dispersed very finely initially, intense agitation with ultrasonics brings this dispersion about, the product being homogenized milk.

The primary consideration in the preparation of colloidal solutions is that the dispersed particles should be within the size range of 1 mμ-200 mμ. The lyophilic sols can be readily prepared. The lyophobic sols require special treatments. The methods consists either in

1. Breaking down the coarser aggregate into particles of colloidal size, or

2. Grouping moleules into larger aggregates of colloidal size.

The methods belonging to these categories are known as *Dispersion* and *Condensation* methods respectively.

Emulsions : Emulsions are colloidal system in which dispersed phase as well as dispersion medium are normally liquids. The examples are *(i)* milk which consists of particles of liquid fat dispersed in water and *(ii)* cod-liver oil emulsion in which particles of water are dispersed is oil. The particles of dispersed phase in emulsions are generally bigger than those in sols and are sometimes visible under microscope.

OBJECTIVE QUESTIONS

1. Adsorption due to strong chemical forces is called
A. Physisorption B. Chemisorption
C. Biosorption D. None

2. The substance that gets adsorbed on the surface of the solid is called
A. Adsorbate B. Adsorbent
C. Micelle D. Inner phase

3. Which of the following substances is not used for preparing lyophilic sols?
A. Starch B. Gelatin
C. Gum D. Metal sulphide

4. The formation of a colloid from suspension is
A. Peptisation B. Condensation
C. Sedimentation D. Fragmentation

5. Arsenic sulphide is a negative sol. The reagent with least precipitating power is
A. $AlCl_3$ B. NaCl
C. CaF_2 D. Glucose

6. Which of the following statement is *true* about Langmuir adsorption?
A. It forms monolayer
B. It is reversible in nature
C. It occurs at low temperature
D. It is not specific in nature

7. When H_2S is passed through nitric acid, the product is
A. Rhombic (S) B. Prismatic (S)
C. Amorphous (S) D. Monoclinic (S)

8. Adsorption is
A. Colligative property
B. Oxidation process
C. Reduction process
D. Surface phenomenon

9. Colloid of which one of the following can be prepared by electrical dispersion as well as reduction method?
A. Sulphur
B. Ferric hydroxide
C. Arsenious sulphide
D. Gold

10. The curve showing the variation of adsorption with pressure at constant temperature is called
A. An isostene B. Adsorption isotherm
C. Adsorption isobar D. All are incorrect

11. Which of the following is *correctly* matched?
A. Emulsion-Curd B. Foam-Mist
C. Aerosol-Smoke D. Solid sol-Cake

12. Which is *correct* in the case of Van der Waal's adorption?
A. High temp, low pressure
B. Low temp, high pressure
C. Low temp, low pressure
D. High temp, high pressure

13. Pt & Pd adsorb large volume of hydrogen under specific conditions. The hydrogen so adsorbed is called
A. Adsorbed hydrogen
B. Reactive hydrogen
C. Occluded hydrogen
D. Atomic hydrogen

14. Which of the following is an incorrect statement for physiosorption?
A. It is a reversible process
B. It requires less heat of absorption
C. It requires activation energy
D. It takes place at low temperature

15. The phenomenon in which adsorption and absorption takes place simultaneously is called
A. Desorption B. Ad-absorption
C. Sorption D. None of these

16. Which of the following is **not** applicable to chemisorption?
A. Effect of pressure is given by Freundlich adsorption isotherm
B. There is formation of monomolecular layer
C. It occurs at high temperature
D. It involves the formation of chemical bonds between adsorbent and adsorbate.

17. Which of the following is a property of physisorption?
A. Non-specific nature
B. High specificity
C. Irreversibility
D. None of above

18. The coagulation of colloidal particles of the sol can be caused by
A. Heating
B. Adding oppositively charged sol
C. Adding electrolyte
D. All of the above

19. The colloidal solution of two immiscible liquids is called
A. Gel B. Aerosol
C. Emulsion D. None of these

20. When adsorption of oxalic acid is carried out on activated charcoal then, activated charcoal is known as,
A. Adsorbate B. Adsorbent
C. Absorber D. Adsorber

21. In the preparation of AgI sol; the excess of $AgNO_3$ is added to potassium iodide solution. The particles of the soil will acquire

A. Negative charge B. Positive charge
C. No charge D. Unpredictable

22. The protective layer of lyophilic sol is
A. Dependent on the size of colloidal particles
B. Expressed in terms of gold number
C. Expressed by *x/m*
D. None of these

23. A metal sulphide sol can be flocculated, by
A. $[Fe(CN)_6]^{4-}$ B. SO_4^{2-}
C. $BaCl_2$ D. Al^{3+}

24. The process of separation of colloids by passing through semipermeable membrane is called
A. Filtration B. Electrophoresis
C. Dialysis D. Ultra-filtration

25. Hydrophillic colloids are stable due to
A. Negative charged particles
B. Large size of particles
C. Small size of particles
D. Layer of dispersion medium on their particles

26. Which of the following is a homogeneous system?
A. Muddy water
B. Bread
C. Concrete
D. A solution of sugar in water

27. The Brownian motion is due to
A. Temperature fluctuation within the liquid phase
B. Attraction and repulsion between charges on the colloidal particles
C. Impact of molecules on the dispersion medium on the colloidal particles
D. Connective currents

28. Gold number is minimum in case of
A. Gelatin B. Egg albumin
C. Gum arabic D. Starch

29. Lyophilic sols are more stable than lyophobic sols because
A. The colloidal particles have positive charge
B. The colloidal particles have negative charge
C. The colloidal particles are solvated
D. There are strong electrostatic repulsions between the negatively charged colloidal particles.

30. The process of froth floatation and chromatography are based on
A. Emulsification B. Adsorption
C. Absorption D. Either of them

31. Which of the following is **not** a property of hydrophilic sols?
A. High concentration of dispersed phase can be easily attained
B. Coagulation is reversible
C. Viscosity and surface tension are nearly same as that of water
D. The charge of the particle depends on the pH value of the medium, it may be positive, negative or even zero.

32. Gelatin is mostly used in making ice-cream in order to
A. Prevent forming the colloidal sol
B. Enrich the fragrance
C. Prevent crystallisation and stabilise the size
D. Modify the taste

33. Difference between colloids and crystalloids is of
A. Diameter B. Particle size
C. Radius D. Solubility

34. Colloidal gold is prepared by
A. Mechanical dispersion
B. Peptisation
C. Bredig's arc method
D. Hydrolysis

35. Alum helps in purifying water by
A. Forming Si complex with clay particles
B. Sulphate part which combines with dirt and removes it
C. Aluminium which coagulates the mud particle
D. Making mud water soluble

36. In Zeiger-Natta polymerisation of ethylene; the active species is
A. $AlCl_3$ B. CH_2CH_2
C. Et_3Al D. Ti'''

37. Cloud or fog is colloidal system in which the dispersed phase and dispersion medium are
A. gas, liquid B. liquid, gas
C. liquid, liquid D. solid, liquid

38. In physical adsorption; the forces of association are

A. Ionic B. Covalent

C. Van der Waal's D. H-bonding

39. Which of the following is an example of homogeneous catalysis?

A. Haber's process of ammonia synthesis

B. Catalytic conversion of SO_2 to SO_3 in contact process

C. Catalytic conversion of water gas to methanol

D. Acid hydrolysis of methyl acetate

40. The heats of absorption in physisorption lies in the range

A. 40-400 kJ/mole

B. 10-40 kJ/mole

C. 40-100 kJ/mole

D. 200-400 kJ/mole

41. The biological catalyst enzymes are

A. Micro-organisms

B. Proteins

C. Inorganic compounds

D. Moulds

42. As_2S_3 sol is

A. Positive colloid B. Negative colloid

C. Neutral colloid D. None of these

43. In chemical reaction, catalyst

A. Alters the amount of the products

B. Lowers the activation energy

C. Decreases the ΔH of forward reaction

D. Increases the ΔH of forward reaction

44. Which of the following sols is hydrophobic?

A. Gum B. Gelatin

C. Strach D. Sulphur

45. Which of the following is less than zero during adsorption?

A. ΔG B. ΔH

C. ΔS D. All of the above

46. In a reversible reaction; a catalyst

A. Increases the rate of forward reaction only

B. Increases the rate of forward reaction to a greater extent than that of backward reaction

C. Increases the rate of the forward reaction and decreases that of backward reaction to different extent

D. Increases the rate of forward & backward reactions equally

47. A catalyst in the finely divided form is most effective because

A. Less surface area is available

B. More active centres are formed.

C. More energy gets stored in the catalyst

D. None of these

48. A catalyst for a reversible reaction is a substance that

A. Supplies energy to the reaction

B. Decreases the time to reach equilibrium

C. Increases the equilibrium concentration of the products

D. Change the equillibrium constant of the reaction

49. Negative catalyst is one

A. Which retards the rate of reaction

B. Takes the reaction in forward direction

C. Promotes the side reaction

D. None of these

50. In homogenous catalytic reactions, the rate of reaction:

A. Depends upon the concentration of catalyst

B. Independent of the concentration of catalyst

C. Depends upon the free energy change

D. Depends upon the physical state of the catalyst

51. For an exothermic reaction:

A. Energy of reactants > energy of products

B. Energy of reactants < energy of products

C. Energy of reactant = energy of products

D. None of these

52. Catalytic poisons act by

A. Coagulating the catalyst

B. Getting adsorbed on the reactive centres on the surface of catalyst

C. Chemical combination with any one of the reactants

D. None of these

53. Protons accelerate the hydrolysis of esters. This is an example of

A. A heterogeneous catalysis

B. An acid base catalysis

C. A promoter

D. A negative catalyst

54. The catalyst used in contact process of sulphuric acid is

A. Copper

B. Iron
C. Vanadium pentoxide
D. Ni

55. Adsorption is accompanied with
A. Decrease in entropy of system
B. Decrease in enthalpy
C. The value of ΔS.T. is negative
D. All of them

56. The enzyme ptylin used for digestion of food is present in
A. Saliva B. Blood
C. Intestine D. Adrenal glands

57. Which type of metals form effective catalysts?
A. Alkali metals
B. Transition metals
C. Alkaline earth metals
D. Radioactive metals

58. Which is an example of auto-catalyst?
A. Hydrolysis of methyl-acetate
B. Decomposition of TNG
C. Oxidation of oxalic acid by $KMnO_4$
D. All of the above

59. A substance which promotes the activity of a catalyst is known as
A. Initiator B. Catalyst
C. Promoter D. Auto-catalyst

60. Which is wrong in case of enzyme catalysis?
A. Enzymes work best at an optimum temperature
B. Enzymes work at an optimum pH
C. Enzymes are highly specific for substrates
D. An enzyme raises activation energy

61. The minimum energy level necessary to permit a reaction to occur is
A. Internal energy
B. Threshold energy
C. Activation energy
D. Free energy

62. Which statement is *correct*?
A. Physical adsorption is multi-layer, non-directional and non-specific
B. Chemical adsorption is unilayer
C. Chemical adsorption is more stronger than physical adsorption
D. All of the above

63. The amount of gas adsorbed physically on charcoal increases with
A. Temperature pressure
B. Temperature decreases with pressure
C. Pressure decreases with temperature
D. None of them

64. The enzyme which can catalyse the conversion of glucose to ethanol is
A. Zymase B. Invertase
C. Maltase D. Diastase

65. Zeolites are
A. Water softener B. Catalyst
C. A & B D. None of these

66. Mutarotation of glucose is an example of
A. Acid-base catalysis
B. Homogeneous catalysis
C. Both A & B
D. None of these

67. Decomposition of urea into NH_3 & CO_2 is followed by the action of enzyme
A. Urease B. Pepsin
C. Trypsin D. None of these

68. Medicines are more effective if they are used in
A. Colloidal state B. Solid state
C. Solution state D. None of these

69. Dust storm is
A. Dispersion of solid in gas
B. Dispersion of gas in solid
C. Dispersion of solid in solid
D. Dispersion of solid in liquid

70. The cementation process is
A. Gel formation B. Emulsion formation
C. Either of them D. None of these

71. The outcome of internal liquid of gels on shear is called
A. Synerisis B. Thixotropy
C. Swelling D. None of these

72. A dilute solution of litmus becomes colourless on shaking with charcoal. This is due to
A. Absorption
B. Adsorption
C. Chemical reaction
D. Both A & B

73. Colloidal solutions are not purified by
A. Dialysis B. Electrodialysis
C. Electrophoresis D. Ultrafiltration

74. The stability of lyophilic colloid is due to
A. Charge on their particles

B. A layer of dispersion medium on their particles
C. The smaller size of their particles
D. The large size of their particles

75. Isoelectric point refers to the H^+ ion concentration at which the colloidal particles
A. Coagulate
B. Becomes electrically neutral
C. Can move to either electrode when subjected to an electric field
D. Reverse their electrical charge

76. Cloud burst due to
A. Attraction towards the electrical charges on the earth
B. Large amount of water present in the cloud
C. Dense clouds are present in the upper atmosphere
D. Mutual discharge of oppositively charged clouds resulting in coagulation

77. Tanning of leather is
A. Colouring of leather by chemicals
B. Drying process to make the leather hard
C. Polishing of leather to make it look attractive
D. Coagulative hardening of leather by chemicals

78. Solid aerosol is an example of colloidal system of
A. Liquid dispersed in gas
B. Gas dispersed in gas
C. Solid dispersed in gas
D. Solid disperssed in liquid

79. Sky looks blue due to
A. Dispersion effect B. Reflection
C. Transmission D. Scattering of light

80. Flocculation value is expressed in terms of
A. Millimole per litre
B. Mol per litre
C. Gram per litre
D. Mol per millilitre

81. Ultramicroscope works on the principle of
A. Light reflection B. Light absorption
C. Light scattering D. Light polarisation

82. The reaction between alkali and fat is called:
A. Saponification B. Hydrolysis
C. Distillation D. Dehydration

83. In which of the following states, the particle size would be greater than 300 μm.
A. Suspensions
B. True solutions
C. Colloidal solutions
D. None of these

84. The detergent action of soap is due to its
A. Alkalinity
B. Solubility in water
C. Emulsifying property
D. Ability to produce lather with water

85. Butter is a colloid formed when
A. Fat is dispersed in water
B. Fat globules are dispersed in water
C. Water is dispersed in fat
D. None of these

86. If dispersed phase is a liquid and the dispersion medium is a solid; the colloid is known as
A. A sol B. A gel
C. An emulsion D. A foam

87. Term catalyst was given by
A. Rutherford B. Berzilius
C. Wohler D. Kolbe

88. Which of the following catalyst is used for preparing toluene by reacting benzene with methyl chloride?
A. Ni B. Anhydrous $AlCl_3$
C. Pd D. Pt

89. Which of the following has the largest protecting power?
A. Gelatin (Gold no. = 0.01)
B. Dextrin (Gold no. = 15)
C. Potato strach (Gold no. ≈ 25)
D. Albumin (Gold no. ≈ 0.25)

90. Which of the following is a Heterogeneous catalysis?
A. $2C_2H_5OH \xrightarrow{\text{Con.}H_2SO_4} C_2H_5OC_2H_5 + H_2O$
B. $2CO + O_2 \xrightarrow{NO} CO_2$
C. $SO_2 + \frac{1}{2}O_2 \xrightarrow{NO} SO_3$
D. $SO_2 + \frac{1}{2}O_2 \xrightarrow{V_2O_5} SO_3$

91. The name *aquadag* is given to the colloidal sol of
A. Copper in water B. Platinum in water
C. Graphite in water D. None of these

92. Which type of molecules form micelles as Non-polar molecules
A. Non-polar molecules
B. Polar molecules
C. Surfactant molecules
D. Any of the above

93. Ferric chloride is applied to stop bleeding because
A. Fe^{3+} ions coagulate blood which is a negatively charged sol
B. Cl^- ions cause coagulation of blood
C. $FeCl_3$ reacts with the constituents of blood
D. Blood absorbs $FeCl_3$

94. The basic principal of cotterell precipitator is
A. Le-Chatelier principle
B. Neutralisation of charge on colloids
C. Peptisation
D. None of the above

95. The extent of physical adsorption
A. Decreases with rise in temperature
B. Increases with rise in temperature
C. Is independent of temperature
D. First increases and decrease with rise in temperature

96. Purple of Cassius is
A. Colloidal solution of gold
B. Colloidal solution of silver
C. Colliodal solution of platinum
D. Oxyacids of gold

97. Which of the following abbreviation is associated with the technology used to determine size of colloids?
A. EM B. HVZ
C. STEM D. None of these

98. Which of the following is *not* heterogeneous?
A. An emulsion B. True solution
C. Suspension D. Colloidal sol

99. The example of heteropolar sol is
A. Starch sol in water
B. Rubber sol in water
C. Protein sol in water
D. Sulphur sol

100. The number of phases of colloidal system are
A. One B. Two
C. Three D. Four

ANSWERS

1	2	3	4	5	6	7	8	9	10
B	A	D	A	D	A	C	D	D	B
11	12	13	14	15	16	17	18	19	20
C	B	C	C	C	A	A	C	C	B
21	22	23	24	25	26	27	28	29	30
B	B	D	C	D	D	C	A	C	D
31	32	33	34	35	36	37	38	39	40
C	C	B	C	C	D	B	C	D	B
41	42	43	44	45	46	47	48	49	50
B	B	B	D	D	D	B	B	A	A
51	52	53	54	55	56	57	58	59	60
A	B	B	C	D	A	B	D	C	D
61	62	63	64	65	66	67	68	69	70
B	D	C	A	C	C	A	A	A	A
71	72	73	74	75	76	77	78	79	80
B	B	C	B	B	D	D	C	D	A
81	82	83	84	85	86	87	88	89	90
C	A	A	C	C	B	B	B	A	D
91	92	93	94	95	96	97	98	99	100
C	C	A	B	A	A	C	B	C	B

6

CHEMICAL KINETICS

Introduction

The branch of chemistry which deals with the study of reaction's rate and their mechanisms is called chemical kinetics. The knowledge of the rate of reactions is very valuable to understand the chemistry of reactions. It is also of great importance in selecting optimum conditions for an industrial chemical process so that it proceeds at a rate to give maximum yield.

Rate of a Chemical Reaction

It may be defined as the speed at which the reactants are converted into products. Quantitatively, the rate of reaction may be expressed in terms of the change in the concentration of any of the reactants or any of the products per unit time.

For example : Consider a hypothetical reaction $A \rightarrow B$.

Now, rate of disappearance of

$$A = \frac{\text{Change in concentration of A}}{\text{Time taken}} = \frac{-\Delta[A]}{\Delta t}$$

Here $\Delta[A]$ is negative, because concentration of A is decreasing with time.

Rate of appearance of B

$$= \frac{\text{Change in concentration of B}}{\text{Time taken}} = \frac{\Delta[B]}{\Delta t}$$

The rate of reaction is, therefore, expressed as

$$\text{Rate} = \frac{-\Delta[A]}{\Delta t} = \frac{\Delta B}{\Delta t}$$

The unit of rate of reaction is mol litre^{-1} sec^{-1}

Examples :

(i) $NO_2 + CO \rightarrow CO_2 + NO$

$$\text{Rate of reaction} = \frac{-\Delta[NO_2]}{\Delta t} = \frac{-\Delta[CO]}{\Delta t} = \frac{\Delta[CO_2]}{\Delta t} = \frac{\Delta[NO]}{\Delta t}$$

(ii) $HI \rightarrow H_2 + I_2$

Rate of reaction

$$= -\frac{1}{2}\frac{\Delta[HI]}{\Delta t} = \frac{\Delta[H_2]}{\Delta t} = \frac{\Delta[I_2]}{\Delta t}$$

Instantaneous Rate of Reaction : The rate of reaction is determined by dividing the total change in concentration by the total time taken for said change. The rate of reaction obtained in this manner is an *average rate* of the reaction. Since rate of reaction varies with time, therefore, it is more appropriate to express the rate of a reaction at a particular moment of time. Such a reaction rate is called *Instantaneous rate*. It is rate of change of concentration at a particular moment of time.

Mathematically, it is expressed by the expression $\frac{dx}{dt}$, where dt is the infinitesimally small time interval and dx is the change in concentration of any of the species in time interval dt.

Rate Law : The rate of a reaction is directly proportional to the reactant concentrations, each concentration being raised to some power. Thus for a substance 'A' undergoing reaction

$$\text{rate } \alpha\ [A]^n \text{ or, rate} = K[A]^n \qquad ...(1)$$

For a reaction,

$$2A + B \rightarrow \text{Products}$$

The reaction rate with respect to A or B is determined by varying the concentration of one reactant keeping that of the other constant. Thus the rate of reaction may be expressed as

$$\text{rate} = K[A]^m[B]^n \qquad ...(2)$$

An expression [such as in eqn. (1) and (2) which shows how the reaction rate is related to concentrations, is called the rate law or rate equation. Rate law for a reaction must be determined by experiment. It cannot be written merely by looking at equation with a background of our knowledge of Law of Mass Action.

The unit of rate of reaction is always mole litre^{-1} time^{-1}.

Molecularity of Reaction

"The total number of molecules present in the reactant(s) of a balanced equation in known as molecularity of the reaction".

Eg. $2HI \rightarrow H_2 + I_2$ (bimolecular)

$PCl_5 \rightarrow PCl_3 + Cl_2$ (unimolecular)

$2NO + O_2 \rightarrow 2NO_2$ (trimolecular

Molecularity of a reaction is always a whole number and can never be zero. Reactions having molecularity of more than three are rare. It is because the chances of simultaneous collisions between three or more particles are rare. In complex reactions (which occur in two or more steps) the slowest step is the rate determining step of the reaction. For example, decomposition of N_2O_5

(i) $2N_2O_5 \rightarrow 2NO_2 + 2NO_3$ (slow)

(ii) $NO_2 + NO_3 \rightarrow NO + NO_2 + O_2$ (slowest)

(iii) $NO + NO_3 \rightarrow 2NO_2$ (fast)

$2N_2O_5 \rightarrow 4NO_2 + O_2$

Step *(ii)* in the above example is the rate determining and has molecularity '2' which could be considered as the molecularity of the decomposition reaction of N_2O_5.

The molecular equation which represents a chemical reaction is also known as 'Stoichiometric equation' but it does not represents the mechanism of the reaction.

Order of a Reaction

It is defined as "the number of molecules whose concentration determines (changes) the rate of reaction. In other words, "it is the sum of the indices to which the concentration terms are raised in the rate equation (rate law).

Order of reaction is an experimentally determined quantity. It cannot be written from the balanced chemical equation. Molecularity and order of a reaction may be same or different.

For a reaction $2A + B \rightarrow$ Products

If the rate law is

$$\text{Rate} = K[A]^m[B]^n$$

Then the order of such a reaction is $(m + n)$. The order of a reaction can also be defined with respect to a single reactant. Thus the reaction order with respect to 'A' in m and with respect to 'B' in n. The overall order $(m + n)$, it ranges from 1 to 3 and can also be fractional.

Zero Order Reaction : A reactant whose concentration does not affect the reaction rate is not included in the rate law. In effect the concentration of such a reactant has the power 0. Thus $[A]^\circ = 0$. A zero concentration is one whose rate is independent of concentration, *e.g.*, rate law for the reaction

$NO_2 + CO \rightarrow NO + CO_2$ at 200°C is

$$\text{Rate} = K[NO_2]^2[CO]^0$$

So the reaction is zero order with respect to CO and second order with respect to NO_2. Many photochemical reactions (*e.g.*, formation of HCl from H_2 and Cl_2) and some heterogenous reactions (*e.g.*, decomposition of hydrogen iodide and ammonia on the surfaces of gold and tungsten) are examples of zero order reactions.

$$H_2(g) + Cl_2(g) \xrightarrow{\text{Sunlight}} 2HCl(g)$$

First Order Reaction : Reactions whose rate is determined by the change of one concentration term only are known as first order reactions. Consider a general reaction of the first order

$$A \rightarrow \text{Products}$$

The rate of such reaction at any moment will thus be given by the expression

where c_A is the concentration of the reactant A at the moment when rate of reaction is determined and K is *rate constant*, *specific rate constant* or *velocity constant*. Thus in the case of first order reaction, the rate of reaction is directly proportional to the concentration of the reacting *substance*.

If the initial concentration of the reactant A (*i.e.* when time $t = 0$) is a moles per litre, and further suppose that after time t, x moles per litre of the reactant has decomposed (reacted), then the remaining concentration of A at time t will be $a - x$ and that of product(s) will be x moles per litre.

At time	0	a	0
		A	→ Product
At time	t	$a - x$	x

Rate of the reaction at time 't' $= K_c$

($c = c_0 - x$, the concentration of reactant left at that instant)

The integrated expression for the rate constant

$$K = \frac{1}{t}\ln\frac{c_0}{c} = \frac{2.303}{t}\log 10\frac{c_0}{c}$$

A plot of 'log c' vs 't' gives straight line with a negative slope $= \left(-\frac{K}{2.303}\right)$

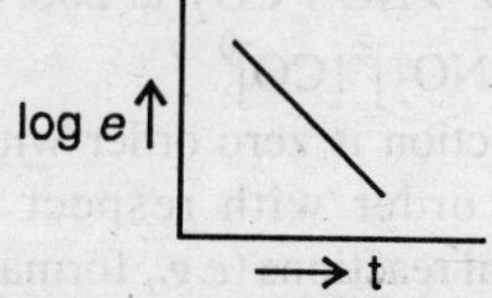

The first order rate constant can also be expressed in the exponential form

$$c = c_0\, e^{-K_t}$$

Unit of K is time^{-1}

Half life period of a reaction

$$t_{1/2} = \frac{0.683}{K}$$

i.e. $t_{1/2}$ is independent of the initial concentration

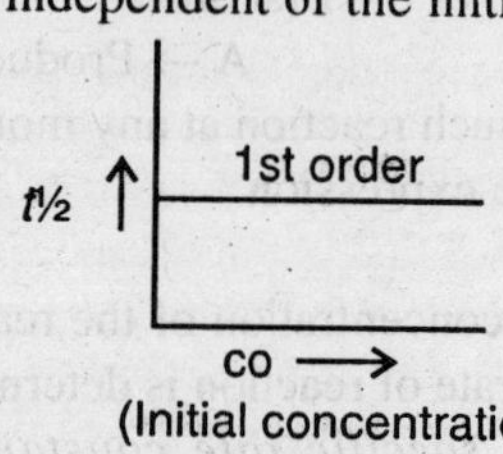

Second Order Reaction

$$K = \frac{1}{t}\cdot\frac{x}{c_0(c_0 - x)} \text{ or } K = \frac{1}{t}\left[\frac{1}{c} - \frac{1}{c_0}\right]$$

(where $c = c_0 - x$)

$c_0 \rightarrow$ initial concentration

and $c \rightarrow$ concentration of a reactant left at that instant.

A plot of '$1/c$' vs 't' gives a straight line with a positive slope = K units of rate constant is litre mole^{-1} time^{-1}

$$\text{Half life time, } t_{1/2} = \frac{1}{c_0 K}$$

where c_0 is initial concentration.

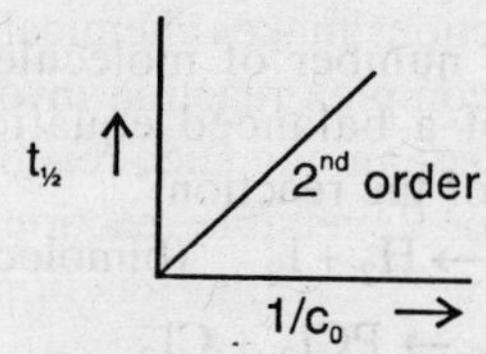

The time taken to complete any fraction of a reaction is inversely proportional to the initial concentration of the reactant.

Fast reaction

The rare of a reaction increases with increse in temperature. In general, for most-reactions, the rate constant doubles with every 10° rise in temperature. Variation in rate constant is of the same degree as the variation of the rate of reaction. Fast reactions are the reactions which take place in just a fraction of a second to complete. The kinetics of fast reactions are expressed is milli seconds ($10^{-3}s$), micro second ($10^{-6}s$), nano seconds (10^{-9}s) and pico seconds ($10^{-12}s$).

The rate of fast reactions can be studied by spectrophotometric techniques band on light absorption and emission i.e., change in the intensity of the colour of the reaction mixture.

Some other techniques based on laser, magnetic properties and electrical conductances are also being used.

Mechanism of Reaction (Only elementary Idea)

Activated complex theory: According to this theory when activation energy is supplied to a reaction, it absorbs to form intermediate activated complex. An activated complex is high energy, unstable intermediate which exists very briefly. Once formed it immediately decomposes to form products of lower energy state or more stability.

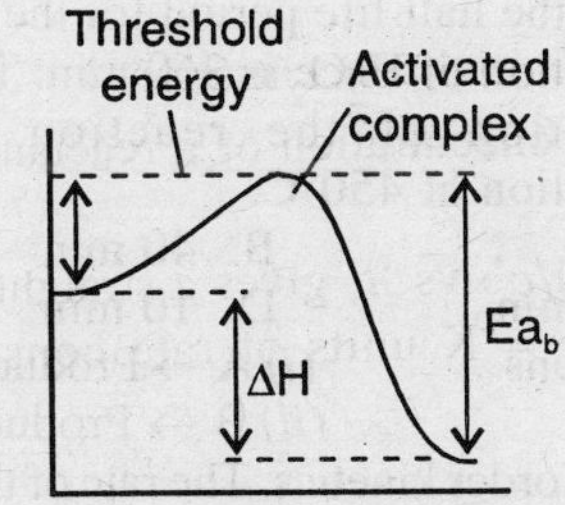

Fig. *Activation energy plot for an exothemic reaction.*

Complex reactions makes chemical kinetics study difficult. There complex reaction involve more than one step. Important among such reactions are

1. Opposing or Reversible reaction.
2. Consecutive reactions-reactions which take plase in two or more steps, one after the other.
3. Competing or parallel Reactions and
4. Chain reaction *(i)* chainintiation
   (ii) propagation
   (iii) inhibition
   (iv) chain termination

Energy Transfer in Photochemical Reactions. Photosensitization & Quenching.

Some chemical reactions take plae not by the absorption of light by one of the reactants but by a third substance which transfers the absorbed energy to the reactants. This third substance which itself does not undergo any change is called *photosensitizer* and the process is known as *photosensitization.* Among the photosensitiger in common one are atomic sensitiger such as mercury, cadmium and zinc and the molecular photosensitizers such as benzophenone and sulphur dioxide molecules.

OBJECTIVE QUESTIONS

1. The progress of the reaction $A \rightleftharpoons nB$ with time is presented in the diagram. Determine
(i) the value of *n*
(ii) the equilibrium constant K, and
(iii) The initial rate of conversion of A

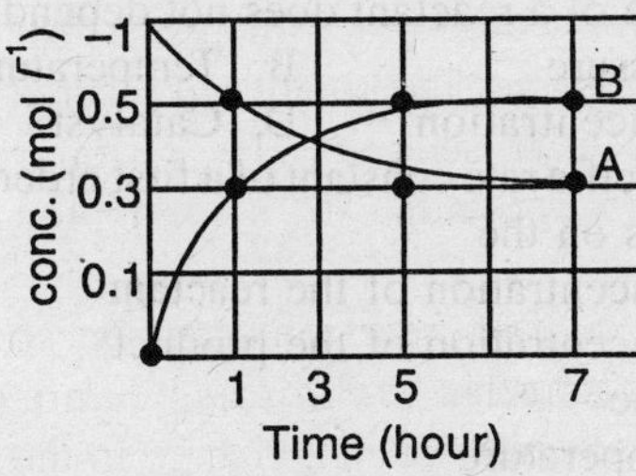

A. *(i)* 2 *(ii)* 0.1 m/*l*/hour *(iii)* 1.2 M
B. *(i)* 2 *(ii)* 1.2 M *(iii)* 0.1 m/*l*/hour
C. *(i)* 2 *(ii)* 1.2 M *(iii)* 0.9 m/*l*/hour
D. None of the above

2. The rate constant for an isomerisation reaction $A \rightarrow B$ is 4.5×10^{-3} min^{-1}. If the initial concentration of A is 1 M; calculate the rate of reaction after 1 h.
A. 4.5×10^{-3} M/min
B. 3.43×10^{-3} M/min
C. 1.24×10^{-5} M/min
D. 2.6×10^{-6} M/min

3. The decomposition of N_2O_5 according to the equation,

$$2N_2O_5(g) \rightarrow 4NO_2(g) + O_2(g)$$

is a first order reaction. After 30 min., from the start of the decomposition is a closed vessel, the total pressure developed is found to be 284.5 mm of Hg and on complete decomposition, the total pressure is 584.5 mm of Hg. Calculate the rate constant of the reaction.
A. 2.5×10^{-2} min^{-1} B. 5.2×10^{-3} min^{-1}
C. 3.6×10^{-4} min^{-1} D. 4.8×10^{-5} min^{-1}

4. A first order reaction has $K = 1.5 \times 10^{-6}$ per second at 200°C. If the reaction is allowed to run for 10 hours, what percentage is found in the product? What is the half life of this reaction?
A. 5.2% and 128.33 hours respectively
B. 2.36% and 117.13 hours respectively
C. 5.2% and 228.34 hours respectively
D. 3.16% and 128.33 hours respectively

5. The gas phase decomposition of dimethyl ether follows first order kinetics :

$$CH_3—O—CH_3(g) \rightarrow CH_4(g) + H_2(g) + CO(g)$$

The reaction is carried out in a constant volume container at 500°C and has a half life is 14.5 minutes. Initially only dimethyl ether is present at a pressure of 0.40 atmosphere. What is the

total pressure of the system after 12 minutes? Assume the ideal gas behaviour.
A. 0.946 atm. B. 0.785 atm.
C. 0.777 atm. D. 0.749 atm.

6. A first order reaction is 20% complete in 10 minutes. Calculate the *(i)* specific rate constant of the reaction and *(ii)* the time taken for the reaction to 75% completion.
A. *(i)* 0.1616 min^{-1} *(ii)* 32.45 minutes
B. *(i)* 0.02231 min^{-1} *(ii)* 36.64 minutes
C. *(i)* 0.3121 min^{-1} *(ii)* 44.45 minutes
D. *(i)* 0.02231 min^{-1} *(ii)* 62.07 minutes

7. In the Arrhenius equation for a certain reaction, the value of A and E_a (activation energy) are 4×10^{13} sec^{-1} and 98.6 kJ mol^{-1} respectively. If the raction is of first order, at what temperature will its half life period be ten minuites?
A. T = 111.53 K B. T = 211.3 K
C. T = 311.35 K D. T = 411.35 K

8. A substance is decomposed by first order reaction. Its velocity constant at 648°K is 2.597×10^{-4} sec^{-1}, what will be its velocity constant at 673°K? E_a = 50,500 per mole and R = 1.987 cal.
A. $K_2 = 1.11 \times 10^{-3}$ sec^{-1}
B. $K_2 = 1.11 \times 10^{3}$ sec^{-1}
C. $K_2 = 1.11 \times 10^{-4}$ sec^{-1}
D. None of the above

9. The time required for 10% completion of a first order reaction at 298 K is equal to that required for its 25% completion at 308 K. If the pre-exponential factor for the reaction is 3.5×10^9 s^{-1}, Calculate its *(i)* rate constant at 318 K. *(ii)* the energy of activation.
A. *(i)* 2.73 *(ii)* 9.22×10^{-4} sec^{-1}
B. *(i)* 2.83 *(ii)* 9.13×10^{-5} sec^{-1}
C. *(i)* 3.13 *(ii)* 10.10×10^{-4} sec^{-1}
D. None of the above

10. The rate constant of a reaction is 1.5×10^7 s^{-1} at 50°C and 4.5×10^7 s^{-1} at 100°C. Evaluate the Arrhenius parameters A and E_a
A. $A = 3.16 \times 10^8$ sec^{-1},
$E_a = 1.16 \times 10^4$ J $mole^{-1}$
B. $A = 5.40 \times 10^{10}$ sec^{-1},
$E_a = 2.199 \times 10^4$ J $mole^{-1}$
C. $A = 6.16 \times 10^{10}$ sec^{-1},
$E_a = 1.16 \times 10^4$ J $mole^{-1}$
D. $A = 5.40 \times 10^{10}$ sec^{-1},
$E_a = 1.11 \times 10^4$ J $mole^{-1}$

11. At 380°C, the half life period for the first order decomposition of H_2O_2 is 360 min. The energy of activation of the reaction for 75% decomposition at 450°C.
A. 60 min B. 40 min
C. 20.34 min D. 10 min

12. The reactions *(i)* A → Products
(ii) B → Products
follow first order kinetics. The rate of the reaction *(i)* is doubled when the temperature is raised from 300 K to 310 K. The half life for this reaction at 310 K is 30 minutes. At the same temperature, B decomposes twice as fast as A. If the energy of activation for the reaction *(ii)* is half of reaction *(i)* calculate the rate of the reaction at 300 K.
A. 3.267×10^{-2} min^{-1} B. 3.267 min^{-1}
C. 3.267×10^{-4} min^{-1} D. 3.267×10^{-6} min^{-1}

13. The correct order indicated against the rate of reaction $A + B \xrightarrow{K}$ is
A. $\frac{d[c]}{dt} = K[A]$ B. $-\frac{d[c]}{dt} = K[A][B]$
C. $-\frac{d[A]}{dt} = K[A][B]$ D. $-\frac{d[A]}{dt} = K[A]$

14. In reversible reaction, both side rates of reaction are
A. Same B. Different
C. One side more D. Reactant rates less

15. The rate of a reactant does not depend upon
A. Pressure B. Temperature
C. Concentration D. Catalyst

16. The specific rate constant of a first order reaction depends on the
A. Concentration of the reactant
B. Concentration of the product
C. Time
D. Temperature

17. Which of the following statements regarding the molecularity of a reaction is wrong?
A. It is the number of molecules of the reactants taking part in a single step chemical reaction
B. It is calculated from the reaction mechanism
C. It may be either a whole number or fraction
D. It depends on the rate of determining step in the reactor

18. For a zero order reaction
A. The reaction rate is double when the initial concentration is doubled
B. The time for half change is half the time taken for completion of the reaction

C. The time for half change is independent of the intial concentration
D. The time for completion of the reaction is independent of the initial concentration.

19. What will be the order of reaction if doubling of the concentration of a reactant increases the rate by a factor of 4 and trepling the concentration of the reactant by a factor of 9?
A. First order B. Zero order
C. Second order D. Third order

20. The rate of reaction between A and B increases by a factor of 100, when the concentration of A is increased 10 folds, the order of reaction with respect to A is
A. 10 B. 1
C. 4 D. 2

21. The temperature coefficient of most of the reactions lies between
A. 1 and 3 B. 2 and 3
C. 1 and 4 D. 2 and 4

22. For an endothermic reaction, where ΔH represents the enthalpy of the reaction in kJ/mole the minimum energy fcr the energy of activation will be
A. Less than ΔH B. Zero
C. More than ΔH D. Equal to ΔH

23. Which of the following is not a characteristic of a catalyst?
A. It changes the equilibrium constant
B. It alters the reaction path
C. It increases the rate of reaction
D. It increases the average K.E. of the molecules

24. In the reversible reaction a catalyst is the substance, which
A. Increases the rate of forward reaction
B. Decreases the value of enthalpy change in the reaction
C. Reduces the time required for reaching the equilibrium state in the reaction
D. Decreases the rate of the reverse reaction

25. According to adsorption theory of catalysis, the speed of the reaction increases because
A. The concentration of reactant molecules at the active centres of the catalyst becomes high due to absorption
B. In the process of adsorption the activation energy of the molecules becomes large
C. Adsorption produces heat which increases the speed of the reaction
D. All of the above

26. In which of the following commerical process a catalyst is not used?
A. Haber's process
B. Deacon's proces
C. Solvay process and Thermite process
D. Lead Chamber process

27. Which of the following statement is wrong?
A. Haber's process of NH_3 requires iron
B. Friedel Craft's reaction uses anhydrous $AlCl_3$
C. Hydrogenation of oil uses iron as catalyst
D. Oxidation of SO_2 to SO_3 requires V_2O_5

28. Enzyme activity is maximum at
A. 2.98 K B. 310 K
C. 320 K D. 330 K

29. The enzyme ptyalin used for the digestion of food is present in
A. Saliva B. Blood
C. Intestine D. Adrenal glands

30. Which of the following statements are correct?
A. The order of reaction is the sum of the components of all the concentration terms in the rate equation
B. The order of reaction with respect of one reactant is the ratio of the change of logarithm of the rate concentration of the particular reactant, keeping the concentration of all other reactants constant.
C. Orders of reactions can be whole numbers or fractional numbers
D. All of the above

31. For a reaction $I^- + OCl^- \rightarrow IO^- + Cl^-$, in an aqueous medium, the rate of the reaction is given by

$$\frac{d[IO^-]}{dt} = K\frac{[I^-][OCl^-]}{[OH^-]}$$

The overall order of reaction is
A. – 1 B. 1
C. Zero D. 2

32. Which of the following graphs best describes the rate at which N_2O_4 decomposes, to NO_2 if the reaction is first order in N_2SO_4?

A. $[N_2O_4]$ 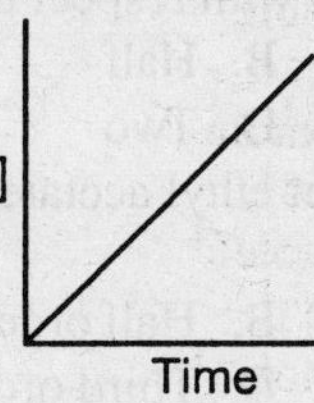

B. $[N_2O_4]$

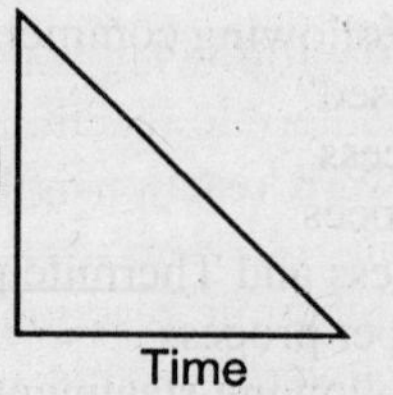

C. $[N_2O_4]$

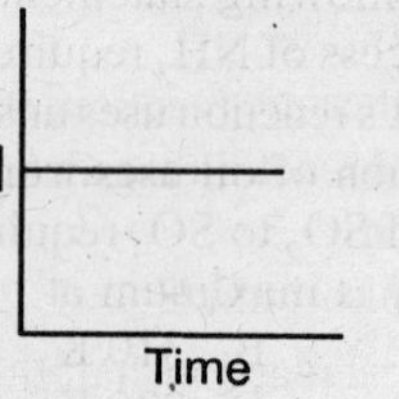

D. $[N_2O_4]$

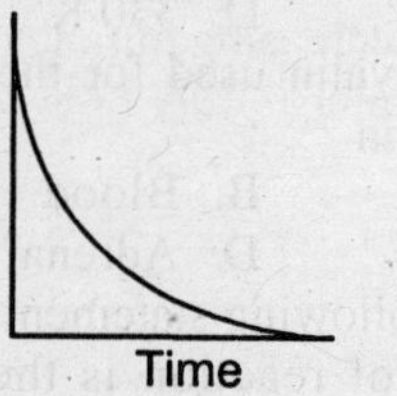

33. The unit of rate constant for an nth order reaction is

A. $L^{n-1}\,(\text{mol})^{-(n-1)}\,s^{-1}$

B. $\text{mol}^{-(n-1)}\,L^{(n-1)}s^{-1}$

C. $\text{mol}^{-(n-2)}\,L^{-(n-1)}s^{-1}$

D. $\text{mol}^{n-1}\,L^{n-1}s^{-1}$

34. The unit of the rate of reaction is same as that of the rate constant for a

A. Zero order reaction

B. First order reaction

C. Second order reaction

D. Half order reaction

35. The half life of a zero order reaction is

A. $t_{1/2} = \frac{1}{2}\frac{K}{a^2}$ B. $t_{1/2} = \frac{2K}{a}$

C. $t_{1/2} = \frac{a^2}{2K}$ D. $t_{1/2} = \frac{a}{2K}$

36. In a chemical reaction, A → B, it is found that the rate of reaction doubles when the concentration of A is increased four times. The order of the reaction with respect to A is

A. Zero B. Half

C. One D. Two

37. The saponification of ethyl acetate is a reaction of the

A. Zero order B. Half order

C. Second order D. Third order

38. Calculate the half life of the first order reaction

$$C_2H_4O(g) \rightarrow CH_4(g) + CO(g)$$

If the initial pressure of $C_2H_4O(g)$ is 80 mm and the total pressure at the end of 20 minutes is 120 mm

A. 40 min B. 120 min

C. 20 min D. 80 min

39. In a particular reaction, the time required to complete half of the reaction was found to increase 16 times whereas the initial concentration of the reactants was reduced to one fourth. What is the order of the reaction?

A. One B. Four

C. Two D. Three

40. For a first order reaction, the time required for 99.9% of the reaction to take place is nearly

A. 10 times that required for half the reaction

B. 100 times that required for thirds of the reaction

C. 10 times that required for one fourth of the reaction

D. 20 times that required half of the reaction

41. Consider the reaction X + Y → Products. If the initial concentration of X is increased to four times its original value, keeping the concentration of Y constant, the rate of reaction increases four folds. When the concentration of X and Y become 16 times their original values, the observed rate law is

A. $K[X]^2[Y]^2$ B. $K[X]^1[Y]^1$

C. $K[X]^1[Y]^2$ D. $K[X]^2[Y]^1$

42. In which of the following ways does an activated complex differ from an ordinary molecule?

A. It is quite unstable and has no independent existence

B. ΔH_f^0 is probably positive

C. The system has more vibrational character

D. The system has no vibrational character

E. A and C

43. The basic theory of Arrhenius's equation is that

A. The number of effective collisions is proportional to the number of molecules above a certain threshold energy

B. As the temperature increases, the number of molecules with energies exceeding the threshold energy increases

C. The rate constant is a function of temperature
D. Activation energy and pre-exponential factors are always temperature independent
E. A, B and C

44. Which of the following is correct?
A. Total collision rate α mean speed α absolute temperature
B. Total collision rate $\alpha \frac{1}{\text{mean speed}} \alpha \frac{1}{\text{absolute temperature}}$
C. Total collision rate $\alpha \, \text{mean speed} \, \alpha \left(\text{absolute temperature}\right)^{1/2}$
D. Total collision rate $\alpha \left(\text{mean speed}\right)^2 \alpha \left(\text{absolute temperature}\right)^3$

45. Which of the following statements is correct for the activation energy of a reaction?
A. It increases with increase in temperature
B. When activation energy is zero, the rate constant is temperature dependent
C. It decreases with decrease in temperature
D. It is nearly independent of temperature, over a wide range

46. The use of catalyst in a reaction cannot change the
A. Rate of reaction
B. Activation energy of a reaction
C. Enthalpy of a reaction
D. Equilibrium constant of a reaction

47. Which of the following is *true* about 1st order chemical reaction?
A. Concentration of product increases linearly with time
B. Concentration of reactant decreases linearly with time
C. Plot of time vs. logarithm of concentration of reactant is straight line passing through origin
D. Concentration of product increases exponentially with time

48. The temperature coefficient of a chemical reaction is 2.5 for a 20°C rise in temperature, the rate increases by a factor of
A. 5 B. 4
C. 6.25 D. 8

49. Which of the following is true?
A. In endothermic reaction, activation energy of forward reaction is less than backward reaction
B. In endothermic reaction, activation energy for backward reaction is less than forward reaction
C. In exothermic reaction, activation energy for forward reaction is greater than for backward reaction
D. At equilibrium, $E_{af} = E_{ab}$

50. In a chemical reaction, half life increases by eight times on decreasing initial concentration to half of initial value. Order of reaction is
A. 0 B. 2
C. 3 D. 4

51. In the reaction $2A \rightarrow B$, the rate of disappearance of A is 0.1 mol $L^{-1}s^{-1}$. The rate of dimerisation is
A. 0.2 mol L^{-1} s^{-1} B. 0.05 mol L^{-1} s^{-1}
C. 0.3 mol L^{-1} s^{-1} D. 0.4 mol L^{-1} s^{-1}

52. The rate constant of a chemical reaction $A \rightarrow B$ is expressed as

$$\log K\,(\text{min}^{-1}) = 31 - \frac{11{,}200}{T}$$

Approximate value of activation energy is
A. 180 kJ/mol B. 280 kJ/mol
C. 220 kJ/mol D. 120 kJ/mol

53. Which of the following is true?
A. Order and molecularity of a reaction are always equal
B. Order of reaction is the sum of stoichiometric coefficients of reactants
C. Order and molecularity of the slowest step of a reaction are same
D. Order of a reaction depends on temperature

54. Concentration of reactant remaining after five half life, in a 1st order reaction is, where *a* is initial concentration
A. $\frac{1}{32}a$ B. $\frac{1}{64}a$
C. $\frac{1}{16}a$ D. $\frac{1}{128}a$

55. Which of the following parameter cannot be used to study the progress of a chemical reaction?

A. Viscosity B. Specific rotation
C. Pressure D. Volume

56. Which one of the following rate laws has an overall order of 0.5 for the reaction $A + B + C \rightarrow$ Product?

A. $R = K[A][B][C]$
B. $R = K[A]^{0.5}[B]^{0.5}[C]^{0.5}$
C. $R = K[A]^{1.5}[B]^{-1}[C]^{0}$
D. $R = K[A][B]^{0}[C]^{0.5}$

57. The specific rate constant of a first order reaction depends on the

A. Concentration of the reactant
B. Concentration of the product
C. Time
D. Temperature

58. If 'K' of a reaction is 1.6×10^{-2} (mol/l) (min^{-1}), the order of the reaction is

A. 0 B. 1
C. 2 D. Cannot be known

59. Which one of the following curves represents a 1st order reaction?

A.
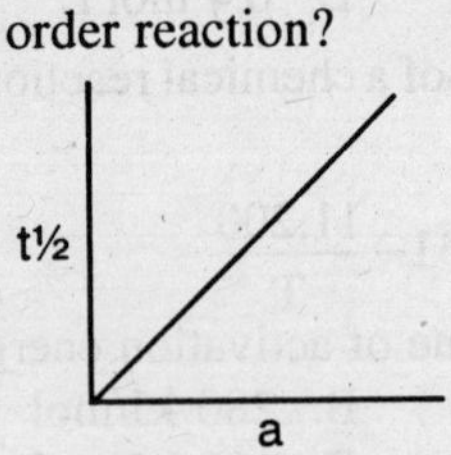

B.
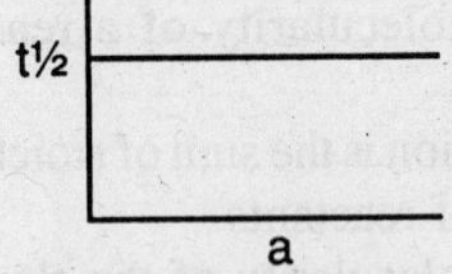

C.
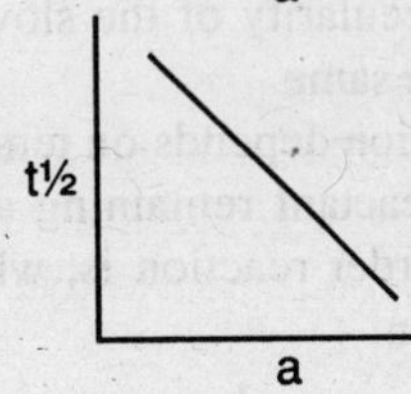

D.
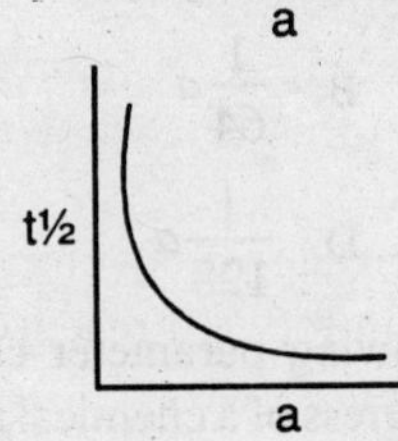

60. The half life for a given reaction was halved as the initial concentration of a reactant was doubled. The order for this reaction is

A. 0 B. 1
C. 2 D. 3

61. The reactions of a higher molecularity are rare because

A. Many body collisions have a low probability
B. Many body collisions are not favoured energetically
C. Activation energy of many body collisions is very large
D. None of the above

62. Increase in the concentration of the reactant leads to change in

A. ΔH
B. Activation energy
C. Collision frequency
D. None of the above

63. The temperature dependence of the rate constant is given by the Arrhenius equation

A. $\ln K = \ln A - E_a/RT$
B. $\ln K = \ln A + E_a/RT$
C. $\ln K = A\,E_a/RT$
D. $\ln K = \ln A + RT \ln E_a$

64. The mechanism of decomposition of ozone $2O_3 \rightarrow 3O_2$ is given as

$O_3 \xrightleftharpoons{K} O_2 + O$ (fast)

$O_3 + O \xrightarrow{K_1} 2O_2$ (slow)

A. $r = K[O_3]$ B. $r = K[O_3]^2$
C. $r = K[O_3]^2[O_2]^{-1}$ D. $r = K[O_3][O_2]$

65. If the rate constant of a first order reaction is 3.465×10^{-3} min^{-1}. Then the half life period for the reaction is

A. 150 min B. 200 min
C. 400 min D. 480 min

66. The rate constant for a first order reaction, whose half life is 480 sec. is

A. 2.88×10^{-3} sec^{-1} B. $1.44 \times$ sec^{-1}
C. 1.44×10^{-3} sec^{-1} D. 0.72×10^{-3} sec^{-1}

67. The alkaline hydrolysis of an ester is represented by

$RCOOR^1 + OH^- \rightarrow RCOO^- + R^1OH$

The reaction is

A. Bimolecular and of second order
B. Bimolecular and of first order
C. Bimolecular but not of second order
D. Second order but not bimolecular

68. Catalytic poisoners act by

A. Coagulating the catalyst
B. Getting adsorbed on the active centres on the surface of catalyst
C. Chemical combination with any one of the reactants
D. None

69. The catalyst used in chamber process of sulphuric acid is

A. Platinum B. Nitric oxide
C. Nickel D. Vanadium pentaoxide

70. Modern theory of heterogeneous catalysis is

A. Intermediate compound formation theory
B. Adsorption theory
C. A combination of two theories, *i.e.* intermediate compound formation and adsoprtion theory.
D. None of the above

71. Which is universally correct for catalyst

A. A catalyst remains unchanged chemically at the end of chemical reaction
B. A catalyst takes part in chemical reaction
C. All kinds of catalysts undergo catalytic poisoning
D. A catalyst physically changes at the end of reaction

72. Which statement is wrong

A. The catalyst does not alter the equilibrium of a reaction
B. Reaction with higher activation energy has higher rate constant
C. In the endothermic reaction, the activation energy of the reaction is higher than that of heat of reaction
D. Half life period of a first order reaction is independent of initial concentration

73. Air can oxidise sodium sulphate in aqueous solution but cannot do so in the case of sodium arsenite. If, however, air is passed through a solution containing both sodium sulphite and sodium arsenite then both are oxidised. This is an example of

A. Positive catalysis B. Negative catalysis
C. Induced catalysis D. Auto-catalysis

74. ZSM-5 is used to convert

A. Alcohol to petrol
B. Benzene to toluene
C. Toluene to benzene
D. Heptane to toluene

75. Radioactive decay follows........order kinetics

A. Zero B. 1
C. 2 D. 3

76. The accompanying figure depicts the change in concentration of species X and Y for the reaction $X \rightarrow Y$, as a function of time. The point of intersection of the two curves represents.

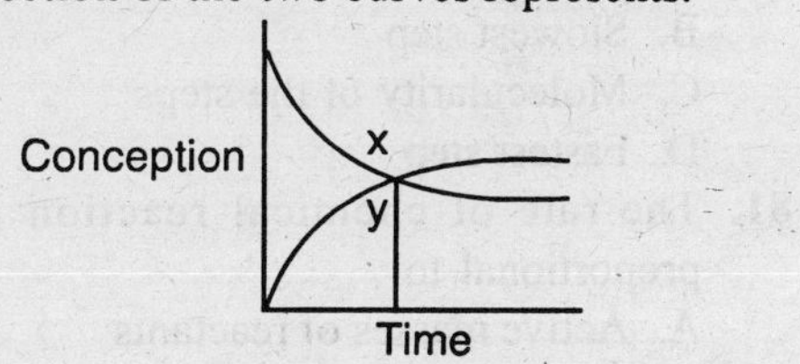

A. $t\frac{1}{2}$
B. $t\frac{3}{4}$
C. $t\frac{2}{3}$
D. Data insufficient to predict

77. On addition of $AgNO_3$ to NaCl white ppt occurs

A. Instantaneously
B. With a measurable speed
C. Slowly
D. None

78. Which statement is not correct?

A. For endothermic reactions, heat of reaction is lesser than energy of activation
B. For exothermic reactions, heat of reaction is more than energy of activation
C. For exothermic reactions energy of activation is less in forward reaction than in backward reaction
D. For endothermic reactions, energy of activation is more in forward reaction than in backward reaction

79. Which curve represents zero order reaction

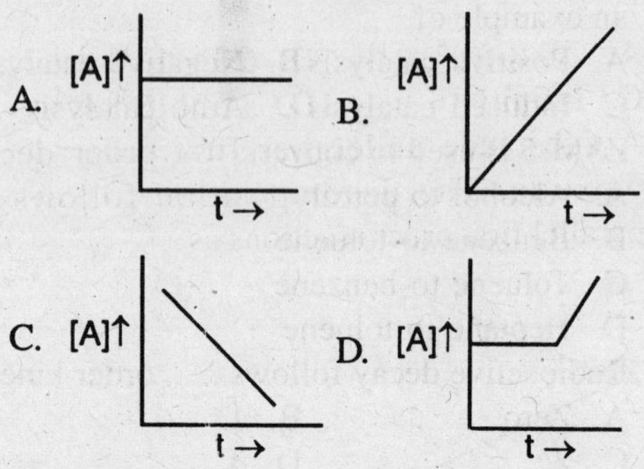

80. In many reactions, the reaction proceeds in a sequence of steps, so the overall rate is determined by

A. Order of different steps
B. Slowest step
C. Molecularity of the steps
D. Fastest step

81. The rate of chemical reaction is directly proportional to

A. Active masses of reactants
B. Equilibrium constant
C. Active masses of products
D. Pressure

82. Point out the incorrect statement

A. Rate law is an experimental value
B. Law of mass action is a theoretical proposal
C. Rate law is more informative than law of mass action for developing mechanism
D. Rate law is always different from the expression of law of mass action

83. Effective collisions are those in which molecules must

A. Have energy equal to or greater than the threshold energy
B. Have proper orientation
C. Acquire the energy of activation
D. All of the above

84. The given example is

$2FeCl_3 + SnCl_2 \rightarrow SnCl_4 + 2FeCl_2$

A. First order reaction
B. Second order reaction
C. Third order reaction
D. Half order reaction

85. In a reaction, the threshold energy is equal to

A. Activation energy + normal energy of reactants
B. Activation energy − normal energy of reactants
C. Activation energy
D. Normal energy of reactants

86. With respect to the figure given below, which of the following statement is correct?

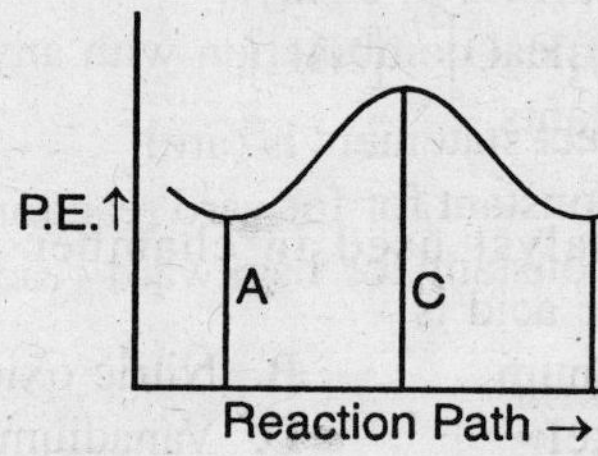

A. ΔE for the forward reaction is C − B
B. ΔE for the forward reaction is B − A
C. $E_{(forward)} > E_{(Backward)}$
D. E(for reverse reaction) = C − A

87. According to the Arrhenius equation, a straight line is to be obtained by plotting the logarithm of the rate constant of a chemical reaction (log K) against

A. T
B. log T
C. 1/T
D. log 1/T

88. Inversion of a sugar follows first order rate equation which can be followed by noting the change in rotation of the plane of polarization of light in the polarimeter. If r_∞, r_t and r_0 are the rotations at $t = \infty$ and t = 0, then first order reaction can be written as

A. $K = \frac{1}{t}\log_e \frac{r_t - r_\infty}{r_0 - r_\infty}$
B. $K = \frac{1}{t}\ln \frac{r_0 - r_\infty}{r_t - r_\infty}$
C. $K = \frac{1}{t}\ln \frac{r_\infty - r_0}{r_\infty - r_t}$
D. $K = \frac{1}{t}\ln \frac{r_\infty - r_t}{r_\infty - r_0}$

89. Milk turns sour at 40°C three times as faster as at 0°C. The energy of activation for souring of milk is

A. 4.693 K cal
B. 2.6 K cal
C. 6.6 K cal
D. None

90. For the reaction

$$\left[Cu(NH_3)_4\right]^{2+} + H_2O \rightleftharpoons \left[Cu(NH_3)_3H_2O\right]^{2+} + NH_3$$

The net rate of reaction at any time is given by

$$\text{net rate} = 2.0 \times 10^{-4}\left[Cu(NH_3)_4\right]^{2+} - 3.0 \times 10^5 \left[Cu(NH_3)_3H_2O\right]^{2+}.[NH_3]$$

Then correct statement is (are)

A. Rate constant for forward reaction = 2×10^{-4}

B. Rate constant for backward reaction = 3×10^5

C. Equilibrium constant for the reaction = 6.6×10^{-10}

D. All of the above

91. The rate constant, the activation energy and the Arrhenius parameter of a chemical reaction at 25°C are $3.0 \times 10^{-4} s^{-1}$, 104.4 kJ mol^{-1} and $6.0 \times 10^{14} s^{-1}$ respectively. The value of the rate constant as $T \to \infty$ is

A. $2.0 \times 10^{18}\ s^{-1}$ B. $6.0 \times 10^{14}\ s^{-1}$

C. Infinity D. $3.6 \times 10^{30}\ s^{-1}$

92. A substance undergoes first order decomposition. The decomposition follows two parallel first order reactions as

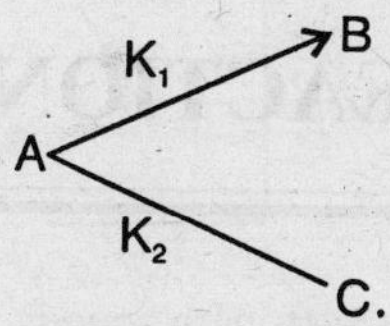

The percentage distribution of B and C are

A. 80% B and 20% C

B. 76.8% B and 23.17% C

C. 90% B and 10% C

D. 60% B and 40% C

93. Hydrogenation of vegetable ghee at 25°C reduces pressure of H_2 from 2 atomosphere to 1.2 atomosphere in 50 minute. The rate of reaction in terms of molarity per second is

A. 1.09×10^{-6} B. 1.09×10^{-5}

C. 1.09×10^{-7} D. 1.09×10^{-5}

ANSWERS

1	2	3	4	5	6	7	8	9	10
B	B	B	A	D	D	C	A	A	B
11	12	13	14	15	16	17	18	19	20
C	A	C	A	A	D	C	B	C	D
21	22	23	24	25	26	27	28	29	30
B	C	A	C	A	C	C	A	A	D
31	32	33	34	35	36	37	38	39	40
B	D	B	A	D	B	C	C	D	A
41	42	43	44	45	46	47	48	49	50
C	E	E	C	D	C	D	C	B	D
51	52	53	54	55	56	57	58	59	60
B	C	C	A	B	C	D	A	B	C
61	62	63	64	65	66	67	68	69	70
A	C	A	C	B	C	B	B	B	C
71	72	73	74	75	76	77	78	79	80
A	B	C	A	B	A	A	B	C	B
81	82	83	84	85	86	87	88	89	90
A	D	D	B	A	B	C	B	A	D
91	92	93							
B	B	B							

7

REDOX REACTION AND ELECTROCHEMISTRY

Oxidation Process

(i) When an element or compound combines with oxygen or any other electronegative atom, the element or the compound is said to be oxidized

$$2Mg + O_2 \rightarrow 2MgO$$
$$Mg + Cl_2 \rightarrow MgCl_2$$
$$3Mg + N_2 \rightarrow MgN_2$$
$$H_2 + Cl_2 \rightarrow 2HCl$$

(ii) The removal of hydrogen or any other electropositive element from a substance is known as oxidation of that substance

$$H_2S + H_2O_2 \rightarrow 2H_2O + S$$
$$2KI + H_2O_2 \rightarrow 2KOH + I_2$$

(iii) According to electronic definition, when any atom, molecule or ions loses electrons, they are said to be oxidised. Hence, *de-electronation* of any species is called oxidation of that species :

$$Na - e^- \rightarrow Na^+$$
$$Al - 3e^- \rightarrow Al^{3+}$$
$$Cl^- - e \rightarrow Cl$$
$$H_2S - 2e^- \rightarrow 2H^+ + S$$
$$Sn^{2+} - 2e^- \rightarrow Sn^{4+}$$
$$Cu^+ - e \rightarrow Cu^{++}$$

(iv) When oxidation number of any chemical species is increased, the species is said to be oxidised. An increase in oxidation number is a tendency of losing electrons.

Reduction Process

(i) The attachment of hydrogen or any electropositive atom to any substance is called reduction of that substance :

$$Cl_2 + H_2 \rightarrow 2HCl$$
$$Cl_2 + 2Na \rightarrow 2NaCl$$
$$O_2 + 2H_2 \rightarrow 2H_2O$$
$$N_2 + 3H_2 \rightarrow 2NH_3$$

(ii) The removal of oxygen or any other electronegative atom from a substance is called reduction of that substance :

$$2MgO \rightarrow 2Mg + O_2$$
$$2HgO \rightarrow 2Hg + O_2$$
$$Fe_2O_3 + 3C \rightarrow 2Fe + 3CO$$

(iii) According to electronic transition any atom, molecule or ion is said to be reduced when accepts electrons

$$F + e^- \rightarrow F^-$$
$$Cl + e^- \rightarrow Cl^-$$
$$S + 2e^- \rightarrow S^{2-}$$
$$Sn^{4+} + 2e^- \rightarrow Sn^{2+}$$
$$Fe^+ + e^- \rightarrow Fe^{2+}$$

(iv) Decrease in oxidation number of any species is called the reduction of that species. The decrease in oxidation number is the tendency of gaining electrons.

Redox Reaction

Since oxidation involves loss of electrons and reduction involves the gain of electrons, it is evident that if one substance loses the electrons, another substance at the same time must gain electrons because the electrons cannot be the products of any chemical change. This means that in any chemical process, oxidation can occur only if reduction is also taking place side by side and *vice versa.* This is the reason that reactions involving oxidation and reduction are called redox reactions.

During redox reaction, there is transference of electrons from the *reducing agent* to the oxidising agent.

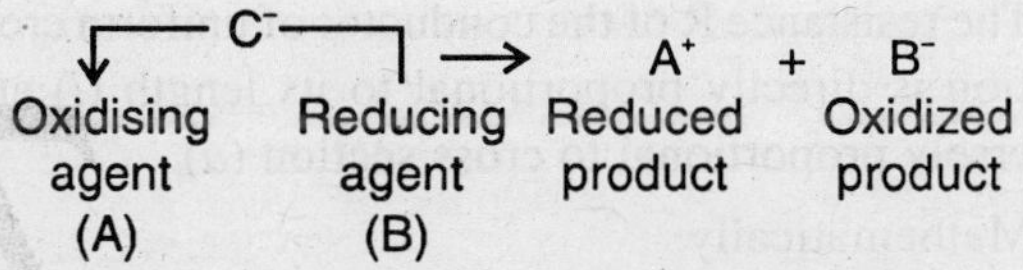

Oxidation → Loss of electrons

Reduction → Gains of electrons

Oxidising Agent → Species which gains electrons and itself is reduced

Reducing Agent → Species which loses electrons and itself is oxidized

We find examples of redox reactions almost every time we analyse the reactions used as a source of either heat or work. When *natural gas* burns, a redox reaction occurs that releases more than 800 kJ/mol of energy.

$$CH_4(g) + 2O_2(g) \rightarrow CO_2(g) + 2H_2O(g)$$

Within our body, a sequence of redox reactions burns sugars, such as glucose, ($C_6H_{12}O_6$) and the fatty acids in the fat use heat

$$C_6H_{12}O_6(g) + 6O_2(g) \rightarrow 6CO_2(g) + 6H_2O(l)$$

$$CH_3(CH_2)_6COOH(aq) + 26O_2(g) \rightarrow 18CO_2(g) + 18H_2O(l)$$

We do not have to restrict ourselves to reactions that can be used as a source of energy, however, to find example of redox reactions. Silver metal is oxidised when it comes in contact with a trace quantity of H_2S or SO_2 in the atmosphere, or food, such as eggs, that are rich in sulphur compounds.

$$4Ag(s) + 2H_2S(g) + O_2(g) \rightarrow 2Ag_2S(s) + 2H_2O(g)$$

The tarnishing of siliver is just one example of a broad class of oxidation-reduction reactions that fall under general heading of *corrosion*.

Another example is the series of reactions that occurs when iron or steel rusts. When heated, iron reacts with oxygen to form a mixture of iron (ii) and iron (iii) oxides :

$$2Fe(s) + O_2(g) \rightarrow 2FeO(s)$$

$$4Fe(s) + 3O_2(g) \rightarrow 2Fe_2O_3(s)$$

Molten iron even reacts with water to form aqueous solution of Fe^{2+} ions and H_2 gas :

$$Fe(l) + 2H_2O(l) \rightarrow Fe^{2+}(aq) + 2OH^-(aq) + H_2O(g)$$

At room temperature all the above three reactions are so slow, they can be ignored.

Iron only corrodes at room temperature in presence of oxygen and water. In the course of this reaction, the iron is oxidized to give a hydrated form of Fe(II) oxide :

$$2Fe(s) + O_2(aq) + H_2O(l) \rightarrow 2FeO.H_2O(s)$$

As the compound $FeO.H_2O$ has same empirical formula as $Fe(OH)_2$, it is often mistakenly called iron (II) or Ferrous hydroxide. The $FeO.H_2O$ formed in this reaction is further oxidized by O_2 dissolved in water to give hydrated form of iron (iii) or ferric oxide:

$$4FeO.H_2O(s) + O_2(aq) + 2H_2O(l) \rightarrow 2Fe_2O_3.3H_2O(s)$$

$FeO.H_2O$ formed at the surface of metal combines with $Fe_2O_3.3H_2O$ to give a hydrated form of magnetic iron oxide (Fe_3O_4) :

$$FeO.H_2O(s) + Fe_2O_3.3H_2O(s) \rightarrow Fe_3O_4.nH_2O(s)$$

Calculation of Oxidation Numbers

Oxidation number of an element in a particular compound may be calculated with the help of the following rules :

(i) The oxidation number of all the atoms in their respective elementary states is taken to be zero. For example, in N_2, Cl_2, H_2, O_2, O_3, Na, P, Zn etc., the oxidation number of each atom is zero.

(ii) The oxidation number of hydrogen is + 1 in all its compounds except metallic hydrides (e.g., NaH, CaH_2, etc.) where it is – 1.

(iii) The oxidation number of oxygen is – 2 in all compounds except peroxides (like H_2O_2, Na_2O_2, BaO_2, etc) where it is – 1, superoxides (the only example of it is KO_2 in which oxidation number of oxygen is – 1/2), oxygen fluoride (OF_2) where it is + 2 and O_2F_2 where it is +1.

(iv) In halides, the oxidation number of halogens is –1.

(v) In sulphides, the oxidation number of sulphur is –2.

(vi) The oxidation number of an ion is the same as its charge. Thus the oxidation number Li^+, Al^{+3}, SO_4^{2-}, and PO_4^{3-} are + 1, + 3, – 2 and – 3 respectively.

(vii) The sum of oxidation numbers of all atoms in the formula of a compound is always zero.

(viii) Alkali metals (group 1 elements of the periodic table *i.e.* Na, K, Li, etc.) and alkaline earth metals (group 2 elements of the periodic table, *i.e.* Mg, Ba, Ca, Sr, etc.) have + 1 and + 2 oxidation states respectively.

(ix) Oxidation number of a metal in carboxyl complex is always zero, *e.g.*, Ni in $[Ni(Co)_4]$.

Elements of group 4, 5, 6 and 7 show a variety of oxidation numbers. Variable oxidation number is more common in transition elements, *e.g.*, managenese can have five different oxidation numbers in different compounds,

+ 2 in $MnCl_2$
+ 3 in $Mn(OH)_3$
+ 4 in MnO_2
+ 6 in K_2MnO_4
+ 7 in $KMnO_4$

(a) Nature of the Electrolyte : Some electrolytes, *e.g.*, mineral acids, such as H_2SO_4, HCl and HNO_3, alkalis such as NaOH and KOH and most salts have a very 'high degree of ionization' (α nearly equal to 1) at all reasonable concentrations. They are known as 'strong electrolytes'. The *number of ions* in solutions of strong electrolytes is large, hence such solutions have high *conductance.*

Some electrolytes, *e.g.*, organic acids, such as acetic acid, propionic acid etc. and bases like ammonium hydroxide have a *low degree of ionization* in solution, they are called weak electrolytes. The *number of ions* in solutions of weak electrolytes is quite small, hence such solutions have *low conductance.*

Conductivity of Solutions of Electrolytes

The strength of current throu e electrolytic as well as metallic conductors is governed by *Ohm's law* which states that the current strength (I) flowing through a conductor at a given temperature is proportional to the potential difference (E) and inversely proportional to the Resistance (R).

Mathematically, $I=\dfrac{E}{R}$ or $R=\dfrac{E}{I}$ ...*(i)*

Resistance : The hind provided by solution in the passage of current expressed in ohm) is known as resistance of solution).

E is expressed in volts and I in amperes.

The resistance R of the conductor of uniform cross section is directly proportional to its length (l) and inversely proportional to cross section (a).

Mathematically,

$$R \propto \rho \frac{l}{a} \text{ or } R = \rho \frac{l}{a} \quad ...(ii)$$

where ρ is a constant, called resistivity or *specific resistance* and may be defined as the 'resistance' in ohms of a conductor of one cm length and one sq cm cross section or the resistance between two opposite faces of one cm cube of metal.

$$\rho = \frac{R.a}{l} = \frac{\text{ohms} \times \text{cm}^2}{\text{cm}} = \text{ohms cm} \quad ...(iii)$$

The reciprocal of specific resistance is called 'specific conductivity' which is represented by χ (Kappa). Thus

$$\chi = \frac{1}{\rho} \quad ...(iv)$$

From equation *(iii)* and *(iv)*

$$\chi = \frac{1}{a \times R} \quad ...(v)$$

Since resistance (R) is reciprocal of

$$R = \frac{1}{c}$$

electrical conductance (c) which is expressed is ohm^{-1}, mho or rho. The unit of electrical conductance is called Siemen (S). Thus equation (v) may also be represented as

$$\chi = \frac{l \times c}{a} \quad ...(vi)$$

Thus, when $l = 1$ cm

$a = 1\ cm^2$ then

$\chi = c.$

Thus specific conductivity is the conductance of 1 cm cube or conductance of 1 cm cube of the solution of an electrolyte.

Since $\dfrac{l}{a}$ is constant for a given conductivity cell is known as *cell constant.*

Thus, equation *(vi)* may also be written as

k = cell constant × observed conductivity ...*(vii)*

Cell constant is determined with the help of a conductivity cell filled with N/50 solution of chemically pure KCl. The cell constant is expressed in cm^{-1}.

Equivalent Conductance (λ) : The conducting power of all the ions present in a solution having 1 g equivalent of electrolyte is called equivalent conductivity

$$\lambda = \chi \times V \text{ in ml}$$

$$= \chi \times \frac{1000}{c} = \chi \times \frac{1000}{N}$$

where V is volume having 1 gm equivalent of electrolyte, c is concentration in eq/litre, λ is expressed in $ohm^{-1}\ cm^2\ eq^{-1}$.

Moler Conductance (μ) : The conducting power of all ions present in a solution having 1 mole of electrolyte.

$$\mu = \chi \times V \text{ in ml}$$

$$= \chi \times \frac{1000}{c} = \chi \times \frac{1000}{M}$$

where V is volume having 1 mole of electrolyte, c is concentration in mole/litre, μ is expressed in $ohm^{-1}\ cm^2\ mole^{-1}$.

Kohlrausch's law of Independent Ionic Conductance : Kohlrausch in 1876 noticed that values of λ_0 for pairs of salts having the same anion showed a constant difference as shown below :

	$^*\lambda_0$		$^*\lambda_0$		$^*\lambda_0$
KCl	0.0150	KBr	0.0152	KNO_3	0.0145
NaCl	0.0127	NaBr	0.0129	$NaNO_3$	0.0121
Difference	0.0023	Difference	0.0023	Difference	0.0024

$^*\lambda_0$ = Equivalent conductance at infinite dilution

These results led him to put forward the law of independent ionic mobilities. "The conductivity of an electrolyte at infinite dilution is the sum of the ionic mobilities of the ions forming the electrolyte and these mobilities are independent of the presence of other ions."

Thus $\lambda_{0NaCl} = \lambda_{0Na^+} + \lambda_{0Cl^-}$

where λ_{0Na^+} and λ_{0Cl^-} are the ionic conductances of the sodium and chloride ions respectively. The ionic conductance is a definite constant for each ion and its value depends only on temperature.

This law can be used to determine λ_0 of a weak electrolyte such as acetic acid. λ_0 of acetic acid cannot be measured directly. So the λ_0 values of HCl, CH_3COONa and NaCl are determined by the extrapolation method.

Then from Kohlrausch law

$$\lambda_0(HCl) + \lambda_0(CH_3COON) - \lambda_0(NaCl)$$

$$= \left(\lambda_{0H^+} + \lambda_{0Cl^-}\right) + \left(\lambda_{0Na^+} + \lambda_{0CH_3COO^-}\right) - \left(\lambda_{0Na^+} + \lambda_{0Cl^-}\right)$$

$$= \lambda_{0H^+} + \lambda_{0CH_3COO^-} = \lambda_{0CH_3COOH}$$

Kohlrausch has shown that the limiting value of equivalent conductance of a solution of a strong electrolyte is best determined by plotting λ against the square root of concentration $(\sqrt{c})$. The plot is linear/or strong electrolytes and the limiting value of λ (i.e. λ_0) as $c \to 0$, is obtained by extrapolation of the line to zero concentration as shown in figure below. In case of weak electrolytes as acetic acid, the plot is not linear. So, it is not possible to determine λ_0 of a weak electrolyte by extropolation. So it is determined indirectly by using Kohlrausch law.

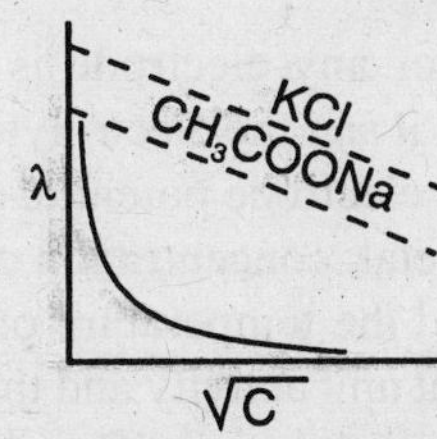

Fig. Plot of λ against $\sqrt{c}$

Cells

An assembly of two half cells or electrode suspended in electrolyte is called a Cell. There are two types of cells, *viz.* electrolytic cells, and electrochemical cells. Electrochemical cells are further of two type, *viz.,* chemical cells and concentration cells.

Electrolytic Cells : In these cells passage of current brings about chemical change and electrical energy is converted into chemical energy.

Electrochemical Cells : In these cells a chemical change brings in passage of current and chemical energy is converted into electrical energy.

Chemical cells : In these cells a net chemical change occurs inside the cell, *e.g.*, Daniell cell

$$Zn|ZnSO_4||CuSO_4|Cu$$

Anode : $Zn \rightarrow Zn^{2+} + 2e^-$

Cathode : $Cu^{2+} + 2e^- \rightarrow Cu$

Redox change : $Zn + Cu^{2+} \rightarrow Zn^{2+} + Cu$

In these cells, a decrease in free energy during the redox change brings in a equivalent amount of work done. The electrode having high standard oxidation potential works as anode *i.e.* negative electrode.

Concentration cells : In these types of cells, no net chemical change occurs *e.g.* $M|M^+(c_1)||M^+(c_2)|M$

$$M \rightarrow M^+(c_1) + e^-$$

$$M^+(c_2) + e^- \rightarrow M$$

Net change : $M^+(c_1) \rightarrow M^+(c_2)$

In these cells, a decrease in free energy during the transfer of concentration from c_1 to c_2 brings in an equivalent amount of electrical work done. The electrode having more dilute surroundings work as an anode.

Electrode Potential

"The potential of any electrode is the potential difference between it and the electrolyte surrounding the electrode". The electrode potential depends upon the nature of the metal, concentration of the metallic ions in solution and the temperature of the solution. When the ions are at unit activity and the temperature is 25°C (298 K) the potential difference is called a standard electrode potential (E^0). The potential of a single electrode cannot be determined but the potential difference between the two electrodes can be accurately measured. Thus an arbitrary standard electrode must be chosen to determine the potential of an electrode.

Electrochemical Series

Arrangement of metals in the order of decreasing tendency of their atoms to give electrons (*i.e.*, undergo oxidation) is known as Electrochemical series as given below.

Note that, this is also the arrangement of metals when arranged in the increasing order of their standard electrode reduction potentials. Electrochemical series exhibits following characterstics :

(i) Metals near the top of the series are strongly electropositive (or weakly electronegative). They lose electrons readily to give cations.

(ii) Weakly electronegative metals in the upper part can displace more electronegative metals below them from their salts. For example, iron displaces copper from $CuSO_4$ solution, Cu displaces silver from silver salt solution, silver displaces gold from gold salt solution as in photography during gold tonning process.

(iii) Hydroxides of metals in the upper part of series are strongly basic and their salts do not undergo hydrolysis. On the other hand, hydroxides of the metals in the lower part of the series are weakly basic and their salts undergo hydrolysis.

(iv) Metals lying above hydrogen are easily rusted. Those situated below are not rusted.

(v) Metals above hydrogen displace hydrogen from dilute acids.

(vi) More weakly electronegative metals like K, Na, Ca, etc. displace hydrogen from water.

(vii) Iron and other metals above it decompose steam and liberate hydrogen.

(viii) Oxides of iron and other metals below it can be reduced only.

(ix) Oxides of manganese and other metals above it are reduced when heated in a current of oxygen.

(x) Oxides of mercury and other metals below it are decomposed on heating.

Calculation of Equilibrium Constant (K_c) from Nernst Equation

During the function of a cell, the EMF of the cell continuously decreases and a stage reaches when the

EMF of the cell becomes zero, *i.e.* there is no flow of electrons. With continuous use of the cell, the concentration of cations around cathode decreases due to reduction and simultaneously the concentration of metal cations around anode increases due to oxidation consequently, the electrode potential of anode increases and that of cathode decreases. Finally, a situation comes when the potential difference ($E_{cathode} - E_{anode}$) reaches zero and the electrochemical cell stops working.

Under these conditions, the cell reaction is said to have attained equilibrium, *e.g.* for the galvanic cell

$$Zn(s)\left|Zn^{2+}(aq)\|Cu^{2+}(aq)\right|Cu(s)$$

The state of equilibrium may be expressed by the reaction

$$Zn(s) + Cu^{+}(aq) \rightleftharpoons Zn^{+2}(aq) + Cu(s)$$

In equilibrium state, the concentration of $Zn^{+2}(aq)$ and $Cu^{2+}(aq)$ will be the equilibrium concentrations and EMF of the cell will be zero.

Therefore, the Nernst equation is modified as

$$0 = E^0_{cell} - \frac{2.303\,RT}{nF}\log\frac{\left[Zn^{2+}(aq)\right]_{equilibrium}}{\left[Cu^{2+}(aq)\right]_{equilibrium}}$$

$$E^0_{cell} = \frac{2.303\,RT}{nF}\log K_c \quad ...(i)$$

$$\because K_c = \frac{\left[Zn^{2+}(aq)\right]_{equilibrium}}{\left[Cu^{2+}(aq)\right]_{equilibrium}}$$

where K_c is the equilibrium constant at 298 K. The value of K_c can be obtained by substituting the standard EMF value in equation *(i)*. At 298 K, the equation *(i)* takes the form

$$E^0_{cell} = \frac{0.0591\,RT}{n}\log K_c$$

$$\log K_c = \frac{n\,E^0_{cell}}{0.0591}$$

$$K_c = \text{Anti}\log\frac{n\,E^0_{cell}}{0.0591}$$

The value of K_c for galvanic cell is found to be about 2×10^7, which shows that the reaction has proceeded almost to completion.

Gibbs Free Energy and Cell Potential

When a cell reaction takes place in an electrochemical cell, the electrical energy generated by the cell can be quantitatively converted into work. So, the EMF of the cell is a measure of the maximum useful work that can be obtained under standard conditions. However, the electrical energy (electrical work) is equal to the product of EMF of the cell and the electrical charge that flows through the external circuit.

$$W_{max} = nFE_{cell} \quad ...(i)$$

Where n = Number of moles of electrons transferred through the wire

F = One Faraday *i.e.* 96500 coulombs

E_{cell} = EMF of the cell

According to thermodynamics, the free energy change (ΔG) for a process is equal to the maximum work that can be derived from a cell, *i.e.*

$$-W_{max} = \Delta G \quad ...(ii)$$

Therefore from equations *(i)* and *(ii)*

$$\Delta G = -nFE^0_{cell} \quad ...(iii)$$

When the cell reaction attains equilibrium,

$$E^0_{cell} = \frac{2.303\,RT}{nF}\log K_c \quad ...(iv)$$

Substituting the value of E^0_{cell} in *(iii)* we get

$$\Delta G^0 = -nF \times \frac{2.303\,RT}{nF}\log K_c$$

$$= -2.303\,RT\log K_c \quad ...(v)$$

Therefore knowing E^0_{cell} the values of the following can be calculated.

(a) Change in free energy (ΔG^0) or maximum useful work (W_{max})

(b) Equilibrium constant (K_c)

OBJECTIVE QUESTIONS

1. The cell reaction for the given cell is spontaneous if

$PtCl_2|Cl^-(1M)||Cl^-(1M)|PtCl_2$
$\quad P_1 \qquad\qquad\qquad\qquad P_2$

A. $P_1 > P_2$ B. $P_1 < P_2$
C. $P_1 = P_2$ D. $P_2 = 1$ atm.

2. Which of the following aqueous solutions remain neutral after electrolysis?

A. $CuSO_4$ B. $AgNO_3$
C. K_2SO_4 D. NaCl

3. Which of the following aqueous solutions remain acidic after electrolysis?

A. $K_2Cr_2O_7$ B. $KMnO_4$
C. CH_3COONa D. $CuCl_2$

4. Which of the following aqueous solutions remain akaline after electrolysis?

A. CH_3COONa B. NaCl
C. KNO_2 D. A and C

5. How many Faradays are required to reduce 1 mol of BrO_3^- to Br^- ?

A. 3 B. 5
C. 6 D. 4

6. How many moles of Zn^{2+} carry the charge of 2×10^{-5}C?

A. 1×10^{-4} B. 4×10^{-10}
C. 4×10^{-5} D. 1×10^{-10}

7. A steady current of 3.0 A for 1 hour corresponds to a passage of

A. 1.8×10^5 C B. 0.11 F
C. 1.08×10^4 electrons D. 1.51 V

8. The number of electrons lost and gained during the elctrolysis of 35.5 g of Cl^- and 65.4 g of Zn^{2+} respectively are

A. 6.02×10^{23} and 3.01×10^{23}
B. 3.01×10^{23} and 3.01×10^{23}
C. 6.02×10^{23} and 6.02×10^{23}
D. 6.02×10^{23} and 3.01×10^{10}

9. During the purification of copper by electrolysis

A. The anode are made of copper ore
B. Pure copper is deposited on the cathodes, with evolution of hydrogen at the anode
C. The impurities such as Ag, Au, Zn and Fe go into solution
D. The voltage is carefully controlled to prevent the deposition of Zn and Fe at the cathode

10. In an electrochemical process, a salt bridge is used

A. To maintain electroneutrality in each solution
B. To complete the circuit so that current can flow
C. As an oxidizing agent
D. As a colour indicator
E. A and B

11. Consider the cell

$Cd(s)|Cd^{2+}(1.0\,M)||Cu^{2+}(1.0\,M)|Cu(s)$

If we wish to make a cell with a more positive voltage using the same substances, we should

A. Increase both $[Cd^{2+}]$ and $[Cu^{2+}]$ to 2.0 M
B. Decrease only the $[Cd^{2+}]$ to 0.1 M
C. Increase only the $[Cu^{2+}]$ to 2.0 M
D. Decrease both $[Cd^{2+}]$ and $[Cu^{2+}]$ to 0.1 M
E. B and C

12. A concentration cell is a galvanic cell in which:

A. The electro material and the solutions in both half-cells are composed of the same substances
B. Only the concentration of the two solutions differ
C. $\Delta E^0_{cell} = 0$
D. The Nernst equation reduces to

$$\Delta E_{cell} = -\left[\frac{0.0592}{n}\right] \log \text{ at } 25°C$$

E. All of the above

13. Calculate the e.m.f. of the following cell at 25°C

$Ag(s)|AgNO_3(0.01 \text{ mol kg}^{-1})||$

$AgNO_3(0.05 \text{ mol kg}^{-1})|Ag(s)$

A. – 0.414 V B. 0.828 V
C. 0.414 V D. 0.0414 V

14. The electrochemical equivalent of copper is 0.0003296 g coulomb^{-1}, calculate the amount

of 0.5 ampere flowing through copper sulphate solution for 50 minutes.

A. 0.894 g B. 0.4944 g
C. 0.1212 g D. 0.2123 g

15. Calculate the mass of aluminium produced in a Hall's cell that possess a current of 1000 amperes for one hour (At wt. of Al = 27)

A. 360 g B. 335.8 g
C. 39.2 g D. 31.02 g

16. How much time is required to reduce 20 g of silver from a solution of silver nitrate, using 20 amps. of current?

A. 432.12 sec. B. 893.52 min.
C. 893.52 sec. D. 432.12 hrs.

17. It is required to electroplate a copper object of total surface area 400 sq. cm. with a layer of silver 0.002 cm thick. If a current of 2 amps. is used, how long will the process take?

A. 2514.0 sec. B. 3756.7 sec.
C. 3121.2 sec. D. 1215.0 sec.

18. The passage of a constant current through a dilute solution of H_2SO_4 with platinum electrodes, for 1 hour resulted in the liberation of 336 ml of mixed hydrogen and oxygen, reduced to STP. Calculate the strength of the current.

A. 96500 amp. B. 0.9125 amp.
C. 0.536 amp. D. 0.919 amp.

19. Silver is electrodeposited on a metallic vessel of surface area 800 cm^2 by passing a current of 0.2 amperes for 3 hours. Calculate the thickness of siliver deposited, given its density as 10.44 g/cc (At wt. of Ag = 107.92)

A. 3.164×10^{-3} cm B. 2.884×10^{-4} cm
C. 2.884×10^{-2} cm D. 3.164×10^{-4} cm

20. 0.5 N solution of a salt between two electrodes 2.1 cm apart and 4.2 sq. cm. in area was found to offer a resistance of 250 ohms. Calculate the equivalent conductivity of the solution

A. 4 ohm^{-1} cm^2/gm. eq.
B. 8 ohm^{-1} cm^2/gm. eq.
C. 9 ohm^{-1} cm^2/gm. eq.
D. None of the above

21. The specific conductivity of dichloroacetic acid at a dilution of 8 litres is 0.0238, λ_0 for this acid is 385, calculate the degree of ionisation at this dilution.

A. 50% B. 45%
C. 49.45% D. 36.02%

22. Calculate λ_0 for acetic acid if λ_0 for HCl, NaCl and CH_3COONa are 380.5, 109.0 and 78.5 $ohm^{-1}cm^2$ respectively

A. 78.5 ohm^{-1} cm^{-1} B. 350 ohm^{-1} cm^2
C. 35 ohm^{-1} cm^{-2} D. 410 ohm^{-1} cm^2

23. Calculate the e.m.f. of the cell

$$Ag|0.01M\,AgNO_3||0.1M\,AgNO_3|Ag \text{ at } 25°C$$

A. 0.36 volt B. 0.059 volt
C. 0.014 volt D. 0.012 volt

24. The voltage operating across the H_2—O_2 cell is 1.23 volts. If the fuel cell operates with 60% efficiency, calculate the number of joules of electrical energy generated per gram of water produced.

A. 3162.5 joules B. 6129.3 joules
C. 7912.6 joules D. 8186.3 joules

25. From the values of Faraday (96500 coulombs) and Avagadro number (6.023×10^{23}), calculate the coulombic charge of an electron

A. 1.6×10^{-18} coulombs
B. 1.1×10^{-19} coulombs
C. 1.6×10^{-10} coulombs
D. 1.6×10^{-23} coulombs

26. Find the charge in coulombs on 1 g ion of N^{-3}

A. 1.60×10^{-19} coulombs
B. 3.6×10^{-19} coulombs
C. 2.89×10^{5} coulombs
D. None of the above

27. A 100 watt, 110 volt incandescent lamp is connected in series with an electrolyte cell containing cadmium sulphate solution. What weight of cadmium will be deposited by the current flowing for 10 hours?

A. 0.339 g B. 19.06 g
C. 21.21 g D. 20.12 g

28. Electrolysis of a solution of $MnSO_4$ in aqueous sulphuric acid is a method for the preparation of MnO_2 as per reaction.

$Mn^{2+}(aq) + 2H_2O \rightarrow Mn_2O(s) + 2H^+(aq) + H_2(g)$. Passing a current of 27 A for 24 hours gives only 1 kg of MnO_2. What is the value of current efficiency?

A. 100% B. 50%
C. 94.8% D. 99%

29. Silver is electrodeposited on a metallic vessel of surface area 800 cm² by passing a current of 0.20 ampere for 3.0 hours. Calculate the thickness of silver deposited, given its density is 10.47 g/cc. [At wt. of Ag = 107.9 Z]

A. 0.000288 cm B. 2.88×10^{-4} cm
C. 3.19×10^{-5} cm D. A and B

30. A current of 1.70 ampere is passed through 300.0 ml of 0.160 M solution of $ZnSO_4$ for 230 sec. with a current efficiency of 90%. Find out the molarity of Zn^{2+} after the deposition of Zn. Assume the volume of the solution to remain constant during the electrolysis.

A. 0.119 M B. 0.154 M
C. 0.167 M D. 0.199 M

31. An acidic solution of Cu^{2+} salt containing 0.4 g of Cu^{2+} is electrolysed until all the copper is deposited. The electrolysis is continued for seven more minutes with the volume of solution kept at 100 ml and the current at 1.2 amp. Calculate the volume of gases evolved at NTP during the entire electrolysis.

A. O_2 = 99.79 ml, H_2 = 48.45 ml
B. O_2 = 87.91 ml, H_2 = 58.48 ml
C. O_2 = 99.79 ml, H_2 = 58.48 ml
D. O_2 = 100 ml, H_2 = 50 ml

32. 19 gram of molten $SnCl_2$ is electrolysed for some time using inert electrodes until 0.119 g of Sn is deposited at the cathode. No substance is lost during the electrolysis. Find the ratio of the weight of $SnCl_2 : SnCl_4$ after electrolysis

A. 81 : 99 B. 78 : 22
C. 71.34 : 1 D. 77.3 : 3.3

33. After electrolysis of a sodium chloride solution with inert electrodes for a certain period of time, 600 ml of the solution was left which was found to be 1 N sodium hydroxide. During the same time, 31.8 g of copper was deposited in a copper voltameter series with the elctrolytic cell. Calculate the percentage of theoretical yield of sodium hydroxide obtained.

A. 40% B. 60%
C. 80% D. 100%

34. A cell contains two hydrogen electrodes. The negative electrode is in contact with a solution of 10^{-6} M hydrogen ions. The EMF of the cell is 0.118 V at 25°C. Calculate the concentration of hydrogen ions at the positive electrode.

A. 10^{-3} M B. 10^{-4} M
C. 10^{-2} M D. 10^{-6} M

35. Zinc granules are added in excess to a 500 ml of 1.0 M nickel nitrate solution at 25°C until the equilibrium is reached. If the standard reduction potential of Zn^{2+}/Zn and Ni^{2+}/Ni are – 0.75 V and – 0.24 V respectively find out the concentration of Ni^{2+} in solution at equilibrium.

A. 3.128×10^{6} mol l^{-1}
B. 5.128×10^{-18} mol l^{-1}
C. 6.117×10^{-15} mol l^{-1}
D. 1.95×10^{-17} mol l^{-1}

36. A cell, $Ag|Ag^+||Cu^{2+}|Cu$, initially contains 1 M Ag^+ and 1 M Cu^{2+} ions. Calculate the change in the cell potential after the passage of 9.65 A of current for 1 h.

A. 68 V B. – 33 V
C. – 0.01355 V D. – 0.0162 V

37. Calculate the equilibrium constant for the reaction

$Fe^{2+} + Ce^{4+} \rightleftharpoons Fe^{3+} + Ce^{3+}$

$$\left(\begin{array}{l}\text{Given } E^0\ Ce^{4+}/Ce^{3+} = 1.44\text{ V} \\ \quad E^0\ Fe^{3+}/Fe^{2+} = 0.68\text{ V}\end{array}\right)$$

A. 6.7×10^{11} B. 7.6×10^{12}
C. 7.7×10^{18} D. 7.8×10^{19}

38. Calculate the equilibrium constant for the reaction, $2Fe^{3+} + 3I^- \rightleftharpoons 2Fe^{2+} + I_3^-$. The standard reduction potential in acidic conditions are 0.77 and 0.54 V respectively for Fe^{3+}/Fe^{2+} and I_3^-/I_3^- couples.

A. 6.12×10^{6} B. 6.26×10^{6}
C. 6.26×10^{7} D. 6.12×10^{7}

39. Find the solubility product of a saturated solution Ag_2CrO_4 in water at 298 K if the e.m.f. of the cell Ag/Ag^+ (satd. Ag_2CrO_4 soln.)||Ag^+ (0.1 M) Ag is 0.164 V at 298 K.
A. 3.14×10^{-10} B. 2.44×10^{-10}
C. 2.44×10^{-12} D. 3.14×10^{-12}

40. Given the following cell,
$Al|Al^{3+}$ (0.1M)||Fe^{2+} (0.2M)| Fe

$$E^0 \frac{Al^{3+}}{Al} = -1.66\text{ V}$$

$$E^0 \frac{Fe^{2+}}{Fe} = -0.44\text{ V}$$

Calculate the maximum work that can be obtained by the cell
A. 648 kJ B. 7.11 kJ
C. 795.6 kJ D. 705.801 kJ

41. Which one of the following statements is not applicable to electrolytic conductors?
A. No products show up at the elctrodes
B. Ions are responsible for carrying the current
C. Show a positive temperature coefficient for conductance
D. A single stream of electrons flows from cathode to anode

42. When electric current is passed through a cell having an electrolyte, the positive ions move towards the cathode and the negative ions towards the anode. If the cathode is pulled out of the solution.
A. The positive and negative ions will move towards the anode
B. The positive ions will start moving towards the anode, the negative ions will stop moving
C. The negative ions will continue to move towards the anode and the positive ions will stop moving
D. The positive and negative ions will start moving randomly.

43. Three Faradays of electricity are passed through molten Al_2O_3 aqueous solution of $CuSO_4$ and molten NaCl taken in different electrolytic cells. The amount of Al, Cu and Na deposited at the cathodes wil be in the ratio of
A. 1 : 2 : 3 moles B. 3 : 2 : 1 moles
C. 1 : 1.5 : 3 moles D. 1.5 : 2 : 3 moles

44. The electric charge for electrode deposition of one gram equivalent of a substance is
A. One ampere per second
B. 96500 coulombs per second
C. One ampere for one hour
D. Charge on one mole of electrons

45. An electric current is passed through an aqueous solution of the following, which one will decompose
A. Urea B. Glucose
C. Silver nitrate D. Ethyl alcohol

46. One the basis of position in the electrochemical series, the metal which does not displace hydrogen from water and acids is
A. Hg B. Al
C. Pb D. Ba

47. The standard reduction potential values of the three metallic cations, X, Y, Z are 0.52, – 3.03, and – 1.18 V respectively. The order of reducing power of the corresponding metal is
A. Y>Z>X B. X>Y>Z
C. Z>Y>X D. Z>X>Y

48. A gas X at 1 atm is bubbled through a solution containing a mixture of 1 MY^- and 1 MZ^- at 25°C. If the reduction potential of Z > Y > X, then,
A. Y will oxidize X and not Z
B. Y will oxidize Z and not X
C. Y will oxidize both X and Z
D. Y will reduce both X and Z

49. Of the following metals that cannot be obtained by electrolysis of the aqueous solution of their salts are
A. Ag and Mg B. Ag and Al
C. Mg and Al D. Cu and Cr

50. A solution containing one mole per litre of each $Cu(NO_3)_2$, $AgNO_3$, $Hg_2(NO_3)_2$, $Mg(NO_3)_2$ is being electrolysed by using inert electrodes. The values of standard electrode potentials in volts (reduction potentials) are

$$Ag|Ag^+ = +0.80, 2Hg|Hg_2^{2+} = -0.79$$

$$Cu|Cu^+ = +0.34, Mg|Mg^{2+} = -2.37$$

With increasing voltage, the sequence of deposition of metals on the cathode will be
A. Ag, Hg, Cu, Mg B. Mg, Cu, Hg, Ag
C. Ag, Hg, Cu D. Cu, Hg, Ag

51. The amount of an ion discharged during electrolysis is not dependent of
A. Resistance of solution
B. Time
C. Current strength
D. Electrochemical equivalent of the element

52. If an iron rod is dipped in $CuSO_4$ solution
A. Blue colour of the solution turns red
B. Brown layer is deposited on iron rod
C. No change occurs in the colour of the solution
D. None

53. When lead storage battery is discharged, then
A. SO_2 is evolved
B. Lead is formed
C. Lead sulphate is consumed
D. Sulphuric acid is consumed

54. Molten NaCl conducts electricity due to the presence of
A. Free electrons B. Free molecules
C. Free ions D. Atoms of Na and Cl

55. Faraday's law of electrolysis fails when
A. Temperature is increased
B. Inert electrodes are used
C. A mixture of electrolytes is used
D. In none of these cases

56. A depolariser used in dry cell batteries is
A. Ammonium chloride
B. Manganese dioxide
C. Potassium hydroxide
D. Sodium phosphate

57. In electrolysis of a fused salt, the weight deposited on an electrode will not depend on
A. Temperature of the bath
B. Current intensity
C. Electrochemical equivalent of ions
D. Time for electrolysis

58. The position of some metals in the electrochemical series in decreasing electropositive character is given below as Mg > Al > Zn > Cu > Ag. What will happen if a copper spoon is used to stir a solution of aluminium nitrate
A. The spoon will get coated with aluminium
B. An alloy of copper and aluminium is formed
C. The solution becomes blue
D. There is no reaction

59. When same electric current is passed through the solution of different electrolytes in series, the amounts of the element deposited on the electrode are in the ratio of their
A. At. no. B. At. wt.
C. Sp. gravity D. Eq. wt.

60. A standard hydrogen electrode has zero electrode potential because
A. Hydrogen is easiest to oxidise
B. This electrode potential is assumed to be zero
C. Hydrogen atom has only one electron
D. Hydrogen is the lightest element

61. In electrochemical corrosion of metals, the metal undergoing corrosion
A. Acts as anode B. Acts as cathode
C. Is reduced D. Either of these

62. Electrolytes when dissolved in water, dissociate into ions, because
A. They are unstable
B. The water dissolves them
C. The forces of repulsion increases
D. The forces of electrostatic attraction are broken down by water

63. If a strip of copper metal is placed in a solution of ferrous sulphate
A. Copper will precipitate out
B. Iron will precipitate out
C. Both copper and iron will be dissolved
D. No reaction will take place

64. If a salt bridge is removed from the two half cells, the voltage
A. Drops to zero B. Does not change
C. Increases gradually D. Increases rapidly

65. The calomel electrode is a
A. Standard hydrogen electrode
B. Reference electrode
C. Platinum electrode
D. Mercury electrode

66. The process in which chemical change accompanies the passage of current is called
A. Conduction

B. Metallic conduction
C. Electrolytic conduction
D. Non-electrolytic conduction

67. Which is correct about fuel cells:
A. Cells continuously run as long as fuels are supplied
B. These are more efficient and free from pollution
C. These are used to provide power and drinking water to astronauts in space programme
D. All of the above

68. Electroplating with chromium is undertaken because:
A. Electrolysis of chromium is easier
B. Chromium can form alloys with other metals
C. Chromium gives a protective and decorative coating to the base metal
D. Of high reactivity of chromium metal

69. The passage of electricity in the Daniell cell when Zn and Cu electrodes are connected is:
A. From Cu to Zn inside the cell
B. From Cu to Zn outside the cell
C. From Zn to Cu outside the cell
D. None of the above

70. More electropositive elements have
A. Positive reduction potential
B. Tendency to gain electrons
C. Negative reduction potential
D. Negative oxidation potential

71. A dilute solution of Li_2SO_4 is electrolysed. The products formed at the anode and cathode respectively are
A. S and Li B. O_2 and Li
C. SO_2 and O_2 D. O_2 and H_2

72. In which cell, electrical energy is converted into chemical energy
A. Water voltameter B. Silver voltameter
C. Coulometer D. Either of these

73. A metal having negative reduction potential when dipped in the solution of its own ions, has a tendency
A. To pass into the solution
B. To be deposited from the solution
C. To become electrically positive
D. To remain neutral

74. Lithium is generally used as an electrode in high energy density batteries. This is because
A. Lithium is the lightest element
B. Lithium has quite high negative reduction potential
C. Lithium is quite reactive
D. Lithium does not corrode easily

75. The electrode potential measures the
A. Tendency of the electrode of gain or lose electrons
B. Tendency of the cell reaction to occur
C. Difference in the ionisation potential of electrode and metal ion
D. Current carried by an electrode

76. The algebraic sum of potentials of two electrodes of a galvanic cell is called
A. Potential difference
B. Ionic difference
C. EMF
D. Electrode difference

77. The product (ampere × second) is equal to the number of
A. Coulombs transferred
B. Electrons transferred
C. Faraday transferred
D. Volt

78. An unit of charge is
A. Volt B. Ampere
C. Coulomb D. None

79. Metals can be prevented from rusting by
A. Connecting iron to more electropositive metal cathodic protection
B. Connecting iron to more electropositive metal anodic protection
C. Connecting iron to less electropositive metal anodic protection
D. Connecting iron to less electropositive metal cathodic protection

80. Stronger the oxidising agent, greater is the
A. Reduction potential
B. Oxidation potential
C. Ionic behaviour
D. None

81. When lead accumulator is charged, it is
A. An electrolytic cell B. A galvanic cell
C. A Daniell cell D. None of the above

82. Hydrogen gas will not reduce
A. Heated cupric oxide
B. Heated ferric oxide
C. Heated stannic oxide
D. Heated aluminium oxide

83. Which is not true for a standard hydrogen electrode
A. The hydrogen ion concentration is 1 M
B. Temperature is 25°C
C. Pressure of hydrogen is 1 atmosphere
D. It contains a metallic conductor which does not absorb hydrogen

84. The value of equilibrium constant for a feasible cell reaction is
A. < 1 B. Zero
C. = 1 D. > 1

85. The electrolytic bath used in gold plating of copper articles contains
A. Molten gold B. $CuSO_4$
C. $AuCl_3$ D. $AuCl_3 + NaCN$

86. Mobility of H^+ (in aq. medium) is high because
A. Of the small size of H^+
B. Of the high hydration energy of H^+
C. It exhibits a Grotthus type of conduction
D. Hydrogen is lightest element

87. A cell with two electrodes, one of grey tin and the other white tin, both dipping in solution of $(NH_4)_2SnCl_6$ showed zero e.m.f. at 18°C, what conclusion may be drawn from this.
A. The e.m.f. developed at the electrode-solution phase boundary cancels the normal e.m.f.
B. Grey tin being non-metallic ceases to provide a reversible electrode reaction
C. Electrode surface develops a protective layer and the cell develops a very large internal resistance
D. The free energy change of the cell becomes zero

88. When an aqueous solution of lithium chloride is electrolysed using graphite electrodes
A. pH of the resulting solution increases
B. pH of the resulting solution decreases
C. As the current flows, pH of solution around the cathode increases
D. None of these

89. The reaction $Cu^{2+}(aq) + 2Cl^-(aq) \rightarrow Cu(s) + Cl_2(g)$ has $E^0_{cell} = 1.03\ V$. This reaction
A. Can be made to produce electricity in voltaic cell
B. Can be made to occur in an electrolytic cell
C. Can occur in acidic medium only
D. Can occur in basic medium only

90. Electrolytic reduction of alumina to aluminium by Halt-Heroult process is carried out
A. In the presence of NaCl
B. In the presence of fluoride
C. In the presence of cryolite which forms a melt with lower melting temperature
D. In the presence of cryolite which forms a melt with higher melting temperature

91. 1 mole of Al is deposited by X coulomb of electricity passing through aluminium nitrate solution. The number of mole of silver deposited by X coulomb of electricity from silver nitrate solution is
A. 3 B. 4
C. 2 D. 1

92. The oxidation potential of a hydrogen electrode at pH = 10 and pH = 1.
A. 0.51 V B. 0.00 V
C. + 0.59 V D. 0.059 V

93. The number of Faraday required to generate 1 g atom of Mg from $MgCl_2$ is
A. 1 B. 2
C. 3 D. 4

94. Normal Al—$AlCl_3$ coupled with normal hydrogen electrode gives an e.m.f. of 1.66 V. The standard oxidation electrode potential of aluminium is
A. – 1.66 V B. + 1.66 V
C. – 0.83 V D. + 0.83 V

95. A certain current liberates 0.504 g of hydrogen in 2 hours. How many gram of copper can be liberated by the same current flowing for the same time in $CuSO_4$ solution.
A. 12.7 B. 16
C. 31.8 D. 63.5

96. The standard reduction potential for $Fe^{2+}|Fe$ and $Sn^{2+}|Sn$ electrode are – 0.44 V and – 0.14 V respectively. For the cell reaction,

$Fe^{2+} + Sn \rightarrow Fe + Sn^{2+}$. The standard e.m.f. is

A. +0.30 V B. −0.58 V
C. +0.58 V D. −0.30 V

97. An electrolytic cell contains a solution of Ag_2SO_4 and platinum electrodes. A current is passed until 1.6 g of O_2 has been liberated at anode. The amount of Ag deposited at cathode would be

A. 1.6 g B. 0.8 g
C. 21.6 g D. 107.88 g

98. The e.m.f. of the cell involving following changes
$Zn(s) + Ni^{2+}(1\ M) \rightarrow Zn^{2+}(1\ M) + Ni(s)$ is 0.5105 V. The standard e.m.f. of the cell is

A. 0.540 V B. 0.4810 V
C. 0.5696 V D. 0.5105 V

99. On passing electricity through dilute H_2SO_4 solution, the amount of substance liberated at the cathode and anode are in the ratio

A. 1 : 8 B. 8 : 1
C. 16 : 1 D. 1 : 16

100. Passage of 96500 coulomb of electricity liberates .... litre of O_2 at NTP during electrolysis

A. 5.6 B. 6.5
C. 22.4 D. 11.2

101. During electrolysis of an aqueous solution of Cu^{2+} sulphate, 0.635 g of copper was deposited at cathode. The amount of electricity consumed in coulomb is

A. 1930 B. 3860
C. 9650 D. 4825

102. 20 g of chlorine are evolved in 6 hours from sodium chloride solution by the current of

A. 5 ampere B. 2.5 ampere
C. 10 ampere D. 50 ampere

103. 13.5 g of Al get deposited when electricity is passed through the solution of $AlCl_3$. The number of Faradays used are

A. 0.50 B. 1.00
C. 1.50 D. 2.00

104. Number of Faraday needed to deposit 0.1 mole of copper from Cu(II) sulphate solution are

A. 0.1 B. 0.2
C. 0.05 D. 0.5

105. Total charge on 1 mole of a monovalent ion is equal to

A. 6.28×10^{18} coulomb
B. 1.6×10^{-19} coulomb
C. 9.65×10^{4} coulomb
D. None

106. The volume of oxygen in mL at STP liberated by 5 ampere current flowing for 193 second through acidulated water is

A. 56 B. 112
C. 224 D. 56

107. Maximum number of mole of oxygen gas that can be obtained by the electrolytic decomposition of 90 g of water will be

A. 1 B. 2.5
C. 5 D. 9

108. An electrochemical equivalent of silver is 0.0011180 g. When an electric current of 0.5 ampere is passed through an aqueous silver nitrate solution for 200 sec., the amount of silver deposited is

A. 1.1180 g B. 0.11180 g
C. 5.590 g D. 0.5590 g

109. During electrolysis of fused sodium chloride, the reaction of the electrodes are

	Anode	*Cathode*
A.	$Na^+ + e \rightarrow Na$	$Cl^- \rightarrow \frac{1}{2}Cl + e$
B.	$Na \rightarrow Na^+ + e$	$\frac{1}{2}Cl_2 + e \rightarrow Cl^-$
C.	$Cl^- \rightarrow \frac{1}{2}Cl_2 + e$	$Na^+ + e \rightarrow Na$
D.	$\frac{1}{2}Cl_2 + e \rightarrow Cl^-$	$Na \rightarrow Na^+ + e$

110. The standard reduction potentials of Cu^{2+}/Cu and Cu^{2+}/Cu^+ are 0.337 and 0.153 V respectively. The standard electrode potential of Cu^+/Cu half cell is

A. 0.184 V B. 0.827 V
C. 0.521 V D. 0.490 V

111. For the cell prepared from electrode A and B,
Electrode A : $Cr_2O_7^{2-}/Cr^{3+}$, $E^0_{red} = +1.33$ V
and Electrode B : Fe^{3+}/Fe^{2+}, $E^0_{red} = 0.77$ V.
Which of the following statements are correct

A. The electrons will flow from B to A when connection are made
B. The e.m.f. of the cell be 0.56 V

C. A will be positive electrode
D. All of these

112. A hydrogen electrode placed in a buffer solution of CH_3COONa and acetic acid in the ratio's $x : y$ and $y : x$ has electrode potential values E_1 volt and E_2 volt respectively at 25°C. The pKa values E_2 are oxidation potentials)

A. $\frac{E_1 + E_2}{0.118}$ B. $\frac{E_2 - E_1}{0.118}0$
C. $-\frac{E_1 - E}{0.118}$ D. $\frac{E_1 - E_2}{0.118}0$

113. The cell reaction for the given cell is

$Pt(H_2)|pH = 2|pH = 3|Pt(H_2)$
$P_1 = 1\,atm$ $P_2 = 1\,atm$

A. Spontaneous B. Non-spontaneous
C. In equilibrium D. Either of these

114. Passage of three Faraday of charge through aqueous solution of $AgNO_3$, $CuSO_4$, $Al(NO_3)_3$ and NaCl will deposit metals at the cathode in the molar ratio of

A. 1 : 2 : 3 : 1 B. 6 : 3 : 2 : 6
C. 6 : 3 : 0 : 0 D. 3 : 2 : 1 : 0

115. Which of the following groups of iodine compounds shows increasing order of oxidation number of iodine?

A. HIO_4, ICl, I_2, HI B. HI, I_2, ICl, HIO_4
C. I_2, HI, HIO_4, ICl D. ICl, HIO_4, HI, I_2

116. Which of the following is a metathesis reactions?

A. $Hg^{2+} + 2OH^- \rightarrow Hg_2O + H_2O$
B. $Hg_2^{2+} + Sn^{2+} \rightarrow 2Hg + Sn^{4+}$
C. $Hg_2^{2+} + H_2S \rightarrow Hg + HgS + 2H^+$
D. None of the above

117. Which of the following reaction is a redox reaction?

A. $PCl_3 + 3H_2O \rightarrow H_3PO_3 + 3HCl$
B. $Co^{3+} + 6NO_2^- \rightarrow Co(NO_2)_6^{3-}$
C. $HgCrO_4 + 2OH^- \rightarrow Hg_2O + CrO_4^{2-} + H_2O$
D. $Br_2 + OH^- \rightarrow Br^- + BrO_3^-$

118. Which of the following pairs of ions cannot coexist in aqueous solution?

A. Cr^{2+} and MnO_4^- B. Fe^{3+} and $Cr_2O_7^{2-}$
C. Cr^{2+} and I_3^- D. Mn^{2+} and Cl^-

119. Which of the following transition metals is strongest reducing agent?

A. Cr B. Mn
C. Ni D. Co

120. Which of the following solutions is strongest oxidising agent?

A. MnO_4^- in acid B. MnO_4^- in base
C. MnO_2 in base D. CrO_4^{2-} in base

121. Which of the following cannot be a reducing agent?

A. Cl^- B. CaH_2
C. Fe^{2+} D. Br_2

122. Which of the following species does not contain hydrogen in negative oxidation state?

A. $LiAlH_4$ B. CaH_2
C. NaH D. N_3H

123. Which of the following compounds have lowest negative oxidation number of oxygen?

A. H_2O_2 B. O_2F_2
C. KO_2 D. $1F_2$

124. The reaction occurring at cathode is

A. Oxidation B. Reduction
C. Hydrolysis D. None of these

125. Compound $(NH_3)_3CrO_4$ is pentagonal bipyramidal in structure involving two peroxo linkages. The oxidation number of chromium atom is

A. 0 B. +2
C. +4 D. +6

126. Which of the following compounds is a product of metathesis reaction between concentrated solution of H_2SO_4 and saturated solution of $K_2Cr_2O_7$ and is known as chromic acid?

A. CrO_3 B. Cr_2O_5
C. Cr_2O_3 D. CrO_2

127. Electrolytic oxidation of K_2MnO_4 leads to the formation of

A. $KMnO_4$ B. Mn_2O_7
C. MnO_4 D. None of these

128. How many moles of Hydrogen are present in 2 grams of Hydrogen

A. 1 mole B. 2 moles
C. 3 moles D. 4 moles

129. How many electrons are there in one mole of electron?

A. 1 B. 10^{23}
C. 6.02×10^{23} D. None of these

130. Number of grams present in one mole of Na_2CO_3 is

A. 106 g B. 40 g
C. 100 g D. 5 g

131. How many molecules are present in 1.0 mole of $KMnO_4$
A. 3.613×10^{23} molecules of $KMnO_4$
B. 6.02×10^{23} molecules of $KMnO_4$
C. 5.418×10^{23} molecules of $KMnO_4$
D. None of these

132. The oxidation number of chromium is + 6 in
A. $FeCr_2O_4$ B. $KCrO_3Cl$
C. $[Cr(OH)_4]^-$ D. None of these

133. In which of the following molecules, bromine shows the maximum oxidation number?
A. $Hg_2(BrO_3)_2$ B. $KBrO_4$
C. Br—Cl D. Br_2

134. A compound contains atoms A, B and C, the oxidation number of A = + 2, B = + 5, C = – 2. The possible formula of the compound is
A. ABC_2 B. $A_2(BC_3)_2$
C. $A_3(BC_4)_2$ D. $A_3(B_4C)_2$

135. The oxidation number of nitrogen varies from
A. – 3 to + 5 B. – 1 to + 1
C. – 3 to – 5 D. – 5 to + 1

136. Phosphorous shows an oxidation number of + 3 in
A. Orthophosphoric acid
B. Orthophosphorous acid
C. Metaphosphoric acid
D. Pyrophosphoric acid

137. A metal ion M^{3+} loses three electrons to produce another cation. The oxidation number of the metal in the cation is
A. +3 B. +4
C. – 3 D. +6

138. A sample of 2.5 mol of hydrazine (N_2H_4) loses 24 mol of electrons on being converted to a new compound X. Assuming that there is no loss of nitrogen in the formation of the new compound, what is the oxidation number of nitrogen in compound X?
A. – 1 B. – 2
C. +3 D. +4

139. In which of the following has the oxidation number of oxygen been arranged in increasing order?
A. $BaO_2 < KO_2 < O_3 < F_2O$
B. $F_2O < KO_2 < BaO_2 < O_3$
C. $BaO_2 < O_3 < F_2O < KO_2$
D. $KO_2 < F_2O < O_3 < BaO_2$

140. In the reaction $3Br_2 + 6CO_3^{2-} + 3H_2O \rightarrow 5Br^- + BrO_3^- + 6HCO_3^-$
A. Bromine is oxidized and the carbonate radical is reduced
B. Bromine is reduced and the carbonate radical is oxidized
C. Bromine is neither reduced nor oxidized
D. Bromine is both reduced and oxidized

141. Which of the following shows agents arranged in order of increasing reducing power?
A. Zn < Al < Mg < Na
B. Al < Mg < Zn < Na
C. Na < Mg < Al < Zn
D. Mg < Na < Zn < Al

142. In the reaction $2Ag + 2H_2SO_4 \rightarrow Ag_2SO_4 + 2H_2O + SO_2$, sulphuric acid acts as
A. An oxidizing agent
B. A reducing agent
C. A catalyst
D. An acid as well as an oxidant

143. The equivalent weight of $KMnO_4$ in an acidic, a slightly alkaline or a neutral medium on the one hand, and an alkaline medium on the other, are respectively (M = molecular weight)
A. M/5, M/2, M B. M/5, M/3, M/2
C. M/5, M/3, M D. M/3, M, M/5

144. The equivalent weight of $Na_2S_2O_3$ in the reaction
$2Na_2S_2O_3 + I_2 \rightarrow Na_2S_4O_6 + 2NaI$ is
A. M B. M/8
C. M/0.5 D. M/2

145. What will be the value of equivalent weight of $KBrO_3$ in the following ionic equation?
$2BrO_3^- + 12H^+ + 10e^- \rightarrow Br_2 + 6H_2O$
A. M/4 B. M/6
C. M/10 D. M/5

146. In the following redox reaction
$xMnO + yPbO_2 + zHNO_3 \rightarrow KMnO_4 + Pb(NO_3)_2 + H_2O$
A. $x = 2, y = 5, z = 10$

B. $x=2, y=7, z=8$
C. $x=2, y=5, z=8$
D. $x=2, y=5, z=5$

147. In the ionic reaction

$xBrO_3^- + yCr^{3+} + zH_2O \rightarrow Br_2 + HCrO_4^- + H^+$

A. $x=6, y=10, z=20$
B. $x=6, y=10, z=22$
C. $x=6, y=10, z=1$
D. $x=5, y=8, z=22$

148. The conversion of sugar $C_{12}H_{22}O_{11} \rightarrow CO_2$ is

A. Oxidation B. Reduction
C. Conversion D. None

149. White phosphorus reacts with caustic soda, the products are PH_3 and NaH_2PO_2. This reaction is an example of

A. Oxidation
B. Reduction
C. Oxidation and Reduction
D. Neutralization

150. The compound which could act both as oxidising as well as reducing agent is

A. SO_2 B. MnO_2
C. Al_2O_3 D. CrO_3

ANSWERS

1	2	3	4	5	6	7	8	9	10
B	C	D	D	C	D	B	A	D	E
11	12	13	14	15	16	17	18	19	20
E	E	C	B	B	C	B	C	B	A
21	22	23	24	25	26	27	28	29	30
C	B	B	C	A	C	B	C	D	B
31	32	33	34	35	36	37	38	39	40
C	C	B	B	B	C	B	C	C	D
41	42	43	44	45	46	47	48	49	50
D	D	C	D	C	A	A	A	C	C
51	52	53	54	55	56	57	58	59	60
A	B	D	C	D	B	A	D	D	B
61	62	63	64	65	66	67	68	69	70
B	D	D	A	B	C	D	C	B	C
71	72	73	74	75	76	77	78	79	80
D	D	A	B	A	C	A	C	A	A
81	82	83	84	85	86	87	88	89	90
A	D	D	D	D	C	D	A	B	C
91	92	93	94	95	96	97	98	99	100
A	C	B	B	B	D	C	D	A	A
101	102	103	104	105	106	107	108	109	110
A	C	C	B	C	A	B	B	C	C
111	112	113	114	115	116	117	118	119	120
D	A	B	C	B	A	D	A	B	A
121	122	123	124	125	126	127	128	129	130
C	D	C	B	C	A	A	A	C	A
131	132	133	134	135	136	137	138	139	140
B	B	C	C	A	B	D	C	A	D
141	142	143	144	145	146	147	148	149	150
A	D	C	A	D	A	B	A	C	A

8

SOLUTIONS

SOLUTION

Solution is a homogeneous mixture of two or more pure substances, whose composition may vary *within certain limits*. In the preparation of a solution, two phases are mixed, *dispersed phase medium* (the phase which is present in relatively smaller amount) and *dispersion medium* (the phase which is present in larger amount). The dispersed phase or the substance which is to be dissolved is called *solute*, while the medium in which the solute is dispersed to get a homogeneous solution is called the *solvent*.

Solute + Solvent = Solution

Substances may be solids, liquids or gases. We are concerned primarily, with solutions prepared from (solid-liquid) and (liquid-liquid) combinations.

The solid substances may be an electrolyte, e.g., NaCl, $BaCl_2$, $Al_2(SO_4)_3$, etc. or a non-electrolytic, e.g., urea, glucose, sucrose, maltose etc.

The liquid substance often used is water but organic liquids are also taken for preparation of solutions for instance, ethanol, benzene, toluene, methanol, chloroform, carbon tetrachloride, *n*-hexane, *n*-heptane etc.

A solution in which relatively a small amount of the solute is present is called a *dilute solution* while a solution in which relatively a large amount of the solute is present is called a *concentrated solution*.

A solution which contains the maximum amount of the solute that can be dissolved in a given amount of the solvent at a particular temperature is called a *saturated solution*.

Binary Solution

A solution may be regarded as a single phase containing more than one components. A *Binary Solution* is composed of two components—the *solute* and *solvent*.

Similarly solutions may be known as Ternary and Quaternary if it is made up of three or four component respectively.

Classification of Solutions

Based upon the physical state of the solvent and solute, solutions are classified into the following types:

(i) **Gaseous Solutions :** Solvent is gas, e.g., Air is gaseous mixture, aerosol is an example of liquid in gas.

(ii) **Liquid Solutions :** Solvent is liquid, e.g., aerated water is an example of gas in liquid, benzene in toluene is an example of liquid in liquid and salt in water etc.

(iii) **Solid Substances :** Solvent is solid. e.g., Hydrogen in palladium is an example of gas in solid and other examples are metal amalgams and alloys.

Types of Solutions

Solvent	*Solute*	*Example*
Gas	Solid	Smoke
Gas	Liquid	Misk
Gas	Gas	Air
Solid	Solid	Alloys
Solid	Liquid	Hg in Zn
Solid	Gas	H_2 in Pd
Liquid	Liquid	Alcohol in water
Liquid	Gas	Aerated drinks
Liquid	Solid	Sugar in water

Solubility

Solubility of a substance may be defined as the amount of a solute dissolved in 100 gm of a solvent to form a saturated solution at a given temperature.

Deciding Factors For Solubility : The solubility of a solute (solid) in a solvent (liquid) depends mostly upon three factors:

(i) Lattice-energy

(ii) Hydration-energy

(iii) Temperature

(i) Lattice-Energy : It is the amount of energy required to separate a mole of crystal into ions. This is an Endothermic Process.

(ii) Hydration Energy : It is the amount of energy liberated when these separated ions get hydrated. This is an Exothermic Process.

Important : *(a)* If lattice energy > hydration energy, the system cools down (insoluble)

(b) If lattice energy < hydration energy, the system heats up (soluble)

(iii) Temperature : Temperature always increases the randomness or disorder of the system. Hence, the solubility increases with increase in the temperature in most of the cases. According to Le-Chatelier's Principle, solubility of a solute in a solvent decreases or increases with the rise in temperature as to whether the dissolution is exothermic or endothermic. Thus

(a) If a substance dissolves with the evolution of heat, the solubility decreases with rise in temperature.

Example : Anhydrous sodium sulphate, CaO, Li_2CO_3, $CaSO_4$, $(CH_3COO)_2Ca$ etc. (Exothermic or heating)

(b) If a substance dissolves with absorption of heat, the solubility increases with rise in temperature.

Example : NH_4Cl, $NaNO_3$, KNO_3, etc. (Endothermic or cooling).

Colligative-Properties

The physical properties of solutions which depend only on the concentration of dissolved particles, ions or molecules, and not on their nature, kind or size, are called "Colligative-Properties". These properties are:

(i) Lowering of Vapour Pressure

(ii) Elevation of Boiling Point

(iii) Depression of Freezing Point

(iv) Osmotic Pressure

Lowering of Vapour-Pressure : Every liquid possesses inherent tendency to escape from its surface. This process is called *evaporation* or *vaporization.*

Vapour pressure is defined as the pressure exerted by the vapour in equilibrium with its liquid at a given temperature.

Why vapour pressure arises? According to the kinetic molecular theory of distribution of energies, some molecules at the surface of the liquid possess kinetic energy greater than the kinetic energy of molecules in the body of the liquid.

Such molecules of surface evaporate to the space above the liquid.

If a liquid is kept in a closed vessel with space above it, the accumulation of vapour builds up pressure on the liquid.

Some vapour-molecules may strike the liquid surface and may get trapped, that is, vapour condenses to liquid.

As evaporation proceeds, the number of molecules in the vapour state increases and the rate of condensation also steadily increases.

A state is reached, when the rate of condensation becomes equal to the rate of evaporation.

We can say, that the liquid and vapour are in *dynamic-equilibrium* and the liquid surface is saturated with its vapour. Thus the pressure exerted by vapour at the equilibrium state is called Vapour-Pressure. The rate of evaporation depends on :

(a) Surface area

(b) Temperature

(c) Pressure above its surface

(d) Intermolecular attraction of liquid molecules

Raoult's Law of Lowering of Vapour-Pressure: The partial pressure of any volatile constituent of a solution at a constant temperature is equal to the vapour pressure of a pure component multiplied by the mole fraction of that constituent in the solution.

Therefore,

$$P_A = \frac{n_A}{n_A + n_B} \times P_A^\circ = X_A . P_A^\circ$$

$$P_B = \frac{n_B}{n_A + n_B} \times P_B^\circ = X_B . P_B^\circ$$

P_A and P_B are partial pressures of two constituents A and B and X_A and X_B are their mole fractions. P_A° and P_B° are vapour-pressures of two pure constituents.

When the solution is prepared by mixing the nonvolatile solute B, and the solvent A :

$$X_A + X_B = 1 \Rightarrow X_B = 1 - X_A$$

X_B = Mole fraction of solute

$$\text{Again,} \quad \frac{P_A}{P_A^\circ} = X_A \text{ or } 1 - \frac{P_A}{P_A^\circ} = 1 - X_A = X_B$$

$$\text{or} \quad \frac{P_A^\circ - P_A}{P_A^\circ} = X_B = \frac{\Delta P}{P_A^\circ}$$

Thus, the relative lowering of vapour pressure of a pure solvent containing a non-volatile solute is equal to the mole fraction of the solute.

Raoult's law may also be stated as : The relative lowering of vapour-pressure of a solvent by dissolving a non-volatile/non-electrolyte (solute) is mole fraction of the solute.

$$\text{Thus,} \quad \frac{\Delta P}{P_A^\circ} = \frac{\text{No. of moles of solute}}{\text{Total moles of solute and solvent}}$$

$$\text{Thus,} \quad \frac{\Delta P}{P_A^\circ} = \frac{P_A^\circ - P_A}{P_A^\circ} = X_B = \frac{n}{n+N}$$

where n and N are the number of moles of solute and solvent respectively,

In a dilute solution, $N >> n$

Hence, $X_B = \frac{n}{N} = \frac{w/m}{W/M}$, where w and W are the weights of solute and solvent and m and M are their molecular weights respectively.

$$\therefore \quad \boxed{\frac{P_A^\circ - P_A}{P_A^\circ} = \frac{\Delta P}{P_A^\circ} = \frac{wM}{Wm}}$$

Raoult's law for solution of two volatile liquids.

Ideal Solution : A solution is called ideal when it follows Raoult's law accurately.

In practice, most of the solutions obey Raoult's law to a good approximation.

Characteristics of an Ideal Solution :

(a) If the solute is solid, non-volatile and non-electrolyte, the solution behaves as an ideal solution.

(b) The amount of solute should be very small that is, the solution should be dilute, and the solute should not associate or dissociate in solution.

(c) $\Delta H_{mixing} = 0$, i.e. there must not be evolution or absorption of heat, when a solution is prepared.

(d) $\Delta V_{mixing} = 0$, i.e., there must not be increase or decrease in volume.

(e) Since, $P_{soln.} = P_{solv.} \times X_{solv.}$ is valid for an ideal solution, a plot of $P_{soln.}$ Vs $X_{solv.}$ gives a straight line passing through the origin.

(f) For two miscible volatile solvents A and B, the intermolecular attraction between A and A molecules, between B and B molecules, and between A and B molecules must be the same.

Raoult's law then may hold for all mole fractions.

Van't Hoff's Factor (*i*)

For strong electrolytes, the dissociation of the solute into ions is essentially complete.

For example, NaCl, $MgCl_2$, Na_3PO_4, and $Al_2(SO_4)_3$ in aqueous solution produce two, three, four and five moles of ions permole of substance respectively. Van't Hoff observed that the osmotic pressure of 1M NaCl solution is two times and of 1M K_2SO_4 solution is three times of the osmotic pressure 1M glucose solution, although molar concentration of all these solutions is the same.

The colligative properties of electrolyte solutions are higher than those for non-electrolyte solutions, though their concentration is equal.

To describe this observation, Van't Hoff introduced the factor (*i*), called Van't Hoff's factor as :

$$i = \frac{\text{Observed colligative property value}}{\text{Expected value for a non-electrolyte}}$$

Important :

For all non-electrolytes, such as urea, glycerol, sucrose, glucose, $i = 1$ and for all electrolytes $i > 1$.

From the value of Van't Hoff's factor (*i*), it is possible to modify the equation for colligative property as :

Elevation of boiling point $(\Delta T_b) = i\,K_b\,m'$

Depression of freezing point $(\Delta T_f) = i\,K_f\,m'$

Osmotic pressure $(\pi) = \frac{inST}{V}$

OBJECTIVE QUESTIONS

1. The molal B.P. constant for water is 0.513°C kg/mol. When 0.1 mol of sugar is dissolved in 200 gm of water, the solution boils under a pressure of 1 atm, at
   A. 100.573°C B. 100.0513°C
   C. 100.2565°C D. 101.025°C
2. Elevation of B.P. was found to be 0.52°C when 6 gm of a compound, X was dissolved in 100 gm of water. Molecular weight of X will be (Given K_b for water per 100 gm is 5.2°C)
   A. 120 B. 60
   C. 600 D. 180
3. If the vapour pressure of water at 20°C is 17 mm, the V.P. of a solution containing 5 gm of urea in 90 gm of water will be
   A. 0.283 mm B. 16.717 mm
   C. 8.358 mm D. None of these
4. The vapour pressure of CCl_4 at 30°C is 143 mm of Hg. If 0.5 gm of a non-volatile solute of mol. wt. 65 is dissolved in 100 ml of CCl_4. The V.P. of the solution will be (Given density of CCl_4 = 1.58 gm/cm^3)
   A. 143.43 mm B. 141.93
   C. 70.86 mm D. None of these
5. Vapour-pressure of a solution of 5 gm of non-electrolyte in 100 gm of water at a particular temperature is 2985 N/m^2. The mol. wt. of solute will be
   A. 60 B. 120
   C. 180 D. 380
6. The no. of moles of water present in 180 gm of water is
   A. 1 B. 18
   C. 10 D. 100
7. The F.P. of a 0.05 molal aqueous solution of a non-electrolyte is
   A. – 1.86°C B. – 0.93°C
   C. – 0.093°C D. + 0.093°C
8. The percentage of oxygen in NaOH is
   A. 40 B. 16
   C. 8 D. 1
9. A solution of 1.25 gm of a non-electrolyte in 20 gm of water freezes at 271.94 K. If K_f is 1.86 k/mol, then the molecular wt. of solute will be
   A. 207.8 gm/mol B. 179.79 gm/mol
   C. 209.6 gm/mol D. 109.66 gm/mol
10. A 0.6% urea solution (mol. wt. 60) would be isotonic with
    A. 0.1 M glucose solution
    B. 0.1 M KCl solution
    C. 0.6% glucose solution
    D. 0.6% KCl solution
11. The molal elevation constant for water is 0.52. The elvation caused in the boiling point of water by dissolving 0.25 mole of a non-electrolyte in 250 gm of water will be
    A. 0.52°C B. 5.2°C
    C. 0.052°C D. None of these
12. The freezing point of benzene is 5.4°C and that of solution containing 2.0 gm of a non-electrolyte per 100 gm of benzene in 4.4°C. The molecular weight of solute will be—(given K_f for benzene = 5)
    A. 30 B. 60
    C. 90 D. 100
13. The osmotic pressure of a 6% urea solution in water at 27°C would be
    A. 12.4 atm B. 30 atm
    C. 24.6 atm D. 10 atm
14. What will be concentration of a glucose ($C_6H_{12}O_6$) solution, if it is isotonic with a solution of urea containing 6 gm per litre?
    A. 18 gm./lit. B. 9 gm./lit.
    C. 3 gm./lit. D. 1 gm./lit.
15. A 0.1 M NaCl solution is found to be isotonic with 1.10% of urea solution at 27°C. The degree of dissociation of NaCl for this solution will be—
    A. 60% B. 70%
    C. 80.4% D. 83.3%
16. When a solute is added to a pure solvent, the
    A. V.P. of the solution becomes lower than the V.P. of the pure solvent.

B. Rate of evaporation of pure solvent is reduced
C. Solute does not affect the rate of condensation.
D. Rate of evaporation of the solution is equal to the rate of condensation of the solution at a lower vapour pressure than for the pure solvent.
E. All of the above

17. According to Raoult's law, the relative decrease in the solvent V.P. over the solution is equal to
A. The mole fraction of the solvent
B. The mole fraction of the solute
C. *i* times the mole fraction of the solute which undergoes dissociation or association in the solvent (*i* = Van't Hoff factor)
D. B and C only

18. The pressure of the water vapour of a solution containing a non-volatile solute is 2% below that of the vapour of pure water. The molality of the solution is
A. 1.134 B. 0.1134
C. 1.051 D. 0.0975

19. Which of the following combinations are correct for a binary solution, in which the solute as well as the solvent are liquid.
A. C_6H_6 and $C_6H_5CH_3$ $\Delta H_{soln.} > 0; \Delta V_{soln.} = 0$
B. CH_3COCH_3 and $CHCl_3$ $\Delta H_{soln.} < 0; \Delta V_{soln.} < 0$
C. H_2O and C_2H_5OH $\Delta H_{soln.} > 0; \Delta V_{soln.} > 0$
D. B and C only

20. The following is a graph plotted between the V.P. of two volatile liquids against their respective mole fraction.

Which of the following combinations are correct?
A. $X_A = 1, X_B = 0$, then $p = p°A$
B. $X_B = 1, X_A = 0$, then $p = p°B$
C. $X_B = 1, X_A = 0$, then $p > p°A$
D. A and B

21. Which of the following statements are correct for a binary solution which shows negative deviation from Raoult's law?
A. The negative deviation from linearity diminishes and tends to zero as the concentration of the solution component approaches unit
B. When solution form, their volumes are smaller than the sum of the volumes of their components.
C. Heat is released during the formation of the solution
D. All of the above

22. A binary liquid (AB) shows positive deviation from Raoult's law when
A. $p_A > p_A^\circ .X_A$ e.q. and $p_A > p_B^\circ .X_B$ liq.
B. Intermolecular forces A – A, B – B > A – B
C. $\Delta V_{mix.} > 0$ and $\Delta H_{mix.} > 0$
D. All of the above

23. A graph is plotted between the V.P. and mole fraction of a solution containing benzene and toluene. Choose the correct options.

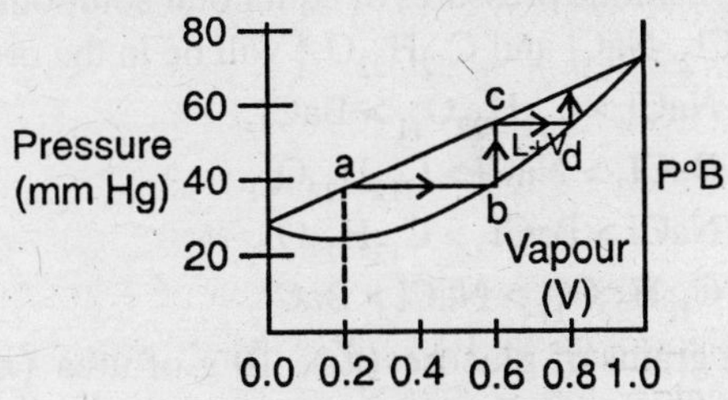

A. At the point *a*, the mole fraction of toluene is 0.80
B. $b \to c$ represents condensation
C. $c \to d$ represents vaporization
D. All of the above

24. The azeotropic solutions of two miscible liquids
A. Can be separated by simple distillation
B. May show positive or negative deviation from Raoult's law
C. Are supersaturated solutions
D. Behave like a simple component and boil at a constant temperature.
E. B and D

25. A deliquescent substance has the vapour pressure.
   A. Equal to the atmospheric pressure
   B. Equal to that of the water vapour in air
   C. Greater than that of the water vapour in air
   D. Less than that of the water vapour in air
26. A substance efflorescences
   A. Due to the formation of a crust on its crystal surface
   B. When the vapour pressure of the substance is greater than that of the water vapour in air.
   C. Till it melts
   D. When all of the above happen
   E. A and B
27. Which of the following aqueous solutions have the highest boiling point?
   A. 0.1 M KNO_3 B. 0.1 M Na_3PO_4
   C. 0.1 M $BaCl_2$ D. 0.1 M K_2SO_4
28. Among the following, the solution which shows the highest osmotic pressure is
   A. 0.05 M NaCl B. 0.10 M $BaCl_2$
   C. 0.05 M $FeCl_2$ D. 0.05 M Na_2SO_4
29. The osmotic pressures of equimolar solutions of $BaCl_2$, NaCl and $C_{12}H_{22}O_{11}$ will be in the order
   A. NaCl > $C_{12}H_{22}O_{11}$ > $BaCl_2$
   B. $BaCl_2$ > NaCl > $C_{12}H_{22}O_{11}$
   C. NaCl > $BaCl_2$ > $C_{12}H_{22}O_{11}$
   D. $C_{12}H_{22}O_{11}$ > NaCl > $BaCl_2$
30. Ten grams of glucose (π_1), 10 g of urea (π_2) and 10 g of sucrose (π_3) are dissolved in 250 ml of water at 300 K. (π = Osmotic pressure of solution). The relationship between the osmotic pressures of the solutions is
   A. $\pi_1 > \pi_2 > \pi_3$ B. $\pi_3 > \pi_2 > \pi_1$
   C. $\pi_2 > \pi_1 > \pi_3$ D. $\pi_2 > \pi_3 > \pi_1$
31. When mercuric iodide is added to an aqueous solution of KI, the
   A. Freezing point is raised
   B. Freezing point is lowered
   C. Boiling point does not change
   D. Freezing point does not change
32. Which of the following pairs of solutions can be expected to be isotonic at the same temperature?
   A. 0.1 M urea and 0.1 M NaCl
   B. 0.1 M urea and 0.2 M $MgCl_2$
   C. 0.1 M NaCl and 0.1 M Na_2SO_4
   D. 0.1 M $Ca(NO_3)_2$ and 0.1 M Na_2SO_4
33. If a solute undergoes dimerization and trimerization, the minimum values of the Van't Hoff factors are
   A. 0.50 and 1.50 B. 1.50 and 1.33
   C. 0.50 and 0.33 D. 0.25 and 0.67
34. In which of the following pairs of solutions will the values of the Van't Hoff factor be the same?
   A. 0.05 M $K_4[Fe(CN)_6]$ and 0.10 M $FeSO_4$
   B. 0.10 M $K_4[Fe(CN)_6]$ and 0.05 M $FeSO_4(NH_4)_2SO_4.6H_2O$
   C. 0.20 M NaCl and 0.10 M $BaCl_2$
   D. 0.05 M $FeSO_4(NH_4)_2SO_4.6H_2O$ and 0.02 M $KCl.MgCl_2.6H_2O$
   E. B and D
35. A solution containing 0.8716 mol L^{-1} of sucrose at 298 K is iso-osmotic with a solution of sodium chloride containing 0.5 mol L^{-1} NaCl. The degree of dissociation of NaCl is
   A. 0.743 B. 0.894
   C. 0.876 D. 0.943
36. Calculate the ebullioscopic constant for water. The heat of vaporization $\Delta H_{vap.}$ is 40.685 kJ mol^{-1}.
   A. 0.512 K kg mol^{-1} B. 1.86 K kg mol^{-1}
   C. 5.12 K kg mol^{-1} D. 3.56 K kg mol^{-1}
37. Calculate the molecular weight of a substance if the freezing point of a solution containing 100 g of benzene and 0.2 g of the substance is 0.17 K below that of benzene. The cryoscopic constant of benzene is 5.16 K kg mol^{-1}.
   A. 70.46 B. 85.66
   C. 60.23 D. 178.25
38. An aqueous solution of NaCl freezes at −0.186°C. Given that $K_b^{H_2O} = 0.512$ K kg mol^{-1} and $K_f^{H_2O} = 1.86$ K kg mol^{-1}. The elevation in boiling point of this solution is
   A. 0.0585 K B. 0.0512 K
   C. 1.864 K D. 0.0265 K
39. The decrease in the freezing point of an aqueous solution of a substance is 1.395 K and that is the

freezing point of a benzene solution of the same substance is 1.280 K. Explain the difference in ΔT. The substance

A. Dissociates in the aqueous solution as well as in the benzene solution
B. Forms complexes in solution
C. Associates in the benzene solution
D. Dissociates in the aqueous solution and not in the benzene solution

40. Determine the molarity of the solution containing 6 millimoles of solute in 60 ml of solution

A. 0.1 B. 0.6
C. 1.0 D. 6.0

41. How many millimoles of solute is present in 250 ml of 0.4 M HCl solution?

A. 100 B. 200
C. 300 D. 400

42. Find the molarity of the solution obtained by mixing 200 ml of water with 300 ml of 0.5 M NaOH.

A. 0.1 M B. 0.2 M
C. 0.3 M D. 0.4 M

43. What volume of water should be added to 300 ml of 0.5 M NaOH solution so as to get a solution of 0.2 M?

A. 700 ml B. 450 ml
C. 350 ml D. 300 ml

44. How many millititres of 0.5 M H_2SO_4 are needed to dissolve 0.5 g of copper (II) carbonate?

A. 7.09 ml B. 8.09 ml
C. 9.09 ml D. 8.86 ml

45. 300 ml of 0.1 M HCl and 200 ml of 0.3 M H_2SO_4 are mixed. Calculate the normality of the resulting mixture.

A. 0.2 N B. 0.3 N
C. 4.0 N D. 3.0 N

46. Calculate the molality of a solution of conc. HCl containing 36.5% by weight of HCl.

A. 1.575% B. 15.75%
C. 157.5% D. 100%

47. 100 ml of 0.2 N KOH solution is mixed with 100 ml of 0.1 M H_2SO_4 solution. What is the normality of the resulting solution.

A. IN B. 2 N
C. 3 N D. 0 N

48. The density of a 3 M sodium thiosulphate solutions is 1.25 g ml^{-1}. Calculate the

(i) % by weight of sodium thiosulphate
(ii) The mole fraction of sodium thiosulphate
(iii) The molalities of Na^+ and $S_2O_3^{-2}$ ions

A. *(i)* 29.28 g *(ii)* 0.65 *(iii)* 7.73 and 1.86
B. *(i)* 37.92 g *(ii)* 0.065 *(iii)* 7.730 and 3.865
C. *(i)* 37.92 g *(ii)* 1.26 *(iii)* 3.30 and 7.70
D. None of the above

49. 8.0575×10^{-2} kg of Glauber's salt is dissolved in water to obtain 1 dm^3 of a solution of density 1077.2 kg m^{-3}. Calculate the molarity, molality and mole fraction of Na_2SO_4 in the solution.

A. 0.25 mol dm^{-3}, 0.24 mol kg^{-1}, 0.0043 respectively
B. 1.0 mol dm^{-3}, 0.26 mol kg^{-1}, 1.14 respectively
C. 3.5 mol dm^{-3}, 24 mol kg^{-1}, 0.0043 respectively
D. None of the above

50. Calculate the normality of a solution containing 0.5 gm of NaOH dissolved in 500 ml solution.

A. 1.25 N B. 0.25 N
C. 0.025 N D. 0.0025 N

51. Calculate the molality of 1 litre solution of 93% H_2SO_4 (weight/volume). The density of the solution is 1.84 g/ml.

A. 1.043 M B. 10.43 M
C. 100.43 M D. 104.3 M

52. A 6.90 M solution of KOH in water contains 30% by weight of KOH. Calculate the density of the solution.

A. 1.118 g ml^{-1} B. 1.288 g ml^{-1}
C. 12.88 g ml^{-1} D. 128.8 g ml^{-1}

53. Upon heating a litre of a $\frac{N}{2}$ HCl solution, 2.675 g hydrogen chloride is lost and the volume of the solution strikes to 750 ml. Calculate *(i)* the normality of the resultant solution, and *(ii)* the number of milliequivalents of HCl in 100 ml of the original solution

A. *(i)* 0.57 N *(ii)* 70 B. *(i)* 0.57 N *(ii)* 80
C. *(i)* 0.35 N *(ii)* 50 D. *(i)* 0.57 N *(ii)* 50

54. The vapour-pressure of pure benzene at a certain temperature is 640 mm Hg. A non-volatile solid weighing 2.175 g is added to 39.0 g of benzene. The V.P. of the solution is 600 mm Hg. What is the molecular weight of the solid substance?

A. 6.525 B. 65.25
C. 650.25 D. 16.525

55. The vapour pressure of water at 20°C is 17.24 mm. When 20 g of a non-ionic substance is dissolved in 100 g of water, the vapour pressure is lowered by 0.30 mm. What is the molecular weight of the substance?

A. 100.8 B. 206.88
C. 216.08 D. 229.13

56. The vapour pressure of pure benzene at 25°C is 639.7 mm of mercury and the vapour pressure of a solution of a solute in benzene at the same temperature is 631.9 mm of mercury. Calculate the molality of the solution.

A. 1.56 mole/kg B. 0.156 mole/kg
C. 0.196 mole/kg D. 1.515 mole/kg

57. What mass of the non-volatile solute, urea (NH_2.CO.NH_2) needs to be dissolved in 100 g of water in order to decrease the vapour-pressure of water by 25%. What will be the molality of the solution?

A. 110 m B. 180 m
C. 18.52 m D. 1.81 m

58. The degree of dissociation of calcium nitrate in dilute aqueous solution containing 7.0 gm of the salt per 100 gm of water at 100°C is 70%. If the vapour pressure of water at 100°C is 760 mm, calculate the vapour pressure of the solution.

A. 123.3 mm of Hg B. 764.3 mm of Hg
C. 98.1 mm of Hg D. 214.2 mm of Hg

59. The vapour-pressure of a dilute aqueous solution of glucose ($C_6H_{12}O_6$) is 750 mm of Hg at 373 K. Calculate *(i)* molality and *(ii)* mole fraction of the solution.

A. *(i)* 0.132 M *(ii)* 7.503 mol kg^{-1}
B. *(i)* 0.0132 M *(ii)* 0.9686 mol kg^{-1}
C. *(i)* 0.0132 M *(ii)* 0.7503 mol kg^{-1}
D. *(i)* 1.132 M *(ii)* 1.17 mol kg^{-1}

60. The vapour pressure of ethanol and methanol are 44.5 and 88.7 mm Hg respectively. An ideal solution is formed at the same temperature by mixing 60 g of ethanol with 40 g of methanol. Calculate the total vapour-pressure of the solution and the mole fraction of methanol in the vapour.

A. 66.17 mm and 0.65 respectively
B. 6.67 mm and 1.65 respectively
C. 1.67 mm and 0.65 respectively
D. None of the above

61. Two liquids A and B form ideal solutions. At 300 K, the vapour pressure of a solution containing 1 mole of A and 3 moles of B is 550 mm of Hg. At the same temperature, if one more mole of B is added to this solution, the vapour-pressure of the solution increases by 10 mm of Hg. Determine the vapour pressure A and B in their pure states.

A. 400 and 500 mm of Hg for A and B respectively
B. 400 and 600 mm of Hg for A and B respectively
C. 400 and 800 mm of Hg for A and B respectively
D. 400 and 1000 mm of Hg for A and B respectively

62. The vapour density (Hydrogen = 1) of a mixture consisting of NO_2 and N_2O_4 is 38.3 at 2.67°C. Calculate the number of moles of NO_2 in 100 gm of the mixture

A. 83 mole B. 0.83 mole
C. 43 mole D. 0.43 mole

63. The boiling point of a solution of 0.1050 gm of a substance is 15.84 gm of ether was found to be 0.100°C higher than that of ether. What is the molecular weight of the substance? (Molal elevation constant of ether per 100 gm = 2.16)

A. 142.18 B. 143.18
C. 144.18 D. 145.18

64. In a cold climate, water gets frozen causing damage to the radiator of a car. Ethylene glycol is used as an antifreezing agent-calculate the amount of ethylene glycol to be added to 4 kg of water to prevent it from freezing at – 6°C (K_f for water = 1.85 K mol^{-1} kg)

A. 80.4 g B. 804.22 g
C. 8.04 g D. 811.23 g

65. Addition of 0.643 g of a compound to 50 ml of benzene (density 0.879 g/ml) lowers the freezing point from 5.51°C to 5.03°C. If K_f, for benzene is 5.12 K kg mol^{-1}, calculate the molar mass of the compound.

A. 136.12 B. 150.01
C. 156.056 D. 186.11

66. A very small amount of a non-volatile solute (this does not dissociate) is dissolved in 56.8 cm^3 of benzene (density 0.889 g cm^{-3}). At room temperature, vapour pressure of this solution is 98.88 mm Hg while that of benzene is 100 mm Hg. Find the molality of this solution. If the freezing temperature of this solution is 0.73 degree lower than that of benzene, what is the value of molal freezing point depression constant of benzene?

A. Molality = 0.1321, K_f = 3.027 K molality^{-1}
B. Molality = 0.1437, K_f = 1.023 K molality^{-1}
C. Molality = 0.1919, K_f = 0.09 K molality^{-1}
D. Molality = 0.1452, K_f = 5.027 K molality^{-1}

67. A solution of a non-volatile solute in water freezes at – 0.30°C. The vapour-pressure of pure water at 298 K is 23.51 mm Hg and K_f for water is 1.86 degree/molal. Calculate the vapour pressure of this solution at 298 K.

A. 23.00 mm Hg B. 23.51 mm Hg
C. 23.44 mm Hg D. 23.19 mm Hg

68. X g of a non-electrolyte compound (molar mass = 200) is dissolved in 1.0 L of 0.05 M NaCl aqueous solution. The osmotic pressure of this solution is found to be 4.92 atm. at 27°C. Calculate the value of X. Assume complete dissociation of NaCl and ideal behaviour of this solution. (R = 0.082 l atm. mol^{-1}K^{-1}).

A. 20 g B. 40 g
C. 60 g D. 80 g

69. 0.85% aqueous solution of $NaNO_3$ is apparently 90% dissociated at 27°C. Calculate its osmotic pressure (R = 0.082 atm. K^{-1}mol^{-1})

A. 4.67 atm. B. 6.47 atm.
C. 8.12 atm. D. 4.14 atm.

70. How much ethyl alcohol must be added to 1.0 litre of water so that the solution will freeze at 14°F (K_f for water = 1.86°C/mole)

A. 114.3 g B. 213.8 g
C. 247.31 g D. 314.13 g

71. Calculate the freezing point of an aqueous solution of a non-electrolyte having an osmotic pressure of 2.0 atm. at 300 K. K_f = 1.86 K kg mol^{-1}, R = 0.081 l atm K^{-1}mol^{-1}

A. 100°C B. 0°C
C. – 0.151°C D. 0.151°C

72. The freezing point of a solution containing 0.2 g of acetic acid in 20.0 g of benzene is lowered by 0.45°C. Calculate the degree of association of acetic acid in benzene.

A. 0.946 B. 1.946
C. 2.946 D. 3.946

73. 2.0 g of benzoic acid dissolved in 250 g of benzene show a depression in freezing point equal to 1.62 K. Molal depression constant (K_f) of benzene is 4.8 K kg mol^{-1}. What is the percentage association of the acid.

A. 80.1% B. 90.2%
C. 99.2% D. 100%

74. Calculate the amount of ice that will separate out on cooling a solution containing 50 g of ethylene glycol in 200 g water to – 9.3°C (K_f for water = 1.86)

A. 30.00 g B. 38.71 g
C. 31.20 g D. 29.10 g

75. Calculate the boiling point of a solution containing 0.61 g of benzoic acid in 50 g of CS_2 assuming 84% dimerisation of the acid. The boiling point and K_b of CS_2 are 46.2°C and 2.3 K kg mol^{-1} respectively.

A. 46.3336°C B. 4.633°C
C. 51.021°C D. 98.11°C

76. A decimolar solution of pot. ferrocyanide is 50% dissociated at 300 K calculate the osmotic pressure of the solution (R = 8.314 JK^{-1} mol^{-1})

A. 70.12 atm. B. 7.4826 atm
C. 0.7482 atm. D. 17.462 atm.

77. In which mode of expression, the concentration of solution remains independent of temperature?

A. Molarity B. Normality
C. Formality D. Molality

78. A molal solution is one that contains one mole of a solute in

A. 1000 g of the solvent

B. One litre of the solvent
C. One litre of the solution
D. 22.4 litres of the solution

79. If 8.50 mole of $BaCl_2$ is mixed with 0.20 mole of Na_3PO_4, the maximum number of moles of $Ba_3(PO_4)_2$ that can be formed in
A. 0.1 B. 0.2
C. 0.5 D. 0.7

80. If 250 ml of 0.25 M NaCl solution is diluted with water to a volume of 500 ml, the new concentration of the solution is
A. 0.167 M B. 0.125 M
C. 0.0833 M D. 0.167 M

81. The volume of 0.2 N base required to completely react with 0.5 litre of 0.1 N acid is
A. 1.00 *l* B. 0.10 *l*
C. 0.25 *l* D. 0.01 *l*

82. An aqueous solution of glucose is 10% in strength. The volume in which 1 gm mole of it is dissolved will be
A. 18 litres B. 9 litres
C. 0.7 litres D. 1.8 litres

83. A 500 g tooth paste sample has 0.2 g fluoride concentration. What is the concentration of F in terms of ppm level?
A. 250 B. 200
C. 400 D. 1000

84. Increasing the temperature of an aqueous solution will cause
A. Decrease in molality
B. Decrease in molarity
C. Decrease in mole fraction
D. Decrease in % w/W

85. Which of the following solutions has the highest normality?
A. 8 g of KOH/*l*
B. N-Phosphoric acid
C. 6 g of NaOH/100 ml
D. 0.5 mH_2SO_4

86. What is the normality of a 1 M solution of H_3PO_4?
A. 0.5 N B. 1.0 N
C. 2.0 N D. 3.0 N

87. Normality of 0.3 M phosphorous acid (a dibasic acid) (H_3PO_3) is
A. 0.3 B. 0.6
C. 0.9 D. 0.1

88. How many grams of dibasic acid (Mol. wt. 200) should be present in 100 ml of its aqueous solutions to give decinormal strength?
A. 1 g B. 2 g
C. 10 g D. 20 g

89. In a solution of 7.8 g of benzene (C_6H_6) and 46 g of toluene ($C_6H_5CH_3$), the mole fraction of benzene is
A. $\frac{1}{6}$ B. $\frac{1}{5}$
C. $\frac{1}{2}$ D. $\frac{1}{3}$

90. Which one of the following solution of sulphuric acid will exactly neutralise 25 ml of 0.2 M sodium hydroxide solution?
A. 12.5 ml of 0.1 M solution
B. 25 ml of 0.1 M solution
C. 25 ml of 0.2 M solution
D. 50 ml of 0.2 M solution

91. A mixture of two completely miscible non-ideal liquids which distil as such without change in its composition at a constant temperature as though it were a pure liquid. This mixture is known as
A. Binary liquid mixture
B. Azeotropic mixture
C. Eutectic mixture
D. Ideal mixture

92. Which one of the following is not a colligative property?
A. Osmotic pressure
B. Elevation of boiling point
C. Vapour pressure
D. Depression of freezing point

93. Ideal solution is formed when its components
A. Have only zero heat of mixing
B. Have only zero volume change
C. Have both zero heat of mixing as well as zero volume change
D. Can be converted into ideal gases

94. Vapour pressure of solution is
A. Directly proportional to the mole fraction of the solvent
B. Inversely proportional to the mole fraction of the solute

C. Inversely proportional to the mole fraction of the solvent
D. Directly proportional to the mole fraction of the solute

95. A mixture of benzene and toluene forms
A. An ideal solution B. Non ideal solution
C. Suspension D. Emulsion

96. Which one of the following pair will not be forming ideal solution?
A. C_6H_6 and CCl_4
B. C_6H_6 and $C_6H_5CH_3$
C. C_2H_5Br and C_2H_5I
D. $(CH_3)_2CO$ and CCl_4

97. An azeotropic solution of two liquids has boiling point higher than either,when it
A. Shows a negative deviation from Raoult's law
B. Shows no deviation from Raoult's law
C. Shows positive deviation from Raoult's law
D. Is saturated

98. Vapour-pressure of a solution of 5 g of non-electrolyte in 100 g of water at a particular temperature is 2985 N/m^2. The vapour-pressure of pure water is 3000 N/m^2, the molecular weight of the solute is
A. 60 B. 120
C. 180 D. 380

99. The molal *b.p.* constant for water is 0.513°C kg mol^{-1}. When 0.1 mole of sugar is dissolved in 200 g of water, the solution boils under a pressure of 1 atm at
A. 100.513°C B. 100.256°C
C. 100.0513°C D. 101.025°C

100. Which of the following solution will have the highest boiling points?
A. 1% glucose B. 1% sucrose
C. 1% NaCl D. 1% $CaCl_2$

101. Which one of the following 0.1 M aqueous solutions will have the lowest freezing point?
A. Potassium sulphate B. Sodium chloride
C. Urea D. Glucose

102. The freezing point for equimolal aqueous solution will be highest for
A. $C_6H_5NH_3^+ + Cl^-$ (aniline hydrochloride)
B. $Ca(NO_3)_2$
C. $Li(NO_3)_3$
D. $C_6H_{12}O_6$ (glucose)

103. What is the freezing point of a solution on containing 8.1 g of HBr in 100 g water assuming the acid to be 90% ionised (K_f for water = 1.86 K mol^{-1})
A. 0.85°C B. – 3.53°C
C. 0°C D. – 0.35°C

104. A liquid is in equilibrium with its vapour at its boiling point. On average, the molecules in the two phases have equal.
A. Intermolecular forces
B. Potential Energy
C. Total Energy
D. Kinetic Energy

105. When mercuric iodide is added to the aqueous solution of potassium iodide, the
A. Freezing point is raised
B. Freezing point does not change
C. Freezing point is lowered
D. Boiling point does not change

106. 0.6 gm of a solute is dissolved in 0.1 litre of a solvent which develops an osmotic pressure of 1.23 atm. at 27°C. The molecular mass of the substance is
A. 149.5 g $mole^{-1}$ B. 120 g $mole^{-1}$
C. 430 g $mole^{-1}$ D. None

107. Osmotic pressure is 0.0821 atm. at temperature of 300 K. Find concentration in mole/litre
A. 0.033 B. 0.066
C. 0.33×10^{-2} D. 3

108. In the depression of freezing point experiment, it is found that
A. The vapour pressure of the solution is less than that of pure solvent
B. The vapour pressure of the solution is more than that of pure solvent
C. Only solute molecules solidify at the freezing point
D. Only solvent molecules solidify at the freezing point
E. A and D

109. The molecular weight of benzoic acid in benzene as determined by depression in freezing point method corresponds to
A. Ionization of benzoic acid

B. Dimerization of benzoic acid
C. Trimerization of benzoic acid
D. Solvation of benzoic acid

110. A use of common salts, e.g. NaCl or $CaCl_2$ anhydrous is made to clear snow on the roads. This causes
A. A lowering of f.p. of water
B. A lowering of m.p. of ice
C. Ice melts at the temperature of atmosphere present at that time
D. All of the above

111. A liquid is kept in a closed vessel. If a glass plate (negligible mass) with a small hole is kept on top of the liquid surface, then the vapour-pressure of the liquid vessel is
A. More than what would be if the glass plate were removed
B. Same as what would be if the glass plate were removed
C. Less than what would be if the glass plate were removed
D. None of the above

112. In which of the following molecular weight determination methods, sensitivity of the measurements decreases as the molecular weight of the solute increases.
A. Elevation of boiling point/depression in freezing point
B. Viscocity
C. Osmotic pressure
D. None

113. Vapour-pressure of a solvent containing non-volatile solute is
A. More than the vapour-pressure of a solvent
B. Less than the vapour pressure of a solvent
C. Equal to the vapour pressure of solvent
D. None

114. If a thin slice of sugar beet is placed in concentrated solution of NaCl then
A. Sugar beet will loose water from its cells
B. Sugar beet will absorb water from solution
C. Sugar beet will neither absorb nor loose water
D. Sugar beet will dissolve in water

115. The osmotic pressure of a solution can be accurately measured in shortest possible time by
A. Berkley and Hartley method
B. Morse and Frazes method
C. Preffer method
D. None of the above

116. Dissolution of a solute is an exothermic process if
A. Hydration energy > Lattice energy
B. Hydration energy < Lattice energy
C. Hydration energy = Lattice energy
D. None of the above

117. Which solution would exhibit abnormal osmotic pressure
A. Aqueous solution of urea
B. Aqueous solution of common salt
C. Aqueous solution of glucose
D. Aqueous solution of sucrose

118. Acetic acid on dissolution in benzene will show
A. Two times of its normal molecular weight
B. Its normal molecular weight
C. Half of its normal molecular weight
D. None of the above

119. Boiling point of a solution is independent of
A. Amount of solution
B. Pressure
C. Nature of solvent
D. Concentration of solution

120. Solubility of solutes which dissolve with the liberation of heat decreases with
A. Decrease in temperature
B. Increase in temperature
C. No change in temperature
D. None

121. When an ideal binary solution is in equilibrium with its vapour, molar ratio of the two components in the solution and in the vapour phase is
A. Same
B. Different
C. May or may not be same depending upon volatile nature of the two components
D. All of the above

122. Blood cells retain their normal shapes in solutions which are
A. Isotonic to Blood
B. Hypotonic to Blood
C. Hypertonic to Blood
D. Equinormal to Blood

123. Which of the following method cannot be used to find out the molecular weight of non-volatile solute
A. Osmotic pressure method
B. Victor Meyer's method
C. Cryoscopic method
D. Ebullioscopic method

124. The highest temperature at which vapour pressure of a liquid can be measured is
A. B. pt of liquid
B. Critical temperature
C. Critical solution temperature
D. Inversion temperature

125. The boiling point of C_6H_6, CH_3OH, $C_6H_5NH_2$ and $C_6H_5NO_2$ are 80°C, 65°C, 184°C, and 212°C respectively which will show highest vapour-pressure at room temperature
A. C_6H_6 B. CH_3OH
C. $C_6H_5NH_2$ D. $C_6H_5NO_2$

126. The phenonmenon in which cells are swelled up and then burst if placed in hypotonic solutions is called
A. Plasmolysis B. Haemolysis
C. Exosmosis D. None

127. Just after slow crystallisation, the solution in contact with the crystal is
A. Dilute B. Unsaturated
C. Saturated D. Super saturated

128. A solution of sulphuric acid in water exhibits
A. Negative deviation from Raoult's law
B. Positive deviation from Raoult's law
C. Ideal properties
D. The applicability of Henry's law

129. The process of getting freshwater from sea water is known as
A. Osmosis B. Filtration
C. Diffusion D. Reverse Osmosis

130. At a suitable pressure near the freezing point of ice, there exists
A. Only ice
B. Ice and water
C. Ice and steam
D. Ice, water and steam, all exists side by side

131. The most suitable method for the determination of molecular weight of oxyhaemoglobin, a compound of high molecular weight is
A. Osmotic pressure method
B. Vapour-pressure lowering method
C. Elevation of boiling point method
D. None

132. The energy that favours dissolution of a solute in water is known as
A. Hydration Energy
B. Lattice Energy
C. Ionisation Energy
D. Exothermic Energy

133. In cold countries, ethylene glycol is added to water in the radiators of cars during winters. It results in
A. Lowering in boiling point
B. Reducing viscocity
C. Reducing specific heat
D. Lowering in freezing point

134. Which has the maximum freezing point
A. 1 M NaCl solution
B. 1 M CCl_4 solution
C. 1 M $CaCl_2$ solution
D. 1 M Urea solution

135. Dry air was passed successively through a solution of 5 g of a solute in 180 g of water. The loss in weight of solution was 2.50 g and that of pure solvent 0.04 g. The molecular weight of the solute is
A. 3.125 B. 31.25
C. 312.5 D. 31205

136. The molal elevation constant of water = 0.52 K molality^{-1}. The boiling point of 1.0 molal aq. KCl solution (assuming complete dilution of KCl, should be
A. 100.52°C B. 101.04°C
C. 99.48°C D. 98.96°C

137. In a solution of 7.8 g benzene (C_6H_6) and 46.0 g toluene ($C_6H_5CH_3$), the mole fraction of benzene is
A. $\frac{1}{6}$ B. $\frac{1}{5}$
C. $\frac{1}{2}$ D. $\frac{1}{3}$

138. At 40°C the vapour-pressure of pure liquids, benzene and toluene, are 160 mm Hg and 60 mm Hg respectively. At the same temperature, the vapour-pressure of an equimolar ideal solution should be

A. 140 mm Hg   B. 110 mm Hg
C. 220 mm Hg   D. 100 mm Hg

139. At 27°C, the osmotic pressure of a solution containing 4.0 g solute (molar mass = 246) per litre at 27°C is
($R = 0.082\ l$ atms. mol^{-1} K)

A. 0.1 atm.   B. 0.9 atm.
C. 0.4 atm.   D. 0.8 atm.

140. The vapour pressure benzene at 90°C is 1020 torr. A solution of 5 g of a solute in 58.5 g benzene has vapour pressure 990 torr. The molecular weight of the solute is

A. 78.2   B. 178.2
C. 206.2   D. 220

141. The freezing point of equimolal aqueous solution will be highest for

A. $C_6H_5NH_3Cl$ B. $Ca(NO_3)_2$
C. $La(NO_3)_3$ D. $C_6H_{12}O_6$

142. The molecular weight of NaCl determined by studying freezing point depression of its 0.5% aq. solution is 30. The apparent degree of dissociation of NaCl is

A. 0.95   B. 0.50
C. 0:60   D. 0.30

143. The depression in freezing point of 0.01 m aq. solution of urea, sodium chloride and sodium sulphate is in the ratio

A. 1 : 1 : 1   B. 1 : 2 : 3
C. 1 : 2 : 4   D. 2 : 3 : 3

144. Azeotropic mixture of HCl and water has

A. 84% HCl   B. 22.4% HCl
C. 63% HCl   D. 20.2% HCl

145. A 5% solution of cane sugar (M. wt. = 342) is isotonic with 1% solution of substance X. The molecular weight of X is

A. 171.2   B. 68.4
C. 34.2   D. 136.2

146. Which term is to be correctly used for expressing concentration of electrolytes in solution

A. Molarity   B. Normality
C. Formality   D. None

147. Which of the following is correct?

A. Mole = molarity = V in mL = $\frac{\text{wt.}}{\text{mol. wt.}}$
B. Millimole = molarity × V in mL = $\frac{\text{wt.}}{\text{mol. wt.}} \times 1000$
C. Mole and millimole of reactants react according to stoichiometric ratio of balanced chemical equation
D. All of the above

148. Molecular weight of NaCl is 58.5.A solution of NaCl containing 5.85 g NaCl per litre is

A. 1 molar   B. 0.1 molar
C. 2 molar   D. 0.58 molar

149. What weight of sodium hydroxide is required to neutralise 100 ml 0.1 N HCl

A. 4.0 g   B. 0.04 g
C. 0.4 g   D. 2.0 g

150. The maximum amount of $BaSO_4$ precipitated on mixing 20 mL of 0.5 M $BaCl_2$ with 20 mL of 1M H_2SO_4 is

A. 0.25 mole   B. 0.5 mole
C. 1 mole   D. 0.01 mole

151. The normality of 0.3 M phosphorous acid (H_3PO_3) is

A. 0.1   B. 0.9
C. 0.3   D. 0.6

ANSWERS

1	2	3	4	5	6	7	8	9	10
C	B	B	B	C	C	C	A	D	A
11	12	13	14	15	16	17	18	19	20
A	D	B	A	D	E	D	A	D	D
21	22	23	24	25	26	27	28	29	30
D	D	D	E	D	E	B	B	B	C

31	32	33	34	35	36	37	38	39	40
A	D	C	C	A	A	C	B	D	A
41	**42**	**43**	**44**	**45**	**46**	**47**	**48**	**49**	**50**
A	C	B	B	B	B	D	B	A	E
51	**52**	**53**	**54**	**55**	**56**	**57**	**58**	**59**	**60**
B	B	D	B	B	B	C	B	C	A
61	**62**	**63**	**64**	**65**	**66**	**67**	**68**	**69**	**70**
B	D	B	B	C	D	B	A	A	C
71	**72**	**73**	**74**	**75**	**76**	**77**	**78**	**79**	**80**
C	A	C	B	A	B	D	A	A	B
81	**82**	**83**	**84**	**85**	**86**	**87**	**88**	**89**	**90**
C	D	C	B	C	D	B	A	A	B
91	**92**	**93**	**94**	**95**	**96**	**97**	**98**	**99**	**100**
B	C	C	A	A	D	C	C	C	D
101	**102**	**103**	**104**	**105**	**106**	**107**	**108**	**109**	**110**
C	D	B	D	C	B	C	E	B	D
111	**112**	**113**	**114**	**115**	**116**	**117**	**118**	**119**	**120**
B	A	B	A	A	A	B	A	A	B
121	**122**	**123**	**124**	**125**	**126**	**127**	**128**	**129**	**130**
C	A	B	B	B	B	D	A	D	D
131	**132**	**133**	**134**	**135**	**136**	**137**	**138**	**139**	**140**
A	A	D	D	B	B	A	B	C	D
141	**142**	**143**	**144**	**145**	**146**	**147**	**148**	**149**	**150**
D	A	B	D	B	C	D	B	C	D
151									
D									

9

Chemical Bonding and Molecular Structure

Introduction

Atoms except those of inert gases, do not have free existence. They readily combine together to form stable clusters or aggregates of atoms. Such aggregates are called molecules and the attraction operating between atoms within the molecule is called Chemical Bond.

The process of combination of atoms, called chemical bonding, involves the union of two or more atoms which in theory is redistribution of electrons in their outermost shell to acquire the stable electronic configuration of noble gases having a state of minimum energy.

Valency

Valency (valentia = power) is the general term used to explain the power or potential which atoms possess to combine with one another for forming a stable molecule. In general valency means the number of chemical bonds and atom forms, which is not necessarily the number of other atoms to which it is bonded. The valency of any element depends upon the electrons present in the outermost orbit. That is why outermost shell or orbit of an atom is termed *valency shell* or *valency orbit*. The elctrons of valency shell, which are involved in chemical bond formation are called Valency Electrons.

Types of Linkages/Valencies/Bonds

***(i)* Electrovalency :** By transfering one or more electrons from one atom to the other atom.

***(ii)* Covalency :** By sharing of electrons by one atom with electrons of other atom (both atoms contributing equal number of electrons).

***(iii)* Co-ordinate valency :** By sharing of electrons between two atoms in such a way that the shared electrons are contributed by one atom only.

Ionic Bond or Electrovalent Linkage : "This bond is formed by complete transfer of one or more electrons from one atom to another atom till a noble gas configuration is attained" by both combining atoms.

Example : Formation of sodium chloride; A sodium atom (atomic no. 11) transfers its valence electron to a chlorine atom (atomic number 17). The sodium atom, by losing an electron, acquires the electronic configuration of neon (2, 8) and becomes sodium ion Na^+, carrying a unit positive charge, while the chlorine atom, by gaining one electron, acquires the stable configuration of argon (2, 8, 8) and becomes the chloride ion, Cl^-, with a unit negative charge. The transfer of electron results in the formation of ionic bond.

$$\underset{[Ne]3s^1}{Na^+} + \underset{[Ne]3s^2sp^5}{:\ddot{Cl}:} \rightarrow \underset{[Ne]}{Na^+} + \underset{[Ar]}{[\overset{\times}{\cdot}\ddot{Cl}:]}$$

Covalent Bond : A covalent bond is formed by the sharing of a pair of electrons between two atoms each atom contributing one electron to the shared pair. From a consideration of wave mechanics, it can be shown that the shared pairs of electrons should spin in opposite directions and they are localized between the two nuclei concerned. A covalent bond is conventionally represented by a short line (i.e., a dash —) between the two atoms.

Sharing of electrons may occur in three ways :

(i) When each atom contributes an electron and hence have two contributed electrons (one pair), one

shared by each atom. The bond formed is known as single bond and is represented as '—'

e.g., (1) H× H or H – H
Hydrogen

(2)
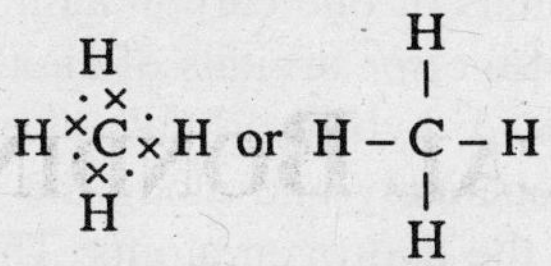
methane

(3)
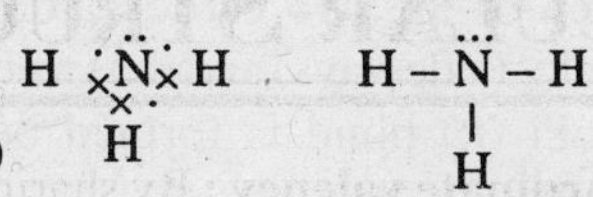
Ammonia

(ii) When each atom contributes two electrons and thus two pair of electrons are shared by each atom. The bond is known as *double bond* and represented by '=', common examples are CO_2, O_2 olefins, etc.

$\dot{O} = C = O$ or $\overset{\times\times}{\underset{\times}{\overset{\times}{}}O}\overset{\times}{\underset{\times}{}}$: C :$\overset{\times\times}{O}$

Carbondioxide

(iii) Similarily triple bond (≡) is formed by sharing of three pairs of electrons (three atoms are contributed by each atom) common examples are N_2, alkenes, etc.

e.g., :N⁝⁝N: or N ≡ N

N_2

Compounds having covalent bond are known as *covalent compounds.*

Coordinate bond/Dative Bond/Semi-Polar Bond:

(i) It is a kind of covalent bond.

(ii) It is shown by an arrow (→), pointing from donor to acceptor.

(iii) Only one of the two atoms involved in the bonding supplies a pair of electrons. This type of bond was suggested by *Langmuir* and named as co-ordinate bond by *Sidwick.*

Example : SO_2, H_3O^+, H_2SO_4, NH_4^+, SO_3, etc.

Characteristics of coordinate bond :

(i) The elements in co-ordinate covalent bond are held firmly by the nuclei of atoms, therefore, they do not ionise in water.

(ii) Coordinate compounds are sparingly soluble in water. Most of them are soluble in organic solvents.

(iii) Co-ordinate covalent bond is rigid and directional and therefore, the molecule having co-ordinate bond show geometrical isomorphism just like covalent compounds.

(iv) A co-ordinate covalent bond results in semipolarity in the molecules. Thus, the co-ordinate compounds lie between electrovalent and covalent compounds in their volatility, melting points, and boiling points.

Dipole Moment (μ) of a polar molecule is defined as a product of particle charges (δ) and the distance between combining atoms (*d*)

$$\mu = \delta \times d$$

Dipole moment is a vector quantity.

The unit of dipole moment is *Debye* which is equal to 1×10^{-18} e.s.u. cm. The molecules having polar bonds need not necessarily be polar molecules.

Molecular Orbital Method : The M.O. method was developed by Hund and Mullikens in 1932. According to this theory an atomic and a molecular orbital can be differentiated as follows :

Atomic Orbital (A.O.) : It is defined as the region in space where there is a probability of finding an electron. An atomic orbital has the following characteristics:

(i) An atomic orbital is distributed around the nucleus of a single atom.

(ii) An atomic orbital can accomodate maximum of the electrons and they should have opposite spins.

(iii) Atomic orbitals are of different shapes and sizes. *s*-orbital is spherically symmetrical while the *p*-orbital is dumb-bell shaped.

(iv) The four quantum numbers *n, l, m* and *s* characterise the atomic orbital.

Molecular Orbital (M.O.) : It is the region in space containing the nuclei of all the bonded atoms where the probability of finding an electron is a maximum. A M.O. has the following characteristics :

(i) A Molecular orbital is formed by the combination of atomic orbitals.

(ii) The number of molecular orbitals formed is the same as the number of atomic orbitals taking part in chemical combination. For example, the combination of the two atomic orbitals give rise to two molecular orbitals.

(iii) Like an atomic orbital, the maximum number of electrons that can be accomodated in a M.O. are two and they should have opposite spins.

(iv) The shape of the M.O. is related to the shape of the A.Os involved.

(*v*) There are two types of M.O.'s, i.e., *bonding* and *antibonding*.

Hybridisation : Merging (mixing) of dissimilar orbitals of similar energies to form new orbitals is known as *hybridisation* and the new orbital formed are known as Hybrid Orbitals. Following points are important in the study of hybridisation.

(A) *sp^3 Hybridisation* (Tetrahedral hybridisation): This type of hybridisation involves mixing of one *s* and 3 pure *p* orbitals to give four equivalent *sp^3 hybrid orbitals*. These orbitals are directed towards the four corners of a regular tetrahedron and separated by an angle of 109° 28' (the normal tetrahedral angle).

In the formation of methane, each of the sp^3 hybrid orbitals overlap axially with the orbital of the hydrogen atom to form four bonds between C and H.

In ammonia, since only three hydrogens overlap with the three sp^3 hybrid orbitals, the fourth sp^3 hybrid orbital, has a lone pair of electrons which repels the electrons involved in bond formation with the result the tetrahedral bond angle of 109° 28' decreases to 106° 45'. Similarly, since water has two lone pair of electrons, repulsion between lone pair and bond pair electrons is more than in ammonia, and hence, bond angle is further distorted to 104° 27'.

Chlorate ion $\left(ClO_3^-\right)$ is also an example where the central atom is sp^3 hybridised and has a lone pair of electrons.

(B) *sp^2 Hybridisation* Trigonal Hybridisation : This type of hybridisation involves of one *s* and two *p* (p_x and p_y) orbitals to give three equivalent sp^2 hybrid orbitals.

The three sp^2 hybrid orbitals are directed towards the three corners of an equilateral triangle with an angle of 120°

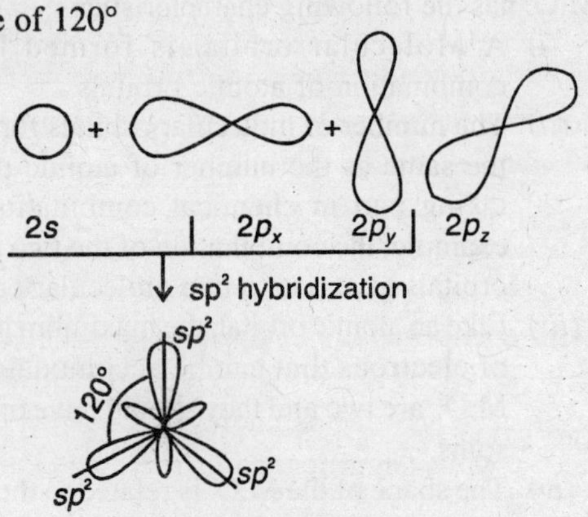

sp^2 hybridization of carbon

The effective size of sp^2 orbitals is slightly smaller than that of sp^3 hybrid orbitals. One *p* orbital remains pure in this type of hybridisation.

In ethylene $H_2C = CH_2$ formation, one of the sp^2 hybrid orbitals of one carbon atom overlaps axially with one of the sp^2 orbitals of another carbon atom. Two of the sp^2 hybrid orbitals of each carbon atom overlaps separately and along the axes with the 1*s* orbitals of the hydrogen atoms. The pure *p* orbitals one on each of the two carbon atoms overlap each other laterally (sideways) and thus a new type of bond, known as Pi (π) bond is formed between the two carbon atoms.

In $SnCl_2$, Sn is also sp^2 hybridised, but here Sn has a lone pair of electrons.

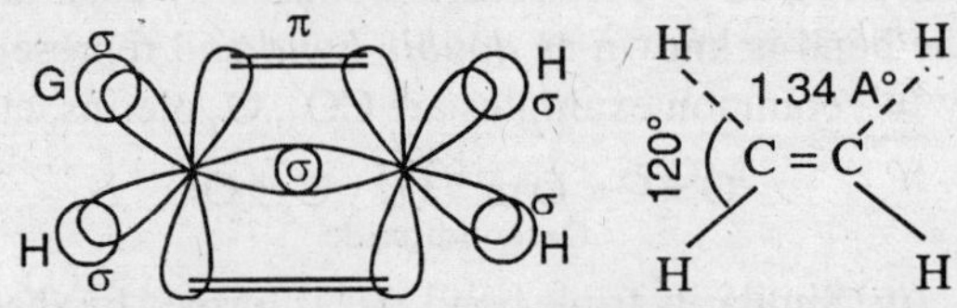

[Ethylene molecule has four C–Hσ, one C–Cσ and one C – Cπ bond)

(C) *sp Hybridisation or Diagonal Hybridisation :* This type of hybridisation involves the intermixing of one *s* and one *p* (say p_x) orbitals to give two equivalent hybrid orbitals, known as *sp* hybrid orbitals. The two *sp* hybrid orbitals are directed diagonally, i.e. in a straight line with an angle of 180° (collinear orbitals). The other two *p*-orbitals (say p_y and p_z) remains pure.

sp Hyrbid orbitals are smaller in size than the sp^3 as well as sp^2 hybrid orbitals. An *sp* hybridised carbon has two *sp* hybrid orbitals and two pure *p*-orbitals. This type of hybridisation takes place in the formation of alkynes (i.e. $C \equiv C$), BeX_2, etc.

In acetylene formation $HC \equiv CH$, one of the *sp* hybrid orbitals of one carbon atom overlaps axially will one of the *sp* hybrid orbital of the other carbon atom, thus a C—Cσ bond is formed second *sp* hybrid orbital of each carbon atom overlaps axially and separately with the 1*s*-orbitals of the two hydrogen atoms and thus two C—Hσ bonds are formed. The remaining two pure *p*-orbitals of one carbon atom overlaps sideways with the corresponding *p*-orbitals of the other carbon atom and thus two C—Cπ bonds are formed.

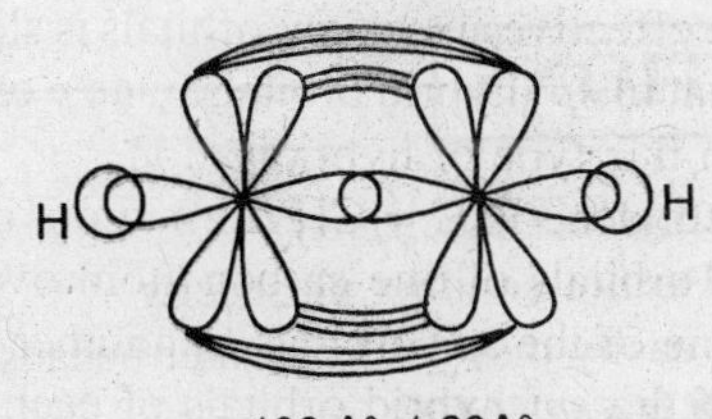

106 A° 1.20A°
H — C ≡ C – H
Acetylene

Single, double and triple covalent bond are formed by sp^3, sp^2 and sp hybridisation.

Geometry of Molecules Containing Only Bond Pairs of Electrons

Type of Hybridi-zations	*Shape of Molecule*	*Bond angle*	*Examples*
sp	Linear	180°	BeH_2, BeF_2, $BeCl_2$, $HgCl_2$, C_2H_2, HCN, CO_2, Cs_2, N_2O, Hg_2Cl_2, etc.
sp^2	Trigonal Plane or Triangular planar	120°	BF_3, BCl_3, C_2H_4, CO_3^{2-}, NO_3^-, SO_3,
sp^3	Tetra hedral	109° 28'	CH_4, SiH_4, $SnCl_4$, $PbCl_4$, $TiBr_4$, CCl_4, SiF_4, $[BeF_4]^{2-}$, $[BH_4]^-$, $[BF_4]^-$, $[NH_4]^+$, $[AlCl_4]^-$, $[PH_4]^+$, $[H_2PO_2]^-$, $[HPO_3]^2$, $[PO_4]^{3-}$, $POCl_3$, $[SO_4]^{2-}$, $[ClO_4]^-$, $[Ni(CO)_4]$, $[Cu(CN)_4]^{3-}$, $[Zn(CN_4)]^{2-}$, $[AsO_4]^{3-}$, $[SeO_{44}]^{2-}$, $[IO_4]^-$, XeO_4
dsp^2	Square Planar	90°	$[Ni(CN)_4]^{2-}$, $[PdCl_4]^{2-}$, $[Pt(NH_3)_4]^{2-}$, $[AuCl_4]^-$
sp^3d	Trigonal bipyramidal	120° and 90°	PCl_5, PFs, AsFs $SbCl_5$, XeO_3F_2
sp^3d^2 or d^2sp^3	Octahedral	90°	SF_6, $[BiCl_6]^-$, $[PF_6]^-$, $[PCl_6]^-$, $[AsF_6]^-$, SeF_6, MoF_6, $[SbCl_6]^-$, TeF_6, WCl_6, UF_6, XeO_2F_4 All six co-ordinated metal complexes
sp^3d^2	Penta-gonal bi pyramidal	90° and 72°	IF_7, $[ZrF_7]^{3-}$, $[UF_7]^{3-}$, $[UO_2F_5]^{3-}$

$[Mo(CN)_8]^{4-}$ is dodecahedral molecule

$[TaF_8]^{3-}$ is square antiprismatic molecule

(C_5H_5) Fe (C_5H_5) is sandwich structure, Thus compared is known as Ferrocene.

Hydrogen Bond

A hydrogen atom is normally univalent. There are however some compounds in which the hydrogen atom exists simultaneously betweeen two atoms, acting as *bridge* between them. In this situation, the hydrogen atom is involved in two bonds, one being the normal covalent bond and the other the hydrogen bond. *A Hydrogen Bond always Formed Between two small, strongly Electro-negative Atoms, Such as Fluorine, Oxygen and Nitrogen and the Size of Electronegative Atom should be Small.*

Hydrogen bond is merely a strong electrostatic attractive force and not a normal chemical bond.

It is very weak (2-10 kcal mol^{-1} of 8.4-42 kJ mol^{-1}) as compared to a covalent bond (strength 50-100 kcal mol^{-1} or 209-418.4 kJ mol^{-1}).

Types of Hydrogen Bonding :

(i) Intermolecular Hydrogen Bonding : In such type of linkages the two or more than two molecules of the same compound combine together to give a polymeric aggregate. Intermolecular Hydrogen bonding increases the boiling point of the compound and also solubility in water.

(ii) Intramolecular Hydrogen Bonding : Sometimes hydrogen bonding may take place with in a *single molecule*, this is known as *intramolecular hydrogen bonding*.

It may lead to the linking of two groups to form a ring, such an effect is known as *Chelation* (the term has a wider significance in the study of complex compounds).

OBJECTIVE QUESTIONS

1. The electronic structures of four elements *a, b, c* and *d* are
   A. $1s^2$ B. $1s^2, 2s^2 2p^2$,
   C. $1s^2, 2s^2 2p^5$ D. $1s^2 2s^2 2p^6$
   The tendency to form electrovalent bond is greatest in (A) (B) (C) (D).
2. Covalent compounds are soluble in
   A. Polar solvents
   B. Non-polar solvents
   C. Concentrated acids
   D. Strong bases only
3. Which of the following is purest covalent bond?
   A. H – Cl B. Cl – Cl
   C. C – Cl D. Na – Cl
4. Which of the following bonds is the most ionic?
   A. (Cs – Cl) B. (Al – Cl)
   C. (C – Cl) D. (H – Cl)
5. The compound which contains both ionic and covalent bonds is
   A. CH_4 B. H_2
   C. KCN D. KCl
6. Which of the following combinations is best explained by the co-ordinate covalent bond?
   A. $(H_2 + I_2)$ B. $\left(Mg + \frac{1}{2}O_2\right)$
   C. (Cl + C) D. $(H^+ + H_2O)$
7. The maximum covalency of an element of the atomic number 7 is
   A. 2 B. 3
   C. 4 D. 5
8. Which of the following molecules does not obey the octet rule?
   A. SiF_4 B. $GeCl_2$
   C. PCl_5 D. C_2Cl_6
9. Molten NaCl conducts electricity due to the presence of
   A. Free electrons
   B. Free ions
   C. Free molecules
   D. Atoms of sodium and chlorine
10. Fused ionic compounds
    A. Are insulators
    B. Are used as semi-conductor
    C. Conduct electricity
    D. Do not conduct electricity
11. KCl easily dissolves in water because
    A. It is a salt of K
    B. It reacts with water
    C. It is an electrovalent compound
    D. Its ions are easily solvated
12. Elements whose electronegativities are 1.2 and 3.0, Bond formed between them would be
    A. Ionic B. Covalent
    C. Coordinate D. Metallic
13. In a double bond connecting two atoms, there is a sharing of
    A. 2 electrons B. 4 electrons
    C. 1 electron D. All electrons
14. The types of bond present is $CuSO_4.5H_2O$ are only
    A. Electrovalent and covalent
    B. Electrovalent and coordinate covalent
    C. Electrovalent, covalent and coordinate covalent
    D. Covalent and coordinate covalent
15. Which of the following contains a coordinate covalent bond?
    A. $N_2H_5^+$ B. $BaCl_2$
    C. HCl D. H_2O
16. Metallic bonds do not play role in
    A. Brass B. Copper
    C. Germanium D. Zinc
17. Iron is tougher than sodium because
    A. Iron atoms are smaller
    B. Iron atoms are more closely packed
    C. Metallic bonds are stronger in iron
    D. All of the above
18. Force present in the crystals of naphthalene is
    A. Electrostatic
    B. Van der Waals forces
    C. Hydrogen bonding
    D. None of the above
19. The ion that is isoelectronic with CO is
    A. CN^- B. O_2^+
    C. O_2^- D. N_2^+

20. A sp^3 hybrid orbital contains

A. $\frac{1}{4}$ *s* character B. $\frac{1}{2}$ *s* character

C. $\frac{2}{3}$ *s* character D. $\frac{3}{4}$ *s* character

21. The mode of hybridization of carbon in CO_2 is

A. *sp* B. sp^2

C. sp^3 D. None

22. Which of the following geometrical configurations corresponds to dsp^2 hybridization?

A. Tetrahedral

B. Pentagonal bipyramidal

C. Square planar

D. Octahedral

23. The shape of sulphate ion is

A. Tetrahedral B. Square planar

C. Trigonal planar D. Hexagonal

24. In diborane, the H—B—H bond angle is 120°, the hybridization of borane is likely to be

A. *sp* B. sp^2

C. sp^3 D. dsp^2

25. XeF_2 involves the following hybridization

A. sp^3 B. sp^3d

C. sp^3d^2 D. *sp*

26. Octahedral molecular shape exists in .... hybridization

A. sp^3d B. sp^3d^2

C. sp^3d^3 D. *sp*

27. Which of the following molecules contain one lone pair of electrons on the central atom?

A. CH_4 B. NH_3

C. CCl_4 D. H_2O

28. The H—O—H angle in water molecule is about

A. 90° B. 180°

C. 105° D. 75°

29. Which of the following molecules does not have a linear arrangement of atoms?

A. H_2S B. C_2H_2

C. BeH_2 D. CO_2

30. The angle between two covalent bonds is maximum is

A. H_2O B. CO_2

C. NH_3 D. CH_4

31. Among the C—X bond, the correct bond energy order is

A. C – Cl > C – Br > C – I

B. C – I > C – Cl > C – Br

C. C – Br > C – Cl > C – I

D. C – I > C – Br > C – Cl

32. Amongst the following molecules, the one with the largest distance between the two adjacent carbon atoms is

A. Ethane B. Ethene

C. Ethyne D. Benzene

33. Excessive solubility of alcohol in water is due to

A. Covalent bond

B. Ionic bond

C. Hydrogen bond with water

D. None of these

34. Which of the following is soluble in water?

A. CS_2 B. C_2H_5OH

C. CCl_4 D. $CHCl_3$

35. The pair of molecules forming strongest intermolecular hydrogen bonds are

A. SiH_4 and SiF

B. $CH_3—\overset{\overset{\large O}{\|}}{C}—CH_3$ and $CHCl_3$

C. $H_3—\overset{\overset{\large O}{\|}}{C}—OH$ and $CH_3—\overset{\overset{\large O}{\|}}{C}—OH$

D. H_2O and H_2O_2

36. The molecular BF_3 and NF_3 both are covalent compounds, but BF_3 is non-polar and NF_3 is polar, because

A. Boron is a metal and nitrogen is a gas in uncombined state

B. B—F bonds have no dipole moments whereas N—F bonds have dipole moments

C. Atomic size of boron is smaller than that of nitrogen

D. BF_3 is planar but NF_3 is pyramidal in shape

37. Which of the following is an electron deficient compound?

A. ICl B. NH_3

C. BCl_3 D. PCl_3

38. Which of the following statement is incorrect?

A. Hybridization is the mixing of atomic orbitals prior of their combining into molecular orbitals

B. sp^2 hybrid orbitals are formed from two *p*-atomic orbitals and one *s*-atomic orbitals

C. dsp^3 hybrid orbitals are all at 90° to one another

D. d^2sp^3 hybrid orbitals are directed towards the corners of a regular octahedral.

39. The molecule having one unpaired electron is

A. NO B. CO
C. CN^- D. O_2

40. Increasing order (lower first) of size of hybrid orbitals is

A. sp, sp^2, sp^3 B. sp^3, sp^2, sp
C. sp^2, sp^3, sp D. sp^2, sp, sp^3

41. Molecular orbital was developed mainly by

A. Neils Bohr
B. T. Seaborg
C. Robert Mullikens
D. Robert Robinson

42. The bond order of a molecule is given by

A. The difference between the number of electrons in bonding and antibonding orbitals

B. Total number of electrons in bonding and antibonding orbitals

C. Twice the difference between the number of electrons in bonding and antibonding orbitals

D. Half the difference between number of electrons in bonding and antibonding orbitals

43. Which of the following has a bond order of 1?

A. H_2 B. O_2
C. N_2 D. He_2

44. Which of the following have identical bond order?

(*i*) CN^- (*ii*) O_2^- (*iii*) NO^+ (*iv*) CN^+

A. (*i*) and (*iii*) B. (*i*) and (*ii*)
C. (*i*) and (*iv*) D. (*ii*) and (*iv*)

45. BeF_2 has zero dipole moment whereas H_2O has a dipole moment became

A. H_2O is a linear molecule
B. H_2O is a bent molecule
C. F is more electronegative than O
D. Hydrogen bonding is present in H_2O

46. Dipole moment is shown by

(*i*) 1, 4 dichlorobenzene
(*ii*) *cis*-1, 2, dichloroethene
(*iii*) *trans*-1, 2 Dichlorethene
(*iv*) *trans*-1, 2, dichloro-2-pentene

A. (*ii*) and (*i*) B. (*ii*) and (*iv*)
C. (*i*) and (*iii*) D. (*i*) and (*iv*)

47. Experiments shows that H_2O has a dipole moment while CO_2 has not. Point out the structures which best illustrates these facts :

A. 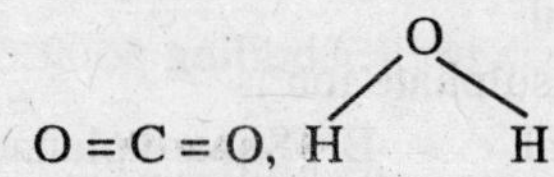

B. O=C=O, H—O—H

C. 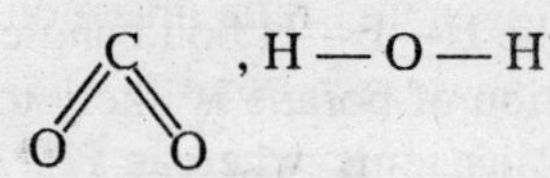

D. 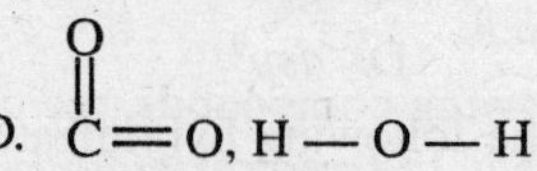

48. Which bond angle, θ would result in the maximum dipole moment for the triatomic molecule YXY?

A. $\theta = 90°$ B. $\theta = 120°$
C. $\theta = 150°$ D. $\theta = 180°$

49. Two elements X and Y have following electronic configuration

$X = 1s^2, 2s^2, 2p^6, 3s^2, 3p^6 4s^2$

$Y = 1s^2, 2s^2, 2p^6, 3s^2, 3p^5$

The expected compound formed by combination of X and Y is

A. XY_2 B. X_5Y_2
C. X_2Y_5 D. XY_5

50. Hybridization of carbon in diamond, graphite and acetylene is

A. sp^3, sp, sp^2 B. sp, sp^2, sp^3
C. sp^3, sp^2, sp D. sp^2, sp^3, sp

51. The number of electrons shared in formation of nitrogen molecule is

A. 6 B. 10
C. 2 D. 8

52. Which one of the following has minimum dipole moment?
A. Butene-1 B. *cis*-Butene-2
C. *trans*-Butene-2 D. 2-Methylpropene

53. Among the following species, identify the iso structural pairs.
NF_3, NO_3^-, BF_3, H_3O^+, HN_3
A. $[NF_3, NO_3^-]$ and $[BF_3, H_3O^+]$
B. $[NF_3, HN_3]$ and $[NO_3^-, BF_3]$
C. $[NF_3, H_3O^+]$ and $[NO_3^-, BF_3]$
D. $[NF_3, H_3O^+]$ and $[HN_3, BF_3]$

54. NH_3 has a much higher boiling point than PH_3 because
A. NH_3 has a larger molecular weight
B. NH_3 undergoes umbrella inversion
C. NH_3 forms hydrogen bond
D. NH_3 contains ionic whereas PH_3 contains covalent bonds

55. Among the following compounds, the one that is a polar and has the central atom with sp^2 hybridization is
A. H_2CO_3 B. SiF_4
C. BF_3 D. $HClO_2$

56. How many π-bonds are there in the nitrogen molecule
A. one B. two
C. three D. four

57. Which of the following has a giant covalent structure?
A. PbO_2 B. SiO_2
C. NaCl D. $AlCl_3$

58. Which of the following has fractional bond order
A. O_2^{2+} B. O_2^{2-}
C. F_2^{2-} D. H_2^-

59. The bonds present in N_2O_5 are
A. Ionic
B. Covalent and coordinate
C. Covalent
D. Ionic and covalent

60. Ionic reactions take place in
A. Liquid state B. Solid state
C. Solution state D. Gaseous state

61. Which of the following statement is incorrect
A. Absolutely pure water does not contain any ion
B. In aqueous solution only electrovalent compounds give ions
C. Very sparingly soluble substances do not dissociate in aqueous solution
D. All of these

62. Which of the following has higher bond energy and stronger bond
A. F_2 B. Cl_2
C. Br_2 D. I_2

63. π-bonding occurs in each of the following except
A. CO_2 B. C_2H_4
C. CN^- D. CH_4

64. Which liquid is not deflected by a non-uniform electrostatic field
A. Water B. Chloroform
C. Nitrobenzene D. Hexane

65. The structure of IF_5 can be best demonstrated as

A. 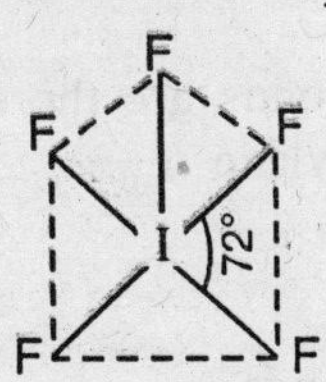

B. 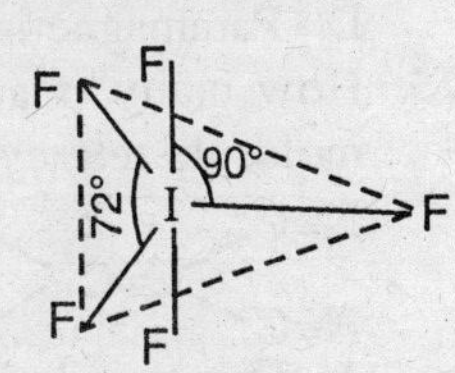

C. 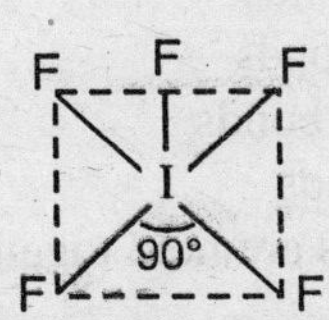

D. None of these

66. Which bond has the highest bond energy
A. Co-ordinate bond B. Sigma bond
C. Multiple bond D. Polar covalent bond

67. The molecule having three folds of axis of symmetry is
A. NH_3 B. PCl_5
C. SO_2 D. CO_2

68. The angle between the overlapping of one *s*-orbital and one *p*-orbital is
A. 180° B. 120°
C. 109° 28' D. 120° 60'

69. Which species does not exist
A. $(SnCl_6)^{2-}$ B. $(CCl_6)^{2-}$
C. $(GeCl_6)^{2-}$ D. $(SiCl_6)^{2-}$

70. CCl_4 is insoluble in water because
A. CCl_4 is non polar and water is polar
B. Water is non polar and CCl_4 is polar
C. Both are polar
D. Both are non polar

71. The equilateral triangle shape has
A. *sp*-hybridization B. *sp*^{2}-hybridization
C. *sp*^{3}-hybridization D. *sp*^{3}*d*-hybridization

72. Which force is strongest
A. Dipole-dipole forces
B. Ion-ion forces
C. Ion-dipole forces
D. Ion-induced dipole forces

73. The pair of species having identical shape is
A. CF_4, SF_4 B. PCl_3, BF_3
C. XeF_2, CO_2 D. PF_5, IF_5

74. Higher is the bond order greater is
A. Bond dissociation energy
B. Covalent character
C. Bond length
D. Paramagnetism

75. How many σ and π bonds are there in the molecule tetracyanoethylene

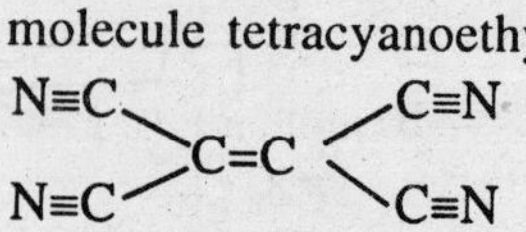

A. Five σ and nine π bonds
B. Nine σ and nine π bonds
C. Five σ and eleven π bonds
D. Five σ and six π bonds

76. In solid argon, the atoms are held together by
A. Ionic bonds
B. Hydrogen bonds
C. Van der Waal's forces
D. Hydrophobic forces

77. Which combination is most likely to form predominantly covalent bonds?
A. Sodium and Hydrogen
B. Magnesium and oxygen
C. Bromine and fluorine
D. Cesium and fluorine

78. The correct order of decreasing polarity is
A. $HF > SO_2 > H_2O > NH_3$
B. $HF > H_2O > SO_2 > NH_3$
C. $HF > NH_3 > SO_2 > H_2O$
D. $H_2O > NH_3 > SO_2 > HF$

79. Ortho and para hydrogen have
A. Same spin of electrons of two H atoms
B. Opposite spin of electrons of two H atoms
C. Different spin of nuclear or proton of two H atoms
D. None

80. An electrovalent compound does not exhibit space isomerism due to
A. Presence of ions
B. High melting point
C. Strong electrostatic forces between constituent ions
D. Non-directional nature of electrovalent bond

81. Which of the following explains that *o*-nitrophenol is more volatile than *p*-nitrophenol
A. Hyper conjugation
B. Steric hinderance
C. Hydrogen bonding
D. Resonance

82. Concept of bond order in the M.O. theory depends on the number of electrons in the bonding and antibonding orbitals. The bond order :
A. Can have a –ve value.
B. Has always an integral value
C. Is a non zero quantity
D. Can assume any +ve value, including zero

83. The bond order of C_2^+ is
A. 1 B. $\frac{3}{2}$
C. 2 D. $\frac{1}{2}$

84. Which will not conduct electricity
A. Aqueous KOH solution
B. Fused NaCl
C. Graphite
D. KCl in solid states

85. The ionisation energy will be maximum for the process
A. $Ba \rightarrow Ba^{2+}$ B. $Be \rightarrow Be^{2+}$
C. $Cs \rightarrow Cs^+$ D. $Li \rightarrow Li^+$

86. Maximum covalence an atom of an element is equal to
A. Number of unpaired electrons in the *s*- and *p*-orbitals of valency shell
B. Number of unpaired electrons in the *p*-orbitals of the valency shell
C. Total number of electrons in the *s*- and *p*-orbitals of the valency shell
D. Total number of electrons in the *p*-orbitals of valency shell

87. The process requiring the absorption of energy is
A. $F \rightarrow F^-$ B. $H \rightarrow H^-$
C. $Cl \rightarrow Cl^-$ D. $O \rightarrow O^{2-}$

88. Intramolecular hydrogen bonding is found in
A. Salicyldehyde B. Water
C. Acetaldehyde D. Phenol

89. Among NaF, NaCl, NaBr, NaI, the NaF has highest melting point because
A. It has maximum ionic character
B. It has minimum ionic character
C. It has associated molecules
D. It has least molecular weight

90. In co-ordinate bond, the acceptor atoms must essentially contain in its valency shell an orbital
A. With paired electron
B. With single electron
C. With no electron
D. With three electrons

91. Electrons having six electrons in its outermost orbital generally form
A. Complex ion B. Negative ion
C. Positive ion D. Zwitter ion

92. The pairs of bases in DNA are held together by
A. Hydrogen bonds
B. Ionic bonds
C. Phosphate groups
D. Deoxyribose groups

93. Solid NaCl is a bad conductor of electricity because
A. In solid NaCl there are no ions
B. Solid NaCl is covalent
C. In solid NaCl there is no velocity of ions
D. In solid NaCl there are no electrons

94. PCl_5 exists but NCl_5 does not because
A. Nitrogen has no vacant 2*d*-orbitals
B. NCl_5 is unstable
C. Nitrogen atom is much smaller than P
D. Nitrogen is highly inert

95. In HCHO, carbon atom has hybridisation
A. sp B. sp^2
C. sp^3 D. sp^3d^2

96. When a chlorine atom becomes a chloride ion, its size
A. Increases B. Decreases
C. Remains same D. None of these

97. Fluorine molecule is formed by the overlapping of
A. $s - p$ orbitals
B. $s - s$ orbitals
C. $p - p$ orbitals by end to end manner
D. $p - p$ orbitals by sides to sides manner

98. In dry ice there are following bond in between molecules
A. Ionic bond B. Covalent bond
C. Hydrogen bond D. None of these

99. In which of the following molecules, the central atom has sp^2-hybridisation
A. BeF_2 B. BF_3
C. C_2H_2 D. NH_3

100. Which of the following molecule is T-shaped
A. BeF_2 B. BCl_3
C. NH_3 D. ClF_3

101. The largest number of unpaired electron is present in
A. Nitrogen B. Fluorine
C. Oxygen D. S^{2-}

102. The increase in bond order results in
A. Decrease in bond length and increase in bond energy
B. Decrease in bond length and bond energy
C. Increase in bond length and bond energy
D. None

103. Most covalent halide of aluminium is
A. $AlCl_3$ B. AlI_3
C. $AlBr_3$ D. AlF_3

104. Which formulae does not correctly represents the bonding capacity of the atom involved

A. 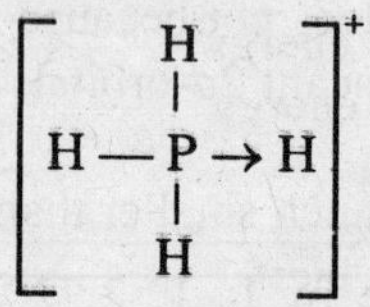 B. 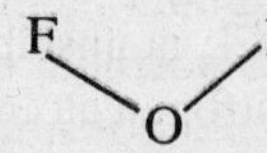

C. 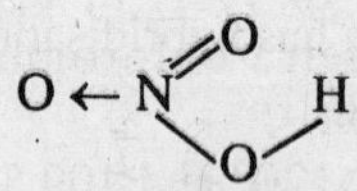 D. 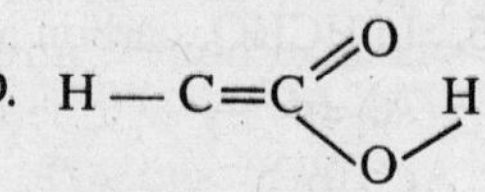

105. For the formation of covalent bond, the difference in the value of electronegativities should be

A. Equal to or less than 1.7
B. More than 1.7
C. 1.7 or more
D. None

106. Bond energy of covalent O—H bond in water is

A. Greater than bond energy of hydrogen bond
B. Equal to bond energy of hydrogen bond
C. Less than bond energy of hydrogen bond
D. None

107. The bond strength increases

A. With increasing bond order
B. With increasing extent of overlapping of orbitals
C. With decreasing difference between energies of overlapping orbitals
D. All of the above

108. If a molecules MX_3 has zero dipole moment the σ-bonding orbitals used by M (at no. < 21) is

A. Pure P B. *sp*-hybrid
C. sp^2-hybrid D. sp^3-hybrid

109. How many bonded electron pairs are present in IF_7 molecule

A. 6 B. 7
C. 5 D. 8

110. When the hybridisation state of carbon atom changes from sp^3 to sp^2 and finally to *sp*, the angle between the hybridised orbitals

A. Decreases gradually
B. Decreases considerably
C. Is not affected
D. Increases progressively

111. At ordinary temperature and pressure, among halogens, the chlorine is a gas, bromine is a liquid and iodine is a solid. This is because

A. The specific heat is in the order $Cl_2 > Br > I_2$
B. Intermolecular forces among molecules of chlorine are the weakest and those in iodine are the strongest
C. The order of density is $I_2 > Br_2 > Cl_2$
D. The order of stability is $Cl_2 > Br_2 > I_2$

112. Which of the following phenomenon will occur when two atoms of an element with same spin of electron in orbitals approach each other

A. Orbitals will overlap
B. Orbitals will not overlap
C. Bonding will take place
D. A diatomic molecule will be formed

113. The pair having similar geometry is

A. BF_3, NH_3 B. BF_3, AlF_3
C. BeF_3, H_2O D. BCl_3, PCl_3

114. The bond between atoms of two elements of atomic number 37 and 53 is

A. Covalent B. Ionic
C. Co-ordinate D. Metallic

115. As compared to ethylene, the bond distance between the two carbon atoms in acetylene is

A. Longer B. Shorter
C. Same D. None

116. Which bond angle, θ would result in the maximum dipole moment for the triatomic molecule XY_2 shown below :

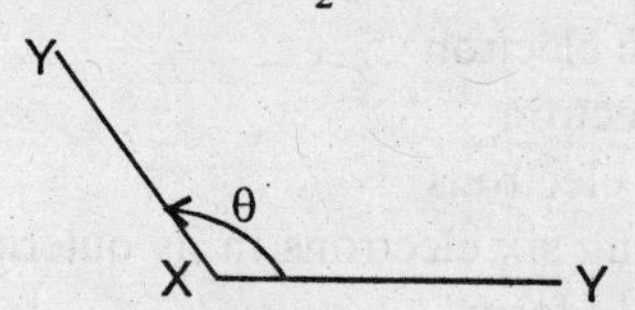

A. $\theta = 90°$ B. $\theta = 120°$
C. $\theta = 150°$ D. $\theta = 180°$

117. Solid CH_4 is

A. Molecular solid B. Ionic solid
C. Covalent solid D. Does not exist

118. The attraction that non polar molecules have for each other is primarily caused by

A. Hydrogen bonding
B. Difference in electronegativities
C. High ionisation energy
D. Van der Waal's forces

119. Which shows the highest lattice energy?

A. RbF B. CsF
C. NaF D. KF

120. Which of the following spacing has four lone pairs of electrons in its outershell

A. I B. O^-
C. Cl^- D. He

121. Which compound does not contain double or triple bond

A. C_2H_4 B. H_2O
C. N_2 D. HCN

122. Which of the following has unchanged valency

A. H B. Na
C. Fe D. O

123. Acetic acid exists as dimer in benzene due to

A. Condensation reaction
B. Hydrogen bonding
C. Presence of Carboxyl group
D. Presence of hydrogen atom at α-carbon

124. Oxygen is divalent, but sulphur exhibit variable valency of 2, 4 & 6 because

A. Sulphur is less electronegative than oxygen
B. Sulphur is bigger atom than oxygen
C. Ionisation potential of sulphur is more than that oxygen
D. Of the presence of *d*-orbitals in sulphur

125. The bond angle between H—O—H in ice is closest to

A. 115° B. 109°28'
C. 110° D. 90°

126. Greater the dipole moment

A. Greater is the ionic nature
B. Lesser is the polarity
C. Smaller the ionic nature
D. None of the above

127. The bond that determines the secondary structure of a protein is

A. Co-ordinate bond B. Covalent bond
C. Hydrogen bond D. Ionic bond

128. Acetate ion contains

A. One C, O single bond and one C, O double bond
B. Two C, O single bond
C. Two C, O double bond
D. None of the above

129. The valency of phosphorous in H_3PO_4 is

A. 2 B. 3
C. 4 D. 5

130. In a crystal the atoms are located at the positions of

A. Maximum potential energy
B. Minimum potential energy
C. Zero potential energy
D. Infinite potential energy

131. The Cl—C—Cl angle in 1, 1, 2, 2, tetra-chloroethene and tetra-chloromethane respectively will be about

A. 109.5° and 90° B. 120° and 109.5°
C. 90° and 109.5° D. 109.5° and 120°

132. The hybridisation of carbon atoms in C—C single bond of

$HC \equiv C - CH = CH_2$ is

A. $sp^3 - sp^3$ B. $sp^2 - sp^3$
C. $sp - sp^2$ D. $sp^3 - sp$

133. In which of the following process, energy is liberated

A. $Cl \rightarrow Cl^+ + e^-$ B. $HCl \rightarrow H^+ + Cl^-$
C. $Cl + e^+ \rightarrow Cl^-$ D. $O^- + e^+ \rightarrow O^{2-}$

134. The cyanide ion, CN^- and N_2 are iso electronic, but as compared to CN^-, N_2 is chemically inert while CN^- is not, because of

A. Low bond energy
B. Absence of bond polarity
C. Unsymmetrical electron distribution
D. Presence of more number of electrons in bonding orbitals

135. For a covalent solid, the units which occupy lattice points are

A. Atoms B. Ions
C. Molecules D. Electrons

136. The total number of valence electrons in 4.2 g of N_3^- ion are

A. 2.2 N B. 4.2 N
C. 1.6 N D. 3.2 N

137. In allene structure, three carbon atoms are joined by

A. 3σ and 3π-bonds B. 2σ and 1π-bond
C. 2σ and 2π-bonds D. 3π-bonds only

138. Which *p*-orbitals overlapping would give the strongest bond

A. 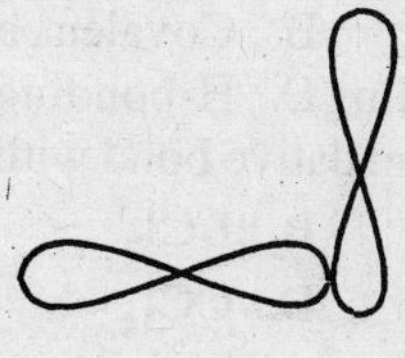

B. 

C. 

D. 

139. Which of the following statement is correct?
A. Polarisation of an anion is maximum by high charged cation
B. Small sized cations minimises the polarisation
C. A small anion brings about a large degree of polarisation
D. A small anion undergoes a high degree of polarisation

140. *p*-orbitals of an atom in presence of magnetic field are
A. Three fold degenerate
B. Two fold degenerate
C. Non-degenerate
D. None

141. The space between proton and electron in H-atom is
A. Full of air B. Full of ether
C. Empty D. None of these

142. The structure $CH_2{=}CH{-}CH{=}CH_2$ in all contains
A. 9σ and 1π bond
B. 8σ and 2π bond
C. 9σ and 2π bond
D. 8σ and 1π bond

143. C—C bond length is 1.54 Å. Which has bond length less than 1.54 Å
A. C—Cl B. C—Br
C. C—I D. C—H

144. Proton can take part in
A. Ionic bonding B. Covalent bonding
C. Co-ordinate bonding D. H-bonding

145. Compound which form dative bond with NH_3 is
A. NaCl B. BCl_3
C. CH_4 D. CCl_4

146. *p*-orbitals can have only.......... unpaired electrons
A. Zero B. 3
C. 2 D. 6

147. Which of the bonds is non-polar
A. C—O in CO_2 B. O—H in H_2O
C. N—N in N_2 D. H—Cl in HCl

148. Ice has an open structure compared to water due to which it floats on water and occupies a greater volume of space. The open structure of ice is due to
A. Solid state of ice B. Its low density
C. Crystalline nature D. Hydrogen bonding

149. A bond with maximum covalent character between non-metallic elements is formed
A. Between identical atoms
B. Between chemically similar atoms
C. Between atoms of widely different electronegativities
D. Between atoms of the same size

150. Which of the following is most stable?
A. Pb^{+2} B. Ge^{+2}
C. Si^{+2} D. Sn^{+2}

151. Shape of molecules is decided by
A. Sigma bond
B. π-bond
C. Both σ and π-bonds
D. None of these

152. Which of the following bond is most stable
A. $1s-1s$ B. $2p-2p$
C. $2s-2p$ D. $1s-2p$

153. Which property is commonly exhibited by a covalent compound
A. High solubility in water
B. Low *m.p.*
C. High electrical conductivity
D. High *b.p.*

154. The molecule having largest dipole moment among the following is
A. CH_4 B. $CHCl_3$
C. CCl_4 D. CHI_3

155. The geometry of H_2S and its dipole moment are
A. Angular and non zero
B. Angular and zero
C. Linear and non-zero
D. Linear and zero

156. As compared to covalent compounds, electrovalent compounds generally have
A. Low melting points and low boiling points
B. Low melting points and high boiling points
C. High melting points and low boiling points
D. High melting points and high boiling points

157. Which of the following bond is the most ionic?
A. Cs—Cl B. Al—Cl
C. C—Cl D. H—Cl

158. In the co-ordinate valency
A. Electrons are equally shared by the two atoms
B. Electrons of one atoms are shared with two atoms
C. Hydrogen bond is formed
D. None of the above

159. The type of bonds present in ammonium chloride are
A. Only ionic
B. Only covalent
C. Only covalent and coordinate
D. Ionic, covalent and coordinate

160. Pick up the iso-electronic structures from the following
I CH_3^+ II H_3O^+
III NH_3 IV CH_3^-
A. I and II B. III and IV
C. I and III D. II, III and IV

161. Beryllium atom in beryllium fluoride is
A. sp^3 hybridised B. sp^2 hybridised
C. sp hybridised D. Unhybridised

162. In $[Cu(NH_3)_4]SO_4$, copper has following hybridisation
A. dsp^2 B. sp^3
C. sp^2 D. sp^3d^2

163. Which has the least bond angle?
A. NH_3 B. BeF_2
C. H_2O D. CH_4

164. In a compound X, all the bond angles are exactly 109°28', is
A. Chloromethane
B. Iodoform
C. Carbon tetrachloride
D. Chloroform

165. If the electron pair forming a bond between two atoms A and B is not in the centre, then the bond is
A. Single bond B. Polar bond
C. Non-polar bond D. π-bond

166. Energy required to dissociate 4 gm of gaseous hydrogen into free gaseous atoms is 208 kcal at 25° C. The bond energy of H—H bond will be
A. 104 kcal B. 10.4 kcal
C. 1040 kcal D. 1.04 kcal

167. What is the maximum number of hydrogen bonds in which a water molecule can participate?
A. 1 B. 2
C. 3 D. 4

168. Which of the following has minimum number of unpaired electrons?
A. O_2 B. O_2^-
C. O_2^+ D. O_2^{2-}

169. The bond between two identical non-metal atoms has a pair of electrons
A. Unequally shared between the two
B. Transferred fully from one atom to another
C. With identical spins
D. Equally shared between them

170. Which of the following is square planar?
A. $[Ni(CN)_4]^{2-}$ B. $[NiCl_4]^{2-}$
C. SO_4^{2-} D. PO_4^{3-}

171. A trigonal bipyramidal molecule has bond angle(s) of
A. 90° B. 109°28'
C. 120° D. 90°, 120°

172. Which of the following cannot exist on the basis of MO theory?
A. H_2^+ B. He_2^+
C. He_2 D. O_2

173. Which of the following has a bond order of 3?
A. H_2 B. Ne_2
C. O_2 D. N_2

174. Which of the following has a bond order of $2\frac{1}{2}$?
A. HCl B. CO
C. CO_2 D. NO

175. Which of the following are paramagnetic?

(i) N_2, NO (ii) NO, O_2^-
(iii) CN^-, NO (iv) O_3, CO

A. (i) and (iii) B. (ii) only
C. (i) and (ii) D. (ii) and (iv)

176. Oxygen molecule is paramagnetic because

A. Bonding electrons are more than antibonding electrons
B. It contains unpaired electrons
C. Bonding electrons are less than antibonding electrons
D. Bonding electrons are equal to anti bonding electrons

177. Which of the following has the highest bond order?

A. O_2 B. O_2^+
C. O_2^- D. O_2^{2-}

178. Which of the following does not have a dipole moment?

A. ClO_2 B. CO_2
C. NO_2 D. SO_2

179. Carbon tetrachloride has no dipole moment it is because of

A. Planar structure
B. Tetrahedral structure
C. Similar size of a C and Cl
D. Similar electron affinity of C and Cl atoms

180. Dipole moment is shown by

A. 1, 4-Dichlorobenzene
B. *cis* 1, 2-Dichloroethene
C. *trans* 1, 2-Dichloroethene
D. *trans* 1, 2-Dichloro-2 pentene]

181. The bond in $K_4[Fe(CN)_6]$ are

A. All ionic
B. All covalent
C. Ionic and covalent
D. Ionic, covalent and coordinate covalent

182. The interatomic distance in H_2 and Cl_2 molecules are 74 and 198 pm respectively. The bond length of HCl is

A. 272 pm B. 136 pm
C. 124 pm D. 248 pm

183. The high boiling point of ethanol (78.2°C) compared to dimethyl ether (– 23.6°C), though having the same molecular formulae C_6H_6O, is due to

A. Hydrogen bonding
B. Ionic bonding
C. Coordinate covalent bonding
D. Resonance

184. Strength of hydrogen bond is intermediate between

A. Van der Waals and covalent
B. Ionic and covalent
C. Ionic and metallic
D. Metallic and covalent

185. The shape of $[OH_3]^+$ is

A. Tetrahedral B. Angular
C. Pyramidal D. Trigonal planar

186. The geometry of $Ni(CO)_4$ and $Ni(PPh_3)_2Cl_2$ are

A. Both square planar
B. Tetrahedral and square planar respectively
C. Both tetrahedral
D. Square planar and tetrahedral respectively

187. The hybridisation state of oxygen in water is

A. sp^2 B. sp^3
C. sp D. sp^3d^2

188. Hydrogen bond energy in around

A. 8.4 kJ mol^{-1} B. 8.4-42 kJ mol^{-1}
C. 42 kJ mol^{-1} D. None of these

189. An electrovalent compound does not exhibit space isomerism because of .... of the electrovalent bond

A. Directional nature
B. Non-directional nature
C. Multidimensional nature
D. None of these

190. When N_2 goes to N_2^+, the N—N bond distance ...., and when O_2 goes to O_2^+, the O—O bond distance ....

A. Decreases, increases
B. Increases, decreases
C. Remains same
D. None of the above

191. Which of the following statement is incorrect?

A. In its covalent compounds, the hydrogen atom has the electronic configuration analogous to that of neon

B. In a solution, all compounds exists in the ionic state
C. A π-bond is stronger than a σ-bond
D. All of the above

192. Calculate the % ionic character of a bond having 1.275 Å its length, and 1.03 D its dipole moment.
A. 1.683% B. 16.83%
C. 168.3% D. None of the above

193. Which of the following statement is correct?
A. In a bond H—X, the hydrogen atom is the positive end of dipole where X is any other than C or H
B. In a bond C—X, the carbon atom is the positive end of the dipole where X is any atom other than carbon
C. Dipole moment is a vector quantity
D. All of the above

194. Which of the following is incorrectly drawn?
A. Sulphuric acid (H_2SO_4)

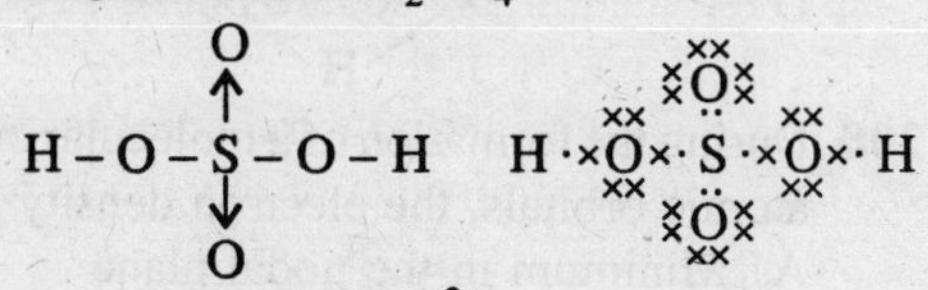

B. Carbonate ion, CO_3^{2-},

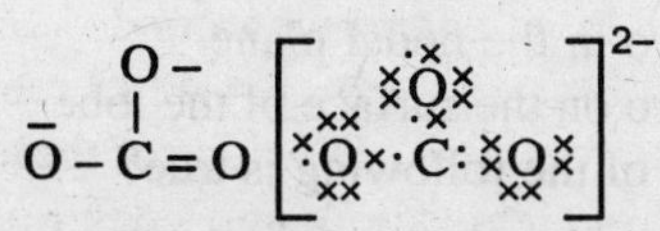

C. Hydrogen peroxide, H_2O_2, H—O—O—H
H ×Ö: Ö× H
D. None of the above

195. For the gaseous reaction
$K + F \rightarrow K^+ + F^-$, $\Delta H = 19$ kcal/mole
under conditions when cations and anions are prevented by electrostatic separation from combining with each other. The IE_1 of K is 4.3 eV, calculate electron affinity of F
A. 3.447 eV B. – 3.447 eV
C. 5.48 eV D. – 5.48 eV

196. The cohesive energy of an ionic crystal is the energy
A. Liberated during the formation of the crystal from individual neutral atoms
B. Absorbed during the formation of the crystal from individual neutral atoms
C. Liberated during the formation of positive ions
D. Absorbed during the formation of negative ions

197. What conclusions can be drawn from the following reactions?
$H_2 + 4.5\,eV \rightarrow H + H$
$H + 13.6\,eV \rightarrow H^+ + e^-$
A. It is more difficult to break up an H_2 molecule than it is to break up a hydrogen atom
B. It is easier to break up an H_2 molecule than it is to break up a hydrogen atom
C. The average energy of formation of H and H^+ are the same
D. Electron and proton attraction in an H_2 molecule as well as an H atom are the same.

198. $AlCl_3$ is covalent while AlF_3 is ionic. This can be justified on the basis of
A. The valence bond theory
B. Fajan's rule
C. The molecular orbital theory
D. Hydration energy

199. Which types of bond are not present in an HNO_2 molecule
A. Covalent
B. Coordinate
C. Ionic
D. Ionic as well as coordinate

200. Which of the following species have the maximum number of resonating structures?
A. PO_4^{3-} B. SO_4^{2-}
C. AsO_3^{2-} D. MnO_4^-

201. Which of the following have a 3-D network structure?
A. SiO_2 B. $(BN)_x$
C. P_4(white) D. CCl_4

202. Polarization involves the distortion of the shape of an anion by an adjacently placed cation. In this context, which of the following statements is correct?
A. Maximum polarization is brought about by a cation of high charge
B. Minimum polarization is brought about by a cation of low radius

C. A large cation is likely to bring about a high degree of polarization

D. The polarizing power of action is less than that of an anion

203. When two ice cubes are pressed together, they join to form one cube. Which of the following forces helps to hold them together

A. Hydrogen bond formation

B. Van der Waals forces

C. Covalent attractions

D. Dipole interaction

204. Which of the following statements are correct?

A. The crystal lattice of ice is mostly formed by covalent as well as hydrogen bonds

B. The density of water increases when heated from 0°C to 4°C due to the change in the structure of the cluster of water molecules

C. Above 4°C the thermal agitation of water molecules increases. Therefore, intermolecular distance increases and water starts expanding.

D. The density of water increases from 0°C to a maximum at 4°C because the entropy of the sytem increases.

E. All of the above

205. Intramolecular hydrogen bonding increases the enthalpy of vaporization of a liquid due to

A. Decrease in the attraction between molecules

B. Increase in the attraction between molecules

C. Decrease in the molar mass of unassociated liquid molecules

D. Increase in the effective molar mass of hydrogen-bonded molecules

206. Orthonitrophenol is steam volatile but paranitrophenol is not because

A. Orthonitrophenol has intramolecular hydrogen bonding while paranitrophenol has intramolecular hydrogen bonding

B. Both ortho-and paranitrophenol have intramolecular hydrogen bonding

C. Orthonitrophenol has intermolecular hydrogen bonding and paranitrophenol has intramolecular hydrogen bonding

D. Van der Waal's forces are dominant in orthonitrophenol

207. The H bond in solid HF can be best represented as

A. H—F- - -H—F- - -H—F

B. 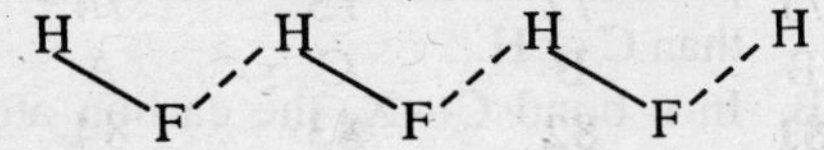

C. 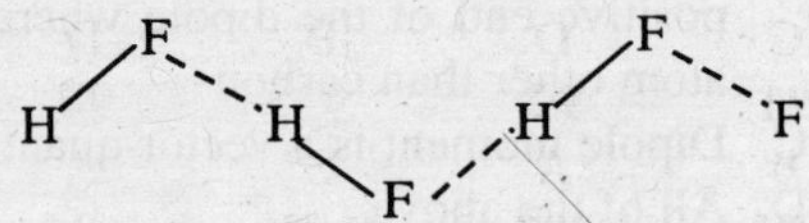

D. 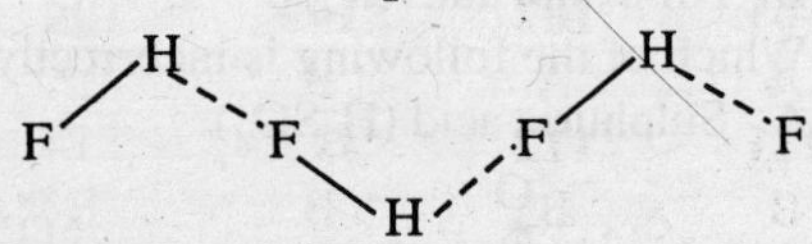

208. During the formation of a molecular orbital from atomic orbitals, the electron density is

A. Minimum in the nodal plane

B. Maximum in the nodal plane

C. Zero in the nodal plane

D. Zero on the surface of the lobe

209. Which of the following is true?

A. Bond order $\propto \frac{1}{\text{bond length}} \propto$ bond strength

B. Bond orders $\propto$ bond length $\propto \frac{1}{\text{bond strength}}$

C. Bond order $\propto \frac{1}{\text{bond length}} \propto \frac{1}{\text{bond strength}}$

D. Bond order $\propto$ bond length $\propto$ bond strength

ANSWERS

1	2	3	4	5	6	7	8	9	10
C	B	B	A	C	D	C	C	B	C
11	**12**	**13**	**14**	**15**	**16**	**17**	**18**	**19**	**20**
D	A	B	C	A	C	C	B	A	A

21	22	23	24	25	26	27	28	29	30
A	C	A	B	B	B	B	C	A	B
31	32	33	34	35	36	37	38	39	40
A	A	C	B	C	D	C	C	A	A
41	42	43	44	45	46	47	48	49	50
C	D	A	A	B	B	A	A	A	C
51	52	53	54	55	56	57	58	59	60
A	C	C	C	A	B	B	D	B	C
61	62	63	64	65	66	67	68	69	70
D	B	D	D	C	C	A	A	B	A
71	72	73	74	75	76	77	78	79	80
B	B	C	A	B	C	C	B	C	D
81	82	83	84	85	86	87	88	89	90
C	D	B	C	B	C	D	A	A	C
91	92	93	94	95	96	97	98	99	100
B	A	C	A	B	A	C	B	B	D
101	102	103	104	105	106	107	108	109	110
A	A	B	D	A	A	D	C	B	D
111	112	113	114	115	116	117	118	119	120
B	B	B	B	B	A	D	B	C	B
121	122	123	124	125	126	127	128	129	130
B	B	D	B	A	C	A	D	B	D
131	132	133	134	135	136	137	138	139	140
C	C	B	A	C	C	C	A	C	C
141	142	143	144	145	146	147	148	149	150
C	D	C	B	B	C	D	A	A	A
151	152	153	154	155	156	157	158	159	160
A	B	B	A	D	A	B	D	D	C
161	162	163	164	165	166	167	168	169	170
A	C	C	B	A	D	C	D	A	D
171	172	173	174	175	176	177	178	179	180
C	D	D	B	B	B	D	B	B	B,D
181	182	183	184	185	186	187	188	189	190
D	B	A	B	C	C	B	B	B	B
191	192	193	194	195	196	197	198	199	200
D	B	D	D	B	A	B	B	D	B
201	202	203	204	205	206	207	208	209	
A, B	A	A	E	B,D	A	C	C	C	

10

THERMODYNAMICS

Heat of Solution or Enthalpy of Solution

It is defined as the change in heat enthalpy when one mole of a substance is dissolved in excess of water so that further dilution does not involve any heat change, e.g.,

$KCl + aq. \rightarrow KCl\ aq.\ \ \Delta H = 4.4$ k cal

$CuSO_4 + aq. \rightarrow CuSO_4.5H_2O$ aq.

$\Delta H = -15.8$ k cal

$CuSO_4.5H_2O + aq. \rightarrow CuSO_4.5H_2O$ aq.

$\Delta H = +2.9$ k cal

The exothermic and endothermic values of heat of solutions for electrolytes dissolution in water are explained as follows :

On dissolution of an electrolyte in water, there occurs two phenomenon :

(i) Heat of ionisation (ΔH_i) is required to separate ions from each other, i.e., $\Delta H_i = +ve$

(ii) Heat of hydration (ΔH_h) is released during hydration of ions, i.e., $\Delta H_h = -ve$

Thus, $\Delta H_{solution} = \Delta H_i + \Delta H_h$;

if $\Delta H_i > \Delta H_h$; $\Delta H_s = +ve$, i.e., endothermic dissolution.

if $\Delta H_i < \Delta H_h$; $\Delta H_s = -ve$, i.e., exothermic dissolution.

Thermodynamics

System : A specific portion of matter under study which is isolated from the rest of the universe with a bounding surface is called a system's surroundings. The rest of the universe which might be in a position to exchange energy and matter with the system is called the surroundings.

Types of Systems :

(a) A system which can exchange mass as well as energy with the surroundings is called "open system", e.g., line kiln, ice in an open beaker.

(b) A system that can exchange energy with the surroundings and not mass is called a 'closed system' i.e. ice in a closed beaker.

(c) A system which can exchange neither mass nor energy with the surroundings is called isolated system e.g. ice. in a thermous flask.

Extensive Property : A property which depends upon the amount of the substance(s) present in the system. e.g. mass, volume, energy, work, internal energy, enthalpy, entropy, etc.

Intensive Property : A property which is independent of amount of substance(s) present in the system is called 'intensive property' e.g. temperature, pressure, density, concentration, viscosity, refractive index, surface tension, specific heat, etc.

State Functions : The thermodynamic parameters which depend only upon initial and final states of the system and are independent of how the change is accomplished are called *state functions*.

Example : Internal energy, enthalpy, entropy, free energy, pressure, temperature, volume, etc. Work and heat energy are not state functions.

Internal Energy (E) : The total energy stored in a substance by virtue of its chemical nature is called its internal energy, i.e. it is the sum of its translational, vibrational, rotational, chemical bond energy, electronic energy, nuclear energy of constituent atoms as potential energy due to interaction with neighbouring molecules is called Internal or Intrinsic Energy :

$$E = E_t + E_r + E_v + E_e + E_n + E_{PE}.$$

Laws of Thermodynamics

First Law of Thermodynamics : It is simply the law of conservation of energy which states that "Energy can neither be created nor destroyed although it can be converted from one from to another".

When work is done by the system

$$\Delta E = Q - W$$

When work is done on the system

$$\Delta E = Q + W$$

In case of small changes

$\delta E = \delta Q - \delta W$ (In case work is done by the system i.e., expansion)

or $\Delta E = \Delta Q - PdV$

$\Delta E = \delta Q + \delta W$ (in case work is done on the system compression) = $\delta Q + PdV$

(i) When $Q = W$, i.e., cyclic process, $\Delta E = 0$

(ii) When volume remains constant $\Delta E = Q_v$ where v indicates constant volume.

(iii) For adiabatic process, $Q = 0$,

$\therefore\ \Delta E = -Wq$ where q indicates constant heat.

(iv) When a gas expands against an external pressure P, the work done by it will be:

$$P\Delta V \quad (\Delta V = V_2 - V_1), \text{ i.e.,}$$
$$W = -P\Delta V$$

(v) When a gas is compressed, work is done on the system and is given by $P\Delta V$.

(vi) When a gas expands into vaccum, work done by it is zero, since $P = 0$, therefore $W = 0$.

(vii) In case of expansion of a gas, maximum work is done, if the process is isothermal and reversible.

Second Law of Thermodynamics : This states that "heat cannot itself pass from a colder to a warmer body." Thus, if heat is to be transferred from the cold to the hot body, work must be provided by an external agency. An alternative and useful expression of the second law is "any system of its own accord will always undergo change in such a way as to increase the entropy."

"Every perfect machine working reversibly between the same temperature of source and sink have the same efficiency whatever be nature of substance used" (Carnot-theorem).

Carnot Cycle : It is a hypothetical scheme for an ideal heat machine. It shows that the maximum efficiency for the conversion of heat into work depends only on the two temperatures between which the heat engine works, and not at all one the nature of substance employed :

$$n = \frac{W}{Q_2} = \frac{Q_2 - Q_1}{Q_2} = \frac{T_2 - T_1}{T_2}$$

Q_2 = heat absorbed from the source
Q_1 = heat returned to the sink
T_2 = Temperature in A° of the source
T_1 = Temperature in A° of the sink
W = Work done
n = Efficiency of the machine

Lord Kelvin Statement : "It is impossible to take heat from a hotter reservoir and convert it completely into work by a cyclic process without transferring a part of it to a cooler reservoir." This statement recognizes the fact that the heat engine can never be 100% efficient.

Clausius Statement : "It is impossible for a cyclic process to transfer heat from a system at a lower temperature to one at higher temperature without applying some work" i.e. without converting some work to heat.

Third Law of Thermodynamics : This states that "for a perfect crystal at about zero on the Kelvin scale, the entropy is zero." This follows the predictions of Einstein (1807) that the specific heats of all substances would approach zero at 0 Kelvin and the conclusion of Planck (1912) that the entropy of all pure solids and liquids approach zero at this temperature.

Entropy (S)

It is a thermodynamic quantity which is a measure of the degree of disorder within any system. The greater the degree of disorder, the higher the entropy. Thus, for a given substance,

$$S_{gas} > S_{liquid} > S_{solid}.$$

Any change taking place which results in an increase in entropy has a positive entropy change (ΔS). Most spontaneous thermodynamic processes are accompanied by an increase in entropy. Entropy has units of joules per degree K per mole.

The entropy of the universe always increase in the course of every natural change i.e.

$\Delta S_{universe} > 0$ and energy of universe is conserved while entropy of universe always increases in any natural or spontaneous process.

Gibbs Free Energy (ΔG)

It is a thermodynamic state function represented by G (after Willard Gibbs). The free energy change (ΔG) in any system is related to the enthalpy and entropy changes by the equation :

$$\Delta G = \Delta H - T\Delta S$$

ΔG is a measure of the maximum amount of useful work which may be obtained from the change under consideration. In any system, the value of the free energy change determines the position of equilibrium in that at equilibrium the free energy ΔG = 0. For substances in their standard state, i.e. 1 mole at 1 atmospheric pressure and a specified temperature, the change in free energy is called the 'standard free energy change, ΔG°_T. This latter quantity is of considerable importance, in that, it determines the thermodynamic feasibility of a reaction. For a reaction to be thermodynamically feasible and thus for more products than reactants to be formed at equilibrium, the value of ΔG° must be negative, i.e. there must be a decrease in standard free energy from reactants to products. ΔG and ΔG° are usually expressed in kilojoules per mole for chemical reactions.

(*i*) For spontaneous process, ΔG is negative

(*ii*) For process in equillibrium, ΔG is zero

(*iii*) For process occuring in backward direction and not in forward direction ΔG is positive.

Standard free energy change (ΔG°) and equillibrium constant are related as below :

$$\Delta G^\circ = -2.303\ RT \log K$$

where ΔG° = (Free energy of formation of products – Free energy of formation of reactants).

Standard enthalpies of formation (ΔH_f°), standard free energies of formation (ΔG_f°) and absolute entropies of selected substances at 298 K are given below :

By definition , all pure elements have

$$\Delta H^\circ_f = 0 \text{ and } \Delta G^\circ_f = 0$$

OBJECTIVE QUESTIONS

1. Which of the following mathematical relations are correct for an ideal gas?

A. $\left(\frac{\delta H}{\delta V}\right)_T = 0$ B. $\left(\frac{\delta H}{\delta p}\right)_T = 0$

C. $\left(\frac{\delta H}{\delta V}\right)_T = 0$ D. None of the above

2. An adiabatic process is a process in which

A. All energy is transferred as heat

B. No energy is transferred as heat

C. The temperature of a gas decreases in a reversible adiabatic expansion

D. B and C

3. If the internal energy of an ideal gas decreases by the same amount as the work done by the system, the process is

A. Cyclic B. Isothermal

C. Adiabatic D. Isolated

4. When the gas is ideal and the process is isothermal, then

A. $P_1V_1 = P_2V_2$ B. $E_1 = E_2$

C. $H_1 \neq H_2$ D. A and B

5. When heat is supplied to an ideal gas in an isothermal process, the

A. Gas will do positive work

B. Gas will do negative work

C. Kinetic energy of gas will increase

D. Gas will not obey the law of conservation of energy

6. Which of the following statements are correct?

A. The work done by the system on the surroundings is negative

B. The work done on the system by the surroundings is positive

C. The heat absorbed by the systems from the surroundings is positive

D. The heat absorbed by the surroundings from the system is negative

E. All of the above

7. Which of the following is a path function dependent as well as an extensive property?

A. Temperature

B. Internal energy

C. Molar heat capacity

D. Heat capacity

E. B and D

8. The molar heat capacity of water in equilibrium with ice at constant pressure is:
A. Negative B. Zero
C. Infinity D. 40.45 kJ $K^{-1}mol^{-1}$

9. For ideal diatomic gases
A. $C_p = \left(\frac{7}{2}\right)R$ B. $C_V = \left(\frac{5}{2}\right)R$
C. $C_p = \left(\frac{3}{2}\right)R$ D. A and C

10. When a solid melts, there will be
A. An increase in enthalpy
B. A decrease in free energy
C. No change in enthalpy
D. Decrease in internal energy
E. A and B

11. Which of the following are thermodynamically stable?
A. C (diamond) B. C (graphite)
C. P_4 (white) D. P_4 (red)
E. B and D

12. Which of the following isomeric hydrocarbons is the most stable on the basis of enthalpy of combustion?
A. 1-Butene B. *trans*-2-Butene
C. 2-Methylpropene D. *cis*-2-Butene

13. Which of the following is exothermic compound with respect to enthalpy of formation?
A. C_2H_2 (g) B. HI (g)
C. HBr (g) D. I_2 (g)

14. Which of the following have maximum standard enthalpy of formation?
A. Glucose B. Sucrose
C. Hexane D. Ethanol

15. The additivity property of ΔH° (formation) value is known as
A. Kirchhoff's law
B. The Lavoisier and Laplace Law
C. Hess's law
D. The Pauling rule

16. Equal volumes of 1 M HCl and 1 M H_2SO_4 are neutralized by a 1 M NaOH solution and x and y kJ/equivalent of heat is liberated respectively. Which of the following relations is correct?
A. $x = 2y$ B. $x = 4y$
C. $x = 3y$ D. $x = \frac{1}{2}y$

17. In which of the following thermochemical reactions is ΔH° always negative?
A. Enthalpy of solution
B. Enthalpy of hydrogenation
C. Enthalpy of reaction
D. Enthalpy of transition

18. For a reversible process, the total change in entropy of the universe is equal to
A. ΔS (system) + ΔS (surroundings)
B. ΔS (system) – ΔS (surroundings)
C. Zero
D. Negative

19. Which of the following statements are correct?
A. The entropy of an isolated system increases in an irreversible process
B. The entropy of an isolated system remains unchanged in a reversible process
C. The entropy can never decrease
D. All of the above

20. In the following table, which are correct?

	ΔH	ΔS	*Nature of Reaction*
1.	(–)	(+)	Spontaneous at all temperature
2.	(+)	(–)	Non-spontaneous regardless of temperature
3.	(+)	(+)	Spontaneous only at high temperature
4.	(–)	(–)	Spontaneous only at low temperature

A. 1, 2 only B. 1, 2 and 4 only
C. 1 and 4 only D. All of the above

21. A gas expands from 3 dm^3 to 5 dm^3 against a constant pressure of 3 atm. The work done during expansion is used to heat 10 mole of water at a temperature of 290 K. Calculate final temperature of water. Specific heat of water = 4.184 J $g^{-1}K^{-1}$
A. 290 K B. 290.81 K
C. 280.67 K D. 276.00 K

22. Combustion of glucose takes place according to the following equation

$$C_6H_{12}O_6(s) + 6O_2(g) \rightarrow 6CO_2(g) + 6H_2O(g)$$

ΔH = – 72 k cal

How much energy will be required for the production of 1.6 g of glucose?

A. 0.94 k cal B. 0.66 k cal
C. 0.64 k cal D. 1.01 k cal

23. An athlete is given 100 g of glucose ($C_6H_{12}O_6$) of energy equivalent to 1560 kJ. He utilizes 50% of this gained energy in the event. In order to avoid storage of energy in the body, calculate the weight of water he would need to perspire. The enthalpy of evaporation of water is 44 kJ/mole.
A. 121 g B. 319.99 g
C. 379.1 g D. 428.2 g

24. The enthalpy change involved in the oxidation of glucose is – 2880 kJ mol^{-1}. Twenty-five per cent of this energy is available for muscular work. If 100 kJ of muscular work is needed to walk one kilometre, what is the maximum distance that a person will be able to walk after taking 120 g of glucose.
A. 3.6 km B. 5.3 km
C. 4.8 km D. 9.1 km

25. The standard heats of formation at 298 K for CCl_4(g), and HCl (g) are – 25.5, – 57.8, – 94.1 and – 22.1 k cal/mole respectively. Calculate the $\Delta H°_{298}$ for the reaction.
A. – 33.0 k cal B. 41.4 k cal
C. + 41.4 k cal D. + 33.0 k cal

26. The molar heats of combustion of C_2H_2(g); C (graphite), and H_2(g) are 310.62 k cal, 94.05 k cal and 68.32 k cal respectively. Calculate the standard heat of formation of C_2H_2(g).
A. 15.31 k cal B. 30.12 k cal
C. 45.31 k cal D. 54.20 k cal

27. The heats of combustion of C_2H_4(g), C_2H_6(g) and H_2(g) are – 1409.5 kJ, – 1558.3 kJ and – 285.6 kJ, respectively. Calculate the heat of hydrogenation of ethylene.
A. – 123.3 kJ B. – 136.8 kJ
C. – 146.11 kJ D. – 151.45 kJ

28. Determine the enthalpy change of the reaction,
$C_3H_8(g) + H_2(g) \rightarrow C_2H_6(g) + CH_4(g)$
at 25°C, using the given heat of combustion values under standard conditions.
Compound (ΔH°(kJ/mole))

H_2(g)	CH_4(g)	C_2H_6(g)	C (graphite)
–285.8	–890.0	–1560.0	–393.5

The standard heat of formation of C_3H_8(g) is – 103.8 kJ/mol.

A. 2609.5 kJ/mol B. + 55.7 kJ/mol
C. – 55.7 kJ/mol D. – 78.6 kJ/mol

29. From the following data, calculate the enthalpy change for the combustion of cyclopropane at 298 K. The enthalpy of formation of CO_2(g), H_2O(*l*) and propene (g) are – 393.5, – 285.8 and 20.42 kJmol^{-1} respectively. The enthalpy of isomerisation of cyclopropane to propene is – 33.0 kJ mol^{-1}.
A. – 1180.5 kJ B. – 857.4 kJ
C. – 2091.32 kJ D. – 3167.64 kJ

30. An intimate mixture of ferric oxide, Fe_2O_3, and aluminium, Al is used in solid fuel rockets. Calculate the fuel value per gram and fuel value per c.c. of the mixture. Heats of formation and densities are as follows :
$H_f(Al_2O_3)$ = 399 k cal/mole
Density of Fe_2O_3 = 5.2 g/cc
$H_f(Fe_2O_3)$ = 199 k cal/mole
Density of Al = 2.7 g/cc
A. 0.1234 k cal/g and 1.26 k cal/cc
B. 0.394 k cal/g and 0.934 k cal/cc
C. 0.9346 k cal/g and 3.94 k cal/cc
D. 0.864 k cal/g and 2.119 k cal/cc

31. Calculate the difference between heats of reaction at constant pressure and constant volume of the reaction at 25°C in kJ.
$2C_6H_6(l) + 15O_2(g) \rightarrow 12CO_2(g) + 6H_2O(l)$
A. – 8.4 kJ B. – 7.4 kJ
C. – 3.6 kJ D. – 5.4 kJ

32. The standard molar enthalpies of formation of cyclohexane (*l*) and benzene (*l*) at 25°C are – 156 and + 49 kJ mol^{-1} respectively. The standard enthalpy of hydrogenation of cyclohexene (*l*) at 25°C is – 119 kJ mol^{-1}. Use these data to estimate the magnitude of the resonance energy of benzene.
A. – 357 kJ/mol. B. – 152 kJ mol^{-1}
C. – 136 kJ mol^{-1} D. – 111 kJ/mol

33. The enthalpy for the following reactions (ΔH°) at 25°C are given below :
(*i*) $\frac{1}{2}H_2(g) + \frac{1}{2}O_2(g) \rightarrow OH(g)$; 10.06 kcal
(*ii*) $H_2(g) \rightarrow 2H(g)$; 104.18 kcal
(*iii*) $O_2(g) \rightarrow 2O(g)$; 118.32 kcal

Calculate the O—H bond energy in the hydroxyl radical.

A. – 101.19 kcal B. + 206.13 kcal
C. – 206.13 kcal D. + 109.19 kcal

34. Estimate the average SF bond energy in SF_6. The standard heat of formation values of $3F_6$(g), S(g) and F(g) are – 1100, 275 and 80 kJ mol^{-1} respectively.

A. 1855 kJ mol^{-1} B. 1482 kJ mol^{-1}
C. 309.6 kJ mol^{-1} D. 716.2 kJ mol^{-1}

35. Compute the heat of formation of liquid methyl alcohol in kilojoules permole using the following data. Heat of vaporisation of liquid methyl alcohol = 38 kJ/mol. Heat of formation of gaseous atoms from the elements in their standard states are
H = 218 kJ mol^{-1}, C = 715 kJ mol^{-1} and O = 249 kJ mol^{-1}. Average bond energies are
C—H = 415 kJ mol^{-1}
C—O = 356 kJ mol^{-1}
O—H = 463 kJ mol^{-1}

A. 266 kJ mol^{-1} B. 316 kJ mol^{-1}
C. – 226 kJ mol^{-1} D. 426 kJ mol^{-1}

36. The bond dissociation energies of gaseous H_2, Cl_2 and HCl are 104, 58 and 103 kcal/mole respectively. Calculate the enthalpy of formation of HCl gas

A. 24 kcal B. – 26 kcal
C. – 22 kcal D. 23 kcal

37. *(i)* Calculate the efficiency of a steam engine operating between 110°C and 25°C.
(ii) What would be the efficiency of the engine if the boiler temperature is raised to 140°C, the temperature of the sink remaining same?

A. *(i)* 22.2% and *(ii)* 27.8% respectively
B. *(i)* 26.1% and *(ii)* 30.1% respectively
C. *(i)* 29.0% and *(ii)* 36.3% respectively
D. *(i)* 46.1% and *(ii)* 73.1% respectively

38. An engine operating between 100°C and 0°C taken 453.6 kcal of heat. How much useful work can be done by it?

A. 316.8 kJ B. 319.8 kJ
C. 508.8 kJ D. 617.9 kJ

39. Identify the intensive quantity from the following:

A. Enthalpy and temperature
B. Volume and temperature
C. Enthalpy and volume
D. Temperature and refractive index

40. When a gas is subjected to adiabatic expansion, it gets cooled due to

A. Fall in temperature
B. Loss in kinetic energy
C. Decrease in velocity
D. Energy spent in doing work

41. The change in internal energy of a system depends on

A. Initial and final states of a system
B. Whether the path is reversible
C. Whether the path is irreversible
D. None of the above

42. The amount of heat measured for a reaction in a bomb calorimeter is

A. ΔG B. ΔH
C. ΔE D. PΔV

43. The enthalpies of elements in their standard states are taken as zero. Hence the enthalpy of formation of a compound

A. Should always be negative
B. Should always be positive
C. Will be equal to twice the energy of combustion
D. May be positive or negative

44. If ΔH is the change in enthlapy and ΔE is the change in internal energy accompanying a gaseous reaction, then

A. ΔH is always greater than ΔE
B. ΔH < ΔE only if the number of moles of products is greater than the number of reactants
C. ΔH is always less than ΔE
D. ΔH < ΔE only if the number of moles of products is less than the number of moles of reactants.

45. From Kirchhoff's equation which factor affects the heat of reaction?

A. Pressure B. Temperature
C. Volume D. Molecularity

46. Which one is not applicable for a thermo-chemical reaction?
A. It tells about the physical state of the reactants and products
B. It tells whether a reaction is exothermic or endothermic
C. It tells about the allotropic form (if any) of the reactant
D. It tells whether a particular reaction is possible or not

47. Evaporation of water is
A. An exothermic change
B. An endothermic change
C. A process where no heat change occurs
D. A process accompanied by chemical reaction

48. Which of the following fuels will have highest calorific value (kJ/kg)?
A. Charcoal B. Kerosene
C. Wood D. Dung

49. Of the reactions stated, the endothermic reactions is
A. Burning sulphur to sulphur dioxide
B. Conversion of monoclinic sulphur to rhombic sulphur
C. Formation of carbon dioxide from carbon and oxygen
D. Melting sulphur

50. Heat of neutralisation of strong acid against strong base is constant and is equal to
A. 13.7 kJ B. 57 kJ
C. 5.7×10^4 J D. All of the above

51. For an endothermic reaction where ΔH represents the enthalpy of the reaction in kJ/mole, the minimum value for the energy available will be
A. Less than ΔH B. Zero
C. More than ΔH D. Equal to ΔH

52. Heat of transition is the heat evolved or absorbed when a substance is converted from
A. Solid to liquid
B. Solid to vapour
C. Liquid to vapour
D. One allotropic form to another allotropic form

53. A spontaneous reaction is impossible if
A. Both ΔH and ΔS are negative
B. Both ΔH and ΔS are positive
C. ΔH is negative and ΔS is positive
D. ΔH is positive and ΔS is negative

54. In which of the following case, entropy decrease
A. Solid changing to liquid
B. Expansion of a gas
C. Crystals dissolve
D. Polymerisation

55. In which case, a spontaneous reaction is impossible at any temperature
A. $\Delta H > 0, \Delta S > 0$ B. $\Delta H < 0, \Delta S < 0$
C. $\Delta H > 0, \Delta S < 0$ D. In all the cases

56. Warming ammonium chloride with sodium hydroxide in a test tube is an example of
A. Closed system B. Isolated system
C. Open system D. None of the above

57. Net work done by a system is given by
A. Decrease in Helmholtz free energy (ΔH)
B. Decrease in Gibb's free energy (ΔG)
C. Decrease in internal energy
D. Decrease in heat enthalpy

58. The work done by a weightless piston in causing an expanstion ΔV (at constant temperature), when the opposing pressure, P is variable, is given by
A. $W = -\int P\Delta V$ B. $W = 0$
C. $W = -P\Delta V$ D. None

59. When an ideal gas is compressed adiabatically and reversibly, the final temperature is
A. Higher than the initial temperature
B. Lower than the initial temperature
C. The same as the initial temperature
D. Dependent on the rate of compression

60. Work done by the system in a cyclic process is equal to
A. Zero B. ΔE
C. ΔH D. q

61. Internal energy of an ideal gas depends on
A. Pressure B. Temperature
C. Volume D. None

62. A spontaneous change is one in which the system suffers
A. An increase in internal energy

B. A lowering of entropy
C. A lowering of free energy
D. No energy

63. It is a general principle that if the energy of system is lesser, it is
A. More stable B. Less stable
C. Unstable D. More unstable

64. Identify the correct statement regarding entropy
A. At absolute zero of temperature the entropy of perfectly crystalline substance is +ve
B. At absolute zero of temperature, entropy of perfectly crystalline substance is taken to be zero
C. At 0°C, the entropy of perfectly crystalline substance is taken to be zero
D. At absolute zero of temperature, the entropy of all crystalline substances is taken to be zero.

65. A reaction taking place with absorption of energy is
A. Burning of a candle
B. Electrolysis of water
C. Digestion of food
D. Rusting of iron

66. Vibrational energy is
A. Partially potential and partially kinetic
B. Only potential
C. Only kinetic
D. None of the above

67. All the naturally occurring processes i.e. spontaneous processes proceed spontaneously in a direction which leads to
A. Decrease of free energy
B. Increase of free energy
C. Decrease of entropy
D. Increase of enthalpy

68. Select the correct limitations of IIIrd law of thermodynamics
A. Glassy solids at zero Kelvin has entropy greater than zero
B. Solids having mixtures of isotopes do not have entropy zero at zero Kelvin
C. Crystals of CO, N_2O, NO, H_2O, etc. do not have zero entropy at zero Kelvin
D. All of the above

69. For which process energy will be absorbed
A. Separation of an electron from an electron
B. Separation of proton from a proton
C. Separation of a neutron from neutron
D. Separation of an electron from a neutral atom

70. When two atoms of hydrogen combine to form a molecule of hydrogen gas, the energy of the molecule is
A. Greater than that of separate atoms
B. Equal to that of separate atoms
C. Lower than that of separate atoms
D. Sometimes lower and sometimes higher

71. On dissolving NaCl in water, there occurs
A. Increase in free energy
B. Increase in entropy
C. Decrease in entropy
D. No change in entropy

72. When hydrogen and oxygen burn to form water in an oxyhydrogen torch, the entropy change is
A. –ve B. +ve
C. 0 D. +ve or –ve

73. If a refrigerator door is kept open, then we get
A. Room cooled
B. Room heated
C. More heat is passed out
D. No effect on room

74. Less random state of water is
A. Ice
B. Liquid water
C. Steam
D. All are present in same random state

75. In a reversible isothermal process, the change in internal energy is
A. Zero B. Positive
C. Negative D. None

76. When the value of entropy is greater, then the ability for work is
A. Maximum B. Minimum
C. Medium D. None of these

77. Human body is an example of
A. Open system B. Closed system
C. Isolated system D. None

78. A closed flask contains water in all its three states, solid, liquid and vapour at 0°C. In this situation the average KE of the water molecule will be

A. Maximum in vapour state
B. Maximum in solid state
C. Greater in the liquid than in vapour state
D. Same in all the three states

79. The internal energy of one mole of gas is

A. $\frac{3}{2}RT$ B. $\frac{kT}{2}$
C. $\frac{RT}{2}$ D. $\frac{3kT}{2}$

80. Work done in reversible adiabatic process is given by

A. $2.303\,RT\log\frac{V_2}{V_1}$ B. $\frac{nR}{(r-1)}(T_2 - T_1)$
C. $2.303\,RT\log\frac{V_1}{V_2}$ D. None

81. The efficiency of a heat engine is maximum when

A. Temperature of source > temperature of sink
B. Temperature of sink > temperature of source
C. Temperature difference of source and sink is minimum
D. Temperature difference of source and sink is maximum

82. Enthalpy of vaporisation for water is 186.5 kJ mol^{-1}. The entropy change during vaporisation is ....kJ $K^{-1}mol^{-1}$

A. 0.5 B. 1.0
C. 1.5 D. 2.0

83. If 50 calorie are added to a system and system does work of 30 calorie on surroundings, the change in internal energy of system is

A. 20 cal B. 50 cal
C. 40 cal D. 30 cal

84. Latent heat of vaporisation of a liquid at 500 K and 1 atm. pressure is 10.0 kcal/mol. What will be the change in internal energy (ΔE) of 3 mole of liquid at same temperature

A. 13.0 kcal B. – 13.0 kcal
C. 27.0 kcal D. – 27.0 kcal

85. A system absrobs 10 kJ of heat at constant volume and its temperature rises from 27°C to 37°C. The ΔE of reaction is

A. 100 kJ B. Zero
C. 10 kJ D. 1 kJ

86. A carnot engine operates between temperature T and 400 K (T > 400 K). If efficiency of engine is 25%, the temperature T is

A. 400 K B. 500 K
C. 533.3 K D. 600 K

87. Boiling point of a liquid is 50 K at 1 atm. and $\Delta H_{vap.} = 460.6$ cal mol^{-1}. What will be its *b.p.* at 10 atm.

A. 150 K B. 75 K
C. 100 K D. 200 K

88. Heat of formation of a compound is equal in magnitude to

A. Heat of that reaction
B. Heat of dissociation
C. Heat of combustion
D. Heat of solution

89. Which phenomenon cannot be described as oxidation

A. Oxidation of coal in air
B. Burning of magnesium in nitrogen
C. Reaction of antimony with chlorine
D. Lighting of an electric lamp.

90. The enthalpies of formation of organic substance can be conveniently determined from

A. Heats of combustion data
B. Boiling point
C. Melting point
D. Heats of neutralisation

91. Which of the following statement is wrong

A. An endothermic reaction must absorb energy before it can take place
B. During an exothermic reaction, heat is evolved
C. After an exothermic reaction, there is no change in the temperature of the reaction mixture
D. None of the above

92. The enthalpy change of a reaction does not depend on

A. State of reactants and products
B. Nature of reactants and products
C. Different intermediate reactions
D. Initial and final enthalpy change of reaction

93. The law of Lavoisier and Laplace is based on

A. The principle of conservation of energy

B. Equivalence of mechanical and thermal energies
C. The principle of conservation of matter
D. Equivalence of mechanical and chemical energies

94. Heat of neutralisation of a strong acid and a strong base is equal to ΔH of
A. $H^+ + OH^- = H_2O$
B. $H_2O + H^+ = H_3O^+$
C. $2H_2 + O_2 = 2H_2O$
D. $CH_3COOH + NaOH \rightarrow CH_3COONa + H_2O$

95. Calorific value of carbohydrate is approximately
A. 4.0 kcal/g B. 20 kcal/g
C. 16.0 kcal/g D. 9.0 kcal/g

96. The bond energy of H_2 is 104.3 kcal mol^{-1}. It means (N = Av. no.)
A. 104.3 kcal heat is required to break N bonds in N molecules of H_2
B. 104.3 kcal heat is required to break up N molecules to 2N atoms of H
C. 104.3 kcal heat is evolved during combination of 2N atoms of H to form N molecules of H_2
D. Heat of formation of H atom = $\frac{1}{2}$ × bond energy of H + 1
E. All of the above

97. The temperature of a 5 ml of strong acid increases by 5°C when 5 ml of each are mixed, temperature should increase by
A. 5°C B. 10°C
C. 15°C D. Cannot be known

98. The enthalpies of formation of N_2O and NO are 28 and 90 kJ mol^{-1} respectively. The enthalpy of the reaction
$2N_2O(g) + O_2(g) \rightarrow 4NO(g)$ is equal to
A. 8 kJ B. 88 kJ
C. – 16 kJ D. 304 kJ

99. Given standard enthalpy of formation of CO (– 100 kJ mol^{-1}) and CO_2 (– 394 kJ mol^{-1}). The heat of combustion when one mole of graphite burns is
A. – 110 kJ B. – 284 kJ
C. – 394 kJ D. – 584 kJ

100. The enthalpy of formation of ammonia is – 46.0 kJ mol^{-1}. The enthalpy change for the reaction,
$2NH_3(g) \rightarrow N_2(g) + 3H_2(g)$ is
A. 46.0 kJ mol^{-1} B. 92.0 kJ mol^{-1}
C. – 23.0 kJ mol^{-1} D. – 92.0 kJ mol^{-1}

101. For the homogeneous gaseous phase reaction,
$C_2H_6 + \frac{15}{2}O_2 \rightarrow 6CO_2 + 3H_2O(g)$, the change in number of moles of gaseous product is
A. 1.5 B. – 1.5
C. 0.5 D. 3

102. For a gaseous reaction,
$A(g) + 3B(g) \rightarrow 3C(g) + 3D(g)$
ΔE is 17 kcal at 27°C. Assuming R = 2 cal K^{-1} mol^{-1}, the value of ΔH for the above reaction will be
A. 15.8 kcal B. 16.4 kcal
C. 18.2 kcal D. 20.0 kcal

103. The enthalpies of combustion of carbon and carbon monoxide – 390 kJ and – 278 kJ respectively. The enthalpy of formation of CO in kJ is
A. 668 B. 112
C. – 112 D. – 668

104. $S + \frac{3}{2}O_2 \rightarrow SO_3 + 2x$ kcal
$SO_2 + \frac{1}{2}O_2 \rightarrow SO_3 + y$ kcal
The heat of formation of SO_2 is
A. $y - 2x$ B. $(2x + y)$
C. $(x + y)$ D. $\frac{2x}{y}$

105. A solution of 200 ml of 1 M KOH is added to 200 ml of 1M HCl and the mixture is well shaken. This rise in temperature T_1 is noted. The experiment is repeated by using 100 ml of each solution and increase in temperature T_2 is again noted. Which of the following is correct?
A. $T_1 = T_2$
B. T_2 is twice as large as T_1
C. T_1 is twice as large as T_2
D. T_1 is four times as large as T_2

ANSWERS

1	2	3	4	5	6	7	8	9	10
D	D	C	D	A	E	E	C	D	E
11	12	13	14	15	16	17	18	19	20
E	C	C	B	C	D	B	C	D	D
21	22	23	24	25	26	27	28	29	30
B	C	C	C	B	D	B	C	C	C
31	32	33	34	35	36	37	38	39	40
B	B	D	C	B	C	A	C	D	D
41	42	43	44	45	46	47	48	49	50
A	C	D	D	B	D	B	B	D	D
51	52	53	54	55	56	57	58	59	60
C	D	D	D	B	C	A	A	C	D
61	62	63	64	65	66	67	68	69	70
B	C	A	B	B	A	A	D	D	C
71	72	73	74	75	76	77	78	79	80
B	A	B	A	A	A	B	D	A	B
81	82	83	84	85	86	87	88	89	90
D	A	A	C	B	C	C	A	D	B
91	92	93	94	95	96	97	98	99	100
C	C	A	A	A	E	A	D	C	B
101	102	103	104	105					
C	C	C	A	A					

11

CLASSIFICATION OF ELEMENTS AND PERIODICITY IN PROPERTIES

The Modern Periodic Law

Moseley's discovery of atomic number proved that atomic number, which represents the number of protons in the nucleus, increases by 1 unit as we pass from one element to the next in the periodic table. Further atomic number also represents the number of electrons in the various shells of an atom. The chemical properties of an element depend only on the extra nuclear electrons and their arrangement. So, atomic number is a more fundamental property than the atomic weight of an element. The periodic law was therefore modified by Moseley, as "the physical and chemical properties of elements are periodic functions of their atomic numbers" (while Mendeleeve's periodic law stated that, the properties of elements are periodic functions of their atomic weights and modern periodic law states that "properties of elements are periodic functions of their electronic configurations".

The concept of atomic number removes the anomaly of inversion of elements and also explains the existence of isotopes.

The Long Form of the Periodic Table (Or Bohr's table)

One of the most frequently used forms of the periodic table, which takes into account both the chemical and electronic relationship is called the "long or extended form" of the periodic table.

This long form of periodic table or Bohr's table, combines, 60th Moseley's and modern periodic laws i.e., arranged according to the increasing order of atomic number.

Like Mendeleev's periodic table, it has seven horizontal rows, called *periods*, denoted by 1 to 7 and 16 vertical columns, called groups or subgroups, denoted by I A to VII A, I B to VII B, VIII and 0. According to IUPAC system's modification adopted is 1984, these are 18 groups in the periodic table (earlier groups, I A, II A and III B to VII B were given numbers 1, 2 and 3 to 7 respectively, group VIII was given number 8, 9 and 10, groups I B and II B were given numbers 11 and 12, groups III A to VII A were given number 13 to 17and zero group was given number 18)

The transition elements fall separately into the middlepoint of table and rare gases are in the extreme right.

Although it is an improvement over Mendeleeve's table, it does not totally eliminate all the defects of the latter (e.g., the position of Lanthanons and actinons is still unsatisfactory). *The following are the advantages of the long form :*

(a) In the long form, separate areas are assigned for the metal and nonmetals with a line of demarcation between them.

(b) Each vertical column contains a group of similar elements.

(c) Using the long form, the electronic configuration of the elements can be easily understood. At the beginning of each period, a new quantum level begins. As we go from left to right in a period, there is a progressive filling up of electronic level according to the Aufbau principle.

Main features of table

(i) The first period is the *shortest period.* It consists of only 2 elements, ${}_1H^1$ and ${}_2He^4$.

(ii) The second and third periods are *short periods* each consisting of 8 elements, viz., $_3$Li to $_{10}$Ne and $_{11}$Na to $_{18}$Ar.

(iii) The fourth and fifth periods are *long periods* each consisting of 18 elements, namely $_{19}$K to $_{36}$Kr and $_{37}$Rb to $_{54}$Xe.

(iv) The sixth period is the *longest* period and consists of 32 elements namely $_{55}$Cs to $_{86}$Rn.

(v) The seventh period is considered to be *incomplete*. It has all other elements, starting with $_{87}$Fr onwards. Elements from 93 onwards are purely synthetic and are called *transuranium elements*.

(vi) Elements of sub-groups I A (1), II A (2) and III A to VII A (13 to 17) have all their inner shells complete and only the outermost shell incomplete. These are called *'normal elements'*.

(vii) Elements sub-group I B (11) II B (12) and III B to VII B (3 to 7) and VIII (8 to 10) have their outermost as well as penultimate (last but one) shells incomplete. These are called *transition elements*.

(viii) Elements of group 0 (or 18) have no incomplete shell and hence they show little reactivity and named as nobel or inert gases.

(ix) Fourteen elements following lanthanum (atomic number 57) and another fourteen elements after actinium (atomic number 89) called as *Lanthanides* and *actinides* respectively are placed in separate rows at the bottom of the periodic table for the sake of convenience.

(A) Characteristics of a Period

(i) Size of the atom decreases from left to right, thus alkali metal is the largest atom and halogen is the smallest.

(ii) Electronegativity increases from left to right.

(iii) Metallic character decreases and their oxides become more and more acidic.

(iv) Each period begins with a new shell (*n*).

(v) The last member in each period is an inert gas.

(vi) The last column of the 7th period is vacant.

(vii) In a period, there is a regular trend in physical and chemical properties as we pass across from one element to another.

(B) Characteristics of a Group

(i) Elements in a given group have similar chemical properties and show gradation in physical properties while going down the group.

(ii) Size of atoms increase, down the group. In group 1, Li is smallest and Cesium is the largest atom.

(iii) Ionisation potential decreases, down the group.

(iv) Electronegativity decreases down the group.

(v) Metallic character increases down the group and their oxides become more and more basic.

Typical Elements : Elements of the third period are known as typical elements, e.g., Na, Mg, Al, Si, P, S and Cl. Properties of all elements present in a particular group (e.g., I A) resembles with the properties of the corresponding typical element (e.g., Na).

Bridge Elements (Diagonal Relationship)

Elements of the second period are known as bridge elements. Properties of bridge elements resemble with the properties of the diagonal elements of the third period. For example, Li resembles Mg, Be resembles Al, boron resembles Si, etc.

	1	2	3	4	5	6	7
2nd period :	Li ↘	Be ↘	B ↘	C ↘	N ↘	O ↘	F
3rd period :	Na	Mg	Al	Si	P	S	Cl

Classification of the elements with respect to *s*, *p* and *d* block

The physical and chemical properties of the elements are dependents to a large extent on their electronic structure. Elements may be classified into *s*-type, *p*-type, *d*-type and *f*-type, based on the electronic sub-level which gets progressively filled up.

(A) *s*-Block elements : They have the electronic structure ns^1 to ns^2, where *n* is the principal quantum number of the outermost occupied level. They consist of helium, Group I-A (hydrogen and alkali metals) and group II A (alkaline earth metals). Their 14 elements are known as *representative elements.*

The *s*-type elements, except H and He and metals. These metals and light (low density) and very reactive chemically and they form mostly ionic compounds.

(B) *p*-Block Elements : These elements have the electronic structure ns^2p^{1-6}. They consist of group III A to VII A and Group 0 (rare gases, except He). These 30 elements are also called *representative* elements.

Of these 30 elements, 20 are non-metals and 10 are metals. The characteristic properties of the non-metals are well known. The 10 metals of this block are not very reactive chemically, except perhaps Al. They generally form covalent compounds.

In these elements *p*-orbitals are being progressively filled.

In the long form of periodic table *p*-block consists of elements of groups 13, 14, 15, 16, 17 and 18 whose outermost energy levels have the configurations ns^2p^1, ns^2p^2, ns^2p^3, ns^2p^4, ns^2p^5 and ns^2p^6 respectively.

Elements of *s*-and *p*-blocks are called Normal or Representative Elements.

(C) *d*-Block Elements : The electronic structure of these elements may be represented as $(n-1)\, s^2p^6d^{1-10}$, ns^{1-2}. These elements in which the filling up of electrons takes place in the last but one quantum level are known as Transition Elments. These 33 elements consist of four series starting with $3d^1$, $4d^1$, $5d^1$ and $6d^1$ in groups III B to II B and VIII. The 6*d* series is incomplete.

3*d* series, Sc to Zn
4*d* series, Y to Cd
5*d* series, La, Hf to Hg
6*d* series, Ac, 104, 105

All the *d*-type transition elements are metals which give rise to coloured paramagnetic ions (containing one or more unpaired electrons). They form a wide variety of co-ordination compounds. These metals and their oxides have catalytic properties.

(D) *f*-Block Elements : *(Inner Transition Elements).*

Elements in which last electron is added in the *f*-orbital (i.e., here *f*-orbitals are being filled progressively) are called *f*-block elements.

In addition to incomplete d-orbitals, (5*d* or 6*d*), their *f*-orbitals (4*f*, 8*f*) are also incomplete. They can be subdivided into two series of 14 elements each on the basis of number of *f*-orbitals (4 or 5) being progressively filled.

(i) Lanthanides, Rare earths or Lanthanones (4*f* series) including Cesium 58 to Lutenium 71.

(ii) Actinides or Actinones (5*f* series) including Thorium 90 to Lawrencium 103

Periodicity in Properties

When elements are arranged in the increasing order of atomic number, *elements with similar properties recur at regular intervals in the periodic table.* This is called *periodicity* in properties. The cause of periodicity in properties is due to recurrence of similar outer electronic configuration at certain regular intervals.

In the periodic table, elements with similar properties recur at certain atomic number intervals namely 2, 8, 18, 18, 32 and 32. These elements with atomic numbers 1, 3, 11, 18, 37, 55 and 87 will have similar properties. Similar is the case with elements having atomic numbers 12, 20, 38, 56, 88; 13, 31, 49 and 81 and so on.

Note : Two adjacent elements placed in a group differ by atomic numbers 2, 8, 18 or 32, these particular numbers are, therefore, called MAGIC NUMBERS.

The existence of these magic numbers can be explained on the basis of following facts :

(i) An orbital can have maximum of two electrons.

(ii) Orbitals are filled in order of their increasing energies.

(iii) Each period begins with a new shell $n = 1$, there is only 1*s* orbital which can accomodate only two electrons $n = 2$. The element with atomic number 3 will lie in next period as 3rd electron enters $n = 2$, hence the first period consists of only 2 elements.

(a) When $n = 2$, there are four orbitals, one *s* and three *p*, hence the second still can have 8 elements.

(b) When $n = 3$, there are 9 orbitals (one 3s, three 3*p*, and five 3*d*) and hence third shell can accomodate 18 electrons but third period has only 8 elements because the energy of 3*d* is higher than that of

4*s*-orbital and hence 4*s*-orbital must be filled completely before the filling of 3*d* starts. The result of this after the filling of 3*p*-orbitals, the next electron goes to 4*s* instead of 3*d* and hence the new (fourth) period starts. Thus the third period has only four orbitals (one *s* and three *p*) and thus 8 elements.

(*c*) When $n = 4$, the number of orbitals actually filled is 9 (one 4*s*, five 3*d* and three 4*p* orbitals) because after filling of 4*p* orbitals the next electrons is added to 5*s* and not to 4*d* due to lower energy of 5*s* than that of 4*d*. Hence the number of elements in the fourth period is 18.

(*d*) When $n = 5$, 9-orbitals, one 5*s*, five 4*d*, three 5*p*, to be filled and hence total elements are 18

(*e*) When $n = 6$ and $n = 7$, sixteen orbitals are to be filled in each case, one 6*s*, seven 4*f*, five 5*d* and three 6*p*.

(*f*) When $n = 6$ and one 7*s*, seven 5*f* and five 6*d* and three 7*p*, where $n = 7$. Hence the sixth and seventh periods have 32 elements each.

Periodic Properties

Periodic properties exhibit a regular variation (increase or decrease) as the atomic number is varied.

The important periodic properties are the following:

(*a*) Related to size:
- (*i*) Atomic volume
- (*ii*) Atomic radius
- (*iii*) Ionic radius

(*b*) Related to energy:
- (*i*) Ionisation energy
- (*ii*) Electronegativity
- (*iii*) Electron affinity

Atomic Radius : Atomic radii is the half of the closest distance of approach of atoms in the structure of the elements. This is easily defined for regular structures, e.g., close-packed metals, but is less easy to define in elements with irregular structures, e.g. As. The values may differ between allotropes (e.g. C – C 1.54 Å in diamond and 1.42 Å in planes of graphite). Atomic radii are very different for ionic and covalent radii.

For a homonuclear diatomic molecule e.g. (I_2), the atomic radius is half the interatomic distance. Interatomic distances can be determined by X-rays or electron diffraction

$$r_A = \frac{\text{Interatomic distances in A} - \text{A}}{2}$$

As we go down a group, atomic radius increases, as atomic number increases. Hence, electrons are placed in higher quantum levels which get far removed from the nucleus. Though, the nuclear charge also increases down a group, this increase in more than compensated by the increasing distance of the outermost electron due to the addition of new electronic levels. Hence atomic radius increases down a group.

As we proceed from left to right along a period, we observe the opposite trend, i.e., a decrease in atomic radius. In a period, with an increase in atomic number, the electrons enter into the same quantum level, where as at the same time the nuclear charge is steadily increasing. This causes the electron cloud to be drawn closer to the nucleus, resulting in the steady decrease of the atomic radius. The atomic radius is found to be additive.

$$\begin{array}{ccccc} r\,\text{Si}-\text{C} & \simeq & r_{\text{Si}} & + & r_{\text{C}} \\ 1.89 & & 1.11 & & 0.77\ (\text{Å}) \end{array}$$

The atomic radius is found to decrease as the bond multiplicity increases.

$$\begin{array}{ccccc} r\,\text{C}-\text{C} & > & r\,\text{C}=\text{C} & > & r\,\text{C}\equiv\text{C} \\ 1.54 & & 1.33 & & 1.2\ (\text{Å}) \\ C_2H_6 & & C_2H_4 & & C_2H_2 \end{array}$$

$$r_C = \frac{\text{C}-\text{C}}{2} \quad \therefore \text{C}-\text{C} = 2r_C \text{ or } r_C + r_C$$

r_C = Single Bond Covalent Radii (SBCR)

Ionic Radius : This is the effective radius of ions in crystal lattices.

The radius of an atom changes appreciably during loss or gain of electrons. When an atom loses an electron and forms a cation, the number of electrons decreases while the nuclear change remains the same. The remaining electrons are drawn more towards the nucleus with the result that a *cation is much smaller than the neutral atom.* When an anion is formed, by the addition of an electron to a neutral atom, the effective nuclear charge is reduced. In other words, the electrostatic attraction exerted by the nucleus is spread over a large number of electrons. *The Anion is always larger than the Neutral Atom.*

Across a period, there is decrease in ionic radius while down a group, there is an increase in ionic radius. In any particular group, the ions of elements increase in size on moving from top to bottom. In case of *isoelectronic ions* (ions having same number of electrons but different nuclear charge), the greater the nuclear charge, the greater is the attraction for electrons and smaller is ionic radius.

Ionisation Energy (Ionisation Potential) : This is the energy required to remove an electron from a free atom or ion in the gaseous state. Normally measured in electron volts or kilo joules per mole.

$$A \xrightarrow{IE_2} A^{+} + e^-$$

$$A \xrightarrow{IE_2} A^{2+} + e^-$$

It is found that,

$$IE_1 < IE_2 < IE_3 < IE_4 < IE_5 < ....$$

This increase is due to strong attraction between the leaving electron and the remaining cation. Also the removal of an electron from a rare-gas type structure is difficult. IE_3 is much greater than IE_2 for magnesium because IE_3 involves removal of an electron from Mg^{2+}, which is isoelectronic with neon and therefore, it is difficult to remove the electron.

For Mg IE_1 = 745 kJ/mol
IE_2 = 1457 kJ/mol
IE_3 = 7732 kJ/mol

The first ionisation energy decreases from top to bottom in a group due to increase in the atomic radii. The first ionisation energy increases from left to right in a period due to decrease in atomic radius.

Electron Affinity : Electron affinity is the energy liberated when an atom in the gaseous state combines with an electron to form an anion.

$$A + e^- \rightarrow A^- + EA$$

$$Cl + e^- \rightarrow Cl^- + 348 \text{ kJ/mol}$$

The halogens have high electron affinities, but the alkali metals have very low values. But the values are unexpectedly low in case of Be, N, Ne in second row and Mg, P and Ar in third row.

The addition of the first electron to an oxygen atom liberates 142 kJ/mole. But, the addition of second electron absorbs 846 kJ/mole due to the repulsion between the negative electron and the negatively charged O^-

$$O + e^- \rightarrow O^- + 142 \text{ kJ/mol (exothermic)}$$

$$O^- + e^- \rightarrow O^{2-} - 846 \text{ kJ/mol (endothermic)}$$

$$\boxed{O + 2e^- \rightarrow O^{2-} - 704 \text{ kJ/mol (endothermic)}}$$

Representative electron affinities (kJ mol^{-1})

			H 73				He – 54	
Li 57	Be – 66	B 15	C 123	N – 31	O 142	F 333	Ne – 99	
Na 21	Mg – 67	Al 26	Si 135	P 60	S 196	Cl 348	Br 340	I 297

Electron affinities may be estimated using a Born-Haber Cycle.

Electronegativity : A measure of the tendency of an atom in a stable molecule to attract electrons within bonds. Thus, in covalently bonded hydrogen chloride, HCl, the electrons are much closer to the chlorine than to the hydrogen, the chlorine being the more electro-negative atom. Numerical values of electronegativity have been calculated by Pauling from bond dissocia-tion energies, ionization energies and electron affinity values using the equation :

$$D_{A-B} = \frac{1}{2}(D_{A-A} + D_{B-B}) + 23(x_A - x_B)^2$$

and

$$125x_A = (\text{ionisation energy} - \text{electron affinity})_A$$

where x is the electronegativity and D is the bond dissociation energy. In general, electronegativity values increases from left to right across each row of the periodic table and decrease down each group.

Oxidation State : The difference (+ve or – ve) between the number of electrons associated with an atom in a compound as compared with an atom of the element. In ions corresponds to the ionic charge, e.g., NaCl [Na (+ 1), Cl (– 1)], in covalent compounds to the formal charge assuming an ionic structure taking account of electronegativity to determine charge, e.g., CCl_4 is assumed to be $C^{4+}4Cl^-$ and thus C (+ 4). Co-ordinate bonds do not affect the oxidation state, e.g., $[CO(NH_3)_6]^{3+}$ contains CO (+ 3) and Fe $(CO)_5$ contains Fe (0). Elements are in the zero oxidation state. Roman numerals is used the oxidation state in systematic nomenclature, e.g. MnO_4^- is manganate (VII).

The oxidation state of most of the representative elements can be predicted from the following facts.

Tendency to attain one of the following stable configurations of the outermost shell.

(a) ns^2p^6 (the stable octet)
(b) $ns^2p^6d^{10}$ (the 18-electron shell)
(c) $(n-1)\ s^2p^6d^{10}$ (the inert pair).

OBJECTIVE QUESTIONS

1. In modern periodic table, elements are arranged in order of
A. Increasing mass
B. Increasing atomic number
C. Increasing volume
D. Increasing density

2. In a period, elements are arranged in strict sequence of
A. Decreasing charges in the nucleus
B. Increasing charges in the nucleus
C. Constant charges in the nucleus
D. Equal charges in the nucleus

3. The elements on the right side of periodic table are
A. Metals B. Metalloids
C. Non-metals D. Transition elements

4. Beryllium resembles much with
A. Zn B. Al
C. Li D. Ra

5. Elements whose atoms have three outermost shells incomplete are called
A. *s*-block elements B. *p*-block elements
C. *d*-block elements D. *f*-block elements

6. Which pair of atomic number represents *s*-block elements?
A. 7, 15 B. 6, 12
C. 9, 17 D. 3, 12

7. Element of atomic number 6 is placed in
A. IV group B. IV period
C. VI group D. III group

8. In the periodic table, going down in fluorine group
A. Reactivity will increase
B. Electronegativity will increase
C. Ionic radius will increase
D. Ionisation potential will increase

9. Which of the following is the biggest ion?
A. Al^{3+} B. Ba^{2+}
C. Mg^{2+} D. Na^+

10. Which one is the *correct* order of the size of the ionic species?
A. $I > I^+ > I^-$ B. $I > I^- > I^+$
C. $I^+ > I^- > I$ D. $I^- > I > I^+$

11. Al^{3+} has a lower ionic radius than Mg^{+2} because
A. Mg atom has less number of neutrons than Al
B. Al^{3+} has a higher nuclear charge than Mg^{++}
C. Their electronegativities are different
D. Al has a lower ionisation potential than Mg atom

12. Which of the following elements will have the lowest ionisation energy?
A. Mg B. Rb
C. Li D. Ca

13. A sudden large jump between the values of second and third ionisation energies of an element would be associated with the electronic configuration
A. $1s^2, 2s^22p^6, 3s^1$
B. $1s^2, 2s^22p^6, 3p^1$
C. $1s^2, 2s^22p^6, 3s^23p^2$
D. $1s^2, 2s^22p^6, 3s^2$

14. As one moves along a given row in the periodic table, ionisation energy
A. Remains same
B. Increases from left to right
C. Frist increases then decreases
D. Decreases from left to right

15. The ionisation energy of nitrogen is more than that of oxygen because
A. Of the extra stability of half-filled *p*-orbitals in nitrogen

B. Of the smaller size of nitrogen
C. The former contains less number of electrons
D. The former is less electronegative

16. How many ionisation energies can carbon have?
A. 1 B. 2
C. 4 D. 6

17. Which of the following statements regarding electronegativity is *correct*?
A. Electronegativity is related to ionisation energy
B. Electronegativity is related to electron affinity
C. Electronegativity is the power of an atom to attract electrons
D. All of the above

18. The statement that is *not correct* for the periodic classification of element is
A. The properties of elements are periodic functions of their atomic numbers
B. Non-metallic elements are lesser in number than metallic elements
C. The first ionisation energies along a period do not vary in a regular manner with increase in atomic number
D. For transition elements, the *d*-sub shells are filled with electrons monotonically with increase in atomic number.

19. Electron affinity is the
A. Energy released when an electron is added to an isolated atom in the gaseous state
B. Energy absorbed when an electron is added to an isolated atom in the gaseous state
C. Energy required to take out an electron from an isolated gaseous atom
D. Power of an atom to attract an electron to itself.

20. Which of the processes mentioned below requires the absorption of energy?
A. $F \rightarrow F^-$ B. $Cl \rightarrow Cl^-$
C. $O \rightarrow O^{2-}$ D. $H \rightarrow H^-$

21. Which of the following does not reflect the periodicity of the elements?
A. Bonding behaviour
B. Electronegativity
C. Ionisation energy
D. Neutron/proton ratio

22. Variable valency is generally shown by
A. Metallic elements
B. Normal elements
C. Transition elements
D. None of the above

23. The electronic configuration of the element which is just above the element with atomic number 43 in the same periodic group is
A. $1s^2\,2s^2\,2p^6\,3s^2\,3p^6\,3d^6\,4s^1$
B. $1s^2\,2s^2\,2p^6\,3s^2\,3p^6\,3d^5\,4s^2$
C. $1s^2\,2s^2\,2p^6\,3s^2\,3p^6\,3d^{10}\,4s^2 4p^5$
D. $1s^2\,2s^2\,2p^6\,3s^2\,3p^6\,3d^{10}\,4s^2 4p^6$

24. The first element of rare earth metals is
A. Cesium B. Actinium
C. Uranium D. Lanthanum

25. Atomic number of next inert gas to be discovered will be
A. 87 B. 104
C. 118 D. 132

26. Elements of Zinc group are called
A. Noble metals
B. Coinage metals
C. Volatile metals
D. Precious metals

27. Elements of third period are known as
A. Typical elements
B. Noble elements
C. Precious metals
D. None of these

28. When metals react with non-metals, the metal atom tends to
A. Lose electrons
B. Gain electrons
C. Share electrons
D. None of these

29. A *p*-block element in which last electron enters into *s*-orbital of valence shell instead of *p*-orbital is
A. As
B. Ga
C. He
D. No such element exists

30. The ground state electronic configuration of an element which is isoelectronic with H_2O is
A. $1s^2\,2s^2\,2p^6$

B. $1s^2\ 2s^2\ 2p^6\ 3s^2$
C. $1s^2\ 2s^2\ 2p^6\ 3s^2\ 3p^2$
D. $1s^2\ 2s^2\ 2p^6\ 3s^2\ 3p^6$

31. An atom becomes ion when there is
A. Gain of electrons
B. Loss of electrons
C. Gain or loss of electrons
D. Neither gain nor loss of electrons

32. The screening effect of *d*-electrons is
A. Equal to *p*-electrons
B. Much more than *p*-electrons
C. Same as *f*-electrons
D. Less than *p*-electrons

33. Which of the following statement is *not true* about the long form of periodic table
A. It reflects the sequence of filling of electrons in order of sub-energy levels *s, p, d* and *f*
B. It helps to predict the stable valency states of the elements
C. If reflects trends is physical and chemical properties of the elements
D. It helps to predict the relative ionicity of the bond between any two elements

34. Pauling's electronegativity values for elements are useful in predicting
A. Polarity of bonds in molecules
B. Position of elements in electromotive series
C. Co-ordination number
D. Dipole moment of various molecules

35. Alkali metals in each period have
A. Largest size
B. Lowest IE
C. Highest IE
D. Highest-Electronegativity

36. Which of the following is isoelectronic with carbon atom
A. Na^+ B. O^{2-}
C. Al^{+3} D. N^+

37. The correct ionic radii order is
A. $N^{3-} > O^{2-} > F^- > Na^+$
B. $N^{3-} > Na^+ > O^{2-} > F^-$
C. $Na^+ > O^{2-} > N^{3-} > F^-$
D. $O^{2-} > F^- > Na^+ > N^{3-}$

38. The attraction that an atom exerts on a pair of electrons that are being shared with another atom for forming covalent bond is referred to as its
A. Electron affinity
B. Electronegativity
C. Ionisation energy
D. Valency

39. The element with strong electropositive nature is
A. Cu B. Cs
C. Cr D. Ba

40. Which configuration represents atom having highest second ionisation energy
A. $1s^2\ 2s^2\ 2p^4$ B. $1s^2\ 2s^2\ 2p^6$
C. $1s^2\ 2s^2\ 2p^6\ 3s^1$ D. $1s^2\ 2s^2\ 2p^6\ 3s^2$

41. Born Haber's cycle is used to determine
A. Lattice energy
B. Electron affinity
C. Ionisation energy
D. Either of them

42. The correct order of radii is
A. $N < Be < B$ B. $F^- < O^{2-} < N^{3-}$
C. $Na < Li^- < K$ D. $Fe^{3+} < Fe^{2+} < Fe^{4+}$

43. Among KO_2, AlO_2^-, BaO_2 and NO_2^+, unpaired electron is present in
A. NO_2^+ and BaO_2 B. KO_2 and AlO_2^-
C. KO_2 only D. BaO_2 only

44. The *incorrect* statement among the following is
A. The first ionisation potential of Al is less than the first ionisation potential of Mg
B. The second ionisation potential of Mg is greater than the second ionisation potential of Na
C. The first ionisation potential of Na is less than the first ionisation potential of Mg
D. The third ionisation potential of Mg is greater than the third ionisation potential of Al

45. The electron affinity of chlorine is highest of all halogen atoms. Which one of the following is strongest oxidising agent?
A. F_2 B. Cl_2
C. Br_2 D. I_2

46. Which of the following molecules will have highest bond angle?
A. H_2O B. OF_2
C. Cl_2O D. ClO_2

47. Screening effect depends on
A. Nuclear charge
B. Number of electrons in valency shell
C. Inner lying electrons between nucleus and outermost shell
D. Number of protons in nucleus

48. Which of the following atomic properties of an element may vary?
A. First electron affinity
B. First ionization potential
C. Electronegativity
D. All of these

49. Which of the following statements is *correct*?
A. Higher the IP and lower the electron affinity of an element, greater will be its electronegativity
B. Higher the IP and electron affinity, greater will be electronegativity of an element
C. Higher the electron affinity, lower will be the IP of an element
D. Lower the effective nuclear charge, greater will be the electronegativity of an element.

50. In which of the following compounds, the electronegativity of carbon atom will be highest?
A. CH_4 B. C_2H_6
C. C_2H_4 D. C_2H_2

51. Which of the following molecules has lowest value of covalent radius of carbon atom?
A. Ethane B. Ethylene
C. Acetylene D. Propane

52. The size of species of isoelectronic series depends on
A. Effective nuclear charge
B. Number of electrons
C. Electronic configuration
D. Number of neutrons present in nucleus

53. Of the pairs mentioned below, choose a pair of elements whose atomic radii are nearly equal
A. Na and K B. He and Ne
C. Zr and Hf D. Cl and I

54. The first ionisation potential in electron volts of nitrogen and oxygen are respectively
A. 14.6 and 13.6 B. 13.6 and 14.6
C. 13.6 and 13.6 D. 14.6 and 14.6

55. Which of the following is *correct* representation of Pauling's formula for determining the electronegativity of elements?

A. $0.208\sqrt{\Delta} = X_A - X_B$

B. $\sqrt{\frac{\Delta}{0.208}} = X_A - X_B$

C. $\Delta\sqrt{0.208} = X_A - X_B$

D. $\Delta = \frac{X_A - X_B}{2}$

56. The strongest reducing agent is
A. K B. Al
C. Mg D. Br

57. Elements upto atomic number 105 have been discovered till now. If an element with atomic number 106 were ever discovered, which of the following electronic configuration will it possess?

A. $[Rn]5f^{14}\,6d^4\,7s^2$

B. $[Rn]5f^{14}\,6d^5\,7s^0$

C. $[Rn]5f^{14}\,6d^6\,7s^0$

D. $[Rn]5f^{14}\,6d^1\,7s^2p^3$

58. Elements with highest *mp* and *bp* respectively are
A. C (diamond) and osmium
B. C (diamond) and rhenium
C. C (Graphite) and rhenium
D. C (diamond)

59. Which of the following elements can have 60th positive and negative oxidation states?
A. F B. H
C. Li D. Cs

60. The element with electronic configuration $1s^2$, $2s^2$, $2p^6$, $3s^2$ would be
A. A metal B. A non metal
C. An inert gas D. A metalloid

ANSWERS

1	2	3	4	5	6	7	8	9	10
B	B	C	B	D	D	A	C	B	D
11	**12**	**13**	**14**	**15**	**16**	**17**	**18**	**19**	**20**
B	B	D	B	A	D	D	C	A	C
21	**22**	**23**	**24**	**25**	**26**	**27**	**28**	**29**	**30**
D	C	B	A	C	C	A	A	C	A
31	**32**	**33**	**34**	**35**	**36**	**37**	**38**	**39**	**40**
C	D	B	A	B	D	A	B	B	C
41	**42**	**43**	**44**	**45**	**46**	**47**	**48**	**49**	**50**
D	B	C	B	A	D	C	C	B	D
51	**52**	**53**	**54**	**55**	**56**	**57**	**58**	**59**	**60**
C	A	C	A	A	A	B	B	B	A

12

INORGANIC CHEMISTRY

Chemistry of Hydrogen : The English chemist Henry Cavendish (1731-1810) first-isolated pure hydrogen. Because the element produces water when burnt in air, the French Chemist Lavoisier gave it the name Hydrogen which means 'water producer'. Hydrogen is the most abundant element in the universe.

Electronic Structure : Hydrogen has the simplest atomic structure of all the elements and consists of a nucleus containing one proton with a charge + 1 and one orbital electron. The electronic structure may be written as $1s^1$. Atoms of hydrogen may attain stability in three different ways.

(i) By forming an electron pair (covalent) bond with another atom. Non-metals typically form this type of bond with hydrogen, e.g., H_2, H_2O, HCl (gas) and CH_4.

(ii) By losing an electron to form hydrogen ion (H^+). A proton is extremely small. Due to very small size, H^+ has high polarizing power and, therefore, distorts the electron clouds on other atoms. Thus protons are always associated with other atoms or molecules. For example, in water or aqueous solution of HCl and H_2SO_4, protons exists as H_3O^+, $H_9O_4{}^+$ or $H(H_2O)_n^+$ ions. Free protons do not exist under normal conditions, though they are found in low pressure gaseous beams, for example in a mass spectrometer.

(iii) By gaining an electron to form hydride ion (H^-) : Crystalline solids such as NaH contain the H^- ions and are formed by highly electropositive metals.

Hydrogen is the first element in the periodic table and is unique. The properties of hydrogen cannot be correlated with any of the main groups in the periodic table, and hydrogen is best considered on its own.

The electronic structure of hydrogen atom is in some ways similar to that of *alkali metals*. The alkali metals belonging to 1st group have just one electron in their outer shell, but they lose this electron in the reactions and form positive ion. Though hydrogen ion (H^+) is known, hydrogen has a much greater tendency to pair the electron and form a covalent bond. The electronic structure of hydrogen atom is also in some ways similar to *halogens* belonging to the 7th group, as both are one electron short of noble gas structure. In many reactions, the halogens gain an electron and form negative ions (X^-). Hydrogen also forms negative hydride ions, and form crystalline hydrides (M^+H^-) with a few highly electropositive metals.

The electronic structure of hydrogen also resembles with the elements of 4th group, as both have the half filled shell of electrons. There are a number of similarities between *hydrides* and *organometallic* compounds since the groups CH_3^- and H^- both have one free valency.

LiH, LiMe, LiEt

NH_3, NMe_3, NEt_3

SiH_4, CH_3SiH_3, $(CH_3)_2SiCl_2$, $(CH_3)_3SiCl$, $(CH_3)_4Si$

Thus, it can be concluded that hydrogen is best treated as a group of its own.

Preparation of Hydrogen :

(i) By passing steam over red hot coke :

$$C + H_2O \xrightarrow{1000°C} \underbrace{CO + H_2}_{\text{Water gas}}$$

Gas mixture is mixed with steam cooled to 400°C and passed over iron oxide in a shift converter giving H_2 and CO_2.

$$CO + H_2 \xrightarrow[Fe_2O_3]{+H_2O} 2H_2 + CO_2$$

The CO_2 formed is removed either by dissolving in water under pressure or treating with K_2CO_3 solution giving $KHCO_3$, and thus giving H_2 gas.

(ii) By catalytic steam-reformation of Hydrocarbons: In todays technology, this method is used to produce largest quantities of hydrogen. The most desirable starting material in natural gas is methane, CH_4.

$$CH_4(g) + H_2O(g) + 206 \text{ kJ} \rightarrow 3H_2(g) + CO(g)$$

The reaction is rapid in the 800°C to 1000°C range and goes nearly to completion. In this process too 'water gas shift' reaction, poisonous CO is converted to CO_2, a nontoxic compound.

$$CO(g) + H_2O(g) \xrightarrow[\text{Fe/Cu}]{400°C} H_2(g) + CO_2(g) + 41 \text{ kJ}$$

The unwanted CO_2 is removed by converting it to carbonate

$$CaO(s) + CO_2(g) \rightarrow CaCO_3(s)$$

Following reactions can also be used to remove carbon dioxide.

$$K_2CO_3 + CO_2 + H_2O \rightarrow 2KHCO_3$$

$$\underset{\text{Ethanolamine}}{2HOCH_2CH_2NH_2} + CO_2 + H_2O \rightarrow (HOCH_2CH_2NH_3)_2CO_3$$

K_2CO_3 or ethanolamine are regenerated simply by heating the reaction products.

(iii) By Electrolysis of water: Very pure hydrogen is made by electrolysis of water or aqueous solutions of NaOH or KOH. This is most expensive method. Water does not conduct electricity well, so it is usual to electrolyse aqueous solutions of NaOH or KOH in a cell with nickel anodes and iron cathodes. The gases produced on anode and cathode compartments must be kept separate.

Anode $\quad 2OH^- \rightarrow H_2O + \frac{1}{2}O_2 + 2e^-$

Cathode $\quad 2H_2O + 2e^- \rightarrow 2OH^- + H_2$

Overall $\quad H_2O \rightarrow H_2 + \frac{1}{2}O_2$

(iv) Laboratory Methods :

(a) Acid + Metal $\rightarrow$ Metal salt + H_2

$$Mg(s) + 2HCl(aq) \rightarrow MgCl_2(aq) + H_2(g)$$

$$Zn(s) + H_2SO_4(aq) \rightarrow ZnSO_4(aq) + H_2(g)$$

(b) Metal + H_2O or base $\rightarrow$ Metal hydroxide or oxide + $H_2(g)$

$$2Na(s) + 2H_2O(l) \rightarrow 2NaOH(aq) + H_2(g)$$

$$2Fe(s) + 3H_2O(l) \rightarrow Fe_2O_3(s) + 3H_2(g)$$

$$2Al(s) + 2NaOH(aq) + 6H_2O(l) \rightarrow 2Na[Al(OH)_4]\, aq + 3H_2(g)$$

(c) Salt like hydride + H_2O $\rightarrow$ Metal Hydroxide + H_2

$$CaH_2(s) + 2H_2O(l) \rightarrow Ca(OH)_2(s) + 2H_2(g)$$

$$LiH(s) + H_2O(l) \rightarrow LiOH(aq) + H_2(g)$$

Isotopes of Hydrogen : Naturally occurring hydrogen contains three isotopes—

(i) Protium ${}^1_1H$ or H

(ii) Deuterium ${}^2_1H$ or D

(iii) Tritium ${}^3_1H$ or T

Naturally, occurring hydrogen contains 99.98% of the ${}^1_1H$ isotope, 0.014% of ${}^2_1H$ and 6×10^{-3}% of ${}^3_1H$, so the properties of hydrogen are essentially those of the lightest isotope. These isotopes have same electronic configuration and have essentially same chemical properties. The only difference in chemical properties are the rates of reaction and equilibrium constants, for example:

(a) H_2 is more rapidly absorbed on to the surfaces of metals than D_2.

(b) H_2 reacts over 13 times faster with chlorine than D_2, because, H_2 has a lower energy of activation. This difference in properties which arises from the differences in mass are called *isotope effect.*

Ortho and Para Hydrogen : The nucleus of an atom has nuclear spin, in a similar way as electron has a spin. In the H_2 molecule, the two nuclei may be spinning in either same direction or in the opposite direction. This gives rise to *spin isomerism* and in this way two forms of H_2 may exist. These are known as ortho and para hydrogen.

(i) When the spin of two nuclei in H_2 molecule are parallel, i.e. in the same direction, the total spin of the nuclei would be $\frac{1}{2} + \frac{1}{2} = 1$. This type of hydrogen molecule is called *ortho hydrogen.*

(ii) When the spins of two nuclei in H_2 molecules are antiparallel, i.e. in opposite direction, the total

spin of the nuclei would be $\frac{1}{2}-\frac{1}{2}=0$. This kind of hydrogen molecule is called *para hydrogen*.

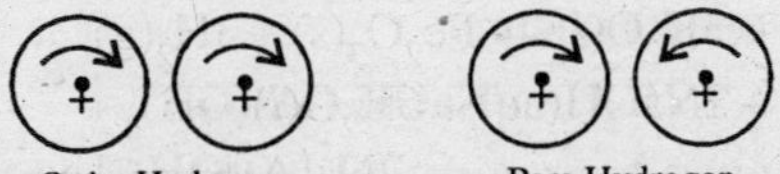

Ortho Hydrogen   Para Hydrogen

Ordinary hydrogen is an equilibrium mixture of ortho and para forms.

$$\text{Ortho form} \rightleftharpoons \text{Para form.}$$

The ratio of ortho to para hydrogen at 300 K and above is 3 : 1. The above equilibrium shifts towards the right on lowering the temperature, i.e. proportion of para form increases on lowering the temperature. The ratio of ortho and para varies with temperature as shown below :

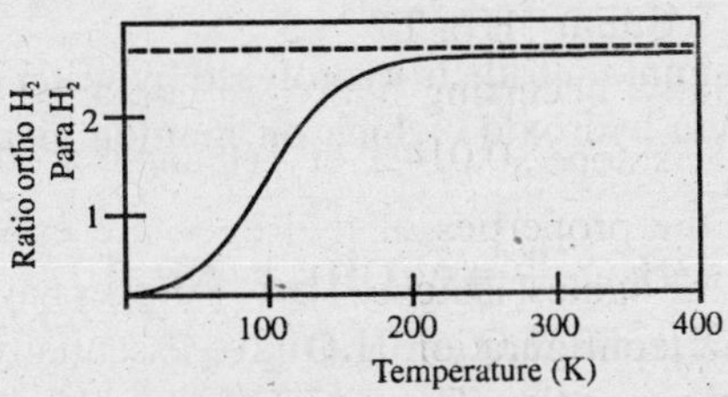

Fig. Variation of the ratio of ortho to para hydrogen with temperature.

There are considerable differences between the physical properties (b.p., specific heat, thermal conductivities) of the ortho and para forms because of difference in their internal energy. There are also differences in the band spectra of the ortho and para hydrogen.

Preparation and Properties

Hydrogen Peroxide

H_2O_2, m.p. – 0.4°C, b.p. 152°C, density 1.45. Colourless syrupy liquid prepared by oxidation of an anthraquinol with oxygen and subsequent reduction of the quinone with hydrogen, also prepared electrolytically via persulphates. The pure liquid is stable but aqueous solutions are unstable and alkalis and dust catalyse decomposition to oxygen and water. Often used as an aqueous solution concentration expressed in volume of O_2 that can be liberated : 6% = 20 vol. It can act as powerful oxidising agent when converted to H_2O and as a reducing agent when converted to O_2. It is the parent compound of peroxides and forms adducts, perhydrates with some salts. It is used in chemicals (33%); pollution control (19%), textiles (17%) paper (13%), and free H_2O_2 is used as a propellant.

Silicones

Polymeric organosilicon derivatives containing Si—O—Si links. Organosilicon halides are prepared RX plus Cu—Si or Ag—Si alloy, RX plus $SiCl_4$ over Zn or Al, $SiCl_4$ or Si—H compounds plus olefins over catalyst (hydrosilylation). These derivatives also formed $SiCl_4$ plus e.g. LiR, RMgX on laboratory scale). The halides are hydrolysed to give polymers with properties depending upon the degree of polymerization (extent of hydrolysis). Silicones are used in greases, hydraulic fluids, sealing compounds, enamels, varnishes, resins, synthetic rubber. Resins are used in electrical insulation and laminates. They are odourless, colourless and inert, immiscible with water and have high flank points.

Preparation : These are prepared from alkyl or aryl chlorosilanes which in turn are obtained from Grignard reagent and silicon tetrachloride.

$$\underset{\text{Methylmagnesium chloride}}{CH_3MgCl} + \underset{\text{Silicon tetrachloride}}{SiCl_4} \rightarrow \underset{\text{Methyl trichlorosilane}}{CH_3SiCl_3} + MgCl_2$$

$$2CH_3MgCl + SiCl_4 \rightarrow \underset{\text{Dimethyl dichlorosilane}}{(CH_3)SiCl_2} + 2MgCl_2$$

$$3CH_3MgCl + SiCl_4 \rightarrow \underset{\text{Trimethyl chlorosilane}}{(CH_3)_3SiCl} + 3MgCl_2$$

Methyltrichlorosilane and dimethyl dichlorosilane are more important, the latter can also be prepared by passing methyl chloride over powdered silicon in the presence of copper catalyst at 275°C-375°C

$$2CH_3Cl + Si \xrightarrow{Cu} (CH_3)_2SiCl_2$$

Silicones may be linear, cyclic or cross linked.

Properties : These are intermediates between organic compounds and silica (SiO_2) as their properties are blend of those of the hydrocarbons, e.g., lubricating properties which are characteristic of hydrocarbon oils, and silica which lies unreactive even at high temperature. They are expensive still used in various ways, as

(i) They are stable to heat upto 200°C and non-volatile on heating. The most heat stable side group is phenyl group, followed by methyl, ethyl and propyl groups in the descending order.

(ii) On heating in air to 300-400°C they are rapidly oxidised and cross-links are formed.

(iii) They are durable and chemically inert. These properties are due to stable silica-like arrangement of Si—O—Si, and very high bond energy (502 kJ mol^{-1}) of the Si—O bond.

(iv) They are non-toxic.

(v) In case of fluids, their viscosity does not change more with temperature.

(vi) They possess good electrical insulating properties, because they are more stable to heat than organic polymers. Any how, if they break down, they do not produce conducting material like carbon.

(vii) Silicones possess outstanding water repellency power. This property is due to the high content of alkyl or aryl radicals.

(viii) Silicone products may be fluids, greasses, resins or rubbers depending upon the size and type of polymer.

Aluminium (Al)

Preparation : Aluminium is the third most abundant element (7.4%) of the earth's crust, the first two are oxygen and silicon. It is found only in combined state.

Extraction of Aluminium from Bauxite

(A) Purification of Bauxite : The ore contains iron (red bauxite) and/or silica (white bauxite) as impurity. Iron is removed by Baeyer's process, while silica by Serpeck's process.

(a) Baeyer's Process : The crushed ore is first heated at low temperature to convert ferrous oxide into ferric oxide and then digested with a strong solution of sodium hydroxide in which alumina dissolves as sodium aluminate while the basic oxide (Fe_2O_3) remains unaffected and hence removed by filtration.

$$Al_2O_3.2H_2O + 2NaOH \rightarrow 2NaAlO_2 + 3H_2O$$

The filtrate containing aluminate is diluted with a crystal of $Al(OH)_3$ to act as *seedling agent.* The mixture is then agitated for few hours when slow hydrolysis of the aluminate occurs.

$$NaAlO_2 + 2H_2O \rightarrow NaOH + Al(OH)_3 \downarrow$$

Aluminium hydroxide is filtered off, wasted and ignited to get anhydrous alumina.

$$2Al(OH)_3 \xrightarrow{\text{Heat}} Al_2O_3 + 3H_2O$$

(b) Serpeck's process : The powdered ore is fused with carbon and heated to 1800°C in a current nitrogen. Aluminium forms its nitride while silica is reduced to silicon which volatilizes off.

$$Al_2O_3 + N_2 + 3C \xrightarrow{1800^\circ C} 2AlN + 3CO\uparrow$$

$$SiO_2 + 2C \rightarrow Si\uparrow + 2CO\uparrow$$

Aluminium nitride is hydrolysed by water to give aluminium hydroxide which on ignition gives pure alumina.

$$AlN + 3H_2O \xrightarrow{\text{Boil}} Al(OH)_3\downarrow + NH_3\uparrow$$

$$2Al(OH)_3 \rightarrow Al_2O_3 + 3H_2O$$

(B) Electrolysis of Alumina : Because of high melting point (2050°C) pure alumina cannot be electrolysed. Hence a mixture of alumina, cryolite (m.p. 1000°C) and calcium fluoride (to lower the temperature of the melt) is electrolysed at about 900°C. The function of cryolite is to increase the electrical conductivity of the electrolyte. The electrolytic cell consists of an iron box line with graphite (carbon) which serves as cathode. A series of graphite rods dipped in the molten electrolyte acts as anode. The charge is covered with a layer of powdered coke to avoid heat loses by radiation. It also slows down the reaction between the carbon of the anode and oxygen. The electrode reactions are very complicated and not properly understood.

$$4AlF_3 \text{ (From cryolite)} \rightleftharpoons 4Al^{3+} + 12F^-$$

At cathode : $4Al^{3+} + 12e^- \rightarrow 4Al$

At anode : *(i)* $12F^- \rightarrow 6F_2 + 12e^-$

(ii) $2Al_2O_3 + 6F_2 \rightarrow 4AlF_3 + 3O_2$

Oxygen evolved at the anode either escapes as such or reacts with carbon of anode to form CO and CO_2 which either burn or escape. Aluminium fluoride goes back, ionises and further amount of Al_2O_3 is exhausted. Aluminium obtained at cathode by this method is 99% pure.

(C) *Electrolytic Refining of Aluminium :* Further purification of aluminium may be done by Hoop's process. The electrolytic cell consists of three liquid layers of different specific gravities.

(a) The top layer of pure aluminium which acts as cathode.

(b) The bottom layer of impure aluminium. It acts as anode.

(c) The middle layer of cryolite and barium fluoride. It acts as electrolyte.

When the current flows, aluminium ionise from the middle layer are discharged at the cathode as pure aluminium while the equivalent aluminium from the anode goes into the electrolyte.

Properties

(A) Physical : It is a silver white metal, capable of taking high polish. It is extremely light with specific gravity 2.7. It is the fourth best good conductor of electricity, the first three being silver, copper and gold. It can be easily welded to cast but can be soldered with a difficulty and also only with a special solder. It is malleable and ductile.

(B) Chemical : Aluminium is a strongly electropositive, very reactive and a powerful reducing agent.

Action of Air : It takes up oxygen to form a protective layer of aluminium oxide. On heating with air to redness it burns with a brilliant white light with the evolution of heat.

$$4Al + 3O_2 \rightarrow 2Al_2O_3 + 772,000 \text{ cal}$$

Action of Water : It corrodes in salt water. It decomposes boiling water.

$$2Al + 6H_2O \text{ (boiling)} \rightarrow 2Al(OH)_3 + 3H_2$$

Action of Acids

(i) $2Al + 6HCl \rightarrow 2AlCl_3 + 3H_2$

(ii) $2Al + 3H_2SO_4 \text{ (dil)} \rightarrow Al_2(SO_4)_3 + 3H_2$

(iii) $2Al + 6H_2SO_4 \text{ (conc.)} \rightarrow Al_2(SO_4)_3 + 3SO_2 + 6H_2O$

(iv) $8Al + 30HNO_3 \text{ (dil)} \rightarrow 8Al(NO_3)_3 + 3NH_4NO_3 + 9H_2O$

Concentrated HNO_3 makes it passive.

Action of Alkalies

$$2Al + 2NaOH + 2H_2O \rightarrow \underset{\text{Sod. metaaluminate}}{2NaAlO_2} + 3H_2$$

$$2Al + 6NaOH \rightarrow \underset{\text{Sod. aluminate}}{2Na_3AlO_3} + 3H_2$$

Aluminium shows amphoteric nature. This is due to the fact that electropositive character of elements in a group increases with the atomic number and since aluminium lies in the middle of the group, it behaves like a metal as well as a non-metal.

Combination with N_2, X_2 & C

(a) $2Al(s) + N_2 \xrightarrow{\Delta} 2AlN \xrightarrow{6H_2O} 2Al(OH)_3 + 2NH_3$

(b) $2Al + 3Cl_2 \xrightarrow{\Delta} 2AlCl_3$

(c) $2Al + 3C \xrightarrow{\Delta} Al_4C_3 \xrightarrow{12H_2O} 4Al(OH)_3 + 3CH_4$

Reducing Action : Due to its great affinity for oxygen, aluminium reduces several metallic oxides like Fe_2O_3, Cr_2O_3, Mn_3O_4 etc.

$$Fe_2O_3 + 2Al \rightarrow Al_2O_3 + 2Fe + \text{Heat}$$

This reaction is the basis of 'thermite welding' (Goldschmidt's aluminothermic process).

Thermite Welding : Thermite (a mixture of 3 parts of Fe_2O_3 and 1 part of powdered aluminium) mixed with a small amount of barium peroxide (added to facilitate ignition) is placed in a crucible lined with magnesia and having a plugged hole at the bottom. The crucible is placed just above the broken ends to be welded. Thermite is ignited by means of a fused magnesium ribbon. Ferric oxide is reduced by aluminium to iron which falls down on the broken ends and since the reaction is exothermic it keeps melting the broken iron which on cooling joins together.

Uses

(i) Being light and good conductor of electricity, aluminium is used to some extent in place of copper (expensive metal) for making electrical transmission cables.

(ii) Because its resistance to corrosion (due to surface oxide formation) aluminium is used in the manufacture of house-hold articles.

(iii) Aluminium is used as a reducing agent for the metallurgy of metals like Cr, W, M etc. whose oxides can't be reduced by carbon.

(iv) Aluminium foil is used as a wrapping material.

(v) Aluminium forms many useful alloys, *e.g.*, magnalium (Al & Mg), duralumin (Al, L_4, Mg & Mn) aluminium bronze (Cu & Al), Y-alloy (Cu, Al, Ni, and Mg) etc. These alloys are light and durable and hence very much used in automobile and aircraft industries.

(vi) Aluminium is also used in thermite welding.

Iron (Fe) : Although small quantities of iron occur in free state, it is mainly found in combined state. It is the second most (first being aluminium) abundant metal occurring in the earth crust (4.5%). It is present in red blood cells of the blood. Its varieties are *(i) Cast iron or Pig iron :* The most impure form containing highest proportion of carbon (2.5 – 4%). After remelting it is called cast-iron.

(ii) *Wrought iron or Malleable Iron :* It is most pure form containing 0.12 – 0.25% carbon.

(iii) *Steel :* It is the most important form of iron and it contains 0.2 – 1.5% carbon. Steels containing 0.2 – 0.5% of carbon are known as *mild steels* while those containing 0.5 – 1.5% are called *hard* steels.

All the three forms of iron differ in their carbon contents. In iron, carbon is found partly in the free form and partly in the form of iron carbide, Fe_3C. Both wrought iron and steel are obtained from cast iron which in turn is obtained from haematite in a blast furnace.

Wrought iron is manufactured from cast iron in a special type of reverberatory furnace called *Puddling furnace.*

(a) Oxidation of Si, Mo and P by haematite and their removal as slag

(Acid Process)

$$2Fe_2O_3 + 3Si \rightarrow 4Fe + 3SiO_2$$

$$Fe_2O_3 + 3Mn \rightarrow 2Fe + 3MnO$$

$$MnO + SiO_2 \rightarrow MnSiO_3 \quad \text{(slag)}$$

(Basic Process)

$$10Fe_2O_3 + 12P \rightarrow 20Fe + 3P_4O_{10}$$

$$P_4O_{10} + 6CaO \rightarrow 2Ca_3(PO_4)_2 \quad \text{(slag)}$$

$$SiO_2 + CaO \rightarrow CaSiO_3$$

$$SiO_2 + MnO \rightarrow MnSiO_3$$

(b) Finally, C and S are oxidised forming volatile gases.

$$Fe_2O_3 + 3C \rightarrow 2Fe + 3CO\uparrow$$

$$2Fe_2O_3 + 3S \rightarrow 4Fe + 3SO_2\uparrow$$

Samples of steel are drawn from time to time and tested for their carbon contents. At the appropriate time, *ferro-manganese* or *Spiegeleisen* are added to the molten mass to obtain mild or hand steel respectively. The process takes 8-10 hours for completion (Bessemmer process takes only 20-30 minutes).

While the molten steel is drawn from the furnace, a little aluminium or ferrosilicon is added to it in order to remove dissolved gases.

Heat Treatment of Steels : It is a process of carefully heating the steel to high temperature followed by cooling to the room temperature under controlled conditions. Heat treatment of steel is done for the following two purposes.

(i) To develop certain special properties like. hardness, strength, ductility etc. without changing the chemical composition.

(ii) To remove some undesirable properties or gases like entrapped gases, internal stresses and strain.

A. Annealing : It is a process of heating steel to redness followed by slow cooling.

B. Quenching or Hardening : It is a process of heating steel to redness followed by sudden cooling by plunging the red hot steel into water or oil.

C. Tempering : It is a process of heating the hardened or quenched steel to a temperature much below redness (200 -350°C) followed by slow cooling.

D. Case Hardening : It is a process of giving a thin coating of hardened steel to wrought iron or to a strong flexible and mild steel by heating it in contact with charcoal followed by quenching in oil.

E. Nitriding : It is a process of heating steels at about 700°C in an atmosphere of ammonia. This process imparts a hard coating of iron nitride on the surface of steel.

Properties

Cast Iron : Carbon is present partly as free carbon in the form of graphite and partly in the form of iron carbide (Fe_3C). Due to presence of impurities, its melting point is low (1100 – 1250°C). The molten iron expands on solidification and hence it produces good castings. It does not rust easily. It can neither be tempered nor magnetised conveniently. Due to high carbon contents, it is hard and brittle and therefore can't be easily welded. It possesses very little ductility and is not suitable for forging.

Wrought Iron : It is extremely tough and melts at about 1500°C. It is highly malleable and ductile. Due to the presence of slag (above 1%), it has fibrous structure and thus can withstand unusual stresses. It softens at about 1000°C and then it can be forged and welded. It can't be tempered and permanently magnetised. It has high magnetic permeability.

Steel : Steel combines the useful properties of cast iron and wrought iron. It is hard and elastic. The properties of steel depend upon its carbon contents with the increase in carbon content, the hardness of steel increases while the ductility decreases. Soft steels contains carbon upto 0.25 percent. Medium carbon steels or mild steels contains 0.25 – 0.5 percent carbon. High carbon or hard steels contain 0.5 – 1.5 percent carbon. Alloy steels or special steels are alloys of steel with Ni, Cr, Co, Mn, V, W etc. For example, stainless steel in an alloy of Fe, Cr and Ni; tool steel is an alloy of Fe, W, V etc.

Pure Iron : Pure iron is a greyish white metal with m.p. 1525°C. It is highly magnetic but loses this property if heated above 766°C. It is malleable and ductile but has a very high tensile strength. Air (dry or moist) has no action on pure iron, but impure iron, when exposed to moist air is covered with a layer of rust, Fe $(OH)_3$. However, finely divided pure iron burns in air or oxygen forming magnetic oxide of iron.

$$3Fe + 2O_2 \rightarrow Fe_3O_4$$

Pure iron decomposes steam at red heat

$$3Fe + 4H_2O \rightarrow Fe_3O_4 + 4H_2$$

Various reactions with acids are

$$Fe + 2HCl \text{ (dil. or conc.)} \rightarrow FeCl_2 + H_2\uparrow$$

$$Fe + H_2SO_4 \text{ (dil.)} \rightarrow FeSO_4 + H_2\uparrow$$

$$Fe + 2H_2SO_4 \text{ (hot conc.)} \rightarrow FeSO_4 + SO_2\uparrow + 2H_2O$$

or $$2Fe + 6H_2SO_4 \text{ (hot conc.)} \rightarrow Fe(SO_4)_3 + 3SO_2\uparrow + 6H_2O$$

$$4Fe + 10HNO_3 \text{ (cold dil.)} \rightarrow 4Fe(NO_3)_2 + NH_4NO_3 + 3H_2O$$

$$Fe + 6HNO_3 \text{ (mode. conc.)} \rightarrow Fe(NO_3)_3 + 3NO_2\uparrow + 3H_2O$$

Cold conc. HNO_3 makes it passive in which state it fails to exhibit the properties of normal iron.

$$Fe + 4HNO_3 \text{ (hot conc.)} \rightarrow Fe(NO_3)_3 + NO\uparrow + 2H_2O$$

Fe + Alkalis $\rightarrow$ No reaction

$Fe + CuSO_4 \rightarrow FeSO_4 + Cu$ *i.e.*, less

Electropositive metals like Cu, Al etc are displaced from their salts.

Fe + Halogens, S, C, P $\rightarrow$ Combines at appropriate temperature

Finely divided iron combines with CO

$Fe + 5CO \rightarrow Fe(CO)_5$ (iron pentacarbonyl)

Passivity of Iron. The inertness exhibited by a substance under conditions in which chemical activity is to be expected is called *passivity.* Passivity of iron is belived to be due to the formation of an extremely thin (almost invisible) and impervious film of ferrous-ferric oxide, Fe_3O_4, on the surface of iron.

Passive iron although does not undergo any change in appearance, it neither liberates hydrogen from H_2SO_4 not precipitates copper from copper sulphate solution. Iron can be rendered passive also by other oxidising agents like $KMnO_4$, $K_2Cr_2O_7$, chloric acid, chromic acid, silver nitrate, dry nitrogen dioxide and anodic oxidation. Passive iron can be rendered active by scratching, immersing in a concentrated alkali solution, heating in a reducing atmosphere of H_2 or CO, or heating in HNO_3 upto 75°C.

Cobalt, nickel and chromium also exhibit the phenomenon of passivity.

Uses

Cast Iron : It is used for small casting for raillings, hot water pipes, electric poles bunsen burner bases and many other purposes where strain is minimum. Wrought iron and steel are manufactured from cast iron.

Wrought iron: It is used for the manufacture of articles capable of withstanding sudden stresses, *e.g.* chairs, nails, hooks, bolts etc. It is used for the manufacture of electromagnets and agriculture implements. It is used for making bars and wines.

Steel : In general steels are used for making machinery parts, girders, tools, knives, razors, household utensils etc. The specific use of steel depends upon the nature of metal added to iron.

Copper (Cu) : Copper was named as cuprum by the Romans because they used to get it from the island of cyprus. Copper occurs in free as well as in combined state.

Extraction : Copper is extracted from the ores (sulphides) by two processes :

I. Pyrometallurgical Process, which is a dry process and is applied to high trade ores (containing 4% or more copper).

II. Hydrometallurgical processes, which is a wet process and is applied to low grade ores.

Extraction from Pyrites (Chalcopyrites) by pyrometallurgical process (Smelting process)

(i) Concentration of Ore : The finely powdered ore is concentrated by froth floatation process.

(ii) Roasting : The concentrated ore is heated strongly in presence of air. Sulphur, arsenic and antimony are removed in the form of their volatile oxides while the proper ore is converted into a mixture of cuprous and ferrous sulphides. These sulphides are partially oxidised to oxides.

$$S + O_2 \rightarrow SO_2\uparrow$$
$$2As_2S_3 + 9O_2 \rightarrow 2As_2O_3\uparrow + 6SO_2\uparrow$$
$$2Sb_2S_3 + 9O_2 \rightarrow 2Sb_2O_3\uparrow + 6SO_2\uparrow$$
$$2Cu_2S + 3O_2 \rightarrow 2Cu_2O + 2SO_2$$
$$2FeS + 3O_2 \rightarrow 2FeO + 2SO_2$$

(iii) Smelting : The roasted ore is mixed with sand (flux) and coke (fuel) and then heated in water jacketed blast furnace called *smelter.* The oxidation of ferrous sulphide which started during roasting now goes a step further. Ferrous oxide formed, reacts with sand to form ferrous silicate (slag). Here some FeS reacts with Cu_2O to form Cu_2S again.

(a) $FeO + SiO_2 \rightarrow FeSiO_3$ (Slag)

(b) $Cu_2O + FeS \rightarrow Cu_2S + FeO$

Slag (forming upper layer) and molten mass consisting of Cu_2S a little Fe (forming lower layer and commonly called matte) are removed from separate holes.

(iv) Bessemerisation : Molten matte is heated in a Bessemer converter and a blast of air mixed with sand is blown through the molten mass. Here iron (FeS) is completely removed as slag, a part of Cu_2S is oxidised to Cu_2O and a part of Cu_2S reduces Cu_2O to metallic copper.

(a) $2FeS + 3O_2 \rightarrow 2FeO + 2SO_2\uparrow$
$FeO + SiO_2 \rightarrow FeSiO_3$

(b) $2Cu_2S + 3O_2 \rightarrow 2Cu_2O + 2SO_2\uparrow$
$2Cu_2O + Cu_2S \rightarrow 6Cu + SO_2\uparrow$

The molten copper is poured off into sand moulds. As it cools, it gives up the dissolved sulphur dioxide which forms blister on the surface of the metal. Hence the metal, thus obtained is called 'blister copper' and contains 98% copper.

(v) Refining of Copper :

(a) Polling : The molten blister copper is heated in presence of air and stirred with green wood poles. Sulphur and Arsenic are oxidised to their volatile oxides, iron is oxidised and forms a scum or slag which is skimmed off. The cuprous oxide is reduced to Cu by CO and H_2 from green wood.

$$Cu_2O + CO \rightarrow 2Cu + CO_2\uparrow$$
$$Cu_2O + H_2 \rightarrow 2Cu + H_2O$$

(b) Electrolytic Refining : This method is used for obtaining copper used in electrical industry. The electrolytic bath contains an acidified solution of copper sulphate impure copper (blister copper) acts as anode while cathode is of pure copper strip. When electric current is poured there is transfer of pure copper from anode to cathode which gradually grows in size. The impurities like Fe, Zn, Ni, Co etc. dissolve in the solution as sulphates and others like Au and Ag settle down below the anode as *anode mud.* The cathode is removed and copper of about 99.99 per cent purity is obtained.

Hydrometallurgical Process : A heap of 100,000 tonnes of crushed and powdered low grade ore is exposed to air and water when copper sulphide is oxidised to copper sulphate. Some iron sulphate and sulphuric acid is also produced. The process is completed in about a year.

(a) $\underset{\text{Copper pyrite}}{CuFeS_2} + 4O_2 \rightarrow CuSO_4 + FeSO_4$

(b) $\underset{\text{Copper glance}}{2Cu_2S} + 5O_2 \rightarrow 2CuSO_4 + 2CuO$

$CuS + 2O_2 \rightarrow CuSO_4$

In case of non-sulphide ores, the crushed ore is leached with dilute sulphuric acid.

(c) $\underset{\text{Malachite}}{CuCO_3.Cu(OH)_2} + 2H_2SO_4 \rightarrow$

$2CuSO_4 + CO_2\uparrow + 3H_2O$

The pale green liquor draining from the bottom of heaps is collected in pans and treated with iron scraps which precipitate out copper.

$CuSO_4 + Fe \rightarrow FeSO_4 + Ca\downarrow$

The precipitated copper is dried melted and refined.

Properties

(A) Physical : It is a reddish coloured lustrous heavy metal (sp. gr. 8.94) which melts as 1080°C and boils at 2325°C. It is highly malleable and ductile. It is best conductor of heat and electricity next to silver. However, presence of traces of other metals reduces conductivity. Molten metals absorbs (occludes) sulphur dioxide which it gives out on cooling.

(B) Chemical : Copper is not affected by dry air at room temperature, but when exposed to moist air having CO_2 it is superficially coated with a green layer of basic carbonate, $CaCO_3.Cu(OH)_2$ called *verdigris.*

$2Cu + H_2O + CO_2 + O_2 \rightarrow CuCO_3.Cu(OH)_2$

Sulphur dioxide present in air may also form basic sulphates (brochanite).

$8Cu + 6H_2O + 2SO_2 + 5O_2 \rightarrow 2[CuSO_4.3Cu(OH)_2]$

When heated with air, it forms cupric and cuprous oxides.

$2Cu + O_2 \xrightarrow{\text{below } 1100°C} 2CuO$ (cupric oxide)

$4Cu + O_2 \xrightarrow{\text{Above } 1100°C} 2Cu_2O$ (cuprous oxide)

It is attacked by steam only at white light.

Cu (red hot) + H_2O (steam) $\rightarrow CuO + H_2\uparrow$

Action of various acids is as non-oxidising acids (HCl & dil H_2SO_4) do not have any effect on copper. However they dissolve the metal in presence of air.

$2Cu + 4HCl$ (conc.) $+ O_2 \rightarrow 2CuCl_2 + 2H_2O$

$2Cu + 2H_2SO_4$ (dil.) $+ O_2 \rightarrow 2CuSO_4 + 2H_2O$

Acids possessing oxidising properties (conc., H_2SO_4 and HNO_3) readily attack the metal.

$Cu + 2H_2SO_4$ (conc.) $\rightarrow CuSO_4 + 2H_2O + SO_2$

$3Cu + 8HNO_3$ (dil.) $\rightarrow 3Cu(NO_3)_2 + 4H_2O + 2NO$

$Cu + 4HNO_3$ (conc.) $\rightarrow Cu(NO_3)_2 + 2H_2O + 2NO_2$

Copper dissolves in aqueous ammonia solution that forming deep blue solution of the complex salt tetrammine copper (II) hydroxide.

$2Cu + 2H_2O + 8NH_3 + O_2 \rightarrow 2[Cu(NH_3)_4](OH)_2$

It dissolves in aqueous solution of potassium cyanide yielding the complex, $[Cu(CN)_4]^{2-}$.

Metal Displacement Reactions: Copper displaces less electropositive metals like Ag, Hg, Au and Pt from their salt solutions. More electropositive metals like Fe and Zn displace copper from copper salt solution.

$2Ag^+ + Cu \rightarrow Cu^{2+} + 2Ag$

$Cu^{2+} + Fe \rightarrow Fe^{2+} + Cu$

Uses : Copper is the second most useful metal (the first being iron) because of its stability in air and water, and excellent conductivity. It is used in the manufacture of electrical wires, cables, vacuum, pans, heating utencils, calorimeters, coinage and ornaments, jewellery etc. It is also used for electroplating and electrotyping. Alloys like bran (Cu + Zn), bronze (Cu + Sn), German silver (Cu + Zn + Ni), bell metal (Cu + Sn), gun metal (Cu + Sn + Zn), Copper coins (Cu + Zn + Sn) etc. are manufactured from copper.

Zinc (Zn) : Zinc is not found in the native state.

Extraction

Reduction Process (Smelting)

(i) Crushing and Concentration: The finely powdered ore is concentrated first by *gravity process* and then by *froth flotation process.* In case, ferric oxide is also present as an impurity, it is removed by *electromagnetic separation.*

(ii) Roasting: The concentrated ore is roasted at about 900°C to convert ZnS and $ZnSO_4$ (formed during roasting) to zinc oxide.

$2ZnS + 3O_2 \rightarrow 2ZnO + 2SO_2$

$ZnS + 2O_2 \rightarrow ZnSO_4$

$2ZnSO_4 \rightarrow 2ZnO + 2SO_2 + O_2$

In case, calamine is used for the extraction of the metal, only calcination (heating at high temperature in absence of air) is required.

$$ZnCO_3 \rightarrow ZnO + CO_2$$

(iii) Reduction: The oxide, obtained above, is mixed with crushed coke and heated to 1400 – 1500°C to get metallic zinc.

$$ZnO + C \rightarrow Zn + CO$$
$$ZnO + CO \rightarrow Zn + CO_2$$

(iv) Purification: Zinc obtained above contains some impurities like Pb, Fe, Cd etc. These impurities may be removed by liquation, fractional distillation and electrolytic process.

Electrolysis is carried out in a cell having acidified $ZnSO_4$ ($ZnSO_4$ + dil H_2SO_4) as electrolyte. The anode is of impure zinc, while cathode is of pure zinc plate.

Electrolytic Process

(i) Concentration is done in reduction process.

(ii) Roasting is done at moderate temperature (700°C)

$$ZnS + 2O_2 \rightarrow ZnSO_4$$
$$2ZnS + 3O_2 \rightarrow 2ZnO + 2SO_2$$

(iii) Leading with sulphuric acid : When ZnO is converted to $ZnSO_4$

$$ZnO + H_2SO_4 \rightarrow ZnSO_4 + H_2O$$

Simultaneously impurities are also converted into their sulphates.

(iv) Removal of Impurities like Cu, Cd, As, Mn, Al, Fe. It is done by treatment with milk of lime, when Fe, Al, As and Sb are removed. Manganese is oxidised to its oxides by a current of air. The less active metals like Cu and Cd are liberated by adding zinc dust.

$$FeSO_4 + Ca(OH)_2 \rightarrow Fe(OH)_2\downarrow + CaSO_4$$
$$CuSO_4 + Zn \rightarrow ZnSO_4 + Cu\downarrow$$

(v) Electrolysis : Zinc sulphate is acidified with H_2SO_4 and then electrolysed between pure Zn or Al as cathode and pure lead as anode. Pure zinc will deposit at cathode. Zinc obtained by this process is 99.9% pure.

Properties

(A) Physical : Zinc is a bluish white metal. It is somewhat brittle at room temperature but becomes malleable and ductile between 100°C and 150°C. At 220°C, the metal becomes brittle and can be easily powdered. Its melting and boiling points are 419°C and 907°C respectively. When molten zinc is poured is cold water, granulated zinc is formed.

(B) Chemical :

Action of Air : Dry air has no action on zinc. In moist air, a protective layer of basic zinc carbonate $ZnCO_3.3Zn(OH)_2$, is formed on the surface of the metal. When heated in presence of air to 500°C, it burns to form a white cloud of zinc oxide.

$$2\,Zn + O_2 \rightarrow 2\,ZnO$$

Action of Water : Pure zinc has no action on water. *Zinc-copper couple* (prepared by allowing zinc dust to stand in a 1% solution of $CuSO_4$) decomposes water liberated H_2. Impure zinc decomposes boiling water slowly and steam quickly.

$$Zn + H_2O \rightarrow ZnO + H_2$$

Action of Acids

$$Zn + 2HCl\ (dil.) \rightarrow ZnCl_2 + H_2$$
$$Zn + H_2SO_4\ (dil.) \rightarrow ZnSO_4 + H_2$$
$$4Zn + 5H_2SO_4\ (mod.\ strong\ \&\ hot) \rightarrow 4ZnSO_4 + H_2S + 4H_2O$$
$$3Zn + 4H_2SO_4\ (mod.\ strong\ \&\ hot) \rightarrow 3ZnSO_4 + S + 4H_2O$$
$$Zn + 2H_2SO_4\ (conc.) \rightarrow ZnSO_4 + SO_2 + 2H_2O$$
$$4Zn + 10HNO_3\ (dil.) \rightarrow 4Zn(NO_3)_2 + NH_4NO_3 + 3H_2O$$
$$3Zn + 8HNO_3\ (mode.\ strong) \rightarrow 3Zn(NO_3)_2 + 2NO + 4H_2O$$
$$Zn + 4HNO_3\ (conc.\ \&\ hot) \rightarrow Zn\,(NO_3)_2 + 2NO_2 + 2H_2O$$

Zinc sulphate crystallises from the aqueous solution as $ZnSO_4.7H_2O$, commonly known as *white vitriol.*

Action of Alkalies

It forms soluble zincates, *e.g.,*

$$Zn + 2NaOH \rightarrow Na_2ZnO_2 + H_2$$

Combination with S & Cl_2

$$Zn + Cl_2 \rightarrow ZnCl_2,\ Zn + S \rightarrow ZnS$$

Displacement of Metals : Zinc being fairly strongly electropositive metal precipitates a number of less electropositive metals from their salt solutions, *e.g.,* Cu from $CuSO_4$ solution, Pb from $PbNO_3$ and silver and gold from respective complex cyanide solutions.

$$CuSO_4 + Zn \rightarrow ZnSO_4 + Cu\downarrow$$

Uses

(i) On account of its resistance to rusting and corrosion, zinc is used to coat iron. This is done by dipping the clean metal in molten zinc or by spraying

molten zinc on the iron sheets, or by electrolytic process in which the iron article is made cathode, zinc rod is anode anode and acidified zinc sulphate is used as electrolyte. This process is known as *galvanisation.* The galvanised iron sheets are used for roofs, gutters, etc. Zinc is used in the preparation of its several important alloys like brass, bronze, and german silver. Zinc is used in the Parke's process for the extraction of silver from lead (desilverization of lead). Zinc dust is used for the precipitation of silver and gold in cyanide process. Zinc dust is used as a reducing agent in the laboratory.

Elements of group 1 (or 1A) and 2 (or IIA) are known as *s-block elements* because elements of these groups contain 1 or 2 electrons in the outermost *s*-orbital.

Some Reactions of Alkali Metals

Reaction	*Comment*
$M + H_2O \rightarrow MOH + H_2$	The hydroxides are the strongest bases known
With excess dioxygen	
$Li + O_2 \rightarrow Li_2O$	Monoxide is formed by Li and to a small extent by Na

Reaction	*Comment*
$Na + O_2 \rightarrow Na_2O_2$	Peroxide formed by Na and to a small extent by Li
$K + O_2 \rightarrow KO_2$	Superoxide formed by K, Rb, Cs
$M + H_2 \rightarrow MH$	Ionic 'salt-like' hydrides
$Li + N_2 \rightarrow Li_3N$	Nitride formed only by Li
$M + P \rightarrow M_3P$	All the metals form phosphides
$M + As \rightarrow M_3As$	All the metals form arsenides
$M + Sb \rightarrow M_3Sb$	All the metals form stibnides
$M + S \rightarrow M_2S$	All the metals form sulphides
$M + Se \rightarrow M_2Se$	All the metals form selenides
$M + Te \rightarrow M_2Te$	All the metals form tellurides
$M + F_2 \rightarrow MF$	All the metals form fluorides
$M + Cl_2 \rightarrow MCl$	All the metals form chlorides
$M + Br_2 \rightarrow MBr$	All the metals form bromides
$M + I_2 \rightarrow MI$	All the metals form iodides
$M + NH_3 \rightarrow MNH_2$	All the metals form amides

Biological Significance of Sodium & Potassium: Sodium cation is major cation of extracellular fluids of animals including human beings. It is supposed to activate certain enzymes in the animal body. Sodium ions are relatively harmless except when present in excess amounts. In excess amounts it may cause hypertension.

The potassium ion is essential to all organisms with the possible exception of blue green algae. It is important cation of intracellular fluid of animal cells.

In view of close resemblance in chemical properties between Na & K, it is surprising that their biological functions are very different. Na^+ ions are actively expelled from cells, whereas K^+ ions are not. This ion transport is called 'Sodium-pump', and it involves both expulsion of Na^+ and take up K^+. In animal cells the concentration of K^+ is about 0.15 M and the concentration of Na^+ is about 0.01 M. In body fluids (*i.e.,* lymph & blood), the concentration of K^+ and Na^+ are about 0.003M and 0.15M respectively. The transport of ions requires energy, and this is obtained by the hydrolysis of one ATP molecule to ADP provides enough energy to move three Na^+ ions out of the cell, and two K^+ and one H^+ ions back into the cell. The mechanism of ion transport involves polyethenes naturally found in organisms.

The difference in the ratio of Na^+ to K^+ inside and outside cells produces an electrical potential across the cell membrane, which is essential for the functioning of nerve and muscle cells. The movement of glucose into cells is associated with Na^+ ions. Potassium ions inside the cell are essential for the metabolism of glucose. The synthesis of proteins, and the activation of some enzymes.

Some reactions of Alkaline earth metals

Action of Water : These metals react slowly with water liberating hydrogen and forming metal hydroxides, *e.g.,*

$$Ca + 2H_2O \rightarrow Ca(OH)_2 + H_2$$

The reaction with water becomes increasingly vigorous on moving down the group. Reaction of beryllium with water is not certain, magnesium reacts only with hot water, while other metals react with cold water, but, of course, not as energetically as the alkali metals.

$$Ba > Sr > Ca > Mg > Be$$
(Reactivity with water)

The inertness of Be & Mg towards water is due to formation of protective thin layer of hydroxide on the surface of the metals.

Action of Hydrogen : All these elements, except beryllium, combine with hydrogen to form hydrides, MH_2. Magnesium hydride (like BeH_2) is a covalent while other hydrides are ionic.

Action of Halogens : All the elements combine with halogens at elevated temperatures forming halides, MX_2. Beryllium halides are covalent, while the rest are ionic and thus dissolves in water and conduct electricity in aqueous solution and in molten state. The solubility of halides (except fluoride) decreases on moving down the group. Fluorides are almost insoluble in water.

Action with Nitrogen : All these elements burn in nitrogen forming nitrides, M_3N_2 which react with water to liberate ammonia.

$$3Ca + N_2 \rightarrow Ca_3N_2$$
$$Ca_3N_2 + 6H_2O \rightarrow 3Ca(OH)_2 + 2NH_3$$

The ease of formation of nitrides decreases on moving down the group.

Action with Acids : On account of their high oxidation potentials, they readily liberate hydrogen from dilute acids.

For examples:

$$Mg + 2HCl \rightarrow MgCl_2 + H_2$$

The reactivity of alkaline earths increases on moving down the group. This is due to increase in electropositive character from Be to Ba. Thus beryllium reacts very slowly, Mg reacts very rapidly while Ca, Sr and Ba react explosively.

Silicon

Silicon, the second most abundant element on the earth crust, is an important constituent of igneous rocks which consists of silicates of magnesium, aluminium potassium and iron. Silicon is also widely present as silica in sand, quartz and flint.

Two allotropic forms, viz., *amorphous* and *crystalline* and prepared artificially.

Amorphous Silicon

It is prepared by heating quartz (SiO_2) with magnesium in presence of a small amount of calcined magnesia.

$$SiO_2 + 2Mg \rightarrow Si + 2MgO$$

Magnesium oxide is soluble in dilute HCl and hence can be removed easily.

By heating potassium silicofluoride with potassium in an iron tube.

$$K_2SiF_6 + 4K \rightarrow 6KF + Si$$

Properties

(i) Amorphous silicon (*sp*. gr. 225) is a brownish powder.

(ii) It burns brilliantly in oxygen but superficially in air

$$Si + O_2 \rightarrow SiO_2$$

(iii) It is soluble in KOH and a mixture of HNO_3 and HF.

$$Si + 2KOH + H_2O \rightarrow K_2SiO_3 + 2H_2$$

(iv) It decomposes steam at red heat

$$Si + 2H_2O(Steam) \xrightarrow{\text{red heat}} SiO_2 + 2H_2$$

(v) It ignites spontaneously in F_2 giving SiF_4. It burns in chlorine on heating forming $SiCl_4$.

(vi) On fusion with sodium carbonate it gives sodium silicate and carbon

$$Na_2CO_3 + Si \rightarrow Na_2SiO_3 + C$$

Crystalline Silicon

By heating potassium silicoflouride with aluminium or zinc in an iron crucible.

$$3K_2SiF_6 + 4Al \rightarrow KF + 4AlF_3 + 3Si$$
$$K_2SiF_6 + 2Zn \rightarrow 2KF + 2ZnF_2 + Si$$

By passing a current of silicon tetrachloride over molten aluminium

$$3SiCl_4 + 4Al \rightarrow 3Si + 4AlCl_3$$

Properties

(i) Crystalline silicon (sp.gr. 2.49) possesses light orange colour and a metallic lustre.

(ii) It is very good and scratches glass.

(iii) It does not burn in oxygen even on strong heating (difference form amorphous silicon).

(iv) When fused with alkali, it gives a silicate.

$$Na_2CO_3 + Si \rightarrow Na_2SiO_3 + C$$

It is also attacked by a mixture of HNO_3 and HI.

$$Si + 2H_2O \rightarrow SiO_2 + 2H_2$$

(v) It combines spontaneously with fluorine in cold but on heating with chlorine

$$Si + 2X_2 \rightarrow SiX_4 \ (X = Cl \text{ or } F)$$

Nitrogen

Occurrence: Air is the most abundant source of free nitrogen. Nitrogen (in free state) forms 75% by weight or 80% by volume of the air. In the combined state it is found as nitrites and ammonium salts. Nitrogen is an essential constituent of all proteins found in animals and plants.

Preparation

By heating a mixture of NH_4Cl and $NaNO_2$ (Laboratory Method)

$$NH_4Cl + NaNO_2 \rightarrow \underset{\text{Unstable}}{[NH_4NO_2]} + NaCl$$

$$NH_4NO_2 \xrightarrow{\text{heat}} N_2 + 2H_2O$$

By oxidation of ammonia

$$8NH_3 + 3Cl_2 \rightarrow 6NH_4Cl + N_2$$

$$2NH_3 + 3CuO \xrightarrow{\text{Heat}} 3Cu + N_2 + 3H_2O$$

By heating ammonium dichromate

$$(NH_4)_2Cr_2O_7 \xrightarrow{\text{Heat}} Cr_2O_3 \downarrow + N_2 + 4H_2O$$

By passing vapours of HNO_3 on strongly heated copper.

$$5Cu + 2HNO_3 \rightarrow 5CuO + N_2 + H_2O$$

Commercially nitrogen is obtained by liquefying air followed by fractional evaporation. Nitrogen, having a lower b.p. (77.3°K), boils off more readily than the less volatile oxygen (b.p. 90.04K).

Properties

Nitrogen is a colourless, tasteless and odourless gas. It is slightly lighter than air. It is only slightly soluble in water. It is neither combustible nor supports combustion. Like CO_2, it is not poisonous but, however, animals die in an atmosphere of N_2 for want of oxygen. It can be liquefied to a colourless liquid (b.p. – 7.3 K)

Combination with hydrogen to form NH_3 (Haber's Process) under pressure 100 – 1000 atmospheres.

$$N_2 + 3H_2 \xrightleftharpoons{\text{Fe + Mo; 400 – 500°C}} 2NH_3$$

Combination with oxygen in presence of electric arc (3500 °C) to form nitric oxide. This reaction is used in 'Birkeland and Eyde Process' for the manufacture of HNO_3.

$$N_2 + O_2 \rightleftharpoons 2NO - 43.2 \text{ kcal}$$

Reaction with Metals

Like Li, Mg, Al, Ca, Si etc. to form nitrides

$$3Mg + N_2 \rightarrow Mg_3N_2$$

$$2Al + N_2 \rightarrow 2AlN$$

These nitrides react with water to form NH_3, and with acids to form salts.

$$Mg_3N_2 + 6H_2O \rightarrow 3Mg(OH)_2 + 2NH_3$$

$$Mg_3N_2 + 8HCl \rightarrow 3MgCl_2 + 2NH_4Cl$$

Reaction with Calcium Carbide

$$CaC_2 + N_2 \xrightarrow[\text{or } 1000°C, \ 1 \text{ atm}]{500–600°C, \ 6.8 \text{ atm}} \underset{\text{Cal. cyanamide}}{CaCN_2} + C$$

Since calcium cyanamide is hydrolysed in the soil to urea and ammonium carbonate, it is used as a fertiliser.

$$NaCN_2 + 3H_2O \rightarrow Ca(OH)_2 + H_2N.CO.NH_2$$

$$\underset{\text{Urea}}{NH_2.CO.NH_2} + 2H_2O \rightarrow \underset{\text{Amm. carbonate}}{(NH_4)_2CO_3}$$

Uses

Nitrogen serves to dilute the action of oxygen in air and thus makes combustion much less rapid. It is used for filling electric lamps and providing in inert atmosphere in certain metallurgical operations. It is used in manufacture of NH_3, HNO_3, $CaCN_2$ and other nitrogen compounds.

Active Nitrogen

Active nitrogen is produced by the action of an electric discharge on nitrogen gas at low pressures. The process is accompanied by a yellow glow which persists for several hours and indicates slow release of energy in the process. It is highly reactive.

Phosphorous

Occurrence: Phosphorous is an extremely active element and hence occurs only in the combined state as phosphate in the rocks and on the soil.

(i) Phosphorite, $Ca_3(PO_4)_2$

(ii) Chlorapatite, $3Ca_3(PO_4)_2.CaCl_2$

(iii) Apatite (Fluorapatite), $3Ca_3(PO_4)_2.\ CaF_2$

Phosphorous is also found in living organisms as phosphoproteins. It is an essential constituent of bores, teeth, blood and nervous tissues. It is necessary for the growth of plants. Bone ash (animal charcoal) contains about 80% calcium phosphate.

Extraction

By heating a mixture of phosphorite (cal. phosphate) coke and silica (sand) in an electric furnace (electrothermic process).

$$2Ca_3(PO_4)_2 + 6SiO_2 \rightarrow 6CaSiO_3 + P_4O_{10}$$

$$P_4O_{10} + 10C \rightarrow P_4 + 10CO$$

Allotropic Forms of Phosphorous

White Phosphorous (Yellow)

It is the most important and most reactive form. When exposed to light, it is covered with a thin coating of red phosphorous giving yellow appearance, hence it is also known as 'yellow phosphorus'. It is very soft and can be cut with a knife. It is extremely poisonous in nature. It is soluble in CCl_4. Molecular weight determination suggests that white phosphorous has the molecular formula P_4 both in solid and vapour states. The four atoms of the molecule are at the corners of a regular tetrahedron. The P – P bond distance on P_4 molecule is 2.21 Å and the P – P – P bond angle are of 60°. However, theoretically the pure *p* – *p* overlap would give bond angle of 90°, hence the low angle in P_4 molecule suggests that the structure is under *strain* and hence unstable.

The strained structure of P_4 molecule is consistent with its high reactivity as it bursts spontaneously in air and is, therefore, stored under water. It glows in the dark on account of oxidation of its vapours (phosphorescence or chemiluminescence) and it is believed that the energy of oxidation is not liberated in the form of heat, rather emitted as light. It is soft, low melting solid (m.p. 44°C) indicating that individual P_4 molecules are held together by weak Van der Waals forces.

Red Phosphorous (Violet)

It is a violet red powder. It is stable variety and obtained by heating white phosphorous at 240 – 250°C. It does not ignite spontaneously in air. It does not show phosphorescence. It is insoluble in CCl_4. It is not poisonous. It is much less reactive than the white phosphorous. It is brittle powder and sublimes on heating giving vapours which when condensed give white phosphorous. It is used in match industry and in making smoke bombs. Red phosphorous is believed to exist as chains on P_4 tetrahedra linked together.

Black Phosphorous

Is a good conductor of electricity like graphite.

Oxygen

Oxygen is found in free state in air as O_2 gas to the extent of 21% by volume or 23% by weight. In the combined state it is present in water (89% by weight), earth's crust (about 50%) and in plants and animal tissues (50 – 70%). Combined oxygen is much more plantiful than free oxygen.

Preparation

By heating oxides of Hg, Pb, Ag, Mn and Ba.

$$2HgO \rightarrow 2Ag + O_2$$

$$2Ag_2O \rightarrow 4Ag + O_2$$

$$2PbO_2 \rightarrow 2PbO + O_2$$

$$2Pb_3O_4 \rightarrow 6PbO + O_2$$

$$3MnO_2 \rightarrow Mn_3O_4 + O_2$$

$$2BaO_2 \rightarrow 2BaO + O_2$$

By heating H_2O_2 and several salts rich in oxygen

$$2H_2O_2 \xrightarrow{MnO_2\text{(catalyst)}} 2H_2O + O_2 \uparrow$$

$$2KNO_3 \xrightarrow{\text{red hot}} 2KNO_2 + O_2 \uparrow$$

$$\underset{\text{Bleaching powder}}{2CaOCl_2} \xrightarrow{\text{Heat}} 2CaCl_2 + O_2 \uparrow$$

$$2KClO_4 \xrightarrow{650°C} 2KCl + 4O_2 \uparrow$$

$$2Pb(NO_3)_2 \xrightarrow{\text{Heat}} 2PbO + 4NO_2 + O_2 \uparrow$$

$$\underset{\text{Pot. permanganate}}{2KMnO_4} \xrightarrow{\text{Heat}} \underset{\text{Pot. manganate}}{K_2MnO_4} + MnO_2 + O_2 \uparrow$$

$$2KClO_3 \xrightarrow[400°C]{MnO_2} 2KCl + 3O_2 \uparrow$$

(Laboratory Method)

$$4K_2Cr_2O_7 \xrightarrow{\text{Heat}} 4K_2CrO_4 + 2Cr_2O_3 + 3O_2 \uparrow$$

By the action of chemical reagent on compounds, rich in oxygen.

$$2Na_2O_2 + 2H_2O \rightarrow 4NaOH + O_2$$

(Laboratory Method)

$$2MnO_2 + 2H_2SO_4 \rightarrow 2MnSO_4 + 2H_2O + O_2\uparrow$$

$$4KMnO_4 + 6H_2SO_4 \rightarrow 2K_2SO_4 + 4MnSO_4 + 6H_2O + 5O_2$$

$$2K_2Cr_2O_7 + 8H_2SO_4 \rightarrow 2K_2SO_4 + 2Cr_2(SO_4)_3 + 8H_2O + 3O_2$$

By the electrolysis of either acidified water using Pt electrodes or alkaline water using Ni electrodes *(Commercial Method).*

(a) $H_2SO_4 \rightleftharpoons 2H^+ + SO_4^{2-}$

At cathode : $2H^+ + 2e^- \rightarrow 2H + H_2\uparrow$

At anode :

$$H_2O + SO_4^{2-} \rightarrow 2H^+ + SO_4^{2-} + O + 2e^-$$

$$O + O \rightarrow O_2\uparrow$$

(b) $Ba(OH)_2 \rightleftharpoons Ba^{2+} + 2OH^-$ (NaOH can also be used)

At cathode :

$$Ba^{2+} + 2H_2O + 2e^- \rightarrow Ba^{+2} + 2OH^- + H_2\uparrow$$

At anode : $2OH^- \rightarrow H_2O + O + 2e^-$

$$O + O \rightarrow O_2\uparrow$$

From Air (Commercial Method)

Air is liquefied by making use of the Joule-Thompson effect (cooling by expansion of the gas). Water vapour and CO_2 are removed by solidification. The remaining constituents of liquid air, *i.e.,* liquid oxygen and liquid nitrogen are separated by means of fractional distillation (b.p. of $O_2 = -183°C$, b.p. of $N_2 = -195.8°C$)

Properties

It is colourless, odourless and tasteless gas slightly soluble in water. It is soluble in alkaline pyrogallol. It is slightly heavier than air. It can be liquefied by cooling under pressure to pale blue liquid. It can also be solidified into a bluish white solid at – 219°C. It is not inflammable but a supporter of combustion. It is paramagnetic. It exists in three isotopic forms with atomic weight 16, 17 and 18. Normally, the three isotopes of atomic weight 16, 17 and 18 are present in the ratio of 10000 : 1 : 8.

Reaction with Metals

Almost all metals burn in air to form oxides most of which are basic in nature.

$$4Na + O_2 \rightarrow 2Na_2O$$

$$3Fe + 2O_2 \rightarrow Fe_3O_4$$

$$2Ca + O_2 \rightarrow 2CaO_2$$

$$4Al + 3O_3 \rightarrow 2Al_2O_3$$

Reaction with Non-Metals

Most of the non-metals also burn in oxygen forming acidic oxides.

$$S + O_2 \rightarrow SO_2$$

$$C + O_2 \rightarrow CO_2$$

$$2H_2 + O_2 \xrightarrow{Pt} 2H_2O$$

$$P_4 + 5O_2 \rightarrow P_4O_{10}$$

Reaction with Compounds

$$2SO_2 + O_2 \xrightarrow{\text{Pt asbestose}} 2SO_3 \text{ (contact process)}$$

$$4NH_3 + 5O_2 \xrightarrow{\text{Pt gauze}} 4NO + 6H_2O \text{ (Ostwald process)}$$

$$4HCl + O_2 \xrightarrow{\text{Cupricchlorides}} 2Cl_2 + 2H_2O \text{ (Deacon's process)}$$

Oxidation of Organic Compounds

On heating in presence of suitable catalyst oxygen oxidises in organic compounds.

$$CH_4 + 2O_2 \rightarrow CO_2 + 2H_2O$$

$$2CH_3OH + O_2 \xrightarrow{Pt} 2HCHO + 2H_2O$$

$$C_6H_{12}O_6 + 6O_2 \rightarrow 6CO_2 + 6H_2O$$

Structure

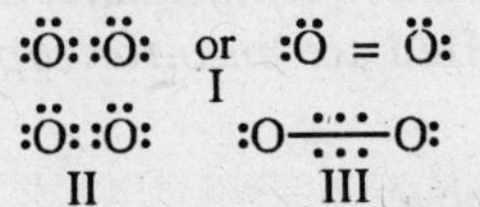

The electronic structure, I for oxygen with no unpaired electron fails to account for the paramagnetic behaviour of oxygen, although it accounts for its high dissociation energy (117 kcal/mole).

The structure II although can explain the paramagnetic behaviour but does not explain the very high dissociating energy of molecule, moreover, this structure does not conform to octet rule.

Pauling suggested structure III in which two oxygen atoms are joined by a covalent bond and by two 3-electron bonds.

The 3-electron bonds have one unpaired electron each and a 3-electron bond has one half the strength of a single bond. Thus this structure can explain the paramagnetic behaviour as well as high dissociation energy of oxygen molecule. However, these properties can better be explained by the molecules orbital structure of oxygen molecule.

Uses

Oxygen mixed with CO_2 or helium is used for artificial respiration. Oxy-hydrogen and oxy-acetylene flames are used for cutting and welding purpose. Liquid oxygen mixed with finely divided carbon is used a substitute for dynamite in coal mining. Liquid oxygen is an important constituent of fuels used in rockets. Oxygen, is used as an oxidising agent in several preparations.

Allotropic Modifications

Allotropic forms of Sulphur

Rhombic, Octahedral or α-sulphur (m.p. 112.8°C, sp.gr. 2.06).

This is the common form of sulphur, all other varieties change into this form on standing. It is prepared by evaporating a solution of sulphur in carbon disulphide. It is soluble in CS_2 and change into β sulphur when heated above 95.5°C.

Monoclinic, Prismatic or β-Sulphur (m.p. 119.2°C, sp.gr. 1.98)

It is prepared by melting rhombic sulphur in a dish followed by cooling till crust is formed. It is stable above 95.5°C below which it is converted into α-form, thus 95.6°C is the transition temperature, and the two sulphurs are called as *enantiotropic* substances.

$$\alpha\text{-sulphur} \xrightleftharpoons{95.6^\circ C} \beta\text{-sulphur}$$

It is soluble in CS_2, α and β sulphur are crystalline variaties (rest being amorphous) and exist as S_8 cyclic molecules.

Plastic or γ-Sulphur (sp.gr. 1.95; no sharp m.p.)

It is obtained by sudden cooling (quenching) by pouring boiling sulphur in a thin stream to cold water. It is dark in colour and insoluble in CS_2. Plastic sulphur may be considered as *supercooled liquid, i.e.,* a liquid which due to rapid cooling below its melting point had no time to settle in a crystalline form.

Milk of Sulphur

It is obtained by boiling milk of lime with sulphur and decomposing the products formed with HCl

$$3Ca(OH)_2 + 12S \rightarrow \underset{\text{Cal.Penta-sulphide}}{2CaS_5} + \underset{\text{Cal.thiosul-phate}}{CaS_2O_3} + 3H_2O$$

$$2CaS_5 + CaS_2O_3 + 6HCl \rightarrow 3CaCl_2 + 3H_2O + 12S\downarrow \text{(white)}$$

Milk of sulphur is soluble in CS_2 and is mainly used in medicine.

Colloidal or δ-Sulphur

It is prepared by passing H_2S through a solution of an oxidising agent (*e.g.,* nitric acid, pot. permanganate etc.) or water, or by treating sodium thiosulphate solution with dil. HCl.

$$2HNO_3 + H_2S \rightarrow 2NO_2 + 2H_2O + S\downarrow$$

$$SO_2 + 2H_2S \rightarrow 2H_2O + 3S\downarrow$$

$$Na_2S_2O_3 + 2HCl \rightarrow 2NaCl + SO_2 + H_2O + S\downarrow$$

On heating or long standing, colloidal sulphur changes into the ordinary form.

Uses

Sulphur is used in the manufacture of SO_2, H_2SO_4, CS_2, gun powder (a mixture of S, charcoal and KNO_3) etc. It is used in match industry and fire works, in vulcanisation of rubber as a disinfectant for houses, in skin medicines and in the manufacture of sulphur dyes.

Fluorine

Occurrence and Properties : Fluorine is found only in the combined state. It is widely distributed. The main ores are *fluorspar* (CaF_2), cryolite ($AlF_3.3NaF$) and *apatite* [$CaF_2.3Ca_3(PO_4)_2$]. Traces of fluorides occur in sea water, bones, teeth, blood, milk etc.

Isolation of fluorine is tough because

(i) It is extremely reactive so it was extracted after hundred of years of its discovery. The reduction potential of fluorine is very high and hence it attacks water giving oxygen, so its production by electrolysis of aqueous solution of fluorides was not possible. It attacks glass carbon and almost all metals including platinum and hence the apparatus could not be made of these usual materials.

(ii) It is most electronegative element so none of the ordinary chemical oxidising agent is capable of extracting electrons from fluoride ions, so preparation of fluorine from fluorides was not possible by ordinary chemical oxidising agents.

Moissan (1886) prepared fluorine by the electrolysis of solution of potassium hydrogen fluoride, KHF_2 in anhydrous hydrogen fluoride. On electrolysis, hydrogen is evolved at the cathode and flourine at the anode.

Now a days, fluorine is obtained commercially by the electrolysis of an equimolar mixture of anhydrous HF and KF at about 250°C. Carbon is used as the anode and a steel vessel serves as the cathode. Hydrogen fluoride is added periodically to maintain the correct composition of the mixture. Following reactions take place at the two electrodes.

$$HF \rightarrow H^+ + F^-$$

At the anode : $2F^- \rightarrow F_2 + 2e^-$

At the cathode : $2H^+ + 2e^- \rightarrow H_2$

Fluorine thus obtained is contaminated with hydrogen fluoride which is removed by passing it over sodium fluoride pellets.

$$NaF + HF \rightarrow \underset{\text{Sod. hydrogen flouride}}{NaHF_2}$$

Uses

It is used in preparation of

(i) Difluorodichloromethane (Freon 12), CF_2Cl_2, which is used in refrigeration and air conditioning in place of NH_3 and SO_2. It is non-toxic and non-inflammable. It is also used as a solvent for D.D.T. and other insecticide.

(ii) Polytetrafluoroethylene (Teflon), $(-F_2C-CF_2)_n$. It is a new plastic. It is resistant to acids alkalies and oxidising agents.

Sodium fluoride and cryolite are used as insecticides.

(iii) Sulphur hexafluoride is used in X-ray and high voltage machines. Its use is due to its high dielectric constant and insulating properties.

(iv) Fluorine, itself, has been used as an oxidising agent in rockets.

Chlorine

It is not found in free state. Main source is NaCl from sea water, other sources are rock salts and other chlorine minerals like *carnallite,* $MgCl_2.KCl.6H_2O$, horn silver AgCl, sylvine, KCl etc.

Preparation

By the action of any oxidising agent (whose oxidation potential is greater than Cl_2) on HCl.

(a) $MnO_2 + 2HCl \rightarrow MnCl_2 + H_2O + [O]$

$2HCl + [O] \rightarrow H_2O + Cl_2$

$MnO_2 + 4HCl \rightarrow MnCl_2 + 2H_2O + Cl_2$

(b) $2KMnO_4 + 6HCl \rightarrow 2KCl + 2MnCl_2 + 3H_2O + 5[O]$

$2HCl + [O] \rightarrow H_2O + Cl_2] \times 5$

$2KMnO_4 + 16HCl \rightarrow 2KCl + 2MnCl_2 + 8H_2O + 5Cl_2$

(c) $K_2Cr_2O_7 + 14HCl \rightarrow 2KCl + 2CrCl_3 + 7H_2O + 3Cl_2$

(d) $PbO_2 + 4HCl \rightarrow PbCl_2 + 2H_2O + Cl_2$

(e) $Pb_3O_4 + 8HCl \rightarrow 3PbCl_2 + 4H_2O + Cl_2$

(f) $CaOCl_2 + 2HCl \rightarrow CaCl_2 + H_2O + Cl_2$

(g) $\underset{\text{Sod.hypochlorite}}{NaOCl} + 2HCl \rightarrow NaCl + H_2O + Cl_2$

(h) $O_3 + 2HCl \rightarrow O_2 + H_2O + Cl_2$

Chlorine can be prepared by heating any chloride with concentrated sulphuric acid and manganese dioxide.

$MnO_2 + 2NaCl + 3H_2SO_4 \rightarrow 2NaHSO_4 + MnSO_4 + 2H_2O + Cl_2$

or $MnO_2 + 4NaCl + 4H_2SO_4 \rightarrow 4NaHSO_4 + MnCl_2 + 2H_2O + Cl_2$

Reaction *(a), (b)* and above are more common in laboratory. Chlorine so obtained is first passed through water for dissolving HCl gas (very soluble) and then through conc. H_2SO_4 for removing moisture.

Manufacture

By the electrolysis brine (aq. solution of NaCl) in Nelson Cell. This is the cheapest method and gives purest chlorine.

$NaCl \rightleftharpoons Na^+ + Cl^-$

$H_2O \rightleftharpoons H^+ + OH^-$

At cathode: $H^+ + e^- \rightarrow H$

$H + H \rightarrow H_2\uparrow$

At anode: $Cl^- \rightarrow Cl + e^-$

$Cl + Cl \rightarrow Cl_2\uparrow$

Deacon's Process (Obsolete Method)

$$\underset{(4\,vol.)}{4HCl} + \underset{(1\,vol)}{O_2}\ (\text{from air}) \xrightarrow[CuCl_2\,(\text{catalyst})]{400-500°C} 2H_2O + 2Cl_2\uparrow$$

The temperature should not be below 350°C because at this temperature oxygen would not decompose hydrochloric acid at all.

Chlorine gas, this obtained, contains N_2 and O_2 and is used for the manufacture of bleaching powder by Hasenclever's process (dilute chlorine process).

Properties

Physical: It is a greenish yellow gas with a suffocating smell and is poisonous in nature. It is about 2.5 times as heavy as air. It can be easily liquefied by cooling under pressure to a yellow liquid (b . p . – 34.6°C and s.p. – 101.6°C). It is fairly soluble in water giving yellowish, strongly smelling liquid called *chlorine water.* A part of chlorine reacts chemically with water forming HOCl which explains its oxidation and bleaching action

$$Cl_2 + H_2O \rightarrow HCl + HOCl$$
$$2HOCl \rightarrow 2HCl + O_2$$

Chemical: *(i) Combination with elements :* It combines with *hydrogen* in light (but not in dark) with explosion to form HCl. However, in presence of charcoal catalyst the reaction is smooth.

$$H_2 + Cl_2 \rightarrow 2HCl$$

It combines directly with all non-metals except N, O and C, and also with many metals, *e.g.,* Na, Fe, Al, Zn, Hg, Cu etc.

$$P_4 + 6Cl_2 \rightarrow 4PCl_3$$
$$S + Cl_2 \rightarrow SCl_2$$
$$2Na + Cl_2 \rightarrow 2NaCl$$
$$P_4 + 10Cl_2 \rightarrow 4PCl_5$$
$$2Sb + 3Cl_2 \rightarrow 2SbCl_3$$
$$Cu + Cl_2 \rightarrow CuCl_2$$

(ii) Affinity for Hydrogen: It decomposes several hydrogen compounds forming HCl.

$$2H_2O + 2Cl_2 \rightarrow 4HCl + O_2$$
$$H_2S + Cl_2 \rightarrow 2HCl + S$$
$$C_6H_6 + 3Cl_2 \rightarrow 6HCl + 6C$$
$$\underset{\text{turpentine oil}}{C_{10}H_{16}} + 8Cl_2 \rightarrow 16HCl + 10C$$

(iii) Oxidising and Bleaching Action : Moist chlorine gives oxygen hence it can act as an oxidising and bleaching agent.

$$Cl_2 + H_2O \rightarrow HCl + HClO$$
$$\underset{\text{Hypochlorous acid}}{HClO} \rightarrow HCl + [O]$$

It takes electron so is an oxidising agent

$$Cl_2 + 2e^- \rightarrow 2Cl^-$$
$$2FeSO_4 + H_2SO_4 + Cl_2 \rightarrow Fe_2(SO_4)_3 + 2HCl$$
$$H_2S + Cl_2 \rightarrow 2HCl + S\downarrow$$
$$SO_2 + 2H_2O + Cl_2 \rightarrow H_2SO_2 + 2HCl$$
$$Na_2SO_3 + H_2O + Cl_2 \rightarrow Na_2SO_4 + 2HCl$$
$$Na_2S_2O_3 + H_2O + Cl_2 \rightarrow Na_2SO_4 + 2HCl + S$$
$$Na_2S_2O_3 + 5H_2O + 4Cl_2 \rightarrow Na_2SO_4 + H_2SO_4 + 8HCl$$
$$2FeCl_2 + Cl_2 \rightarrow 2FeCl_3$$
$$SnCl_2 + Cl_2 \rightarrow SnCl_4$$
$$2HBr + Cl_2 \rightarrow 2HCl + Br_2$$
$$2KI + Cl_2 \rightarrow 2KCl + I_2$$

Owing to liberation of oxygen from water, moist chlorine bleaches vegetable colouring matter like litmus, indigo, linen, woodpulp, cotton fabric etc.

$$Cl_2 + H_2O \rightarrow 2HCl + [O]$$

Coloured matter + [O] → colourless matter

Bleaching done by Cl_2 is permanent and the colour is not restored on standing. However, it can't be used for bleaching delicate articles (*e.g.,* straw, silk, wool etc.) which are damaged by it.

(iv) Action of Alkalies :

$$2NaOH(cold) + Cl_2 \rightarrow NaCl + \underset{\text{Sod. hypochlorite}}{NaClO} + H_2O$$
$$6NaOH\ (hot) + 3Cl_2 \rightarrow 5NaCl + \underset{\text{Sod. chlorate}}{NaClO_3} + 3H_2O$$

With milk of lime (paste of lime in water), chlorine reacts as above but with slacked lime it forms bleaching powder, $CaOCl_2$.

$$Ca(OH)_2 + Cl_2 \rightarrow CaOCl_2 + H_2O$$

(v) Action of Ammonia :

$$8NH_3\ (excess) + 3Cl_2 \rightarrow 6\ NH_4Cl + N_2$$
$$NH_3 + 3Cl_2\ (excess) \rightarrow NCl_3 + 3HCl$$

(vi) Formation of addition compounds:

$$SO_2(dry) + Cl_2 \rightarrow \underset{\text{Sulphuryl chloride}}{SO_2Cl_2}$$
$$CO + Cl_2 \rightarrow \underset{\text{Carbonyl chloride}}{COCl_2}$$

(vii) Action on organic compounds:

$$CH_4 + Cl_2 \rightarrow CH_3Cl + HCl \quad \text{(Substitution Reaction)}$$
$$C_2H_4 + Cl_2 \rightarrow \underset{\text{Ethylene chloride}}{C_2H_4Cl_2} \quad \text{(addition reaction)}$$

Uses

Chlorine is used as a bleaching agent, in sterilisation of drinking water, in swimming pools as germicide and disinfectant. It is also used in preparation of domestic antiseptic solutions (NaOCl), in the manufacture of bleaching powder, chlorates, bromine, HCl, $CHCl_3$, CCl_4, CH_2Cl_2, DDT, synthetic plastics, rubbers etc. In the extraction of gold and platinum also chlorine is used. Its one more important use is in warfare for the manufacture of poisonous gases like phosgene ($COCl_2$), tear gas ($CCl_3.NO_2$) and mustard gas ($ClC_2H_4 - S - C_2H_4Cl$)

Bromine

It is found only in combined state.

Bromides of Na, K and Mg are found in sea water and certain mineral springs. Carnallite, $KCl.MgCl_2.6H_2O$, contains about 0.01 to 0.1 bromine as $MgBr_2$.

Preparation

Laboratory Method

By heating a mixture of MnO_2, conc. H_2SO_4 and a bromide

$$2KBr + 3H_2SO_4 + MnO_2 \rightarrow 2KHSO_4 + MnSO_4 + 2H_2O + Br_2$$

By passing chlorine through a solution of potassium bromide

$$2KBr + Cl_2 \rightarrow 2KCl + Br_2$$

Commercial Method

(i) *From Carnallite :* The mineral carnallite is dissolved in water and KCl and $MgCl_2$ are crystallised out. The mother liquor contains about 0.25% of bromine as $MgBr_2$ and is known as bittern. Bittern is treated with chlorine gas

$$MgBr_2 + Cl_2 \rightarrow MgCl_2 + Br_2$$

Purification : Bromine contaminated with H_2O, Cl_2 and I_2 is distilled over a mixture of KBr and zinc oxide to remove Cl_2 and I_2 respectively.

$$2KBr + Cl_2 \rightarrow 2KCl + Br_2$$

$$2ZnO + 2I_2 \rightarrow 2ZnI_2 + O_2$$

Water is removed by distilling over conc. H_2SO_4.

(iii) *From Sea Water :* Sea water contains about 0.006% by weight of bromine as $MgBr_2$. It is liberated by passing chlorine gas.

$$MgBr_2 + Cl_2 \rightarrow MgCl_2 + Br_2$$

Bromine vapours led by current of air are absorbed in Na_2CO_3 to form bromide-bromate mixture.

$$3Na_2CO_3 + 3Br_2 \rightarrow 5NaBr + NaBrO_3 + 3CO_2\uparrow$$

Bromine is now liberated from this mixture by means of dil. HCl or dil. H_2SO_4.

$$5NaBr + NaBrO_3 + 6HCl \rightarrow 6NaCl + 3H_2O + 3Br_2$$

$$5NaBr + NaBrO_3 + 3H_2SO_4 \rightarrow 3Na_2SO_4 + 3H_2O + 3Br_2$$

Purification : Method is same as is done in preparation from carnallite.

Properties

Physical: It is reddish brown, heavy density (3.2) liquid, b.p. is 58°C and is poisonous. It colours starch paper yellow. It is highly soluble in water to form *bromine water,* a part of which reacts to form HOBr which on heating liberates oxygen.

$$H_2O + Br_2 \rightarrow HOBr \xrightarrow{\text{Heat}} HBr + O$$

Combination with Elements

Bromine has greater affinity for hydrogen. It combines with hydrogen at 200°C or at room temperature in the presence of platinum (catalyst). Bromine reacts with most of the metals and some of the non-metals such as S, P etc.

$$H_2 + Br_2 \rightarrow 2HBr$$

$$2K + Br_2 \rightarrow 2KBr$$

$$2Al + 3Br_2 \rightarrow 2AlBr_3$$

$$2As + 3Br_2 \rightarrow 2AsBr_3$$

Oxidation and Bleaching Action

Bromine reacts with water liberating oxygen. Hence bromine can act as an oxidising and bleaching agent. This reaction also explains why bromine loses its colour on standing.

$$2H_2O + 2Br_2 \rightarrow 4HBr + O_2$$

Thus like chlorine, it oxidises $FeSO_4$ + dil. H_2SO_4, H_2S, moist SO_2, Na_2SO_3, $Na_2S_2O_3$ and KI to the corresponding substance.

Action of Alkalies

Similar to that of Cl_2

$$2NaOH\,(cold) + Br_2 \rightarrow NaBr + NaBrO + H_2O$$

$$8NaOH\,(hot) + 3Br_2 \rightarrow 5NaBr + NaBrO_3 + 3H_2O$$

Action of Ammonia

Similar to that of Cl_2

$$8NH_3 + 3Br_2 \rightarrow 6NH_4Br + HBr$$

Action on Organic Compounds

Similar to that of Cl_2

$$CH_4 + Br_2 \rightarrow CH_3Br + HBr$$

$$CH_2 = CH_2 + Br_2 \rightarrow CH_2Br.\,CH_2Br$$

Uses

It is used in the preparation of ethyl bromide which is used in the manufacture of tetraethyl lead (TEL), an important anti-knock compound in the petroleum industry

$$C_2H_6 + Br_2 \rightarrow C_2H_5Br + HBr$$

$$4C_2H_5Br + 4Na - Pb \rightarrow (C_2H_5)_4Pb + 4NaBr + 3Pb$$

It is used in the preparation of ethylene bromide (used to increase the efficiency of TEL), dyestuffs, NaBr and KBr (used in medicine as sedatives), AgBr (used in photography), etc. It is also used as an oxidising agent.

Iodine

It is the rarest of all the halogens. It occurs only in the combined state. Its main source is Relp (Varee), the ash obtained on burning sea-weeds, which contains about 1% iodine as iodides of alkali metals. Caliche (crude chile saltpetre, $NaNO_3$) contains iodine as sodium iodate.

Preparation

By heating a mixture of MnO_2, H_2SO_4 and iodide (laboratory method)

$$2KI + 3H_2SO_4 + MnO_2 \rightarrow 2KHSO_4 + MnSO_4 + 2H_2O + I_2$$

By passing chlorine gas through a solution of potassium iodide

$$2KI + Cl_2 \rightarrow 2KCl + I_2$$

Commercial Methods

(i) From Sea Weeds : The ash of sea-weeds is extracted with water, sulphates and chlorides of Na and K present in it are removed by crystallisation. The mother liquor is now heated with MnO_2 and conc. H_2SO_4 in a cast iron retort and iodine vapours are collected in earthen jars called aludels or udells.

$$2NaI + 3H_2SO_4 + MnO_2 \rightarrow 2NaHSO_4 + MnSO_4 + 2H_2O + I_2$$

(ii) From Caliche (Crude Salt Petre) : Its hot solution is cooled to remove crystals of $NaNO_3$. The mother liquor is treated with a calculated amount of sodium bisulphite when iodine is precipitated out due to reduction of sodium iodate ($NaIO_3$) present in caliche.

$$2NaIO_3 + 5NaHSO_3 \rightarrow 2Na_2SO_4 + 3NaHSO_4 + H_2O + I_2\downarrow$$

$NaHSO_3$ (if present in excess) will react with iodine to form HI.

$$NaHSO_3 + I_2 + H_2O \rightarrow NaHSO_4 + 2HI$$

Purification : The precipitated iodine is contaminated with iodine chloride (ICl), iodine bromide (IBr) and water. It is distilled over potassium iodide to remove ICl and IBr.

$$KI + ICl \rightarrow KCl + I_2,$$

$$KI + IBr \rightarrow KBr + I_2$$

Water is removed by distilling over conc. H_2SO_4. Further purification may be done by sublimation.

Properties

Physical : It is a black (dark violet) shining solid which sublimes on heating giving violet coloured vapours. It is only sparingly soluble in water but readily soluble in sodium or potassium iodide due to the formation of triodide.

$$KI + I_2 \rightleftharpoons KI_3$$

However, this solution behaves as a simple mixture of KI and free I_2. Tincture of iodine contains 1/2 ounce I_2, $\frac{1}{4}$ ounce KI and 1 pint of rectified spirit. Iodine is soluble many organic solvents. Its solution in CS_2 and $CHCl_3$ is violet in colour, while its solution in other solvents, *e.g.*, alcohol, ether and CCl_4 is brown.

Combination with Elements

Iodine is least reactive among halogens.

Iodine reacts slowly even in the presence of platinum catalyst. Antimony catches fire when sprinkled in jar of iodine vapours. Phosphorus and potassium explode in contact with iodine.

$$H_2 + I_2 \overset{Pt}{\rightleftharpoons} 2HI$$

$$2Sb + 3I_2 \rightarrow 2SbI_3$$

$$P_4 + 6I_2 \rightarrow 4PI_3$$

Oxidising Property

It acts as an oxidising agent. It oxidises $FeSO_4$ + dil. H_2SO_4, H_2S, moist SO_2, Na_2SO_3, potassium nitrite and sod. arsenite to the corresponding compounds. Chemical reactions are similar to that of chlorine. Iodine does not act as a bleaching agent but is used as a disinfectant.

It does not displace chlorine or bromine from the solution of their salts, yet displaces them from their oxy-salts (difference frorm Cl_2 and Br_2)

$$\underset{\text{Pot. chlorate}}{2KClO_3} + I_2 \rightarrow 2KIO_3 + Cl_2$$

$$2KBrO_3 + I_2 \rightarrow 2KIO_3 + Br_2$$

Action of Sodium thiosulphate : It forms sodium tetrathionate (difference from Cl_2 and Br_2)

$$2Na_2S_2O_3 + I_2 \rightarrow Na_2S_4O_6 + 2NaI$$

Action of Alkalies

Similar to Cl_2 and Br_2.

Action of Ammonia

Different from Cl_2 and Br_2

$$2NH_3 + 3I_2 \rightarrow NI_3.NH_3 + 3HI$$

$NI_3.NH_3$ is a mild explosive and decomposes as below.

$$8NI_3.NH_3 \rightarrow 5N_2 + 9I_2 + 6NH_4I$$

Action of Nitric Acid

Dilute nitric acid does not attack any halogen, while conc. HNO_3 attacks only iodine which is relatively more basic in character.

$$I_2 + 10HNO_3 \rightarrow 2HIO_3 + 10NO_2 + 4H_2O$$

Action on Organic Compounds

$$CH_4 + I_2 \rightleftharpoons CH_3I + HI$$

($\because$ HI is a strong reducing agent)

$$C_2H_4 + I_2 \rightarrow C_2H_4I_2$$

When warmed with alcohol and alkali, iodine gives iodoform (iodoform reaction)

$$C_2H_5OH + 6KOH + 4I_2 \rightarrow HCOOK + CHI_3 + 5KI + 4H_2O$$

CHI_3 is iodoform.

Similar reaction is also given by chlorine and bromine.

Uses

It is used in tincture of iodine, iodex, iodoform, iodole and certain iodides. Solutions of iodine in KI are used in the treatment of goitre. It is used as a reagent in the laboratory. It is also used to increase production of eggs.

Ozone

It is highly unstable triatomic allotropic form of oxygen. It is present in the atmosphere about 20 km above sea level. It is formed from oxygen present there, under the influence of UV light from the sun. Ozone can absorb UV light to give back oxygen. Thus the ozone layer acts as a screen and prevents the harmful UV radiations from reaching the surface of earth where we live.

Structure

It is considered as a resonance hybrid of the following two structures

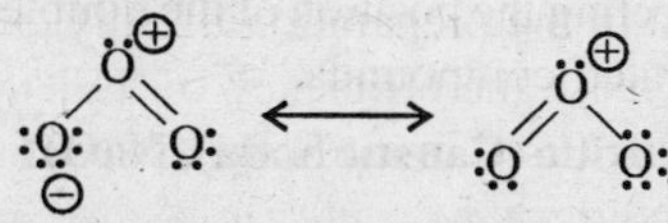

Ozone molecule is angular, the angle between the three oxygen atoms being 116.8° and the O – O distance being 1.28 Å.

It has a strong rotten smell. It turns an alcoholic solution of benzidine brown. Metallic mercury loses its fluidity in contact with ozone (tailing of Mercury). It turns starch iodide paper blue. It turns an alcoholic solution of tetramethyl base violet.

Preparation

It is prepared by passing a silent-electric discharge through dry, pure and cold oxygen in special type of apparatus called ozoniser (Siemen's and Brodie's ozoniser)

$$3O_2 \rightleftharpoons 2O_3, \Delta H_2 = +68 \text{ kcal}$$

Since formation of ozone is an endothermic reaction (hence ozone is an example of endothermic compound), it must be carried out at high temperatures. Hence, it is prepared by means of silent electric discharge, otherwise sparking would generate heat and decompose ozone. Silent electric discharge acts as UV light and decomposes ozone molecules into oxygen atoms which then recombine with the dissociated oxygen molecules forming ozone. The mixture obtained (having 5 – 10% ozone by volume) is called ozonised oxygen.

Properties

It is a pale blue gas (b.p. – 111°C) with a characteristic fishy smell. It condenses at –120°C as a dark blue liquid. It is poisonous gas, more than 100 ppm of ozone in breathing air causes headache and breathing trouble. Ozone is a dangerous gas because of its destructive action on body tissues and being explosive. Ozone is heavier than air and slightly soluble in water. It turns starch iodide paper blue.

Uses

It is mostly used as a sterilising agent for water, and for improving the atmosphere of crowded places like cinema halls, underground, tunnels etc. It is used as mild bleaching agent for bleaching oils, ivory, starch, flour, wax and delicate fabrics. It is also used in manufacture of permanganate (from potassium manganate), artificial silk and synthetic camphor. It is used for detecting the position of the double bond(s) in the unsaturated compounds.

Sodium Hydroxide (Caustic Soda), NaOH

Preparation

(i) Causticizing Process (Gossage Process) : It is an old process involving heating of a 10% solution of Na_2CO_3 with a little excess of milk of lime, $Ca(OH)_2$

$$Na_2CO_3 + Ca(OH)_2 \rightarrow CaCO_3\downarrow + 2NaOH$$

(ii) Electrolytic Method : Caustic soda is manufactured by the electrolysis of a concentrated solution of sodium chloride. Since chlorine is one of the by-products, it may react with NaOH forming NaCl and sodium hypochlorite. To avoid reaction between NaOH and Cl_2 specially designed electrolytic cells are used.

(a) Nelson Cell (or Diaphragm Cell) : In this cell, salt solution is percolated through the porous diaphragm.

$$NaCl(aq) \rightleftharpoons Na^+ + Cl^-$$

$$H_2O \rightleftharpoons H^+ + OH^-$$

At cathode (perforated steel) : $2H^+ + 2e^- \rightarrow H_2$

At anode (carbon red) : $2Cl^- \rightarrow Cl_2 + 2e^-$

The solution remained behind contains Na^+ and OH^- ions and thus about 10 – 15%. NaOH is obtained. It is concentrated under vacuum to 50% when NaCl (being less soluble) is most separated. The filterate is evaporated and dry mass is fused and cast into sticks.

(b) Mercury Cathode Process (Castner-Kellner Cell) :

$$NaCl(aq.) \rightleftharpoons Na^+ + Cl^-$$

At cathode (mercury) : $2Na^+ + 2e^- \rightarrow 2Na$

$$Na + Hg \rightarrow \underset{\text{Sod. amalgam}}{NaHg}$$

At anode (graphite): $2Cl^- \rightarrow Cl_2 + 2e^-$

Here H^+ ions of H_2O are not discharged because of the high over potential of halogen over mercury.

Sodium amalgam is removed from the cell. It is then decomposed in a separate cell by water giving NaOH, hydrogen and mercury. Mercury is recirculated to the cell.

$$Hg_xNa_2 + 2H_2O \rightarrow 2NaOH + xHg + H_2\uparrow$$

Commercial sodium hydroxide, besides other impurities, invariably contains some amount of sodium carbonate owing to the absorption of atmospheric CO_2. However, it may be purified (as required in acid-alkali titration) by dissolving it in alcohol in which impurities including Na_2CO_3 are insoluble. The fitrate may be used as pure NaOH solution or may be evaporated in a silver brain to get solid NaOH.

Physical Properties : M.P. 318°C, b.p. 1390°C, density 2.13, white, translucent, hygroscopic solid. It absorbs moisture and CO_2 from the atmosphere forming sodium carbonate.

$$2NaOH + CO_2 \rightarrow Na_2CO_3 + H_2O$$

It is highly soluble in water and the solution is bitter to taste, corrosive and soapy to touch. It is only sparingly soluble in alcohol (KOH dissolves in alcohol considerably).

Chemical Properties

(i) Reaction with Acids : It is a strong alkali and neutralized all acids or acidic oxides forming salts

$$NaOH + HCl \rightarrow NaCl + H_2O$$

$$NaOH + SO_2 \rightarrow NaHSO_3 \text{ or } Na_2SO_3$$

$$2NaOH + Al_2O_3 \rightarrow \underset{\text{Sod. aluminate}}{2NaAlO_2} + H_2O$$

(ii) Reaction with Salts : NaOH reacts with metallic salts to form hydroxides which may be insoluble or soluble in excess of NaOH. Some of the hydroxides are unstable and decompose to insoluble oxides.

(a) Formation of insoluble hydroxide, *e.g.*,

$$FeCl_3 + 3NaOH \rightarrow Fe(OH)_3\downarrow + 3NaCl$$

(iii) Action of Non-Metals : Non-metals like B, Si, P (white), S, and halogens react with NaOH forming sod. salt of the corresponding oxy-acid.

$$2B + 6NaOH \rightarrow \underset{\text{Sod.borate}}{2Na_3BO_3} + 3H_2$$

(iv) Action on Metals : Weakly electropositive metals like Zn, Al and Sn, dissolve in NaOH solution to liberate hydrogen gas.

$Zn + 2NaOH \rightarrow Na_2ZnO_2 + H_2$

(v) *Reaction with Sand, SiO_2*

$$\underset{\text{Sod. sillicate (glass)}}{2NaOH + SiO_2 \rightarrow Na_2SiO_3 + H_2O}$$

(vi) *Action of carbon monoxide*

$$NaOH + CO \xrightarrow[5-10\text{ atm}]{150-200°C} \underset{\text{Sod.formate}}{HCOONa}$$

(vii) Caustic Property : Sodium hydroxide is a powerful cautery and breaks down proteins of the skin and flesh to a pasty mass, therefore, it is commonly known as *caustic soda.*

Uses : Sodium hydroxide is used in the manufacture of sodium metal, soap (from oils and fats), rayon, paper, dyes and drugs. It is used in petroleum refining, for mercerizing cotton to make cloth unshrinkable, and as a reagent in the laboratory.

Sodium Carbonate, Na_2CO_3

It is manufactured in the ammonia-soda or Solvay process. Brine (NaCl solution in water) has added NH_3 then CO_2. $NaHCO_3$ is precipitated which decomposes to Na_2CO_3 at 175°C, NH_3 is recovered by treating the NH_4Cl solution with $Ca(OH)_2$ slurry forms hydrates, Anhydrous Na_2CO_3 is known as soda ash, $Na_2CO_3.10H_2O$ is washing soda. Na_2CO_3 occurs naturally as trona. It is used in glass (55%), soap, chemical detergents and paper industries.

It exists in various forms, namely anhydrous sodium carbonate Na_2CO_3 (soda-ash), monohydrate, $Na_2CO_3.H_2O$ (crystal carbonate), heptahydrate, $Na_2CO_3.7H_2O$ and decahydrate, $Na_2CO_3.10H_2O$ (washing soda or sal soda). It occurs in the form of *reh* and *sajji matti* in U.P. & Bihar.

Solvay Process (Ammonia Soda Process):

$$NH_3 + CO_2 + H_2O \rightarrow NH_4HCO_3$$

$$NH_4HCO_3 + NaCl \xrightarrow{30°C} \underset{\text{Sod.bicarbonate}}{NaHCO_3} \downarrow + NH_4Cl$$

$$2NaHCO_3 \xrightarrow{250°C} Na_2CO_3 + H_2O + \underset{\text{(used again)}}{CO_2}$$

$$\underset{\text{Amm. chloride}}{2NH_4Cl} + \underset{\text{Slaked lime}}{Ca(OH)_2} \rightarrow CaCl_2 + 2H_2O + \underset{\text{(used again)}}{2NH_3}$$

Properties

$$Na_2CO_3.10H_2O \xrightarrow[\text{air}]{\text{dry}} Na_2CO_3.H_2O + 9H_2O$$

On heating, the monohydrate changes to anhydrous salt (m.p. 853°C) which does not decompose on further heating even to redness.

$$Na_2CO_3 + 2H_2O \rightleftharpoons \underset{\text{(Weal acid)}}{H_2CO_3} + \underset{\text{(Strong alkali)}}{2NaOH}$$

$$CaCl_2 + Na_2CO_3 \rightarrow CaCO_3 \downarrow + 2NaCl$$

$$2MgCl_2 + 2Na_2CO_3 + H_2O \rightarrow MgCO_3.Mg(OH)_2 \downarrow + 4NaCl + CO_2$$

It reacts with carbonates of metals like Al, Fe, Sn etc. When formed are immediately hydrolysed to hydroxides.

$$Fe_2(SO_4)_3 + 3Na_2CO_3 \rightarrow Fe_2(CO_3)_3 \xrightarrow{3H_2O} 2Fe(OH)_3 + 3CO_2$$

$$Na_2CO_3 + H_2O + CO_2 \rightarrow \underset{\text{Sod. bicarbonate}}{2NaHCO_3}$$

Sodium Bicarbonate or Baking Soda, $NaHCO_3$, Sodium hydrogen Carbonate.

Prepared CO_2 into Na_2CO_3 solution, also in Solvay process for sodium carbonate. It is sparingly soluble in water. Decomposes to Na_2CO_3 on heating used in Na_2CO_3 manufacture, as an ingredient of baking powders, pharmaceutically, and in fire extinguishers, in the preparation of effervescent drinks and fruit salts, as antacid.

Its aqueous solution is alkaline in nature (gives yellow colour with methyl orange but no colour with phenopthalein.

$$NaHCO_3 + H_2O \rightleftharpoons H_2CO_3 + NaOH$$

$$2NaHCO_3 \xrightarrow{\text{above}100°C} Na_2CO_3 + H_2O + CO_2 \uparrow$$

$$NaHCO_3 + HCl \rightarrow NaCl + H_2O + CO_2 \uparrow$$

$$NaHCO_3 + H_2SO_4 \rightarrow NaSO_4 + H_2O + CO_2 \uparrow$$

It precipitates out certain metal salts as normal carbonates which are precipitated by Na_2CO_3 as basic carbonates, *e.g.*, Zn^{2+} and Mg^{2+} salts.

$$ZnCl_2 + 2NaHCO_3 \rightarrow ZnCO_3 \downarrow + 2NaCl + H_2O + CO_2$$

When equimolecular amounts of Na_2CO_3 and $NaHCO_3$ are dissolved in water and the resulting solution cooled to 35°C, crystals of sodium sesquicarbonate, Na_2CO_3. $NaHCO_3.2H_2O$ separate out. It is neither deliquescent nor efflorescent and is used for wool washing.

Sodium Chloride : NaCl M.P. 801°C, b.p. 1439°C, density 2.17.

Occurs naturally as rock salt which is widely distributed and occurs extensively in thick beds and to about 3% in sea water. Obtained commercially by solar evaporation of sea water, by mining or usually as brine by passing water into underground deposits. The brine contains Ca^{2+}, Fe^{2+}, Mg^{2+} as impurities, these are removed by precipitation with Na_2CO_3 and NaOH. Pure NaCl is obtained by passing HCl gas into a saturated aqueous solution of NaCl. Sodium chloride is used for the formation of NaOH and Na_2CO_3 (for the alkali and glass industries) and chlorine (for the chlorocarbon industry) and is one of the chemical industries most important raw materials. Solid NaCl is used for the removal of ice and snow and as a preservative. The sodium chloride structure is cubic with octahedral co-ordination about Na and Cl (both are ccp). Many other MX compounds crystallizes with this structure.

Calcium Hydroxide (Slaked Lime), $Ca(OH)_2$

The powder from the action of an equivalent quantity of water on CaO is slaked lime, a suspension with excess water is milk of lime, a clear solution of $Ca(OH)_2$ in water is lime water. Used as an industrial alkali and in the preparation of mortar which sets to a solid by reconversion of the $Ca(OH)_2$ to $CaCO_3$.

Preparation :

(i) $CaO + H_2O \rightarrow Ca(OH)_2$

(ii) Caustic alkali + a soluble calcium salt $\rightarrow Ca(OH)_2$

Properties : It is a white amorphous powder, only sparingly soluble in water. Its solubility decreases with the increase in temperature. When dried and heated to redness, it loses a molecule of water and converted into calcium oxide (lime). Lime water [Lime + $H_2O \rightarrow Ca(OH)_2$] is frequently used for the detection of CO_2 gas as CO_2 gas turns lime water milky due to formation of $CaCO_3$.

$$Ca(OH)_2 + CO_2 \rightarrow CaCO_3\downarrow + H_2O.$$

However, the precipitate disappears on prolonged treatment with CO_2 because of the conversion of $CaCO_3$ (insoluble) to calcium bicarbonate (soluble).

$$\underset{\text{Insoluble}}{CaCO_3} + H_2O + CO_2 \rightarrow \underset{\text{Soluble}}{Ca(HCO_3)_2}$$

The above solution, if heated, again gives turbidity due to decomposition of calcium bicarbonate to calcium carbonate.

$$Ca(HCO_3)_2 \xrightarrow{\text{Heat}} CaCO_3 + CO_2 + H_2O$$

With chlorine it gives different products under different conditions.

(i) $3Ca(OH)_2 + 2Cl_2 \xrightarrow{\text{below } 35°C} \underset{\text{Bleaching powder}}{Ca(OCl)_2.CaCl_2.Ca(OH)_2.H_2O} + H_2O$

(ii) $2Ca(OH)_2 + 2Cl_2 \xrightarrow{\text{Red heat}} 2CaCl_2 + 2H_2O + O_2\uparrow$

(iii) $\underset{\text{Milk of lime}}{2Ca(OH)_2} + 2Cl_2 \xrightarrow{\text{Cold}} CaCl_2 + \underset{\text{Calcium hypochlorite}}{Ca(OCl)_2} + 2H_2O$

(iv) $\underset{\text{Milk of lime}}{6Ca(OH)_2} + 6Cl_2 \xrightarrow{\text{Heat}} 5CaCl_2 + \underset{\text{Cal. chlorate}}{Ca(ClO_3)_6} + 6H_2O$

Uses : Its main uses are manufacture of bleaching powder, caustic soda, white washing, for softening of water and in preparation of *soda lime* (mixture of cal. hydroxide and caustic soda) which is a good absorbent for a number of gases. Soda lime is also used in decarboxylation of sodium salts of fatty acids.

Calcium Carbonate, $CaCO_3$

Found in nature as limestone, marble, coral, ice land spar, calcite, chalk, dolomite etc.

Preparation

(i) By dissolving marble or limestone in hydrochloric acid followed by precipitation with sodium or ammonium carbonate as *precipitated chalk.*

$$CaCO_3 + 2HCl \rightarrow CaCl_2 + H_2O + CO_2$$

$$CaCl_2 + (NH_4)_2CO_3 \rightarrow CaCO_3 + 2NH_4Cl$$

(ii) In the laboratory it is prepared by passing CO_2 through lime water or by adding sodium or ammonium carbonate solution to $CaCl_2$.

$$Ca(OH)_2 + CO_2 \rightarrow CaCO_3\downarrow + H_2O$$

Properties : It is a white powder existing in two crystalline forms, *calcite* and *araganite.* It is insoluble in water but dissolves in the presence of CO_2 due to the formation of calcium bicarbonate

$$CaCO_3 + H_2O + CO_2 \rightarrow Ca(HCO_3)_2.$$

Uses : It is used for the manufacture of lime, cement, washing soda, glass and as a flux since CaO obtained from its decomposition combines with silica to form calcium silicate, $CaSiO_3$. Marble is used for building purposes and in the laboratory for the production of CO_2 gas. Chalk is used in paints (white ash) and distempers and in the production of CO_2 in the laboratory. Precipitated chalk is used in tooth pastes and powders, in medicine for indigestion, in adhesives and in cosmetic powder and also to deacidify wines.

Nitric Acid, HNO_3 : It was first called aqua *fortis*, meaning strong water, because, it attacks nearly all the metals.

The structure of nitric acid can be best explained by assuming that nitric acid is a resonance hybrid of the following two structures.

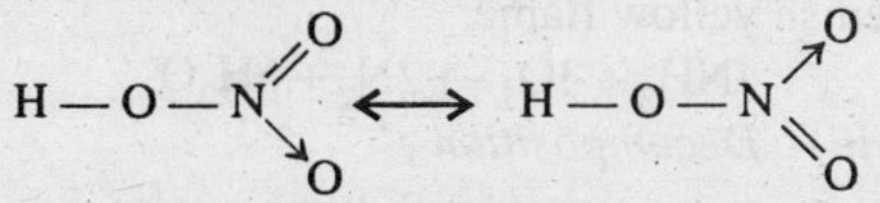

The nitrate ion, NO_3^- has a planar and symmetrical structure with the sp^2 hybridized nitrogen atom at the centre and the oxygen atoms at the corners of an equilateral triangle. The shorter the N–O bond length (1.22 Å) than the single nitrogen-oxygen bond length (1.39 Å) and the equivalence of all N–O bonds suggests that nitrate ion is a resonance hybrid of the following three structures:

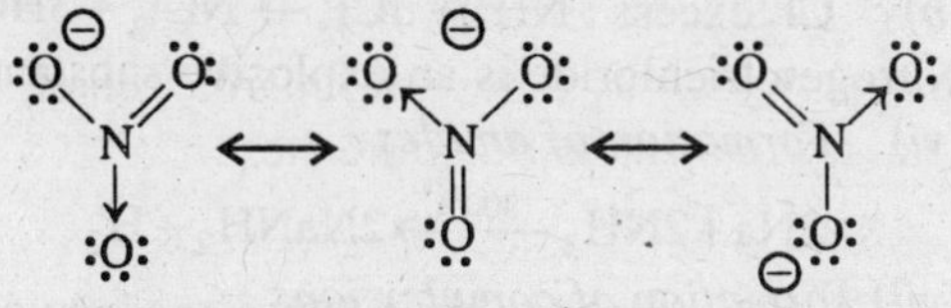

Preparation

(i) By distilling sodium nitrate or potassium nitrate (nitre) with conc. sulphuric acid (Laboratory Method)

$$NaNO_3 + H_2SO_4 \xrightarrow{200°C} NaHSO_4 + HNO_3$$
$$NaHSO_4 + NaNO_3 \rightarrow Na_2SO_4 + HNO_3$$

(ii) From air (Birkeland Eyde electric arc process)

$$N_2 + O_2 \underset{}{\overset{\text{electicarc}}{\rightleftharpoons}} 2NO - 43.2 \text{ kcal}$$
$$2NO + O_2 \xrightarrow{50°C} 2NO_2$$
$$2NO_2 + H_2O \rightarrow HNO_2 + HNO_3$$
$$3HNO_2 \rightarrow HNO_3 + H_2O + 2NO$$

(iii) By catalytic oxidation of ammonia (1. vol.) with oxygen (9 vol. of air)

[Ostwald Process]

$$4NH_3 + SO_2 \xrightarrow[800–900°C]{\text{Ptguage}} 4NO + 6H_2O + 21.5 \text{ kcal}$$
$$2NO + O_2 \rightarrow 2NO_2$$
$$4NO_2 + 2H_2O + O_2 \rightarrow 4HNO_3$$

Concentration of Nitric Acid : Dilute nitric acid (50–60%) thus obtained is concentrated by distillation till it forms a constant boiling mixture (b.p. 121°C). This is the ordinary concentrated HNO_3 (sp.gravity 1.414) and is 68% in strength. Fuming HNO_3 (98% HNO_3, sp.gr. 1.51) is obtained by distilling this acid with conc. H_2SO_4. Fuming nitric acid may also be obtained by dissolving excess of NO_2 in conc. HNO_3. Crystals of pure HNO_3 may be obtained by cooling fuming HNO_3 is a freezing mixture.

Properties : Pure nitric acid is a colourless fuming liquid having a pungent smell. The yellow colour of the usual nitric acid is due to the presence of nitrogen dioxide, NO_2 (formed by decomposition of HNO_3 in sunlight) in it.

$$4HNO_3 \xrightarrow[\text{or heat}]{\text{Sunlight}} 4NO_2 + 2H_2O + O_2$$

However, the yellow colour of the acid may be decolourised by warming it to 60-80 °C and bubbling dry air through it.

Ammonia, NH_3

It is the most important of the nitrogen hydrides. It is a colourless gas with a characteristic smell. Readily liquefied by cooling or compression. B.P. is –33.5 °C and m.p. is –77.7 °C. It is very soluble in water, the saturated solution at room temperature has density 0.88 ('0.99 ammonia'); hydrates $NH_3.H_2O$ and $2NH_3.H_2O$ are known. NH_3 occurs naturally in some gases from hot springs. It is manufactured by the Haber's process and is used to produce HNO_3 (25%) urea (15%), NH_4NO_3 (15%), Nylon (10%), the ultimate products being fertilizers (80%), explosives (5%) and plastics, foams and films (10%). It just burns in oxygen; NH_3 : O_2 mixture give N over catalysts; oxidized to N_2 over heated metal oxides NH_3 co-ordinates to many elements and forms ammines; reacts with Na or K to give amides MNH_2. Liquid ammonia is a good ionizing solvent (self dissociation $2NH_3 \rightleftharpoons NH_4^+ + NH_2^-$ pK = 30; NH_4^+ salts acids, NH_2^- salts bases). It is generally a better solvent for organic compounds (unless NH_3 complexes formed. Metals frequently dissolve to give blue reducing solutions containing solvated electrons. It is detected by smell; blackening of $Hg_2(NO_3)_2$ paper and Nessler's reagent. Since nitrogen is the third most electonegative element, ammonia readily forms hydrogen bonding with itself and also with water. It is a covalent molecule and its simple electronic structure may be represented as :

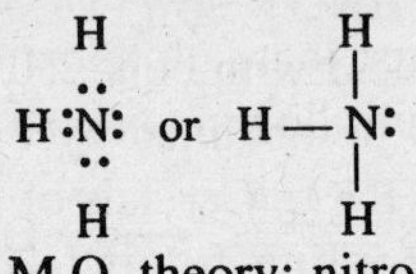

According to M.O. theory; nitrogen of ammonia involves sp^3 hybridisation. Since one pair of electrons on nitrogen remains free; the ammonia molecule gets distorted and acquires, a pyramidal structure instead of a regular tetrahedron. The bond angle H—N—H is $\approx 107°$.

Preparations

(i) By heating ammonium salt with a base, *e.g.*, slaked lime (lab. method).

$$2NH_4Cl + Ca(OH)_2 \rightarrow CaCl_2 + 2H_2O + 2NH_3\uparrow$$

The gas so formed is dried with quick lime, CaO. NH_3 reacts with other dehydrating agents;

$$2NH_3 + H_2SO_4 \rightarrow CaCl_2.\ 4NH_3$$

$$CaCl_2 + 4NH_3 \rightarrow CaCl_2.\ 4NH_3$$

$$P_4O_{10} \xrightarrow{2H_2O} 4HPO_3 \xrightarrow{4NH_3} 4NH_4PO_3$$

so these agents can't be used during its preparation.

(ii) By the action of water on nitrides of Ca, Mg and Al

$$Ca_3N_2 + 6H_2O \rightarrow 3Ca(OH)_2 + 2NH_3$$

$$AlN + 3H_2O \rightarrow Al(OH)_3 + NH_3$$

(iii) Cyanamide Process (Commercial Method)

$$CaO + 3C \xrightarrow{800-1000°C} CaC_2 + CO\uparrow$$

$$CaC_2 + N_2 \rightarrow \underset{\text{Cal.Cyanamide Nitrolim}}{CaCN_2} + C$$

$$CaCN_2 + 3H_2O\,(\text{steam}) \xrightarrow{3\ \text{atm.}} CaCO_3 + 2NH_3$$

(iv) *Haber's Process* (from air) Commercial Method.

$$N_2 + 3H_2 \xrightarrow[300\text{atm}]{500°C,\ \text{catalyst FetMO}} 2NH_3$$

(The H_2 is generally from steam-reforming process.)

Reactions : (i) Basic Nature : It behaves as a strong Lewis base since nitrogen of ammonia has a lone pair of electrons. Its solution in water is best described as *aqueous ammonia* or NH_3 (aq.) Its ionisation in water is represented as

$$NH_3(aq.) + H_2O \rightleftharpoons NH_4^+ + OH^-$$

Because of its ability to give hydroxyl ions, aqueous ammonia has basic character and thus turns red litmus blue and phenophthalein pink. It reacts with HCl to give white fumes of ammonium chloride.

(ii) *Combustion :* Ordinarily it is neither combustible or supporter of combustion. However, a jet of NH_3 can be made to burn in oxygen with greenish yellow flame.

$$4NH_3 + 3O_2 \rightarrow 2N_2 + 6H_2O$$

(iii) *Decomposition :*

$$2NH_3 \xrightarrow[\text{spark}]{\text{red hot or electric}} N_2 + 3H_2$$

(iv) *Oxidation :* (Reducing Property)

(a) $3CuO + 2NH_3 \rightarrow 3Cu + N_2 + 3H_2O$

(b) $4NH_3 + 5O_2 \xrightarrow[800°C]{\text{Pt guaze}} 4NO + 6H_2O$

(v) *Reaction with Chloride :*

(a) NH_3 excess : $8NH_3 + 3Cl_2 \rightarrow 6NH_4Cl + N_2$

(b) Cl_2 excess : $NH_3 + 3Cl_2 \rightarrow NCl_3 + 3HCl.$

Nitrogen trichloride is an explosive substance.

(vi) *Formation of amides*

$$2Na + 2NH_3 \xrightarrow{300°C} 2NaNH_2 + H_2$$

(vii) Formation of complex ions :

Ammonia combines with certain cations like Ag^+, Ca^{2+}, Hg^{2+}, etc., to form very stable soluble complex cations.

(a) $AgCl + 2NH_4OH\,(\text{excess}) \rightarrow$

$$\underset{\text{Silver ammine chloride}}{[Ag(NH_3)_2]Cl} + H_2O$$

(b) $CuSO_4 + 2NH_4OH \rightarrow Cu(OH)_2\downarrow + (NH_4)_2SO_4$

$Cu(OH)_2 + 4NH_4OH\,(\text{excess}) \rightarrow$

$$\underset{\text{Cuprammine hydroxide (soluble in water)}}{[Cu(NH_3)_4](OH)_2} + 4H_2O$$

(c) $HgCl_2 + 2NH_4OH \rightarrow$

$$\underset{\text{Mercuriammine chloride}}{[Hg(NH_2)]Cl\,NH_4Cl} + 2H_2O$$

(viii) Reaction of Hydroxyl ions :

$$HCl + NH_4OH \rightarrow NH_4Cl + H_2O$$

$$FeCl_3 + 3NH_4OH \rightarrow \underset{\text{(Brown ppt)}}{Fe(OH)_3\downarrow} + 3NH_4Cl$$

$$ZnSO_4 + 2NH_4OH \rightarrow \underset{\text{white ppt}}{Zn(OH)_2\downarrow} + (NH_4)_2SO_4$$

(ix) Reaction with Nessler's Reagent

$HgCl_2 + 2KI \rightarrow 2KCl + HgI_2$ (red ppt)

$HgI_2 + 2KI \rightarrow K_2HgI_4$ (Nessler's reagent)

$$2K_2HgI_4 + NH_3 + 3KOH \rightarrow H_2N.HgO.HgI\downarrow + 7KI + 2H_2O$$

It is used as a laboratory reagent and in preparation of nitric acid (Ostwald process), sodium bicarbonate (Solvay process), ammonium sulphate and ammonium calcium phosphate which are used as fertilizers and also used in preparation of ammonium nitrate which is used as explosive. On account of high dielectric constant (22), anhydrous liquid ammonia (like water) is a good solvent for ionic compounds and on account of large heat of evaporation, liquid ammonia is commonly used in refrigeration.

Sulphur Dioxide, SO_2

Preparation : It is prepared by

(i) Heating copper turnings with conc. H_2SO_4 (Lab. method). H_2SO_4 is reduced by Cu.

$$Cu + 2H_2SO_4(\text{conc.}) \xrightarrow{\text{Heat}} CuSO_4 + SO_2 + 2H_2O$$

(ii) By the reduction of H_2SO_4 with carbon or sulphur

$$C + 2H_2SO_4 \rightarrow CO_2 + 2SO_2 + 2H_2O$$

$$S + 2H_2SO_4 \rightarrow 3SO_2 + 2H_2O$$

(iii) Manufacture of SO_2 :

(a) By burning sulphur in air

$$S + O_2 \rightarrow SO_2$$

(b) By roasting zinc blend or iron pyrites.

$$2ZnS + 3O_2 \rightarrow 2ZnO + 2SO_2$$

$$4FeS_2 + 11O_2 \rightarrow 2Fe_2O_3 + 8SO_2$$

(c) By heating anhydrite ($CaSO_4$) obtained from gypsum with carbon above 1000 °C.

$$2CaSO_4 + C \rightarrow 2CaO + 2SO_2 + CO_2$$

Sulphur dioxide has a planar triangular (V-shaped- which is in accordance with its dipole (1.60 D) moment) structure involving sp^2 hybridisation of the sulphur atom. In SO_2 molecules each oxygen atom is ionised to sulphur, by a σ and a π-bond. The σ-bonds between S and O are formed by sp^2-p overlap while one of the π-bonds arises from *pπ-pπ* overlap and the other from *pπ-dπ* overlap. The bond angle O–S–O is slightly reduced from 120° to 119.5° because of the presence of a lone pair of electrons on sulphur.

It is important to note that SO_2 molecule has two different types of π-bonds (*pπ-pπ* and *pπ-dπ*). But even then both of the S–O bonds are identical (1.43 Å). This indicates that sulphur dioxide is a resonance hybrid of the following two structures.

$$O \underset{p\pi - p\pi}{\overset{p - sp^2}{=\!=\!=}} S \underset{d\pi - p\pi}{\overset{sp^2 - p}{=\!=\!=}} \longleftrightarrow O \underset{p\pi - d\pi}{\overset{p - sp^2}{=\!=\!=}} S \underset{p\pi - p\pi}{\overset{sp^2 - p}{=\!=\!=}} O$$

Molecule here is drawn in a linear fashion only for the sake of convenience,

SO_2 is a gas and forms discrete molecule even in the solid state.

Reactions : (i) Due to presence of lone pair of electrons, it acts as a *Lewis* base.

(ii) Decomposition, $3SO_2 \xrightarrow{\text{Heat}} 2SO_3 + S$

(This is example of disproportionation *i.e.*, oxidation of two molecules of the same compound at the expense of the third which is reduced).

$$4SO_2 \underset{}{\overset{\text{elect. discharge}}{\rightleftharpoons}} 2S_2O + 3O_2$$

(iii) Combustion : It is neither combustible nor a supporter of combustion but strongly burning, K, Mg and C continues to burn in it. It is because SO_2 decomposes into S and O_2 by means of heat of burning metal.

$$SO_2 + 2Mg \rightarrow 2MgO + S;$$

$$SO_2 + C \rightarrow CO_2 + S$$

(iv) Acidic Nature : It dissolves in H_2O forming sulphurous acid, hence the gas is known as *sulphurous anhydride.* Thus SO_2 is an acidic oxide and combines with basic oxides forming salts.

$$2NaOH + 2SO_2 \rightarrow 2NaHSO_3$$

$$2NaOH + SO_2 \rightarrow Na_2SO_3 + H_2O$$

$$BaO + SO_2 \rightarrow BaSO_3$$

(v) Reducing Property ; In presence of moisture it can liberate nascent hydrogen or in presence of an oxidising agent it can easily take an oxygen atom.

$$SO_2 + Cl_2 + 2H_2O \rightarrow H_2SO_4 + 2HCl$$

$$SO_2 + 2HNO_3 \rightarrow H_2SO_4 + 2NO_2$$

$$SO_2 + 2FeCl_3 + 2H_2O \rightarrow H_2SO_4 + 2HCl + 2FeCl_2$$

$$5SO_2 + 2KMnO_4 + 2H_2O \rightarrow K_2SO_4 + 2MnSO_4 + 2H_2SO_4$$

$$3SO_2 + K_2Cr_2O_7 + H_2SO_4 \rightarrow K_2SO_4 + Cr_2(SO_4) + H_2O$$

$$5SO_2 + 2KIO_3 + 4H_2O \rightarrow 2KHSO_4 + 3H_2SO_4 + I_2$$

$$SO_2 + 2CuCl_2 + 2H_2O \rightarrow H_2SO_4 + 2CuCl + 2HCl$$

(vi) Oxidising Property :

$$2H_2S + SO_2 \rightarrow 2H_2O + 3S\downarrow$$

$$4Na + 3SO_2 \rightarrow Na_2SO_3 + Na_2S_2O_3$$

$$3Fe + SO_2 \rightarrow 2FeO + FeS$$

Similarly, K and Mg are also oxidised at high temperature.

$$2CO + SO_2 \rightarrow 2CO_2 + S\downarrow$$

(vii) Combination with O_2, Cl_2, PbO_2 and BaO_2

$$2SO_2 + O_2 \xrightarrow{Pt} 2SO_3$$

$$SO_2 + PbO_2 \rightarrow PbSO_4$$

$$SO_2 + Cl_2 \xrightarrow[\text{camphor}]{\text{Sunlight or}} \underset{\text{Sulphuryl chloride}}{SO_2Cl_2}$$

$$SO_2 + BaO_2 \rightarrow BaSO_4\downarrow$$

$$SO_2 + CaO \rightarrow CaSO_3\downarrow$$

(viii) Bleaching Property : It acts as bleaching agent in the following two ways.

(A) In the presence of water, it is oxidised with the liberation of nascent hydrogen which reduces the colouring matter to colourless.

$$SO_2 + 2H_2O \rightarrow H_2SO_4 + 2[H]$$

$$\text{Colouring matter} + 2[H] \underset{\text{air}}{\rightleftharpoons} \text{Colourless compound}$$

Since colourless (reduced) compound is reoxidised by air to coloured compound; bleaching by SO_2 is temporary.

Difference from bleaching action of chlorine.

(a) Bleaching action of chlorine is an oxidation process

$$Cl_2 + H_2O \rightarrow 2HCl + [O]$$

$$\text{Colouring matter} + [O] \rightarrow \text{Colourless compound.}$$

(b) Since it is not reversible, bleaching is permanent.

(c) In case of SO_2 bleaching, H_2SO_4 is produced which is harmful to fibres.

(B) In certain cases, bleaching by SO_2 takes place *via* the formation of colourless sulphites and bisulphites. The colour can be restored by dipping the bleached matter in dilute acids.

$$\underset{\text{coloured compound}}{X-OH} + SO_2 \rightarrow \underset{\text{colourless compound}}{X-HSO_3}$$

$$\underset{\text{coloured compound}}{X-HSO_3} + HCl \rightarrow X-Cl + H_2O + SO_2$$

$$X-Cl + H_2O \rightarrow \underset{\text{coloured compound}}{X-OH} + HCl$$

SO_2 is used as a bleaching agent for delicate articles like wool, silk and straw. It is used as an antichlor for removing excess of chlorine from a fabric after bleaching. It is used in the preparation of H_2SO_4 and bisulphites. Liquid SO_2 is used as a solvent for many organic and inorganic compounds. It is used in refining of petroleum and sugar. It is used as a disinfectant for killing disease germs, fungi and certain moulds.

OBJECTIVE QUESTIONS

1. The raw material used in Solvay process for manufacture of sodium carbonate comprises
   A. Sodium chloride and carbon dioxide
   B. Ammonia and carbon dioxide
   C. Sodium chloride, limestone and ammonia
   D. Sodium chloride, limestone and carbon dioxide
2. Alkali metal atoms show the oxidation states
   A. + 1 B. + 2
   C. − 1 D. − 2
3. The degree of hydration of alkali metal ions are in the order
   A. $Li^+ > Na^+ > K^+ > Rb^+ > Cs^+$
   B. $Li^+ > Rb^+ > Cs^+ > Na^+ > K^+$
   C. $Rb^+ > Cs^+ > Li^+ > Na^+ > K^+$
   D. $Na^+ > K^+ > Li^+ > Rb^+ > Cs^+$
4. Alkali metals react with hydrogen forming ionic hydrates. The reactivity of alkali metals with hydrogen decreases in the order
   A. Li > Na >K > Rb > Cs

B. Na > K > Rb > Cs > Li
C. Rb > Cs > Li > Na > K
D. Cs > Rb > K > Na > Li

5. Which of the following alkali metals is used in photoelectric cells?
A. Na B. K
C. Li D. Cs

6. A solution of sodium metal in liquid ammonia is blue and is a strong reducing agent due to the presence of
A. Sodium atoms B. Sodium hydride
C. Sodium amide D. Solvated electrons

7. Soda ash is
A. $Na_2CO_3.H_2O$ B. $NaHCO_3$
C. Na_2CO_3 D. NaOH

8. Sodium thiosulphate is used in photography to
A. Convert metallic silver to silver salt
B. Reduce silver bromide to silver salt
C. Remove unreduced silver
D. Remove undecomposed AgBr as a soluble silver thiosulphate complex

9. Sodium carbonate reacts with SO_2 in an aqueous medium to give
A. Na_2SO_4 B. $NaHSO_4$
C. Na_2SO_3 D. $NaHSO_3$

10. In a nuclear reactor, molten sodium is used to
A. Absorb neutrons for controlling the chain reaction
B. Absorb the heat generated by nuclear fission
C. Slow down fast neutrons
D. Extract radioisotopes produced in the reactor

11. Addition of excess KCN to an aqueous solution of $CuSO_4$ gives
A. $Cu(CN)_2$ B. $K_2[Cu(CN)_4]$
C. $K_3[Cu(CN)_4]$ D. $K[Cu(CN)_2]$

12. Sodium thiosulphate is prepared by
A. Boiling an Na_2SO_3 solution with S in an acidic medium
B. Boiling an NaOH solution with S
C. Neutralizing an H_2SO_3 solution with NaOH
D. Boiling Na_2SO_3 with S in an alkaline medium
E. B & D

13. Dolomite is
A. $MgCO_3$ B. $MgCO_3.CaCO_3$
C. MgO D. $CaSO_4$

14. Plaster of Paris is
A. $CaSO_4.2H_2O$ B. $(CaSO_4)_2.H_2O$
C. $CaSO_4.MgO$ D. $CaSO_4.5H_2O$

15. Epsom salt is
A. $MgSO_4.7H_2O$ B. $Na_2SO_4.10H_2O$
C. $MgCO_3.CaCO_3$ D. $Al_2O_3.H_2O$

16. The main constituent of bones is
A. CaF_2 B. $CaSO_4$
C. $Ca_3(PO_4)_2$ D. $CaSO_4$

17. In comparison to alkali metals, alkaline earth metals are
A. Less reactive B. Less basic
C. More reactive D. Less reducing
E. B & D

18. The most electropositive among the alkaline earth metals is
A. Beryllium B. Barium
C. Magnesium D. Calcium

19. The order of solubility of the sulphates of alkaline earth metals in water is
A. Be > Mg > Ca > Sr > Ba
B. Mg > Be >> Ba > Ca > Sr
C. Be > Ca > Mg > Ca >> Sr
D. Mg > Ca > Ba >> Be > Sr

20. Neutrons are produced by
A. Ra B. Ba
C. Sr D. Be

21. Which of the following has the highest electrode potential?
A. Be B. Mg
C. Ca D. Ba

22. Which of the following forms the least ionic chloride?
A. Mg B. Ca
C. Sr D. Be

23. Electrolysis of carnallite ($KCl.MgCl_2.6H_2O$) yields
A. Potassium ions
B. Magnesium ions
C. Magnesium and chlorine
D. Potassium and chlorine

24. Which of the following can be extracted from sea-water?
A. Ca B. Cl
C. Mg D. None

25. Which of the following is the weakest base?
A. NaOH B. KOH
C. $Ca(OH)_2$ D. $Zn(OH)_2$

26. A mixture of MgO and $MgCl_2$ is called
A. Sorel cement B. Portland cement
C. Double salt D. None

27. The crimson light in fireworks is due to the presence of
A. Ca B. Sr
C. Ba D. Na

28. Calcium is obtained by the
A. Roasting of limestone
B. Reduction of calcium chloride with carbon
C. Electrolysis of an aqueous solution of calcium chloride
D. Electrolysis of molten calcium chloride

29. In case of alkaline earth metals; which of the following increases with atomic number?
A. The solubility of their hydroxides
B. The solubility of their sulphates
C. Electronegativity
D. Ionization energy

30. The thermal stability of alkaline earth metal carbonates decreases in the order
A. $BaCO_3 > SrCO_3 > MgCO_3 > CaCO_3$
B. $BaCO_3 > SrCO_3 > CaCO_3 > MgCO_3$
C. $MgCO_3 > CaCO_3 > SrCO_3 > BaCO_3$
D. $CaCO_3 > SrCO_3 > MgCO_3 > BaCO_3$

31. Which of the following are commonly used in making toothpaste?
A. $Mg(OH)_2$ B. $MgCO_3$
C. $CaCl_2$ D. $Ca(NO_3)_2$
E. A & B

32. The fluxes that can be used for the removal of basic impurities like CaO and FeO from an ore are
A. SiO_2 B. $Na_2B_4O_7.10H_2O$
C. $MgCO_3$ D. $CaCO_3$
E. A & B

33. In the extraction of which of the following metals is amalgamation used?
A. Ag B. Au
C. Cu D. Fe
E. A & B

34. The reducing property of alkali metals follows the order
A. $Na < K < Rb < Cs < Li$
B. $K < Na < Rb < Cs < Li$
C. $Li < Cs < Rb < K < Na$
D. $Rb < Cs < K < Na < Li$

35. Which of the following will react with sodium to give hydrogen gas?
A. Methane B. Ethane
C. Ethylene D. Acetylene

36. Which of the following metals will form a monoxide on reaction with oxygen?
A. La B. Na
C. K D. Rb

37. Chlorides of which of the following metals crystallize from an aqueous solution as hydrates?
A. Li B. Na
C. K D. Mg
E. A & D

38. A salt is soluble in water if its
A. Hydration energy is less than its lattice energy
B. Hydration energy is greater than its lattice energy
C. Hydration energy is equal to its lattice energy
D. The solubility of a salt does not depend on the relation between its hydration energy and lattice energy

39. Which of the following is the least stable?
A. $MgCO_3$ B. $CaCO_3$
C. $SrCO_3$ D. $BeCO_3$

40. The oxide of which of the following metals is amphoteric?
A. Be B. Al
C. Mg D. A & B

41. Na_2SO_4 is soluble in water while $BaSO_4$ is sparingly soluble because
A. The lattice energy of $BaSO_4$ is more than its hydration energy
B. The hydration energy of Na_2SO_4 is less than its lattice energy
C. The hydration energy of Na_2SO_4 is more than its lattice energy

D. The hydration energy and the lattice energy have no role to play
E. A & C

42. Which of the following metals can be obtained by the electrolysis of an aqueous solution of their salts?

A. Ca B. Al
C. Na D. None of the above

43. The lattice energies of the carbonates of Mg, Ca, Sr and Ba follow the order

A. $MgCO_3 > CaCO_3 > SrCO_3 > BaCO_3$
B. $CaCO_3 > SrCO_3 > BaCO_3 > MgCO_3$
C. $BaCO_3 > SrCO_3 > CaCO_3 > MgCO_3$
D. $SrCO_3 > MgCO_3 > CaCO_3 > BaCO_3$

44. For compounds will the same anion the hydration energies of Na^+, K^+, Rb^+, Cs^+ and Li^+ follows the order

A. $Cs^+ > Rb^+ > K^+ > Na^+ > Li^+$
B. $Li^+ > Na^+ > K^+ > Rb^+ > Cs^+$
C. $K^+ > Na^+ > Li^+ > Cs^+ > Rb^+$
D. $Li^+ > K^+ > Na^+ > Cs^+ > Rb^+$

45. The metallic lustre exhibited by sodium is explained by

A. Diffusion of sodium ions
B. Oscillation of loose electrons
C. Excitation of free protons
D. Existence of body centred cubic lattice

46. Four alkali metals A, B, C & D are having, respectively, standard electrode potentials as –3.05, –1.66, –0.40 and 0.80 V. Which one will be the most reducing

A. A B. B
C. C D. D

47. A solution of sodium metal in liquid ammonia is strongly reducing due to the presence of

A. Sodium atoms B. Sodium hydride
C. Sodium amide D. Solvated electrons

48. Potassium metal is kept under

A. Water B. Alcohol
C. Ammonia D. Kerosene

49. K, Ca and Li metals may be arranged in the decreasing order of their standard electrode potential as

A. K, Ca, Li B. Li, K, Ca
C. Li, Ca, K D. Ca, Li, K

50. Alkali metals give colour in Bunsen flame due to

A. Low ionization potential
B. Low melting point
C. Softness
D. One electron in outermost orbit

51. The alkali metal that reacts with nitrogen directly to form nitride is

A. Li B. Na
C. K D. Kb

52. A solution of sodium sulphate in water is electrolysed using inert electrodes. The products at the cathode and anode are respectively

A. H_2, O_2 B. O_2, Na
C. O_2, H_2 D. O_2, SO_2

53. Electrolysis of molten sodium chloride leads to the formation of

A. Na & H_2 B. Na & O_2
C. H_2 & O_2 D. Na & Cl_2

54. When NaCl is dissolved in water, the sodium ion is

A. Oxidised B. Reduced
C. Hydrolysed D. Hydrated

55. Which of the following does not illustrate the anomalous properties of Li?

A. The m.p. & b.p. of Li are comparatively high
B. Li is much softer than the other group I metals
C. Li forms a nitride Li_3N unlike group I metals
D. The ion of Li and its compounds are more heavily hydrated than those of the rest of the group

56. Molten sodium chloride conducts electricity due to the presence of

A. Free electrons
B. Free ions
C. Free molecules
D. Atoms of sodium & chloride.

57. Which of the following is purely ionic?

A. Sodium chloride
B. Beryllium chloride
C. Lithium chloride
D. Carbon tetrachloride

58. Among NaCl, NaBr, NaF and NaI; NaF is the highest melting halide because it has

A. Minimum ionic character
B. Maximum ionic character

C. Highest oxidising power
D. Lowest polarity

59. Which one of the following is formed in Solvay process?
A. Na_2CO_3 B. $NaHCO_3$
C. $CaCl_2$ D. All

60. Sodium carbonate reacts with SO_2 in aqueous medium to give
A. $NaHSO_3$ B. Na_2SO_3
C. $NaHSO_4$ D. Na_2SO_4

61. $Na_2CO_3.10H_2O$ is prepared by
A. Castner process B. Solvay process
C. Ostwald's process D. Haber's process

62. Molten sodium is used in nuclear reactors to
A. Absorb neutrons in order to control the chain reaction
B. Slow down the fast neutrons
C. Absorb the heat generated by nuclear fission
D. Extract radio-isotopes produced in the reactor

63. Squasher are stored by adding
A. Citric acid B. KCl
C. Na_2SO_3 D. Sod. metabisulphite

64. Fire extinguishers contain H_2SO_4 and
A. $NaHCO_3$ & Na_2CO_3
B. $NaHCO_3$ solution
C. Na_2CO_3
D. $CaCO_3$

65. Which of the following pair can't exist in solution?
A. $NaHCO_3$ & NaOH
B. Na_2CO_3 & NaOH
C. Na_2CO_3 & NaCl
D. $NaHCO_3$ & NaCl

66. Chile salt petre is
A. $NaNO_3$ B. Na_2SO_4
C. KNO_3 D. $Na_2S_2O_3$

67. Which of the following imparts violet colouration of the Bunsen burner non-luminous flame?
A. NaCl B. $BaCl_2$
C. $CaCl_2$ D. KCl

68. K_2CS_3 can be called potassium
A. Sulphocyanide B. Thiocarbide
C. Thiocarbonate D. Thiocyanate

69. Which of the following is most basic in character?
A. RbOH B. KOH
C. LiOH D. NaOH

70. Which of the following has highest electrode potential?
A. Be B. Mg
C. Ca D. Ba

71. Of the metals Be, Mg, Ca and Sr of group IIA in the periodic table, the least ionic chloride would be formed by
A. Be B. Mg
C. Ca D. Sr

72. Mixture of $MgCl_2$ & MgO is called
A. Portland cement B. Sorrels cement
C. Double salt D. None

73. The increasing order of solubility is
A. $CaCO_3$, $KHCO_3$, $NaHCO_3$
B. $NaHCO_3$, $KHCO_3$, $CaCO_3$
C. $KHCO_3$, $NaHCO_3$, $CaCO_3$
D. $CaCO_3$, $NaHCO_3$, $KHCO_3$

74. In India at the occasion of marriage, the fireworks used give green flame. Which one of the following radicals may be present?
A. Na^+ B. K^+
C. Ba^{2+} D. Ca^{2+}

75. Gypsum is
A. $MgSO_4.2H_2O$ B. $CaSO_4.2H_2O$
C. $2CaSO_4$ D. $CaSO_4.3H_2O$

76. Setting of cement is an
A. Exothermic reaction
B. Endothermic reaction
C. None
D. Both

77. Setting (hardening) of plaster of paris involves
A. Oxidation with atmospheric oxygen
B. Combination with atmospheric CO_2
C. Dehydration
D. Hydration to yield another hydrate.

78. Of the following the commonly used as a laboratory desiccator is
A. Na_2CO_3 B. $CaCl_2$
C. CaCl D. None

79. Which of the following is not a drying and dehydrating agent?
A. Silica gel B. P_2O_5
C. Conc. H_2SO_4 D. Hydrated $CaCl_2$

80. Which is quick lime?
A. $Ca(OH)_2$ B. CaO
C. $CaCO_3$ D. $Ca(OH)_2 + H_2O$

81. Which mineral was used in isolation of radium?
A. Lime stone B. Pitch blende
C. Rutile D. Haematite

82. Alkali metals are powerful reducing agents because
A. These are metals
B. These are monovalent
C. Their ionic radii is large
D. Of low ionization potential value.

83. When a crystal of caustic soda is exposed to air, a liquid layer is deposited because
A. Crystal melts
B. Crystal loses water
C. Crystal absorbs moisture and CO_2
D. Crystal sublimes

84. The products of the electrolysis of concentrated aqueous solution of common salt are :
A. $Na + Cl_2$ B. $H_2 + O_2$
C. $NaOH + H_2 + Cl_2$ D. $NaOH + Cl_2 + O_2$

85. The principle products obtained on heating iodine with caustic soda solution are
A. $NaOI + NaI$
B. $NaIO_3 + NaI$
C. $NaOI + NaIO_3 + NaI$
D. $NaIO_4 + NaI$

86. Sodium metal is obtained by
A. The electrolysis of concentrated NaCl (aq.)
B. Heating Na_2O with H_2
C. Heating fused sodium chloride
D. Electrolysis of fused sodium chloride

87. Brine is chemically
A. Conc. solution of Na_2CO_3
B. Conc. solution of Na_2SO_4
C. Conc. solution of NaCl
D. Conc. solution of alum

88. On heating sodium metal in a current of dry ammonia gas the compound formed is
A. Sodium nitrate B. Sodium hydride
C. Sodium amide D. Sodium azide

89. Sodium reacts with water less vigorously than potassium because
A. It has higher atomic weight
B. It is less electropositive
C. It is more electropositive
D. It is a metal

90. The most homogenous family in Periodic Table is of
A. Alkali metals B. Alkaline earth metals
C. Volatile metals D. Coinage metals

91. Which element of IA group is most-abundantly found in combined state :
A. Li B. Na
C. Cs D. K

92. NO_2 is obtained by heating
A. $CsNO_3$ B. KNO_3
C. $LiNO_3$ D. $NaNO_3$

93. Lithium is the only alkali metal which is not placed in kerosene but is wrapped in paraffin wax, because
A. It reacts with kerosene
B. It floats to the surface of kerosene because of low density
C. It does not react with air and H_2O
D. None

94. Gun powder is
A. KNO_3 + Charcoal + S
B. $NaNO_3 + KNO_3 + S$
C. $NaNO_3 + S$
D. None

95. Black ash is
A. $NaOH + CaS$ B. $NaHCO_3 + CoS$
C. $Na_2CO_3 + CaS$ D. $Na_2CO_3 + CoS$

96. The electrolyte employed in the extraction of sodium by Down's electrolysis method is
A. An aqueous solution of NaCl
B. Molten NaCl
C. Molten NaOH
D. A molten mixture of $MgCl_2$ & NaCl

97. Alkali metals are soft and have relatively low m.p. and low density. This is because
A. Interatomic bonds are weak
B. Interatomic bonds are strong
C. Of their ionization potential
D. Of their position in the periodic table

98. Fusion of AgCl with Na_2CO_3 gives:
A. Ag_2CO_3 B. Silver carbide
C. Ag D. Ag_2

99. Tin dissolves in boiling caustic soda solution because of the formation of soluble
A. $Sn(OH)_2$ B. $Sn(OH)_4$
C. Na_2SnO_3 D. None

100. Sodium metal cannot be stored under
A. Benzene B. Kerosene
C. Alcohol D. Toluene

101. NaOH is prepared by the electrolysis of
A. Aqueous solution of sodium chloride with platinum electrode
B. Molten sodium chloride with graphite anode and iron cathode
C. Sodium carbonate with platinum electrodes
D. Sodium carbonate with nickel electrodes

102. When carbon monoxide is passed over solid caustic soda heated to 200 °C, it forms
A. Na_2CO_3 B. $NaHCO_3$
C. HCOONa D. None

103. If NaOH is added to an aqueous solution of Zn^{2+} ions, a white precipitate appears and on adding excess NaOH, the precipitate dissolves. In this solution zinc exists in the
A. Cationic part
B. Anionic part
C. Both A & B
D. There is no zinc left in the solution

104. Addition of excess of sodium hydroxide solution to a solution of nickel sulphate results in the formation of a
A. Green precipitate B. Pink colouration
C. Blue ppt D. Violet colouration

105. Water glass is
A. Another name for sodium silicate
B. A special form of glass to store water only
C. Hydrated form of glass
D. Hydrated silica

106. Which one of the following is formed on dissolving I_2 in aqueous solution of KI.
A. KIO_4 B. KIO
C. KI_3 D. KIO_3

107. Pearl ash and caustic potash are chemically
A. K_2CO_3 & KOH B. KOH and K_2CO_3
C. Na_2CO_3 & KOH D. Na_2CO_3 & NaOH

108. Sodium metabisulphite is not
A. An antichlor
B. A bleaching agent
C. An oxidising agent
D. A reducing agent

109. The main reason for using a mercury electrolytic cell in NaOH manufacture is that
A. Hg is toxic
B. Na^+ is discharged at cathode
C. Hg has a high vapour pressure
D. Hg is a good conductor of electricity

110. Which substance gives a different flame colouration from the other
A. Nitre
B. Caustic potash
C. Potassium chloride
D. Table salt

111. The by-product of Solvay process is
A. CO_2 B. $CaCl_2$
C. NH_3 D. $CaCO_3$

112. Manufacture of NaOH is done by
A. Castner-Kellner process
B. Solvay process
C. Bire process
D. Monel process

113. An ore of potassium is
A. Carnallite B. Cryolite
C. Bauxite D. Dolomite

114. Acidic field solution of sodium thiosulphate are unstable because in thiosulphate
A. The sulphur atoms are at unstable oxidation state of + 2
B. The two sulphur atoms are at different oxidation states of + 6 and – 2
C. The S–S bond are unstable bonds
D. Thio compounds contain sulphur in zero oxidation state.

115. Washing soda is
A. Na_2CO_3 B. $Na_2CO_3.H_2O$
C. $Na_2CO_3.7H_2O$ D. $Na_2CO_3.10H_2O$

116. Common table salt becomes moist and does not pour easily in rainy season because :
A. It contains magnesium chloride
B. It contains magnesium carbonate
C. It melts slightly in rainy season
D. Sodium chloride is hygroscopic

117. Sodium chloride imparts a golden yellow colour to the Bunsen flame. This can be interpreted due to
A. Low ionization potential of sodium
B. Photosensitivity of sodium
C. Sublimation of metallic sodium to give yellow vapour
D. Emission of excess of energy absorbed as a radiation in the visible region

118. Which of the following has minimum values of cation-anion size ratio?
A. NaCl B. KCl
C. $MgCl_2$ D. CaF_2

119. The alkali metals
A. Form salt like hydrides
B. Form salts which are predominantly covalent
C. Show decreased chemical reactivity with dry oxygen in going from Li to Cs
D. Show increasingly electronegativity from Li to Cs

120. Which of the following statements is false regarding saline hydrides?
A. In the molten state they conduct electricity
B. They dissolve in water giving off hydrogen
C. They are used as reducing agents
D. They are covalent in nature

121. Sodium thiosulphate, $Na_2S_2O_3.5H_2O$ is used in photography to
A. Reduce the silver bromide grains to metallic silver
B. Convert the metallic silver to silver salt
C. Remove undercomposed AgBr as soluble silver thiosulphate complex
D. Remove reduced silver

122. Which of the following compounds on reaction with NaOH and H_2O_2 gives yellow colour?
A. $Zn(OH)_2$ B. $Cr(OH)_3$
C. $Al(OH)_3$ D. None

123. Dissolving metallic zinc in excess of NaOH produces
A. $Zn(OH)_2$ B. Na_2ZnO_2
C. ZnO D. $Zn(OH)_2$ & Na_2ZnO_2

124. Among the following, which has minimum solubility in water?
A. KOH B. CsOH
C. LiOH D. RbOH

125. Hypo is used in photography for
A. Fixing B. Developing
C. Printing D. Tonning

126. The reaction of sodium with water is highly exothermic. The rate of reaction is lowered by
A. Lowering the temperature
B. Mixing with alcohol
C. Mixing with acetic acid
D. Making an amalgam

127. Oxone is the name given to :
A. Ozone B. Sodium peroxide
C. Sodium oxide D. Sodamide

128. The nitride ion in lithium nitride is composed of
A. 7 protons + 7 electrons
B. 10 protons + 7 electrons
C. 7 protons + 10 electrons
D. 10 protons + 10 electrons

129. Elements of group I and group VI in the periodic table have one thing common. That is with the increasing atomic number, the
A. Maximum valency increases
B. Reactivity increases
C. Atomic radius increases
D. Oxidising power increases

130. The metallic lustre exhibited by sodium is due to
A. Diffusion of Na^+ ions
B. Oscillation of loose electrons
C. Excitation of free protons
D. Excitation of body centred cubic lattice

131. Solubility of NaCl in heavy water is
A. More than ordinary water
B. Less than ordinary water
C. Same as in ordinary water
D. None

132. Francium was discovered by
A. Perry B. Davy
C. Rutherford D. Sheele

133. Compared with alkaline earth metals, the alkali metals exhibit
A. Smaller ionic radii
B. Greater hardness
C. High boiling point
D. Lower ionisation energies

134. In a sodium chloride crystal, each chloride ion is surrounded by

A. $4Na^+$ ions B. $6Na^+$ ions
C. One Na^+ ion D. $2Na^+$ ions

135. The stability of the following alkali metal chlorides follows the order
A. LiCl > KCl > NaCl > CsCl
B. CsCl > KCl > NaCl > LiCl
C. NaCl > KCl > LiCl > CsCl
D. KCl > CsCl > NaCl > LiCl

136. When CO_2 is bubbled into an aqueous solution of Na_2CO_3 the following is formed
A. H_2O B. OH^-
C. $NaHCO_3$ D. NaOH

137. Sodium carbonate contains
A. 5 molecules of crystalline water
B. 10 molecules of crystalline water
C. 3 molecules of crystalline water
D. No molecule of crystalline water

138. Sodium peroxide in contact with moist air turns white due to the formation of
A. Na_2O B. Na_2CO_3
C. $NaHCO_3$ D. NaOH

139. In which of the following, sodium carbonate is not used :
A. In soap making B. In paper making
C. In tyre making D. In baking of bread

140. Which of the following alkali metal ion in aqueous solution is the best conductor of electricity?
A. Li^+ B. Na^+
C. Cs^+ D. K^+

141. Li, Na among alkali metals show properties of
A. Noble gases
B. Transition metal
C. Inner transition metal
D. Representative elements

142. Alkali metal chloride soluble in pyridine is
A. LiCl B. CsCl
C. NaCl D. KCl

143. The chloride ion is isoelectronic with potassium. The size of chloride ion is
A. Larger than K^+ ion
B. Smaller than K^+ ion
C. Same as that of K^+ ion
D. None

144. IA group elements react violently with water and the solution becomes
A. Acidic B. Basic
C. Neutral D. Amphoteric

145. Siedlitz powder contains
A. $CaCO_3$ B. $MgCO_3$
C. $NaHCO_3$ D. KNO_3

146. Which does not form peroxide on heating in air
A. Na B. Ba
C. Ca D. Li

147. Which one is not known to form compounds in more than one oxidation state :
A. Noble gases B. Halogens
C. Alkali metals D. Transition metals

148. Which one has the highest lattice energy?
A. NaBr B. NaF
C. NaCl D. NaI

149. Which metal does not form ionic hydride?
A. Na B. Rb
C. Ca D. Be

150. Which ion has closed shell electronic configuration?
A. Li B. Li^+
C. Li^{2+} D. Li^-

151. Hypo is used in
A. Iodimetric titrations
B. Iodometric titrations
C. Photography
D. All of the above

152. An aqueous solution of KI does not give a precipitate with
A. Mg^{2+} B. Pb^{2+}
C. Hg^{2+} D. Ca^{2+}

153. Property of the alkaline earth metals that increases with their atomic number is
A. Ionisation energy
B. Solubility of their hydroxides
C. Solubility of their sulphates
D. Electronegativity

154. Plaster of Paris hardens by
A. Giving off CO_2
B. Changing into $CaCO_3$
C. Uniting with water
D. Giving out water

155. Alloys of which metal are light and strong and are used in the manufacture of aeroplane parts
A. Cr B. Sn
C. Fe D. Mg

156. Flash bulbs contain wire or foil of Mg packed in an atmosphere of
A. SO_3 B. O_2
C. Air D. N_2

157. Magnesium metal is prepared by
A. Reduction of MgO by coke
B. Electrolysis of aqueous solution of $Mg(NO_3)_2$
C. Displacement of Mg by iron from magnesium sulphate solution
D. Electrolysis of molten magnesium chloride

158. The Plaster of Paris is
A. $CaSO_4.2H_2O$ B. $CaSO_4$
C. $2CaSO_4.2H_2O$ D. $2CaSO_4.H_2O$

159. Mortar is a mixture of
A. $CaCO_3$ & CaO
B. Slaked lime and water
C. Slaked line, sand and water
D. None

160. Gypsum on heating at 120 – 130 °C gives
A. Hemihydrate B. Monohydrate
C. Dihydrates D. Anhydrous salt

161. Gypsum is added to clinker during cement manufacture to
A. Decrease the rate of setting of cement
B. Make the cement impervious
C. Bind the particles of calcium silicate
D. To facilitate the formation of colloidal gel

162. Hesenclever's process is a method for the manufacture of
A. NaOH B. HNO_3
C. H_2SO_4 D. Bleaching powder

163. Oxygen is obtained from bleaching powder by
A. The action of dilute acid
B. The action of alkali
C. Heating it with lime
D. Heating it with cobalt salt

164. A chloride dissolves appreciably in cold water. When placed on a platinum wire in Bunsen flame; no distinctive colour is noticed. Which one is cations?
A. Mg^{++} B. Ba^{++}
C. Pb^{++} D. Ca^{++}

165. Portland cement does not contain:
A. $CaSiO_4$ B. Ca_2SiO_5
C. $Ca_2Al_2O_6$ D. $Ca_3(PO_4)_2$

166. Slaked lime is used in the manufacture of
A. Cement B. Fire bricks
C. Pigment D. White-wash

167. Salt used as a purgative is
A. NaCl B. $MgSO_4.7H_2O$
C. $Ca_3Al_2O_6$ D. $MgCl_2.6H_2O$

168. Ra is placed at the bottom of the alkaline earth metals. The element should
A. Have the highest atomic volume
B. Possess the minimum density
C. Be less easily ionizable
D. Be least electropositive

169. At high temperature nitrogen combines with CaO_2 to give
A. Calcium cyanide
B. Calcium cyanamide
C. Calcium carbonate
D. Calcium nitride

170. Which represents nitrolime
A. $CaCN_2 + C$
B. $CaC_2 + N_2$
C. $Ca(CN)_2 + Ca(NO_3)_2$
D. None

171. Which removes temporary hardness of water and is used in the manufacture of bleaching powder?
A. Slaked lime B. Plaster of Paris
C. Epsom D. Hydrolith

172. Superphosphate of lime is a mixture of
A. Primary calcium phosphate and epsom
B. Primary magnesium phosphate and epsom
C. Primary magnesium phosphate and gypsum
D. Primary calcium phosphate gypsum

173. Which gives apple green colour in fireworks?
A. Na B. K
C. Ba D. Ca

174. One of the important use of quick lime is
A. As a purgative
B. In bleaching silk
C. In drying gases and alcohol
D. In dyeing cotton

175. Calcium is extracted by the electrolysis of
A. Fused mixture of $CaCl_2$ and CaF_2
B. $CaCl_2$ solution
C. Fused mixture of $CaCl_2$ and NaF
D. $Ca_3(PO_4)_2$ solution

176. Lithophone is a mixture of
A. Barium sulphate and zinc sulphide
B. Barium sulphite and zinc sulphide
C. Calcium sulphate and zinc sulphide
D. Calcium sulphide and zinc sulphide

177. Baryta water is
A. BaO B. $Ca(OH)_2$
C. $Ba(OH)_2$ D. $BaSO_4$

178. The main constituent of egg-shells is
A. $CaCO_3$ B. $CaSiO_3$
C. $CaSO_4 \frac{1}{2} H_2O$ D. $CaSO_4.2H_2O$

179. The compound insoluble in acetic acid is
A. Calcium oxide
B. Calcium carbonate
C. Calcium hydroxide
D. Calcium oxalate

180. The compound which is not soluble in dil. HCl is
A. $BaSO_4$ B. MnS
C. ZnS D. $BaCO_3$

181. Electric cookers have a coating of that protects them against fire
A. Heavy lead B. Magnesium oxide
C. Zinc oxide D. Sodium sulphate

182. Which of the following represent calcium chlorite
A. $Ca(ClO_2)_2$ B. $CaClO_2$
C. $Ca(ClO_3)_2$ D. $Ca(ClO_4)_2$

183. The highly efficient method of obtaining beryllium is
A. Reduction of beryllium halide with Mg
B. Reduction of beryllium oxide with carbon
C. Electrolysis of fused beryllium chloride
D. Dissociation of beryllium carbide

184. Beryllium shows diagonal relationship with aluminium. Which of the following similarity is incorrect?
A. Be_2C like AlC_3 yields methane on hydrolysis
B. Be like Al is rendered passive by HNO_3
C. $Be(OH)_2$ like $Al(OH)_3$ is basic
D. Be forms beryllates and Al forms aluminates.

185. Sedimentary rocks laid down under water mainly contain
A. CaO B. $Ca(OH)_2$
C. $CaCO_3$ D. $CaSO_4$

186. Dead burnt is
A. $CaSO_4$
B. Na_2CO_3
C. Anhydrous Na_2SO_4
D. Anhydrous $CuSO_4$

187. Which decomposes on heating
A. K_2CO_3 B. Rb_2CO_3
C. Na_2CO_3 D. $MgCO_3$

188. Alkaline earth metals are
A. Reducing agent B. Oxidizing agent
C. Amphoteric D. Acidic

189. Barium is extracted from its ore
A. Dolomite B. Witherite
C. Carnallite D. Gypsum

190. Anhydrous magnesium chloride can be prepared by heating $MgCl_2.2H_2O$.
A. In a current of dry HCl gas
B. With carbon
C. Until it fumes
D. With lime

191. Which component of cement sets at the slowest rate?
A. Dicalcium silicate
B. Tricalcium silicate
C. Tricalcium aluminate
D. Tetracalcium alumino ferrite

192. Substance which absorbs CO_2 and violently reacts with H_2O with sound is
A. $CaCO_3$ B. CaO
C. H_2SO_4 D. ZnO

193. Which one is most soluble in water?
A. $Mg(OH)_2$ B. $G(OH)_2$
C. $Ca(OH)_2$ D. $Ba(OH)_2$

194. Electrolysis of fused $KCl.MgCl_2.6H_2O$ gives
A. Potassium only
B. Magnesium only
C. Magnesium and chlorine
D. Potassium, magnesium and chlorine

195. Which compound gives acetylene on reaction with water?
A. Al_4C_3 B. Mg_3N_2
C. CaC_2 D. CaH_2

196. Chemical A is used for water softening to remove temporary hardness. A reacts with sodium carbonate to generate caustic soda. When CO_2 is bubbled through A; it turns cloudy. What is the chemical formula of A?
A. $CaCO_3$ B. CaO
C. $Ca(OH)_2$ D. $Ca(HCO_3)_2$

197. Which substance is used in the laboratory for a fast drying of neutral gases?
A. P_2O_5
B. Active charcoal
C. Anhydrous calcium chloride
D. Na_3PO_4

198. A sudden jump between the values of second and third ionisation energies of an element would be associated with the electronic configuration

A. $1s^2, 2s^2, 2p^6, 3s^1$
B. $1s^2, 2s^2, 2p^6, 3s^2\ 3p^1$
C. $1s^2, 2s^2, 2p^6. 3s^2, 3p^2$
D. $1s^2, 2s^2, 2p^6, 3s^2$

199. Thermal decomposition of which compound yields a basic and acidic oxide simultaneously
A. $KClO_3$ B. NH_4NO_3
C. $NaNO_3$ D. $CaCO_3$

200. Mg burns with a brilliant flame. This property is used in
A. Fire-works
B. Military signals
C. Photographic flash bulbs
D. All of the above

201. Which alkaline earth metal is the most abundant in the earth's crest?
A. Mg 111 B. Ca Ca
C. Sr D. Ba 111

202. Melting point is highest for
A. Be B. Mgaa
C. Sr D. Ca

203. Thermal stability of $BaCO_3$, $CaCO_3$ & $MgCO_3$ is
A. $CaCO_3 > MgCO_3 > BaCO_3$
B. $MgCO_3 > CaCO_3 > BaCO_3$
C. $BaCO_3 > MgCO_3 > CaCO_3$
D. $BaCO_3 > CaCO_3 > MgCO_3$

204. BeF_2 is soluble in water whereas fluorides of other alkaline earth metals are insoluble because of
A. Ionic nature of BeF_2
B. Covalent nature of BeF_2
C. Greater hydration energy of Be^{2+} ion as compared to its lattice energy
D. None

205. When $SiCl_4$ vapours are poured over hot Mg, the products formed are
A. $SiCl_2 + MgCl_2$ B. $MgSi + Cl_2$
C. $Si + MgCl_2$ D. $MgSiCl_6$

206. Element found in plant-systems which forms an important constituent of photosynthesis is
A. Fe B. Cu
C. Na D. Mg111

207. The function of sand in mortar is
A. To decrease the hardness
B. To make the mass compact
C. To decrease the plasticity of the mass
D. To prevent the excess shrinkage because of which cracks may result

208. Which of the following will liberate hydrogen by its reaction with hydrochloric acid?
A. Copper B. Phosphorus
C. Mercury D. Magnesium

209. The first-ionisation energies of alkaline earth-metals are higher than those of alkali metals because of :
A. There is increase in the nuclear charge of the alkaline earth melts
B. There is decrease in the nuclear charge of the alkaline earth metals
C. Therė is no change in the nuclear charge
D. None of the above

210. The formula of Norweign saltpetre is
A. $NaNO_3$ B. KNO_3
C. $Ca(NO_3)_2.CaO$ D. $Ba(NO_3)_2$

211. On heating Al at 800 °C in air, Al_2O_3 is formed. The reaction is
A. An endothermic reaction
B. An exothermic reaction
C. Reduction of aluminium
D. None

212. Borax is
A. $Na_2B_4O_7$ B. $Na_2B_4O_7.4H_2O$
C. $Na_2B_4O_7.7H_2O$ D. $Na_2B_4O_7.10H_2O$

213. Sapphire is a mineral of
A. Cu B. Zn
C. Al D. Hg

214. Borax on heating with cobalt oxide forms a blue bead of
A. $CO(BO_2)_2$ B. $CoBO_2$
C. $CO_3(BO_3)_2$ D. $Na_3CO(BO_3)_2$

215. Aluminium on heating with carbon in nitrogen atmosphere gives :
A. Al + CO B. $Al + CO_2$
C. AlN + CO D. $Al + CO + N_2$

216. Hoope's process is used in the refining of
A. Al B. Zn
C. Ag D. Ca

217. The correct order of decreasing hardness of the following compound is
A. Diamond > Borazon > Carborundrum > Corundum
B. Borazon > Diamond > Carborundum > Corundum
C. Corundum > Carborundum > Borazon > Diamond
D. Diamond > Carborundum > Borazon > Corundum

218. Which of the following has the minimum heat of dissociation?
A. $(CH_3)_3N \rightarrow BF_3$
B. $(CH_3)_3N \rightarrow B(CH_3)F_2$
C. $(CH_3)_3N \rightarrow B(CH_3)_2F$
D. $(CH_3)_3N \rightarrow BC(CH_3)_3$

219. Aluminium becomes passive in nitric acid because it
A. Is a noble metal
B. Forms a thin film of oxide
C. Has positive reduction potential
D. None

220. Aluminium reduces most of the metallic oxides due to its greater affinity for
A. Oxygen B. Metals
C. Electrons D. Protons

221. Aluminium is mainly extracted from
A. Magnetite B. Bauxite
C. Alumina D. Haematite

222. Which is not a mineral of aluminium?
A. Anhydrite B. Bauxite
C. Corundum D. Diaspore

223. Thermite, a mixture used for welding, is
A. Fe & Al
B. Ferric oxide and aluminium powder
C. Barium peroxide and magnesium powder
D. Copper and aluminium

224. Alumino-thermy is a process involving
A. Reduction of oxide of a metal by heating with sodium
B. Exo-thermic reduction of metal oxides by heating with Al
C. Reduction of oxides of a metal by heating with carbon
D. None

225. Al and Ga have the same covalent radii because of
A. Greater shielding power of *s*-electrons of Ga atoms
B. Poor shielding power of *s*-electrons of Ga atoms
C. Poor shielding power of *d*-electrons of Ga atoms
D. Greater shielding power of *d*-electrons of Ga atoms.

226. Al-Bronze contains Al and
A. Zn B. Sb
C. Cu D. Ni

227. Which is used as a mordant?
A. $AlCl_3$ B. $Al_2(SO_4)_3$
C. Alum D. Al_2O_3

228. Corundum is
A. SiO_2 B. Al_2O_3
C. CaF_2 D. Cr_2O_3

229. Aqueous solution of potash alum is
A. Alkaline B. Acidic
C. Neutral D. Soppy

230. All alums contain
A. One monovalent and one trivalent metal
B. Both monovalent metals
C. One divalent and one monovalent metal
D. Both divalent metals

231. The strongest Lewis acid is
A. BF_3 B. BCl_3
C. BBr_3 D. BI_3

232. The protective film of oxide on the surface of Al metal may be strengthened by
A. Galvanizing B. Cathodizing
C. Sheradizing D. Anodizing

233. The blue coloured mineral 'Lapis Lazuli' used as semi precious stone is
A. Sodium alumino silicate
B. Zinc cobaltate
C. Prussian blue
D. Basic copper carbonate

234. The purification method used for mineral $Al_2O_3.2H_2O$ is
A. Froth floatation B. Leaching
C. Liquation D. Magnetic separation

235. Purification of alumina is essential because
A. Impure alumina has a very poor conductor of electricity
B. Impure alumina has a very high melting point
C. Impure alumina cannot react with the oxidizing agent
D. It is difficult to purify aluminium metal

236. Boron carbide, B_4C is widely used for
A. Making acetylene
B. Making Plaster of Paris
C. As a hardest substance after diamond
D. Making boric acid

237. Which reaction cannot give anhydrous $AlCl_3$?
A. Heating of $AlCl_3.6H_2O$
B. Passing dry HCl over heated aluminium powder

C. Passing dry Cl_2 over heated aluminium powder
D. Heating a mixture of alumina and coke in a current of dry Cl_2

238. Which one is explosive?
A. PCl_5
B. $Pb(NO_3)_2$
C. NH_4NO_3 + Al powder
D. $C_6H_5—NO_2$

239. Which of the following is alum?
A. $Na_2SO_4.Al_2(SO_4)_3.24H_2O$
B. $(NH_4)_2SO_4.FeSO_4.6H_2O$
C. $KCl.MgCl_2.6H_2O$
D. $FeSO_4.(NH_4)_2SO_4.6H_2O$

240. The process used for purification of bauxite ore containing iron oxide impurity is known as
A. Hoope's process B. Serpek's process
C. Baeyer's process D. Electrolytic process

241. Alum is used by dyer of cloth
A. For fire-proofing fabrics
B. As first-aid for cuts
C. For softening hard water
D. As mordant

242. IUPAC name of complex $K_3[Al(C_2O_4)_3]$ is
A. Potassium alumino-oxalate
B. Potassium trioxalato aluminate (III)
C. Potassium aluminium (III) oxalate
D. Potassium trioxalatoaluminate (VI)

243. Chemically borax is
A. Sodium metaborate
B. Sodium orthoborate
C. Sodium tetraborate
D. Sodium tetraborate decahydrate

244. Chief core of Al is
A. Cryolite B. Kaolin
C. Bauxite D. Feldspar

245. Alum is not used
A. As a mordant in dyeing
B. As an insecticide
C. In the purification of water
D. In tanning of leather

246. Aluminium is obtained by
A. Reducing Al_2O_3 with coke
B. Electrolysing Al_2O_3 dissolved in Na_3AlF_6
C. Reducing Al_2O_3 with chromium
D. Heating Al_2O_3 and cryolite

247. Aluminium vessels should not be washed with materials containing washing soda because
A. Washing soda is expensive
B. Washing soda is easily decomposed
C. Washing soda reacts with aluminium to form soluble aluminate
D. Washing soda reacts with aluminium to form insoluble aluminium oxide

248. Which statement is not true about potash alum?
A. It's empirical formula is $KAl(SO_4)_2.12H_2O$
B. It's aqueous solution is basic in nature
C. It is used in dyeing industries
D. On heating it melts and loses its water of crystallization

249. The role of flourspar (CaF_2) which is added in small qualities in the electrolytic reduction of alumina dissolved in fused cryolite (Na_3AlF_6) is
A. As a catalyst
B. To make the fused mixture very conducting
C. To increase the temperature of the melt
D. To decrease the rate of oxidation of carbon at anode

250. In Gold Schmidt reaction, certain metallic oxides are reduced to the metallic state by heating with
A. Metallic magnesium
B. Metallic aluminium
C. Metallic ion
D. Sodium metal

ANSWERS

1	2	3	4	5	6	7	8	9	10
C	A	A	A	D	D	C	D	D	B
11	12	13	14	15	16	17	18	19	20
C	E	B	B	A	C	E	D	A	A
21	22	23	24	25	26	27	28	29	30
B	D	C	C	D	A	B	D	A	B

31	32	33	34	35	36	37	38	39	40
E	E	E	A	D	A	E	A	D	D
41	**42**	**43**	**44**	**45**	**46**	**47**	**48**	**49**	**50**
E	D	A	B	B	A	D	D	B	A
51	**52**	**53**	**54**	**55**	**56**	**57**	**58**	**59**	**60**
A	A	D	D	A	B	A	B	D	A
61	**62**	**63**	**64**	**65**	**66**	**67**	**68**	**69**	**70**
B	D	D	A	A	A	D	C	A	B
71	**72**	**73**	**74**	**75**	**76**	**77**	**78**	**79**	**80**
A	B	D	C	B	A	D	B	D	B
81	**82**	**83**	**84**	**85**	**86**	**87**	**88**	**89**	**90**
B	D	C	C	B	D	C	C	B	A
91	**92**	**93**	**94**	**95**	**96**	**97**	**98**	**99**	**100**
B	C	B	A	C	B	A	C	C	C
101	**102**	**103**	**104**	**105**	**106**	**107**	**108**	**109**	**110**
B	C	B	A	A	C	A	C	B	D
111	**112**	**113**	**114**	**115**	**116**	**117**	**118**	**119**	**120**
B	A	A	B	D	A	D	C	A	D
121	**122**	**123**	**124**	**125**	**126**	**127**	**128**	**129**	**130**
C	B	B	C	B	D	B	C	C	B
131	**132**	**133**	**134**	**135**	**136**	**137**	**138**	**139**	**140**
B	A	D	B	D	C	B	D	C	C
141	**142**	**143**	**144**	**145**	**146**	**147**	**148**	**149**	**150**
D	A	A	C	C	D	C	B	D	B
151	**152**	**153**	**154**	**155**	**156**	**157**	**158**	**159**	**160**
C	C	B	C	D	B	D	D	C	A
161	**162**	**163**	**164**	**165**	**166**	**167**	**168**	**169**	**170**
A	D	A	B	D	A	B	A	B	A
171	**172**	**173**	**174**	**175**	**176**	**177**	**178**	**179**	**180**
A	D	C	C	A	A	C	B	D	A
181	**182**	**183**	**184**	**185**	**186**	**187**	**188**	**189**	**190**
B	A	C	B	C	A	D	A	C	A
191	**192**	**193**	**194**	**195**	**196**	**197**	**198**	**199**	**200**
A	B	C	B	C	C	C	B	B	D
201	**202**	**203**	**204**	**205**	**206**	**207**	**208**	**209**	**210**
C	A	D	C	A	D	D	D	A	C
211	**212**	**213**	**214**	**215**	**216**	**217**	**218**	**219**	**220**
A	D	C	A	A	A	A	D	B	A
221	**222**	**223**	**224**	**225**	**226**	**227**	**228**	**229**	**230**
B	A	B	B	C	C	C	B	B	A
231	**232**	**233**	**234**	**235**	**236**	**237**	**238**	**239**	**240**
D	D	A	A	A	C	B	B	A	B
241	**242**	**243**	**244**	**245**	**246**	**247**	**248**	**249**	**250**
D	B	D	C	B	C	C	B	A	B

13

Co-Ordination Compounds and Organometallics

Coordination Compounds : These are the addition compounds which retain their identity in the solid as well as in the solution forms. In these compounds the individual properties of constituents are generally lost. For example, when aqueous copper sulphate is mixed with aqueous solution of ammonia, a deep blue coloured solution is obtained. The deep blue colour does not show the presence of Cu^{2+} ion. Instead it shows the presence of cupro-ammonium ions, $\left[Cu(NH_3)_4\right]^{2+}$ which are formed by combination of Cu^{2+} ion and four ammonia molecules. Such ions are known as 'complex ions'. Similarly, a complex ferrocyanide $[Fe(CN)_6]^{4-}$ ion is formed when aqueous solution of $Fe(CN)_2$ and KCN are mixed together. The salts of these complex ions are known as 'complex compounds' or 'coordination compounds'. The term coordination is given to these addition compounds because in all these compounds, the central metal ion forms 'dative' or 'coordinate' bonds with the species surrounding it.

A coordination compound generally contains one or more complex ions. For example—

$\left[Cu(NH_3)_4\right]SO_4$ contains $\left[Cu(NH_3)_4\right]^{2+}$ complex ion

$\left[Ag(NH_3)_2\right]Cl$ contains $\left[Ag(NH_3)_2\right]^{+}$ complex ion

$Na\left[Ag(CN)_2\right]$ contains $\left[Ag(CN)_2\right]^{-}$ complex ion

$K_4\left[Fe(CN)_6\right]$ contains $\left[Fe(CN)_6\right]^{4-}$ complex ion

$K_3\left[Fe(CN)_6\right]$ contains $\left[Fe(CN)_6\right]^{3-}$ complex ion

$\left[Co(NH_3)_6\right]\left[Cr(CN)_6\right]$ contains $\left[Co(NH_3)_6\right]^{3+}$ and $\left[Cr(CN)_6\right]^{3-}$ complex ions.

A complex ion is thus an electrically charged radical or ion carrying positive or negative charge in which the central atom or ion is surrounded by a suitable number of neutral molecules or negative ions called LIGANDS. The chemistry of metal ions in the solution is essentially the chemistry of their complexes. A complex compound which on ionisation gives a complex cation, is known as 'cationic complex'.

For example :

$$\left[Co(NH_3)_6\right]Cl_3 \rightarrow \underset{\text{Complex cation}}{\left[Co(NH_3)_6\right]^{3+}} + 3Cl^-$$

Similarly, a complex compound which on ionization gives a complex anion, is known as *anionic complex.* e.g.

$$K_4\left[Fe(CN_6)\right] \rightarrow 4K^+ + \underset{\text{Complex anion}}{\left[Fe(CN)_6\right]^{4-}}$$

Ligand : The neutral molecules or ions that surround the metal ion in a complex are known as ligands. Term ligand is derived from Latin word *ligase* meaning to bind. Ligands are normally polar molecules such as NH_3, H_2O or anions such as Cl^-, OH^-, CN^-, etc. which have atleast one unshared pair of valence electrons. They get attached to the central metal ion by a coordinate or dative bond. The atom is the ligand which is involved in the formation of coordinate bond while the central metal ion is called coordinating atom or donor atom. A ligand may contain one or more donor sites. Depending upon the number of donor sites, the ligands may be classified as:

Monodentate, having one donor atom
Bidentate, having two donor atoms

Tridentate, having three donor atoms
Tetradentate, having four donor atoms
Hexadentate, having six donor atoms.

The ligands having more than one donor atoms or sites are collectively known as *multidentate ligands*. When a multidentate ligand simultaneously coordinate to a metal ion by more than one donor site, then a ring like structure is obtained. It is called a *chelate ring* and the ligand is known as *chelating ligand* (From Greek word *chele* meaning claws). The chelate ring like structure formed by Cu(II) with ethylenediamine—

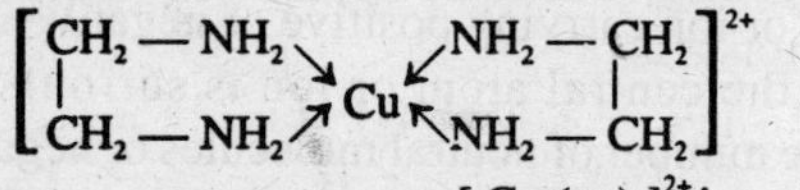

$[Cu(en)_2]^{2+}$ ion

The category of coordination compounds which is formed by chelating ligands is known as *Chelates*. The chelates find important application in micro detection and determination of metal ions in analytical chemistry.

Werner's Theory

Werner's coordination theory in 1893 was the first attempt to explain the bonding in coordination complexes. It must be noted that this imaginative theory was put forth before the electron had been discovered by J.J. Thomson, in 1896 and before the *electronic theory of valency*. This theory won Alfred Werner the Nobel Prize for Chemistry in 1913. The chemists wondered about how and why does a stable salt like $CoCl_3$ react with varying number of stable molecules of a compound like NH_3 to give several new compounds.

Werner was able to explain the nature of bonding in complexes. The brief outlines of Werner's theory are as :

Metal shows two different kinds of valencies :

***(i)* Primary Valency :** This is non-directional and ionizable. The modern explanation of primary valency is as follows :

The primary valency is the number of +ve charges on the metal atom. Primary valencies are satisfied by negative ions. The primary valency applies equally well to simple salt and to complexes. In $CoCl_2$, there are two primary valence, *i.e.*, two ionic bonds.

The complex $[Co(NH_3)_6]Cl_3$, actually exists as $[Co(NH_3)_6]^{3+}$ and $3Cl^-$. Thus, the primary valency of Co is 3, as there are three ionic bonds.

***(ii)* Secondary Valency :** This valency is directional and non-ionizable. In modern terms the number of secondary valencies equals the number of ligand atoms coordinated to the metal. This is now called the *co-ordination number* of the metal.

Ligands are commonly negative ions such as Cl^-, CN^-, etc. or neutral molecules such as NH_3, H_2O, CO, NO, etc. Less commonly, the ligands may be positive ions such as NO^+. Each metal has a characteristic number of secondary valencies. Thus, in $[Co(NH_3)_6]Cl_3$, the three Cl^- are held by primary valencies and six NH_3 groups by secondary valencies.

According to the modern concept, the primary valencies of metal indicate the oxidation number of the metal ion, whereas, secondary valencies refer to as the *coordination number* of metal ion. Every metal atom has a tendency to satisfy its both primary as well as secondary valencies when an ion replaces a neutral molecule in the coordination sphere, it loses its electrovalent character and gets attached to central metal ion by non-ionizable valency. The coordination compounds $[Co(NH_3)_5Br]SO_4$ and $[Co(NH_3)_5SO_4]Br$ have the same molecular formula. The former gives white precipitate with $BaCl_2$ while latter does not. The former does not give brown precipitate with $AgNO_3$ while latter does.

Shape of Complexes

(A) Octahedral Complexes : These complexes result from d^2sp^3 (inner orbital) or sp^3d^2 (outer orbital) hybridization.

***(a)* Inner Orbital Complexes :** In these complexes, the *d*-orbitals used are of lower quantum numbers, *i.e.* $(n - 1)$

(i) Formation $[Cr(NH_3)_6]^{3+}$ ion : Chromium is in + 3 oxidation state.

$$Cr_{24}\ [Ar]\ 3d^5 4s^1, Cr^{3+}\ [Ar]\ 3d^3$$

The two 3*d*, one 4*s* and three 4*p* orbitals (all of a nearly equal energy) hybridize to give six d^2sp^3 hybrid orbitals. The resulting six d^2sp^3 hybrid orbitals are occupied by the electron pairs donated by six ligand molecules, each donating one lone pair.

d^2sp^3 hybridization leads to octahedral geometry, the complex will be octahedral in shape. It has 3 unpaired electrons so is *paramagnetic* also.

Other such examples are $[Cr(CN)_6]^{3-}$ and $\left[Cr(H_2O)_6\right]^{3+}$.

(ii) Formation of Ferrocyanide ion, $[Fe(CN)_6]^{4-}$: The electronic configuration of the central atom Fe and the ion Fe^{2+} present in ferrocyanide ion is as

(i) $Fe_{26} = [Ar]\ 3d^6 4s^2$

(ii) $Fe^{2+} = [Ar]\ 3d^6$

Fe^{+2} ion does not contain any empty 3*d* orbital and hence should not form complex ion but it is not so. In the presence of cyanide ligand, the electrons in the 3*d*-orbitals are forced to pair up against the Hund's rule of maximum multiplicity in order to accomodate the electrons donated by the ligands. Thus, after pairing up against Hund's rule, the electronic configuration of the Fe^{2+} becomes as

(iii) Fe^{2+} (after rearrangement)

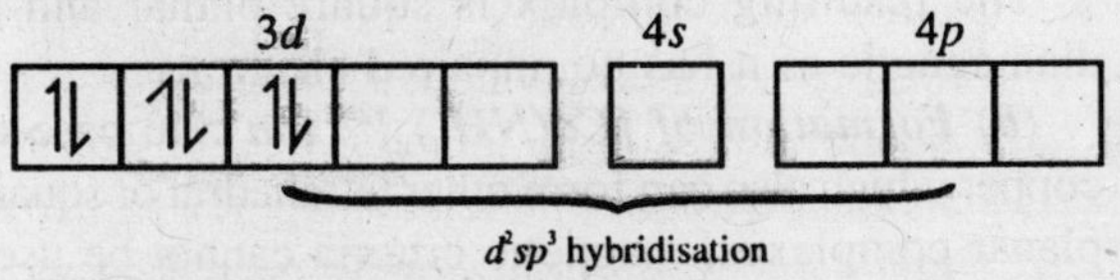

In this state Fe^{2+} undergoes d^2sp^3 hybridiration to form six d^2sp^3 hybrid orbitals, each of which accept electron pair donated by CN^- ions.

The resulting complex is inner octahedral and it should be diamagnetic, as it has no unpaired electron.

Formation of $\left[Co(NH_3)_6\right]^{3+}$ takes place in the same manner.

(iii) Formation of Ferricyanide $[Fe(CN)_6]^{3-}$:

(i) Fe atom At no. 26, $3d^6\ 4s^2\ 4p$

(ii) Fe^{3+} ion $3d^5\ 4s\ 4p$

(iii) Fe^{3+} (after rearrangement in the presence of CN^-)

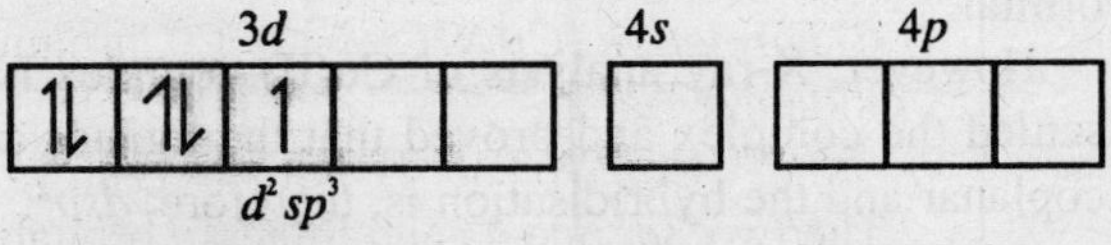

The resulting complex will be octahedral due to d^2sp^3 hybridisation and paramagnetic due to one unpaired electron.

(b) Outer Orbital Complexes : In these complexes *s, p* as well as *d*-orbitals involved in hybridisation belong to the highest quantum number (*n*). Complexes formed by the use of inner orbitals are diamagnetic or have reduced paramagnetism. They are called *low-spin* or *spin-paired complexes*. On the other hand, complexes formed by the use of outer *nd*-orbitals will be paramagnetic. These complexes are called *high-spin* or *spin-free complexes*. The outer orbital complexes have greater number of unpaired electrons.

Formation of $[CoF_6]^{3-}$: The electronic configurations of cobalt (At. number 27) and Co^{3+} ion is as

(i) Co atom (at. no. 27)

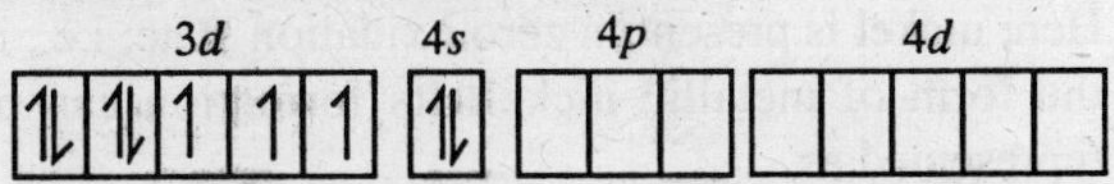

(ii) Co^{3+} ion

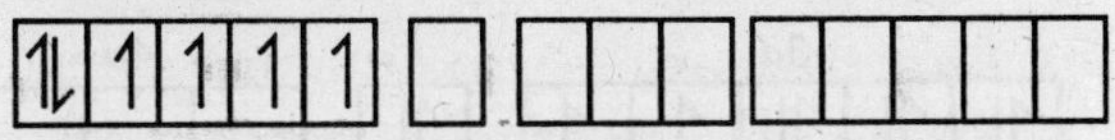

Physical experiments show that $[CoF_6]^{3-}$ ion has paramagnetic character corresponding to the presence of four unpaired electrons in 3*d*-orbital. Thus to get six hybrid orbitals, none of the 3*d*-orbital is involved in hybridisation. This is also in accordance with the fact that fluoride ion is a weak ligand and cannot force the pairing up of electrons against Hund's rule. Here one 4*s*, three 4*p* and two 4*d*-orbitals mix to give six equivalent (sp^3d^2) hybrid orbitals which can accept six lone pairs donated by six ligands (*i.e.*, F^- ions) to form $[CoF_6]^{3-}$ ion.

Other examples of outer orbital complexes are : $[FeF_6]^{3-}$, $\left[Fe(NH_3)_6\right]^{2+}$, $\left[Ni(NH_3)_6\right]^{2+}$, $\left[Cu(NH_3)_6\right]^{2+}$, $\left[Cr(H_2O)_6\right]^{2+}$, $\left[Fe(H_2O)_6\right]^{3+}$, etc.

(B) Tetrahedral Complexes : These are formed by sp^3 hybridisation.

(a) Example: Zn (Atomic no. 30) :

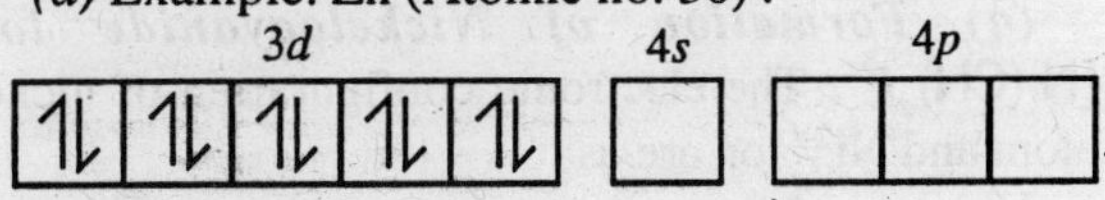

Zn^{+2} :

Since the 3*d*-orbitals are fully occupied and only four ligands are to be accommodated by the Zn^{2+} ion, it is obvious that the vacant one 4*s* and three 4*p* orbitals mix together to form four sp^3-hybrid orbitals. Each sp^3-hybrid orbital takes up on electron pair from ammonia ligand forming $\left[Zn(NH_3)_4\right]^{2+}$. Since the complex is formed by sp^3 hybridisation, it is tetrahedral, as it does not have any unpaired electron it is diamagnetic. Similar tetrahedral complexes (diamagnetic or paramagnetic) are formed by Cd^{2+}, Hg^{2+}, Ag^{+}, Ni^{2+} and Co^{2+} ions all of which have the structure as that of Zn^{2+}, $[FeCl_4]^-$, $[MnCl_4]^2$, and $[Ni(CO)_4]$ are also tetrahedral.

(b) Formation of nickel tetracarbonyl, $[Ni(CO)_4]$. Here nickel is present in zero oxidation state, i.e., in the form of metallic nickel. Its formation can be represented as

Ni (At. No. 28) :

3d					4s	4p		
↑↓	↑↓	↑↓	↑	↑	↑↓			

Ni (after rearrangement) :

3d					4s	4p		
↑↓	↑↓	↑↓	↑↓	↑↓				

In the presence of CO ligand, rearrangement takes place and the electrons are paired up against the Hund's rule *i.e*, the two 4*s* electrons go to the 3*d* orbitals in order to vacate the 4*s* orbital for electrons donated by the ligand CO.

The empty 4*s* and three 4*p* orbitals mix (sp^3 hybridisation) to form four equivalent hybrid orbitals each of which accepts an electron pair from CO molecule forming $Ni(CO)_4$. Thus nickel tetracarbonyl is tetrahedral and diamagnetic in nature.

(C) Square Planar Complexes : These are formed by the dsp^2 hybridisation. These complexes tend to be formed when the central ion has only one *d*-orbital available in the inner shell.

(a) Formation of Nickelocyanide ion $[Ni(CN)_4]^{2-}$: The electronic configuration of nickel atom and Ni^{2+} ion are as :

Ni (at. no. 28):

3d					4s	4p		
↑↓	↑↓	↑↓	↑	↑	↑↓			

Ni^{2+} :

3d					4s	4p		
↑↓	↑↓	↑↓	↑	↑				

Since the coordination number of Ni in this complex is 4, the configuration of Ni^{2+}, at first sight, shows that the complex is formed by sp^3 hybridisation and is paramagnetic as it has two unpaired electrons. However, experiments show that the complex is diamagnetic, *i.e.*, it does not have any unpaired electrons. This is possible when the 3*d* electrons rearrange against the Hund's rule as shown below. This is also in accordance with the fact that the ligand involved here is a strong CN^- ion

Ni^{2+} (after rearrangement)

3d					4s	4p		
↑↓	↑↓	↑↓	↑↓					

Hence, now dsp^2 hybridisation, involving one 3*d*, one 4*s* and two 4*p* orbitals, takes place leading to four dsp^2-hybrid orbitals, each of which accepts an electron pair from (CN^- ion forming $[Ni(CN)_4]^{2-}$ ion.

The resulting complex is square planar and is diamagnetic as it has no unpaired electrons.

(b) Formation of $[Ca(NH_3)_4]^{2+}$ ion : In case of copper which also can form other tetrahedral or square planar complexes, magnetic criteria cannot be used successfully since both the types of hybridisation will give unpaired electron in the 3*d* or 4*p* orbital.

	3d					4s	4p		
Cu (at. no. 29)	↑↓	↑↓	↑↓	↑↓	↑↓	↑			
Cu^{2+}	↑↓	↑↓	↑↓	↑↓	↑				
Cu^{2+} (tetrahedral)	↑↓	↑↓	↑↓	↑↓	↑				

(sp^3 Hybridised: 4s and 4p)

Note that the unpaired electron is present in 3*d* orbital.

	3d							
Cu^{2+} (square planar)	↑↓	↑↓	↑↓	↑↓				↑

(dsp^2 Hybridisation)

In this case the unpaired electron is present in 4*p* orbital.

However, X-ray analysis of Cu(II) complex has settled the complex and proved that the ligands are coplanar and the hybridisation is, therefore, dsp^2.

Isomerism in Coordination Compounds

(1) Ionization Isomerism : This type of isomerism is due to the exchange of groups or ion between the coordinating sphere and the ionization sphere and thus such type of isomers yield different ions in solution, since only the ion from ionisation sphere is released in solution.

(2) Hydrate Isomerism : These are isomers differing in the number of water molecules attached to the metal ion as ligands in the coordination sphere.

(3) Linkage, Structural or Salt Isomerism : This type of isomerism arises due to the presence of two different donor atoms in the same ligand which may thus attach through either of two atoms.

(4) Coordination Isomerism : This type of isomerism occurs when both cation and anion are complex. The isomerism is caused by the interchange of ligands between the two complex ions of the same complex.

(5) Stereoisomerism : It is the type of isomerism in which two substances of the same composition and even constitution differ only in the relative position in space assumed by certain of their constituent atoms or groups. It is of two types, geometrical and optical.

Nomenclature (I.U.P.A.C.) of Coordination Compounds : The essential features of the system are as given below :

(1) Like simple salts, the positive parts of the coordination compound is named first followed by the negative part. In case, the complex is non-ionic or molecular species, one word name is given to it, *e.g.*

$\left[Co(NH_3)_3Cl_3\right]$ *Cobalt (III) triamminetrichloro.*

(2) Naming of the Coordination Sphere : While naming a coordination sphere, ligands are named first and then the metal. Following points are followed while naming ligands and the central metal.

(i) (a) The *neutral ligands* are named as the molecule, *e.g.*

C_5H_5N pyridine $(C_6H_5)_3P$ triphenylphosphine

$NH_2CH_2CH_2NH_2$ ethylenediamine

However, following neutral ligands are named as below and not as molecule.

H_2O aquo	CO carbonyl
NH_3 ammine	NO nitrosyl

(b) The name of negative ligands end in —O, *e.g.*

Cl^- chloro	NO_2^- nitro
NH_2^- amido	ONO^- nitrito
SO_4^{2-} sulphato	OH^- hydroxo
NH^{2-} imido	$C_2O_4^{2-}$ oxalato
NO_3^- nitrato	CO_3^{2-} carbonato

(c) The names of positive ligands end in -ium, *e.g.*

NO_2^+ nitronium $\quad NO^+$ nitrosonium

(ii) If there are several ligands in the coordination sphere, these are listed in alphabetical order. In case, simple ligands like chloro, nitro, amido, ammine, aquo, etc. are present more than once, their number is indicated by the prefixes : di-, tri-, tetra- etc. On the other hand the number of other ligands which already have prefixes, di-, tri-, etc. in their names, as ethylenediamine, is indicated by the prefixes bis-, tris, tetrakis- etc.

When ligands are listed alphabetically, spellings (alphabet) of their proper names are taken into consideration and not the spellings of the prefixes di-, tri-, etc. Thus, di-amine should be listed under '*a*' and not under '*d*'.

(iii) When the coordination sphere is either a cation or a neutral molecule, the name of the central atom remains as such and the oxidation state of the metal is shown by Roman numeral in bracket immediately following the name of the metal. For example:

$\left[Co(NH_3)_6\right]Cl_3$ Hexamminecobalt (III) chloride

$\left[Cr(H_2O)_4Cl_2\right]Cl$ Tetraquodichlorochromium (III) chloride

$\left[Pt(NH_3)_2Cl_4\right]$

Diamminetetrachloroplatinum (IV)

$\left[Co(NH_3)_3Cl_3\right]$

Triamminetrichlorocobalt (III)

When the coordination sphere is an anion, the name of the metal ends in -ate, the oxidation state is then indicated in the last by the Roman numeral in bracket. For example:

$K_3\left[Co(NO_2)_6\right]$ Potassium hexanitrocobaltate (III)

$Na_3[Fe(CN)_5NO]$ Sodium pentacyanonitrosylferrate (III)

$K_3[Fe(CN)_5CO]$ Potassium carbonyl pentacyanoferrate (II)

Note that whole of coordination sphere is written as one word, *i.e.* without any space throughout.

Illustration of IUPAC Nomenclature of complexes:

$[Cu(NH_3)_4]^{2+}$ Tetramminecopper (II) ion

$[PtCl_2(NH_3)_2]$ Diamminedichloroplatinum (II)

$K[Ag(CN)_2]$ Potassium dicyanoargentate (I)

$[Cr(en)_3]Cl_3$ Tris-(ethylenediamine)-chromium (III) -chloride

$Na_3[Fe(CN)_5(NO)]$ Sodium pentacyanonitrosyl ferrate (II)

OBJECTIVE QUESTIONS

1. The number of ions formed when cuprammonium sulphate is dissolved in water is
A. 1 B. 2
C. 4 D. Zero

2. Ligands in a complex salt are
A. Anions linked by coordinate bonds to a central metal atom or ion
B. Cations linked by coordinate bonds to a central metal atom or ion
C. Molecules linked by coordinate bonds to a central metal atom or ion
D. Ions or molecules linked by coordinate bonds to a central atom or ion

3. A group of atoms can function as a ligand only when
A. It is a small molecule
B. It has unshared electron pair
C. It is negatively charged ion
D. It is positively charged ion

4. Which of the following is a hexadentate ligand?
A. 2, 2-Dipyridyl
B. Ethylenediamine
C. Ethylenediamine tetracetate ion
D. None of the above

5. $K_4[Fe(CN)_6]$ is called
A. Potassium hexacyanoferrate (II)
B. Potassium ferricyanide
C. Potassium hexacyanoferrate
D. Prussian blue

6. The atomic number of copper is 29, its EAN in $[Cu(NH_3)_4]^{2+}$ is
A. 35 B. 36
C. 49 D. 40

7. The valency of Cr in the complex $[Cr(H_2O)_4Cl_2]^+$ is
A. 3 B. 1
C. 6 D. 5

8. The oxidation number of Pt is $[Pt(C_2H_4)Cl_3]^-$ is
A. +1 B. +2
C. +3 D. +4

9. Among the following ions, which one has the highest paramagnetism?
A. $[Cr(H_2O)_6]^{3+}$ B. $[Fe(H_2O)_6]^{2+}$
C. $[Cu(H_2O)_6]^{2+}$ D. $[Zn(H_2O)_6]^{2+}$

10. Which one of the following is expected to be a paramagnetic complex?
A. $[Ni(H_2O)_6]^{2+}$ B. $[Ni(CO)_4]$
C. $[Zn(NH_3)_4]^{2+}$ D. $[Co(NH_3)_6]$

11. The compound which does not show paramagnetism is
A. $[Cu(NH_3)_4]Cl_2$ B. $[Ag(NH_3)_2]Cl$
C. NO D. NO_2

12. Amongst $Ni(CO)_4$, $[Ni(CN)_4]^{2-}$ and $[NiCl_4]^{2-}$
A. $Ni(CO)_4$ and $[NiCl_4]^{2-}$ are diamagnetic

B. $[NiCl_4]^{2}$ and $[Ni(CN)_4]^{2-}$ are diamagnetic
C. $Ni(CO)_4$ and $[Ni(CN)_4]^{2-}$ are diamagnetic
D. $Ni(CO)_4$ is diamagnetic

13. Identify the complexes which are expected to be coloured
A. $[Ti(NO_3)_4]$
B. $[Cu(NC)(CH_3)_4]^+ BF_4^-$
C. $[Cr(NH_3)_6]^{3+} 3Cl^-$
D. $K_3[VF_6]$
E. (C) and (D)

14. $[Co(NH_3)_4Cl_2]NO_2$ and $[CO(NH_3)_4Cl.NO_2]Cl$ are isomers of which type
A. Geometrical B. Optical
C. Linkage D. Ionization

15. Hypo is used in photography because it is
A. A strong oxidising agent
B. A strong reducing agent
C. A strong complexing agent
D. None of the above

16. AgCl dissolves in NH_4OH due to the formation of
A. $[Ag(NH_4)_2]Cl$ B. $[Ag(NH_4)_3]Cl$
C. $[Ag(NH_3)_2]Cl$ D. $[Ag(NH_3)_2OH]$

17. The metal hydroxide which is soluble in excess of ammonium hydroxide is
A. $Fe(OH)_2$ B. $Fe(OH)_3$
C. $Al(OH)_3$ D. $Cu(OH)_2$

18. The most probable formula of prussian blue is
A. $Fe_3[Fe(CN)_6]_2$ B. $Fe_2[Fe(CN)_6]_3$
C. $Fe_4[Fe(CN)_6]_3$ D. $Fe_3[Fe(CN)_6]_4$

19. The formula of sodium nitroprusside is
A. $Na_4[Fe(CN)_5NOS]$
B. $Na_2[Fe(CN)_5NO]$
C. $NaFe[Fe(CN)_6]$
D. $Na_2[Fe(CN)_6NO_2]$

20. Trunbull's blue is
A. Ferricyanide B. Ferrous ferrocyanide
C. Ferrous cyanide D. Ferriferrocyanide

21. Tollen's reagent is
A. $[Ag(NH_3)_2]^+$ B. Ag_2O
C. $[Cu(OH)_4]^{2-}$ D. Cu_2O

22. Prussian blue is formed when
A. Ferrous sulphate reacts with $FeCl_3$
B. Ferric sulphate reacts with $K_4[Fe(CN)_6]$
C. Ferrous ammonium sulphate reacts with $FeCl_3$
D. Ammonium sulphate reacts with $FeCl_3$

23. The number of ligands attached to the central atom is termed the .... of the central atom.
A. Oxidation number
B. Coordination number
C. Effective atomic number
D. Hybridization number

24. Which of the following have square-planar structures?
A. $[Ni(CN)_4]^{2-}$ B. $[NiCl_4]^{2-}$
C. $[Cu(NH_3)_4]^{2+}$ D. $Ni(CO)_4$

25. Cu^{2+} is
A. sp^3-hybridized B. sp^3d-hybridized
C. dsp^2-hybridized D. sp^3d^2-hybridized

26. Which of the following have a tetrahedral geometry?
A. $[Ni(CN)_4]^{2-}$ B. $Fe(CO)_5$
C. $[Cu(NH_3)_4]^{2+}$ D. $[Co(NH_3)_6]^{3+}$

27. Which of the following is/are bidentate ligands?
A. SCN^-
B. $H_2NCH_2—CH_2NH_2$
C. $H_2N–CH_2–CH_2–NH–CH_2–CH_2–NH_2$
D. All of the above

28. Dimethylglyoxime is an example of a
A. Monodentate ligand
B. Bidentate ligand
C. Tridentate ligand
D. Hexadentate ligand

29. Which of the following oxide is neutral?
A. CO B. SiO_2
C. CO_2 D. ZnO

30. Which of the following will produce a white precipitate upon reacting with $AgNO_3$?
A. $[Co(NH_2)_6]Cl_3$ B. $[Co(NH_3)_3Cl_3]$
C. $K_2[Pt(en)_2Cl_2]$ D. $[Fe(en)_3]Cl_3$
E. (A) and (D)

31. In which of the following does the central atom exhibit an oxidation state of 3?
A. $K[Ni(CN)_4]$
B. $K_4[Fe(CN)_6]$
C. $[Ni(CO_4)]$
D. $[Co(NO_3)_2(Py)_2(NH_3)_2]NO_3$
E. (A) and (B)

32. The central atom has a coordination number of 6 in
A. $[Fe(C_2O_4)_3]^{3-}$
B. $[Ag(CN)_2]^-$
C. $[Co(NH_3)_4Cl_2]Cl$
D. (A) and (C)

33. In which of the following does Fe have an oxidation number of 3?
A. $[Fe(C_2O_4)_3]^{3-}$ B. $[Fe(CN)_6]^{3-}$
C. $K_4[Fe(CN)_6]$ D. (A) and (B)

34. Which of the following compound is pink?
A. $CoCl_3.5NH_3.H_2O$
B. $CoCl_3.6NH_3$
C. $CoCl_3.5NH_3$
D. $CoCl_3.4NH_3$

35. The oxidation state and coordination number cobalt in the $CoCl_3.5NH_3$ complex are, respectively
A. 3 and 6 B. 6 and 3
C. 6 and 2 D. 5 and 3

36. The total number of ions in a solution of complex is five. The complex can be
A. $[Pt(NH_3)_5Cl]Cl_3$
B. $[Pt(NH_3)_4Cl_2]Cl_2$
C. $[Pt(NH_3)_6]Cl_4$
D. $[Pt(NH_3)_2Cl_4]$

37. Which of the following pairs are coordination isomers?
A. $[Co(NH_3)_5Br]SO_4$ and $[Co(NH_3)_5SO_4]Br$
B. $[Co(en)_2(H_2O)Cl]Cl_2$ and $[Co(en_2)Cl_2]Cl.H_2O$
C. $[Co(NH_3)_6][Cr(CN)_6]$ and $Cr(NH_3)_6][Co(CN)_6]$
D. $[Co(NH_3)_5(NO_2)]Cl_2$ and $[Co(NH_3)_5(ONO)]Cl_2$

38. $[Co(NH_3)_5CO_3]Cl$ and $[Co(NH_3)_5Cl]CO_3$ are
A. Optical isomers
B. Ionization isomers
C. Geometrical isomers
D. Coordination isomers

39. The IUPAC name of $K_2[Ni(CN)_4]$ is
A. Nickel tetracyanokalium (I)
B. Potassium tetracyanonickelate (II)
C. Tetracyanonickelkalium (I)
D. Potassium nickel tetracyanide

40. A complex involving sp^3d^2-hybridization has
A. Tetrahedral geometry
B. Square planar geometry
C. Octahedral geometry
D. Trigonal geometry

41. The stabilities of coordination compounds containing the ions Cu^{2+}, Ni^{2+}, Co^{2+}, Fe^{2+} and Mn^{2+} follow the order.
A. $Mn^{2+} > Fe^{2+} > Co^{2+} > Ni^{2+} > Cu^{2+}$
B. $Ni^{2+} > Cu^{2+} > Fe^{2+} > Co^{2+} > Mn^{2+}$
C. $Cu^{2+} > Ni^{2+} > Co^{2+} > Fe^{2+} > Mn^{2+}$
D. $Fe^{2+} > Mn^{2+} > Ni^{2+} > Co^{2+} > Cu^{2+}$

42. Which of the following are π - bonded organometallic compounds?
A. Ferrocene
B. Diethyl zinc
C. Ethylmagnesium iodide
D. (A) and (D)

43. Which of the following are paramagnetic and have tetrahedral geometry?
A. $[Ni(CO)_4]$ B. $[NiCl_4]^{2-}$
C. $[Ni(CN)_4]^{2-}$ D. None of the above

44. The IUPAC name of $[Co(NH_3)_5ONO]Cl_2$ is
A. Nitrito penta amine cobalt (III) chloride
B. Nitrito amino cobalt chloride
C. Penta amine nitrito cobalt (III) chloride
D. Amino nitrito cobalt chloride

45. A coordination compound of platinum chloride and ammonia gives a white precipitate with

$AgNO_3$, and on ionization gives four ions. Its formula is

A. $[Pt(NH_3)_2Cl_4]$

B. $[Pt(NH_3)_3Cl]Cl_3$

C. $[Pt(NH_3)_4Cl_2]Cl_2$

D. $[Pt(NH_3)_3Cl_3]Cl$

46. Diethylene triamine is

A. Chelating agent B. Polydentate ligand

C. Tridentate ligand D. All of the above

47. The IUPAC name of $[Cr(NH_3)_4Cl_2]NO_3$ is

A. Tetramino dichloro chromium nitrate

B. Tetramino dichloro chromium (III) nitrate

C. Dichloro tetra ammine chromium (III) nitrate

D. Tetra amino dichloro chromium (II) nitrate

48. The number of isomers possible for square planar complex $K_2[PdClBr_2SCN]$ is

A. 2 B. 3

C. 4 D. 6

49. The colour of $FeSO_4.(NH_4)_2SO_4.6H_2O$ is

A. Red B. White

C. Green D. Blue

50. According to effective atomic number rule, the central metal acquires

A. Inert gas configuration

B. Duplet

C. Octet

D. Quartet

51. The groups satisfying the secondary valencies of a cation in a complex are called

A. Ligands B. Radicals

C. Primary valencies D. None

52. Complex forming tendency increases with

A. Increase in size of cation

B. Decrease in size of cation

C. Increase in size of anion

D. None

53. EAN of Cr in $[Cr(NH_3)_6]Cl_3$ is

A. 32 B. 33

C. 34 D. 35

54. Exchange of co-ordination group by a water molecule in complex molecule results in

A. Ionisation isomerism

B. Ligand isomerism

C. Hydration isomerism

D. Geometrical isomerism

55. $[Cr(H_2O)_6]^{3+}$ ion has *d*-electrons equal to

A. 2 B. 3

C. 4 D. 5

56. An imperfect complex of a complex compound is 100% ionised, the compound is called

A. Double salt B. Complex salt

C. Acid salt D. Normal salt

57. Addition of KI to HgI_2 forms complex $K_2[HgI_4]$ having

A. Red colour B. Blue colour

C. Violet colour D. Colourless nature

58. If a compound absorbs violet colour from the sunlight, then the observed colour is

A. Yellow B. Orange

C. Blue D. Green

59. The coordination number of Cu in copper ammonium sulphate is

A. 2 B. 3

C. 1 D. 4

60. Which ligand is expected to be bidentate?

A. $C_2O_4^{2-}$ B. $CH_3C\equiv N$

C. Br^- D. CH_3NH_2

61. Which complex is likely to show optical activity?

A. Trans-$[Co(NH_3)_4Cl_2]^+$

B. $[Cr(H_2O)_6]^{3+}$

C. Cis $[Co(NH_3)_2(en)_2]^{3+}$

D. Trans $[Co(NH_3)_2(en)_2]^{3+}$

62. Pick a poor electrolytic conductor complex in solution

A. $K_2[PtCl_6]$ B. $[Co(NH_3)_3](NO_2)_3$

C. $K_4[Fe(CN)_6]$ D. $[Co(NH_3)_4]SO_4$

63. Oxidation number of Fe in $K_3[Fe(CN)_6]$ is

A. +3 B. +2

C. +10 D. 1

64. Glycinato ligand is

A. $CH_2 \langle^{\ddot{N}H_2}_{COO^-}$

B. Bidentate ligand

C. Two donar sites N and O^-

D. All

65. Which is not a π-bonded complex

A. Zeise salt

B. Ferrocene

C. Dibenzene chromium

D. Tetraethyl lead

66. In haemoglobin, the iron shows oxidation state

A. +2 B. +3

C. +1 D. +4

67. The number of ions formed when copper ammonium sulphate is dissolved in water is

A. 1 B. 2

C. 4 D. Zero

68. The brown ring complex compound is formulated as $[Fe(H_2O)_5NO]SO_4$. The oxidation state of Fe is

A. +1 B. +2

C. +3 D. 0

69. The number of *d*-electrons of Cr (Z = 24) in $[Cr(H_2O)_6]^{3+}$ ion is

A. 2 B. 3

C. 4 D. 5

70. The oxidation state of Mo in its oxo-complex species $[Mo_2O_4(C_2H_4)_2(H_2O)_2]^{2-}$ is

A. +2 B. +3

C. +4 D. +5

71. A complex shown below can exhibit

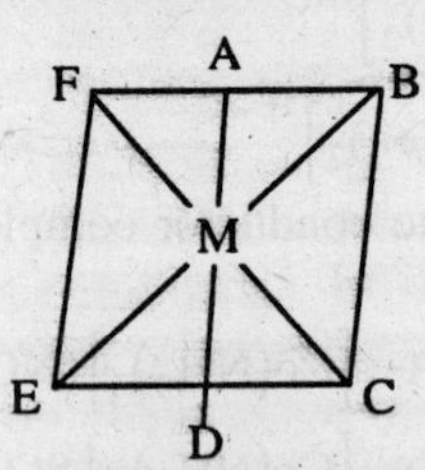

A. Optical isomerism only

B. Geometrical isomerism only

C. Both (A) and (B)

D. None

72. Which of the following compounds is not coloured?

A. $Na_2[CuCl_4]$ B. $Na_2[CdCl_4]$

C. $K_4[Fe(CN)_6]$ D. $K_3[Fe(CN)_6]$

73. Magnetic moment of $[Ag(CN)_2]^-$ is zero. How many unpaired electrons are there?

A. Zero B. 4

C. 3 D. 1

74. The hardness of water is estimated by

A. Conductivity method

B. EDTA method

C. Titrimetric method

D. Distillation method

75. K_3CoF_6 is high spin complex. What is the hybrid state of Co atom in this complex?

A. sp^3d B. sp^3d^2

C. d^2sp^3 D. dsp^2

76. A complex of cobalt has five ammonia molecule, one nitro group and two chlorine atoms for each cobalt atom. One mole of this compound produces three moles ions in aqueous solution which on treating with excess of $AgNO_3$ give two mole of AgCl. The formula of the compound is

A. $[Co(NH_3)_4NO_2Cl][(NH_3)Cl]$

B. $[Co(NH_3)_5Cl][ClNO_2]$

C. $[Co(NH_3)_5NO_2]Cl_2$

D. $[Co(NH_3)_5][(NO_2)_2Cl_2]$

77. In lithium tetrahydroaluminate, the ligand is

A. Al^+ B. H

C. H^- D. None

78. In which of the following compounds does the central atom obey EAN rule?

A. $K_3Fe(CN)_6$ B. $K_4Fe(CN)_6$

C. $Cu(NH_3)_4SO_4$ D. All

79. The formula of dichlorobis (urea) copper (II) is

A. $[Cu(O=C(NH_2)_2)]Cl_2$

B. $[CuCl_2\{O=C(NH_2)\}]$

C. $[Cu\{O=C(NH_2)_2\}Cl]Cl$

D. $[CuCl_2][O=C(NH_2)_2]H_2$

80. Out of the following, the metal which forms poly-nuclear carbonyl is

A. Na B. Mg
C. Mn D. All

81. Name the metal M which is extracted on the basis of following reactions

$$4M + 8CN^- + 2H_2O + O_2 \rightarrow 4[M(CN)_2]^- + 4OH^-$$
$$2[M(CN_2)]^- + Zn \rightarrow [Zn(CN)_4]^{2-} + 2M$$

A. Nickel B. Silver
C. Copper D. Mercury

82. If NH_4OH is added to the $(PtCl_4)^{2-}$ ion, the complex formed represents

A. Zero dipole B. Finite dipole
C. Infinite dipole D. All of the above

83. The possible number of isomers for the complex $[MCl_2Br_2]\ SO_4$ is

A. 1 B. 2
C. 4 D. 5

84. The number of *d*-electrons in $\left[Cr(H_2O)_6\right]^{3+}$ is

A. 2 B. 4
C. 3 D. 5

85. $Fe_2(CO)_9$ is diamagnetic. Which of the following reasons is correct?

A. Presence of one CO as bridge group
B. Presence of monodentate ligand
C. Metal metal (Fe-Fe) bond in molecule
D. Resonance hybridisation of CO

86. The geometry of $Ni(CO)_4$ and $Ni(PPH_3)_2Cl_2$ are

A. Both square planar
B. Tetrahedral and square planar respectively
C. Both tetrahedral
D. Square planar and tetrahedral respectively

87. Which of the following represents a chelating ligand?

A. Cl^- B. DMG
C. OH^- D. H_2O

88. Which of the following will be able to show cis-trans isomerism?

A. MA_3B B. $M(AA^1)_2$
C. MA_2BCD D. MA_4

(AA^1 : is unsymmetrical bidentate ligand. ABCD are unidentate ligand.)

89. $\left[(C_6H_5)_2Pd(SCN)_2\right]$ and $\left[(C_6H_5)_2Pd(NCS)_2\right]$ are

A. Linkage isomers
B. Co-ordination isomers
C. Ionisation isomers
D. Geometrical isomers

90. The co-ordination number and oxidation number of X in the following compound $\left[X(SO_4)(NH_3)_5\right]Cl$ will be

A. 10 and + 3 B. 2 and + 6
C. 6 and + 3 D. 6 and + 4

91. The IUPAC name of $K_2[Zn(OH)_4]$ is

A. Potassium tetrahydroxy zinc (II)
B. Potassium tetrahydroxy zincate (II)
C. Potassium tetrahydroxy zincate (VI)
D. Potassium hydroxy zinc (II)

92. The correct IUPAC name of the complex

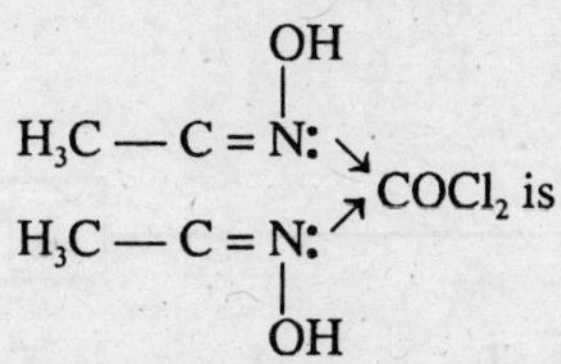

A. Dichlorodimethylglyoximato cobalt (II)
B. Bis (dimethylglyoxime) dichloro cobalt (II)
C. Dimethylglyoxime cobalt (II) chloride
D. Dichloromethyl glyoxime—N, N-cobalt (II)

93. The correct name of 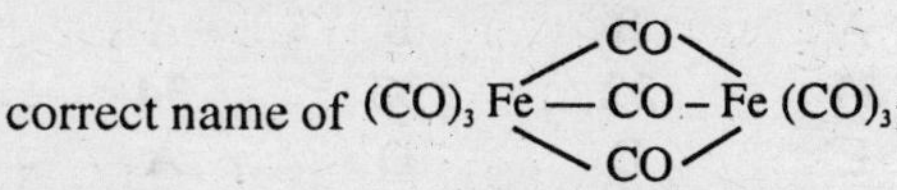

A. Tri-μ carbonyl bis (tricarbonyl) iron (0)
B. Hexacarbonyl iron (III) μ-tricarbonyl ferrate (0)
C. Tricarbonyl iron (0) μ-tricarbonyl iron (0) tricarbonyl
D. Nonacarbonyl iron

94. Lithium tetrahydridoaluminate is correctly repre-sented as

A. $Al[LiH_4]$ B. $Al_2[LiH_4]_3$
C. $Li[AlH_4]$ D. $Li[AlH_4]_2$

95. The two complexes given below are :

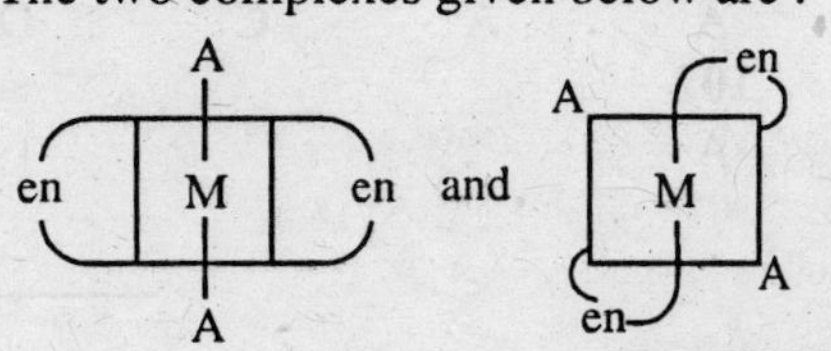

A. Geometrical isomers
B. Position isomers
C. Optical isomers
D. Identical

96. Hexafluoroferrate (III) ion is an outer orbital complex. The number of unpaired electrons present in it is
A. 1 B. 5
C. 4 D. unpredictable

97. K_3CoF_6 is high spin complex. What is the hybrid state of Co atom in this complex?
A. sp^3d B. sp^3d^2
C. d^2sp^3 D. dsp^2

98. Geometrical isomerism is found in co-ordination compounds having co-ordination number
A. 2 B. 3
C. 4 (tetrahedral) D. 6

99. Cis-trans isomerism is found in square planar complexes of the molecular formula (*a* and *b* are monodentate ligands)
A. Ma_4 B. Ma_3b
C. Ma_2b_2 D. Mab_3

100. A reagent used for identifying nickel ion is
A. Potassium ferrocyanide
B. Phenophthalein
C. Dimethyl glyoxime
D. EDTA

101. In the complex $Fe(CO)_x$, the value of *x* is
A. 3 B. 4
C. 5 D. 6

102. In solid $CuSO_4.5H_2O$ copper is co-ordinated to
A. 4 water molecules
B. 5 water molecules
C. One sulphate molecule
D. One water molecule

ANSWERS

1	2	3	4	5	6	7	8	9	10
B	B	B	C	A	A	A	B	B	A
11	12	13	14	15	16	17	18	19	20
B	C	E	D	C	C	D	C	B	B
21	22	23	24	25	26	27	28	29	30
A	B	B	A	C	C	B	B	A	E
31	32	33	34	35	36	37	38	39	40
E	D	D	A	A	C	C	B	B	C
41	42	43	44	45	46	47	48	49	50
C	E	B	C	B	D	C	C	C	A
51	52	53	54	55	56	57	58	59	60
A	B	B	C	B	A	D	A	B	A
61	62	63	64	65	66	67	68	69	70
C	D	A	D	D	A	B	A	B	B
71	72	73	74	75	76	77	78	79	80
A	B	A	B	B	C	C	B	B	C
81	82	83	84	85	86	87	88	89	90
B	B	D	B	C	B	B	C	A	C
91	92	93	94	95	96	97	98	99	100
A	A	A	C	D	B	B	D	C	C
101	102								
C	A								

14

Hydrocarbons: Alkanes, Alkenes and Alkynes, Aromatic Hydrocarbons

Homologous Series

"A homologous series is a series of compounds in which adjacent members differ by a CH_2 unit". The individual members are called 'Homologs'.

The general characteristics of a homologous series are :

1. All compounds in the series contain the same elements and the functional group.
2. All compounds in the series can be represented by a general formula.
3. The molecular formula of such homolog differs from one *above* and one *below* it by a CH_2 unit.
4. All compounds in the series can be prepared by similar methods.
5. All compounds in the series have similar chemical properties.
6. There is a gradual variation in physical properties with increasing molecular weight.

Example : The homologous series of alcohols can be represented as :

General formula is ROH or $C_nH_{2n+1}OH$

n	*R*	*Formula*
1	CH_3^-	CH_3OH
2	$CH_3CH_2^-$	CH_3CH_2OH
3	$CH_3CH_2CH_2^-$	$CH_3CH_2CH_2OH$
4	$CH_3CH_2CH_2CH_2^-$	$CH_3CH_2CH_2CH_2OH$
5	$CH_3CH_2CH_2CH_2CH_2^-$	$CH_3CH_2CH_2CH_2OH$

Isomerism

"Compounds having the same molecular formula but differing from each other in physical or chemical properties are called *isomers* and this phenomenon is called *isomerism*. Isomerism is of two main types.

(A) Structural isomerism.

(B) Stereo isomerism.

(A) Structural Isomerism : When the isomerism is due to difference in the arrangement of atoms within the molecule, without any reference to space, the phenomenon is called 'Structural Isomerism'. In other words, "Structural isomers are the compounds that have the same molecular formula but different structural formulas". Structural isomerism is of five types.

(*i*) Chain Isomerism.

(*ii*) Position Isomerism.

(*iii*) Functional Isomerism

(*iv*) Metamerism.

(*v*) Tautomerism.

(i) Chain isomerism : "Chain isomers have the same molecular formula but differ in the order in which the carbon atoms are bonded to each other".

Example 1 : *n*-Butane & Isobutane

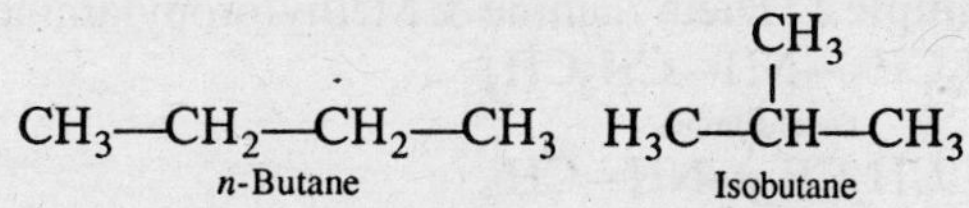

n-Butane Isobutane

Example 2 : 2-Methylbutane & 2,2 Dimethyl propane.

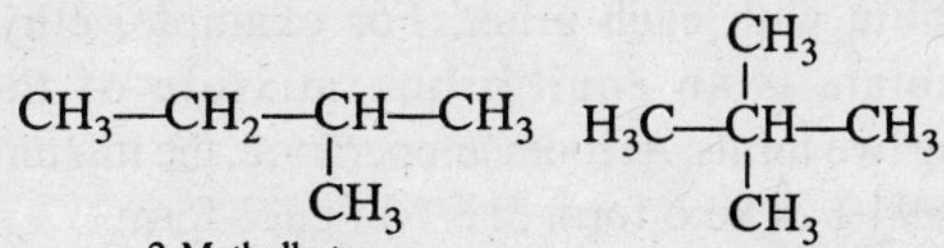

2-Methylbutane 2,2-Dimethylpropane

(ii) Position isomerism : "Position isomers have the same molecular formula but differ in the position of a functional group on the carbon chain".

Example 1 : *n*-Propyl alcohol & Isopropyl alcohol.

$CH_3—CH_2—CH_2—OH$ (*n*-Propyl alcohol) $H_3C—CH(OH)—CH_3$ (Isopropyl alcohol)

Example 2 : 1-Butene & 2-Butene.

$CH_3CH_2CH{=}CH_2$ (1-Butane) $CH_3CH{=}CHCH_2$ (2-Butane)

Example 3 : o-Dichlorobenzene & *m*-Dichlorobenzene

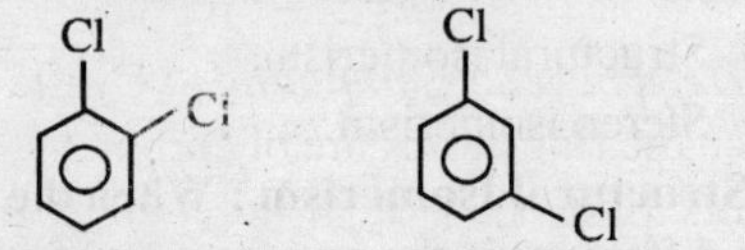

o - Dichloro benzene m - Dichloro benzene

(iii) Functional isomerism : "Functional isomers have the same molecular formula but different functional groups".

Example 1 : Ethyl acohol & Dimethyl ether

CH_3CH_2OH (Ethyl alcohol) $H_3C—O—CH_3$ (Dimethyl ether)

Example 2 : Acetic acid & Methyl formate.

$H_3C—C(=O)—OH$ (Acetic acid) $H—C(=O)—CH_3$ (Methyl formate)

(iv) Metamerism : This type of isomerism is due to unequal distribution group. Members belong to the same homologous series.

Example 1 : Diethyl ether & Methyl propyl ether.

$CH_3CH_2—O—CH_2CH_3$ (Diethyl ether) $CH_3—O—CH_2CH_2CH_3$ (Methyl propyl ether)

Example 2 : Diethylamine & Methylpropylamine.

$CH_3CH_2—NH—CH_2CH_3$ (Diethylamine)

$CH_3CH_2CH_2—NH—CH_3$ (Methylpropylamine)

(v) Tautomerism : It is a special type of functional isomerism in which the isomers are in dynamic equilibrium with each other. For example, ethyl acetoacetate is an equilibrium mixture of the following two forms. At room temperature, the mixture contains 94% of keto form & 6% of enol-form.

$$CH_3—C(=O)—CH_2COOC_2H_5 \rightleftharpoons CH_3—C(OH)=CH—COOC_2H_5$$

Keto form Enol form

(B) Stereo Isomerism : When isomerism is caused by the different arrangements of atoms or groups in space, the phenomenon is called 'Stereoisomerism', "The stereoisomers have the same structural formulas but differ in arrangement of atoms in space". *i.e.* they differ in configuration. (The term refers to the three dimensional arrangement of atoms that characterise a particular compound). Stereoisomerism is of two types:

(i) Geometrical or *cis-trans* Isomerism.

(ii) Optical Isomerism.

(i) Geometrical isomerism : When two carbon atoms of a compound, containing two different atoms or groups are linked by a double bond the independent rotation of the carbon atoms is not possible and position of groups or atoms becomes fixed in the space.

This type of isomerism arises due to the presence of a double bond about which there is no free rotation, is called geometrical isomerism and the compounds showing this type of isomerism are known as *cis*–trans isomers.

This also, results from a restriction in rotation about single bonds in cyclic compounds.

Examples :

$H—C—COOH \;\|\; H—C—COOH$ — Maleic acid (*cis*-form)

$HOOC—C—H \;\|\; H—C—COOH$ — Fumatic acid (*trans*-form)

$CH_3—C—H \;\|\; CH_3—C—H$ — Butene-2 (*cis*-form)

$CH_3—C—H \;\|\; H—C—CH_3$ — Butene-2 (*trans*-form)

Oximes also show *cis-trans* isomers as.

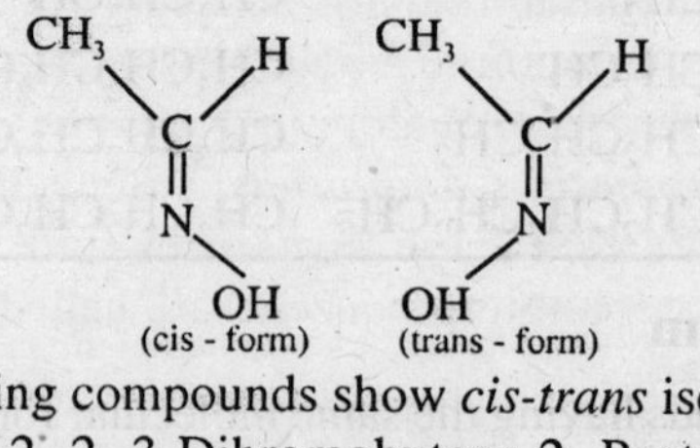

(cis - form) (trans - form)

Following compounds show *cis-trans* isomerism. Butene-2, 2, 3-Dibromobutene-2, Pentene-2, 1-Chloropentene-1, Hexene-2.

Generally, the geometrical isomer which undergoes the process of cyclisation easily on heating is *cis* form while other is *trans* form.

The dipole moment of *cis* form is always higher than that of *trans* form. The trans isomer of some alkene derivatives have zero dipole moment. *Cis*-isomers have low melting point and high boiling point and they are soluble in water due to their dipole moments. The trans isomers have high melting points and low boiling points and they are sparingly soluble in water.

IUPAC Nomenclature

There are 3 million organic compounds: In dealing with such a large number of compounds some classification is essential. There are five main types of organic compounds:

(i) Aliphatic Compounds : Compounds which consist of open chain of carbon atoms are called aliphatic compounds. There is no limit to the number of atoms involved.

Examples are :

Ethane	$CH_3—CH_3$
Propane	$CH_3—CH_2—CH_3$
Ethyl alcohol	$CH_3—CH_2—OH$
Acetic Acid	$CH_3—COOH$
n-Butylamine	$CH_3—CH_2—CH_2—CH_2—NH_2$

(ii) Saturated and Unsaturated Compounds : Compounds which contain only carbon and hydrogen are called Hydrocarbons. A hydrocarbon is said to be saturated if it contains only C—C single bonds. A hydrocarbon is said to be *unsaturated* if it contains C═C or C ≡ C multiple bonds.

Examples are :

Ethane	$CH_3—CH_3$	(saturated)
Ethylene	$CH_2 = CH_2$	(unsaturated)
Acetylene	$HC \equiv CH$	(unsaturated)

The term unsaturation is also sometimes used to describe a compound containing multiple bonds between other pairs of atoms, *e.g.* C═O, C ≡ N.

(iii) Aromatic Compounds : Benzene and all compounds that have structures and chemical properties resembling benzene are called aromatic compounds.

Examples are :

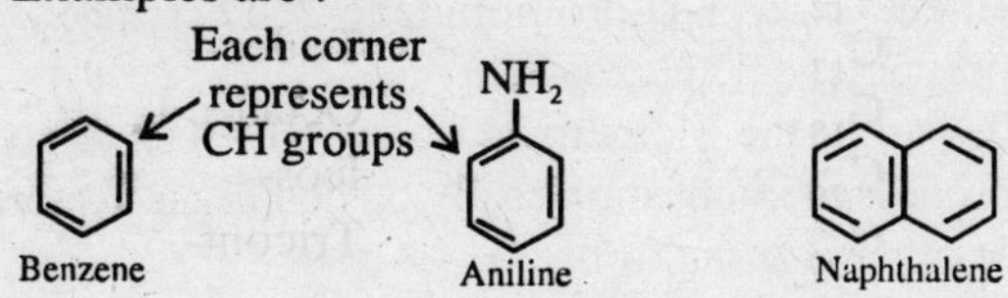

(iv) Alicyclic Compounds : Cyclic compounds which consists only of carbon atoms are called alicyclic or carbocyclic compounds. Examples are :

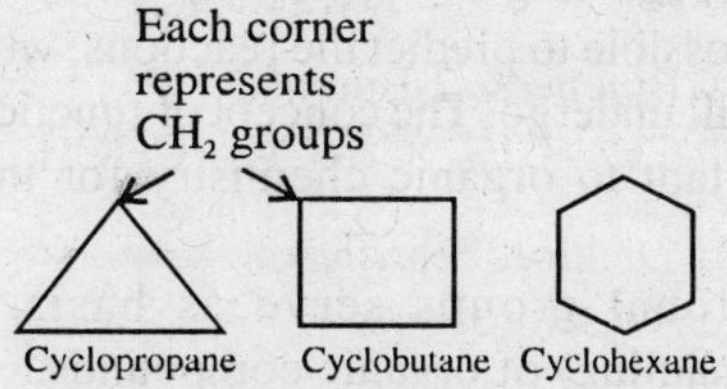

(v) Heterocyclic Compounds : Cyclic compounds in which the ring atoms are of carbon and some other elements like N, S or O are called heterocyclic compounds. Examples are :

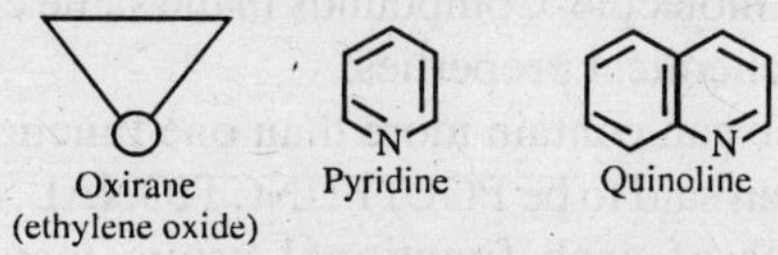

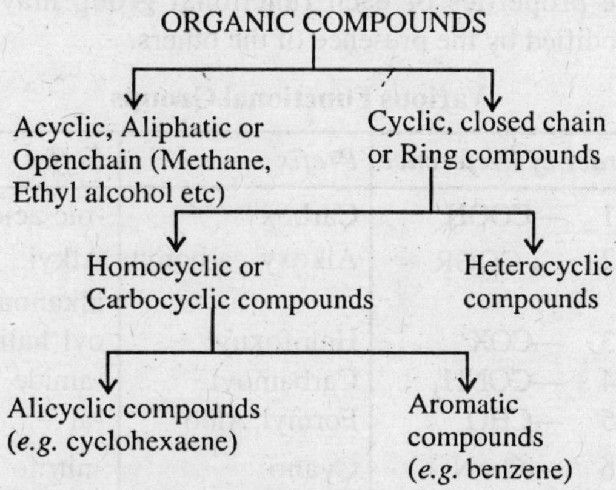

Functional Group Concept : "A functional group is an atom or group of atoms in a molecule that gives the molecule its characteristic chemical properties". Double and Triple bonds are functional groups, other examples are given below. It should be remembered that the functional group is the **action group**. The hydrocarbon portion remains inert.

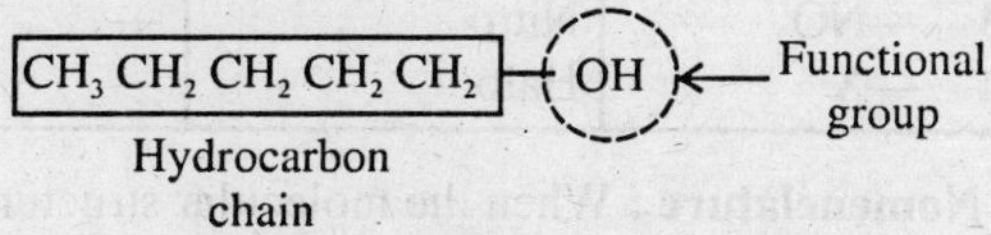

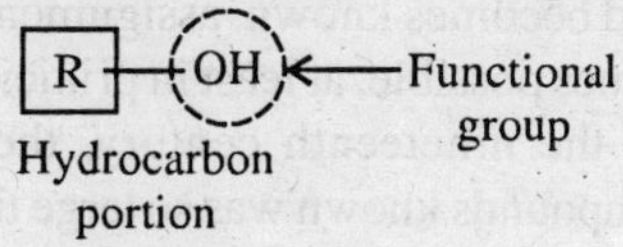

R- is used to represent the hydrocarbon portion to which the functional group is attached.

Each functional group undergoes characteristic reactions. By recognising the functional group in a molecule, it is possible to predict the reactions, which that molecule will undergo. The concept of functional group is important to organic chemistry for three reasons.

(a) Functional groups serve as basis for nomenclature (naming) of organic compounds.

(b) Functional groups serve to classify organic compounds into classes/families. All compounds with the same functional group belong to the same class.

(c) A functional group is a site of chemical reactivity in a molecule. Compounds in the same class have similar chemical properties.

A molecule can contain more than one functional group. It is then said to be POLYFUNCTIONAL, and the properties of each functional group may be modified by the presence of the others.

Various Functional Groups

Order of Preference	*Prefix*	*Suffix*
1 —COOH	Carboxy	-oic acid
2 →COOR	Alkoxy carbonyl	Alkyl alkanoate
3 —COX	Halofoxnyl	oyl halide
4 $—CONH_2$	Carbamoyl	-amide
5 —CHO	Formyl, Aldo	-al
6 —C≡N	Cyano	-nitrile
7 •C═O	Keto, Oxo	-one
8 —OH	Hydroxy	-ol
9 $—NH_2$	Amino	-amine
10 >C═C	—	-ene
11 —C≡C—	—	-yne
12 —O—	Epoxy	—
13 $—NO_2$	Nitro	—
14 —X	Halo	—

Nomenclature : When the molecular structure of a compound becomes known, assignment of a logical name becomes possible, at least in priniciple. Towards the end of the nineteenth century, the number of organic compounds known was so large that it became difficult to remember individual names of the organic compounds. In order to rationalise the system of nomenclature, an international congress of chemists was held in *Geneva* in 1892. It led to the development of comprehensive system of nomenclature known as *Geneva System.* There was further improvement in *Geneva System* in 1931 by *International Union of Chemists.* The improved system was known as *IUC System.* The IUC System was futher revised by 'International Union of Pure and Applied Chemistry' in the light of practical difficulties. This system of nomenclature was accepted all over the world and is known as IUPAC System of nomenclature.

1. *Nomenclature of aliphatic compounds :* According to IUPAC system, the name of organic compounds, in general, comprises of the following constituents :

(a) Word root
(b) Primary suffix
(c) Secondary suffix
(d) Prefix

(a) Word Root : The word root represents the number of carbon atoms in the parent chain. The parent chain in the compound is selected by applying certain rules. For chain up to four carbon atoms special word roots are used, but for the chains having more than four carbon atoms, Greek numerals are used. The general word root for different aliphatic compounds is *alk.* The word root for different lengths of carbon chains are given below :

Chain Length	*Word Root*
C_1	Meth-
C_2	Eth-
C_3	Prop-
C_4	But-
C_5	Pent-
C_6	Hex-
C_7	Hept-
C_8	OCl-
C_9	Non-
C_{10}	Dec-
C_{11}	Undec-
C_{12}	Dodec-
C_{13}	Tridec-
C_{18}	Octadec-
C_{20}	Icos-
C_{30}	Tricont-

(b) Primary Suffix : Primary suffix is used to show saturation or unsaturation in the carbon chain. When writing the name, primary suffix is added to the word root. Some examples are given below :

Carbon Chain	*Primary Suffix*
Saturated Carbon Chain	-ane
Unsaturated Carbon Chain	
One C=C bond	-ene
Two C=C bond	-a diene
Three C=C bond	-a triene
One C≡C bond	-yne
Two C≡C bond	-adiyne

(c) Secondary Suffix : Secondary suffix is used to indicate the functional group in the organic compound. It is added to primary suffix by dropping its terminal letter. Secondary suffixes for various functional groups are given below.

If the name of the secondary suffix starts with a consonant, then the terminal 'e' of primary suffix is not dropped while adding secondary suffix to it. The terminal 'e' is also retained if some numerical prefixes like di, tri etc. are used before the secondary suffix.

(d) Prefix : Prefix is the part of the name which is added before the word root. Prefixes are used to represent the names of alkyl groups in branch chain or some *functional groups* which are regarded as substituents as discussed below :

(i) Alkyl Groups : These groups are formed by removing H atom from alkanes. They are represented by general formula C_nH_{2n+1} or R. Some alkyl groups along with their prefixes are mentioned below :

Alkane	*Alkyl Groups*	*Abbreviation*	*Prefix*
CH_4	CH_3	Me	Methyl
C_2H_6	$CH_3—CH_2—$	Et	Ethyl
C_3H_8	$CH_3CH_2CH_2—$	*n*Pr	*n*-Propyl
		Iso—Pr	Isopropyl or (1-Methyl ethyl)

(ii) Some Functional Groups used as Prefixes : Following functional groups are always used as prefixes :

Functional Groups	*Prefix*	*Family of Compound*	*IUPAC Name*
—NO	Nitroso	R—NO	Nitroso alkane
$—NO_2$	Nitro	$R—NO_2$	Nitro alkane
$—OR^1$	Alkoxy	$R—OR^1$	Alkorcy alkane
—X	Halo	R—Cl	Halo alkane

(iii) Poly Functional Compounds : In compounds having more than one functional groups, one of the functional groups is treated as principal functional group and is indicated by secondary suffix whereas other functional groups are treated as substituents and are indicated by the prefixes. The prefixes of various groups are given below :

Functional Group	*Prefix*
—OH	Hydroxy
—CN	Cyano
—NC	Isocyano
—CHO	Foromyl
—SH	Mercapto
—SR	Alkylthio
—COOH	Carboxy
—COOR	Carboalkoxy
$—CONH_2$	Carbanoyl
—COCl	Chloroformyl
$—NH_2$	Amino
=NH	Imido
>C = O	Keto or Oxo

2. *Rules for writing IUPAC names :*

(1) Alkanes : Alkanes are hydrocarbons that contain only single bonds.

Methane (1 carbon)	CH_4
Ethane (2 carbons)	C_2H_6
Propane (3 carbons)	C_3H_8
Butane (4 carbons)	C_4H_{10}
Pentane (5 carbons)	C_5H_{12}
Hexane (6 carbons)	C_6H_{14}
Heptane (7 carbons)	C_7H_{16}
Octane (8 carbons)	C_8H_{18}
Nonane (9 carbons)	C_9H_{20}
Decane (10 carbons)	$C_{10}H_{22}$

Group of Organic Compound	*General Formula*	*Functional Group*	*Suffix*	*IUPAC name of Family word root + p. suffix + Sec. Suffix*
Alcohols	R— OH	–OH	– ol	Alka nol
Thioalcohols	R— SH	—SH	-thriol	Alkane thiol
Aldehydes	R— CHO	— CHO	-al	Alkan al
Ketones	R— COR	$>C=O$	-one	Alkan one
Amines	R— NH_2	$—NH_2$	-amine	Alkan amine
Carboxylic acid	R— COOH	$-\overset{\overset{O}{\parallel}}{C}-OH$	-oic acid	Alkan oic acid
Amides	R— $CONH_2$	$-\overset{\overset{O}{\parallel}}{C}-NH_2$	-amide	Alkan amide
Acid chlorides	R— COCl	$-\overset{\overset{O}{\parallel}}{C}-Cl$	-oyl	Alkan oyl chloride
Esters	R— COOR	$-\overset{\overset{O}{\parallel}}{C}-OR$	-oate	Alkyl alkan oate
Nitrites	R— $C\equiv N$	$—C\equiv N$	-nitrite	Alkane nitrile

In the common system all isomeric alkanes have the same parent name. Two isomeric C_4H_{10} alkanes are known as butanes. The prefixes indicate the type of branching present in the molecule

Prefix	*Meaning of the Prefix*
n-	Alkane is unbranched
iso-	Alkane contains $(CH_3)_2CH\cdot$ and no other branches.
neo-	Alkane contains $(CH_3)_3C—$ and no other branches.

$CH_3CH_2CH_2CH_3$

n-Butane

$CH_3CH_2CH_2CH_2CH_3$

n-Pentane

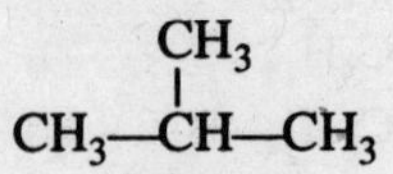

Isobutane

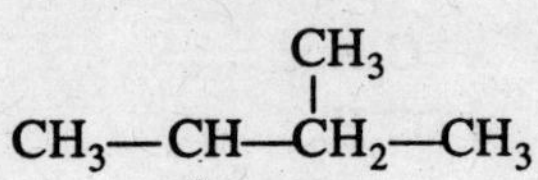

Isopentane

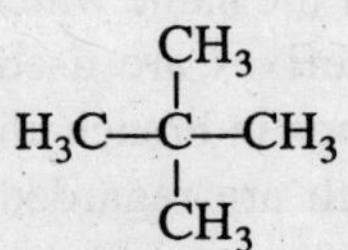

Neopentane

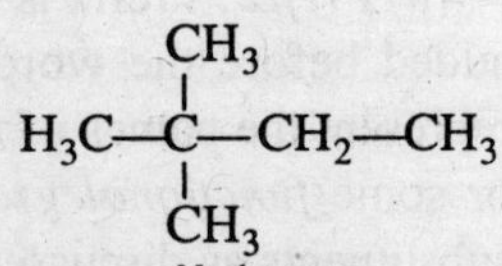

Neohexane

Classification of Carbon Atoms

The structural formula of alkanes contain four types of carbons :

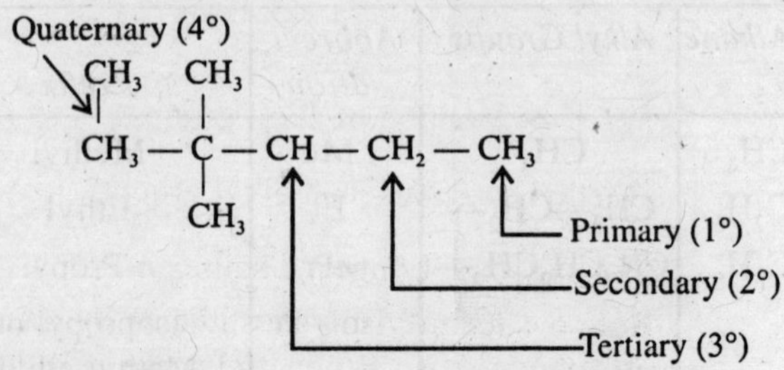

1° (Primary) → A carbon atom attached to one other (or no other) carbon atoms.

2° (Secondary) → A carbon atom attached to two other carbon atoms.

3° (Tertiary) → A carbon atom attached to three other carbon atoms.

4° (Quaternary) → A carbon atom attached to four other carbon atoms.

IUPAC Rules for Naming Alkanes

Rule 1 : Select the longest continuous carbon chain.

Rule 2 : Name the longest chain.

Rule 3 : Number the longest chain : The carbon atoms in the longest chain are numbered. The numbering is started from that end which will give numbers having the lowest value to carbons carrying substituents.

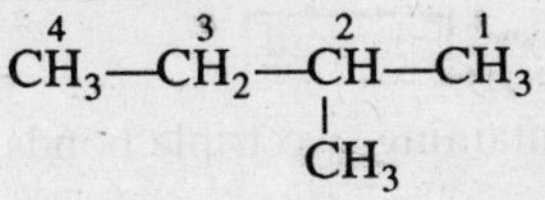 and not

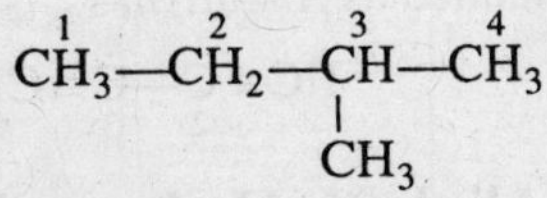

Rule 4 : Identify the substituent : Name the substituent. Indicate its position by the number of carbon atom to which it is attached.

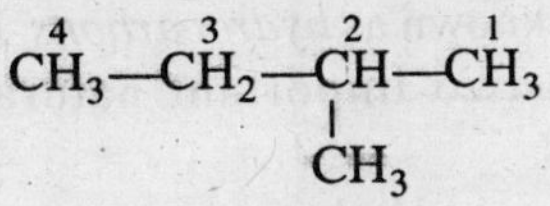

The attached group is located on carbon 2 of the chain and it is a methyl group.

Rule 5 : Prefix the position number and name of the substituent into the parent name. The whole name is written as one word. Notice that the number and name of substituent are separated by a hyphen.

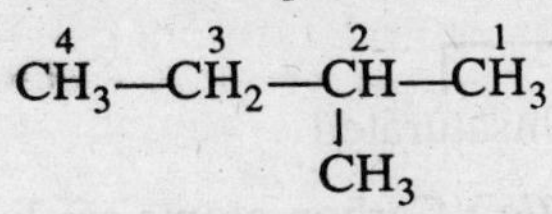

2-Methylbutane

[2–] → Position of alkyl groups.

[Methyl] → Attached alkyl group.

[Butane] → Longest Chain.

Rule 6 : Identify the substituents by names and *position numbers* : When the same substituent is present two or more times in the molecule, prefixes di-, tri-, tetra-, penta- etc. are used. Position of each substituent is indicated by a separate number. These position numbers, separated by commas, are put just before the name of the substituent, with the hyphen before and after the numbers when necessary.

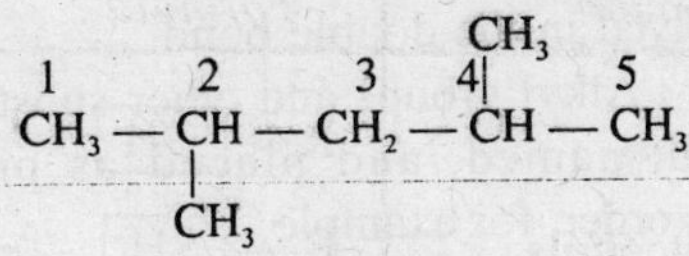

2, 4-Dimethyl pentane

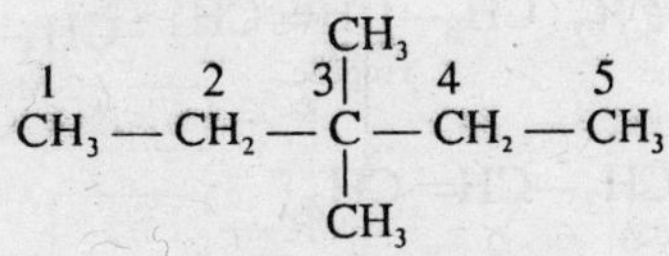

3, 3-Dimethyl pentane

Rule 7 : When two or more different substituents are present, their names are arranged in alphabetic order and added to the name of the parent alkane, again as one word.

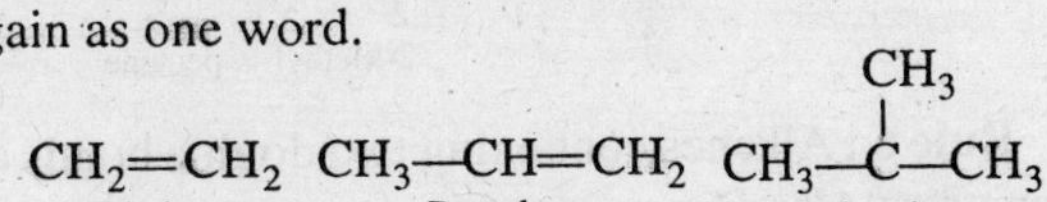

Ethylene Propylene Isobutylene

Cycloalkanes : Cycloalkanes are alkanes in which carbon atoms are arranged in a ring. They are named by attaching the prefix cyclo- to the name of the alkane having the same number of carbons as in the ring

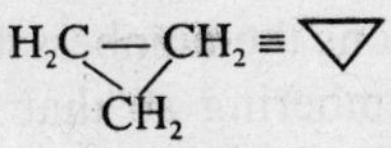

Cyclopropane

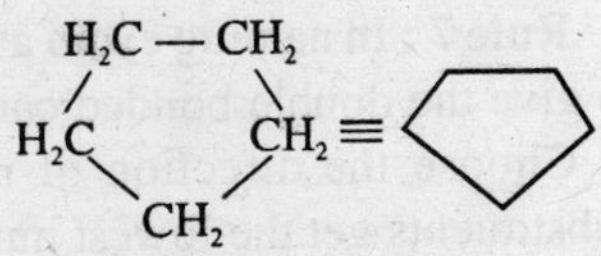

Cyclohexane

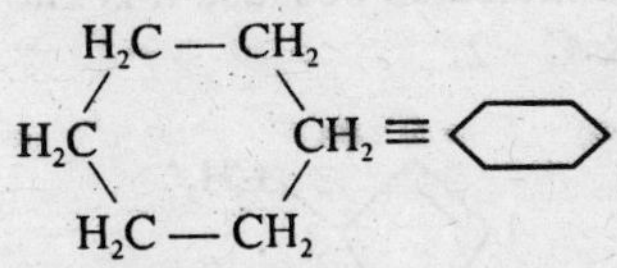

Cyclopentane

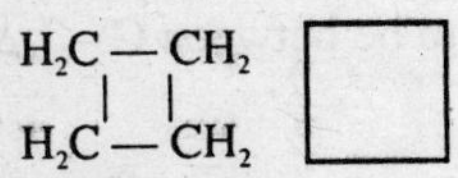

Cyclobutane

Substituted cycloalkanes are named as Alkylcyclo alkanes.

IUPAC Rules for Naming Alkenes

Rule 1 : Select the longest carbon chain containing the double bond. This is the parent chain.

Rule 2 : Name the longest chain. The name is obtained by dropping the final– e from the name of the corresponding alkane, and adding the ending – ene.

Alkane – e + ene = Alkene

Rule 3 : Number the chain from the end closer to the double bond.

Rule 4 : Indicate the position of the double bond by the number of the first (lowest numbered) carbon atom involved in the double bond.

Rule 5 : Alkyl groups and other substituents are numbered, named, and placed as prefixes in alphabetic order, for example

$CH_2{=}CH_2$ (Ethene) $\quad CH_3{-}CH{=}CH_2$ (Propene) $\quad CH_3{-}\overset{\overset{\Large CH_3}{|}}{C}{=}CH_2$ (2-Methylpropene)

$\underset{4}{CH_3}{-}\underset{3}{CH_2}{-}\underset{2}{CH}{=}\underset{1}{CH_2}$

1-Butene

$\underset{1}{CH_3}{-}\underset{2}{\overset{\overset{\Large CH_3}{|}}{C}}{=}\underset{3}{CH}{-}\underset{4}{CH_2}{-}\underset{5}{CH_3}$

2-Methyl-2-pentene

Rule 6 : Alkenes containing two double bonds are named as *Alkadienes.*

$\overset{1}{CH_2}{=}\overset{2}{C}{=}\overset{3}{CH_2}$

1, 2 Propadiene

$\overset{1}{CH_2}{=}\overset{2}{CH}{-}\overset{3}{CH}{=}\overset{4}{CH_2}$

1, 3 Butadiene

Rule 7 : In naming cyclo alkenes, number the ring to give the double bonded carbons the numbers 1 & 2. Choose the direction of numbering so that the substituents get the lowest numbers. The position of the double bond is not indicated because it is known to be between C – 1 & C – 2.

Cyclohexane

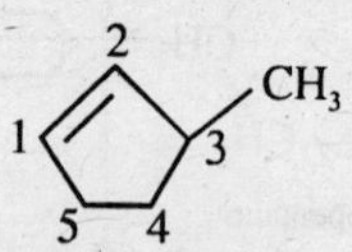

3 - Methyl cyclopentene

IUPAC Rules for Naming Alkynes

Rule 1 : Select the longest carbon chain containing the triple bond. This is the parent chain.

Rule 2 : Name the longest chain. The name is obtained by dropping the final – e from the name of the corresponding alkane, and adding the ending–yne.

Alkane – e + yne = Alkyne.

Rule 3 : Number the chain from end closer to the triple bond.

Rule 4 : Indicate the position of the triple bond by the number of the first (lowest numbered) carbon atom involved in the triple bond.

Rule 5 : Alkyl groups and other substituents are numbered, named and placed as prefixes in alphabetic order. For example,

$HC\equiv CH$ (Ethyne) $\quad CH_3{-}C\equiv CH$ (Propyne) $\quad \overset{4}{CH_3}\overset{3}{C}\equiv \overset{2}{C}\overset{1}{CH_3}$ (2-Butyne)

$\underset{1}{CH_3}{-}\underset{2}{C}\equiv \underset{3}{C}{-}CH_2{-}\overset{\overset{\Large CH_3}{|}}{CH}{-}CH_3$

5-Methyl-2-hexyne
(not 2-methyl-4 hexyne)

Rule 6 : Alkynes containing two triple bonds are named as *Alkadiynes.*

$\underset{1}{HC}\equiv \underset{2}{C}{-}\underset{3}{C}\equiv \underset{4}{CH}$ 1, 3-Butadiyne.

Aliphatic Hydrocarbons

Alkanes, Alkenes and Alkynes: Preparation and Properties

Properties : Compounds containing only carbon and hydrogen are known as *hydrocarbons.* Petroleum and coal are the two important natural sources as hydrocarbons.

- Hydrocarbons
  - Aliphatic or Open chain
    - Saturated
    - Unsaturated
  - Alicyclic
  - Aromatic

(A) Aliphatic : Carbon atoms are linked together to form an open chain.

(a) Saturated : All four valencies of carbon atom(s) are satisfied by four atoms or groups. They are also called *paraffins* and in IUPAC system alkanes.

(b) Unsaturated : Two carbon atoms are linked together by double (in case of olefins) or triple (in case of acetylenes) bond *i.e.* they do not have the maximum possible number of hydrogen atoms.

(B) Alicyclic : Those cyclic compounds which resemble aliphatic hydrocarbons in several respects are known as alicyclic. These are also called as *cyclic* *aliphatic hydrocarbons*, cycloalkanes, cycloparaffins or polymethylenes, *e.g.* cyclohexane.

(C) Aromatic : Those hydrocarbons which have at least one six membered carbocyclic ring with alternate single and double bonds (benzene ring) are called aromatic. Most of these have fragrant odour and possess distinctive properties from those of the aliphatic compounds.

1. Alkanes : Alkanes form a homologous series of hydrocarbons which can be represented by general formula, C_nH_{2n+2}. As they are comparatively inert towards the most of the reagents, they are also known as paraffins (Latin : param, little; affini, affinity). They are also referred to as saturated acyclic hydrocarbons, as they are open chain compounds which are almost saturated among themselves. All the atoms in the molecules of alkanes are linked by single C—C and C—H bonds. Many of these substances are familiar because of their widespread use. Methane is a major component of natural gas and is used for home heating and in gas stoves and hot water heaters. Propane is the *component* of bottled gas used for home heating cooking in areas where natural gas is not available. Butane is used in disposable lighters and in fuel caninsters for gas camping stoves and lanterns. Alkanes with 5-12 carbon atoms per molecule are found in *gasoline*. Petroleum and natural gas are the principal sources of alkanes. A few alkanes have been detected in waxy constituents of certain plants. For example *n*-nonacosane, $C_{29}H_{60}$ has been isolated from cabbage leaves and *n*-heptane, C_7H_{16} in found to be present in pinus species.

The natural gas from petroleum wells contains alkanes with low molecular weight, *i.e.*, more volatile alkanes. It's chief constituent being methane and other hydrocarbons like ethane, propane and higher alkanes which are present in progressively low proportions. A sample of natural gas from *Pennsylvania* contains methane, ethane and propane in the ratio 12 : 2 : 1 with higher alkanes making up only 3% of total. Crude petroleum contains large quantities of liquid hydrocarbons along with little solid paraffin wax dissolved in it. Paraffin wax is a mixture of higher solid hydrocarbons.

1. Structure of Alkanes

Methane (CH_4) : In methane, carbon forms single bonds with four hydrogen atoms. Since the carbon atom is attached to four other atoms, it uses sp^3 hybrid orbitals to form these bonds. Each C—H bond is the result of the overlap of an sp^2 orbital from carbon and a *s*-orbital from hydrogen. All C—H bonds are σ-bonds.

The saturated Hydrocarbons or Alkanes

Name	*Molecular Formula*	*Melting Point (°C)*	*Boiling Point (°C)*	*State at 25°C*
Methane	CH_4	– 182.5	– 164	Gas
Ethane	C_2H_6	– 183.3	– 88.6	Gas
Propane	C_3H_8	– 189.7	– 42.1	Gas
Butane	C_4H_{10}	– 138.4	– 0.5	Gas
Pentane	C_5H_{12}	– 129.7	36.1	Liquid
Hexane	C_6H_{14}	– 95	68.9	Liquid
Heptane	C_7H_{16}	– 90.6	98.4	Liquid
Octane	C_8H_{18}	– 56.8	124.7	Liquid
Nonane	C_9H_{20}	– 51	150.8	Liquid
Decane	$C_{10}H_{22}$	– 29.7	174.1	Liquid
Undecane	$C_{11}H_{24}$	– 24.6	195.9	Liquid
Do decane	$C_{12}H_{26}$	– 9.6	216.9	Liquid
Eicosane	$C_{20}H_{42}$	36.8	343	Solid
Triacontane	$C_{30}H_{62}$	65.8	449.9	Solid

As the four sp^3 orbitals are directed to the four corners of a *tetrahedron*, the methane molecule is tetrahedral rather than uniplanar.

C—H bond length is 1.09 Å (109 pm) and each H—C—H bond angle is 109.5°.

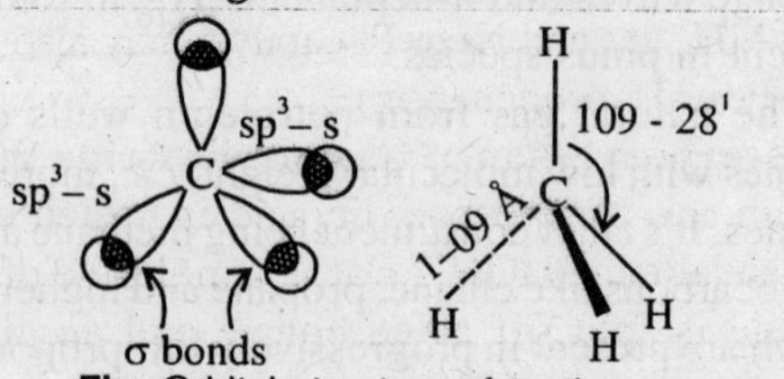

Fig. Orbital structure of methane

Ethane (C_2H_6) : It has a multiplanar structure with each carbon having a tetrahedral arrangement of bonds. The C—C bond in ethane is formed by overlap of sp^3 hybrid orbitals of each carbon atom. The six C—H bonds are formed by the overlap of sp^3 orbitals of each carbon and the 1s orbitals of hydrogen atoms. The C—C and C—H bonds in ethane are all strong σ-bonds. The length of C—H bond is similar to that of methane, *i.e.*, 1.09 Å (109 pm). The different bond angles are also tetrahedral angles, *i.e.*, 109.5°. The C—C bond length in ethane is 1.54 Å (154 pm)

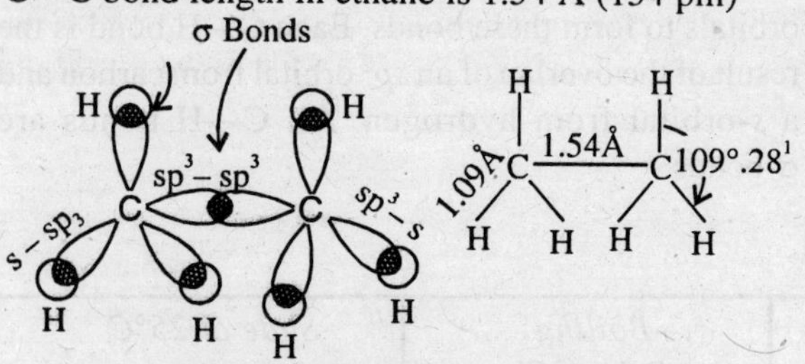

Fig. Orbital structure of ethane

Hydrocarbon Fractions from Petroleum

Fraction	*Size Range of Molecules*	*Boiling Point Range (°C)*	*Uses*
Gas	C_1 to C_5	– 160 to 30	Gaseous fuel production of H_2
Straight-run gasoline	C_5 to C_{12}	30 to 200	Motor fuel
kerosene, fuel oil	C_{12} to C_{18}	180 to 400	Diesel fuel, furnace fuel
Lubricants	C_{10} and up	350 and up	Lubricants
Paraffins	C_{20} and up	Low melting solids	Candles, matches
Asphalt	C_{36} and up	Gummy residues	Surfacing of roads

Cycloalkanes : When open chain aliphatic hydrocarbons close up to forming, cyclic aliphatic hydrocarbons are formed. They are commonly known as *alicyclic hydrocarbons* (ali-from aliphatic and cyclic from their ring structures.) The alicyclic hydrocarbons corresponding to alkanes are the cyclic counterparts of alkanes and, therefore, they are known as *cycloalkanes* or *cycloparaffins*. Some examples are

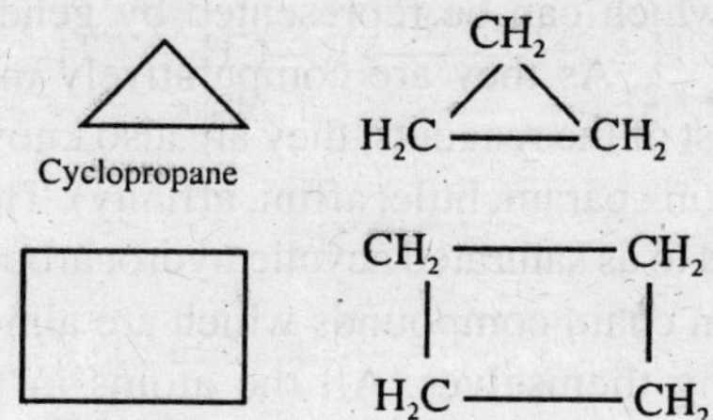

Cyclopropane

Cyclobutane

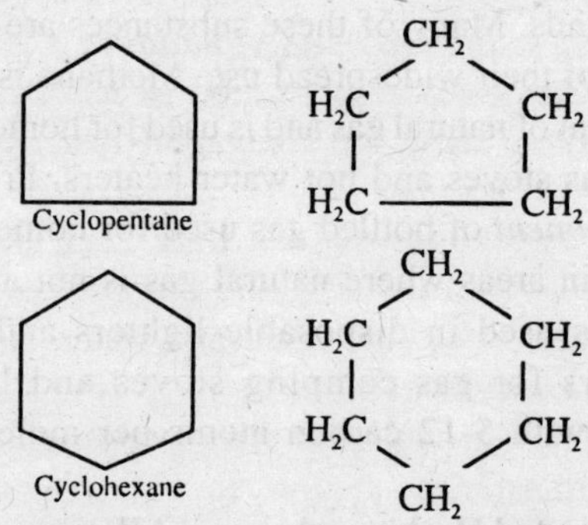

Cyclopentane

Cyclohexane

The cycloalkanes which contain a number of methylene groups joined together to form a ring are sometimes referred to as *polymethylenes*. Thus cyclopropane and cyclobutane are named as trimethylene and tetramethylene respectively.

2. *Natural sources of alkanes* : The two main sources of alkanes are natural gas and petroleum. Both of these substances are frequently found together in underground deposits. Natural gas contains about 80% methane and 10% ethane the remaining 10% being a mixture of higher members. Petroleum is a chief source of alkanes containing upto 40 carbons.

Methods of Preparation : Alkanes are prepared by the following methods :

Catalytic Hydrogenation of unsaturated *hydrocarbons* (*alkenes* or *alkynes*)

Alkenes or alkynes react with hydrogen in the presence of nickel catalyst at 200-300°C to form alkanes. Other catalysts which can be used are platinum and palladium.

(*i*) $\underset{\text{Alkene}}{R{-}CH{=}CH_2} + H_2 \xrightarrow[\Delta]{Ni} \underset{\text{Alkane}}{R{-}CH_2{-}CH_3}$

$$\underset{\text{Ethylene}}{CH_2{=}CH_2} + H_2 \xrightarrow[\Delta]{Ni} \underset{\text{Ethane}}{CH_3{-}CH_3}$$

$$\underset{\text{Propene}}{CH_3{-}CH{=}CH_2} + H_2 \xrightarrow[\Delta]{Pt} \underset{\text{Propane}}{CH_3{-}CH_2{-}CH_3}$$

(*ii*) $\underset{\text{Alkyne}}{R{-}C \equiv CH} + 2H_2 \xrightarrow[\Delta]{Ni} \underset{\text{Alkane}}{R{-}CH_2{-}CH_3}$

$$\underset{\text{Acetylene}}{CH \equiv CH} + 2H_2 \xrightarrow[\Delta]{Ni} \underset{\text{Ethane}}{CH_3{-}CH_2}$$

(*a*) Using nickel catalyst in this reaction is called *Sabatier-Senderen's* reaction.

(*b*) Methane cannot be prepared by this method.

3. *Direct reduction of alkyl halides :*

(*a*) This reaction is termed as *hydrogenolysis* since it brings about the cleavage (-lysis) of C—X bond by hydrogen.

(*b*) Reducing agents used are Zinc and acetic acid or hydrochloric acid, zinc -copper couple and alcohol, magnesium amalgam and water, palladised charcoal and hydrogen.

(*c*) The mechanism of this reaction involves the electrons transfer as

$$\text{Reducing agent } : + R - X \rightarrow R:^{\ominus} + :X^{\ominus}$$

(*d*) The reduction of the iodo derivative, can also be carried out by use of HI in the presence of phosphorous

$$C_2H_5I + HI \xrightarrow[432K]{P} C_2H_6 + I_2$$

The function of red phosphorous is to remove iodine formed during the reaction

$$2P + 3I_2 \rightarrow 2PI_3$$

Alkyl halides undergo reduction with nascent hydrogen to form alkanes

$$\underset{\text{Alkyl halide}}{R{-}X} + 2H \rightarrow \underset{\text{Alkane}}{R{-}H} + HX$$

$$\underset{\text{Methyl iodide}}{CH_3{-}I} + 2H \rightarrow \underset{\text{Methane}}{CH_4} + HI$$

$$\underset{\text{Ethyl bromide}}{CH_3OH_2{-}Br} + 2H \rightarrow \underset{\text{Ethane}}{CH_3{-}CH_3} + HBr$$

The hydrogen for reduction may be obtained by using any of the following reducing agents :

Zn + HCl,

Zn + CH_3COOH.

Zn—Cu couple in ethanole or

$LiAlH_4$ gas and Ni or Pt catalyst may also be used (Catalytic Hydrogenation)

Decarboxylation of Carboxylic Acid : When the sodium salt of a carboxylic acid is heated strongly with sodalime (NaOH + CaO); a molecule of carbon dioxide is split off as carbonate and an alkane is formed.

Important : Alkane so produced contains one carbon less than the original acid

$$R{-}COONa + NaOH \xrightarrow{\Delta} \underset{\text{Alkane}}{RH} + Na_2CO_3$$

$$\underset{\text{Sod. acetate}}{CH_3{-}COONa} + NaOH \xrightarrow{\Delta} \underset{\text{Methane}}{CH_4} + Na_2CO_3$$

4. *Wurtz reaction :* Higher alkanes are produced by heating an alkyl halide (RX) with sodium metal in dry ether solution. Two molecules of alkyl halide lose their hydrogen atoms as NaX. The net result is the joining of two alkyl groups to yield a symmetrical alkane (R—R type) having an even number of carbon atoms.

$$R{-}\overline{X} + \overline{2Na} + \overline{X}{-}R \xrightarrow{Ether} \underset{\substack{\text{Symmetrical}\\ \text{alkane}}}{R{-}R} + 2NaX$$

$$\underset{\substack{\text{Methyle}\\ \text{bromide}}}{CH_5{-}\overline{Br}} + \overline{2Na} + \overline{Br}{-}CH_3 \xrightarrow{Ether} \underset{\text{Ethane}}{CH_3{-}CH_3} + 2NaBr$$

The mechanism involves the formation of an extremely reactive organosodium intermediate.

$$RX + 2Na \rightarrow [RNa] + NaX$$

$$RX + [RNa] \rightarrow R{-}R + NaX$$

The reaction between two different alkyl halides and sodium gives a mixture of products that are difficult to separate. For example, methyl chloride and ethyl chloride when treated with sodium give three products as :

$$C_2H_5I + 2Na + I{-}CH_3 \xrightarrow[Ether]{Dry} \underset{\text{Propane}}{C_2H_5{-}CH_3} + 2NaI$$

$$C_2H_5{-}I + 2Na + I{-}C_2H_5 \xrightarrow[Ether]{Dry} \underset{\text{Butane}}{C_2H_5{-}C_2H_5} + 2NaI$$

$$CH_3—I + 2Na + I—CH_3 \xrightarrow[\text{Ether}]{\text{Dry}} CH_3—CH_3 + 2NaI$$

Limitations :

(i) The separation of these alkanes is not always easy because of a little difference in their boiling points, thus usefulness of this method is limited to the preparation of only symmetrical alkanes.

(ii) Also this method is not suitable to prepare alkanes containing odd number of carbon atoms.

(iii) Methane cannot be prepared by this method.

Hydrolysis of Grignard Reagents : Alkyl magnesium halides (Grignard reagents) are obtained by treating alkyl halides with magnesium in anhydrous ether. These on treatment with water gives alkanes.

$$RX + Mg \xrightarrow{\text{Ether}} \underset{\text{Alkylmagnesium halide}}{RMgX}$$

$$RMgX + HOH \rightarrow \underset{\text{Alkane}}{RH} + MgX(OH)$$

$$\underset{\text{Methylmagnesium iodide}}{CH_3MgI} + HOH \rightarrow \underset{\text{Methane}}{CH_4} + MgX(OH)$$

Corey-House Alkane Synthesis : This method was developed in late 1960s. An alkyl halide is first converted to lithium dialkyl cuperate, LiR_2Cu. This is then treated with an alkyl halide to give an alkane.

$$\underset{\text{Methyl Bromide}}{CH_3Br} + 2Li \xrightarrow{\text{Ether}} \underset{\text{Methyllithium}}{CH_3Li} + LiBr$$

$$2CH_3Li + CuI \rightarrow \underset{\text{Lithiumdimethyl Cuperate}}{Li(CH_3)_2Cu} + LiI$$

$$\underset{\text{Ethyl bromide}}{CH_3CH_2Br} + Li(CH_3)_2Cu \rightarrow \underset{\text{Propane}}{CH_3CH_2—CH_3} + CH_3Cu + LiBr$$

This method is particularly suitable for the preparation of unsymmetrical alkanes, *i.e.*, those of the type R—R′.

5. *Kolbe's synthesis :* When a concentrated solution of sodium salt, a carboxylic acid is eletrolysed, an alkane is formed.

$$2RCOO^-Na^+ + 2H_2O \rightarrow \frac{R—R + 2CO_2}{\text{At anode}} + \frac{2NaOH + H_2}{\text{At cathode}}$$

$$2CH_3COONa^+ + 2H_2O \rightarrow \frac{CH_3—CH_3 + 2CO_2}{\text{At anode}} + \frac{2NaOH + H_2}{\text{At cathode}}$$

This reaction is only suitable for the preparation of symmetrical alkanes, *i.e.* those of the type, R—R.

From Salts of Fatty Acids :

(A) Soda-lime decarboxylation of sodium salt of fatty acids :

$$RCOONa + NaOH \xrightarrow{\text{CaO}} \underset{\text{Alkane}}{R—H} + Na_2CO_3$$

(B) Electrolytic decarboxylation of potassium salt of carboxylic acid

$$CH_3COOK \rightarrow CH_3COO^- + K^+$$

At anode : $CH_3COO^- - e^- \rightarrow CH_3CO\dot{O}$

$$CH_3CO\dot{O} \rightarrow \dot{C}H_3 + CO_2$$

$$\dot{C}H_3 + \dot{C}H_3 \rightarrow \underset{\text{Ethane}}{CH_3—CH_3}$$

At cathode :

$$2H_2O + 2e^- \rightarrow 2OH^- + H_2$$

Important :

(a) The soda lime acid in Method (A) is a mixture of NaOH and CaO in the ratio 3 : 1

(b) CaO in this reaction does not participate as such but helps in fusion of reaction mixture.

(c) Method (B) is useful for preparing ethane and higher members but methane cannot be prepared by this method.

6. *Reduction of fatty acids with HI :* COOH group is reduced to CH_3 group

$$\underset{\text{Acetic acid}}{CH_3COOH} + 6HI \rightarrow \underset{\text{Ethane}}{CH_3—CH_3} + 2H_2O + 3I_2$$

$$\underset{\text{Acetic acid}}{C_2H_5COOH} + 6HI \rightarrow \underset{\text{Propane}}{C_2H_5—CH_3} + 2H_2O + 3I_2$$

Physical Properties of Alkanes :

1. First four alkanes are gases. Next thirteen members (C_5 to C_{17}) are colourless liquids. Higher alkanes are solids.

2. Liquid alkanes are lighter than water.

3. Alkanes are insoluble in water but dissolve freely in organic solvents like ether, acetone and carbon tetrachloride.

4. In general, the boiling points and specific gravities of alkanes increase with rise of molecular weight.

2. Alkenes or Olefins : Alkenes are unsaturated hydrocarbons. Their molecules have two hydrogen atoms less than the corresponding members of alkanes. Their general formula is C_nH_{2n}. The characteristic features of alkanes is the presence of carbon-carbon double bond (C═C) in their molecules. Alkenes are also known as *olefins* (derived from *Greek* word *Olefiant* (means oil forming). Alkenes are reactive due to pi (π) electrons of the multiple bond the pi (π) electrons of the multiple bond can be used to form addition sigma (σ) bonds.

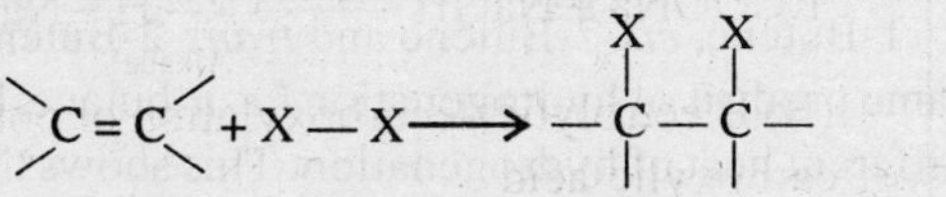

These compounds are often the building blocks used by chemical industry to synthesize new compounds. As such they represent a class of organic compounds of considerable economic importance.

Alkanes seldom occur free in nature. They are, however, produced in large amounts by cracking of petroleum.

Structure	*Systematic Name*	*Common Name*	*b.p. (°C)*	*m.p. (°C)*
$CH_2{=}CH_2$	Ethene	Ethylene	– 104	–169
$CH_3CH{=}CH_2$	Propene	Propylene	– 48	–185
$CH_3CH_2CH{=}CH_2$	2-Butene	—	– 6	–185
$CH_3CH{=}CHCH_3$	2-Butene	—	3.7	139.3
	2-Methyl propene	Iso-butylene	– 7	–140
	2-Methyl 2-butene	—	39	–134
	2-Methyl-1 3-butadiene	Isoprene	34	–146

Bonding, Structure and Isomerism : From the VSEPR theory and from the experimental observations, it is confirmed that substituents of a carbon atom doubly bonded to another carbon will be arranged in a planar triangle.

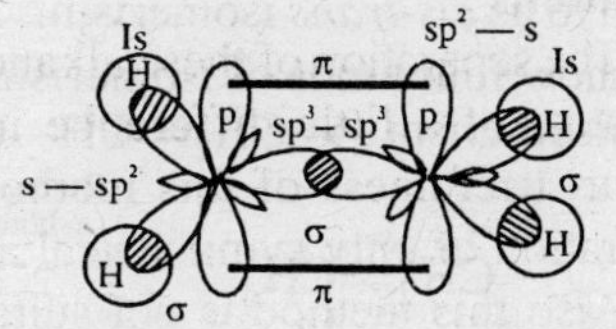

Fig. The σ and π bond in ethane

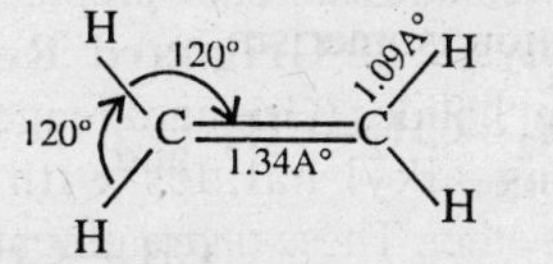

Fig. Geometry of the molecule

This means that carbon atoms must be sp^2 hybridised and the pi (π) bond can be formed by using the unhybridised *p*-orbitals, one on each carbon atom.

One of the most important aspects of alkane chemistry is to recognize the effect of π-bond on the molecular structure. Ordinarily when two carbon atoms are bonded only by σ (sigma) bond, the groups at the end of the bond rotate rapidly around C—C.

However, the effect of the carbon-carbon π-bond is to prevent rotation about C = C bond axis. The rotation of ends of the molecules can occur if the two C atoms are joined by only a σ-bond. This means that rotation can occur in alkenes ($R_1C = CR_2$) only if π-bond is broken, and this would require considerable energy. Therefore, if a chlorine atom is attached at each carbon atom in ethylene, there are two possible permanent arrangments.

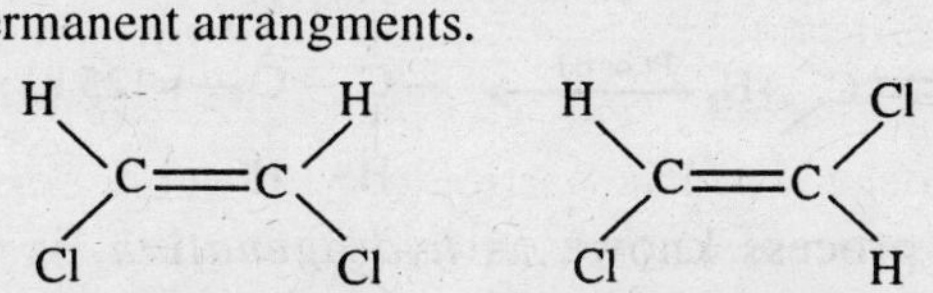

CB–1, 2-dichloro ethene m.p. –80°C, 6 p. 60°C   trans–1, 2-dichloro ethene m.p. –50°C, 6 p. 48°C

The above two molecules have the same formula, but restricted rotation about the C═C bond causes them to have different structure and different properties. Hence, these are *isomers*, since they have the same molecular formula but the atoms are arranged in different manner. The isomer with chlorine atoms on opposite sides of the bond is called the *trans-*

isomer and that with the chlorine atoms on the same side is called the *cis*-isomer. This form of isomerism is often referred to as *cis-trans* isomerism.

Alkenes show four kinds of isomerism.

(*a*) Chainisomerism → $CH_2{=}CH{-}CH_2{-}CH_3$
Butene-1 (*n*-butene)

$CH_2{=}CH_3$ (with CH_3 on the second carbon)
2-Methyl Propane (Isobutene)

(*b*) Position isomerism →

$CH_2{=}CH_2{-}CH_2{-}CH_3$ and
Butene–1

$CH_3{-}CH{=}CH{-}CH_3$
Butene–2

(*c*) Geometrical isomerism → $H{-}C{-}CH_3$ ‖ $H{-}C{-}CH_3$
cis-2-Butene

and $H{-}C{-}CH_3$ ‖ $H_3C{-}C{-}H$
trans-2-butene

(*d*) Ring-chain isomerism → $CH_3{-}CH{-}CH_2$
Propene

and 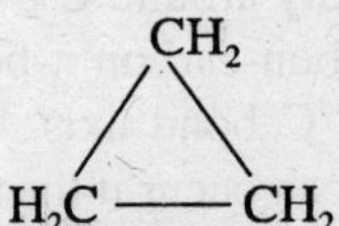
cyclo propene

Relative Stability of Alkenes : The relative stability of alkenes is related with the heats of hydrogenation.

$$>C{=}C< + H_2 \xrightarrow{\text{Pt or pd}} -\underset{H}{\overset{H}{C}}-\underset{H}{\overset{H}{C}}- \approx 125\text{ kJ}$$

This process known as *hydrogenation*, is a quantitative basis of the method for determining the number of carbon-carbon double bonds in the organic compound. One mole, *i.e.*, 22.4 litre of H_2 is consumed at STP for each double bond per mole.

The amount of heat evolved when one mole of an unsaturated compound is hydrogenated is known as heat of hydrogenation. Almost every alkene has the heat of hydrogenation of about 125 kJ mol^{-1} for each double bond present in one mole of an alkane.

Alkene	*Heat of hydrogenation (kJ mol^{-1})*
Ethene	137.2
Propene	125.9
1-Butene	126.8
cis-2-Butene	119.6
trans-2-Butene	115.5
2-Methyl-1-Butene	119.2
2-Methyl-2-Butene	112.1

1-Butene, *cis*-2-Butene and *trans*-2-Butene yields same product of hydrogenation *i.e. n*-butane, but have different heat of hydrogenation. This shows that these alkenes must have different heat of hydrogenation and different stability. An alkene which has a lower heat of hydrogenation must have less energy and hence, greater stability than its isomers.

Important : (*i*) Heats of hydrogenation of some alkenes are as :

Unsubstituted alkene $CH_2{=}CH_2$ 137.2 kJ mol^{-1}

Monosubstituted alkene $RCH{=}CH_2$ 125.0 kJ mol^{-1}

Disubstituted alkene $RCH{=}CHR$ 117 kJ mol^{-1} or $R_2C{=}CHR$ 113 kJ mol^{-1}

(*ii*) From the above values it may be concluded that greater the number of alkyl groups attached to the doubly bonded carbon atoms, more stable is the alkene. Following is decreasing order of stability

$$R_2C{=}CR'_2 > R_2C{=}CHR > R_2C{=}CH_2 > RCH{=}CHR' > RCH{=}CH_2 > CH_2{=}CH_2$$

This order of stability can be described in the light of Hyperconjugation. The greater the degree of substitution in an alkene, the greater will be the number of *hyperconjugative forms* and hence greater the stability.

(*iii*) A *trans*-form is slightly more stable than the corresponding *cis*-isomer. In a *trans*-form, the bulky groups or atoms are farther apart than in *cis*-isomer. There is, therefore, less steric hindrance and less Van der Waals strain in the trans-isomer. Consequently, the trans-isomer must be more stable than the *cis*-isomer.

Preparation of Alkenes : Most of the methods of preparation of alkenes involve elimination of atoms or groups from two adjacent carbon atoms.

$$-\underset{X}{\overset{|}{\underset{|}{C}}}-\underset{Y}{\overset{|}{\underset{|}{C}}}- \rightarrow \underset{\text{Alkene}}{-\overset{|}{C}=\overset{|}{C}-} + XY$$

Dehydration of Alcohols : Protonic acids like conc. H_2SO_4 and H_3PO_4 and Lewis acids like zinc chloride, alumina, etc. *dehydrate* alcohols to alkenes under suitable experimental conditions

$$\underset{\text{Ethanol}}{H_2\overset{1}{C}-\overset{2}{C}H_2} \xrightarrow[623\text{-}633\,K]{Al_2O_3} \underset{\text{Ethane}}{CH_2=CH_2} + H_2O$$

$$RCH_2CH_2OH \xrightarrow{H^+} RCH=CH_2 + H_2O$$

$$\underset{\text{1-Propanol}}{CH_3-\underset{H}{\underset{|}{CH}}-\underset{OH}{\underset{|}{CH_2}}} \xrightarrow[170°]{H_2SO_4} \underset{\text{Propene}}{CH_3-CH=CH_2} + H_2O$$

$$\underset{\text{Ethyl alcohol}}{CH_3-CH_2-OH} \xrightarrow[170°]{H_2SO_4} \underset{\text{Ethylene}}{CH_2=CH_2} + H_2O$$

The ease of dehydration of alcohols is

3° alcohol > 2° alcohol > 1° alcohol

In case of unsymmetrical secondary or tertiary alcohols, elimination can proceed in two ways and a mixture of alkene is formed. For example, dehydration of 2-butanol gives 2-butene (major product) and 1-butene (minor product)

$$\underset{\text{2-Butanol}}{CH_3-\underset{H}{\underset{|}{CH}}-\underset{OH}{\underset{|}{CH}}-CH_3} \xrightarrow[\Delta]{H_2SO_4} \underset{\text{2-Butene 80\%}}{CH_3-CH=CH-CH_3}$$

$$\underset{\text{2-Butanol}}{CH_3-CH_2-\underset{OH}{\underset{|}{CH}}-\underset{H}{\underset{|}{CH_2}}} \xrightarrow[\Delta]{H_2SO_4} \underset{\text{1-Butene 20\%}}{CH_3-CH_2-CH=CH_2}$$

This is in accordance with *Saytzeff's Rule*. The rule states that "when alternative exists, hydrogen is preferentially elminated from the carbon atoms with fewer number of hydrogen atoms."

Other dehydrating agents are phosphorous pentoxide (P_2O_5) and phosphoric acid (H_3PO_4).

Mechanism of Dehydration of Alcohols

$$H_2SO_4 \rightarrow H^+ + HSO_4^-$$

(i) Protonation of Alcohol

$$CH_3CH_2\ddot{O}H + H \rightleftharpoons CH_3CH_2\overset{\overset{H}{|}}{\underset{\cdot\cdot}{O}}{}^{\oplus}H$$

(ii) Loss of water molecule

$$CH_3CH_2-\overset{\overset{H}{|}}{O}{}^{\oplus}-H \rightarrow CH_3-\overset{\oplus}{C}H_2 + H_2O$$

(iii) Loss of H^+ ions by carbocation

$$H-\underset{H}{\overset{H}{\overset{|}{\underset{|}{C}}}}-\overset{H}{\overset{|}{\underset{\oplus}{C}}}-H \xrightarrow{HSO_4^-} \underset{\text{Alkene}}{CH_2=CH_2} + H_2SO_4$$

By Dehydrohalogenation of Alkyl Halides : The dehydrohalogenation is carried with the help of alcoholic caustic potash. In this reaction halogen atom is lost from α-carbon atom and H atom from β-carbon and double bond is formed between α and β carbon atoms.

$$\underset{\text{Ethylbromide}}{CH_3CH_2Br} + \underset{\text{(alcoholic)}}{KOH} \rightarrow \underset{\text{Ethene}}{CH_2=CH_2} + KBr + H_2O$$

$$\underset{n\text{-Propylbromide}}{CH_3CH_2CH_2Br} + \underset{\text{(alcoholic)}}{KOH} \xrightarrow{360\,K} \underset{\text{Propene}}{CH_3CH=CH_2} + KBr + H_2O$$

$$\underset{\text{Iso-propylbromide}}{CH_3-\overset{\overset{CH_3}{|}}{C}HBr} + KOH(\text{alcoholic}) \xrightarrow{363\,K} \underset{\text{Propene}}{CH_3CH=CH_2} + KBr + H_2O$$

The ease of dehydrohalogenation of alkyl halides is

3° alkyl halide > 2° alkyl halide > 1° alkyl halide.

By Dehalogenation of Vicinal Dihalides : When a vicinal dihalide is treated with zinc the alkene is formed as

$$R-\underset{Br}{\underset{|}{CH}}-\underset{Br}{\underset{|}{CH}}-R' + Zn \rightarrow RCH=CHR' + ZnBr_2$$

Important : This reaction is more suitable for purification of compounds containing carbon-carbon double bond or for the protection of carbon-carbon double bonds.

By Controlled Hydrogenation of Alkynes :

(A) When alkyne is made to react with the calculated amount of hydrogen in the presence of palladised charcoal partially deactivated with sulphur compounds or quinoline (Lindlar's catalyst) *cis*-alkenes are formed.

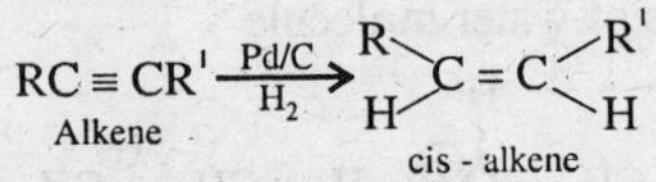

(B) When alkynes are reduced with sodium in liquid ammonia, trans-alkenes are formed predominantly.

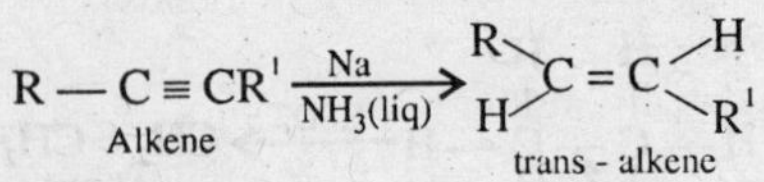

Important : The reactions are *Stereo Selective Reactions.*

By Cracking of Alkanes : Alkanes when heated at 500-700°C in the absence of air decompose to yield lower molecular weight alkenes, alkanes and hydrogen.

$$\underset{\text{Ethane}}{CH_3{-}CH_3} \xrightarrow{600°C} \underset{\text{Ethylene}}{CH_2{=}CH_2} + CH_4 + H_2$$

$$\underset{\text{Propane}}{CH_3{-}CH_2{-}CH_3} \xrightarrow{600°C} \underset{\text{Propane}}{CH_3{-}CH{=}CH_2}$$

$$+\underset{\text{Ethylene}}{CH_2{=}CH_2} + \underset{\text{Methane}}{CH_4} + H_2$$

By Electrolysis of Potassium Salt of Dicarboxylic Acids : This is also known as *Kolbe's reaction.*

$$\begin{matrix} CH_2COOK \\ | \\ CH_2COOK \end{matrix} + 2H_2O \xrightarrow{\text{Electrolysis}} \begin{matrix} CH_2 \\ || \\ CH_2 \end{matrix} + 2CO_2 + H_2 + 2KOH$$

Physical Properties :

(i) The first three members (ethene, propene and butenes) are gases at ordinary temperature, the next fourteen members are liquids, and the alkenes with more than 18 carbon atoms in the molecule are solids. They are colourless and odourless, except ethene which has a rather pleasant odour.

(ii) They are only slightly soluble in water but dissolve freely in organic solvents.

(iii) Their boiling points, melting points and specific gravities, in general, rise with increase of molecular weight in homologous series. The melting points and boiling points of some 1-alkenes are given in following table.

The boiling points of two successive members differ by about 20°-30°C

Name	*Formula*	*m.p. °C*	*b.p. °C*
Ethylene	$CH_2{=}CH_2$	– 169	– 104
Propene	$CH_2{=}CHCH_3$	– 185	– 47
1-Butene	$CH_2{=}CHCH_2CH_3$	– 130	– 65
1-Pentene	$CH_2{=}CH(CH_2)_2CH_3$	– 138	32
1-Hexene	$CH_2{=}CH(CH_2)_3CH_3$	– 141	64

The branched chain alkenes have lower boiling points than corresponding straight chain alkenes.

(iv) *Cis*-alkenes as compared to *trans*-alkenes have a higher dipole moment. *cis*-alkenes, therefore, boil at somewhat higher temperature than *trans*-isomer.

(v) *Cis*-alkenes have poor symmetry and as such they do not fit into crystalline lattice as properly as *trans*-alkenes do. Consequently, *trans*-alkenes have generally higher melting point than corresponding *cis*-isomers.

(vi) IR spectra of alkenes show C—H stretching absorptions at 3000-3100 cm^{-1}. Carbon-carbon double bonds give stretching absorption peaks at 1620-1680 cm^{-1}. Absorptions arising from C—H bending vibrations are at 600-1000 cm^{-1}.

Chemical Properties of Alkenes : Alkenes are more reactive than alkanes because :

(i) The π-electons of a double bond are located much farther from the carbon nuclei and are thus less firmly bound to them.

(ii) The overlap of atomic orbitals in forming a π-bond is not as effective as that in σ-bonds.

Thus a π-bond is weaker than a σ-bond and more easily broken.

The most important reactions of alkenes are the *addition reactions*. In these reactions the π-bond is broken and is replaced by two new σ-bonds. For example, when an alkene, reacts with E—Nu, the carbon-carbon π-bond is broken and a new C—E σ-bond and C—Nu σ-bond are formed.

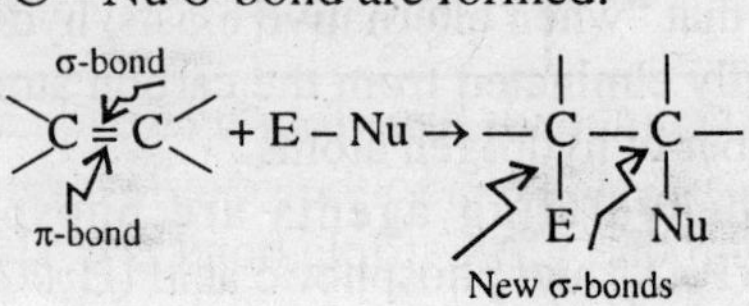

• The most important reactions of alkenes are electrophilic addition and free-radical addition reactions. They also undergo free radical substitution reactions.

3. Alkynes or Acetylenes

Alkynes are unsaturated hydrogens containing one or more C≡C bonds. The simplest alkyne is acetylene (C_2H_2), a highly reactive molecule. When acetylene is burnt in a stream of oxygen in an oxyacetylene torch, the flame reaches a very high temperature, about 3200 K. Alkynes in general are highly reactive molecules. Due to their high reactivity, they are not as widely distributed in nature as alkenes. However, they are important intermediates of many industrial processes.

At one time most synthetic organic compounds were divided from coal and acetylene (HC≡CH) was an important intermediate in organic synthesis. However, its method of preparation involved high temperature processes and therefore costly.

(i) $CaO(s) + 3C(s) + heat \rightarrow CO(g) + CaC_2(s)$

$CaC_2(s) + 2H_2O(l) \rightarrow HC\equiv CH(g) + Ca(OH)_2(s)$

(ii) $2CH_4(g) + Heat \rightarrow HC\equiv CH(g) + 3H_2(g)$

When relatively inexpensive ethylene became available from petroleum and natural gas, about 40 years ago, acetylene was almost completely replaced by the alkene.

Some Simple Alkynes

Structure	*IUPAC Name*	*Common Name*	*b.p.(°C)*
H—C≡C—H	Ethyne	Acetylene	– 75
$CH_3C\equiv CH$	Propyne	Methyl-acetylene	– 23
$CH_3CH_2C\equiv CH$	1-Butyne	Ethyle-acetylene	9
$CH_3C\equiv CCH_3$	2-Butyne	Dimethyl-acetylene	27
	3-Methyl-1-butyne	*iso*-Propyl-acetylene	40

These compounds have four hydrogen atoms less than the parent alkane, so the generic formula for an alkyne with one C≡C triple bond is C_nH_{2n-2}.

Structure of Alkynes : The structure-pair geometry around the carbon atoms is clearly linear, so each carbon is *sp*-hybridized. This means that two half-filled *p*-orbitals remain on each carbon after hybridization and are available for π-bond formation. Two *sp*-hybridized orbitals on each carbon atom are used for C—H and C—C sigma (σ) bond formation.

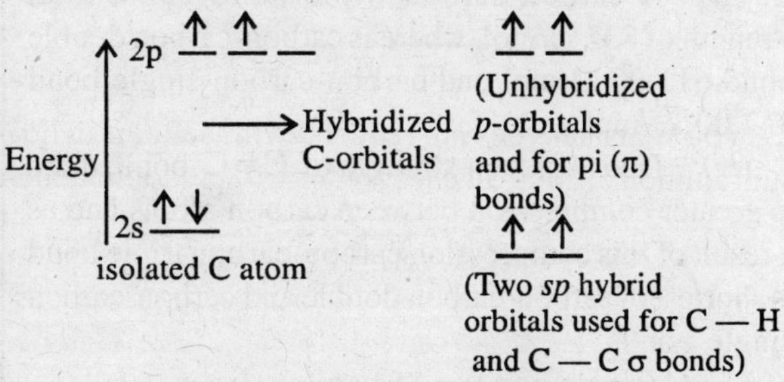

The orbitals about each C atom are pictured as :

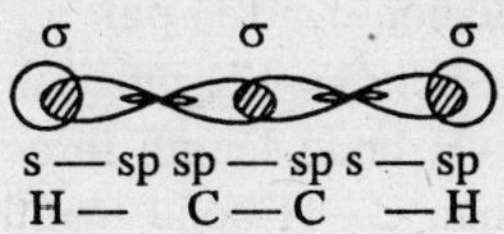

Orbital picture of acetylene depicting σ-bonds only

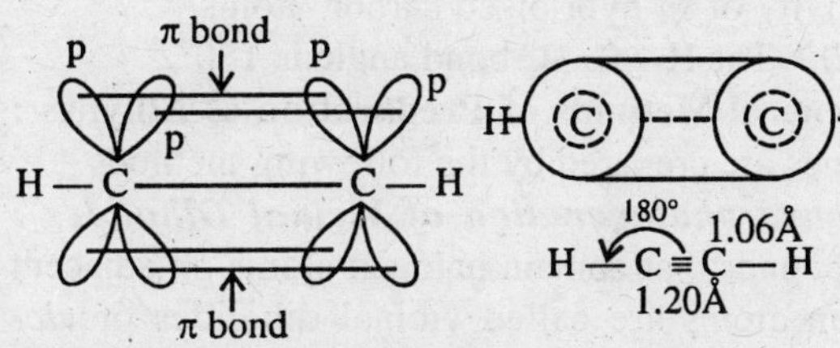

Fig. Orbital picture of acetylene depicting the formation of π-bonds.

The two *sp*-orbitals are 180° apart, and two unhybridized *p*-orbitals are 90° apart and lie in planes perpendicular to the *sp*-axis. The *sp*-hybrid orbitals are used for C—C and C—H σ-bond formation, and the pure *p*-orbitals overlap sideways to produce two carbon-carbon (π) pi bonds.

Important : *(i)* The carbon-carbon triple bond in alkynes is made up of one σ-bonds and two π-bonds.

(ii) Like alkenes, alkynes undergo addition reactions. These reactions are due to the availability of more exposed π-electrons.

Important : *(i)* If one π-cloud in acetylene lies above and below the line joining two nuclei, the other π-cloud will be in front and at the back of the line. The four lobes of two π-bonds merge to form a single electron cloud which is symmetrical (cylindrical) about the internuclear axis.

(ii) The π-bonds formed by poor sideways overlapping of 2*p*-orbitals are comparatively weaker than σ-bond formed by an efficient overlapping of *sp*-*sp* orbitals.

(iii) A carbon-carbon triple bond has a total strength of 837 kJ/mol, whereas carbon-carbon double bond 611.00 kJ/mol and carbon-carbon single bond 347.00 kJ/mol.

(iv) Due to greater strength of C≡C bond, there is greater compression between carbon atoms and as a result of this compression carbon-carbon triple bond is shortest of carbon-carbon double and carbon-carbon single bonds.

C—C (single bond) = 154 pm
C═C (double bond) = 134 pm
C≡C (tripple bond) = 121 pm

(v) The C—H bond length in acetylene (108 pm) is shorter than C—H bond length in ethylene (110.3 pm). This is due to the increased electronegativity of *sp*-hybridized carbon atoms.

(vi) The H—C—C bond angle is 180°.

General Methods of Preparation of Alkynes : Alkynes are prepared by the following methods :

Dehydrohalogenation of Vicinal Dihalides : Compounds that contain halogen atoms on adjacent carbon atoms are called vicinal dihalides or *vic*-dihalides. Alkynes are obtained by treatment of vicinal dihalides with alcoholic KOH followed by sodium amide ($NaNH_2$). This is a useful method since the vicinal dihalides are readily prepared from alkenes by the addition of halogen.

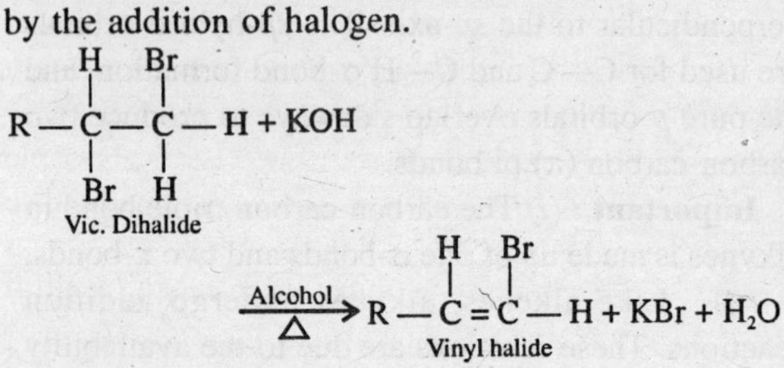

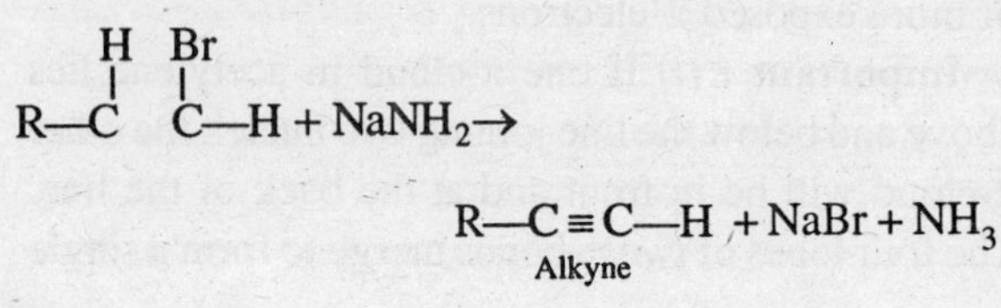

Notice that the product of the first HBr elimination is a substituted vinyl bromide. The vinyl halides are unreactive and a stronger base ($NaNH_2$) is used to remove the second HBr molecule.

Acetylene and propyne can be prepared by this method as follows :

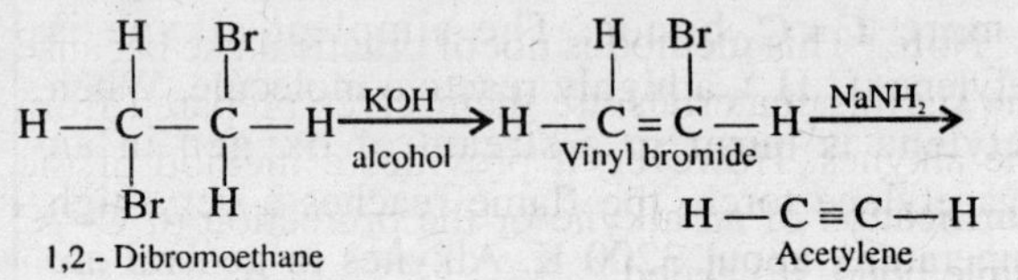

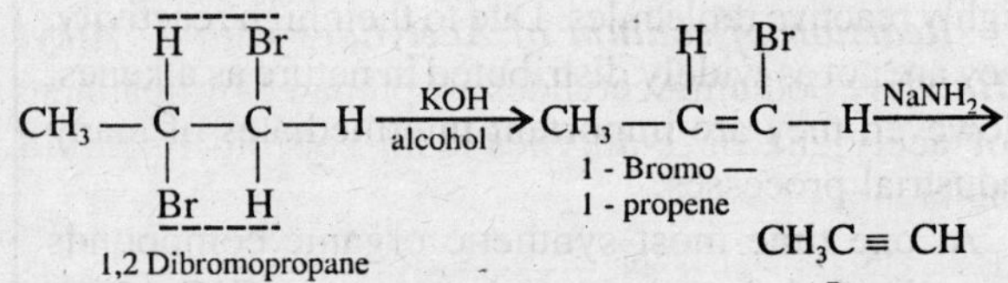

The *vic*-dihalides may be directly treated with $NaNH_2$ to give alkynes.

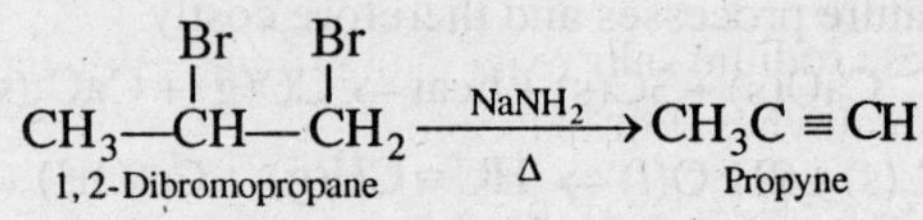

Important : *(i)* Dehydrohalogenation is carried out in two steps as :

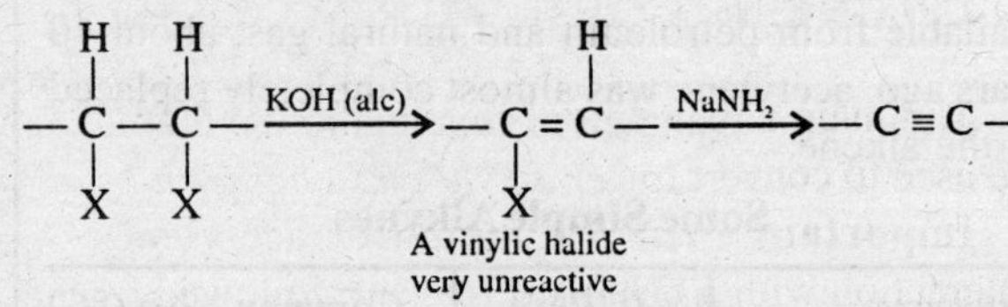

Vinylic halides are very stable. Under mild condition therefore, dehydrohalogenation stops at vinylic stage, more vigorous conditions (use of a stronger base) are required for alkyne formation.

(ii) Conversion of smaller alkynes into larger ones is done by use of metal acetylides.

Dehalogenation of Tetrahalides : By the action of zinc on tetrahalides, alkynes are obtained.

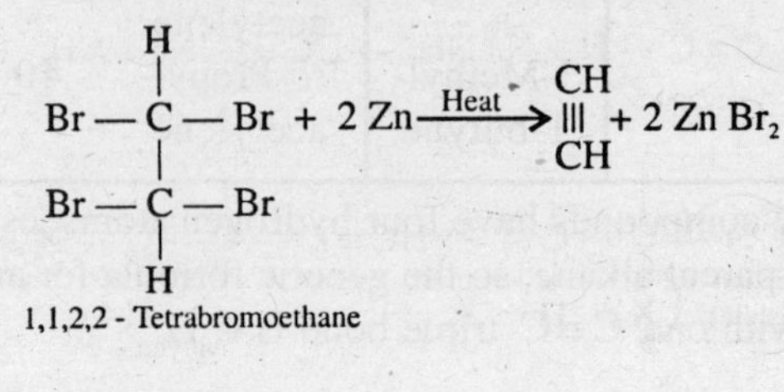

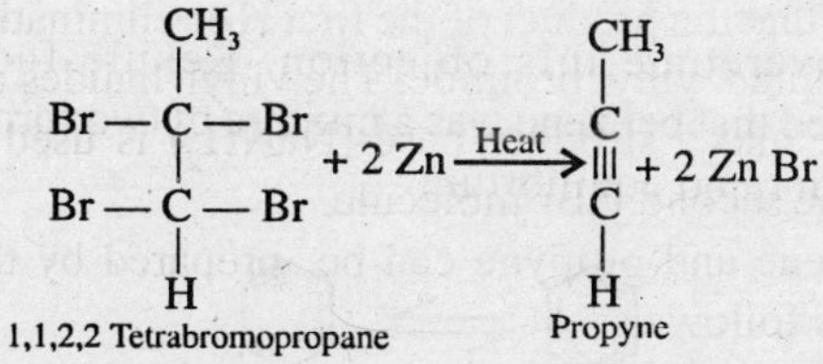

Note : This method is not of practical use because the starting materials are themselves prepared from the alkynes. However, it provides a method of the purification of an alkyne or the protection of C—C triple bond, if needed.

Reaction of sodium of Acetylides with 1° Alkyl Halides : Sodium Acetylides are prepared by treatment of acetylene or 1-alkynes with sodium in liquid ammonia.

$$\underset{\text{Acetylene}}{H—C\equiv C—H} + Na \xrightarrow[NH_3]{\text{Liquid}} \underset{\text{Sod acetylide}}{H—C\equiv \bar{C}{:}\overset{+}{Na}} + ½\,H_2$$

$$\underset{\text{1 - Alkyne}}{R—C\equiv C—H} + Na \xrightarrow[NH_3]{\text{Liquid}} R—C\equiv \bar{C}{:}\overset{+}{Na} + ½\,H_2$$

These sodium salts react with primary alkyl halides to form alkynes. For example,

$$\underset{\text{Sod acetylide}}{H—C\equiv \bar{C}{:}\overset{+}{Na}} + \underset{\substack{\text{Ethyl bromide}\\(1°\text{ halide})}}{C_2H_5\,Br} \rightarrow \underset{\text{1 - Butyne}}{H—C\equiv C—C_2H_6} + NaBr$$

$$C_2H_6C\equiv \bar{C}{:}\overset{+}{Na} + C_2H_5Br \rightarrow \underset{\text{3 - Hexyne}}{C_2H_5C\equiv CC_2H_5} + NaBr$$

The main advantage of this method is that it can be used to convert *lower alkynes into higher alkynes.*

Important : *(a)* Alkylation of acetylenes on interaction with a Grignard reagent, followed by the action of alkyl halide, also give similar results :

$$R—C\equiv CH + CH_3MgI \rightarrow R—C\equiv \bar{C}\,\overset{+}{Mgl} \xrightarrow{R'X} R—C\equiv CR'$$

(b) Alkylation of acetylenes is a nucleophilic displacement of halogen from alkyl halide. Acetylide ion is a nucleophile being a strong base

$$\underset{\text{Acetylene}}{H—C\equiv C—H} + \overset{+}{Na}\,\overset{-}{N}H_2 \rightarrow HC\equiv \bar{C}{:}\overset{+}{Na} + NH_3$$

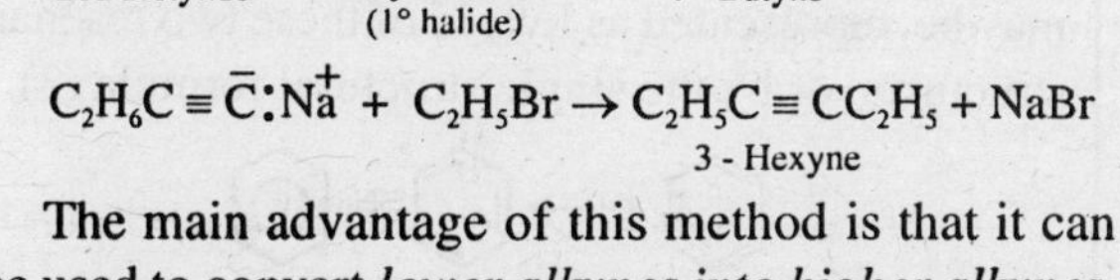

(c) Acetylide ion is a strong base and a competing elimination reaction is also likely. Since the decreasing order of elimination alkyl halide is tertiary > secondary > primary. The method is most useful and successful with primary alkyl halides.

Acetylene can also be prepared by following methods :

Reaction of Calcium Carbide with H_2O : Calcium carbide reacts with water to yield acetylene

$$\underset{\text{Cal.carbide}}{CaC_2} + H_2O \rightarrow \underset{\text{Acetylene}}{H—C\equiv C—H} + Ca(OH_2)$$

Synthesis from Carbon and Hydrogen : By passing a stream of hydrogen through electric arc struck between carbon electrodes.

$$2C + H_2 \xrightarrow[2773\,K]{\text{Electric arc}} \underset{\text{Acetylene}}{HC\equiv CH}$$

Physical Properties of Alkynes :

(i) The first three members are gases, next eight are liquids, and the higher alkynes are solids. They are all colourless except acetylene which has a garlic odour.

(ii) They are only slightly soluble in water but dissolve readily in organic solvents such as benzene, acetone and ethyl alcohol.

(iii) Their boiling points, melting points and specific gravities show a regular increase with the increase in molecular weights.

Structure of Benzene : The structure of benzene has been derived as follows :

(i) Molecular Formula : Elemental analysis and molecular weight determination showed that benzene had the molecular formula C_6H_6. This indicated that benzene was a highly unsaturated compound (compare it with n-hexane, C_6H_{14}).

(ii) Straight Chain Structure Not Possible : Benzene could be constructed as a straight chain or ring compound having double (C=C) and/or triple (C≡C) bonds. But benzene did not behave like alkenes or alkynes. It did not decolourise bromine in carbon tetrachloride or cold aqueous potassium permanganate. It did not add water in the presence of acids.

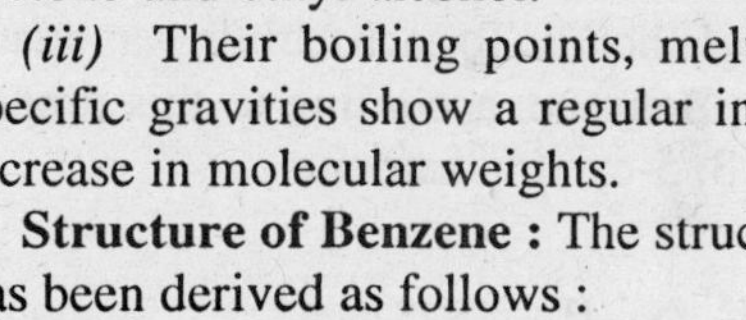

(iii) Evidence of Cyclic Structure :

(a) Substitution of Benzene : Benzene reacted with bromine in the presence of $FeBr_3$ (catalyst) to form *monobromobenzene.*

$$\underset{\text{Benzene}}{C_6H_6} + Br_2 \xrightarrow{FeBr_3} \underset{\text{Bromobenzene}}{C_6H_5Br} + HBr$$

The fact that only one monobromo and no isomeric products were obtained indicated that all six hydrogen atoms in benzene were identical. This could be possible only if benzene had a cyclic structure of six carbons and to each carbon was attached an hydrogen.

(b) Addition of Hydrogen : Benzene added three moles of hydrogen in the presence of nickel catalyst to give cyclohexane

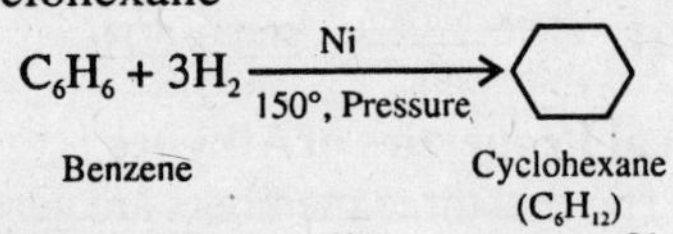

This confirmed the cyclic structure of benzene and also showed the presence of three carbon-carbon double bonds.

(iv) Kekule's Structure for Benzene : In 1865, August Kekule suggested benzene consisted of a cyclic planar structure of six carbons with alternate double and single bonds. To each carbon was attached one hydrogen. Benzene, according to this proposal, was simple 1, 3, 5-cyclohexatriene

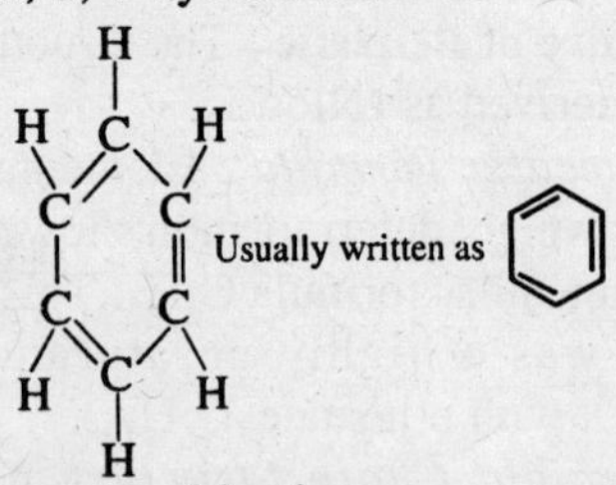

There were two objections :

(I) If the Kekule's structure was correct, there should exist two ortho isomers of dibromobenzene. In one isomer, the two bromine atoms should be on carbon that are connected by a double bond, as shown in structure *(a)*. In the other isomer, the bromines should be on carbons connected by a single bond, as shown in structure *(b)*. In fact, only one ortho-dibromobenzene could be prepared.

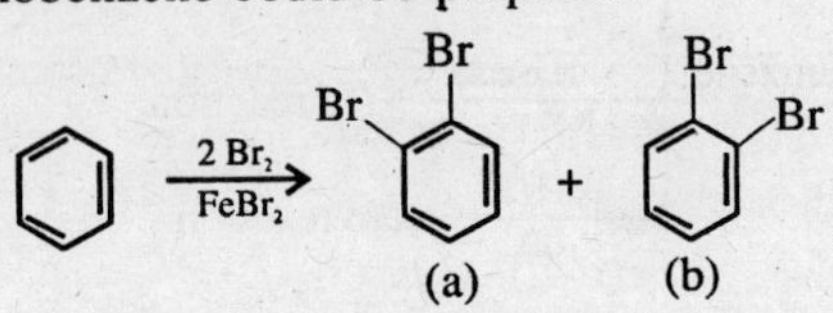

To overcome this objection, Kekule further suggested that benzene was a mixture of two forms (1 and 2) in rapid equilibrium.

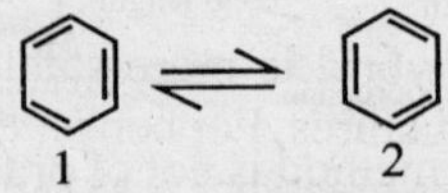

1 2

(II) Kekule's structure failed to explain why benzene with three double bonds did not give addition reaction like other alkenes. For example, benzene did not react with HBr or Br_2 in CCl_4.

(v) Resonance Description of Benzene : The phenomenon in which two or more structures can be written for a substance which involve identical positions of atoms is called *Resonance*. The actual structure of the molecule is said to be *Resonance Hybrid* of various possible alternative structures. The alternative structures are referred to as the *Resonance Structures* or *Contributing Forms*. A double headed arrow (↔) between the resonance structure is used to represent the resonance hybrid. Thus in the case of benzene, Kekule's structures (1) and (2) represent the resonance structures. Actual structure of the molecule may be represented as hybrid of these two resonance structures, or by the single structural formula (3).

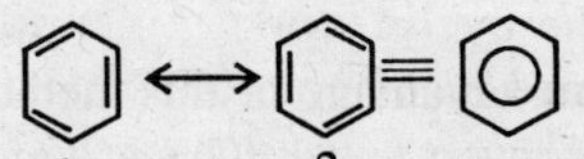

1 2

It should be clearly understood that the resonance structures (1) and (2) are not the actual structures of benzene molecule. They exist only in theory. None of these structures adequately represent the molecule. In resonance theory, we view the benzene molecule (which of course is a real entity) as being hybrid of these two hypothetical resonance structures. All single bonds in structure (1) are double bonds in structure (2), that is considered a hybrid of them, then the carbon-carbon bonds in benzene are neither single bonds nor double bonds. Rather, they are something halfway between. This is exactly what we find experimentally. Spectroscopic measurement show that benzene is planar and that all of its carbon-carbon bonds are of equal length, 1.40Å. This value lies in between the carbon-carbon single bond length (1.54 Å) and the carbon-carbon double bond length (1.34 Å)

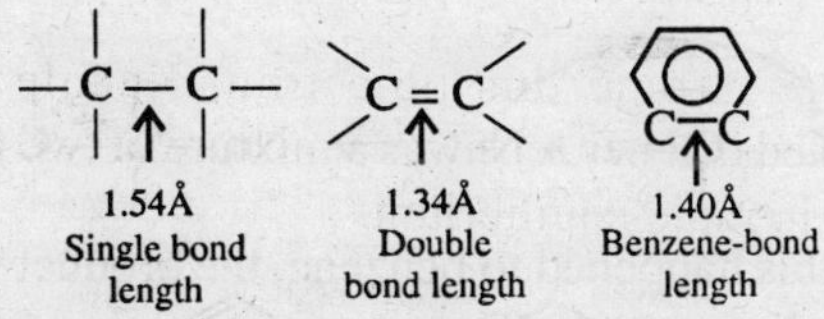

Resonance hybrid is more stable than any of its contributing structures. For benzene, the stability due to resonance is so great that π-bonds of the molecule will normally resist breaking. This explains lack of reactivity of benzene towards addition.

Aromaticity : The aromatic compounds apparently contain alternate double and single bonds in a cyclic structure, and resemble benzene in chemical behaviour. They undergo substitution rather addition reactions. This characteristic behaviour is called *Aromatic character* or *aromaticity*. Aromaticity is, in fact, a property of the sp^2-hybridized planar rings in which the *p*-orbitals (one on each atom) allow cyclic delocalisation of π-electrons.

Criteria for Aromaticity

Following are criteria to know whether a particular compound is aromatic or non-aromatic.

1. An aromatic compound is cyclic and planar.
2. Each atom in an aromatic ring has a *p*-orbital. These *p*-orbitals must be parallel so that a continuous overlap is possible around the ring.
3. The cyclic π-molecular orbital (electron cloud) formed by overlap of *p*-orbitals must contain $(4n + 2)$ π-electrons where n = integer 0, 1, 2, 3, etc. This is known as HUCKEL RULE.

Let us apply these rules to the following examples:

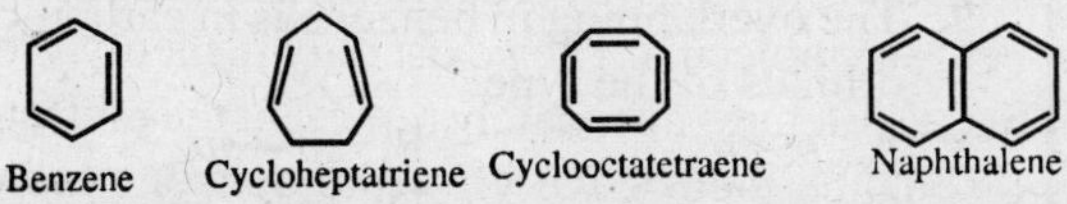

Benzene : It is a cyclic and planar compound. It has a *p*-orbital on each carbon of the ring involved in a double bond. It has three double bonds and six π-electrons, which is in accordance with Huckel rule.

$4n + 2 = 6$ or $4n = 6 - 2$

$\therefore 4n = 4$ and $n = 1$

Cycloheptatriene : It is a cyclic and planar. It has three double bonds and six π-electrons. But one of the carbons is saturated and does not possess a *p*-orbital. Hence a continuous overlap around the ring is not possible. The compound is, therefore, non-aromatic.

Cyclooctatetraene : It is cyclic and has a *p*-orbital on each atom of the ring. The Huckel rule is not satisfied, since there are 8 π-electrons.

$4n + 2 = 8$ equal $4n = 6$

$\therefore \; n = 1.5$

The compound is non-aromatic. Moreover, it has been determined that it is not planar but tube shaped.

***(a)* Electrophilic Substitution Reactions :** Benzene undergoes electrophilic substitution reactions. The benzene ring with delocalised π-electrons is an electron-rich system. It is attacked by electrophiles, giving substitution products. These reactions can be represented as

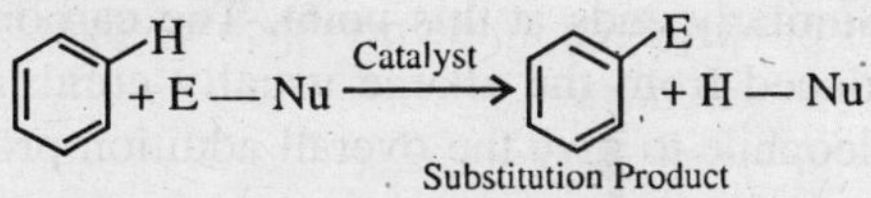

where E^+ is any electrophile and Nu^-: is a nucleophile. Such reactions in which hydrogen atom of the aromatic ring is replaced by an electrophile are called electrophilic aromatic substitution reactions.

General Mechanism : All electrophilic aromatic substitution reactions follow the same three-step mechanism :

Step 1 : Formation of an Electrophile :

$E — Nu + \text{ Catalyst } \rightarrow E^+ + Nu — \text{ catalyst}$

Step 2 : The electrophile attacks the aromatic ring to form a carbonium ion.

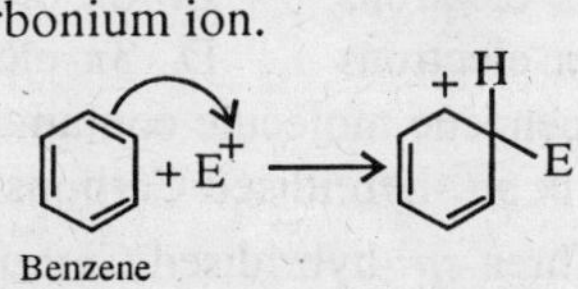

The intermediate ion is resonance stabilised. It is a hybrid of the following three structures:

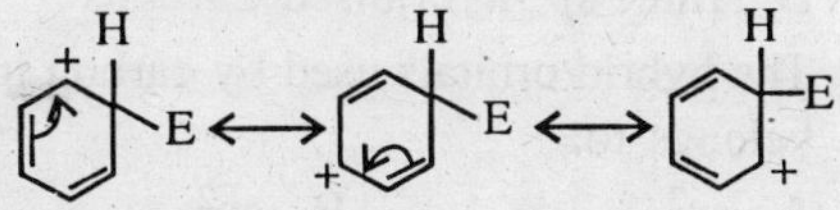

Step 3 : Loss of proton gives the substitution product.

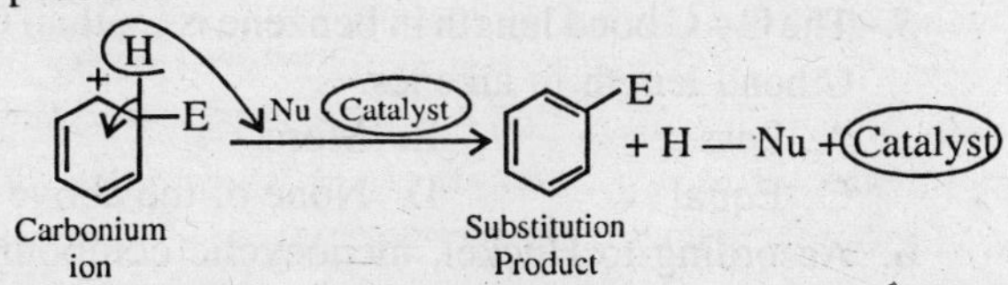

Important : Benzene undergoes Electrophilic substitution reactions whereas alkenes undergo addition reactions.

Both, benzene and alkenes are susceptible to electrophilic attack because of their exposed π-electrons. Both react with electrophiles to form stable carbonium ions.

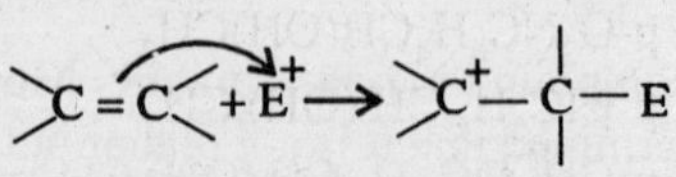

Electrophilic Addition to an Alkene

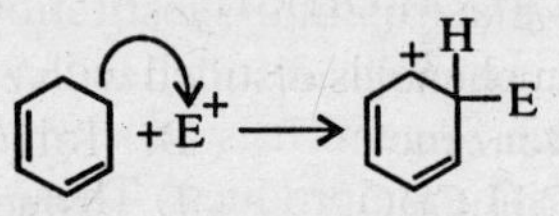

Electrophilic Addition to Benzene

Similarly ends at this point. The carbonium ion produced from the alkene usually combines with nucleophile to give the overall addition product :

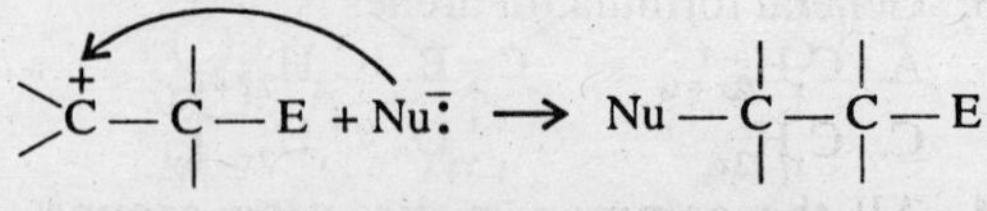

If this happened to benzene, the product would no longer be aromatic. The resonance energy (stabilising energy) of benzene would be lost. Instead, the nucleophile removes a proton from the carbonium ion intermediate. The loss of proton allows the electrons from the C—H bond to go back into the ring and regenerate the aromatic π system. Net change in the replacement of a hydrogen atom by an electrophile.

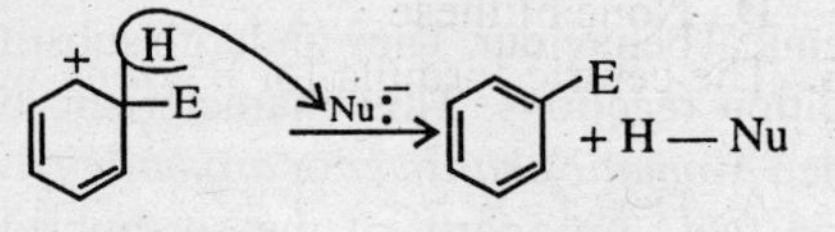

OBJECTIVE QUESTIONS

1. Aromatic hydrocarbons are the derivatives of:
A. Benzene
B. Methane
C. Normal series of Paraffins
D. None of the above

2. In benzene there are:
A. 2π electrons B. 6π electrons
C. 8π electrons D. 3π electrons

3. The benzene molecule contains :
A. Six sp^2-hybridised Carbons
B. Three sp^3-hybridised Carbons
C. Six sp^3-hybridised Carbons
D. Three sp^3-hybridised Carbons

4. The hybrid orbitals used by carbon in benzene belongs to:
A. sp^3 B. sp^2
C. sp D. dsp^3

5. The C – C bond length in benzene is..... than C – C bond length in alkenes.
A. Less B. More
C. Equal D. None of the above

6. According to Huckel, menocyclic compounds will show aromaticity when:
A. It has 4π electrons
B. It has no π electron
C. It has 4π + 2 electrons
D. It has $(4n + 2)\pi$ electrons

7. Carbon in benzene undergoes sp^2-hybridisation and the bond angle is 120°. The shape of benzene molecule is:
A. Linear B. Planar
C. Pyramidal D. Planar hexagonal

8. According to Huckel rule, the number of π electrons in anthracene is:
A. 12 B. 14
C. 10 D. 20

9. The overlapping in benzene is in carbon-carbon orbitals of the type:
A. $p - p$ B. $sp - sp$
C. $sp^2 - sp^2$ D. $sp^3 - sp^3$

10. C – C bond length in benzene is:
A. 1.54 Å B. 1.20 Å
C. 1.39 Å D. 1.48 Å

11. C – C bond length in benzene is.....than C – C bond length in alkanes.
A. Less B. More
C. Equal D. None of the above

12. The correct structure for benzene was first proposed by:
A. Faraday B. Kekule
C. Wohler D. Davy

13. General formula for arenes is:
A. C_xH_{2x+6} B. C_xH_{2x+6y}
C. C_xH_{2x} D. C_xH_{2x-6y}

14. All the common m-directing groups.....the benzene ring towards electrophilic substitution reactions.
A. Deactivate B. Activate
C. Both (A) and (B) D. None of the above

15. *o, p*-directing groups are generally:
A. Activating groups
B. Deactivating groups
C. Neutral groups
D. None of these

16. The centric formula for benzene was proposed by:
A. Dewar
B. Armstrong and Baeyer
C. Ladenberg
D. Kekule

17. The end product of the reaction

$C_6H_6 + Cl_2 \xrightarrow{\text{Sunlight}}$ is:
A. C_6H_5Cl B. o-$C_6H_4Cl_2$
C. $C_6H_6Cl_6$ D. p-$C_6H_4Cl_2$

18. Which of the following is expected to undergo nitration more easily and reality to furnish the corresponding nitro derivatives employing the usual nitrating mixture:
A. C_6H_6 B. $C_6H_5NO_2$
C. $C_6H_5CH_3$ D. $C_6H_5.CCl_3$

19. Which of the following species is most stable:
A. $P-O_2N-C_6H_4-\overset{+}{C}H_2$
B. $C_6H_5-\overset{+}{C}H_2$
C. $P-Cl-C_6H_4-\overset{+}{C}H_2$
D. $P-CH_3O-C_6H_4-\overset{+}{C}H_2$

20. Which of the following is explosive:
A. Nitrobenzene B. Nitrophenol
C. Nitromethane D. Trinitrobenzene

21. The reaction, $C_6H_6 + CH_3Cl \xrightarrow[AlCl_3]{\text{Anhydrous}}$ $C_6H_5CH_3 + HCl$ is an example of:
A. Friedel-Crafts reaction
B. Kolbe's synthesis
C. Wurtz reaction
D. Grignard Synthesis

22. Which of the following alcohols is dehydrated most readily with conc. H_2SO_4:
A. p-$O_2NC_6H_4CH(OH)CH_3$
B. p-$ClC_6H_4CH(OH)CH_3$
C. p-$CH_3OC_6H_4CH(OH)CH_3$
D. $C_6H_5CH(OH)CH_3$

23. When phenol is distilled with zinc dust, it gives:
A. Benzene B. Toluene
C. C_6H_5CHO D. None of the above

24. Rate of substitution in phenol is:
A. Slower than as in benzene
B. Faster than as in benzene
C. Equal to that as in benzene
D. None of these

25. Amongst the following the comound that can be most readily sulphonated is:
A. Benzene B. Methoxy benzene
C. Toluene D. Chlorobenzene

26. Which compound is least soluble in water:
A. Phenol B. Benzene
C. Ethanol D. Benzoic acid

27. Chlorine reacts with benzaldehyde to give:
A. Benzyl chloride B. Benzal chloride
C. Benzoyl chloride D. Chlorobenzene

28. Nitrosobenzene can be isolated from nitrobenzene under:
A. Metal and acid
B. Zn dust and NH_4Cl
C. Alkaline sodium arsenite
D. None of the above

29. Bakelite is obtained from phenol by reacting with:
A. Acetaldehyde B. Formaldehyde
C. Baking soda D. Formic acid

30. The major product obtained when 3-Phenyl-1, 2-Propane-diol is heated with H_2SO_4 is:
A. $C_6H_5-CH_2-CO-CH_3$
B. $C_6H_5-CH_2-CH_2-CHO$
C. $C_6H_5-CH_2-CH=CH_2$
D. $C_6H_5-CH_2-CH-CH_2$ (with O bridging the two CH carbons)

31. Dyes are formed when diazonium salts reacts with:

A. Phenols B. Aldehydes

C. Ketones D. Alcohols

32. Chlorobenzene is prepared commercially by:

A. Grignard reaction

B. Reaschig Process

C. Wurtz-Fittig reaction

D. Friedel-Crafts reaction

33. Benzene reacts with CH_3COCl in the presence of $AlCl_3$ to give:

A. C_6H_5Cl B. C_6H_5COCl

C. $C_6H_5CH_3$ D. $C_6H_5COCH_3$

34. Which of the following compounds is formed when an aqueous acidic solution of benzene diazonium chloride is bailed:

A. Chlorobenzene B. Benzene

C. Aniline D. Phenol

35. Dry distillation of calcium benzoate with calcium formate gives:

A. Acetaldehyde B. Benzoic acid

C. Benzaldehyde D. Benzoic anhydride

36. For benzaldehyde which of the following is incorrect:

A. It is an aromatic aldehyde

B. It is used in perfumery

C. On oxidation it yields benzoic acid

D. On reduction it yields phenol

37. The reaction, $C_6H_5N_2Cl \xrightarrow{Cu_2Cl_2/HCl} C_6H_5Cl + N_2$ is called:

A. Etard's reaction

B. Sandmeyer's reaction

C. Wurtz-Fittig reaction

D. Perkin's reaction

38. Which of the following ion is produced when we prepare nitrating mixture by mixing together con-centrated HNO_3 and concentrated H_2SO_4:

A. NO_2^- B. $\overset{+}{N}O_2$

C. NO_3^- D. $\overset{+}{S}O_3H$

39. The correct order of reactivity towards electrophilic substitution is:

A. Phenol > Benzene > Chlorobenzene > Benzoic acid

B. Benzoic acid > Chlorobenzene > Benzene > Phenol

C. Phenol > Chlorobenzene > Benzene > Benzoic acid

D. Benzoic acid > Phenol > Benzene > Chlorobenzene

40. Among the following statements on the nitration of aromatic compounds, the false one is:

A. The rate of nitration of benzene is almost the same as that of hexadeuterobenzene

B. The rate of nitration of toluene is greater than that of benzene

C. The rate of nitration of benzene is greater than that of hexadeuterobenzene

D. Nitration is an electrophilic substitution reaction

41. Which among the following is the strongest ortho-para directing group:

A. –OH B. –Cl

C. $-OCH_3$ D. $-CH_3$

42. 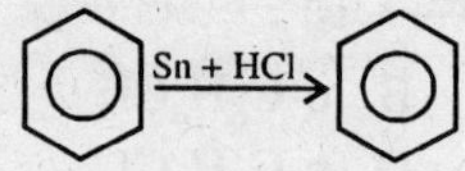

In the above reaction '*x*' stands for

A. NH_2 B. Cl

C. $SnCl_2$ D. $N^+.H_3Cl^-$

43. 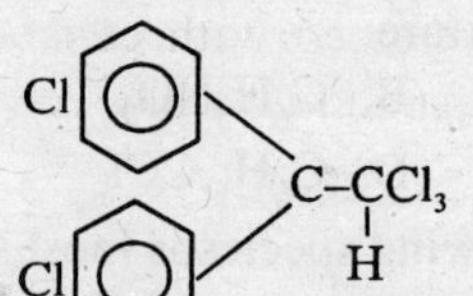

The above structural formula refers to:

A. BHC B. DNA

C. DDT D. RNA

44. Aromatic compounds most easily

A. Nucleophilic substiturion

B. Electrophilic substitution

C. Nucleophilic addition

D. Electrophilic addition

45. Benzyl alcohol is obtained from benzaldehyde by:

A. Fittig's reaction B. Cannizzaro's reaction

C. Kolbe's reaction D. Wurtz's reaction

46. Nitration of benzene is:

A. Nucleophilic substitution
B. Electrophilic substitution
C. Electrophilic addition
D. Nucleophilic addition

47. The correct sequence of activating power of a group in benzene is:
A. $-NH_2 > -NHCOCH_3 > -CH_3$
B. $-NH_2 < -NHCOCH_3 < -CH_3$
C. $-NH_2 > -NHCOCH_3 < -CH_3$
D. $-NH_2 < -NHCOCH_3 > -CH_3$

48. Nitrobenzene on reduction with Zn and aq. NH_4Cl gives:
A. Aniline
B. Nitrosobenzene
C. N-Phenyl hydroxylamine
D. Hydrazobenzene

49. Activation of benzene ring by-NH_2 in aniline can be reduced by treating with:
A. Dil. HCl B. Ethyl alcohol
C. Acetic acid D. Acetyl chloride

50. Wurtz-Fittig reaction is used to prepare:
A. Alkyl benzene B. Alkanes
C. Alkenes D. Alkynes

51. When benzoic acid is heated with soda lime, we get:
A. Phenol B. Benzyl alcohol
C. Benzene D. Benzaldehyde

52. When benzene is treated with concentrated HNO_3 at room temperature it will give:
A. CO_2 and H_2O
B. Nitrochlorobenzene
C. Will become dark red
D. Dinitrobenzene

53. Which of the following is phenol:
A. Benzene B. Cresol
C. Catechol D. All of the above

54. In phenols:
A. –OH group is attached in side chain
B. –OH group is directly attached to benzene nucleus
C. Both (A) and (B)
D. None of the above

55. Carbolic acid is the name used for:
A. Opium B. Phenol
C. Chloroform D. H_2CO_3

56. Phenol is:
A. A base weaker than NH_3
B. An acid stronger than carbonic acid
C. An acid weaker than carbonic acid
D. Neutral

57. In chlorobenzene the –Cl group:
A. Activates the benzene ring more via resonance effect than deactivating it via inductive effect
B. Deactivates the benzene ring more via inductive effect than activating it via resonance effect
C. Activates the benzene ring via resonance effect and deactivates it via inductive effect. Both these effects are more evenly matched
D. None of the above

58. Chlorobenzene on heating with NaOH at 300° C under pressure gives:
A. Phenol B. Benzaldehyde
C. Chlorophenol D. None of the above

59. The IUPAC name of picric acid is:
A. 2, 4, 6-trinitrophenol
B. 2, 4, 6-trinitro-1-hydroxy hexane
C. 2, 4, 6-trinitro-1-hydroxy benzene
D. 1, 3, 5-trinitro-6-hydroxy benzene

60. Which of the following is explosive:
A. PCl_5 B. HNO_3
C. C_6H_5OH D. 2, 4, 6-trinitrophenol

61. Phenol reacts with Br_2 in CCl_4 at low temperature to give:
A. *m*-bromophenol
B. *o*- and *p*-bromophenol
C. *p*-bromophenol
D. 2, 4, 6-tribromophenol

62. Between P-nitrophenol and salicylaldehyde, solubility in base is:
A. Almost nil in both cases
B. Higher in P-nitrophenol
C. Higher for salicylaldehyde
D. Equal in nature

63. An aromatic amine (A) was treated with alcoholic potash and another compound (Y) when a foul smelling gas was formed with formula C_6H_5NC. Y was formed by reacting a compound Z with Cl_2 in presence of slaked lime. Compound Z is:
A. $C_6H_5NH_2$ B. CH_3OH
C. CH_3COCH_3 D. $CHCl_3$

64. Which concept best explains that *o*-nitrophenol is more volatile than *p*-nitrophenol?
A. Resonance
B. Hydrogen bonding
C. Hyper conjugation
D. Steric hindrance

65. Identify Z in the change:

$$C_6H_5NH_2 \xrightarrow[280\ K]{NaNO_2/HCl} X \xrightarrow{CuBr/HBr} Z$$

A. 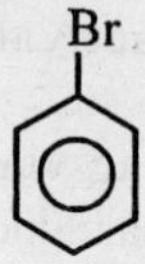
B. 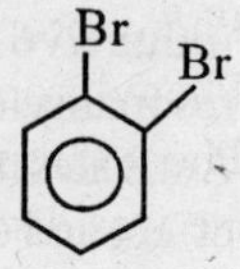
C. 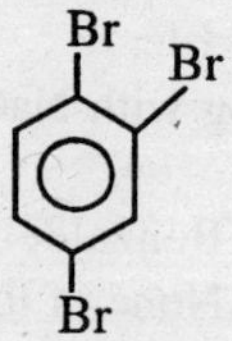
D. 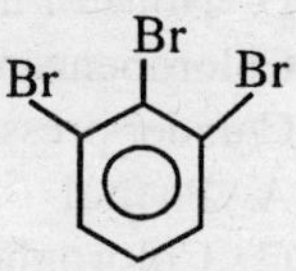

66. Identify *y* in the change:

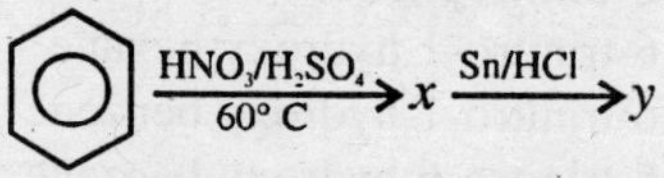

A. 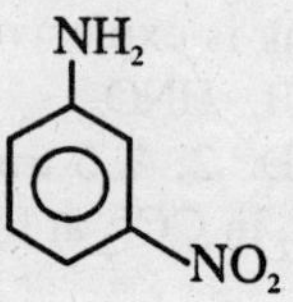
B. 
C. 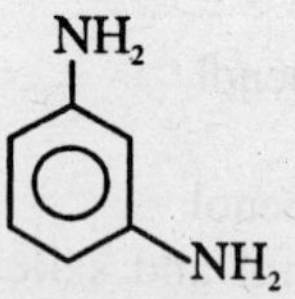
D. 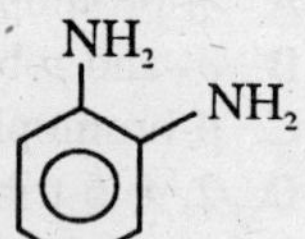

67. When phenol is reacted with chloroform and an alkali like NaOH, the compound formed is salicylaldehyde. If we use Pyrene in place of chloroform the product obtained is:
A. Salicylaldehyde B. Phenolphthalan
C. Salicylic acid D. Cyclohexanal

68. Which represents Reimer-Tiemann reaction?

A. 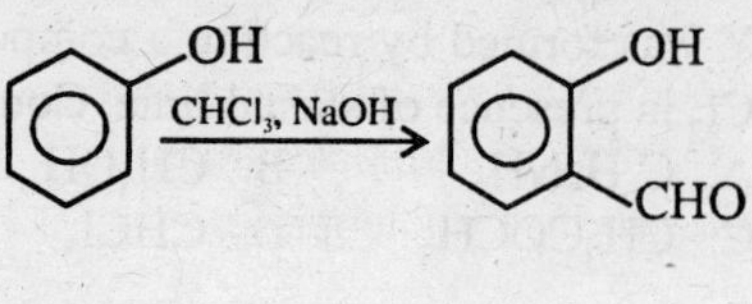
B. 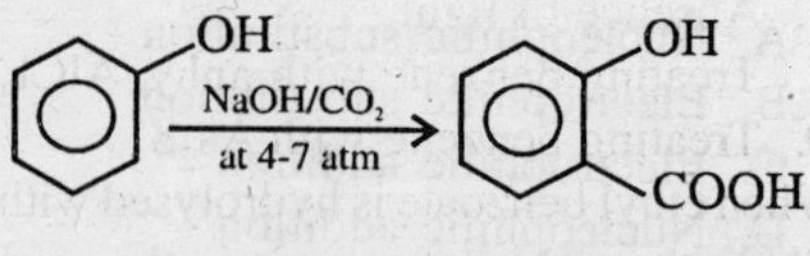
C. 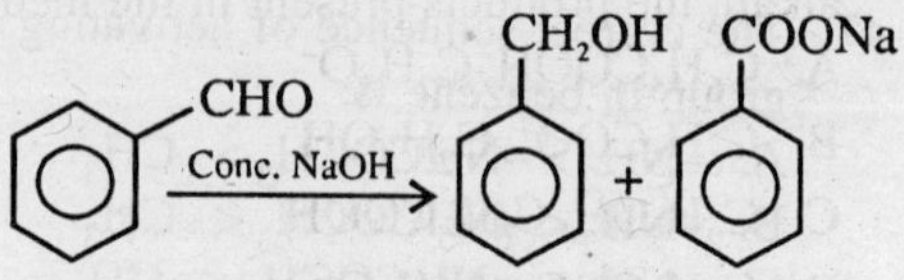
D. 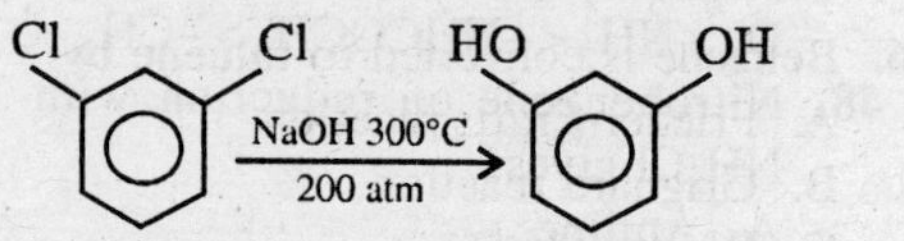

69. Phenol with dilute HNO_3 gives:
A. Meta and Para nitrophenol
B. Ortho and Para nitrophenol
C. Trinitrophenol
D. Ortho and Meta nitrophenol

70. An aromatic primary amine with cold nitrous acid leads to the formation of:
A. Alcohol B. Nitrite
C. Diazonium salt D. Benzene

71. Which of the following molecules/species are aromatic in character:

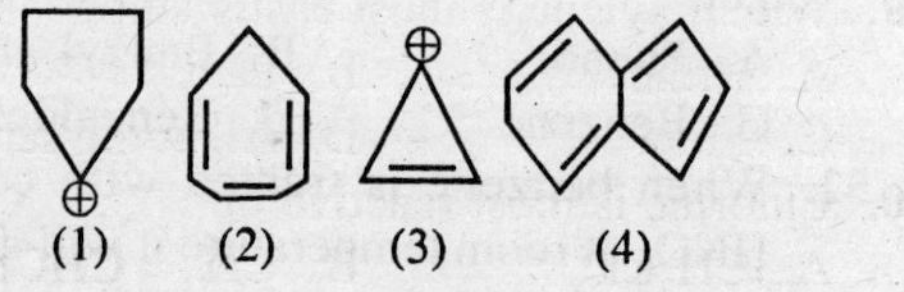

(1) (2) (3) (4)

A. 2 B. 3
C. 4 D. 1

72. Aniline reacts with excess of bromine to give:
A. Benzyl bromide and hydrobromic acid
B. 2, 4, 6-tribromoaniline
C. 2-bromotoluene and hydrobromic acid
D. 2-bromophenol and hydrobromic acid

73. In Etard's reaction toluene is oxidised to benzaldehyde using:
A. H_2O_2
B. Cl_2
C. Chromium trioxide or CrO_2Cl_2
D. $KMnO_4$

74. Benzyl chloride is formed by treating toluene with Cl_2 in:
A. Presence of light

B. Absence of light
C. Treating benzene with anhy. $AlCl_3$
D. Treating benzene with As_2S_3

75. When ethyl benzoate is hydrolysed with aqueous alkali, the products present in the medium are:
A. $C_6H_5COOH, C_2H_5O^-$
B. $C_6H_5COO^-, C_2H_5OH$
C. C_2H_5OH, C_6H_5COOH
D. $C_6H_5COO^-, C_2H_5O^-$

76. Benzene is converted to toluene by:
A. Friedel-Crafts reaction
B. Grignard reaction
C. Wurtz reaction
D. Perkin reaction

77. The chlorination of toluene in presence of ferric chloride gives predominantly:
A. Benzyl chloride
B. *m*-chlorotoluene
C. Benzal chloride
D. *o*- and *p*-chlorotoluene

78. Among the following group, which deactivates benzene ring for electrophilic substitution?
A. Methyl B. Amine
C. Hydroxyl D. Chlorine

79. Which xylene is most easily sulphonated?
A. Ortho B. Para
C. Meta D. All at the same rate

80. Chlorine is most reactive in:
A. CH_3Cl B. $CH_2=CHCl$
C. C_6H_5Cl D. $C_6H_5CH_2Cl$

81. Chlorine is least reactive in:
A. CH_3Cl B. $CH_2=CHCl$
C. C_6H_5Cl D. C_2H_5Cl

82. In which of the following P electrons of the halogens are not involved in delocalisation:
A. Chlorobenzene B. Bromobenzene
C. Allyl chloride D. Vinyl chloride

83. The most basic compound among the following is:
A. Benzylamine B. Aniline
C. Acetanilide D. p-nitro aniline

84. *m*-chlorobenzaldehyde on reaction with conc. KOH at room temperature gives:
A. Potassium *m*-chlorobenzoate and *m*-hydroxy benzaldehyde
B. *m*-hydroxy benzaldehyde and *m*-chlorobenzyl-alcohol
C. *m*-chlorobenzylalcohol and *m*-hydroxy benzyl-alcohol
D. Potassium *m*-chlorobenzoate and *m*-chlorobenzyl alcohol

85. 1-phenyl, 2-chloropropane on treatment with aqueous KOH gives mainly:
A. 1-Phenylpropane
B. 3-Phenylpropane
C. 1-Phenylpropan-2-ol
D. 1-Phenylpropan-3-ol

86. Benzene was discovered by:
A. Cavendish B. Faraday
C. Berzelius D. Wohler

87. Formylchloride has not been prepared so far. Which can function as formylchloride in formylation?
A. $HCHO+HCl$ B. $HCOOCH_3+HCl$
C. $CO+HCl$ D. $HCONH_2+HCl$

88. Aniline on heating with conc. H_2SO_4 at 460K gives:
A. Aniline sulphate
B. Benzene sulphonic acid
C. Sulphanilic acid
D. None of the above

89. What are the products formed when an equimolar mixture of benzaldehyde and formaldehyde is heated with concentrated NaOH?
A. C_6H_5-CH_2-OH and H-COONa
B. C_6H_5-COONa and CH_3-OH
C. C_6H_5-CH-COONa
D. C_6H_5-COOH and CH_3-ONa

90. The nitro group in nitrobenzene is:
A. Ortho directing
B. Meta directing
C. Para directing
D. Ortho and Para directing

91. The function of anhydrous aluminium chloride in the Friedel-crafts reaction is:
A. To absorb water
B. To absorb hydrochloric acid
C. To produce an electrophile
D. To produce nucleophile

92. The chemical name of DDT is:
A. Dichlorodinitrotoluene
B. Dichlorodimethyltoluene
C. P, P'-dichlorodiphenyltrichloroethane
D. None of these

93. Which one of the following compounds when dissolved in water gives a solution with pH more than 7?
A. $C_6H_5NH_2$ B. C_6H_5OH
C. C_2H_5OH D. CH_3COCH_3

94. In the halogenation of aromatic nucleus, the halogen carrier is used to generate the species:
A. Cl B. Cl^+
C. Cl^- D. Cl

95. Gammexane (*an*-isomer of) is:
A. BHC
B. Benzene hexachloride
C. Lindane
D. All of the above

96. Aniline is separated by:
A. Fractional crystallisation
B. Fractional distillation
C. Steam distillation
D. Vacuum distillation

97. Picric acid is a yellow coloured compound. Its chemical name is:
A. *m*-nitrobenzoic acid
B. 2, 4, 6-trinitrophenol
C. Trinitrotoluene
D. Trinitroaniline

98. The reaction involving condensation of acetic anhydride with an aromatic aldehyde by a carboxylate ion giving α–β unsaturated acid is an example of:
A. Aldol condensation
B. Benzoin condensation
C. Perkin reaction
D. Wurtz reaction

99. Which does not have a carboxyl group?
A. Picric acid B. Ethanoic acid
C. Aspirin D. Benzoic acid

100. When aniline is heated with benzaldehyde the product is:
A. Benzoin B. Schiff's base
C. Unsaturated acid D. Azoxy benzene

101. Which one of the following is most reactive towards aqueous NaOH:
A. C_6H_5Cl B. $C_6H_5CH_2Cl$
C. C_6H_5Br D. BrC_6H_5Br

102. When sodium benzene sulphonate is fused with sodium hydroxide (solid), followed by hydrolysis the product formed is:
A. Benzene
B. Sod. phenoxide
C. Benzene thiophenol
D. Phenol

103. Pure aniline is a:
A. Brown coloured liquid
B. Colourless liquid
C. Brown coloured solid
D. Colourless solid

104. The strongest acid among the following aromatic compounds is:
A. Orthonitrophenol B. Parachlorophenol
C. Paranitrophenol D. Metanitrophenol

105. When phenol is treated with excess bromine water. It gives:
A. *m*-bromophenol
B. *o*- and *p*-bromophenol
C. 2, 4-dibromophenol
D. 2, 4, 6-tribromophenol

106. Among the following –Phenol, benzoic acid, nitrobenzene and toluene, the compound that undergoes nitration readily is:
A. Benzoic acid B. Toluene
C. Phenol D. Nitrobenzene

107. Benzene reacts with sulphuric acid only when the acid is:
A. Dilute and cold
B. Dilute and hot
C. Hot and concentrated
D. Mixed with HNO_3

108. In 'nitration mixture' concentrated sulphuric acid is used:
A. As sulphonating agent
B. As dehydrating agent
C. For the formation of nitronium ions
D. As a solvent

109. Which of the following reacts with KCN to form benzoin?

A. C_6H_5CHO B. C_6H_5Cl
C. C_2H_5Cl D. $C_6H_5CH_3$

110. Sulphonation of benzoic acid produces mainly:
A. *o*-sulphobenzoic acid
B. *m*-sulphobenzoic acid
C. *p*-sulphobenzoic acid
D. *o, p*-disulphobenzoic acid

111. The product of oxidation of aniline with $K_2Cr_2O_7$ and conc. H_2SO_4 will be:
A. *p*-amino phenol
B. *p*-benzoquinone
C. Aniline black dye
D. Phenyl hydroxylamine

112. Phenol on treatment with dil. HNO_3 at room temperature gives:

A. 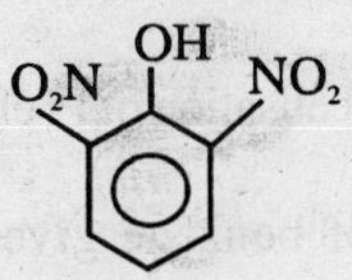

B. 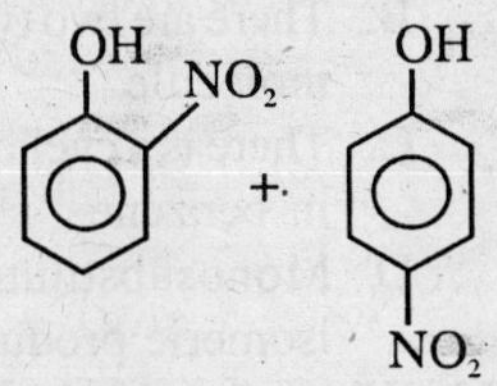

C. 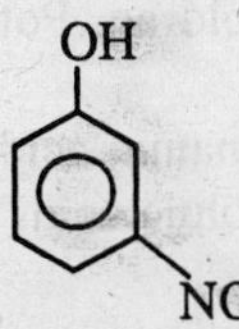

D. 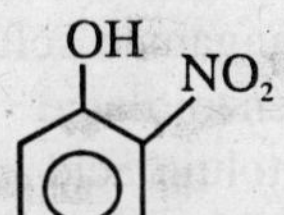

113. In the reaction of *p*-chlorotoluene with KNH_2 in liq. NH_3 the major product is:
A. *o*-toluidine B. *m*-toluidine
C. *p*-toluidine D. *p*-chloranniline

114. Benzaldehyde, when heated with concentrated KOH solution, gives:
A. $C_6H_5CH_2OH$
B. C_6H_5COOH
C. C_6H_5CHO
D. Mixture of C_6H_5 COOK and $C_6H_5CH_2OH$

115. Which aromatic acid among the following is weaker than simple benzoic acid:

A. 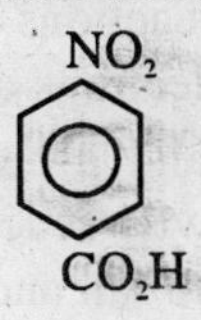

B. 

C. 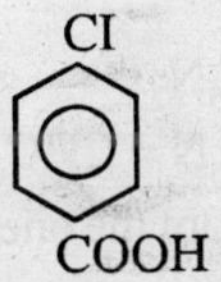

D. 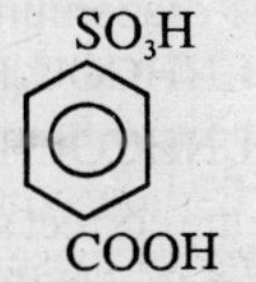

116. The reaction, $C_6H_5NH_2.HCl + HNO_2$. $\xrightarrow{\text{About } 5°C} C_6H_5N_2Cl + 2H_2O$ is known as:
A. Diazotisation
B. Perkin's reaction
C. Cannizzaro's reaction
D. Coupling reaction

117. Phenol and ethanol can be distinguished by using:
A. NaOH B. PCl_5
C. $FeCl_3$ D. Benzoic acid

118. Chlorination of toluene in the presence of light and heat followed by treatment with aqueous NaOH gives:
A. *o*-Cresol
B. *p*-Cresol
C. 2, 4-dihydroxytoluene
D. Benzoic acid

119. Benzaldehyde can be obtained by the hydrolysis of:
A. Benzyl chloride B. Benzal chloride
C. Benzonitrile D. Benzoic acid

120. Increasing order of acid strength among *p*-methoxyphenol, *p*-methylphenol and *p*-nitrophenol
A. *p*-methyl phenol < *p*-methoxy phenol < *p*-nitro- phenol
B. *p*-methoxy phenol < *p*-methyl phenol < *p*-nitro phenol
C. *p*-nitro phenol < *p*-methoxy phenol < *p*-methyl-phenol
D. *p*-nitrophenol < *p*-methylphenol < *p*-methoxy phenol

121. Which represents an example of Friedel Crafts reaction:
A. $C_6H_6 + C_2H_5Cl \xrightarrow{AlCl_3} C_6H_5C_2H_5 + HCl$
B $C_2H_5OH + HCl \xrightarrow{ZnCl_2} C_2H_5Cl + H_2O$
C. $C_6H_5Cl + CH_3COCl \xrightarrow{AlCl_3} C_6H_5COCH_3 + Cl_2$
D. $C_2H_5Br + Mg \xrightarrow{Ether} C_2H_5MgBr$

122. Benzene diazonium salt is:

A. $C_6H_5NHCOC_6H_5$ B. $C_6H_5N_2x$

C. $C_6H_5NHCOCH_3$ D. $C_6H_5N=CHC_6H_5$

123. Choose the correct statement from the ones given below for two anilium in:

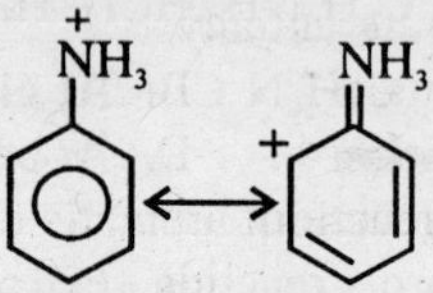

(I) (II)

A. It is not an acceptable canonical structure because carbonium ions are less stable than ammonium ions

B. It is not an acceptable canonical structure because it is non-aromatic

C. It is not an acceptable canonical structure because the nitrogen has 10 valence electrons

D. It is an acceptable canonical structure

124. Which statement is not correct regarding aniline?

A. It is less basic than ethyl amine

B. It can be steam distilled

C. It reacts with sodium to give hydrogen

D. It is soluble in water

125. Anhydrous aluminium chloride is used in Friedel-Crafts reaction because it is:

A. Electron rich

B. Soluble in ether

C. Ionizable to chloride and aluminium ions

D. Electron deficient molecule

126. Benzoic acid reacts with $SOCl_2$ to give:

A. Chlorobenzene B. Dichlorobenzene

C. Benzoyl chloride D. Benzyl chloride

127. On boiling with conc. hydrobromic acid, Phenyl ethyl ether will yield:

A. Phenol and ethyl bromide

B. Bromobenzene and ethanal

C. Phenol and ethane

D. Bromobenzene and ethane

128. Benzene reacts with *n*-Propyl chloride in the presence of anhydrous $AlCl_3$ to give predominantly:

A. Isopropyl benzene

B. No reaction

C. *n*-Propylbenzene

D. 3-Propyl-1-chlorobenzene

129. Which compound burns with a sooty flame?

A. $C_6H_5CH_2OH$ B. C_6H_5COOH

C. CH_3OH D. $CH_3COC_2H_5$

130. The correct symbol relating the two Kekule structures of benzene is:

A. $\rightarrow$ B. $\rightleftharpoons$

C. $\leftrightarrow$ D. $\rightleftarrows$

131. The number of double bonds in BHC (gammexane) is:

A. 1 B. 2

C. 3 D. Zero

132. The true statement about benzene is:

A. Because of unsaturation benzene easily undergoes molecule

B. There are two types of C - C bonds in benzene molecule

C. There is a cyclic delocalisation of Pi electrons in benzene

D. Monosubstitution of benzene gives three isomeric products

133. Which would decolourise cold aq. Potassium Permanganate solution?

A. Benzoic acid B. Cinnamic acid

C. *p*-toluic acid D. *m*-toluic acid

134. Which represents amide:

A. 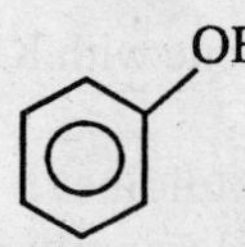 B. 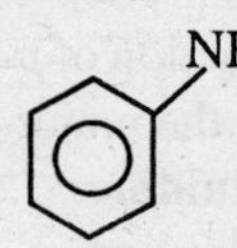

C. 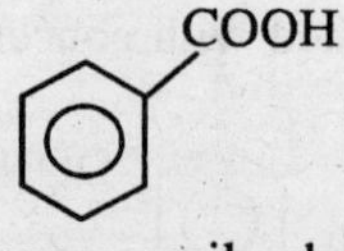 D. 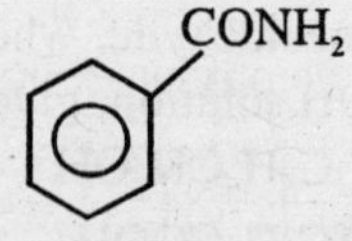

135. Benzene easily shows:

A. Ring fission reactions since it is unstable

B. Addition reactions since it is unsaturated

C. Electrophilic substitution reactions due to stable ring and high Pi electron density

D. Nucleophilic substitution reactions due to stable ring and minimum electrons density

136. Among acetic acid, Phenol and *n*-hexanol, which of the compound(s) will react with $NaHCO_3$ solution to give sodium salt and CO_2?

A. Acetic acid and phenol
B. Acetic acid
C. Phenol
D. *n*-hexanal

137. Which of the following statements regarding phenol is not correct:
A. Phenols are stronger acid than water and alcohols
B. Phenols are weaker acids than carboxylic acids
C. Phenols are soluble in both aqueous NaOH and aqueous $NaHCO_3$
D. Phenoxide ions are more stable than the corresponding phenols

138. C_6H_5Cl on treating with NaOH at 300°C gives phenol. However the yield is poor because of side reaction producing:
A. C_6H_5Na
B. $C_6H_5OCH_3$
C. $C_6H_5OC_6H_5$
D. None of the above

139. Dipole moment of *p*-nitroaniline, when compared to nitrobenzene (*x*) and aniline (*y*) will be:
A. Greater than (*x*) and (*y*)
B. Smaller than (*x*) and (*y*)
C. Greater than (*x*) but smaller than (*y*)
D. Equal to zero

140. 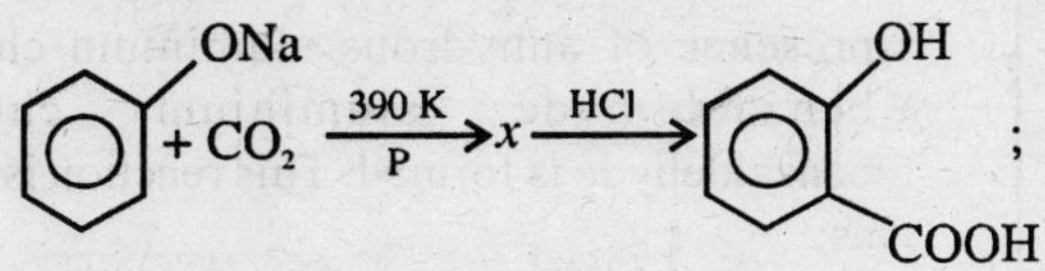

;

The product *x* in the reaction is:

A. 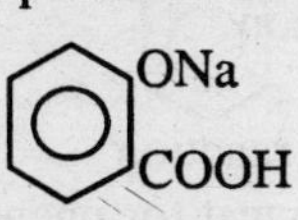

B. 

C. 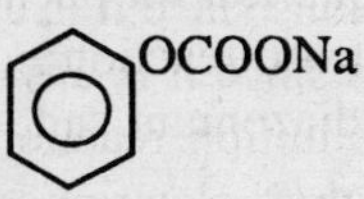

D. 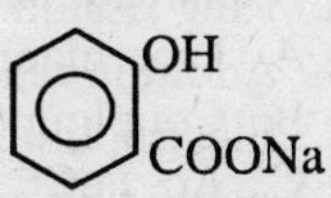

141. Amongst the following carboxylic acids the strongest acid is:
A. Benzoic acid
B. *o*-methoxybenzoic acid
C. *m*-nitrobenzoic acid
D. *p*-nitrobenzoic acid

142. 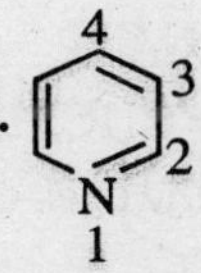

undergoes electrophilic substitution reaction preferentially:
A. At position 2 B. At position 3
C. At position 4 D. At positions 2 and 4

143. The main source of aromatic compounds is:
A. Wood B. Petroleum
C. Coal D. (B) and (C) both

144. Chlorobenzene gives DDT when it reacts with:
A. Phenol B. Naphthalene
C. Chloral D. Acetaldehyde

145. Among the compounds

A. 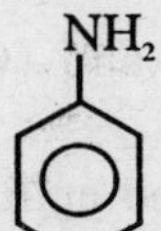

B. Et_3N

C. 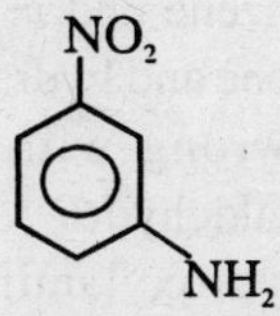

D. 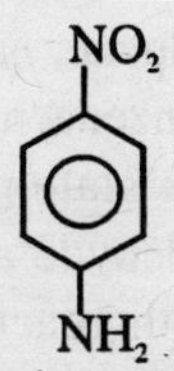

the order of basicity is:
A. $d > c > b > a$ B. $b > a > c > d$
C. $c > d > b > a$ D. $a > c > d > b$

146. When toluene is treated with acidic $KMnO_4$, we get:
A. Benzoic acid B. Benzyl alcohol
C. Benzaldehyde D. Benzene

147. Reimer-Tiemann reaction involves a;
A. Carbonium ion intermediate
B. Carbene intermediate
C. Carnonion intermediate
D. Free radical intermediate

148. Toluene can be oxidized to benzoic acid by:
A. $KMnO_4$ (acidic) B. $K_2Cr_2O_7$(alk)
C. Any of these D. None of these

149. Identify 'Z' in the reaction given below:

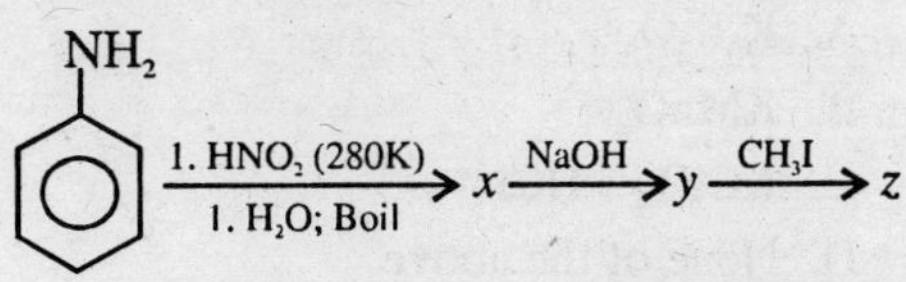

A. 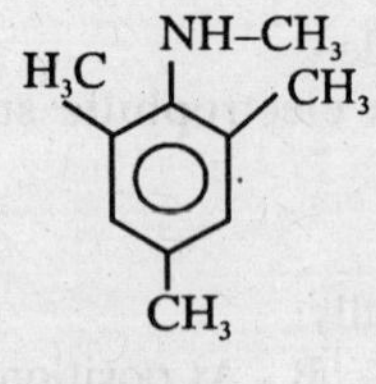 B. 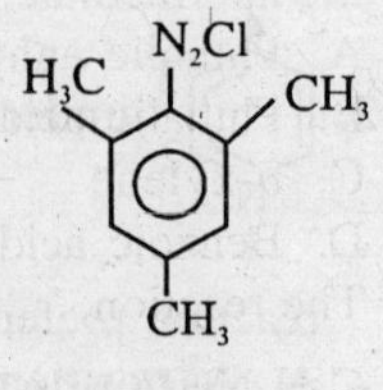

C. 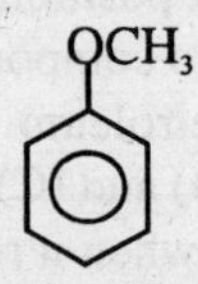 D. 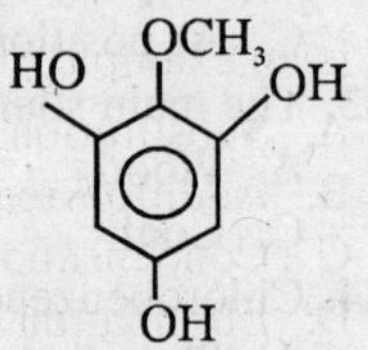

150. In the reaction,

$$\text{Phenol} \xrightarrow[\text{Distillation}]{\text{Zn}} (A) \xrightarrow[\text{Conc. } HNO_3 \text{ at } 60^\circ C]{\text{Conc. } H_2SO_4} (B) \xrightarrow[\text{NaOH aq.}]{\text{Zn}} (C)$$

The compounds (A), (B) and (C) are the following:

A. Benzene nitrobenzene and aniline
B. Benzene, dinitrobenzene and *m*-nitro aniline
C. Toluene, *m*-nitrobenzene and *m*-toluidine
D. Benzene, nitrobenzene and hydrazobenzene

151. Which statement is wrong with regard to acetaldehyde and benzaldehyde?

A. Both react with hydroxylamine to form oximes
B. Both react with HCN to form cyanohydrin
C. Both react with NaOH to form polymers
D. Both react with hydrazine to form hydrazones

152. In the following compound, the order of acidity is:

 I  II 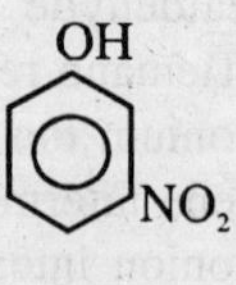 III  IV

A. III > IV > I > II B. I > IV > III > II
C. II > I > III > IV D. IV > III > I > II

153. Phenol on oxidation gives chloranil. The oxidant used is:

A. $K_2S_2O_8$
B. $KMnO_4$
C. $KClO_3 + HCl$
D. None of the above

154. Which of the following will be aromatic?

A. 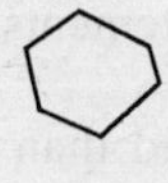 B. 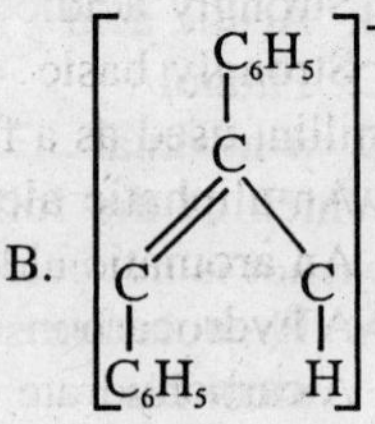

C. 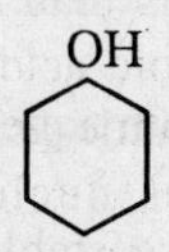 D. 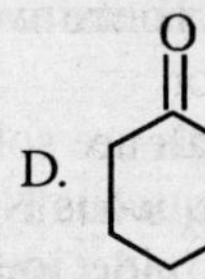

155. Nitration of aniline is done in:

A. Acidic medium
B. Alkaline medium
C. Neutral medium
D. In acidic medium by first converting it into acetanilide before nitration

156. When chlorine is passed in boiling toluene in presence of light, the reaction that takes place is:

A. Hydrogen is substituted by chlorine in the nucleus
B. Hydrogen is substituted by chlorine in the side chain
C. Side chain is oxidised
D. Nucleus is reduced

157. When benzene is treated with CO and HCl in presence of anhydrous aluminium chloride, benzalde-hyde aluminium chloride, benzaldehyde is formed. This reaction is known as:

A. Friedel-Crafts reaction
B. Rosenmund reaction
C. Stephen reaction
D. Gattermann Koch reaction

158. A characteristic group test for phenolic gp. is:

A. Libermann's nitroso reaction
B. Coupling with diazonium salt
C. Aq. $FeCl_3$
D. All of the above

159. Nitration of toluene takes place is:

A. Ortho position
B. Meta position
C. Para position
D. Both ortho and para position

160. Phenol is:
A. Strongly acidic B. Weakly acidic
C. Strongly basic D. Weakly basic

161. Vanillin, used as a flavouring agent is:
A. An aliphatic alcohol
B. An aromatic aldehyde
C. A hydrocarbon
D. A carbohydrate

162. Moth balls contain:
A. Camphor B. Benzoic acid
C. Naphthalene D. Cinnamic acid

163. The halide which undergoes nucleophilic substitution most readily is:
A. p-$H_3CC_6H_4Cl$ B. o-$H_3COC_6H_4Cl$
C. p-ClC_6H_4Cl D. p-$O_2NC_6H_4Cl$

164. Benzyl chloride ($C_6H_5CH_2Cl$) can be prepared from toluene by chlorination with
A. SO_2Cl_2 B. $SOCl_2$
C. S_2Cl_2 D. NaOCl

165. Friedel-Crafts reaction of bromobenzene with methyl iodide gives:
A. *o*-bromotoluene
B. *p*-bromotoluene
C. *o*-and *p*-bromotoluenes
D. *m*-bromotoluene

166. In the reaction,

$C_8H_6O_4 \xrightarrow{\Delta} x \xrightarrow{NH_3}$ 

the intermediate '*x*' is :
A. Phthalic anhydride
B. Phthalic acid
C. *o*-xylene
D. Benzoic acid

167. The reaction,

$C_6H_5NHCOCH_3 \xrightarrow{B_2/Fe} BrC_6H_4NHCOCH_3$

is an example of:
A. Substitution reaction
B. Addition reaction
C. Condensation reaction
D. Elimination reaction

168. Benzene is formed by the electrolysis of:
A. Benzyl chloride
B. Sodium benzoate
C. Chlorobenzene
D. None of these

169. Action of benzoic acid with hydrazoic acid in presence of N_3H gives:
A. Aniline
B. Benzamide
C. Phenyl cyanide
D. All of the above

170. In the reaction

$C_6H_5CH_3 \xrightarrow{\text{oxidation}} A \xrightarrow{\text{NaOH}} B \xrightarrow{\text{Soda lime}}$ C the product C is:

A. C_6H_5OH B. C_6H_6
C. C_6H_5COONa D. C_6H_5ONa

ANSWERS

1	2	3	4	5	6	7	8	9	10
A	B	A	B	B	D	D	B	C	C
11	12	13	14	15	16	17	18	19	20
A	B	D	A	A	B	C	C	D	D
21	22	23	24	25	26	27	28	29	30
A	B	A	B	B	B	C	C	B	D
31	32	33	34	35	36	37	38	39	40
A	B	D	D	C	D	B	B	A	A
41	42	43	44	45	46	47	48	49	50
A	A	C	B	B	B	A	C	D	A
51	52	53	54	55	56	57	58	59	60
C	C	D	D	B	C	C	A	A	D

61	62	63	64	65	66	67	68	69	70
B	B	C	B	A	B	C	A	B	C
71	72	73	74	75	76	77	78	79	80
B	B	C	A	B	A	D	D	C	D
81	82	83	84	85	86	87	88	89	90
C	C	A	D	C	B	C	C	A	B
91	92	93	94	95	96	97	98	99	100
C	C	A	B	D	C	B	C	A	B
101	102	103	104	105	106	107	108	109	110
B	D	B	C	D	C	C	C	A	B
111	112	113	114	115	116	117	118	119	120
B	B	B	D	B	A	C	D	B	A
121	122	123	124	125	126	127	128	129	130
A	B	C	D	D	C	A	A	B	D
131	132	133	134	135	136	137	138	139	140
D	C	B	D	C	B	C	C	A	D
141	142	143	144	145	146	147	148	149	150
D	B	D	C	B	A	B	C	C	D
151	152	153	154	155	156	157	158	159	160
C	D	C	B	D	B	D	D	D	B
161	162	163	164	165	166	167	168	169	170
B	C	D	A	C	D	B	D	A	C

15

ENVIRONMENTAL CHEMISTRY

Environment: The term *environment* is sometimes used to denote a certain set of circumstances surrounding a particular occurrernce. The environment of an organism includes:

(i) The purely physical or abiotic milieu in which it exists, e.g. geographic location, climatic conditions and terrain.

(ii) The organic or biotic milieu including non-living organic matter and all other organisms, plants and animals in the region including the particular population to which the organism belongs. Human environment includes the abiotic factors of land, water, atmosphere, climate, sound, odours, and taste; bacteria, viruses and the social factors of aesthetics. Energy components are solar energy, geochemical, thermochemical, hydroelectric and nuclear energy. All energy supply and consumption affects the local environment to some extent of particular importance has been air and water pollution from various sources.

Environmental Pollution : The disturbance of the natural environment resulting directly and indirectly from human activities often involving substances being in the wrong place at the wrong time, in the wrong amounts, and in the wrong physical and chemical forms. Environmental pollution harms human life, life of other desirable species natural resources, cultural assets and industries contamination in presence of harmful organisms or their toxins that cause discomfort or disease.

Natural Pollution : It is the pollution caused by natural sources e.g., volcanic eruptions, release of methane by paddy field and cattle, release of carbon dioxide by plants and animals, emission of natural gas, soil erosion, durt storms cosmic rays; ultra violet rays etc.

Manmade or Artificial Pollution : It is the pollution resulting from human activities like burning of fossil fuels, deforestation, mining, sewage, industrial effluents, pesticides, fertilizers etc. Amount of man-made atmospheric pollution is hardly 0.05% of total but is more dangerous because of its concentration in certain localities. Pollution can be atmospheric, soil & water.

Pollutant : A contaminant causing damage to the environment. These substances may be useful for some process but harmful to others or may be disposed off waste product.

Primary Pollutant : Pollutant persisting in the environment in the form it is produced e.g. Carbon monoxide.

Secondary Pollutant : Pollutant formed from a primary one through change or reaction. Nitrogen oxides and hydrocarbons react photochemically to produce peroxyacyl nitrates and ozone. The secondary pollutants may be more toxic than the primary ones.

Degradable Pollutants : These pollutants degrades after some time either automatically (e.g. heat) or through the agency of micro organisms (e.g. sewage is biodegradable)

Nondegradable Pollutants : These pollutants does not get degraded or broken down into harmless material e.g. DDT, plastics.

Soil Pollution

Soil : It is product of weathering of the bedrock before removal by erosion. It forms the upper layer of the mantle rock of the earth; consisting mainly of very small particle of inorganic mineral matter plus humus. The depth of soil varies upto several metres and is the material from which roots derive both food and moisture. Top soil is fertile for plant cultivation. Top soil contains more organic matter. Soil pollution is alteration in soil caused by removal or addition of substances and factors which decreases its productivity, quality of plants and ground water, *Negative soil pollution* is reduction in soil productivity due to erosion and over use. *Positive soil Production* is reduction in soil productivity due to addition of undesirable substances (e.g., pesticides, fertilizers, industrial waste, air pollutants washed down by rain, faulty sanitation). *Landscape/third pollution* is converting fertile land into barren one by dumping wastes (e.g. ash, sludge, garbage, rubbish, industrial wastes.

Pesticides : All chemical agents used to kill animal and vegetable life which interfere with agricultural productivity. They include insecticides, fungicides, algicides, rodenticides and weedicides. Pesticides are generally broad spectrum and function as *biocides.*

Water Pollution : It is the degradation of quality of water due to addition of substances (inorganic, organic, biological, radiological), factors (e.g. heat) and deprivation that makes it health hazard, unfit for human use and growth of aquatic biota. It is of two types:

(a) **Natural Sources of Water Pollution :** Clay and silt from soil erosion, leaching of minerals, falling of organic matter from banks.

(b) **Manmade Sources of Water Pollution :** Domestic waste, sewage, soaps and detergents run-off from agriculture fields having fertilizers and pesticides, industrial wastes, meat waste from animal sheds and slaughter houses, oil pollution, etc.

Air Pollution : Introduction of air pollutants into the atmosphere causes air pollution. Each day an adult inhales a volume of air normally in the range of 10 to $15m^3$. While the lungs provide a very effective means of absorbing oxygen into the blood stream. They provide similar facilities for many other gaseous impurities in the air. Also, any small solid particles in the atmosphere can be drawn into the lungs with each breath and a proportion may be deposited on the lung surface. Occupational diseases such as silicosis, which can arise among workers subjected to high levels of dust have been recognized for many years.

Air Pollutants : Uncommon constituents of the air that in certain concentrations be hazardous to animal and plant life, including human beings. Examples are CO, CO_2, nitrogen oxides, sulphur, inorganic and organic acids, hydrocarbons, inorganic particulate, trace elements and their compounds, insecticides, bacteria, viruses, dust, coal smoke, formaldehyde, aerolin, radioactive emissions and many more.

Air Pollution Index : Air arbitrary function of the concentration of one or more pollutants that is taken as a measure of the severity of pollution.

Pollution Standard Index (PSI) : In air pollution control, a measurement of the air quality mandated by the amendments to the clean Air Act, in order to allow standardization of comparisons of pollutant levels from community to community. The PSI is handed on five criteria pollutants, SO_2, NO_2, O_3, CO and total suspended particulates. Each of these pollutants is assigned a number from 0 to 100 on its measured level takes as percentage of regulatory standard for health effects. For example, if the ambient level of sulphur dioxide is 45% of that judged to be harmful to human health, the SO_2 number would be 45. The five numbers are then added together to obtain PSI. The values below 100 are regarded as healthful; from 100 to 199, unhealthful from 200 to 299 very unhealthful and over 300, hazardous.

Major Atmospheric Pollutants (Including Industrial Air Pollution) : Its is the addition of particulate matter, gases and other ingredients into air, which can produce adverse effect on human beings, animals, vegetation; human assets and resources. Major sources of atmospheric pollution are:

(i) Combustion of fossil fuels in homes, factories, thermal plant, automobiles, aircrafts, railways etc.

(ii) Mining and processing

(iii) Chemical industries

(iv) Processing industries etc.

Nearly 52% of air pollution is caused by CO, 18% by SO_2, 12% by hydrocarbons, 10% by particulates; 6% by nitrogen oxides and 2% by the remaining factors.

Acid Rain : The term was coined by Robert Augus (1872). In polluted atmosphere, rainfall occurs when atmospheric water vapours combine with oxides of sulphur and nitrogen or other acidic species present in the atmosphere. These pollutants result from burning of fossil fuel, especially in thermal power station, but they can also be caused by factories and car exhausts.

In relatively unpolluted atmosphere, acidity of rainwater is mainly due to the dissolved carbon-dioxide.

Once in the atmosphere, pollutants can be washed down to earth by rainfall in the form of sulphuric and nitric acids. The oxides and other species of nitrogen and sulphur can be incorporated into liquid water droplets in several different ways. They may be soluble enough to dissolve in water, may attach through diffusional processes may be incorporated through interactions and collisions and acid aerosol species may act as nuclei for water droplet formation.

Green House Effect : Green house effect in the selective energy absorption by CO_2, CH_4, NO_x(acids of nitrogen), water vapour etc., present in the atmosphere. Objects at a higher temperature (say of the sun) emit shorter I. R. radiations while objects at a lower temperature (say of the hot earth) emit longer I.R. radiations. These gases and vapour allow the shorter wavelength I.R. radiations from the sun to pass through but do not allow longer wavelength I.R radiations emitted by earth. As a result of Green House effect; heat from the sun can reach the earth but cannot be radiated back into the space. This results in the steady increase in the temperature of the earth resulting in global warming. Such global warming can result in major climatic changes on the earth, including melting of the polar ice caps. It is estimated that such melting of polar ice caps may raise the mean sea level by 0.5 to 1.5 m in next 100 years. Apart from carbondioxide, there are more than 35 gases that could contribute to possible green house effect or global warming. These include nitrogenous species, sulphur compounds, chlorofluorocarbons, ozone and aldehydes.

Ozone And Its Reactions Causing Ozone layer depletion and effects of the depletion of ozone layer: O_3, is a colourless gas, soluble in cold water and in alkalis. Liquid ozone is dark blue in colour and is diamagnetic (dioxygen, O_2 is paramagnetic). The gas is made by passing oxygen through a silent electric discharge and is usually and in mixtures with oxygen. It is produced in the stratosphere by the action of high energy ultraviolet radiations on oxygen and its presence thus acts as a screen for ultraviolet radiation. It is a powerful oxidizing agent and is used to form ozonides by reaction with alkenes and subsequently by hydrolysis to carbonyl compounds. Ozone layer occur 15-50 km above the earth's surface and is virtually synonymous with the stratosphere. In this layer, most of the sun's ultra voilet radiations are absorbed by the ozone molecules causing a rise in the temperature of the stratosphere and preventing vertical mixing so that the stratosphere forms a stable layer. By absorbing most of the solar ultraviolet radiations, the ozone layer protects living organisms on earth. The fact that the ozone layer is thinner at the equator is believed to account for the high equatorial incidence of skin cancer as a result of exposure to unabsorbed solar ultraviolet radiation. *Ozone hole* has been found to have develop over Antarctica each spring as the so called 'polar stratospheric clouds' (PSCs) disperse. The size of the hole waxes and waves in almost perfect correspondence with the concentration of CFCs in the polar atmosphere.

OBJECTIVE QUESTIONS

1. Atmospheric pollutant is
A. CO_2 B. CO
C. O_2 D. N_2

2. Biodegradable pollutant is
A. Domestic waste B. DDT
C. Mercury salt D. Aluminium foil

3. Water pollution is mainly due to
A. Agricultural discharges
B. Sewage and other wastes
C. Industrial effluents
D. All of the above

4. Photochemical smog always contain
A. O_3 B. CO
C. CO_2 D. CH_4

5. Water is often treated with chlorine to
   A. Increase oxygen content
   B. Kill germs
   C. Remove hardness
   D. Remove suspended particles
6. Result of ozone hole is
   A. Green house effect
   B. UV rays reaching the earth
   C. Global warming
   D. Acid rain
7. Photochemical smog is caused by
   A. CO B. CO_2
   C. O_3 D. NO_2
8. Atmosphere of big/meteropolitian cities is polluted most by
   A. Automobile exhaust
   B. Pesticide residue
   C. Household waste
   D. Radioactive fall out
9. Carbon monoxide is a pollutant as it
   A. Inactivates nerves
   B. Inhibits glycolysis
   C. Combines with oxygen
   D. Combines with haemoglobin and replaces O_2
10. Chief air pollutant which is likely to deplete ozone layer is
    A. Oxygen
    B. Fluorsive
    C. Nitrogen oxides and chlorofluorocarbons
    D. All of them
11. Gas released during *Bhopal Gas tragedy* was
    A. Potassium isothiocyanate
    B. Calcium chloride
    C. Methyl isocyanate
    D. Hydrogen sulphide
12. SO_2 & NO_2 produce pollution by increasing
    A. Alkalinity B. Acidity
    C. Neutrality D. Buffer action
13. Air pollutant that produce photochemical oxidants include
    A. CO_2, CO & SO_2
    B. Nitrous oxide, nitric oxide & nitric acid
    C. Oxygen, chlorine & nitric acid
    D. Ozone, chlorine & sulphur dioxide
14. Minamata disease is due to pollution of
    A. Organic waste into drinking water
    B. Oil spill in water
    C. Industrial waste mercury into fishing water
    D. Arsenic into the atmosphere
15. Chlorofluorocarbon release a chemical harmful to ozone is
    A. Iodine B. Hydrocarbons
    C. Chorine D. Fluorine
16. A secondary pollutant is
    A. PAN B. CO
    C. CO_2 D. Aerosol
17. DDT is
    A. Biodegradable pollutant
    B. Nondegradable pollutant
    C. An antibiotic
    D. None of the above
18. Measurement of rate of oxygen utilisation by a unit volume of water over a period of time is to measure
    A. Fermentation
    B. Biogas generation
    C. Biosynthetic pathway
    D. Biological oxygen demand
19. Most hazardous metal pollutant of automobile exhaust is
    A. Mercury B. Lead
    C. Cadmium D. Copper
20. Increasing skin cancer and high mutation rate are due to
    A. Acid rain B. Ozone depletion
    C. CO pollution D. CO_2 pollution
21. Peeling of ozone umbrella is due to
    A. CFCs B. PAN
    C. CO_2 D. Coal Burning
22. As it paves into food chain; the concentration of DDT
    A. Remains the same
    B. Decreases
    C. Increases
    D. Unpredictable
23. Methane gas producing field is
    A. Wheat field B. Paddy field
    C. Cotton field D. Groundnut field
24. Water is often treated with chlorine to
    A. Increase oxygen content

B. Kill germs
C. Remove hardness
D. Remove suspended particles

25. Environmental pollution affects
A. Biotic components
B. Plants only
C. Man only
D. Biotic & abiotic components of environment

26. Sewage water is purified by
A. Micro orgnisms B. Light
C. Fishes D. Aquatic plants

27. Ozone hole is maximum over
A. Europe B. Antarctica
C. Africa D. India

28. Phosphate pollution is caused by
A. Weathering of phosphate rocks only
B. Agricultural fertilizers
C. Phosphate rocks and sewage
D. Sewage and agricultural fertilizers

29. Cyclone collector is used for minimising
A. Radioactive pollution
B. Air pollution
C. Noise pollution
D. Water pollution

30. Ultra violet light causes
A. Formation of pyrimidines
B. Sticky metaphores
C. Sticky anaphores
D. Destruction of hydrogen bonds between complementary DNA strands.

31. Burning of fossil fuels is the main source of pollution due to
A. Nitrogen oxide B. Nitric oxide
C. Nitrous oxide D. Sulphur dioxide

32. Sulphur dioxide affects
A. Cell-wall B. Plasmodesmata
C. Nervous system D. All membrane system

33. Model of controlling pollution in large cities include
A. Cleanness and less use of insecticides
B. Proper disposal of organic wastes, sewage and industrial effluents
C. Broader roads and shifting of factories out of the residential areas
D. All

34. Increased asthmatic attacks in certain season is related to
A. Eating of seasonal vegetables
B. Varying temperature
C. Inhalation of seasonal pollens
D. None of above

35. Ozone depletion in stratosphere will result in
A. Forest fires
B. Increased incidence of skin cancer
C. Global warming
D. None of above

36. Ultraviolet radiation from sun causes a reaction that produces
A. Fluorides B. Carbon monoxide
C. Sulphur dioxide D. Ozone

37. Classical smog occurs in places of
A. Excess SO_2 B. Low temperature
C. High temperature D. Excess NH_3

38. Which of the following is **not** a pollutant from exhaust of motor vehicle?
A. Hydrocarbons B. Fly ash
C. NO_x D. CO

39. Air pollution is not caused by
A. Pollen grains B. Hydroelectric power
C. Industries D. Automobiles

40. Disease caused by eating fish found in water contaminated with industrial waste having mercury is
A. Minamata disease
B. Bright's disease
C. Hashimoto's disease
D. Osteosclerosis

41. Fish die in water bodies polluted by sewage due to
A. Pathogens
B. Clogging of gills by silt
C. Reduction in oxygen
D. Foul smell

42. Drained sewage has B.O.D.
A. More than that of water
B. Less than that of water
C. Equal to that of water
D. None of the above

43. *Taj Mahal* is threatened by pollution from
A. Chlorine B. Sulphur dioxide
C. Hydrogen D. Oxygen

44. Which one is the most toxic?

A. Carbon B. SO_2
C. CO D. CO_2

45. Soil salinity can be measured by

A. Calorimeter
B. Potometer
C. Porometer
D. Conductivity meter

46. Eutrophication causes reduction in

A. Dissolved hydrogen
B. Dissolved oxygen
C. Dissolved salts
D. All of the above

ANSWERS

1	2	3	4	5	6	7	8	9	10
B	A	D	A	B	B	D	A	D	C
11	**12**	**13**	**14**	**15**	**16**	**17**	**18**	**19**	**20**
C	B	B	C	B	A	B	D	B	B
21	**22**	**23**	**24**	**25**	**26**	**27**	**28**	**29**	**30**
A	C	B	B	D	A	B	D	B	D
31	**32**	**33**	**34**	**35**	**36**	**37**	**38**	**39**	**40**
D	D	D	C	B	D	B	B	B	A
41	**42**	**43**	**44**	**45**	**46**				
C	C	B	C	D	B				

16

HALOALKANES AND HALOARENES; ALCOHOLS & PHENOLS

Halogen Derivatives

Compounds derived from hydrocarbons by the replacement of one or more hydrogen atom(s) by the halogen atom(s) are known as *halogen derivatives.* The halogen derivatives of alkanes, alkenes, alkynes and arenes are known as *alkyl halides* (haloalkanes), *alkenyl halides* (haloalkenes), alkynyl halides (haloalkynes) and aryl halides (halobenzenes) respectively.

Halogen derivaties may be classified in several ways depending upon the type of the halogen atom, number of halogen atom(s) and position of the halogen atom. Thus alkyl halides may be primary, secondary or tertiary depending on whether the halogen is attached to a *primary, secondary* or *tertiary* carbon atom.

Example of alkylhalide

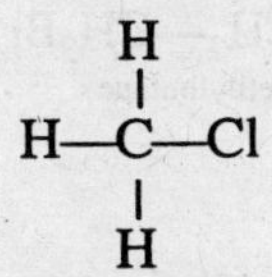

Methyl chloride

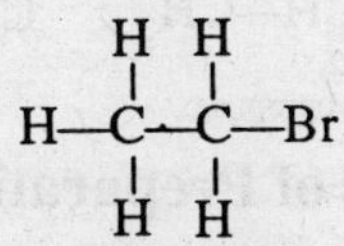

Ethyl bromide

They have the general formula

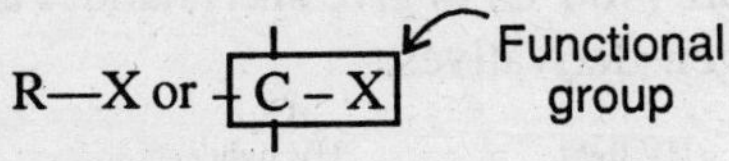

R = alkyl group

X = Cl, Br, I or F.

The halogen atom bonded to carbon in the functional group of alkyl halides.

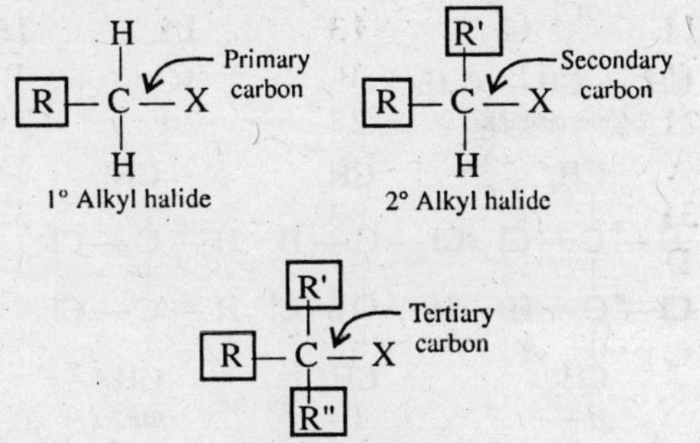

Alkyl halides are among the most useful organic compounds. They are frequently used to introduce alkyl groups into other molecules.

Structure

In alkyl halide like methyl chloride, for example, the carbon atom is sp^3-hybridized. The chlorine atom has a half-filled *p*-orbital in its valence shell. The C—Cl bond is formed by the overlap of an sp^3-orbital of carbon and the half-filled *p*-orbital of chlorine atom. Each C—H bond is formed by the overlap of an sp^3-orbital of carbon and the *s*-orbital of hydrogen. All bonds are σ-bonds. The H—C—H and H—C—Cl bond angles are approximately tetrahedral.

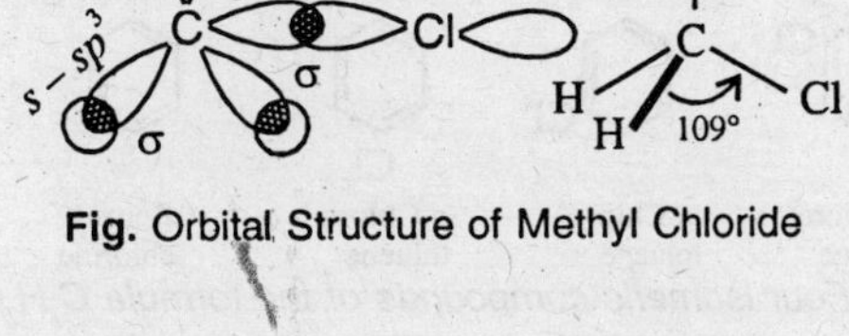

Fig. Orbital Structure of Methyl Chloride

Isomerism

Alkyl halides having three or more carbon atoms exhibit *chain* and *position isomerism. Sec-* and *ter-* alkyl halides may also show optical isomerism. Few examples of optical isomerism are given below: (* denotes asymmetric carbon atom)

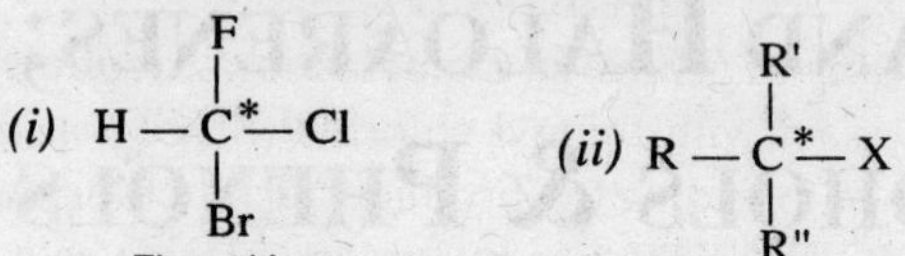

(i) Fluorochloro bromomethane (ii) ter-alkyl halide

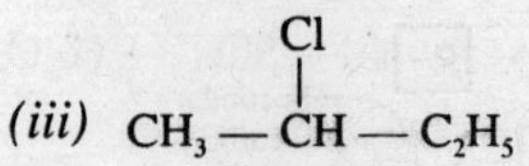

(iii) 2-Chlorobutane

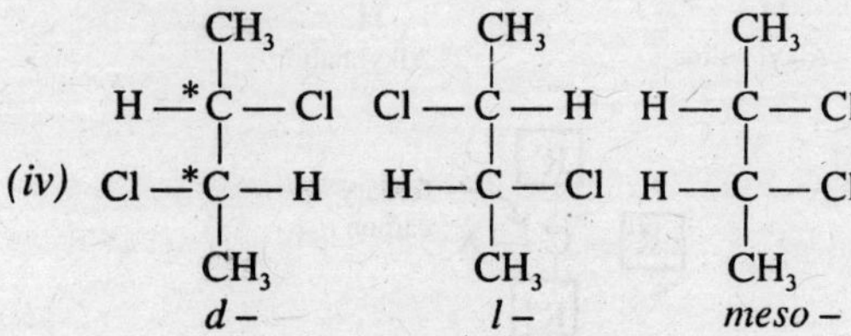

(iv) *d* – *l* – *meso* –

Optical isomers of 2,3 dichlorobutane

Certain alkenyl halides show geometrical isomerism. For example, 1-chlropropene, 1, 2-dichloroethene, etc.

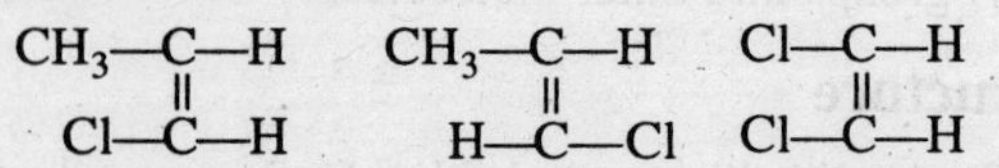

cis-1-chloropropene (high dipole moment) *trans*-1-chloropropene (less dipole moment) *cis*-1, 2, Dichloro-ethylene (definite dipole moment)

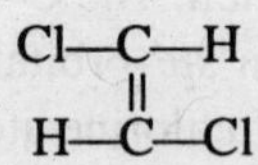

trans-1, 2-Dichloro-ethylene (dipole moment = 0)

The *trans*-isomers has low dipole moment than the corresponding *cis*-isomes; *trans* -isomer of symmetrical olefins has zero dipole moment.

Aryl halides also show isomerism. For example;

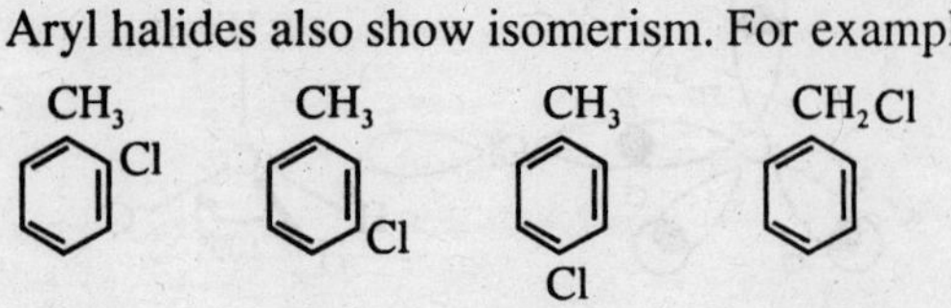

o-Chloro toluene *m*-Chloro toluene *p*-Chloro toluene Benzyl chloride

Fig. *Four isomeric compounds of the formula C_7H_7Cl*

p-Isomers have lower dipole moment, *p*-isomers of the symmertical compounds, e.g., *p*-dichloro-benzene has zero dipole moment,.

Nomenclature

Alkyl halides are named in two ways :

1. Common System : In this system, the alkyl group attached to the halogen atom is named first. This is then followed by an appropriate word chloride, bromide or fluoride. Notice that the common names of alkyl halides are TWO-WORDS names.

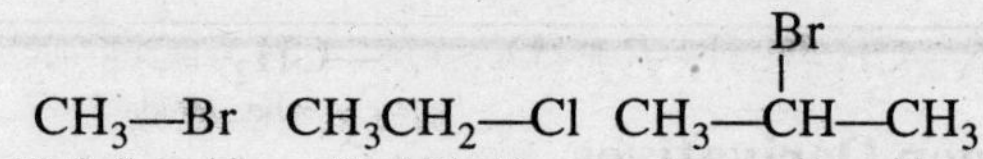

Methylbromide Ethylchloride Isopropyl bromide

2. IUPAC System : Following rules are used:

(i) Select the longest carbon chain containing the halogen atom and name the alkyl halide as a derivative of the corresponding hydrocarbon.

(ii) Number the chain so as to give the carbon carrying the halogen atom the *lowest* possible number.

(iii) Indicate the position of the halogen atom by a number and by the fluoro-, chloro-, bromo-, or iodo.

(iv) Name other substituents and indicate their positions by the numbers.

The examples given below show how these rules are applied. Notice that the IUPAC names of alkyl halides are ONE-WORD names.

CH_3CH_2Br — Bromoethane $CH_3CH_2CH_2—I$ — 1-Iodopropane

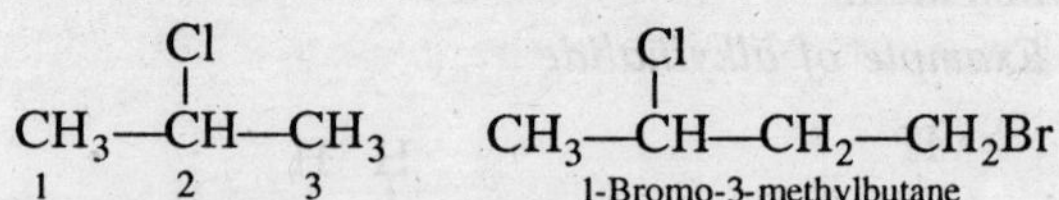

2-chloropropane 1-Bromo-3-methylbutane

Methods of Preparation

1. Direct Halogenation of Alkanes : Alkanes react with Cl_2 or Br_2 in the presence of UV light or at high temperature (400°C) to give alkyl halides along with polyhalogen derivatives.

$$\underset{\text{Methane}}{CH_4} + Cl_2 \xrightarrow[-\text{HCl}]{\text{UV light}} CH_3Cl \xrightarrow[-\text{HCl}]{+Cl_2,\ \text{UV light}} CH_2Cl_2 \xrightarrow[-\text{HCl}]{+Cl_2,\ \text{UV light}} CHCl_3 \xrightarrow[-\text{HCl}]{+Cl_2,\ \text{UV light}} CCl_4$$

This method is not used in the laboratory because of the difficulty of separating the products.

Chlorination beyond monochlorination may be suppressed by controlling the ratio of chlorine to alkane. In absence of high temperature catalyst $CuCl_2$, $FeCl_3$, $FeBr_3$, etc,. can be used.

2. Addition of Halogen Acids to Alkenes : Halogen acids (HCl, HBr, HI) add to alkenes to yield alkyl halides. The mode of addition follows *Markovnikov Rule*, except for the addition of HBr in the presence of organic peroxides (R—O—O—R).

$$\underset{\text{2-Alkene}}{R—CH{=}CH—R} + HX \rightarrow \underset{\text{Alkyl halide}}{R—CH_2—\overset{\overset{\large X}{|}}{C}H—R}$$

$$\underset{\text{Ethylene}}{CH_2{=}CH_2} + HI \rightarrow \underset{\text{Ethyl iodide}}{CH_3—CH_2—I}$$

$$\underset{\text{1-Alkene}}{R—CH{=}CH_2} + HBr \rightarrow R—\overset{\overset{\large Br}{|}}{C}H—CH_3$$

$$\underset{\text{Propene}}{CH_3—CH{=}CH_2} + HBr \rightarrow \underset{\substack{\text{2-Bromopropane}\\\text{(Markovnikov product)}}}{CH_3—\overset{\overset{\large Br}{|}}{C}H—CH_3}$$

$$\underset{\text{Propene}}{CH_3—CH{=}CH_2} + HBr \xrightarrow{\text{Peroxide}} \underset{\substack{\text{1-Bromopropane}\\\text{(anti-Markovnikov product)}}}{CH_3—CH_2—CH_2Br}$$

3. Action of Halogen Acids on Alcohols : Alcohols react with HBr or HI to produce alkyl bromides or alkyl iodides Alkyl chlorides are produced by the action of dry HCl in the presence zinc-chloride catalyst.

$$\underset{\text{Alcohol}}{R—OH} + \underset{\substack{\text{Halogen}\\\text{acid}}}{H—X} \rightarrow \underset{\text{Alkyl halide}}{R—X} + H_2O$$

$$\underset{\text{Ethyl alcohol}}{CH_3CH_2OH} + \underset{\text{(dry)}}{HCl} \xrightarrow{ZnCl_2} \underset{\text{Ethyl chloride}}{CH_3CH_2Cl} + H_2O$$

$$\underset{n\text{-Propyl alcohol}}{CH_3CH_2CH_2OH} + HBr \rightarrow \underset{n\text{-Propyl bromide}}{CH_3CH_2CH_2Br} + H_2O$$

4. Action of Phosphorus Halides on Alcohols : Alcohols react with phosphorus halides (PX_5 or PX_3) to form alkyl halides.

$$\underset{\text{Alcohol}}{R—OH} + PX_5(\text{or } PX_3) \rightarrow \underset{\text{Alkyl halide}}{R—X}$$

$$\underset{\text{Ethyl alcohol}}{2CH_3CH_2OH} + PCl_5 \rightarrow \underset{\text{Ethyl chloride}}{2CH_3CH_2Cl} + POCl_3 + H_2O$$

$$3CH_3CH_2OH + PBr_3 \rightarrow \underset{\text{Ethyl bromide}}{3CH_3CH_2Br} + H_3PO_3$$

$$\underset{\text{Methyl alcohol}}{3CH_3OH} + PI_3 \rightarrow \underset{\substack{\text{Methyl}\\\text{iodide}}}{3CH_3I} + H_3PO_3$$

PBr_3 or PI_3 are produced *in situ* by the addition of Br_2 and I_2 to red phosphorus.

$$2P + 3Br_2 \rightarrow 2PBr_3$$

$$2P + 3I_2 \rightarrow 2PI_3$$

5. Action of Thionyl Chloride on Alcohols : Alcohols react with thionyl chloride ($SOCl_2$) in the presence of pyridine to produce alkyl chlorides. Pyridine (C_6H_5N) absorbs hydrogen chloride as it is formed.

$$\underset{\text{Alcohol}}{R—OH} + SOCl_2 \xrightarrow{\text{Pyridine}} \underset{\text{Alkyl chloride}}{R—Cl} + SO_2 + H_2O$$

$$\underset{\text{Ethyl alcohol}}{C_2H_5OH} + SOCl_2 \xrightarrow{\text{Pyridine}} \underset{\text{Ethyl chloride}}{C_2H_5Cl} + SO_2 + HCl$$

6. Halogen Exchange Reaction : This reaction is particularly suitable for preparing alkyl iodides. The alkyl bromide or chloride is heated with a concentrated solution of sodium iodide in acetone.

$$\underset{\text{Ethyl bromide}}{CH_3—CH_2—Br} + NaI \xrightarrow[\Delta]{\text{Acetone}} \underset{\text{Ethyl iodide}}{CH_3CH_2I} + NaBr$$

Alkyl fluorides are also prepared by treating an alkyl chloride or bromide with inorganic fluorides.

$$\underset{\text{Methyl chloride}}{2CH_3—Cl} + Hg_2F_2 \rightarrow \underset{\substack{\text{Methyl}\\\text{fluoride}}}{2CH_3—F} + Hg_2Cl_2$$

7. Hunsdiecker Method :

$$CH_3COOAg + Br_2 \rightarrow CH_3Br + CO_2 + AgBr$$

Physical Properties

(i) CH_3Cl, CH_3Br, CH_3F and CH_3CH_2Cl are gases at room temperature. Other alkyl halides upto C_{18} are colourless liquids. Those beyond C_{18} are colourless solids.

(ii) Alkyl halides are insoluble in water but soluble in organic solvents. The insolubility in water is due to their inability to form hydrogen bonds with water.

(iii) Alkyl bromides and iodides are denser than water. Alkyl chlorides and fluorides are lighter than water.

(iv) Alkyl halides have higher boiling points than alkanes of comparable molecular weight. For a given halogen atom, the boiling points of alkyl halides increase with the increase in the size of the alkyl group. For a given alkyl group, the boiling points of alkyl halides follow the order

$$RI > RBr > RCl > RF$$

(v) Alkyl iodides, on standing become violet or brown because of their decomposition in presence of light to give iodine

$$2R—I \xrightarrow{\text{Light}} R—R + I_2$$

Chemical Properties

Alkyl halides are very reactive compounds. They undergo substitution, elimination, and reduction reactions. Alkyl halides also react with metals to form organometallic compounds.

Because of high electronegativity of the halogen atom, the carbon-halogen (C—X) bond is highly polarised covalent bond. Polarity in C—X bonds produces dipole moment. The dipole moment of alkyl halides is in the order of 2 – 2.2 D. Vinyl chloride and chlorobenzene showing resonance have lower dipole moments.

Thus the carbon atom of the C—X bond becomes a good site for attack by electron rich species (*nucleophiles* or *nucleophilic* reagents). In fact, *nucleophilic substitution* (replacement of the halide ion by a nucleophile) *reactions are the most common reactions of alkyl halides.*

$$\overset{\ominus}{Nu}: + R — X \rightarrow R — Nu + \overset{\ominus}{X}:$$

The common nucleophiles are OH^-, CN^-, NO_2^-, SH^-, NH_2^-, OR^- and $RCOO^-$.

1. Substitution : The carbon-halogen bond in alkyl halides is polar because of the high electronegativity of the halogen atom relative to carbon. The carbon atom is therefore a good target for the attack by nucleophiles (electron rich species). In fact, the nucleophilic substitution reactions are the most common reactions of alkyl halides. They may be represented as

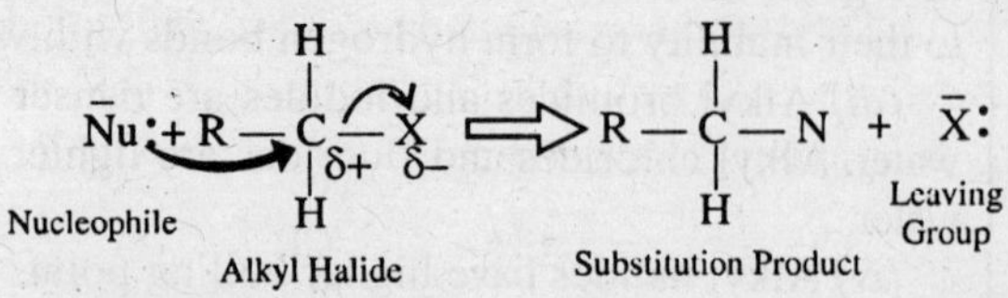

Alkyl halides can undergo nucleophilic substitution by two mechanisms :

S_N2 Mechanism : S_N2 stands for bimolecular nucleophilic substitution. In this mechanism, the attack of the nucleophile and the ejection of the halide ion takes place simultaneously. The reactants on their way to products pass through a transition state where the C—OH bond is half-formed and the C—X bond is half-broken. Consider the example of hydrolysis of methyl bromide by aqueous NaOH. The reaction and the transition states are shown below :

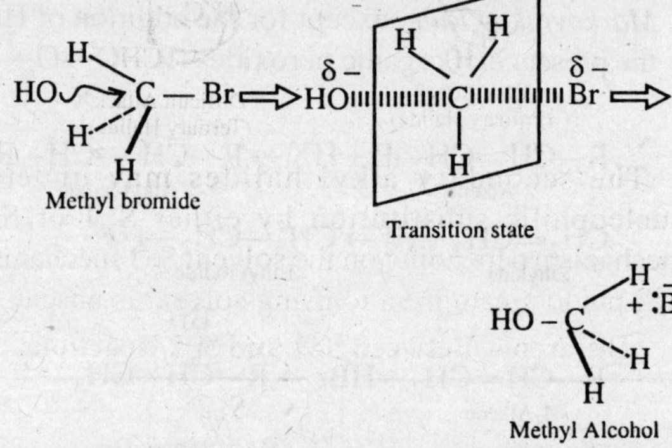

Fig. Nucleophilic substitution by S_N2 mechanism.

S_N1 Mechanism : S_N1 stands for unimolecular nucleophilic substitution. This mechanism involves two steps. Consider the hydrolysis of *tert*-butyl bromide with aqueous NaOH.

Step 1 : The alkyl halide ionises to give a planar carbonium ion. The carbonium ion is planar because the central positively charged carbon atom is sp^2 hybridized.

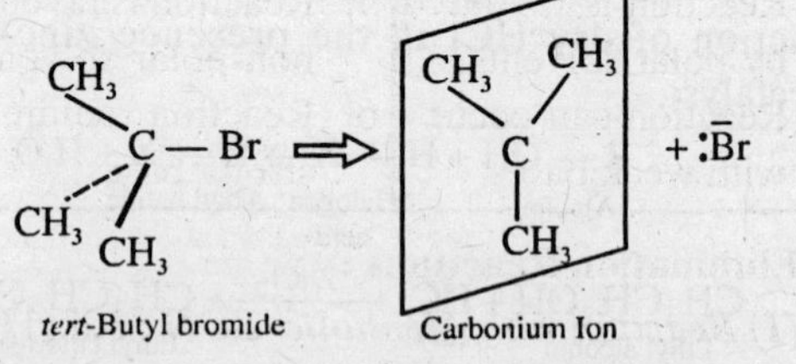

Step 2 : The nucleophile can attack the planar carbonium ion from either side to give the product.

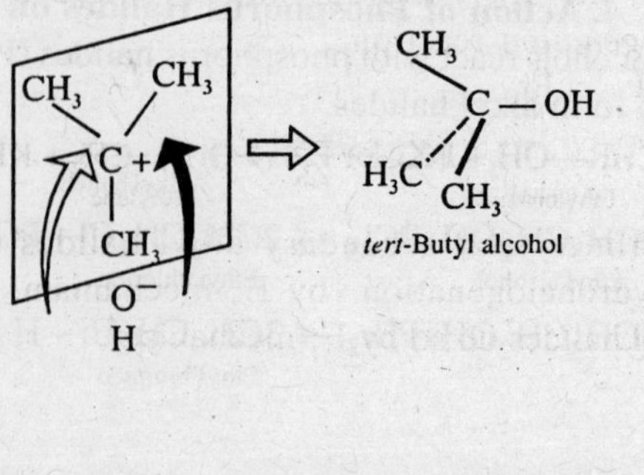

Important : Primary alkyl halides undergo substitution by S_N2 mechanism. The tertiary alkyl halides undergo substitution by S_N1 mechanism. This is because the attack of the nucleophile on the crowded tertiary alkyl halide is quite difficult.

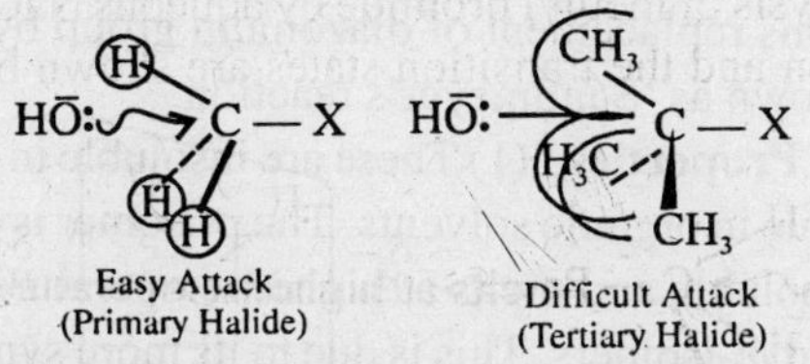

The secondary alkyl halides may undergo nucleophilic substitution by either S_N1 or S_N2 mechanism depending on the solvent S_N1 mechanism will predominate if an ionising solvent is absent.

Difference Between S_N1 and S_N2 Reactions

S_N1 *Reactions*	S_N2 *Reactions*
1. It is a two-step mechanism.	1. It is a one-step mechanism.
2. Rate depends only upon the concentration of alkyl halide.	2. Rate depends on concentration of alkyl halide and nucleophile.
3. It is unimolecular	3. It is bimolecular
4. Rate depends on structure of halide : $3° > 2° > 1° > CH_3X$	4. Rate depends on structure of halide : $CH_3X > 1° > 2° > 3°$
5. Reaction is favoured by polar solvents.	5. Reaction is favoured by non-polar solvents.
6. Reaction can occur with weak bases.	6. Reaction requires strong bases.

Elimination Reactions :

(1) Reaction with Alcoholic KOH : Alkyl halides react with alcoholic potassium hydroxides to form alkenes. The reaction involves the elimination of HX from the alkyl halides and is called *Dehydrohalogenation* reaction.

$$\underset{\text{Ethylbromide}}{\underset{|}{\overset{}{\text{H}}}\!\!\!\!\!\!\!\!\quad CH_2 - \underset{}{CH_2}}\ (\text{H on } CH_2,\ \text{Br on } CH_2) + KOH \xrightarrow[\Delta]{\text{Ethanol}} \underset{\text{Ethylene}}{CH_2 = CH_2} + KBr + H_2O$$

Primary and secondary alkyl halides undergo dehydrohalogenation by E_2 mechanism. Tertiary alkyl halides do so by E_1 mechanism.

Saytzeff Rule : If the dehydrohalogenation of an alkyl halide can yield more than one alkene, then, according to the Saytzeff Rule, the main product is the most highly substituted alkene. For example, two alkenes are possible when 2-bromobutane is heated with alcoholic KOH.

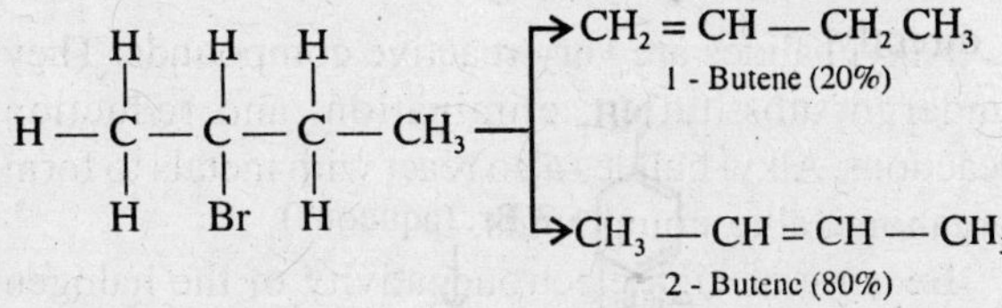

Major product is 2-butene, a disubstituted alkene.

Aryl Halides

1. Preparation :

(1) Nuclear Halogenation : Aryl chloride and bromides can be prepared by treating the arenes with chlorine or bromine at low temperature in the absence of sunlight and in the presence of halogen carrier (Lewis acid) like $AlCl_3$, $FeCl_3$, etc.

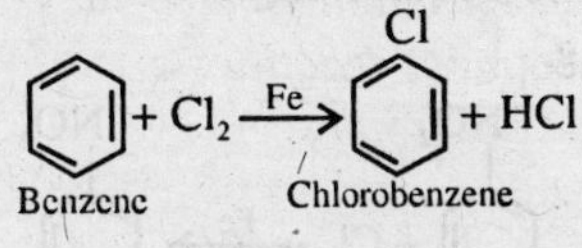

Iron reacts with Cl_2 to form $FeCl_3$ which acts as Lewis acid. Due to deactivating influence of the halogen atom on the aromatic ring, chlorination generally stops at the monosubstitution stage. However, if chlorine is used in excess, further chlorination takes place to form a mixture of *o*- and *p*-dichlorobenzenes.

(i) Halogenation of activated Compounds : Benzene ring having activating group (*o, p*-directing groups except halogen) are halogenated easily as compared to benzene itself, the product formed is a mixture of *o*- and *p*-substituted products. Thus toluene undergoes chlorination easily in presence of iron to form *o*- and *p*-chlorotoluenes.

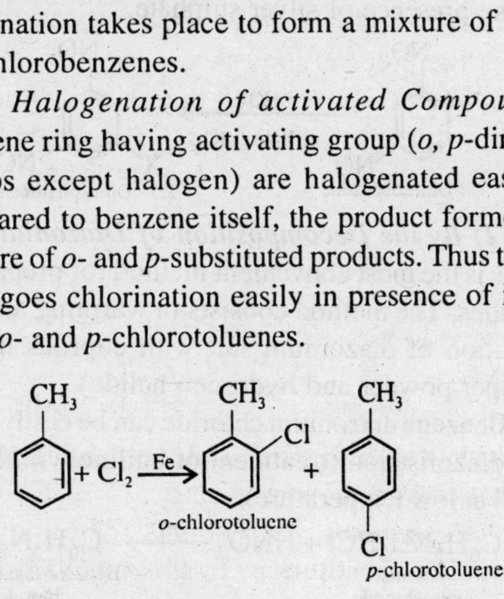

Highly activated compounds like amines and phenols undergo halogenation so easily that they do not require any Lewis acid catalyst, the reaction occurs readily simply by treating the compound with dilute aqueous solution of chlorine or bromine. Moreover, the polyhalogenated product is formed directly.

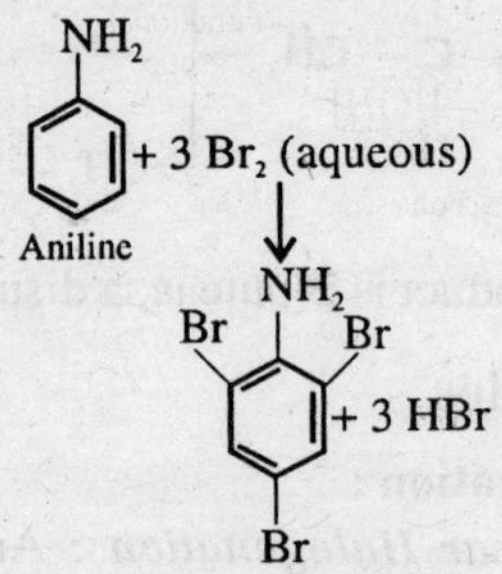

2, 4, 6 — Tribromoaniline
(*Sym* – Tribromoaniline)

(ii) Halogenation of deactivated Compounds :

(a) Deactivated aromatic compounds like nitrobenzene require high temperature as well as catalyst, e.g.

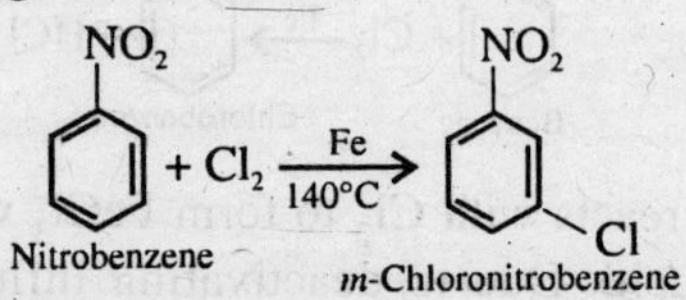

(b) Strongly deactivated compounds like di- and poly- nitro compounds are halogenated by an acidified solution of hypohalous acid or by halogen in the presence of silver sulphate.

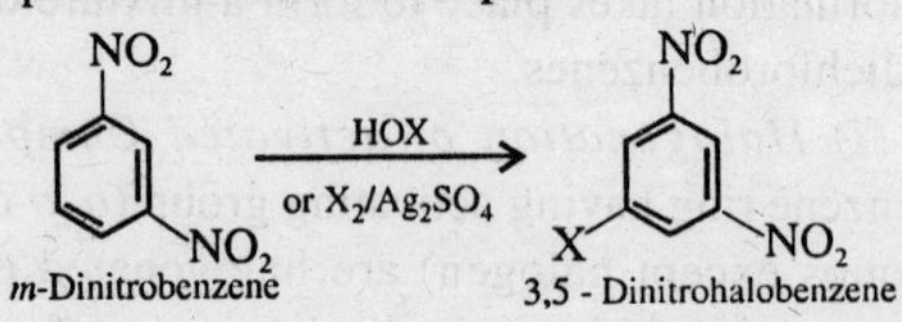

(2) By the Decomposition of Diazonium Salts : This is the most convenient method for preparing aryl halides. The method consists in warming an aqueous solution of diazonium salt with cuprous halide (or copper powder and hydrogen halide).

Benzene diazonium chloride can be easily prepared by diazotisation (treatment of aniline with $NaNO_2$ + HCl at low temperature).

$$\underset{\text{Aniline hydrochloride}}{C_6H_5NH_2HCl} + HNO_2 \xrightarrow{0°C} \underset{\text{Benzene diazonium chloride}}{C_6H_5N_2Cl}$$

$$N_2 + \underset{\text{Bromobenzene}}{C_6H_5Br} \xleftarrow[\text{Cu + HBr (Warm)}]{\text{CuBr}} \underset{\text{Benzene diazonium chloride}}{C_6H_5N_2Cl} \xrightarrow[\text{or Cu + HCl (Warm)}]{\text{CuCl}} \underset{\text{Chlorobenzene}}{C_6H_5Cl} + N_2$$

This replacement of diazonium group by halogen is known as 'Sandmeyer's reaction.'

2. Properties : (1) These are insoluble in water but soluble in organic solvents. The p-isomer is generally less soluble and melts at higher temperature than the *o-* and *m-*isomers. This is due to its more symmetrical structure and hence its ability to fit better into the crystalline structure.

(2) *Nucleophilic Substitution :* 'Unlike alkyl halides, but-like vinyl halides, aryl halides do not undergo nucleophilic substitution under ordinary conditions. Thus, the halogen atom of aryl halides is not replaced by —OH, —NH_2, —CN, etc. When aryl halides are treated with aq. NaOH, NH_3 and KCN respectively. The low reactivity of halogen atom in aryl halides is due to resonance

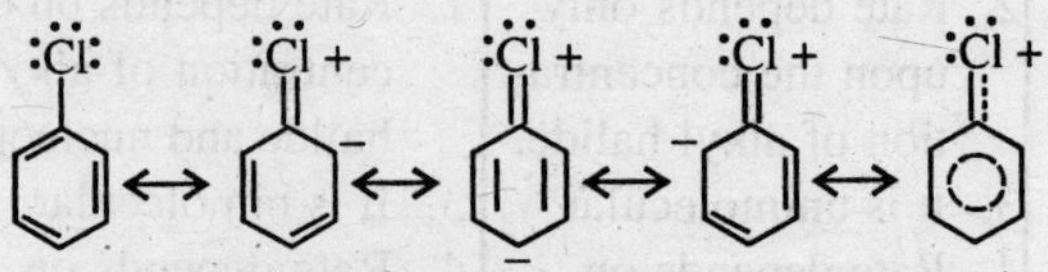

Resonating Structures of Chlorobenzene

$$CH_2 = CH - \ddot{\underset{..}{Cl}}: \leftrightarrow \bar{C}H_2 - CH = \overset{+*}{\underset{..}{Cl}}:$$

Resonating structure of Vinyl chloride

* The unusual positive charge on Cl decreases its electronegativity and thus polarity of the bond. Hence resonance decreases the dipole moment of chlorobenzene and vinyl chloride are 1.7 D and 1.4 D respectively. Dipole moment of alkyl halides lie in the range of 2-2.2 D.

"Due to resonance, carbon-chlorine bond acquires partial double bond character, hence it becomes shorter and stronger and thus cannot be easily replaced by nucleophiles." However, aryl halides can be made to undergo nucleophilic substitution either under drastic conditions (like the use of high temperature, pressure of electron withdrawing group (e.g. —NO_2, —COOH, etc.) in the *o-* and *p-*position to the nuclear halogen.

(3) Like alkyl halides, aryl halides undergo Wurtz-Fitting reaction (condensation of arylhalides and alkyl halides with sodium in presence of dry ether). Ullmann reaction (heating of aryl halides, with copper powder), formation of Grignard reagent and reduction.

(i) $\underset{\text{Bromobenzene}}{C_6H_5Br} + 2Na + \underset{\text{Methyl bromide}}{BrCH_3} \xrightarrow[\text{ether}]{\text{dry}} \underset{\text{Toluene}}{C_6H_5CH_3} + 2NaBr$

(ii) $\underset{\text{Bromobenzene}}{C_6H_5Br} + 2Na + \underset{\text{Bromobenzene}}{BrC_6H_5} \xrightarrow[\text{ether}]{\text{dry}} \underset{\text{Diphenyl}}{C_6H_5C_6H_5} + 2NaBr$

(iii) $\underset{\text{Iodobenzene}}{C_6H_5I} + 2Cu + \underset{\text{Iodobenzene}}{IC_6H_5} \xrightarrow{\text{heat}} \underset{\text{Diphenyl}}{C_6H_5C_6H_5} + 2CuI$

Aryl chlorides and aryl bromides undergo Ullmann reaction only if they have electron withdrawing group like —NO_2 in *o*- or *p*-position to the halogen.

(iv) $\underset{\text{Bromobenzene}}{C_6H_5Br} + Mg \xrightarrow{\text{dry ether}} \underset{\text{Phenyl mag. bromide}}{C_6H_5MgBr}$

Aryl chlorides form Grignard reagents in tetrahydrofuran (THF) instead of ether.

(v) $\underset{\text{Bromobenzene}}{C_6H_5Br} + 2[H] \xrightarrow[\text{(Reduction)}]{\text{Ni—Al/NaOH}} \underset{\text{benzene}}{C_6H_6} + HBr$

(4) *Electrophilic Substitution :* Aryl halides undergo the typical electrophilic substitution reactions in the *o*- and *p*-positions, though less readily than benzene because halogens have a deactivating influence as the aromatic ring. Again, it is important to note that inspite of being deactivators, the halogens are *o*-, *p*-directors (difference from other *o*-, *p*-directing groups which are activating groups).

(5) *Reactions of the Side Chain :* Side chain if present may undergo

(i) oxidation to —COOH groups

(ii) halogenation in presence of light.

For example :

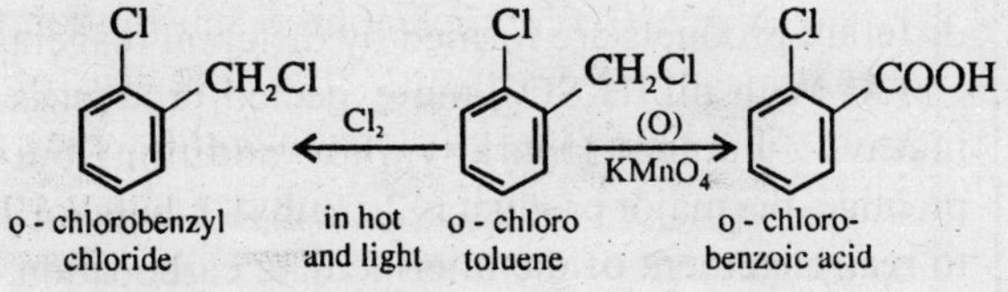

HYDROXY COMPOUNDS
(Alcohols and Phenols)

Alcohols

Alcohols are compounds in which a hydroxyl (—OH) group is attached to saturated carbon atom.

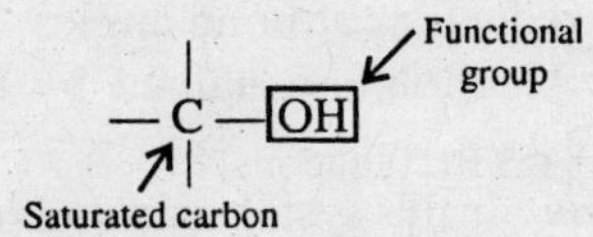

R — OH
General formula

The hydroxyl group is the functional group of alcohols.

Alcohols are :

Monohydric—Containing one hydroxyl group

Dihydric—Containing two hydroxyl groups

Trihydric—Containing three hydroxyl groups

and Polyhydric—Containing many hydroxyl groups

C_2H_5OH Ethyl alcohol (Monohydric)

CH_2OH—CH_2OH Glycol (Dihydric)

CH_2OH—CH_2OH—CH_2OH Glycerol (Trihydric)

CH_2OH—$(CHOH)_4$—CH_2OH Sorbitol (Polyhydric)

Monohydric alcohols are classified as primary (1°), secondary (2°) or tertiary (3°) depending upon whether the —OH group is attached to a primary, secondary or tertiary carbon.

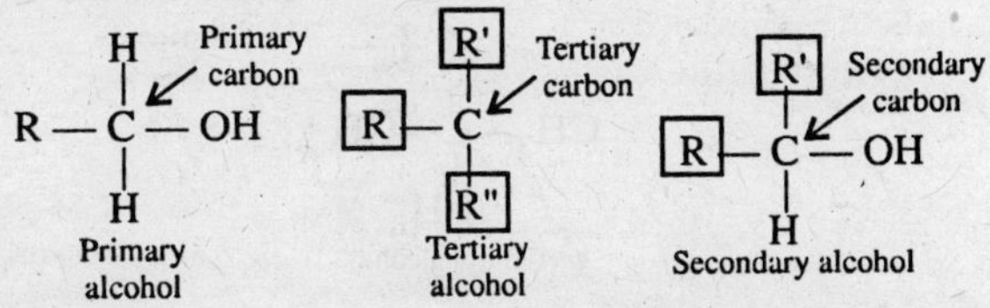

Structure : Considering the structure of methyl alcohol (CH_3OH), we find that both oxygen and carbon are sp^3-hybridized. Two of the sp^3-orbitals of oxygen are completely filled and cannot take part in bond formation.

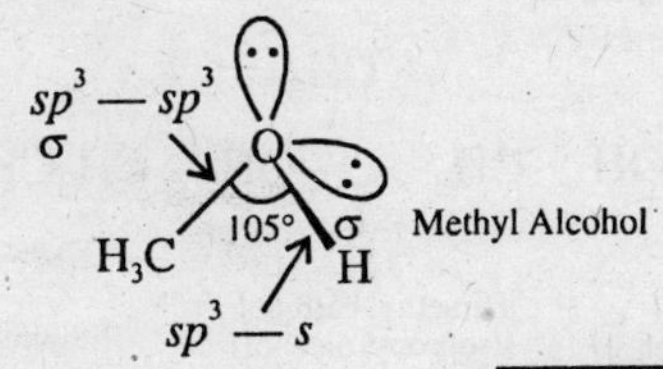

The C—O bond in methyl alcohol is formed by overlap of an sp^3-orbital of carbon and an sp^3-orbital of oxygen. The O—H bond is formed by overlap of an sp^3-orbital of oxygen and *s*-orbital of hydrogen. The C—O—H bond angle is 105°. It is less than the normal tetrahedral angle. This is because the two completely filled sp^3-orbitals of oxygen repel each other. This results in reduction of bond angle.

Nomenclature : Alcohols are named by three systems.

(1) Common System : In this system, alcohols (R—OH) are named as *Alkyl Alcohols.* The alkyl group attached to the —OH group is named and 'alcohol' is added as a separate word. For example,

$CH_3—OH$ (Methyl alcohol) $CH_3CH_2—OH$ (Ethyl alcohol)

$CH_3CH_2CH_2—OH$ (*n*-Ethyl alcohol) $CH_3—CH(CH_3)—OH$ (Isopropyl alcohol)

As we go higher in the series, it becomes necessary to indicate whether a particular alcohol is primary (1°), secondary (2°) or tertiary (3°). The prefix secondary is abbreviated as *sec-* and *tertiary* as *tert* or *t-*. Examples are :

$CH_3CH_2CH_2CH_2OH$ (*n*-Butyl alcohol) $CH_3CH_2CH(CH_3)OH$ (*sec*-Butyl alcohol)

$CH_3—C(CH_3)_2—OH$ (*tert*-Butyl alcohol)

(2) Carbinol System : In this system alcohols are considered as derivatives of methyl alcohol which is called *carbinol*. The alkyl group attached to the carbon carrying the —OH group are named in alphabetic order. Then the suffix *carbinol* is added. For example:

$H—CH_2—OH$ Carbinol (Methyl alcohol) $CH_3—CH(H)—OH$...

$$H_3C—OH \qquad CH_3—CH_2—OH\ (CH_3—C(H)(CH_3)—OH) \qquad CH_3CH_2—C(H)(CH_3)—OH$$

Carbinol (Methyl alcohol) Dimethyl carbinol (Isopropyl alcohol) Ethylmethyl-carbinol (*sec*-Butyl alcohol)

Preparation : Alcohols are prepared by following methods :

Hydrolysis of Alkyl Halides : Alkyl halides react with aqueous sodium hydroxide to form alcohols

$$\underset{\text{Alkyl Halide}}{R—X} + NaOH \xrightarrow[\Delta]{H_2O} \underset{\text{Alcohol}}{R—OH} + NaX$$

$$CH_3CH_2—Br + NaOH \xrightarrow[\Delta]{H_2O} \underset{\text{Ethyl alcohol}}{CH_3CH_2—OH} + NaBr$$

This reaction is of limited use, because the alkyl halides themselves are obtained from alcohols.

Hydration of Alkenes : Alkenes react with sulphuric acid to produce alkyl hydrogen sulphates (Markovnikov rule is followed). Alkyl hydrogen sulphates on hydrolysis give alcohols. For example,

$$\underset{\text{Propylene}}{CH_3—CH{=}CH_2} + \overset{+}{H}OSO_3H \rightarrow \underset{\text{Isopropyl hydrogen sulphate}}{CH_3—CH(OSO_3H)—CH_3}$$

$$CH_3—CH(OSO_3H)—CH_3 + H—O—H \xrightarrow{\Delta} \underset{\text{Isopropyl alcohol}}{CH_3—CH(OH)—CH_3} + H_2SO_4$$

The overall result of the above reaction appears to be Markovnikov addition of H_2O (Hydration) to a double bond.

$$\underset{\text{Propylene}}{CH_3—CH{=}CH_2} + H—OH \xrightarrow[\Delta]{H^+} \underset{\text{Isopropyl alcohol}}{CH_3—CH(OH)—CH_3}$$

It is not possible to make primary alcohol, by this method (ethyl alcohol is the only exception).

$$CH_2{=}CH_2 + \underset{98\%}{H_2SO_4} \rightarrow \underset{\text{Ethyl hydrogen sulphate}}{CH_3CH_2HSO_4} \xrightarrow{\text{boil}} \underset{\text{Ethyl alcohol}}{CH_3CH_2OH} + H_2SO_4$$

It is important to note that when an unsymmetrical olefin, e.g. $(CH_3)_2CHCH{=}CH_2$ is hydrated, different products are formed by different reagents.

(A) With dil. H_2SO_4, the expected product is 3-methyl-2-butanol (Markovnikov addition) but in practice, the major product is 2-methyl-2-butanol due to rearrangement of the intermediate carbocation.

$$\underset{\text{3-Methyl butene-1}}{(CH_3)_2CHCH=CH_2} \xrightarrow[CH_2O]{H^+} \underset{2^\circ\text{ carbocation}}{(CH_3)_2CH\overset{+}{C}HCH_3}$$

$$\xrightarrow{\text{rearrangement}} \underset{3^\circ\text{ carbocation}}{(CH_3)_2\overset{+}{C}CH_2CH_3}$$

$$\xrightarrow[(-H+)]{H_2O} \underset{\text{2-Methyl-2 butanol}}{(CH_3)_2C(OH)—CH_2CH_3}$$

(B) With B_2H_6, hydration (Hydroboration-oxidation) gives 3-methyl-1-butanol (anti-Markovnikov addition). The positive part of BH_3 is the boron and negative is hydrogen.

$$\underset{\text{3-Methylbutene-1}}{(CH_3)_2CHCH{=}CH_2} + (BH_3)_2$$

$$\longrightarrow \left[(CH_3)_2CHCH_2CH_2\right]_3B$$

$$\xrightarrow{H_2O_2} \underset{\text{3-Methyl-1-butanol}}{(CH_3)_2CHCH_2CH_2CH}$$

Important : Trialkylboranes are used for making primary alcohols by reaction with alkaline aqueous solution of Hydrogen peroxide.

(C) With mercuric acetate, the product is 3-methyl-2-butanol (Markovnikoff addition with no rearrangement)

$$\underset{\text{3-Methylbutene-1}}{(CH_3)_2CHCH=CH_2} \xrightarrow[H_2O]{Hg(OCOCH_3)_2} \underset{\text{not isolated}}{(CH_3)_2CH\,CH(OH)\,CH_2HgOCOCH_3}$$

$$\xrightarrow{NaBH_4} \underset{\text{3-Methyl-2 butanol}}{(CH_3)_2CH\,CH(OH)\,CH_3}$$

Hydrolysis of Esters : Alcohols may be prepared by base or acid-catalysed hydrolysis of esters.

$$\underset{\text{Ester}}{R'—\overset{O}{\overset{||}{C}}—OR} + H—OH \xrightarrow[\Delta]{H^+} \underset{\text{Acid}}{R'—\overset{O}{\overset{||}{C}}—OH} + \underset{\text{Alcohol}}{R—OH}$$

Alkaline hydrolysis of esters is known as Saponification.

Hydrolysis of Ethers : With hot dil. H_2SO_4 under pressure

$$C_2H_5—O—C_2H_5 + H_2O \xrightarrow[\text{pressure}]{\text{dil. }H_2SO_4} 2C_2H_5OH$$

By the action of nitrous acid on aliphatic primary amines.

$$C_2H_5NH_2 + HONO \rightarrow C_2H_5OH + N_2 + H_2O$$

Reduction of Aldehydes and Ketones : Aldehydes and ketones can be reduced with H_2/Ni or lithium aluminium hydride to form the corresponding alcohols. Aldehydes give primary alcohols. Ketones give secondary alcohols.

$$\underset{\text{Aldehyde}}{R—\overset{O}{\overset{||}{C}}—H} + H_2 \xrightarrow[\Delta]{Ni} \underset{1^\circ\text{ Alcohol}}{R—CH_2—OH}$$

$$\underset{\text{Ketone}}{R—\overset{O}{\overset{||}{C}}—R'} + 2[H] \xrightarrow{LiAlH_4} \underset{2^\circ\text{ Alcohol}}{R—\overset{OH}{\overset{|}{C}H}—R'}$$

$$CH_3CHO + 2H \xrightarrow{Na/C_2H_5OH} CH_3CH_2OH$$

$$(CH_3)_2CO + 2H \xrightarrow{Na/C_2H_5OH} \underset{\text{2-Propanol}}{(CH_3)_2CHOH}$$

$$CH_3CHO \xrightarrow[NaBH_4]{LiAlH_4\text{ or}} CH_3CH_2OH$$

$$CH_3CHO + H_2 \xrightarrow[\text{Heat}]{PtO_2\text{ catalyst}} CH_3CH_2OH$$

$LiAlH_4$ is used in anhydrous ether while $NaBH_4$ can be used in protic solvents like ROH and H_2O.

Reduction of unsaturated aldehydes.

$$\underset{\text{Acrolein}}{H_2C{=}CHCH_2OH} \xleftarrow{NaBH_4} \underset{\text{Alkyl alcohol}}{CH_2{=}CHCHO}$$

$$\xrightarrow{H_2/Ni} CH_3CH_2CH_2OH$$

By Fermentation :

1. Fermentation is the slow decomposition of complex organic compounds into simpler compounds in the presence of suitable *micro-organism* which are the source of biochemical catalyst known as *enzymes*."

(*a*) $\underset{\text{Glucose}}{C_6H_{12}O_6} \xrightarrow[\text{(yeast)}]{\text{Zymase}} 2C_2H_5OH + 2CO_2$

(*b*) $\underset{\text{Starch}}{(C_6H_{10}O_5)_n} \rightarrow \underset{n\text{-Butyl alcohol}}{CH_3.CH_2.CH_2.CH_2OH} + CH_3.CO.CH_3$

Addition of Grignard Reagents to Aldehyde and Ketones : Grignard reagents react with aldehydes or ketones to form an addition compound which on hydrolysis with dilute acid gives the corresponding alcohol.

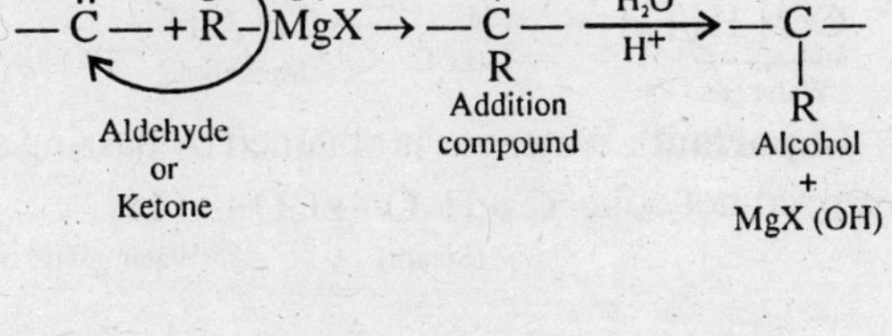

Primary Alcohols are obtained by treating a Grignard reagent with formaldehyde

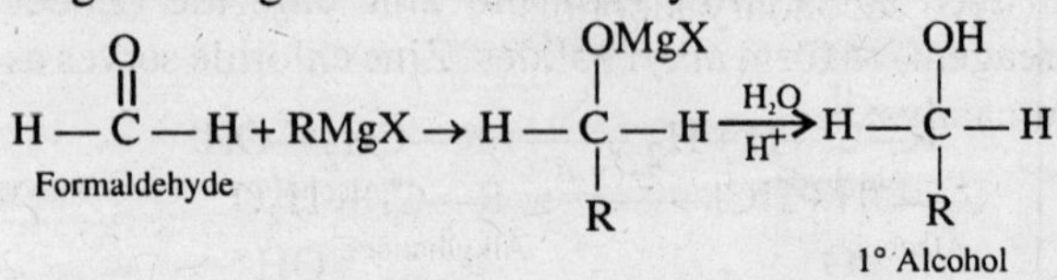

Secondary Alcohols are obtained by treating a Grignard reagent with aldehydes other than formaldehyde

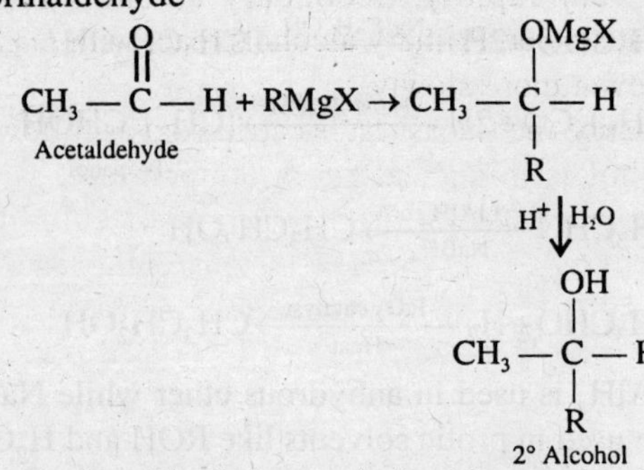

Tertiary Alcohols are obained by treating Grignard reagents with ketones

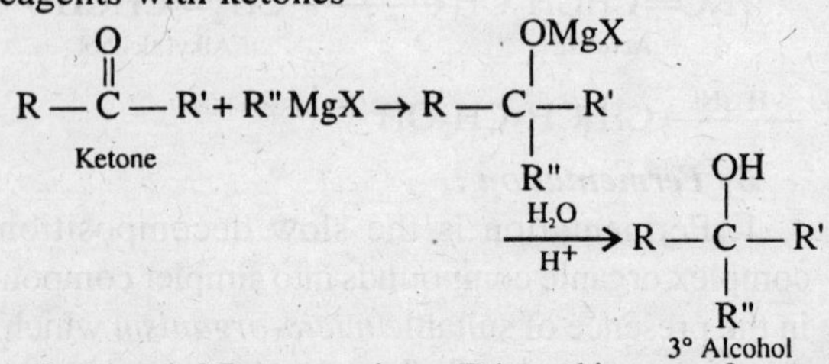

Industrial Preparation : Ethanol is manufactured by

(i) the hydration of ethylene in the presence of H_2SO_4 and

(ii) fermentation of sugars present in the form of starch (e.g. potato, maize, barley, rice, etc.) or cane sugar (e.g. molasses).

Methanol is manufactured

(i) as a by product by the destructive distillation of wood during the manufacture of charcoal or

(ii) By heating a mixture of water gas (a mixture of CO and H_2 in equimolar ratio) with half its volume of hydrogen in presence of catalyst.

$$\underbrace{CO + H_2}_{\text{Water gas}} + H_2 \xrightarrow[300°C]{Cr_2O_3-ZnO} \underset{\text{Methanol}}{CH_3OH}$$

Important : Water gas is obtained by passing steam over red hot coke $C + \underset{\text{(Steam)}}{H_2O} \rightarrow \underset{\text{(Water gas)}}{CO + H_2}$

Properties of Alcohols :

Physical Properties :

(1) Lower alcohols are colourless, toxic liquids. They have a characteristic smell. Higher alcohols having more than 12 carbon atoms are solids. They are colourless neutral substances having burning taste.

(2) The lower alcohols are readily soluble in water and the solubility decreases with the increase in molecular weight. The solubility of alcohols in water can be explained due to the formation of hydrogen bond between the highly polarised —OH groups present both in alcohol and water.

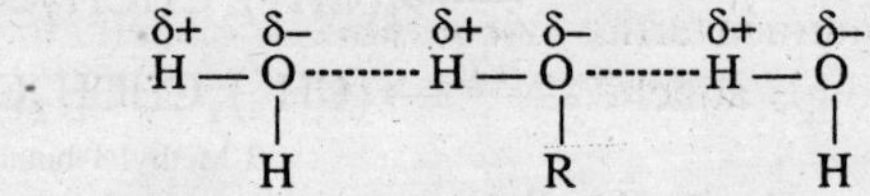

Hydrogen bonding between alcohol and water molecules.

However, in higher alcohols the hydrocarbon character (alkyl chain) of the molecule increases and thus alcohols tend to resemble hydrocarbon (which are insoluble in water) and hence the solubility in water decreases. When the ratio of C to CH is more than 4, alcohols have little solubility in water.

Chemical Properties of Alcohols : Alcohols are reactive compounds. They are attacked by polar or ionic reagents. This is because :

(i) The C—O and O—H bonds of alcohols are polar and as oxygen is highly electronegative.

(ii) The oxygen atom of alcohols is an electron rich centre because it has two unshared pairs of electrons.

Alcohols undergo the following general reactions:

(A) Reactions involving only the hydrogen atom of *the —OH group.*

These are reactions involving cleavage of oxygen-hydrogen bond, —O—H. All such reactions (1 to 4) follow the following order :

Primary > Secondary > Tertiary

(1) Action of Alkali Metals : Alcohols react with sodium or potassium to form alkoxide with the liberation of hydrogen gas.

$$\underset{\text{Alcohol}}{ROH} + 2Na \rightarrow \underset{\text{Sodium alkoxide}}{2R\overset{-}{O}\overset{+}{Na}} + H_2\uparrow$$

$$\underset{\text{Ethyl alcohol}}{2CH_3CH_2OH} + 2Na \rightarrow \underset{\text{Sodium ethoxide}}{2CH_3CH_2\overset{-}{O}\overset{+}{Na}} + H_2\uparrow$$

The above reaction shows that alcohols are acidic in nature. The reason for this is that the O—H bond in alcohols is polar and allows the release of the hydrogen atom as proton (H^+). However, alcohols are weaker acids ($K_a = 10^{-16}$ to 10^{-18}) than water. This is because the alkyl groups in alcohols have a + I effect. They release electrons towards the oxygen atom so that it becomes negatively charged. This negative charge on oxygen makes the release of the positive proton more difficult.

Tertiary alcohols are less acidic than secondary alcohols. The secondary alcohols are less acidic than primary alcohols. This is because the + I effect would be maximum in tertiary alcohols, as they contain three alkyl groups attached to the carbon bearing the — OH group.

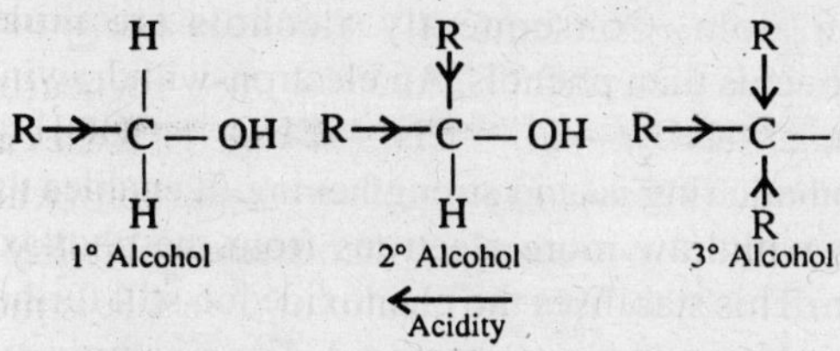

Alcohols are not acidic enough to react with aqueous NaOH or KOH.

$$R—OH + NaOH \rightarrow \text{No reaction}$$

The decreasing order of acidic character of few such compounds is

$H_2O > CH_3OH > 1° > 2° > 3°$ alcohol $> RC{\equiv}CH > RCH_3$.

(2) Action of Acids (Esterification): Alcohols react with organic and inorganic acids (except halogen acids) in presence of a dehydrating agent like H_2SO_4 or dry halogen chloride gas to form esters. The process is known as esterification.

(a) With organic acids :

$$CH_3COOH + HOC_2H_5 \xrightleftharpoons{H_2SO_4} \underset{\text{Ethyl acetate}}{CH_3COOC_2H_5} + H_2O$$

In general,

$$RCOOH + HOR \xrightleftharpoons{H_2SO_4} RCOOR' + H_2O$$

Distinction between Primary, Secondary and Tertiary Alcohols : The following tests are used to distinguish between primary, secondary and tertiary alcohols.

(1) Lucas Test : In this test, alcohols are treated with a solution of HCl and zinc chloride (Lucas reagent) to form alkyl halides. Zinc chloride serves as a catalyst.

$$\underset{\text{Alcohol}}{R—OH} + HCl \xrightarrow{ZnCl_2} \underset{\text{Alkylhalide}}{R—Cl} + H_2O$$

The three types of alcohols undergo this reaction at different rates. Tertiary alcohols react with *Lucas reagent* very rapidly. Secondary alcohols react somewhat slower. Primary alcohols react with *Lucas reagent* even more slowly.

In practice the Lucas test is carried out as follows: An alcohol is mixed, at room temperature, with concentrated HCl and $ZnCl_2$. The alkyl chloride, which is formed is insoluble in the medium. It causes the solution to become cloudy before it separates as a distinct layer.

(a) With 3° alcohol, cloudiness appears immediately.

(b) With 2° alcohol, cloudiness appears in 5 minutes.

(c) With 1° alcohols, the solution remains clear. This is because primary alcohols do not react with *Lucas reagent* at room temperature. High temperatures are needed.

Phenols

"Phenols are compounds containing an —OH group attached directly to an aromatic ring". Like alcohols, they may be monohydric or polyhydric according to the number of —OH groups that they contain. Phenols are usually named by common system or as derivatives of the parent phenol (C_6H_5OH). Examples are :

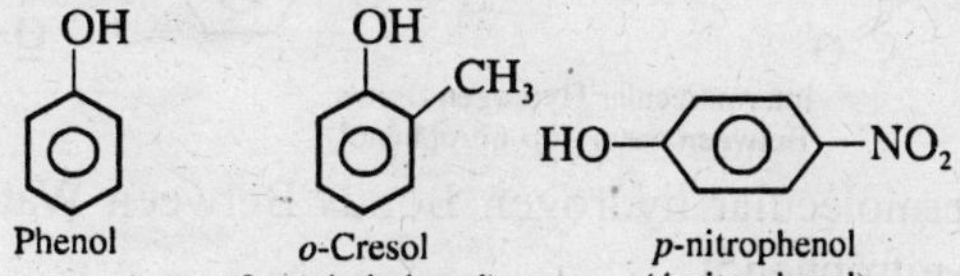

Phenol — *o*-Cresol (2-methyl phenol) — *p*-nitrophenol (4-nitrophenol)

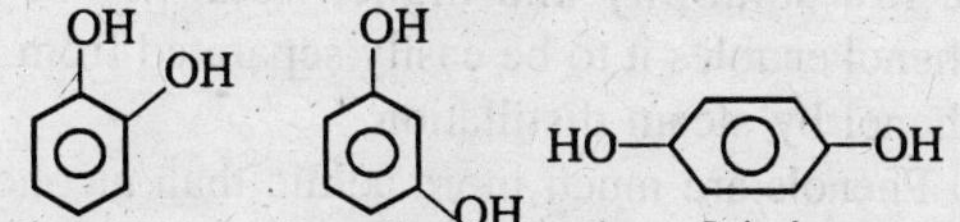

Catechol — Resorcinol — Quinol

Compounds which contain an —OH group in a side chain attached to an aromatic ring are not phenols. They are called 'aromatic alcohols'. Examples are :

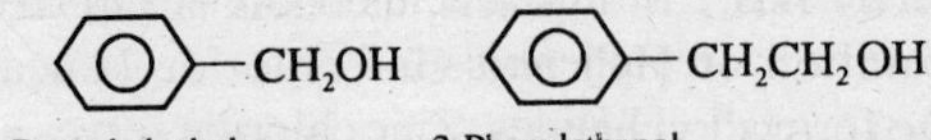

Benzyl alcohol 2-Phenylethanol

Physical Properties of Phenols :

(i) Most pure alcohols are colourless liquids or solids, although they are often found to contain a red tinge owing to the presence of oxidation products.

(ii) Phenols have a characteristic 'Carbolic' odour which in case of phenol itself is highly toxic.

(iii) The boiling points of phenols are higher than aliphatic alcohols of comparable molecular weights. This is due to stronger intermolecular hydrogen bonding in phenols relative to alcohols.

Compound	*m.w.*	*b.p. °C*
Phenol	94	182
Cyclohexanol	100	162
1-Haxanol	102	157

The introduction of a hydroxyl group into an already substituted aromatic ring, especially in the *para*-position to methyl, halogen or nitro group, produces a marked increase in the boiling point. The greater volatility of the ortho isomer is due to *intramolecular hydrogen* bonding whereas the higher boiling point of the para isomer is due to intermolecular hydrogen bonding. Also *p*-nitrophenol is more soluble in water than *o*-nitrophenol. This is because *p*-nitrophenol can associate with itself and also with water molecules. *o*-Nitrophenol cannot form intermolecular hydrogen bonds.

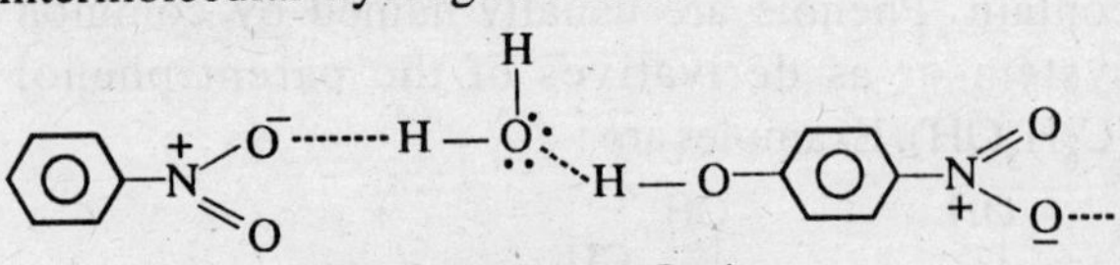

Intermolecular Hydrogen Bonds Between water & *p*-nitrophenol

Intermolecular hydrogen Bonds Between Water and *p*-nitrophenol

The low solubility and higher volatility of *o*-nitrophenol enables it to be easily separated from *p*-nitrophenol by steam distillation.

(iv) Phenols are much more acidic than alcohols but less so than carboxylic acids or even carbonic acid. Phenols are acidic due to the formation of stable phenoxide ions in aqueous solutions. For example, phenol itself gives phenoxide ion on dissociation.

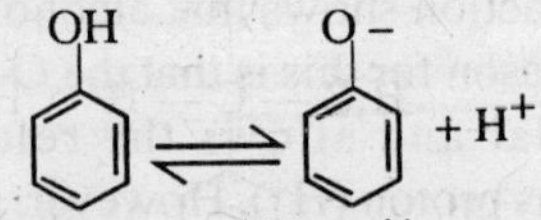

Phenol Phenoxide Ion

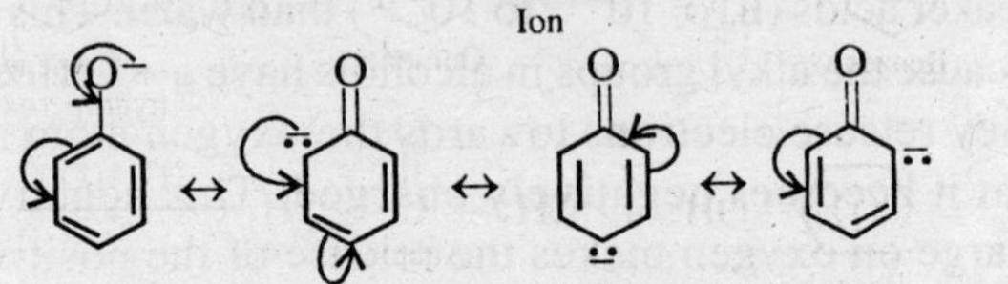

Resonating Structures of Phenoxide ion

Negative charge is spread throughout the benzene ring, and thereby effectively dispersed. This charge delocalisation is a stabilising factor in the phenoxide ion. On the other hand, no resonance is possible in alkoxide ions (RO^-) derived from alcohols. The negative charge is concentrated (localised) on a single oxygen atom. Consequently alcohols are much weaker acids than phenols. An electron-withdrawing group e.g. —NO_2, —Cl. —CN, —CHO, —COOH on the aromatic ring is acid strengthening. It enables the ring to withdraw more electrons from the phenoxy oxygen. This stabilises the phenoxide ion still further and results in the stronger acid. For example, *p*-nitrophenol is more acidic than phenol.

An electron-releasing group e.g. —CH_3, —OCH_3, —NH_2) on the aromatic ring is acid weakening. It strengthens the negative charge on phenoxy oxygen and inhibits the charge delocalization due to resonance, this stabilises the phenoxide ion and results in a weaker acid. For example, *p*-cresol is less acidic than phenol.

Preparation :

From chlorobenzene (Dow's Process) : This involves the hydrolysis of chlorobenzene with aqueous NaOH at high temperature and pressure followed by treatment with dilute HCl.

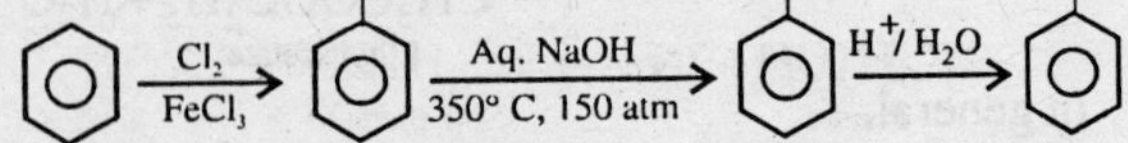

Benzene Chlorobenzene Sodium phenoxide Phenol

This process was first introduced by Dow Chemical Company of U.S.A. in 1928.

From Cumene Process : This involves air-oxidation of cumene (Isopropyl-benzene) followed by treatment with dilute HCl

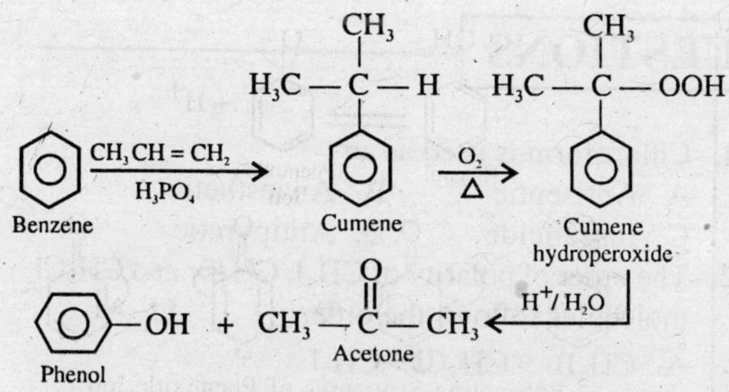

This process accounts for 80% of the total world production of phenol. The success of this method is due to the availability of benzene and propene from petroleum and to the formation of acetone, a valuable by-product.

From Sodium Benzene Sulphonate : This involves fusion of sodium benzene-sulphonate with solid NaOH at 300°C followed by treatment with dil. HCl.

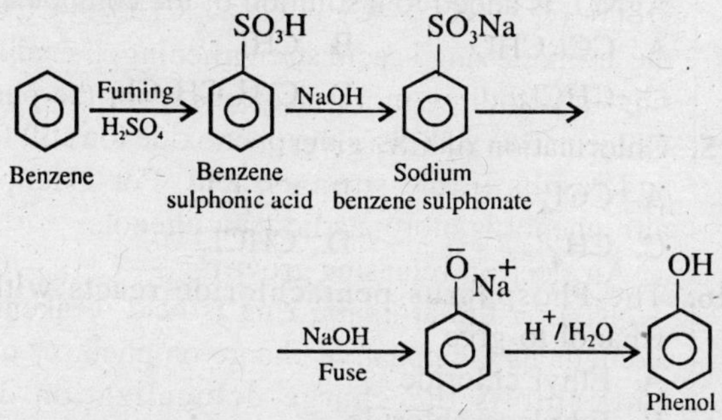

This process was once used for phenol manufacture but is now obsolete.

Properties Chemical of Phenols

(1) Acidic Character (Salt formation) : Unlike alcohols, phenols are acidic in nature and react with alkali metals and their hydroxides to form salts known as 'phenoxides' or 'phenates'. However, phenols do not react with weak alkalies like carbonates or bicarbonates (difference from carboxylic acids).

$$\underset{\text{Phenol}}{2C_6H_5OH} + 2Na \rightarrow \underset{\text{Sod. phenate}}{2C_6H_5ONa} + H_2$$

$$C_6H_5OH + NaOH \rightarrow C_6H_5ONa + H_2O$$

Salts of phenols are decomposed by aqueous mineral acids, carboxylic acids or even carbonic acids to give back free phenols.

$$C_6H_5ONa + \underset{\substack{\text{Carbonic acid}\\\text{(stronger acid)}}}{H_2O + CO_2} \rightarrow \underset{\substack{\text{Phenol}\\\text{(Weaker acid)}}}{C_6H_5OH} + NaHCO_3$$

This indicates that phenols are very weak acids, weaker than carboxylic acids or even carbonic acids. In short, 'phenols are stronger acids than alcohols but weaker than the carboxylic acids and even carbonic acids'.

(2) Action of Ferric Chloride : Phenol gives purple colouration with one or two drops of neutral ferric chloride solution due to the formation of a complex. This reaction is given by most phenols. Reaction of phenols with ferric chloride is used in analytical chemistry for distinguishing phenols from carboxylic acids.

(3) Reduction with Zinc Dust : Phenols, when distilled with zinc dust give aromatic hydrocarbons (alcohols are reduced to hydrocarbons with hydriodic acid)

$$\underset{\text{Phenol}}{C_6H_5OH} + Zn \xrightarrow{\text{ditill.}} \underset{\text{Benzene}}{C_6H_6} + ZnO$$

Important : Phenols differs from alcohols in above three reactions, numbered 1, 2 and 3.

(4) Alkylation : (Ether formation).

(a) Phenols react with alkyl halides in alkali solution to form phenyl ethers. The alkali first forms the phenoxide ion which then reacts with the alkyl halide.

$$C_6H_5OH + NaOH \rightarrow \underset{\text{Sodium phenate}}{C_6H_5\overset{-}{O}\overset{+}{Na}} + H_2O$$

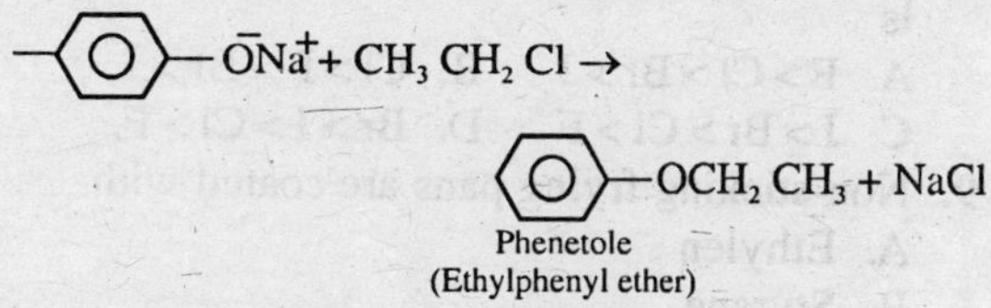

$$C_6H_5ONa + ICH_3 \rightarrow \underset{\substack{\text{Phenyl methyl}\\\text{ether}\\\text{(Anisole)}}}{C_6H_5.O.CH_3} + NaI$$

OBJECTIVE QUESTIONS

1. A Grignard reagent is prepared by reacting magnesium with
   A. Methyl amine B. Diethyl ether
   C. Ethyl iodide D. Ethyl alcohol
2. Fires result from the combustion of alkali metals can be extinguished by
   A. CCl_4 B. HCl
   C. Water D. Kerosene
3. The S_{N_2} reactivity order for halides
   A. R—F > R—Cl > R—Br > R—I
   B. R—I > R—Br > R—Cl > R—F
   C. R—Br > R—I > R—Cl > R—F
   D. R—Cl > R—Br > R—F > R—I
4. Reaction of chloroform with alcoholic KOH in presence of a primary aromatic amine is called
   A. Hydrolysis B. Reduction
   C. Wurtz reaction D. Carbylamine reaction
5. Ethyl bromide reacts with lead-sodium alloy to form
   A. Tetraethyl lead B. Tetraethyl bromide
   C. Both (A) and (B) D. None
6. Grignard reagent shows addition on
   A. >C=O B. —C≡N
   C. >C=S D. All
7. Which is ethyl-dihalide?
   A. $CH_3.CHBr_2$
   B. $CH_2Br.CH_2Br$
   C. $CH_3.CHBr.CH_2Br$
   D. None *[CPMT 1988]*
8. The reactivity order of halide ion in alkyl halide is
   A. F > Cl > Br > I B. Cl > F > Br > I
   C. I > Br > Cl > F D. Br > I > Cl > F
9. Non-sticking frying pans are coated with
   A. Ethylen
   B. Styrene
   C. Tetrafluoro ethylene (Teflon)
   D. Chlorofluoro methane
10. Pick up the correct statement about alkyl halides
    A. They show H-bonding
    B. They are soluble in water
    C. They are soluble in organic solvents
    D. They do not contain any polar bond
11. Chloroform is used as an
    A. Antiseptic B. Anaesthetic
    C. Insecticide D. Antipyretic
12. The order of polarity of CH_3I, CH_3Br and CH_3Cl molecules follows the order
    A. $CH_3Br > CH_3Cl > CH_3I$
    B. $CH_3I > CH_3Br > CH_3Cl$
    C. $CH_3Cl > CH_3Br > CH_3I$
    D. $CH_3Cl > CH_3I > CH_3Br$
13. A silver salt of fatty acid on heating with alkyl halide gives
    A. Ether B. Aldehyde
    C. Ester D. Alcohol
14. A yellow precipitate is obtained when aqueous $AgNO_3$ is added to a solution of the compound
    A. CCl_3CHO B. CHI_3
    C. $CHCl_3$ D. $C_6H_5CH_2Cl$
15. Chlorination of CS_2 gives:
    A. CCl_4 B. CS_2Cl_2
    C. CH_4 D. $CHCl_3$
16. The Phosphorus pentachloride reacts with ethanol to give
    A. Ethyl chloride
    B. Ethylene chloride
    C. Ethylidene chloride
    D. None of these
17. Freon is used as
    A. Refrigerant B. Antiseptic
    C. An algesic D. Insecticide
18. Sodium ethoride reacts with ethyl iodide to yield
    A. CH_3CH_3 B. $C_2H_5OCH_3$
    C. $C_2H_5OC_2H_5$ D. None of these
19. The shape of $CHCl_3$ molecule is
    A. Pyramidal B. Linear
    C. Tetrahedral D. Trigonal pyramidal
20. 20% aqueous solution of sodium chloride containing ethyl alcohol on electrolysis gives
    A. Ethyl chloride B. Chloral
    C. Acetaldehyde D. Chloroform
21. When iodoform is heated with silver powder it forms

A. Acetylene B. Ethylene
C. Methane D. Ethane

22. Chloroform on reaction with conc. HNO_3 gives
A. Chloropicrin B. Nitromethane
C. Picric acid D. Acetylene

23. The compound which gives negative iodoform test is
A. CH_3CHO B. CH_3CH_2OH
C. $C_6H_5COCH_3$ D. $C_6H_5CH_2CH_2OH$

24. Which compound gives the iodoform reaction?
A. Formaldehyde B. Acetaldehyde
C. CH_3OH D. CH_3COOH

25. Which set of reagents will produce CCl_2F_2?
A. $C + F_2 + Cl_2$
B. $CH_3Cl + F_2$
C. $CCl_4 + HF \xrightarrow{SbCl_5}$
D. $CCl_4 + F_2 \rightarrow$

26. Chloroform is kept in dark coloured bottles because
A. It is inflammable
B. It gives a peroxide
C. It undergoes rapid chlorination
D. It is oxidised to poisonous phosgene

27. If chloroform is left open in air in presence of sun-rays
A. Explosion takes place
B. Poisonous phosgene gas is formed
C. Polymerisation takes place
D. No reaction takes place

28. Which statement is correct?
A. C_2H_5Br reacts with alcoholic KOH to form C_2H_5OH
B. C_2H_5Br when treated with metallic sodium gives ethane
C. C_2H_5Br when treated with sodium ethoxide forms diethyl ether
D. C_2H_5Br with AgCN forms ethyl cyanide

29. CH_3NH_2 reacts with CH_3MgX to give
A. Acetone B. Alcohol
C. Methane D. Ethane

30. Methyl chloride reacts with silver acetate to yield
A. Acetic acid B. Methyl acetate
C. Acetyl chloride D. Acetaldehyde

31. Ethyline dichloride (CH_3CHCl_2) can be prepared by the addition of hydrogen chloride on
A. C_2H_6 B. C_2H_4
C. C_2H_2 D. All of the above

32. $(CH_3)_3$ CMgCl on reaction with D_2O gives
A. $(CH_3)_3CD$ B. $(CH_3)_3OD$
C. $(CD_3)_3CD$ D. $(CD_3)_3OD$

33. Ethyl iodide on treatment with alcoholic potash, gives
A. Ethyl alcohol B. Ethane
C. Acetylene D. Ethylene

34. The reactivity order of alkyl halides depends upon
A. Nature of alkyl group only
B. Nature of halogen atom only
C. Nature of both alkyl group and halogen atoms
D. None of these

35. An alkyl iodide on standing darkens, due to
A. Hydrolysis
B. Conversion into ether
C. Liberation of iodine
D. Formation of alkanes

36. The given reaction is an example of $C_2H_5Br + KCN\ (aq) \rightarrow C_2H_5CN + KBr$
A. Elimination
B. Nucleophilic substitution
C. Electrophilic substitution
D. Redox change

37. When propylene reacts with HBr in the presence of a peroxide, the product formed is
A. *n*-propyl alcohol B. Propylene peroxide
C. *n*-propyl bromide D. Isopropyl bromide

38. In the following sequence of reactions,
$CH_3CH_2CH_2I \xrightarrow{KOH(alc.)} (A) \xrightarrow{KOH(alc.)} (B) \xrightarrow{NaNH_2/NH_3} (C)$
The end product (C) is
A. Alkene B. Alkanal
C. Alkyne D. Alkyl amine

39. In the following sequence of reactions,

$$CH_3CH_2CH_2Br \xrightarrow{KOH\,(alc.)} (A) \xrightarrow{HBr} (B) \xrightarrow{KOH(aq.)} (C)$$

The product (C) is

A. Propene B. Propyne

C. Propan-1-01 D. Propan-2-ol

40. Chloroform on reduction with Zn and HCl (alc.) gives

A. Formic acid

B. Chlorotone

C. Chloropicrin

D. Methylene dichloride

41. Freon is

A. CCl_2F_2 B. $CHCl_3$

C. CH_3F D. CHF_3

42. Chloropicrin (nitro chloroform) used as an insecticide and a war gas, is

A. CH_2ClCCl_3 B. CCl_3NO_2

C. $CH_2(OH)CH_2Cl$ D. CHI_3

43. Westrosol is

A. Acetylene tetrachloride

B. Acetylene dichloride

C. Trichloroethyne

D. 1, 1, 2-trichloroethane

44. When a solution of $AgNO_3$ is added to pure CCl_4

A. A pale yellow precipitate is formed

B. Curdy white precipitate is formed

C. No precipitate is formed

D. None of these

45. The bad smelling substance formed by the action of alcoholic caustic patash on chloroform and aniline is

A. Phenyl isocyanide

B. Nitrobenzene

C. Acetylene

D. Chlorobenzene

46. Optically active compound is

A. 2-chloropropane B. 2-chlorobutane

C. 3-chloropentane D. None of these

47. Propyl iodide and isopropyl iodide are

A. Functional isomers

B. Chain isomers

C. Metamers

D. Position isomers

48. In alkyl nitrites the oxygen of —O—N=O group is linked with carbon. An alkyl nitrite is:

A. An ester B. A nitro compound

C. An amide D. A nitrile

49. Iodoform can be used in medicine as

A. Anaesthetic B. Antiseptic

C. Analgesic D. Antifebrin

50. Chlorotone used as a drug is prepared by the reaction of acetone with

A. Chlorine B. Ethyl chloride

C. Chloroform D. Ethylene dichloride

51. Which would be obtained by boiling $CHCl_3$ with caustic soda?

A. CH_3COONa B. $HCOONa$

C. $Na_2C_2O_4$ D. CH_3OH

52. The starting material for the preparation of CHI_3 is

A. C_2H_5OH B. CH_3OH

C. C_2H_5CHO D. $HCHO$

53. Most readily hydrolysed halide is

A. C_6H_5Cl B. $(C_6H_5)_2CHCl$

C. $C_2H_5CH_2Cl$ D. $(C_2H_5)_3CCl$

54. The coupling of alkyl halides to form an alkane is called

A. Wurtz synthesis

B. Kolbe's synthesis

C. Claisen condensation

D. Friedel-craft's reaction

55. Iodoform is formed on warming iodine and sodium hydroxide with

A. C_2H_5OH B. CH_3OH

C. $HCOOH$ D. C_6H_6

56. An alkyl halide may be converted into an alcohol by

A. Addition

B. Substitution

C. Dehydrohalogenation

D. Elimination

57. A sample of chloform before being used as an anaesthetic is tested by

A. $AgNO_3$ solution

B. $AgNO_3$ solution after boiling with alc. KOH

C. Fehling's solution

D. Ammoniacal Cu_2Cl_2

58. CCl_4 is insoluble in water because

A. Water is non-polar

B. CCl_4 is non-polar

C. Water and CCl_4 are polar
D. None of the above

59. A magnesium alkyl halide is known as
A. Grignard's reagent
B. Fenton's reagent
C. Twitchell's reagent
D. Schweitzer's reagent

60. Which is finally produced when acetylene reacts with HCl?
A. $CH_2 = CHCl$ B. CH_3CHCl_2
C. $ClCH = CHCl$ D. None of these

61. PCl_2 reacts with propanone, to give
A. Gem-dichloride B. Vic-dichloride
C. Propanal D. Propane chloride

62. Haloform reaction is used for preparing
A. Halogens B. CCl_4
C. $CHCl_3$ D. Halides

63. Ethylene dichloride and ethylidene chloride are isomeric compounds. Identify the statement which is not applicable to both of them.
A. React with alcoholic potash
B. React with aqueous potash and give the same products
C. Are dihalides
D. Answer Beilstein's test

64. In the reaction,
$CH_3C \equiv C^-Na^+ + (CH_3)_2CHCl \rightarrow$ the product formed is
A. 4-methyl-2 pentyne
B. Propyne
C. Propyne and propene
D. None of these

65. Chloral is
A. CCl_3CHO B. $CCl.C.CH_3$
C. $CCl_3.CO.CCl_3$ D. $CCl_3.CH_2OH$

66. A true organometallic compound is
A. Sodium carbonate
B. Sodium methoxide
C. Sodium amide
D. Sodium acetylide

67. Which process does not occur during formation of $CHCl_3$ from C_2H_5OH and bleaching powder?
A. Hydrolysis B. Oxidation
C. Elimination D. Chlorination

68. The reaction between ethyl bromide and sodium in dry ether to form butane is called
A. Friedel-crafts reaction
B. Wurtz reaction
C. Cannizzaro's reaction
D. Williamson's reaction

69. Reagent not used to prepare an alkyl halide from an alcohol is
A. $HCl + ZnCl_2$ B. NaCl
C. PCl_5 D. $SOCl_2$

70. Compound that gives a positive iodoform test is
A. 1-pentanal B. 2-pentanone
C. 3-pentanone D. Pentanal

71. Alkye halides give alcohols on hydrolysis with
A. NaOH aq. B. Alc. NaOH
C. Both of these D. None of these

72. Methyl chloride on treatment with potassium cyanide followed by hydrolysis yields
A. HCOOH B. CH_3COOH
C. CH_3CN D. CH_3COOK

73. Compounds formed when ethyl amine is heated with chloroform in the presence of KOH is
A. Ethyl chloride B. Ethyl isocyanide
C. Ethanal D. Diethyl ether

74. Isobutyl chloride and butyl chloride are
A. Position isomers
B. Chain isomers
C. Functional isomers
D. Metamers

75. When chloroform is heated with aniline and caustic potash, we get a compound having
A. Rose odour
B. Jasmine odour
C. Bitter almond odour
D. Obnoxious odour

76. Phosgene is a common name for
A. CO_2 and PH_3
B. Phosphoryl chloride
C. Carbonyl chloride
D. Carbon tetrachloride

77. For a given alkyl group, the densities/b.pt./m.pt. are in the order:
A. $RI < RBr < RCl$ B. $RI < RCl < RBr$
C. $RBr < RI < RCl$ D. $RCl < RBr < RI$

78. Carbylamine test is performed by heating alc.

KOH with

A. $CHCl_3$ and Ag

B. Trihalogenated methane and primary amine

C. CH_3Cl and $C_2H_5NH_2$

D. RCN and RNH_2

79. Alkyl halides on treatment with a suspension of Ag_2O moist in ether gives

A. Alkanal B. Alkanal

C. Alkanes D. Alkoxy alkane

80. Which will give carbylamine test?

A. Urea B. Alkanal

C. Alkanes D. Alkoxy alkane

81. A salt solution is treated with chloroform drops and is shaken with chlorine water. Chloroform layer becomes violet, solution contains

A. NO_2^- B. NO_3^-

C. Br^- D. I^-

82. Strong reducing agent converts $CHCl_3$ into

A. C_2H_2 B. C_2H_6

C. C_2H_4 D. CH_4

83. A compound containing two —OH groups attached with one carbon atom is unstable but which one of the following is stable

A. 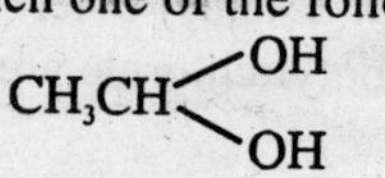

B. 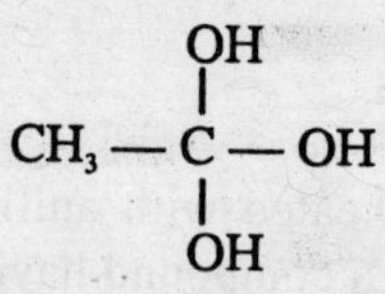

C. 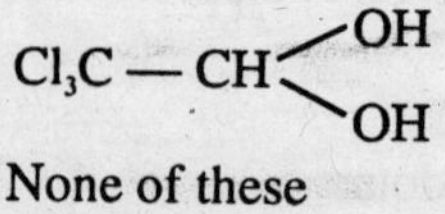

D. None of these

84. The compound having no dipole moment is

A. CH_3Cl B. CCl_4

C. CH_2Cl_2 D. $CHCl_3$

85. Chloroform when treated with benzene in presence of anhydrous $AlCl_3$, the product formed is

A. Chlorobenzene

B. Toluene

C. Mixture of ortho and para chlorotoluene

D. Triphenyl methane

86. 1-chlorobutane on reaction with alcoholic KOH gives

A. 1-butene B. 1-butanal

C. 2-butene D. 2-butanal

87. Which of the following can be used as local anaes-thetic:

A. $CHCl_3$ B. C_2H_4 with O_2

C. C_2H_5Cl D. C_2H_5OH

88. Chlorine is most reactive towards NaOH in

A. CH_3Cl B. $CH_2=CHCl$

C. C_6H_5Cl D. $C_6H_5CH_2Cl$

89. 1-phenyl, 2-chloropropane on treating with alc. KOH gives mainly

A. 1-Phenyl propene

B. 2-Phenyl propene

C. 1-Phenyl propene-2-ol

D. 1-Phenyl propene-1-ol

90. The reaction of ethyl alcohol and methyl magnesium bromide gives

A. CH_4 B. C_2H_6

C. C_3H_8 D. None of these

91. $CHCl_3$ can be obtained from

A. Methanal B. Methanol

C. Propanal-1 D. Propanal-2

92. Which is most reactive for S_N2 reactions?

A. CH_3I B. C_2H_5I

C. C_3H_7I D. C_4H_9I

93. Chloral hydrate is

A. $CCl_3CH(OH)_2$ B. CCl_3COCH_3

C. CCl_3COCCl_3 D. CCl_3CH_2OH

94. $C_2H_5Br \xrightarrow{KCN} (A) \xrightarrow{Hydrolysis} (B)$

The compound (B) in above reaction is

A. Ethylene chloride B. Acetic acid

C. Propionic acid D. Ethyl cyanide

95. Formation of alkane by the action of Zn on alkyl halide is called

A. Wurtz reaction

B. Kolbe's reaction

C. Cannizzaro's reaction

D. Frankland's reaction

96. Alcoholic solution of KOH is used for

A. Dehalogenation

B. Dehydrohalogenation

C. Dehydration

D. Dehydrogenation

97. *n*-propyl bromide reacts with ethanol KOH to form:

A. $C_6H_5C \equiv N$

B. $C_6H_5N \equiv C$

C. $CH_3—O—C \equiv N$

D. $CH_3—N=C=O$

98. *n*-propyl bromide reacts with ethanolic KOH to form

A. Propane B. Propene

C. Propyne D. Propyl alcohol

99. Which one is true organometallic compounds

A. Lithium methoxide

B. Lithium acetate

C. Lithium dimethyl amide

D. Methyl lithium

100. Monohalogen derivative of alkanes with alcoholic KOH gives

A. Alkane

B. Alkene

C. Alkyne

D. Alicyclic hydrocarbon

ANSWERS

1	2	3	4	5	6	7	8	9	10
C	A	B	D	A	D	A	C	C	C
11	12	13	14	15	16	17	18	19	20
A	C	C	B	A	A	A	C	B	D
21	22	23	24	25	26	27	28	29	30
A	A	D	B	C	D	B	C	C	B
31	32	33	34	35	36	37	38	39	40
D	A	D	B	C	C	B	C	D	D
41	42	43	44	45	46	47	48	49	50
A	B	D	C	A	B	D	A	B	C
51	52	53	54	55	56	57	58	59	60
B	A	D	A	A	B	B	B	A	B
61	62	63	64	65	66	67	68	69	70
A	C	B	A	A	D	C	B	B	B
71	72	73	74	75	76	77	78	79	80
A	B	B	B	D	C	D	B	D	C
81	82	83	84	85	86	87	88	89	90
D	D	C	B	D	A	C	D	A	A
91	92	93	94	95	96	97	98	99	100
D	A	A	C	D	B	B	B	D	B

17

ALDEHYDES, KETONES AND CARBOXYLIC ACIDS

Aldehydes and Ketones

Aldehydes and ketones contain a carbon-oxygen double bond (>C=O). This unit is referred to as the *Carbonyl Group*.

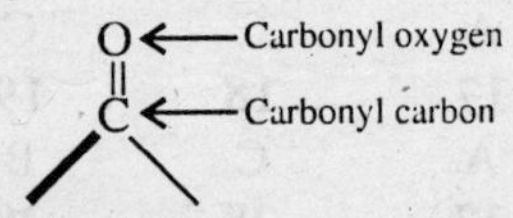

Carbonyl group

Aldehydes and ketones are collectively called Carbonyl Compounds. In aldehydes, the carbonyl carbon is bonded to one hydrogen and one alkyl group. Formaldehyde, HCHO, in which the carbonyl carbon is bonded to two hydrogen atoms is an exception. In ketones, the carbonyl carbon is always bonded to two alkyl groups. These alkyl groups may be same or different.

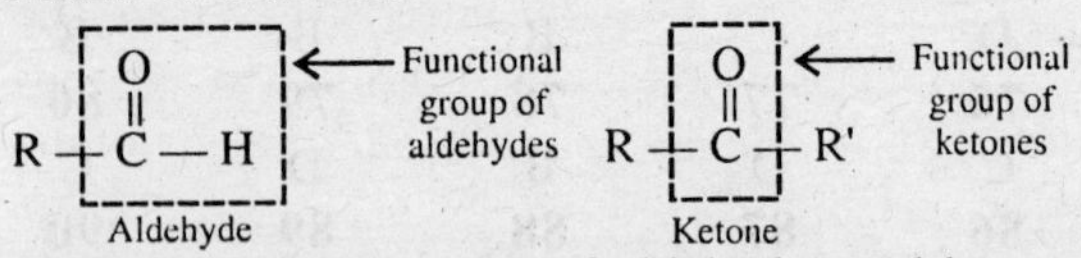

Most of the properties of aldehydes and ketones are a result of the presence of the carbonyl group.

Structure of the Carbonyl Group

The carbonyl group, like the carbon-carbon double bond of alkenes, is composed of one σ-bond and one π-bond.

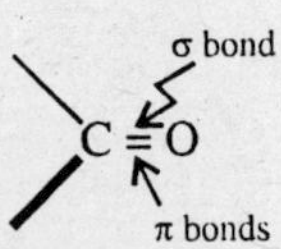

Both the carbon and oxygen are sp^2-hybridized. The σ-bond is formed by the overlap of an sp^2-orbital of carbon and an sp^2-orbital of oxygen. The π-bond is formed by the overlap of unhybridized p-orbitals of the two atoms. The two unshared electron pairs of oxygen occupy the sp^2-hybrid orbitals of oxygen. Because the carbonyl carbon is sp^2-hybridized, the three atoms attached to it lie in the same plane. The bond angles between the attached atoms are approximately 120°.

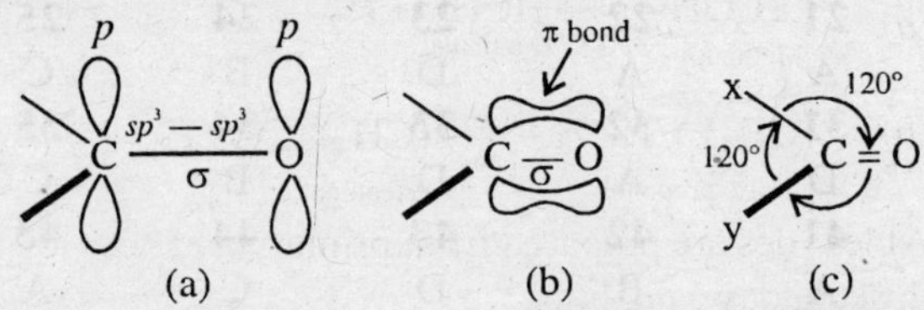

The electrons in the π-bond of the carbonyl group are not equally shared. In fact, they are pulled more towards the more electronegative oxygen atom. As a result, the bond is polarized, with the oxygen atom being slightly negative (δ–) and the carbon atom being slightly positive (δ+). This is often indicated as

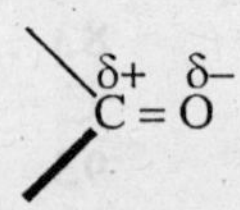

Alternatively, the polar nature of the carbonyl group can also be indicated by the following resonance structure.

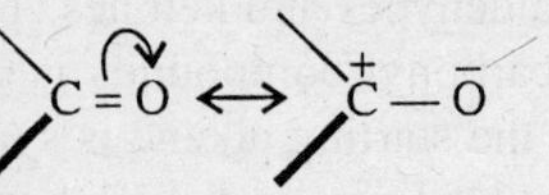

Preparation

1. Oxidation of Alcohols : Primary alcohols form aldehydes while secondary alcohols form ketones.

$$\underset{\text{Ethyl alcohol}}{CH_3CH_2OH} \xrightarrow[\text{[O]}]{K_2Cr_2O_7 + \text{dil. } H_2SO_4} \underset{\text{Acetaldehyde}}{CH_3CHO} + H_2O$$

$$\underset{\text{Isopropyl alcohol}}{CH_3CHOHCH_3} \xrightarrow[\text{[O]}]{K_2Cr_2O_7 + \text{dil. } H_2SO_4} \underset{\text{Acetone}}{CH_3.CO.CH_3}$$

Ketones are not easily oxidised further and can be obtained in high yield by this method.

Alternatively, ketones can be obtained from secondary alcohols by *Oppenauer Oxidations*. In this process, the appropriate secondary alcohol refluxed with excess of acetone in the presence of aluminium tertiary butoxide, $AlOC(CH_3)_3$, catalyst

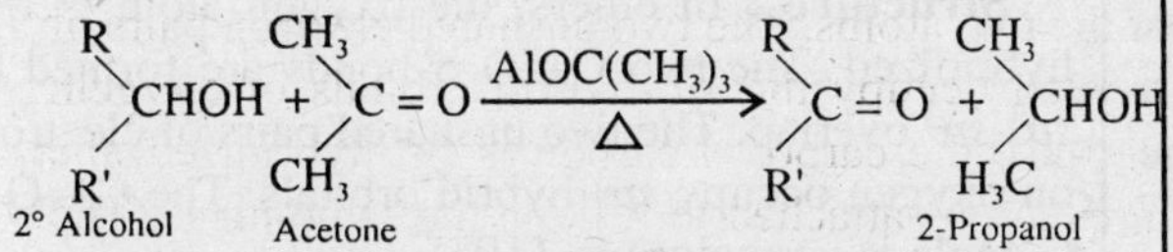

2. Catalytic Dehydrogenation of Alcohols :

(a) $\underset{\text{Methanol}}{CH_3OH} \xrightarrow[300°C]{Cu} \underset{\text{Methanal}}{HCHO} + H_2$

(b) $\underset{\text{Iso-propanol}}{(CH_3)_2CHOH} \xrightarrow[300°C]{Cu} \underset{\text{Acetone}}{(CH_3)_2CO} + H_2$

Aldehydes are prepared from primary and ketones from secondary alcohols.

3. Oxidation of Alkenes (Ozonolysis) : Aldehydes and ketones can be obtained by ozonolysis of alkenes. This involves the treatment of alkenes with ozone to give ozonides. The ozonides are not isolated because they are often explosive in dry state. They are decomposed with Zn + H_2O to form aldehyde and ketones.

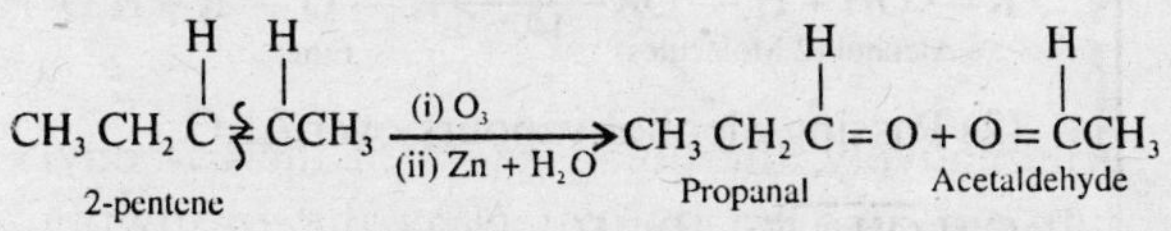

Ozonolysis of alkenes is not a good preparative method for aldehydes and ketones. This is because a mixture of carbonyl compounds is often produced. However, if the starting alkene is symmetrical, only one carbonyl compound will be obtained. For example,

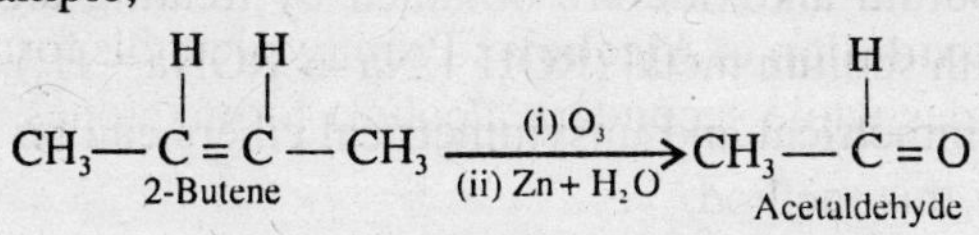

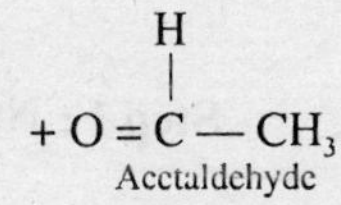

Properties

1. Physical Properties :

(i) Formaldehyde is a gas at room temperature. Acetaldehyde boils at 20°C. Other lower aldehydes and ketones are colourless liquids.

(ii) Lower aldehydes possess rather unpleasant, pungent smells, whereas the ketones have pleasant, sweet odours.

(iii) Density of aldehydes and ketones is less than that of water.

(iv) Aldehydes and ketones are polar compounds. They have higher boiling points than alkanes and other non-polar compounds of the same molecular weight. However, since aldehydes and ketones cannot form hydrogen bonds with each other, they have lower boiling points than the corresponding alcohols.

(v) Lower aldehydes and ketones are soluble in water. This is because of their ability to form hydrogen bonds with water molecules. Higher members containing more than five carbons are virtually insoluble in water.

(vi) Carbonyl groups of aldehydes and ketones give rise to very strong C = O stretching bonds in the 1665-1780 cm^{-1} region of the infrared spectrum. The —CHO group of aldehydes also gives two weak bands in the 2700-2775 and 2820-2900 cm^{-1} region of the infrared spectrum.

2. Chemical Properties Nucleophilic Addition Reactions : The carbonyl group of aldehydes and ketones is a highly polar group. It may be represented as

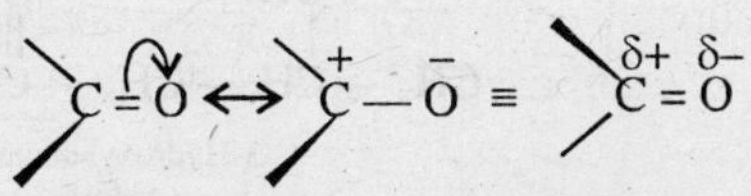

The positively charged carbon is readily attacked by electron-rich *nucleophiles*. The negatively charged oxygen is attacked by electron-deficient electrophiles.

Aldehydes and ketones undergo nucleophilic addition reactions by the following general mechanism.

Step 1 : 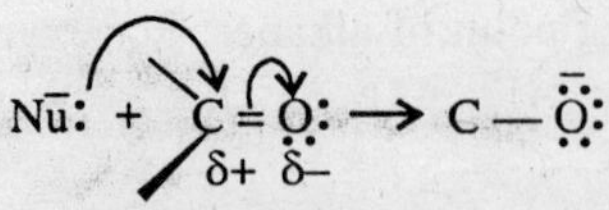

Step 2 : The electrophile (e.g. H^+) attacks the negatively charged oxygen to form the addition product.

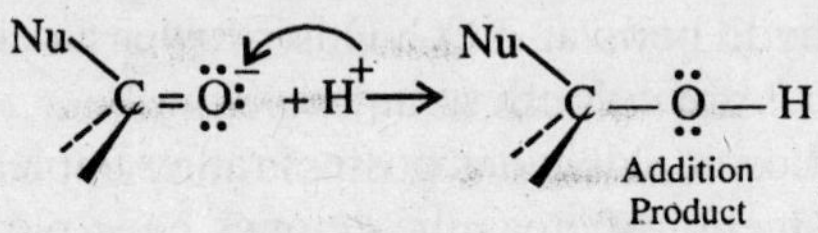

The nucleophilic addition reactions of carbonyl compounds may be catalysed by acids or bases.

Base-catalysed Addition : Bases convert a weak neutral nucleophile to a strong one by removing a proton. The strong nucleophile then adds to the carbonyl group as shown above

$$\underset{\text{Neutral nucleophile (weak)}}{\text{Na—H}} + \text{B} \rightarrow \underset{\text{Anionic nucleophile (Strong)}}{\text{Nu}:^-} + \overset{+}{\text{BH}}$$

(1) Aldol Condensation : Aldehydes containing α-hydrogens undergo self addition in the presence of a base to form products called Aldols. The reaction is called Aldol Condensation. The term aldol is derived from the combination of the words **Aldehyde** and **Alcohol**, the two functional groups present in the product. For example, two molecules of acetaldehyde combine with each other in the presence of dilute NaOH to form 3-Hydroxybutanal.

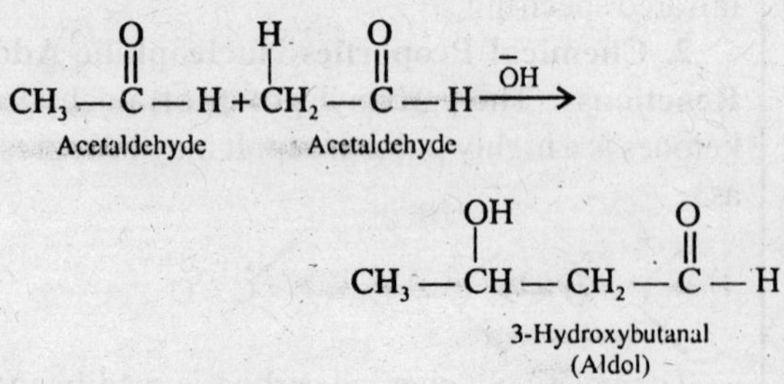

Ethers and Epoxides

Ethers (Alkoxyalkanes)

The functional group of ethers is C—O—C. Ethers are a class of compounds which contain an oxygen atom bonded to two alkyl groups. They are further designated as *Symmetrical Ethers* or *Unsymmetrical Ethers* according as the two alkyl groups attached to the oxygen atom are same or different.

$$\underset{\text{Symmetrical Ether}}{R-\ddot{O}-R} \qquad \underset{\text{Unsymmetrical Ether}}{R-\ddot{O}-R'}$$

Ethers may be considered as derivatives of water in which both halogen atoms have been replaced by alkyl groups. They may also be considered to be derivatives of alcohols in which the hydroxyl hydrogen has been replaced by an alkyl group.

$$\underset{\text{Water}}{H-O-H} \qquad \underset{\text{Ether}}{R-O-R'} \qquad \underset{\text{Alcohol}}{R-O-H}$$

Structure : In ethers, the oxygen atom is sp^3-hybridized. The two C—O σ-bonds are formed by sp^3-sp^3 overlap. The two unshared pairs of electrons on oxygen occupy sp^3-hybrid orbitals. The C—O—C angle is very close to 110°.

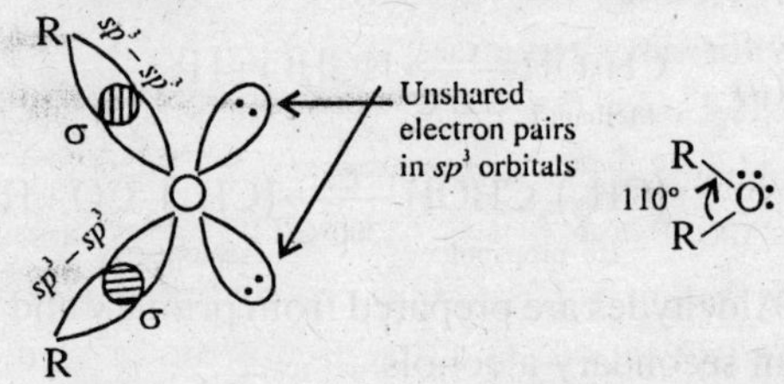

Fig. Orbital structure of an ether molecule

Preparation :

(1) Dehydration of Alcohols : Symmetrical ethers are prepared by heating an excess of alcohol with concentrated H_2SO_4 at 140°C.

$$\underset{\text{Alcohol (2 Molecules)}}{R-OH+H-OR} \xrightarrow[140^\circ]{H_2SO_4} \underset{\text{Ether}}{R-O-R} + H_2O$$

(2) Passing alcohol vapours over Al_2O_3

$$\underset{\text{Ethanol}}{C_2H_5OH} + \underset{\text{Ethanol}}{H-OC_2H_5} \xrightarrow[250^\circ]{Al_2O_3} \underset{\text{Diethyl ether}}{C_2H_5-O-C_2H_5} + H_2O$$

(3) Williamson-Ether Synthesis : This involves the treatment of a sodium alkoxide with an alkyl halide. Sodium alkoxide are obtained by treating alcohols with sodium metal ($ROH + Na \rightarrow RONa + H_2$). Both symmetrical and unsymmetrical ethers can be made by this method.

$$\underset{\text{Sod. alkoxide}}{R{-}\overset{-}{O}\overset{+}{Na}} + \underset{\text{Alkyl halide}}{R'{-}X} \rightarrow \underset{\text{Ether}}{R{-}O{-}R'} + NaX$$

$$\underset{\text{Sod. ethoxide}}{C_2H_5{-}\overset{-}{O}\overset{+}{Na}} + \underset{\text{Bromoethane}}{C_2H_5{-}Br} \rightarrow \underset{\text{Diethyl ether}}{C_2H_5{-}O{-}C_2H_5} + NaBr$$

Mechanism : The Williamson synthesis involves a displacement of halide ion from an alkyl halide by an alkoxide. It follows S_N2 mechanism.

$$\underset{\text{Sodium ethoxide}}{CH_3CH_2\overset{-}{O}\overset{+}{Na}} + \underset{\text{Bromoethane}}{CH_3CH_2{-}Br} \xrightarrow{S_N2} \underset{\text{Diethyl ether}}{CH_3CH_2{-}O{-}CH_2CH_3} + NaBr$$

Yields of ethers are highest when the halide ion is displaced from a primary rather than secondary or tertiary halides.

(4) Heating Alkylhalides with Dry silver oxide : (only for simple ethers).

$$C_2H_5I + Ag_2O + IC_2H_5 \rightarrow C_2H_5.O.C_2H_5 + 2AgI$$

Remember that reaction of alkyl halides with moist silver oxide ($Ag_2O + H_2O = AgOH$) gives alcohols.

(5) Action of Diazomethane on Alcohols : Methyl ethers can be obtained by treatment of primary or secondary alcohols with diazomethane. Fluoroboric acid (HBF_4) is used as a catalyst

$$R{-}O{-}H + CH_2N_2 \xrightarrow{HBF_4} R{-}O{-}CH_3 + N_2$$

$$\underset{\text{Ethyl alcohol}}{CH_3CH_2{-}O{-}H} + CH_2N_2 \xrightarrow{HBF_4} \underset{\text{Ethyl methyl ether}}{CH_3CH_2{-}O{-}CH_3} + N_2$$

Properties :

Physical :

(1) Dimethyl ether and ethyl methyl ether are gases. All others are colourless liquids with pleasant odours.

(2) Lower ethers are highly volatile and very flammable.

(3) Boiling points of ethers show a gradual increase with the increase in molecular weight.

(4) Ethers have lower boiling points than isomeric alcohols. This is because ether molecules cannot form hydrogen bonds with each other as they have no —OH groups. The boiling points of ethers are close to the boiling point of alkanes. For example, diethyl ether (MW = 74) boils at 35°C, *n*-pentane (MW = 72) boils at 36°C.

(5) Ethers are slightly soluble in water, as they can form hydrogen bonds with water.

(6) Ethers show a strong broad band due to C—O stretching in the 1060-1300 cm^{-1} range.

(7) Since the two C—O bonds in ethers are not linear (180°) but they are at an angle of about 110°, i.e. the molecule is bent, the dipole moment of the two C—O bonds do not cancel each other. Consequently, ethers are slightly polar and have a small net dipole moment (e.g. 1.80 D for diethyl ether).

Chemical : Ethers are much less reactive than compounds containing other functional group. They do not react with active metals like Na, strong base like NaOH, reducing or oxidising agents.

(1) Formation of Peroxides : On standing in contact with air, ethers are converted into unstable peroxides ($R_2O \rightarrow O$) which are highly explosive even in low concentrations.

(2) Basic Nature : Owing to the presence of unshared electron pairs on oxygen, ethers are basic. Hence they dissolve in strong acids (e.g. conc. HCl, conc. H_2SO_4) at low temperature to form oxonium salts.

$$\underset{\text{Diethyl ether}}{(C_2H_5)_2O} + H_2SO_4 \rightarrow \underset{\text{Diethyl oxonium hydrogen sulphate}}{\left[(C_2H_5)_2OH\right]} + HSO_4^-$$

On account of this property, ether is removed from ethyl bromide by shaking with conc. H_2SO_4.

The oxonium salts are stable only at low temperatures and in a strongly acidic medium. On dilution, they decompose to give back the original ether and acid. Ethers also form coordination complexes with Lewis acids like BF_3, $AlCl_3$, RMgX, etc.

(a) $R_2\ddot{O}{:} + BF_3 \rightarrow R_2O \rightarrow BF_3$

(b) $2R_2O + RMgX \rightarrow R_2O \rightarrow Mg(R)(X) \leftarrow OR_2$

"It is for this reason that ethers are used as solvent for Grignard reagents".

(3) Action of dilute H_2SO_4 (Hydrolysis) :

$$C_2H_5-O-C_2H_5 \xrightarrow[\text{pressure}]{\text{dil. } H_2SO_4 \text{ heat}} 2C_2H_5-OH$$

(4) Action of concentrated H_2SO_4

$$C_2H_5-O-C_2H_5 + H_2SO_4(\text{conc.}) \xrightarrow{\text{Heat}} \underset{\text{Ethyl alcohol}}{C_2H_5OH} + \underset{\text{Ethyl hydrogen sulphate}}{C_2H_5HSO_4}$$

(5) Action of conc. HI or HBr :

(a) (i) $C_2H_5-O-C_2H_5 + HI(\text{cold}) \rightarrow \underset{\text{Ethyl alcohol}}{C_2H_5OH} + \underset{\text{Ethyl iodide}}{C_2H_5I}$

(ii) $C_6H_5-O-C_2H_5 + HI \rightarrow C_6H_5OH + C_2H_5I$

In case of mixed ethers, the halogen atom attaches itself to the smaller alkyl group.

(b) $C_2H_5-O-C_2H_5 + 2HI \xrightarrow{\text{Heat}} \underset{\text{Ethyl iodide}}{2C_2H_5I} + H_2O$

The order of reactivity of halogen acids is HI > HBr > HCl.

HI is preferred over HBr because it is a stronger acid than HBr and thus gives a greater concentration of the oxonium ion, RO^-HR. Moreover, I^- ions is a better nucleophile in S_N2 reaction than Br^- ion.

The reaction of ethers with HI forms the basis of *Ziesel method* for the detection and estimation of alkoxy group in a compound, which is

$$C_2H_5OC_2H_5 + 2HI \xrightarrow{\text{Heat}} 2C_2H_5I$$

$$C_2H_5I + AgNO_3(\text{alc.}) \rightarrow AgI\downarrow$$

Silver iodide can be detected and estimated.

(6) Action of phosphorus pentachloride :

$$C_2H_5-O-C_2H_5 + PCl_5 \rightarrow \underset{\text{Ethyl chloride}}{2C_2H_5Cl} + POCl_3$$

(7) Action of Acid chlorides and acid anhydrides :

$$\underset{\text{Diethyl ether}}{C_2H_5-O-C_2H_5} + \underset{\text{Acetyl chloride}}{CH_3COCl} \xrightarrow[\text{or anhy. } AlCl_3]{\text{anhy. } ZnCl_2} \underset{\text{Ethyl chloride}}{C_2H_5Cl} + \underset{\text{Ethyl acetate}}{CH_3COOC_2H_5}$$

Uses : Ether is used :

(i) as a general anaesthetic.

(ii) as refrigerant since it produces cooling on evaporation.

(iii) as solvent for oils, fats, resins, etc.

(iv) for providing inert medium in Wurtz-reaction.

(v) for preparing Grignard reagents.

(vi) in perfumery.

Carboxylic Acids and Acid Derivatives

Organic compounds which contain the carboxyl functional group (—COOH) are called the *Carboxylic acids*. Their general formula is

$$R-\overset{\overset{\displaystyle O}{\|}}{C}-OH \text{ or } R-COOH \text{ or } R-CO_2H$$

where R is an alkyl group.

The name *carboxyl* is derived from Carbonyl (C=O) and hydroxyl (—OH) because in the carboxyl group these two groups are directly bonded to each other. The properties of the carboxyl group are not simply those of carboxyl and hydroxyl groups combined, the two groups interact to give carboxylic acids their own distinctive properties. Carboxylic acids are futher classified as *monocarboxylic acids*, *dicarboxylic acids*, *tricarboxylic acids*, etc., according as the number of —COOH groups present in the molecules is 1, 2, 3, or more. The long chain monocarboxylic acids are commonly called fatty acids because many of them are obtained by the hydrolysis of animal fats or vegetable oils. Examples are palmitic acid and stearic acid, etc.

Nomenclature of Monocarboxylic Acids : There are three ways of naming carboxylic acids :

(1) Common System : The simple carboxylic acids are better known by their common names. The common names are usually derived from the *Latin* or *Greek* word that indicates the original source of the acid. They do not follow any rule except that all common names of acids end in -ic acid.

Examples are,

$HCOOH$	Formic acid
CH_3COOH	Acetic acid
CH_3CH_2COOH	Propionic acid
$CH_3CH_2CH_2COOH$	Butyric acid
$CH_3CH_2CH_2CH_2COOH$	Valeric acid

In the common system, Greek letters (α, β, γ, δ etc.) are used to indicate the position of substituents. The carbon atom adjacent to the carboxyl carbon is assigned the letter α, the next carbon on the chain β, the next γ and so on.

For example,

$$\overset{\delta}{C}-\overset{\gamma}{C}-\overset{\beta}{C}-\overset{\alpha}{C}-COOH$$

$$CH_3-\underset{}{\overset{CH_3}{\overset{|}{C}H}}-COOH \qquad CH_3-\overset{CH_3}{\overset{|}{C}H}-CH_2-COOH$$

α-Methylpropionic acid (Isobutyric acid) β-Methylbutyric acid (Isovaleric acid)

Preparation :

By the oxidation of alcohols, aldehydes and ketones:

$$\underset{\text{Ethanol}}{CH_3CH_2OH} \xrightarrow[H_2SO_4]{K_2Cr_2O_7} \underset{\text{Acetaldehyde}}{CH_3CHO} \xrightarrow{[O]} \underset{\text{Acetic acid}}{CH_3COOH}$$

$$\underset{\text{iso-Propanol}}{(CH_3)_2CHOH} \xrightarrow[H_2SO_4]{K_2Cr_2O_7} \underset{\text{Acetone}}{(CH_3)_2CO}$$

$$\xrightarrow{[O]} \underset{\text{Acetic acid}}{CH_3COOH}$$

Aryl nitrites may easily be prepared by fusing the alkali salt of sulphonic acid with KCN or by *Sandmeyer reaction.*

$$\underset{\text{Pot. Benzene sulphonate}}{C_6H_5SO_3K} + KCN \rightarrow \underset{\text{Phenyl cyanide}}{C_6H_5CN} \xrightarrow[KCN]{Cu_2(CN)_2}$$

$$\underset{\text{Benzene diazonium chloride}}{C_6H_5N_2Cl}$$

By the hydrolysis of cyanides (nitriles) :

$$\underset{\text{Methyl cyanide}}{CH_3.C\equiv N} \xrightarrow{\text{acid or alkali}} \underset{\text{Acetamide}}{CH_3CONH_2} \xrightarrow{H_2O}$$

$$\underset{\text{Acetic acid}}{CH_3COOH} + NH_3$$

By the hydrolysis of esters with alkali (saponification) :

$$CH_3COOC_2H_5 + H_2O \xrightarrow{KOH} \underset{\text{Pot. acetate}}{CH_3COOK} + C_2H_5OH$$

$$2CH_3COOK + H_2SO_4 \rightarrow 2CH_3COOH + K_2SO_4$$

Esters may also be hydrolysed in presence of acids or even in neutral medium, i.e. simply by water.

$$CH_3COOC_2H_5 + H_2O \xrightarrow{H^+} CH_3COOH + C_2H_5OH$$

$$CH_3COOC_2H_5 + H_2O \rightarrow CH_3COOH + C_2H_5OH$$

In the latter case, i.e. hydrolysis in neutral medium, the reaction is slow in the beginning but becomes faster after some time. The reason being the fact that the acetic acid formed in the reaction gives H^+ which catalyses the hydrolysis of ester.

From Grignard reagent and carbon dioxide (dry ice) :

$$\underset{\text{Carbon dioxide}}{\overset{O}{\overset{||}{C}}=O} \xrightarrow{CH_3MgI} CH_3-\overset{O}{\overset{||}{C}}-OMgI$$

$$\xrightarrow{\text{hydrolysis}} \underset{\text{Acetic acid}}{CH_3-\overset{O}{\overset{||}{C}}-OH}$$

Acid formed by this method contain one more carbon than the original Grignard reagent. Organolithium compound may also be used in place of Grignard reagents.

By the oxidation of alkyl benzenes : In addition to the above methods, aromatic carboxylic acids can also be prepared by the oxidation of an alkyl group attached to benzene nucleus which will be oxidised to —COOH group irrespective of the size of the alkyl group. For example,

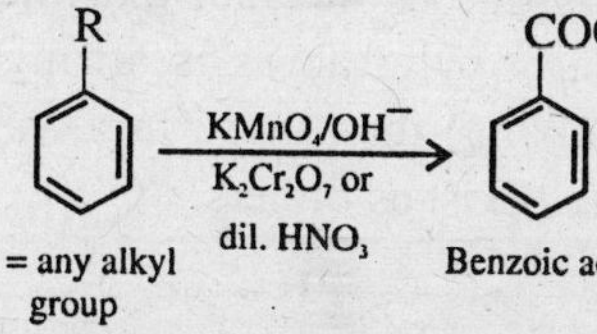

Aromatic carboxylic acids can also be prepared by Friedel-Craft reaction and hydrolysis of the side chain halogen derivatives. e.g.

(a) $$C_6H_6 + \underset{\text{Carbonyl chloride}}{COCl_2} \xrightarrow{\text{Anhy. AlCl}_3} \underset{\text{Benzoyl chloride}}{C_6H_5COCl}$$

$$\xrightarrow{H_2O} C_6H_5COOH$$

Note : Carbonyl chloride should be used in excess otherwise benzophenone may be formed as the main product.

$$C_6H_6 + COCl_2 + C_6H_6 \xrightarrow{\text{Anhy. AlCl}_3}$$

$$\underset{\text{Benzophenone}}{C_6H_5.CO.C_6H_5} + 2HCl$$

(b) $$\underset{\text{Benzotrichloride}}{C_6H_5CCl_3} \xrightarrow{\text{aq. NaOH}} \underset{\text{Unstable}}{C_6H_5(COH)_3}$$

$$\rightarrow \underset{\text{Benzoic acid}}{C_6H_5COOH}$$

Properties :

Physical Properties :

(1) The first three members (C_1 to C_3) are colourless, pungent smelling liquids, the next-three (C_4 to C_6)

have unpleasant odour. Acids with 7 or more carbon atoms have no distinct smell because of low volatility.

(2) Carboxylic acids upto C_5 are freely soluble in water due to hydrogen bonding with water molecules.

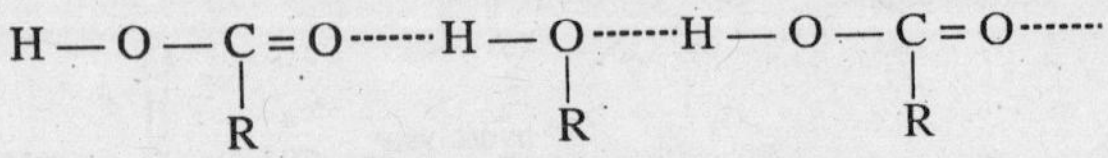

The solubility of higher members decreases rapidly with the increase in the size of the alkyl group due to increased influence of hydrocarbon part which is non-polar and lyophobic. Benzoic acid is nearly insoluble in cold water because here also the hydrocarbon part (C_6H_5) outweighs the influence of the polar part.

(3) Boiling points of the carboxylic acids, particularly lower members, are higher than alcohols of comparable molecular masses. The higher b.p. (low volatility) of lower carboxylic acids including benzoic acid is due to the fact that the hydrogen bonding in carboxylic acids is stronger (due to formation of a ring) than those in alcohols. These carboxylic acids exist as dimers.

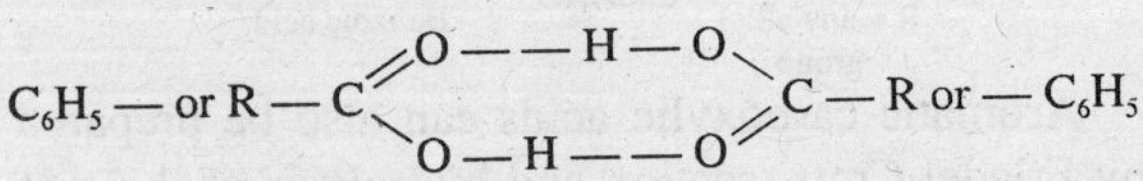

The behaviour of 'formic acid is exceptional'. It exists as a dimer in vapour state and as a polymer in liquid and solid states.

(4) In normal carboxylic acids, the even members have markedly higher melting points than the odd members preceeding or following it. This is because in the case of even membered acids the carboxyl and terminal methyl groups are on opposite sides of the zig-zag carbon chain and hence fit better in the crystal lattice. This results in increase is intermolecular forces which in turn increase melting point. On the other hand, the odd membered acids have carboxylic and terminal methyl groups on the same side of the zig-zag chain.

(5) Lower carboxylic acids (up to C_{10}) are liquids with sharp or disagreeable odours while higher are wax-like solids and almost odourless.

(6) Carboxylic acids show a broad O—H stretching vibrations at 2500-3300 cm^{-1}, which overlaps the normally sharp C—H stretching band. They also show carbonyl (C=O) stretching frequency at 1710-1720 cm^{-1}.

(7) *Acidity of Carboxylic Acids :* Carboxylic acids are acidic in nature. They can donate a proton and form salts with bases.

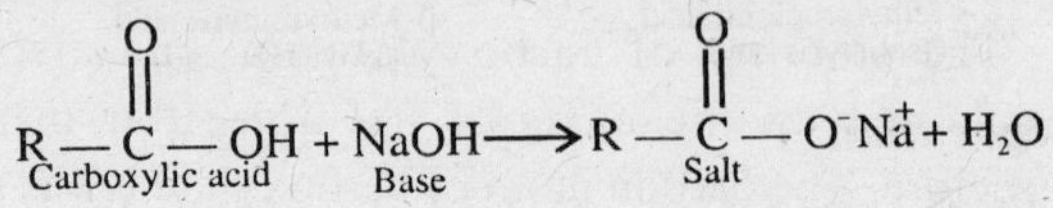

Strong acids i.e. inorganic acids like HCl or H_2SO_4 completely ionise in aqueous solution but carboxylic acids are weak acids compared to them. They are only partially ionised in aqueous solution and an equilibrium exists between the ionised and un-ionised forms.

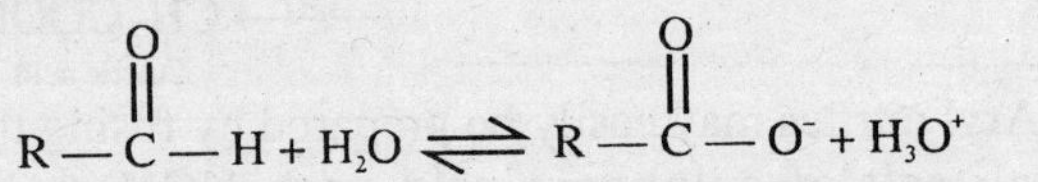

The extent of ionisation is described by an equilibrium constant K_a, which is known as Acidity Constant. It is defined as the concentration of the products of ionsation in moles per litre divided by the concentration of the un-ionised acid.

$$K_a = \frac{[RCOO^-][H_3O^+]}{[RCOOH]}$$

The acidity constant describes the relative strength of a weak acid. Stronger acids will have higher numerical value of acidity constants.

Reason of Acidity : Carboxylic acids are acidic and lose a proton readily because the carboxylate ion formed by ionisation or reaction with a base is stabilized by resonance.

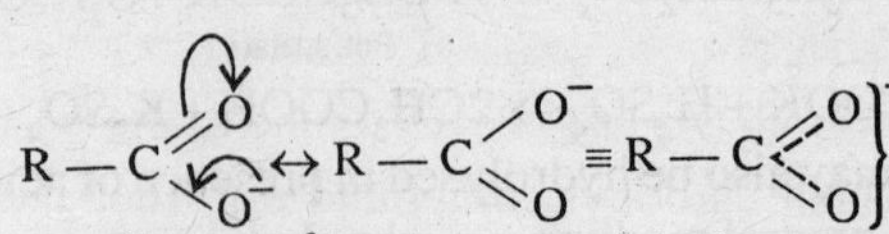

Resonance forms of carboxylate ion — Resonance hybrid

X-ray studies support the fact that carboxylate ion exists as a resonance hybrid. For example, in formic acid the carbon-oxgen bonds have different lengths whereas in sodium formate, the two carbon-oxygen bond lengths are identical and intermediate in lengths between those of normal double and single carbon-oxygen bonds.

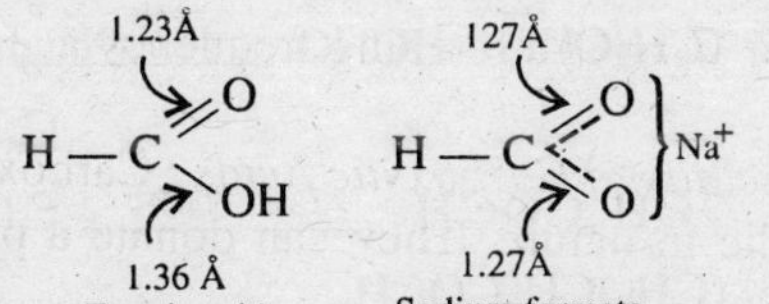

Formic acid   Sodium formate

The stability of carboxylate ion can also be explained on the basis of its molecular orbital structure. The carbon atom of carboxylate ion is sp^2-hybridized. It is bound to each oxygen atom by a σ-bond. The unused *p*-orbital overlaps with *p*-orbitals of both oxygen atoms to form stable delocalized (spread-out) molecular orbital.

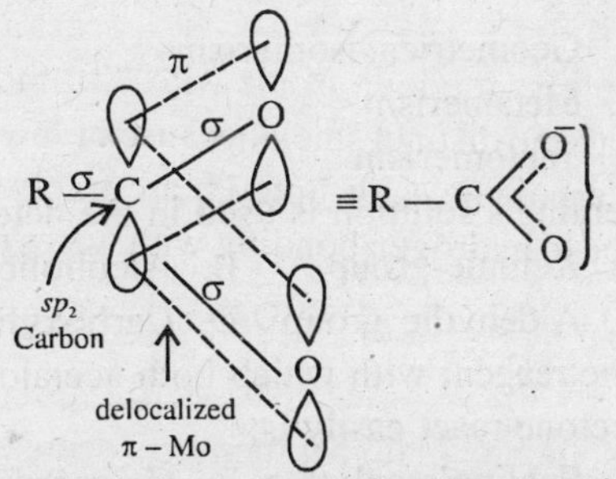

Fig. *Orbital structure of carboxylate ion*

Notice that the four electrons are bound to three atoms (1 carbon + 2 oxygens). This delocalization of π-electrons is responsible for the extra-stability of the carboxylate ion.

OBJECTIVE QUESTIONS

1. General formula of carbonyl compound is:
A. $C_nH_{2n}O$ B. $C_nH_{2n+2}O$
C. $C_nH_{2n+1}O$ D. $C_nH_{2n+2}O_2$

2. The IUPAC name of CH_3CHO is:
A. Ethanal B. Acetaldehyde
C. Ethanol D. Methyl aldehyde

3. Hybridisation of carbon in carbonyl group is:
A. *sp* B. sp^2
C. sp^3 D. None of these

4. Carbonyl group undergoes:
A. Electrophilic addition reactions
B. Nucleophilic addition reactions
C. Both (A) and (B)
D. None of these

5. Aldehydes and ketones both give addition reaction with:
A. HCN B. $NaHSO_3$
C. Both (A) and (B) D. None of these

6. Which carbonyl compound does not undergo aldol condensation?
A. HCHO B. CH_3CHO
C. CH_3CH_2CHO D. CH_3COCH_3

7. Most reactive carbonyl compound is:
A. HCHO B. CH_3CHO
C. CH_3COCH_3 D. C_2H_5CHO

8. Isopropyl alcohol on passing over heated copper at 300°C gives:
A. Propylene B. Acetaldehyde
C. Acetone D. None of these

9. Formaldehyde is not used in:
A. Adhesives B. Bakelite
C. Tooth powders D. Explosives

10. Which can show haloform reaction?
A. HCHO B. $(CH_3)_2CO$
C. $CH_3—O—CH_3$ D. CH_3CH_2Cl

11. Aldol condensation between the following compounds followed by dehydration gives methyl vinyl ketone:
A. Methanal and ethanal
B. Two mole of formaldehyde
C. Methanal and propanone
D. Two mole of ethanol

12. The reagent of choice for the selective reduction of a ketone in the presence of an ester is:
A. Lithium aluminium hydride
B. Sodium borohydride
C. Hydrogen and palladium on carbon
D. Sodium in ethanol

13. At room temperature formaldehyde is:
A. Gas B. Liquid
C. Solid D. None of these

14. Acetaldehyde reacts with HCN followed by hydrolysis forms a compound which shows:
A. Optical isomerism

B. Geometrical isomerism
C. Metamerism
D. Tautomerism

15. Fehling's solution is used in the detection of:
A. Ketonic group B. Alcoholic group
C. Aldehydic group D. Carboxylic group

16. The reagent with which both acetaldehyde and acetone react easily is:
A. Fehling's solution B. Grignard reagent
C. Schiff's reagent D. Tollen's reagent

17. Carbon atom of carbonyl gp, in adehyde is of:
A. 1° B. 2°
C. 3° D. None of these

18. Carbon atom of carbonyl group in ketone is of:
A. 1° B. 2°
C. 3° D. None of these

19. An aldehyde on oxidation gives:
A. An alcohol B. A ketone
C. An acid D. An amine

20. When formaldehyde is heated with ammonia the compound formed is:
A. Methyl amine
B. Amino formaldehyde
C. Hexamethylene tetramine
D. Formalin

21. A ketone on reduction gives:
A. Primary alcohol
B. Secondary alcohol
C. A dihydric alcohol
D. A mixture of above all three

22. $RCH=O + 2H \rightarrow RCH_2OH$
For this reaction catalyst is
A. Ni only B. Pd only
C. Pt only D. Any of the above

23. Which compound is oxidised to prepare ethyl methyl ketone?
A. Propanal-2 B. Butanal-1
C. Butanol-2 D. Tert butyl alcohol

24. Which of the following is an example of aldol condensation?
A. $2CH_3CHO \xrightarrow{\text{dil. NaOH}} CH_3CHOHCH_2CHO$
B. $HCHO \xrightarrow{\text{dil. NaOH}} CH_3OH$
C. $C_6H_5CHO + HCHO \xrightarrow{\text{dil. NaOH}} C_6H_5CH_2OH$
D. $2CH_3COCH_3 \xrightarrow{\text{Conc.NaOH}} CH_3C(OH)(CH_3)CH_2COCH_3$

25. Which of the following has most acidic proton?
A. CH_3COCH_3 B. $(CH_3)_2C=CH_2$
C. $CH_3COCH_2COCH_3$ D. $(CH_3.CO)_3CH$

26. Cyclohexane is subjected to reduction by $NaBH_4$. The product formed is:
A. Cyclohexane B. Cyclohexanal
C. Cyclohexadiene D. Cyclohexanol

27. In the following sequence of reactions the end product is:

$$H\equiv CH \xrightarrow[H_2SO_4]{Hg^{2+}} A \xrightarrow[[H_2O]]{CH_3MgX} B \xrightarrow{[O]} C$$

A. Acetaldehyde B. Isopropyl alcohol
C. Acetone D. Ethyl alcohol

28. Which of the following has most acidic hydrogen?
A. 3-hexanone B. 2, 4-hexanedione
C. 2, 5-hexanedione D. 2, 3-hexanedione

29. Acetaldehyde on treatment of few drops of H_2SO_4 gives:
A. Ethyl acetate B. Ethyl alcohol
C. Ethyl methylamine D. Paraldehyde

30. When propyne is treated with aqueous sulphuric acid in presence of mercuric sulphate, the major product is:
A. Propanal
B. Propyl hydrogen sulphate
C. Propanol
D. Acetone

31. In the following sequence of reactions, the end product is:

$$CH_3CHO \xrightarrow{HCN} A \xrightarrow{H_2O} B$$

A. CH_3COOH B. $CH_3CHOHCOOH$
C. $CH_3CH_2NH_2$ D. CH_3CONH_2

32. Formaldehyde can be distinguished from acetaldehyde by the use of:
A. Schiff's reagent B. Tollen's reagent
C. Fehling's solution D. NaOH and iodine

33. The enolic form of acetone contains:
A. 9σ-bonds, 1π-bond and 2 lone pairs

B. 8σ-bonds, 2π-bonds and 2 lone pairs
C. 10σ-bonds, 1π-bond and 1 lone pair
D. 9σ-bonds, 2π-bond and 1 lone pair

34. Methyl ketones are characterised through:
A. The Tollen's reagent
B. The iodoform test
C. The Schiff's test
D. The Benedict's reagent

35. Treatment of propionaldehyde with dil. NaOH gives:
A. $CH_3CH_2COOCH_2CH_2CH_3$
B. $CH_3CH_2CHOHCH_2CH_2CHO$
C. $CH_3CH_2CHOHCH(CH_3)CHO$
D. $CH_3CH_2COCH_2CH_2CHO$

36. When acetaldehyde is heated with Fehling's solution, it gives a red precipitate at:
A. Cu B. CuO
C. $Cu + Cu_2O + CuO$ D. Cu_2O

37. Fehling's solution is:
A. Acidified copper sulphate solution
B. Ammoniacal cuprous chloride solution
C. Copper sulphate, Rochelle salt + NaOH
D. None of these

38. The formation of cyanohydrin from a ketone is an example of:
A. Electrophilic addition
B. Nucleophilic addition
C. Nucleophilic substitution
D. Electrophilic substitution

39. Schiff's reagent is:
A. Magenta solution decolourised with sulphurous acid
B. Magenta solution decolourised with chlorine
C. Ammoniacal cobalt chloride solution
D. Ammoniacal manganese sulphate solution

40. Acetone when saturated with dry acid gives:
A. Diacetone alcohol B. Mesityl oxide
C. Mesitylene D. Propane

41. If oxygen is attached to a secondary carbon, the compound is known as:
A. Aldehyde B. Ketone
C. Acid D. Ester

42. Which of the following will react with water?
A. $CHCl_3$ B. CCl_3CHO
C. CCl_4 D. $CH_2Cl.CH_2Cl$

43. Which of the following reaction is a condensation reaction?
A. HCHO → paraformaldehyde
B. $CH_3CHO \rightarrow$ Paraldehyde
C. $CH_3COCH_3 \rightarrow$ Mesityl oxide
D. $CH_2 = CH_2 \rightarrow$ polyethylene

44. Among the given compounds, the most susceptible to nucleophile attack at the carbonyl group is:
A. MeCOCl B. MeCHO
C. MeCOOMe D. MeCOOCOMe

45. A plastic bakelite is a compound of HCHO with:
A. Benzene B. Phenol
C. Ammonia D. Hydrocarbon

46. In a Cannizzaro's reaction, the intermediate that will be best hydride donor is:

A. 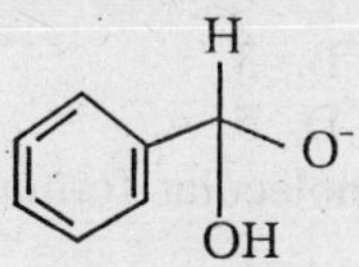

B. 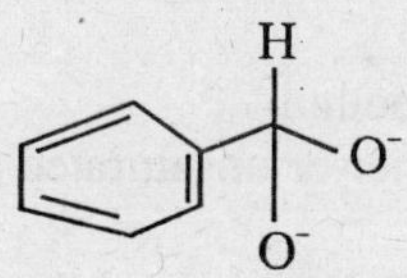

C. 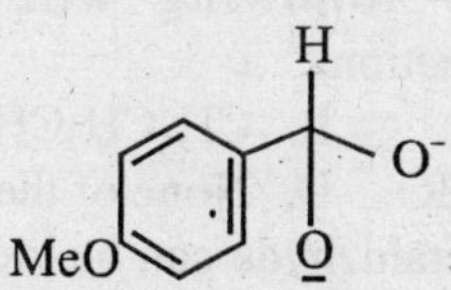

D. 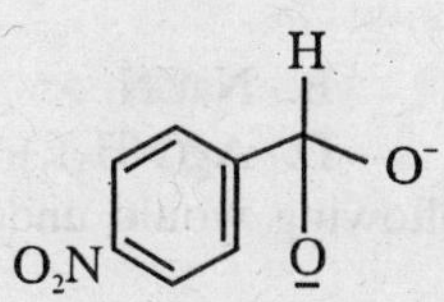

47. The following reaction is known by the name of:

$$CH_3COCl + H_2 \xrightarrow[Pd/BaSO_4]{[H]} CH_3CHO + HCl$$

xylene.
A. Stephen's reduction
B. Rosenmund's reaction
C. Cannizzaro's reaction
D. None of these

48. When vapours of acetic acid are passed over.....at 300°C we get acetone.
A. Al_2O_3 B. CuO
C. MoD D. Cu

49. Which of the following is correct for carbonyl compounds?

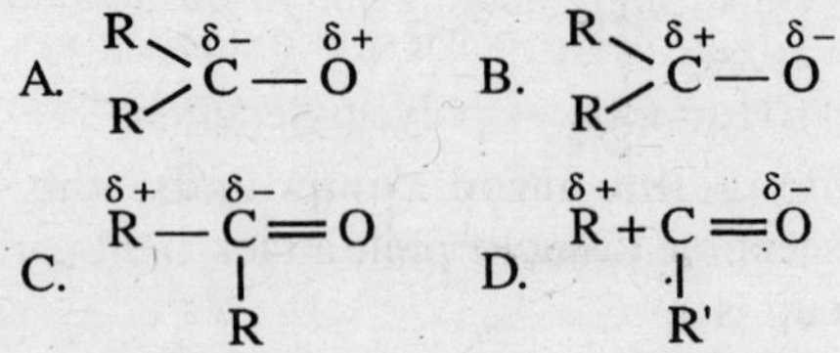

50. $\begin{matrix} CHO \\ | \\ CHO \end{matrix} \xrightarrow{OH^-} x$; The product *x* is:
A. $CH_3OH + CH_3OH$ B. $CH_2OH - COO^-$
C. $CH_3OH + HCOOH$ D. $\bar{O}OC - CO\bar{O}$

51. The number of aldehydes of molecular formula $C_5H_{10}O$ is:
A. 2 B. 3
C. 4 D. 5

52. Compound having molecular formula C_3H_6O may be:
A. Cyclic ether
B. Carbonyl compound
C. Unsaturated ether or unsaturated alcohol
D. All

53. Which of the following will undergo Cannizzaro's reaction?
A. CH_3CHO B. CH_3CH_2CHO
C. $(CH_3)_2CHCHO$ D. None of these

54. Acetone and acetaldehyde can be identified by treatment with:
A. $NaHSO_3$ B. NaCN
C. $NaOH + I_2$ D. $Ag(NH_3)_2+$

55. Which of the following would undergo aldol condensation:
A. CCl_3CHO B. 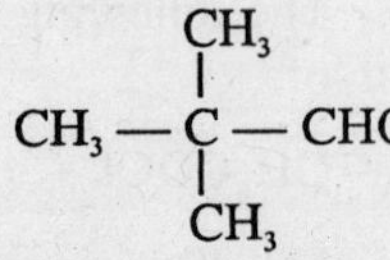
C. CH_3CH_2CHO D. HCHO

56. In the Cannizzaro's reaction given below:
$2Ph - CHO \xrightarrow{OH^-} Ph - CH_2OH + PhCOO^-$
the slowest step is:
A. The attack of OH^- at the carbonyl group
B. The transfer of hydride to the carbonyl group
C. The abstraction of proton from the carboxlic acid
D. The deprotonation of $ph - CH_2OH$

57. Which of the following aldehyde will respond to Cannizzaro's reaction when treated with strong alkali solution?
A. Benzaldehyde B. Acetaldehyde
C. Propionaldehyde D. All of the above

58. Paraldehyde is:
A. A trimer of formaldehyde
B. A trimer of acetaldehyde
C. A hexamer of formaldehyde
D. A hexamer of acetaldehyde

59. Paraldehyde is used as a:
A. Saporific B. Poison
C. Polymer D. Dye

60. Methylene chloride on hydrolysis yields:
A. HCHO B. CH_2CHO
C. CH_3COCl D. None of these

61. Aldehydes having no α-hydrogen atoms undergo:
A. Friedel-Craft's reaction
B. Reimer-Tiemann reaction
C. Cannizzaro's reaction
D. Rosenmund's reaction

62. The reaction of acetaldehyde with Tollen's reagent gives:
A. Methyl alcohol B. Silver acetate
C. Silver mirror D. Formaldehyde

63. Tollen's reagent is:
A. Ammoniacal cuprous chloride
B. Ammoniacal cuprous oxide
C. Ammoniacal silver nitrate
D. Ammoniacal silver nitrate

64. Which gives positive haloform test and positive Fehling's solution test?
A. Acetone B. Acetaldehyde
C. Ethanol D. Formaldehyde

65. A mixture of calcium acetate and calcium formate on heating gives:
A. CH_3COCH_3 B. CH_3CHO
C. HCHO D. All of the above

66. The structural formula of the compound isomeric with acetone is:

A. CH_3CH_2CHO B. CH_3CHO
C. CH_3CH_2OH D. None of these

67. Which of the following compounds will give a mixed ketone on oxidation?
A. $(CH_3)_3COH$
B. $CH_3CH_2CH_2OH$
C. $CH_3CH_2CH(OH)CH_3$
D. $(CH_3)_2CHCH_2OH$

68. When acetylene is passed through H_2SO_4 containing $HgSO_4$ it gives:
A. Ethyl alcohol B. Acetone
C. Acetaldehyde D. Ethylene

69. A typical compound undergoes Cannizzaro's reaction and aldol condensation. It is:
A. $(CH_3)_2CHCHO$ B. HCHO
C. C_6H_5CHO D. CH_3CHO

70. Aldol condensation is given by:
A. Aldehydes only having α-hydrogen atom
B. Aldehydes and ketones having α-hydrogen atom
C. Ketones only having α-hydrogen atom
D. Aldehydes having on α-hydrogen atom

71. Formaldehyde when treated with KOH gives methanol and potassium formate. The reaction is known as:
A. Perkin's reaction
B. Claisen's reaction
C. Cannizzaro's reaction
D. Knoevenagel's reaction

72. Magenta is:
A. Alkaline phenolphthalein
B. Red litmus
C. P-rosaniline hydrochloride
D. Methyled

73. C_2H_5CHO and CH_3COCH_3 can be distinguished by testing with:
A. Phenyl hydrazine
B. Hydroxylamine
C. Fehling's solution
D. Sodium bisulphate

74. If acetyl chloride is reduced in presence of $BaSO_4$ + Pd, the product formed is:
A. CH_3CHO B. CH_3CH_2OH
C. CH_3COOH D. CH_3COCH_3

75. Formalin is an aqueous solution of:
A. Formica acid B. Formaldehyde
C. Fluorescein D. Furfuraldehyde

76. Schiff's reagent gives pink colour with:
A. Alcohols B. Acetaldehyde
C. Ketone D. Mesitylene chloride

77. On strongly heating anhydrous calcium acetate gives:
A. Acetone B. Ether
C. Acetic anhydride D. CO

78. Boiling point of acetone is:
A. 100°C B. 60°C
C. 56°C D. 90°C

79. Urotropine has the composition:
A. $(CH_2)_4N_6$ B. $(CH_2)_5N_5$
C. $(CH_2)_6N_4$ D. $(CH_2)_6N_5$

80. In the reaction, P is:

$$\begin{matrix} CH_3 \\ CH_3 \end{matrix}\!\!>CO \xrightarrow{SeO_2} P + Se + H_2O$$

A. CH_3COCHO B. CH_3COOCH_3
C. CH_3COCH_2OH D. None of these

81. Which can be used to distinguish aldehydes and ketones?
A. Fehling's solution B. H_2SO_4 solution
C. $NaHSO_3$ D. NH_3

82. Clemmensen's reduction of a ketone is carried out in presence of:
A. H_2 with Pd as catalyst
B. Glycol with KOH
C. $LiAlH_4$ in ether
D. Zn — Hg with HCl

83. Acetaldehyde reacts with PCl_5, to give:
A. Ethyl chloride
B. Ethylene chloride
C. Ethylidene dichloride
D. Trichloroacetaldehyde

84. Aldehydes and ketones form addition products with:
A. Phenyl hydrazine B. Hydrazine
C. Semicarbazide D. Hydrogen cyanide

85. The aldol condensation of acetaldehyde results in the formation of:
A. $CH_3\underset{\underset{O}{||}}{C}\underset{\underset{OH}{|}}{CH}CH_3$

B. $CH_3CH(OH)CH_2CH(=O)$ (i.e. $CH_3\,CHCH_2\,CH$ with OH on the second carbon and =O on CH)

C. $CH_3CH_2CH(OH)—CH(=O)$

D. $CH_3CH_2OH + CH_3COOH$

86. Which one of the following aldehydes will not form an aldol when treated with dilute NaOH?

A. CH_3CHO B. CH_3CH_2CHO

C. $(CH_3)_3CCHO$ D. $C_6H_5CH_2CHO$

87. The correct order of reactivity of >CO group in given compounds is:

A. $(CH_3)(H)>CO$ > $(CH_3)(CH_3)>CO$ > $(C_6H_5)(CH_3)>CO$

B. $(C_6H_5)(CH_3)>CO$ > $(CH_3)(CH_3)>CO$ > $(CH_3)(H)>CO$

C. $(CH_3)(CH_3)>CO$ > $(CH_3)(H)>CO$ > $(C_6H_5)(CH_3)>CO$

D. $(CH_3)(CH_3)>CO$ > $(C_6H_5)(CH_3)>CO$ > $(CH_3)(H)>CO$

88. In an alkaline medium acetaldehyde undergoes:

A. Benzoin condensation

B. Aldol condensation

C. Polymerisation

D. Cannizzaro's reaction

89. Ketones can be obtained in one step by:

A. Hydrolysis of ester

B. Oxidation of primary alcohols

C. Reaction of acid halide with alcohols

D. Oxidation of secondary alcohol

90. Which is obtained by the oxidation of propionaldehyde:

A. Acetic acid

B. Formic acid and acetic acid

C. Propanoic acid

D. *n*-propyl alcohol

91. Acetone when treated with conc. H_2SO_4 gives mesitylene which has the following formula:

A. $(CH_3)_2C=CHCOCH_3$

B. $(CH_3)_2C(OH)CH_2COCH_3$

C. 1, 3, 5-trimethylbenzene

D. $(CH_3)_2C=CHCOCH=C(CH_3)_2$

92. Compound (A) $C_5H_{10}O$ forms a phenyl hydrazone and gives negative Tollen's and iodoform tests. Compound (A) on reduction gives *n*-pentane compound (A) is:

A. A primary alcohol

B. An aldehyde

C. A ketone

D. A secondary alcohol

93. Acetaldehyde can not exhibit:

A. Iodoform test B. Benedict's test

C. Tollen's test D. Lucas test

94. The figure given below describes a condensation polymer which can be obtained in two ways. Either treating 3 molecules of acetone (CH_3COCH_3) with conc. H_2SO_4 or passing propyne ($CH_3C \equiv CH$) through a red hot tube. The polymer is:

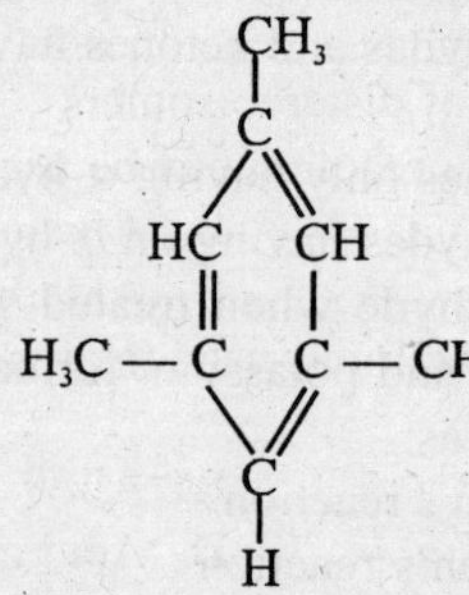

A. Pharone B. Mesityl oxide

C. Diacetonyl alcohol D. Mesitylene

95. Wolff Kishner's reduction is:

A. Reduction of carbonyl compound into hydrocarbons

B. Reduction of carbonyl compound into alcohols

C. Reduction of nitrobenzene into aniline

D. Reduction of carbohydrates to alcohols

96. The Cannizzaro's reaction is not given by:

A. Trimethylacetaldehyde

B. Acetaldehyde

C. Benzaldehyde

D. Formaldehyde

97. When sodium formate is heated it gives:

A. Hydrogen B. Water

C. Sodium hydroxide D. Carbon dioxide

98. Stephen's reaction is the reduction of:
A. Alkyl cyanide with $LiAlH_4$
B. Alkyl cyanide with $SnCl_2$ and HCl
C. Alkyl isocyanide with Na and alcohol
D. Acyl halide in the $LiAlH_4$

99. When acetone is heated with hydroxylamine the compound formed is:
A. Cyanohydrin B. Oxime
C. Semicarbazone D. Hydrazone

100. When HCHO is heated with C_6H_5CHO in presence of NaOH, the products are:
A. CH_3OH and HCOONa
B. $C_6H_5CH_2OH$ and C_6H_5COONa
C. CH_3OH and C_6H_5COONa
D. HCOONa and $C_6H_5CH_2OH$

101. $C_6H_5CHO + HCN \rightarrow C_6H_5CH(CN)OH$; the product is:
A. Optically active
B. A meso compound
C. Recemate
D. Mixture of distereoisomers

102. Rosenmund's reaction can be used to obtain:
A. Alkanes B. Alkenes
C. Alcohols D. Aldehydes

103. Stephen's reaction is used to prepare aldehydes from:
A. Alcohol B. Alkyl cyanides
C. Alkenes D. Acid chlorides

104. Formaldehyde can be distinguished from acetaldehyde by:
A. Fehling's solution
B. Schiff's reagent
C. Ammonia
D. Ammoniacal $AgNO_3$

105. Which aldehyde can not be obtained by Rosenmund's reaction?
A A. CH_3CHO B. HCHO
C. CH_3CH_2CHO D. All of the above

106. An aldehyde can be distinguished from a ketone by the use of the reagent:
A. Grignard's reagent B. Schiff's reagent
C. Hydroxylamine D. Hydrazine

107. Aldehydes behave as:
A. Oxidising agent
B. Reducing agent
C. Dehydrating agent
D. Oxidising as well as reducing agent

108. Acetaldehyde on treatment with HCN forms a cyanohydrin. What will be the product if this cyanohydrin is further hydrolysed:
A. CH_3COOH
B. $(CH_3)_2C{=}O$
C. $CH_3-CH(OH)COOH$
D. CH_3CH_2OH

109. Which gives a ketone with a Grignard's reagent?
A. Formaldehyde B. Ethyl alcohol
C. Methyl cyanide D. Methyl iodide

110. In Tischenko's reaction an aldehyde is heated with catalyst......
A. NaOH B. $Al(OC_2H_5)_3$
C. Al_2O_3 D. Mg/Hg

111. Which of the following reagents reacts in same manner with HCHO, CH_3CHO, CH_3COCH_3?
A. HCN B. NH_2OH
C. $C_6H_5NHNH_2$ D. All of the above

112. Aldehyde used in the manufacture of perfumes is:
A. HCHO B. CH_3CHO
C. C_6H_5CHO D. CCl_3CHO

113. Formalin is:
A. Formaldehyde
B. Formaldehyde + methanol
C. Formaldehyde + methanol + water
D. Formaldehyde + water

114. Acrolein on complete reduction gives
A. Allyl alcohol B. Propanol
C. Propanal D. None of these

115. Fehling's solution consists of two separate alkaline solution. If one is $CuSO_4$, the other is:
A. $NaHCO_3$ B. Na_2SO_4
C. $NaKC_4H_6O_8$ D. $NaKC_2O_4$

116. Formaldehyde on condensation in presence of $Ca(OH)_2$ gives:
A. Formose B. Fructose
C. Maltose D. Xylose

117. Doctors detect diabetes disease by testing the presence of glucose in urine with:
A. Nessler's reagent B. Fehling's solution
C. Fenton's reagent D. Silver nitrate solution

118. Acetals are:
A. Aldehyde B. Diethers
C. Ketones D. Hydroxy aldehydes

119. Chloral is prepared industrially by the chlorination of:
A. Propanone B. Formaldehyde
C. Ethanol D. Chloroform

120. Ketones are first oxidation product of:
A. Primary alcohols
B. Secondary alcohols
C. Dihydric alcohols
D. Trihydric alcohols

121. Aldehydes are first oxidation product of:
A. Primary alcohols B. Secondary alcohols
C. Tertiary alcohols D. Dihydric alcohols

122. Alkaline hydrolysis of $R_2C.Cl_2$ forms:
A. Propanone B. Propane
C. Alkanone D. Alkanal

123. Alkaline hydrolysis if 1,1-dichloroalkane yields:
A. Alkanal B. Alkanol
C. Alkanone D. Alkyne

124. Ketones are prepared by:
A. Clemmensen's reduction
B. Rosenmund's reduction
C. Oppenauer's oxidation
D. Cannizzaro's reaction

125. When propanone reacts with chlorine it forms:
A. Trichloro propanone
B. Hexachloro propanone
C. Trichloro ethanol
D. Trichloro propanal

126. Chlorine does not react with:
A. Methanal B. CH_3CHO
C. Propanone D. C_6H_5CHO

127. Both acetaldehyde and ketone react with:
A. Ammonical $AgNO_3$
B. Rochelle Salt
C. 2, 4-dinitrophenylhydrazine
D. All of the above

128. Two molecules of an aldehyde react with a concentrated solution of caustic soda and produces one molecule of an alcohol and acid each, which one is the aldehyde?
A. Acetaldehyde B. Formaldehyde
C. Propionaldehyde D. Butyraldehyde

129. Which compounds will not reduce Fehling's solution?
A. Methanal B. Ethanal
C. Trichloroethanal D. Benzaldehyde

130. Which is highly soluble in water?
A. Methanal B. Propanal
C. Propanone D. Butanone

131. Aldehydes are produced in atmosphere by:
A. Oxidation of secondary alcohols
B. Reduction of alkenes
C. Reaction of oxygen atoms with hydrocarbons
D. Reaction of oxygen atoms with O_3

132. $\begin{matrix} R \\ R' \end{matrix}\!\!>C{=}O \xrightarrow{HCN} (A) \xrightarrow{NH_3} (B) \xrightarrow{\text{Hydrolysis}}$ (C) compound (C) in above reaction is:
A. α-hydroxy acid
B. α-amino acid
C. α-amino alkanal
D. α-amino β-hydroxy acid

133. Which reactant is more effective to convert but-2-enal to but-2-enol?
A. $K_2Cr_2O_7/H_2SO_4$ B. $KMnO_4$
C. H_2/Pt D. $NaBH_4$

134. Which structural unit is possessed by aldehyde and not ketone?
A. α-H atom
B. H-atom and carbonyl group
C. OH and carbonyl group
D. None of these

135. A compound A has molecular formula C_2Cl_3 OH. It reduces Fehling's solution and on oxidation gives a monocarboxylic acid B. A is obtained by action of Cl_2 on ethyl alcohol. A is
A. Chloral B. $CHCl_3$
C. CH_3Cl D. Chloro acetic acid

136. Which is most easily oxidised and passes more reactivity for nucleophilic addition?

A. Methanal B. Ethanal
C. Propanal D. Propanone

137. Carbonyl compounds when treated with sodium bisulphite solution generally a crystalline sodium bisulphite addition product is formed but which of the following carbonyl compound not forms crystalline addition product:

A. HCHO B. CH_3CHO
C. CH_3COCH_3 D. $C_2H_5COC_2H_5$

138. Main product of the reaction, are,

$$\begin{matrix} CH_3 \\ CH_3 \end{matrix}\!\!>CO \xrightarrow[\text{Catalyst}]{\text{Pt, } H_2}$$

A. $CH_3COOH + H_2$ B. CH_3CH_2COOH
C. $CH_3CH(OH)CH_3$ D. CH_3CH_2OH

139. Cannizzaro's reaction involves:

A. Conversion of aldehyde into acid only
B. Conversion of aldehyde into alcohol only
C. Redox system reaction
D. Aromatic transformation

140. The final products of oxidation of isopropyl alcohol are:

A. $CH_3COCH_3 + HCOOH$
B. $CH_3CH_2COOH + HCOOH$
C. $CH_3COOH + HCOOH$
D. $CH_3COOH + CH_3CH_2COOH$

141. Phorone is obtained by condensation of:

A. Two molecules of acetaldehyde
B. Two molecules of acetone
C. Two molecules of CH_3CHO + One molecule of CH_3COCH_3
D. 3 molecules of acetone

142. Formaldehyde gives an additive product with methyl magnesium iodide. Which on aqueous hydrolysis gives:

A. Isopropyl alcohol B. Ethyl alcohol
C. Methyl alcohol D. Propyl alcohol

143. $(CH_3)_2C = CHCOCH_3$ can be oxidised to $(CH_3)_2C=CHCOOH$ by:

A. Cu at 300°C B. $KMnO_4$
C. Chromic acid D. NaOI

144. Which of the following substances will not react with PCl_5?

A. Methyl alcohol B. Acetic acid
C. Acetaldehyde D. Ethane

145. Reduction of aldehydes with HI gives:

A. Primary alcohol B. Secondary alcohol
C. Alkane D. Tertiary alcohol

146. Identify Z in the series,

$$CH_3CHO \xrightarrow[\text{dil. } H_2SO_4]{MnO_4^-} X \xrightarrow{SOCl_2} Y \xrightarrow[\text{heat}]{CH_3COONa} Z$$

A. $CH_3.CO.CH_2COONa$
B. $(CH_3CO)_2O$
C. $CH_2Cl.CO.O.COCH_3$
D. $CHCl_2.CO.O.COCH_3$

147. Base catalysed aldol condensation occurs with:

A. Propionaldehyde
B. Benzaldehyde
C. 2, 2-dimethyl propionaldehyde
D. None of these

148. Which statement is incorrect in the case of acetaldehyde and acetone?

A. Both react with hydroxylamine to form oximes
B. Both react with sodium bisulphite to form addition product
C. Both reduce ammoniacal silver nitrate to silver
D. Both react with hydrazine to form hydrazones

149. Which will form two oximes with NH_2OH?

A. CH_3COCH_3 B. $CH_3CH_2COCH_3$
C. $CH_3CH_2COCH_2CH_3$ D. $\begin{matrix} H \\ H \end{matrix}\!\!>C{=}O$

150. Identify x,

$$H_3C-\overset{\displaystyle CH_3}{\overset{|}{C}}{=}O \xrightarrow[\text{dry ether}]{CH_3MgI} (A) \xrightarrow{H_2O} x$$

A. CH_3OH B. CH_3CH_2OH
C. $CH_3CHOHCH_3$ D. $CH_3C(OH)(CH_3)_2$

151. Acetone may be produced from starch by the action of:

A. Acid B. Certain bacteria
C. Oxidising agents D. None of the above

152. The reaction given below is called,

$$\begin{matrix}R \\ R\end{matrix}\!\!>\!CHOH + \begin{matrix}CH_3 \\ CH_3\end{matrix}\!\!>\!CO \xrightarrow{[(CH_3)_3\,CO]_3\,Al} \begin{matrix}R \\ R\end{matrix}\!\!>\!CO + \begin{matrix}CH_3 \\ CH_3\end{matrix}\!\!>\!CHOH$$

A. Tischenko's reaction
B. Perkin's reaction
C. Oppemuer oxidation
D. Schmidt reaction

153. Ethanal reacts with alkali to give 3-hydroxybutanal. This reaction is:

A. Polymerisation
B. Claisen condensation
C. Reimer-Tiemann reaction
D. Aldol condensation

154. The term hypnone is used for:

A. Benzophenone B. Acetophenone
C. Acetaldehyde D. None of these

155. Collin's reagent causes the conversion:

A. $>CO \rightarrow >CHOH$
B. $>CHO \rightarrow —COOH$
C. $>CHOH \rightarrow >CO$
D. $>CHOH \rightarrow —COOH$

156. An organic compound $C_5H_{10}O$ forms phenyl hydrazone, give positive iodoform test and undergoes Wolff-Kishner reaction to give isopentane. It is:

A. Pentanal B. Pentan-2-one
C. Pentan-3-one D. 3-methylbutan-2-one

157. $3CH_3COCH_3 \xrightarrow{HCl}$ $\begin{matrix}(CH_3)_2C = CH \\ | \\ CO \\ | \\ (CH_3)_2\,C = CH\end{matrix} + 2H_2O$

This polymer is obtained when acetone is saturated with hydrogen chloride gas. Polymer is:

A. Phorone
B. Formose
C. Diacetonyl alcohol
D. Mesityl oxide

158. In presence of dry HCl gas, CH_3CHO condenses with C_2H_5OH to give:

A. Aldol B. Paraldehyde
C. Ethyl acetate D. Acetal

159. C_6H_5CHO on reacting with Cl_2 gives:

A. $C_6H_5CHCl_2$ B. C_6H_5COOH
C. $C_6H_5CH_2OH$ D. C_6H_5COCl

160. Among the following compounds which will react with acetone to give a product containing $>C=N—$:

A. $C_6H_5NH_2$ B. $C_6H_5NHNH_2$
C. $(CH_3)_3N$ D. $C_6H_5NHC_6H_5$

161. Identify x in the sequence,

$$x \xrightarrow[2.\ H_2O/H^+]{1.\ CH_3MgCl} C_5H_{12}O \xrightarrow[575\ K]{Cu} C_5H_{10}$$

A. $CH_3 — \underset{\underset{O}{\|}}{C} — CH_2 — CH_3$

B. $CH_3CH_2CH_2CHO$
C. $(CH_3)_2CHCHO$
D. $CH_3CH_2CH_2CH_2OH$

162. Dialkyl cadmium reacts with a compound to form a ketone. The compound is:

A. Acid B. Acid chloride
C. Ester D. CO

163. Treatment of acetaldehyde with ethyl magnesium bromide and subsequent hydrolysis gives:

A. 1-butanol B. 2-butanol
C. 1-propanol D. Tert. butanol

164. Ketones are less reactive than aldehydes because:

A. $C=O$ group is less polar in ketones
B. of electromeric effect
C. of steric hindrance to the attacking reagent
D. None

165. Acetaldehyde reacts with:

A. Only nucleophiles
B. Both electrophiles and nucleophiles
C. Only electrophiles
D. Only free radicals

166. The final product formed when acetaldehyde is reduced with sodium and alcohol is:

A. Ethylene B. Ethyl alcohol
C. Ethene D. All of these

167. Benzaldehyde and acetaldehyde can be distinguish by:
A. Iodoform test
B. 2-4 DNP test
C. NH_3 reaction
D. Wolff Kishner's reduction

168. Which of the following shows electromeric effect?
A. Aldehyde B. Alkane
C. Alkyl amines D. Alkyl halides

169. The polymer 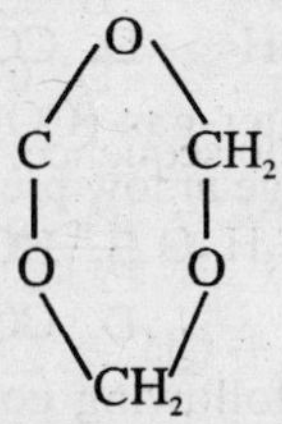 is obtained when HCHO is allowed to stand. It is a white solid. The polymer is:
A. Trioxane
B. Formose
C. Paraformaldehyde
D. Metaldehyde

170. CH_3COCH_3 can be obtained by:
A. Heating acetaldehyde with methanol
B. Oxidation of propyl alcohol
C. Oxidation of isopropyl alcohol
D. Reduction of propionic acid

171. When an aldehyde was heated with alkali, a part of it was converted into alcohol an a part of it into an acid. The aldehyde is:
A. An aliphatic aldehyde other than HCHO
B. An aliphatic aldehyde or salicylaldehyde
C. An aromatic aldehyde other than salicylaldehyde
D. An aromatic aldehyde or HCHO

172. Hexamethylene tetramine is used as an:
A. Analgesic
B. Antipyretic
C. Urinary antiseptic
D. All of these

173. Aldol condensation takes place in:
A. Acid medium B. Basic medium
C. Neutral medium D. None of these

174. Calcium propanoate on refluxing yields:
A. Propanol-2 B. Propanone-2
C. Pentanone-3 D. Pentanone-2

175. Cannizzaro's reaction is possible with:
A. Ketones
B. Carboxylic acids
C. Aldehydes containing α-H atom
D. Aldehydes containing no α-H atom

176. With hot conc. KOH brown black resinous product is given by:
A. CH_3CHO B. C_2H_5OH
C. HCHO D. CH_3COCH_3

177. Which of the following is correct?
A. All aldehydes undergo Cannizzaro's reaction
B. Aldehydes are more susceptible to oxidation than ketones
C. Aldehydes are more susceptible to oxidation than ketones
D. Formaldehyde forms $CH_2(OH)NH_2$ with NH_3

178. The important step in Cannizzaro's reaction is the intermolecular shift of:
A. Proton B. H-atom
C. Hydride ion D. Hydronium ion

179. HCHO and HCOOH are distinguished by treating with:
A. Tollen's reagent
B. $NaHCO_3$
C. Fehling's solution
D. Benedict's solution

180. CH_3CH_2CHO is produced when the following is hydrolysed:
A. $CH_3CH_2CH_2Cl$ B. $CH_3CHClCH_2Cl$
C. $CH_3CH_2CHCl_2$ D. $CH_3C.Cl_2.CH_3$

181. Formula of diacetone alcohol is:
A. $(CH_3)_2C(OH)CH_2COCH_3$
B. $CH_3CHOHCH_2COCH_3$
C. $(CH_3)_2CHOHCH_2COCH_3$
D. None of these

182. The reducing agent in Wolff Kishner reaction is:
A. $LiAlH_4$ B. $NaBH_4$
C. NH_2NH_2 + Base D. Zn – Hg/HCl

183. Formaldehyde can be manufactured from:
A. Natural gas B. Water gas
C. Both (A) and (B) D. None of these

184. A powerful sedative made from acetaldehyde is:
A. Acetic anhydride
B. Paraldehyde
C. Acetic acid
D. Acetamide

185. Pinacole is:
A. 2, 3-dimethyl-2,3-butandiol
B. 3, 3-dimethyl-2-propanone
C. 3-methyl butan-2-ol
D. None of these

186. The compound obtained by the reduction of propionaldehyde by Zn/Hg and conc. HCl is:
A. Propanol B. Propane
C. Propene D. None of these

187. Which of the following forces explain the boiling point of aldehydes and ketones?
A. Hydrogen bonding
B. Van der Waals' forces
C. Dipole-dipole attraction
D. None of these

188. Which reaction is used for detecting the presence of carbonyl group?
A. Reaction with hydrazine
B. Reaction with phenyl hydrazine
C. Reaction with hydroxylamine
D. All of these

189. The class of compounds that are reduced to primary alcohols and also respond to Fehling's solution are known as:
A. Aliphatic aldehydes
B. Aliphatic Ketones
C. Aromatic amines
D. Aromatic Ketones

190. Acetone is used in:
A. Face creams
B. Vanilla
C. Nail polishes
D. Sweet smelling erasers

191. Aldehydes can be oxidised by:
A. Tollen's reagent
B. Fehling's solution
C. Benedict's solution
D. All of these

192. Benedict's solution provides:
A. Ag^+ B. Cu^{2+}
C. Ba^{2+} D. Li^+

193. Choral belongs to the class of:
A. Alcohols B. Aldehyde
C. Amides D. Ketones

194. The molecular formula of chlorinated acetone produced in the distillation with bleaching powder is:
A. CH_3COCl B. CCl_3COCl_3
C. $CH_2ClCOOH$ D. CCl_3COCH_3

195. By passing water gas ($CO + H_2$) through an electric discharge at low pressure, we get:
A. HCHO B. HCOOH
C. CH_3CHO D. CO_2 and H_2O

196. Which of the following combinations give t-butyl alcohol when treated with Grignard's reagent?
A. $CH_3MgBr + CH_3COCH_3$
B. $C_2H_5MgBr + CH_3COCH_3$
C. $CH_3MgBr + (CH_3)_3C.OH$
D. $CH_3MgBr + CH_3CH_2CHO$

197. An olefin *x* on ozonolysis gives, CH_3CH_2CHO + HCHO. The olefin is:
A. 1-butene B. 2-butene
C. 2-pentene D. 1-pentene

198. The alkene which on ozonolysis yields acetone is:
A. $CH_2 = CH_2$
B. $CH_3 - CH = CH_2$
C. $(CH_3)_2C = C(CH_3)_2$
D. $CH_3 - CH = CH - CH_3$

199. An organic compound contains hydrogen and oxygen and a single carbon atom and responds positively to Tollen's reagent. The compound is:
A. HCHO B. CH_3OH
C. CH_3CHO D. None of these

200. Jone's reagent is:
A. Acidified $KMnO_4$
B. $K_2Cr_2O_7 + H_2SO_4$ or Chromic acid + H_2SO_4
C. Alkaline $K_2Cr_2O_7$
D. None of these

ANSWERS

1	2	3	4	5	6	7	8	9	10
A	A	B	B	C	A	A	C	D	B
11	12	13	14	15	16	17	18	19	20
C	B	A	A	C	B	A	B	A	C
21	22	23	24	25	26	27	28	29	30
B	B	D	C	C	D	C	B	D	D
31	32	33	34	35	36	37	38	39	40
B	D	A	B	C	D	C	B	A	B
41	42	43	44	45	46	47	48	49	50
B	B	C	B	B	D	B	A	B	B
51	52	53	54	55	56	57	58	59	60
C	D	C	D	C	A	A	B	A	A
61	62	63	64	65	66	67	68	69	70
C	C	C	B	D	A	C	C	A	B
71	72	73	74	75	76	77	78	79	80
C	C	C	A	B	B	A	C	C	A
81	82	83	84	85	86	87	88	89	90
A	D	C	D	B	C	A	B	D	C
91	92	93	94	95	96	97	98	99	100
C	C	D	D	A	B	A	B	B	D
101	102	103	104	105	106	107	108	109	110
C	D	B	C	B	B	B	C	C	B
111	112	113	114	115	116	117	118	119	120
D	C	C	B	C	A	B	B	C	B
121	122	123	124	125	126	127	128	129	130
A	C	A	C	A	A	C	B	D	A
131	132	133	134	135	136	137	138	139	140
C	B	D	B	A	A	D	C	C	C
141	142	143	144	145	146	147	148	149	150
D	B	D	D	C	B	A	C	B	D
151	152	153	154	155	156	157	158	159	160
B	C	D	B	C	D	A	D	D	B
161	162	163	164	165	166	167	168	169	170
A	B	B	C	A	B	A	A	A	C
171	172	173	174	175	176	177	178	179	180
D	C	B	C	D	A	C	C	B	C
181	182	183	184	185	186	187	188	189	190
A	C	C	B	A	B	C	D	A	C
191	192	193	194	195	196	197	198	199	200
D	B	B	D	A	A	A	C	A	B

18

AMINES (ORGANIC COMPOUNDS CONTAINING NITROGEN)

Amines

Amines are derivatives of ammonia (NH_3) in which one or more hydrogen atoms have been replaced by alkyl group.

$$CH_3-\overset{\overset{H}{|}}{N}-H \qquad CH_3-\overset{\overset{CH_3}{|}}{N}-H \qquad CH_3-\overset{\overset{CH_3}{|}}{N}-CH_3$$

Methylamine Primary (1°) — Dimethylamine Secondary (2°) — Trimethylamine Tertiary (3°)

A primary amine has only one alkyl group directly attached to the nitrogen. A secondary amine has two alkyl groups directly attached to the nitrogen. A tertiary amine has three alkyl groups directly attached to the nitrogen.

Structure : Taking example of methylamine we find that both nitrogen and carbon are sp^3-hybridized. One of the sp^3-orbitals of nitrogen is completely filled and cannot take part in bond formation. The C—N σ-bond in methylamine is formed by overlap of an sp^3-orbital of carbon and an sp^3-orbital of nitrogen. Each N—H σ-bond is formed by the overlap of an sp^3-orbital of nitrogen and *s*-orbital of hydrogen. Each C—H σ-bond is formed by overlap of an sp^3-orbital of carbon and *s*-orbital of hydrogen. All bond angles are approximately tetrahedral.

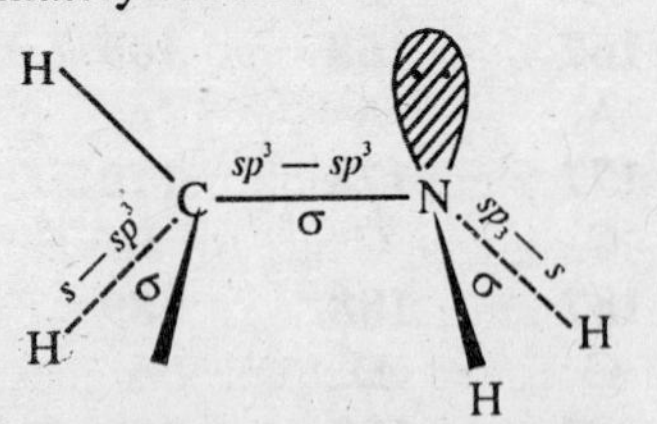

Fig. Structure of Methylamine

Nomenclature : The following rules are applied in naming amines.

(i) Amines are named by naming the alkyl groups attached to the nitrogen atom followed by the ending *-amine*. Notice that the names are written as one word.

$$CH_3-NH_2 \qquad CH_3CH_2-NH_2 \qquad CH_3CH_2CH_2-NH_2$$

Methylamine — Ethylamine — *n*-Propylamine

(ii) When two or three identical alkyl groups are attached to the nitrogen atom, the prefix di- or tri- is added to the name of the amine.

$$CH_3-\overset{\overset{CH_3}{|}}{N}-H \qquad CH_3-\overset{\overset{CH_3}{|}}{N}-CH_3$$

Dimethylamine — Trimethylamine

(iii) When two or three different alkyl groups are attached to the nitrogen atom, they are named in alphabetical order

$$CH_3-\overset{\overset{H}{|}}{N}-CH_2CH_3 \qquad CH_3CH_2-\overset{\overset{CH_3}{|}}{N}-CH(CH_3)_2$$

Ethylmethylamine — Ethylisopropylmethylamine

Isomerism

Amines show *chain isomerism* (*n*-butylamine and isobutylamine), *position isomerism* (*n*-propylamine and isopropylamine), *metamerism* (diethyl, methyl-*n* propyl and methyl-isopropyl amines) and functional isomerism (*n*-propylamine, ethylmethylamine and trimethylamine). Thus, C_3H_9N can exist in four isomeric forms.

$$n\text{-}C_3H_7NH_2 \qquad CH_3\overset{\overset{NH_2}{|}}{C}H\cdot CH_3 \qquad \begin{matrix} CH_3 \\ C_2H_5 \end{matrix}{>}NH \qquad (CH_3)_3N$$

n-Propylamine, Isopropylamine (1° Amine) — Ethyl methyl amine (2° Amine) — Tri methyl amine (3° Amine)

Preparation :

(A) Methods yielding Mixtures of Amines :

(1) Reaction of Alkyl Halides with Ammonia (Hofmann Method) : Amines can be prepared by heating an alkyl halide with alcoholic ammonia in a seated tube. A mixture of primary, secondary, tertiary amines and quaternary ammonium salt is obtained.

$$\underset{\text{Methyliodide}}{CH_3I} + H{-}NH_2 \rightarrow \underset{\text{Methylamine}}{CH_3NH_2} + HI$$

Di-, tri- and tetra-alkylation (exhaustive methylation) takes place as below :

$$\underset{\substack{\text{Methyl amine}\\(1°)}}{CH_3NH_2} \xrightarrow{ICH_3} \underset{\substack{\text{Dimethyl}\\\text{amine}\\(2°)}}{(CH_3)_2NH} \xrightarrow[-HI]{ICH_3} \underset{\substack{\text{Triethyl}\\\text{amine}\\(3°)}}{(CH_3)_3N} \xrightarrow[-HI]{ICH_3} \underset{\substack{\text{Tetramethyl}\\\text{ammonium iodide}}}{(CH_3)_4\overset{+}{N}\overset{-}{I}}$$

The amines however, at once react with the hydrogen halide produced in the reaction to form salts.

$$CH_3\overset{+}{N}H_3\overset{-}{I};\ (CH_3)_2\overset{+}{N}H_2\overset{-}{I};\ \text{and}\ (CH_3)_3\overset{+}{N}H\overset{-}{I}$$

Thus, in actual practice, the resulting mixture consists of different amine salts and the quaternary ammonium salt.

This method is not suitable for laboratory synthesis because the mixture is often difficult to separate. On industrial scale, the mixture is separated by adding alkali to liberate the free amines and fractionally distilling. The primary, secondary, and tertiary amines pass over, while the quaternary ammonium salt is left behind.

(2) Reaction of Alcohols with Ammonia : Amines can be prepared by passing the vapours of alcohol and ammonia over heated alumina at 400°C. A mixture of primary, secondary and tertiary amines is produced

$$\underset{\text{Methanol}}{CH_3OH} + HNH_2 \xrightarrow{Al_2O_3} \underset{\text{Methylamine}}{CH_3NH_2} + H_2O$$

$$CH_3NH_2 + CH_3OH \rightarrow \underset{\text{Dimethylamine}}{(CH_3)_2NH} + H_2O$$

$$(CH_3)_2NH + CH_3OH \rightarrow \underset{\text{Trimethylamine}}{(CH_3)_3N} + H_2O$$

The primary amines may be obtained as the main product by using a large excess of ammonia.

Mixtures can be separated from each other by means of benzene sulphonyl chloride, $C_6H_5SO_2Cl$ (Hinsberg method), diethyl oxalate, $COOC_2H_5COOC_2H_5$ (Hofmann method) and fractional distillation.

However 1° amines can be prepared in good yield by using excess of ammonia.

This is one of the industrial methods for preparing aniline.

$$\underset{\text{Phenol}}{C_6H_5OH} + \underset{\text{Ammonia}}{HNH_2} \xrightarrow[300°C]{ZnCl_2} \underset{\text{Aniline}}{C_6H_5NH_2} + H_2O$$

Physical Properties

(i) Lower amines are gases or low-boiling liquids, possess a characteristic ammonia like smell.

(ii) Amines have higher boiling points than the compounds of similar molecular weights. This is because amines are polar compounds and form intermolecular hydrogen bonds. For example, ethylamine, $C_2H_5NH_2$, boils at + 17°C and propane C_3H_8 at – 42°C

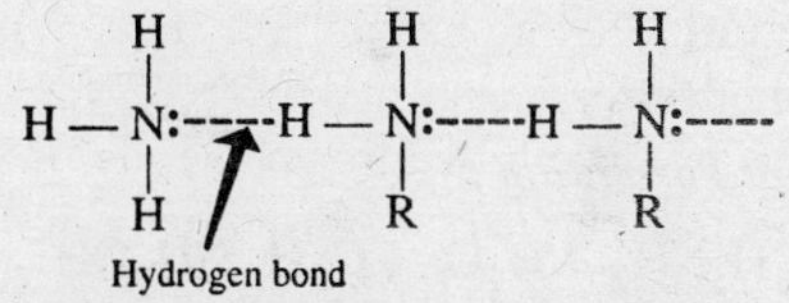

Hydrogen Bonding in Amine Molecules

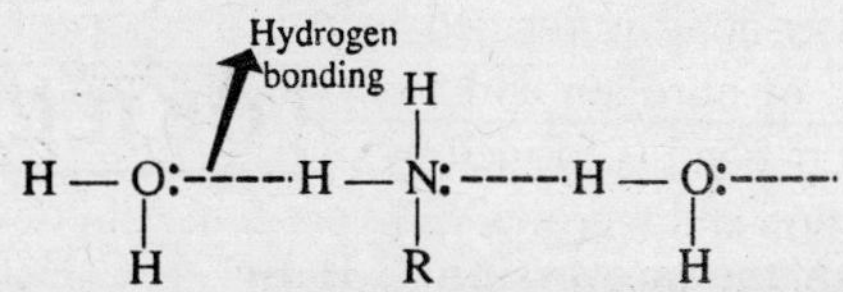

Hydrogen Bonding Between Amine and Water Molecules

(iii) Amines are soluble in water, because of formation of hydrogen bonds. Amines are also soluble in benzene and ether.

(iv) The infrared spectrum of amines show N—H stretching as 3330 to 3570 cm^{-1}. Primary amines have two sharp peaks in this region, secondary amines only one and tertiary amines none (as no N—H bonds are there). The N—H bending frequency occur at 1550 to 1650 cm^{-1}.

Chemical Properties

Nitrogen atom of all the three types of amines has a lone pair of electrons which is responsible for most of the reactions of amines.

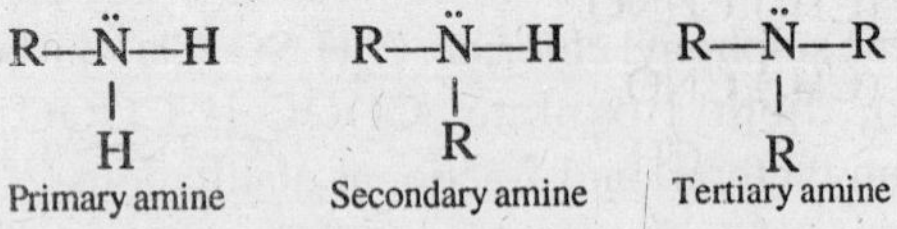

This lone pair of electrons is available for donation to electron-seeking reagents and thus amines act as nucleophilic reagents. However, due to presence of different number of hydrogen atoms on nitrogen, the three amines differ each other in some of their properties.

(1) Basicity of Amines : Amines are basic in nature. This is because they possess an unshared pair (lone pair) of electrons on nitrogen.

This lone pair of electrons is available for the formation of a new bond with a proton or Lewis acids. Thus amines react with acids to form salts.

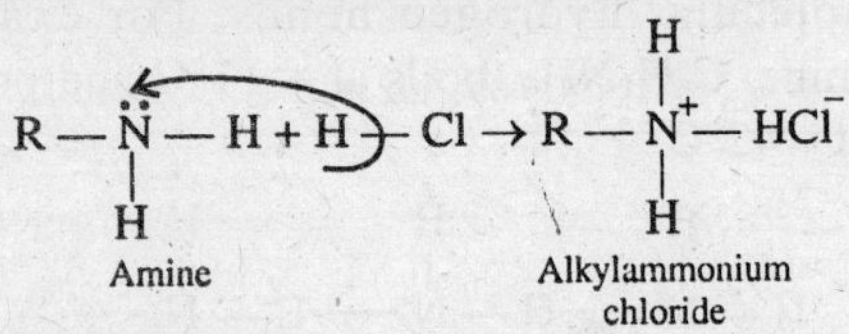

(2) Salt Formation :

(i) $C_6H_5NH_2 + H_2O \rightarrow C_6H_5\overset{+}{N}H_3OH^-$
Aniline — Anilinium hydroxide

(ii) $C_6H_5NH_2 + HCl \rightarrow C_6H_5\overset{+}{N}H_3Cl^-$ or
Anilinium chloride or
$C_6H_5NH_2.HCl$
Anilinehydro-chloride

Amine salts are generally soluble in water, but insoluble in organic solvents like ether because amines (except lower aliphatic amines) are insoluble in water but soluble in organic solvents.

(3) Reaction with Alkyl Halides : When an amine is treated with an alkyl halide, hydrogen atoms of the N-atom are successively replaced by alkyl groups. In the final step, the tertiary amine adds one molecule of the alkyl halide to yield a *Quaternary ammonium salt.*

$$\underset{1^\circ \text{ Amine}}{RNH_2} \xrightarrow[-HX]{RX} \underset{2^\circ \text{ Amine}}{R_2NH} \xrightarrow[-HX]{RX} \underset{3^\circ \text{ Amine}}{R_3N} \xrightarrow[-HX]{RX} \underset{\text{Quaternary salts}}{R_4N^+X^-}$$

(4) Reaction with Acid Chlorides : (Acylation)

(a) Primary amines react with acid chlorides or acid anhydrides to form N-substituted amides. For example:

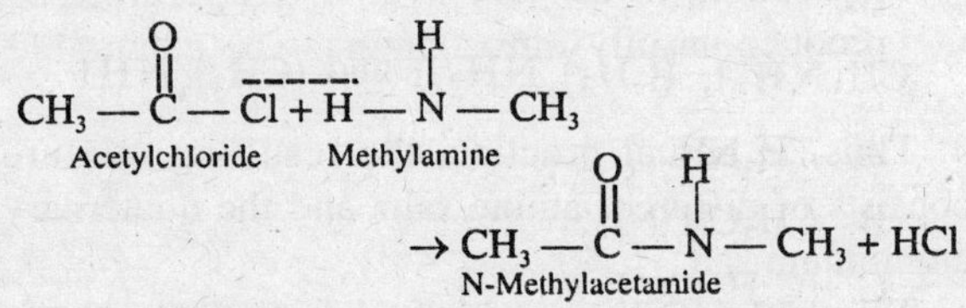

OBJECTIVE QUESTIONS

1. In the conversion $C_2H_5Br \rightarrow C_2H_5CN$, the reagent used is

A. alc. KCN B. alc. AgCN
C. NH_3 D. None of these

2. The reduction of methyl cyanide with sodium and alcohol gives

A. Methylamine B. Ethylamine
C. Acetic acid D. Methyl alcohol

3. An aliphatic organic compound containing C, H and N reacts with dilute HCl to produce formic acid. It is reduced to dimethylamine by Pt or Ni and it undergoes an addition reaction with chlorine and sulphur. The compound can be

A. CH_3NC
B. CH_3CN
C. CH_3NH_2
D. A mixture of (A) and (B)

4. Ethyl isocyanide is prepared by the reaction between

A. C_2H_5Br and KCN
B. C_2H_5Br and AgCN

C. C_2H_5Br and HCN
D. C_2H_5Br and NH_3

5. In the reaction between C_2H_5Br and alcoholic $AgNO_2$ the product obtained is
A. Nitroethane
B. Ethane
C. Ethyl nitrite
D. Ethyl isocyanide

6. In the reaction between CH_3HC and HgO, the product obtained is
A. Methyl isothiocyanate
B. Methyl isocyanate
C. Methylamine
D. Methyl cyanide

7. Which of the following reactions will produce methyl nitrite as the major product?
A. $CH_3I + AgNO_2 \rightarrow$
B. $CH_3I + NaNO_2 \rightarrow$
C. Both (A) and (B)
D. None of these

8. An organic amino compound reacts with aqueous nitrous acid at low temperature to produce an oily nitrosoamine. The compound is
A. CH_3NH_2
B. $CH_3CH_2NH_2$
C. $(C_2H_5)_2NH$
D. $(C_2H_5)_3N$

9. In the nitration of benzene with conc. HNO_3 and conc. H_2SO_4, the electrophile is
A. NO_2^+ B. NO_2^-
C. NO_2 D. Nitric oxide

10. A nitroalkane reacts with nitrous acid to yield a product which is insoluble in alkali, and gives a blue colour on treatment with alkali. The nitroalkane could be
A. $CH_3CH_2NO_2$
B. $(CH_3)_2CHNO_2$
C. $(CH_3)_3CNO_2$
D. $CH_3CH(CH_3)-CH_2NO_2$

11. A nitroalkane produces a ketone when it is boiled with HCl. The nitroalkane could be
A. $CH_3CH_2NO_2$
B. $(CH_3)_2CHNO_2$
C. $(CH_3)_3CNO_2$
D. $CH_3-C(CH_3)_2-CH_2NO_2$

12. The electrolytic reduction of nitrobenzene in a strongly acidic medium produces
A. aniline
B. phenylhydroxylamine
C. *p*-aminophenol
D. azoxybenzene

13. The electrolytic reduction of nitrobenzene in a weakly acidic medium produces
A. aniline
B. phenylhydroxylamine
C. *p*-aminophenol
D. azoxybenzene

14. Which of the following will give only one mono-substituted product?
A. *o*-dinitrobenzene
B. *m*-dinitrobenzene
C. *p*-dinitrobenzene
D. none of these

15. The oxidation of aniline with $K_2Cr_2O_7/H_2SO_4$ produces
A. benzoic acid
B. benzene
C. *p*-benzoquinone
D. *p*-nitrophenol

16. How many isomeric amines with the formula C_7H_9N contain a benzene ring?
A. Two B. Three
C. Four D. Five

17. How many isomeric amines can have the formula $C_4H_{11}N$?
A. Five B. Six
C. Seven D. Eight

18. Which among the following has the highest b.p.?
A. $CH_3CH_2CH_2NH_2$

B. $CH_3CH_2-NH-CH_3$

C. $CH_3-N(CH_3)-CH_3$

D. CH_3NH_2

19. The N atom in anines involves
A. sp^3-hybridization
B. sp^2-hybridization
C. sp^2-and sp^3-hybridization
D. None of these

20. Arrange the following in decreasing order of basic strength
$(C_2H_5)_2NH, C_2H_5HN_2, (C_2H_5)_3N$
A. $(C_2H_5)_2NH > C_2H_5HN_2 > (C_2H_5)_3N$
B. $C_2H_5NH_2 > (C_2H_5)_2NH > (C_2H_5)_3N$
C. $(C_2H_5)_3N > (C_2H_5)_2NH > C_2H_5NH_2$
D. $(C_2H_5)_3N > C_2H_5HN_2 > (C_2H_5)_2NH$

21. Arrange aniline (I) *p*-nitroaniline (II) and *p*-metho-xyaniline (III) in decreasing order of basic strength
A. III > I > II B. I > II > III
C. II > I > III D. III > II > I

22. Arrange *p*-methylaniline (I) *m*-methylaniline (II) aniline (III) and *o*-methylaniline (IV) in decreasing order of basic strength
A. II > I > III > IV B. IV > III > II > I
C. I > II > III > IV D. III > II > I > IV

23. In the reaction
$$CH_3NH_2 \xrightarrow{\text{excess } CH_3Cl} X \xrightarrow[\text{moist}]{Ag_2O} Y \xrightarrow{\Delta} Z,$$
the final product Z is
A. $(CH_3)_3N$ B. $(CH_3)_4N^+Cl^-$
C. $(CH_3)_4N^+OH^-$ D. $(CH_3)_2NH$

24. In the reaction
$$C_6H_5NH_2 + C_6H_5CHO \rightarrow X \xrightarrow{\text{Raney Ni}} Y,$$ the product Y is
A. $C_6H_5N=CHC_6H_5$
B. $C_6H_5NHCH_2C_6H_5$
C. $(C_6H_5NH)_2CHC_6H_5$
D. None of these

25. Aniline produces a schiff base on reaction with
A. ammonia B. acetyl chloride
C. benzaldehyde D. acetone

26. In the reaction $C_2H_5NH_2 + HNO_2 \rightarrow$, the products obtained are
A. $C_2H_5NO_2$ B. C_2H_5OH, N_2, H_2O
C. $C_2H_5N_2^+Cl$ D. C_2H_5NHOH, NH_2

27. The presence of primary amines can be confirmed by
A. Reaction with HNO_2
B. Reaction with $CHCl_3$ and alc. KOH
C. Reaction with Grignard reagent
D. Reaction with acetyl chloride

28. Dimethylamine reacts with HNO_2 to produce
A. CH_3OH B. $N_2 + CH_3OH$
C. $(CH_3)_2NH^+NO_2^-$ D. $(CH_3)_2NNO$

29. Benzenediazonium chloride reacts with hypophosphorus acid to produce
A. Benzene B. A phenol
C. Cyanobenzene D. Chlorobenzene

30. In piperidine, the N atom involves the hybridization
A. *sp* B. sp^2
C. sp^3 D. dsp^2

31. In the reaction $C_6H_5NH_2 + CS_2 \xrightarrow[\Delta]{HgCl_2}$....., the product obtained is
A. phenyl cyanide
B. phenyl isocyanide
C. phenyl isothiocyanate
D. *p*-aminobenzene sulphonic acid

32. In the reaction $CH_3CH_2NH_2 + CH_3MgBr \rightarrow X$, the product is
A. CH_3CH_3 B. $CH_3CH_2CH_3$
C. $CH_3CH_2CH_2CH_3$ D. CH_4

33. Diethylamine reacts with HNO_2 to produce
A. $(C_2H_5)_2NH^+NO_2^-$
B. $(C_2H_5)_2NNO$
C. $N_2 + C_2H_5OH$
D. C_2H_5OH

34. The product obtained in the reaction $CH_3CH_2CONH_2 \xrightarrow[\text{(ii) KOH}]{\text{(i) bromine water}} X$ is

A. CH_3CH_2COOH B. $CH_3CH_2CH_2NH_2$
C. $CH_3CH_2NH_2$ D. $CH_3CH_2COONH_4$

35. Arrange *p*-toluidine (I) N,N-dimethyl-*p*-toluidine (II), *p*-nitroaniline (III) and aniline (IV) in order of decreasing basicity.

A. I > IV > III > II B. I > II > III > IV
C. II > I > IV > III D. III > I > II > IV

36. Arrange methylamine (I) dimethylamine (II) aniline (III) and N-methylaniline (IV) in order of decreasing basicity.

A. I > II > III > IV B. II > I > IV > III
C. III > II > I > IV D. IV > III > II > I

37. Gabriel phthalimide synthesis is used for the preparation of

A. Primary aromatic amines
B. Primary aliphatic amines
C. Secondary amines
D. Tertiary amines

38. Consider the following structure for the anilium ion

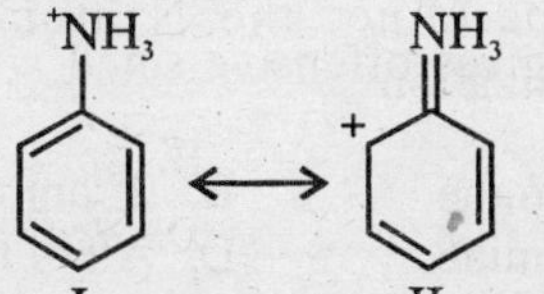

I II

Which of the statement are correct regarding this structure?

A. It is not an acceptable canonical structure because it is nonaromatic
B. It is not an acceptable canonical structure because here nitrogen has ten valence electrons
C. It is an acceptable canonical structure
D. It is not an acceptable canonical structure because carbonium ions are less stable than ammonium ions

39. Arrange phenol (I), *p*-cresol (II), *m*-nitrophenol (III) and *p*-nitrophenol (IV) in order of acidity.

A. II > I > III > IV B. IV > III > I > II
C. III > IV > I > II D. I > IV > III > II

40. The major product of the reaction between *p*-chlorotoluene and KNH_2 in liquid NH_3 is

A. *o*-toluidene B. *m*-toluidine
C. *p*-toluidene D. *p*-chloroaniline

41. Which of the following is a Sandmeyer reaction?

A. $C_6H_5N_2Cl \xrightarrow[\Delta]{\text{cuprous chloride}} C_6H_5Cl + N_2$
B. $2C_6H_5Cl \xrightarrow{CuCl_2/HCl} C_6H_6 + Cl_2$
C. $C_6H_5OH \xrightarrow{\text{Zn dust}} C_6H_6 + ZnO$
D. $C_6H_5NO_2 + 6H \xrightarrow{Sn + HCl} C_6H_5NH_2 + 2H_2O$

42. Which of the following compounds will produce a *p*-nitroso derivative on treatment with $NaNO_2$/HCl at 0–5°C?

A. Aniline B. N-methylaniline
C. *o*-methylaniline D. N,N-dimethylaniline

43. Which of the following reaction will produce benzenesulphonic acid?

A. Benzene $\xrightarrow{\text{conc. } H_2SO_4\text{, 80°C}}$
B. Benzene $\xrightarrow{\text{fuming sulphuric acid, 200–250°C}}$
C. Benzene $\xrightarrow{\text{chlorosulphonic acid}}$
D. Benzene $\xrightarrow{\text{sulphuryl chloride pyridine}}$

44. Nitrobenzene can be converted into azoxybenzene by

A. Reduction with $Na_3AsO_3/NaOH/H_2O$
B. Reduction with $Zn/NaOH/CH_3OH$
C. Reduction with Sn + HCl
D. Reduction with $Zn/NH_4Cl/H_2O$

45. Benzenediazonium chloride can be converted into phenol by treating it with

A. H_3PO_3, H_2O, CuCl
B. H_2O, heat
C. Alcohol, heat
D. HBF_4 and $NaNO_2$/Cu

46. Arrange CH_3NH_2 (I), CH_3CONH_2 (II) and NH_2CH_2COOH (III) in decreasing order of basicity.

A. I > III > II B. III > II > I
C. II > I > III D. II > III > I

47. The bond angles in methane (I), ammonia (II) and trimethyl amine (III) increase in the order

A. I>III>II B. I>II>III
C. II>I>III D. III>II>I

48. Arrange the following compounds in order of decreasing basic strength.

CH_3NH_2 (I) $(CH_3)_2NH$ (II) $(CH_3)_3N$ (III) NH_3 (IV)

A. I>II>III>IV B. II>I>III>IV
C. IV>III>II>I D. II>III>I>IV

49. How many structures are possible for a compound having the molecular formula $C_3H_7NO_2$?
A. One B. Two
C. Three D. Four

50. A nitrogenous substance *x* is treated with HNO_2 and the product so formed is further treated with NaOH solution, which produces blue colouration. *x* can be:
A. $CH_3CH_2NH_2$ B. $CH_3CH_2NO_2$
C. CH_3CH_2ONO D. $(CH_3)_2CHNO_2$

51. The name urea was given by:
A. Wholer B. Berzelius
C. Roulle D. Lemery

52. Urea when heated slowly, product formed is :
A. N_2
B. CO
C. Biuret
D. Ammonium carbamate

53. Urea when heated, a white residue is formed. Its alkaline solution when treated with few drops of $CuSO_4$ solution gives:
A. Red colour B. Violet colour
C. Green colour D. Yellow colour

54. The diamide of carbonic acid is:
A. Acetamide B. Formamide
C. Benzamide D. Urea

55. Reaction, $CH_3CONH_2 \rightarrow$ NaOBr gives:
A. CH_3Br B. CH_4
C. CH_3OBr D. CH_3NH_2

56. Amides may be converted into amines by reaction named after:
A. Perkin B. Claisen
C. Hofmann D. Kolbe

57. Benzaldehyde reacts with methyl amine to give:
A. $C_6H_5NH_2$
B. $C_6H_5CH_2NH_2$
C. $C_6H_5CH=NCH_3$
D. $C_6H_5CONH_2$

58. A compound which on reaction with aqueous nitrous acid gives an oily nitrosamine is:
A. Methylamine B. Ethylamine
C. Diethylamine D. Triethylamine

59. Gabriel Phthalimide reaction is used to prepare:
A. *p*-amine B. *s*-amine
C. *t*-amine D. All of these

60. CH_3CONH_2 is dehydrated by P_2O_5 to give:
A. CH_3NH_2
B. CH_3CN
C. CH_3CHO
D. $CH_3-CH_3+CO+NH_3$

61. Grignard reagent and acetyl chloride does not react with:
A. RNH_2 B. R_2NH
C. R_3N D. None of these

62. Which one of the following compound when heated with KOH and Primary amines gives carbylamine test?
A. $CHCl_3$ B. CH_3Cl
C. CCl_4 D. CH_3NC

63. Which gives offensive smell with $CHCl_3$ and KOH?
A. 1° amine B. 2° amine
C. 3° amine D. All of these

64. General formula of an amine is:
A. C_nH_{2n+1n} B. C_nH_{2n+2n}
C. C_nH_{2n+3n} D. $C_nH_{2n}N$

65. Amine may contain:
A. $-NH_2$ gp B. >NH gp
C. $\rightarrow$N gp D. All of these

66. *p*-amine and *s*-amine are distinguished by:
A. Br_2/KOH B. HClO
C. HNO_2 D. NH_3

67. The pri-, Sec. and ter. Amines can be distinguished.
A. Hinsberg's reagent
B. Grignard's reagent
C. Fehling's solution
D. Tollen's reagent

68. The correct order of basicities of the following compounds is:

$CH_3-C(=NH)NH_2$ (1) $\quad CH_3CH_2NH_2$ (2)

$(CH_3)_2NH$ (3) $\quad CH_3-C(=O)-NH_2$ (4)

A. $2>1>3>4$ B. $1>3>2>4$

C. $3>1>2>4$ D. $1>2>3>4$

69. Alkanamide, which on Hofmann's reaction gives 1- Phenylethylamine, is:

A. 2-Phenylpropanamide

B. 3-Phenylpropanamide

C. 2-Phenylethanamide

D. N-Phenylethanamide

70. Ethyl amine can be prepared by the action of Br_2 and NaOH on:

A. Acetamide B. Propionamide

B. Methylamine D. Methyl cyanide

71. Gas evolved during the reaction of sodium metal on ethyl amine is:

A. N_2 B. C_2H_2

C. H_2 D. CO_2

72. Ethyl amine undergoes oxidation in the presence of $KMnO_4$ followed by hydrolysis to form:

A. An acid B. An alcohol

C. An aldehyde D. A N–oxide

73. Indicate the correct statement:

A. $C_2H_5N^+H_3OH^-$ is acidic

B. $C_2H_5NH_2$ is less basic than NH_3

C. $C_2H_5NH_2$ is a stronger base than NH_3

D. $C_2H_5NH_2$ forms salts with bases

74. Which of the following reactions does not yield an amine?

A. $R-X+NH_3$

B. $R-C(H)=N-OH+[H]\xrightarrow[C_2H_5OH]{Na}$

C. $R-CN+H_2O\xrightarrow{H+}$

D. $R-C(=O)-NH_2+4[H]\xrightarrow{LiAlH_4}$

75. What is the end product in the following sequence of reactions?

$$C_2H_5NH_2\xrightarrow{HNO_2}A\xrightarrow{PCl_5}B\xrightarrow{NH_3}C$$

A. Ethyl cyanide B. Ethylamine

C. Methylamine D. Acetamide

76. A positive carbylamine test is given by:

A. N, N-dimethyl aniline

B. 2, 4-dimethyl aniline

C. N-methyl –*o*– methyl aniline

D. P-methyl benzyl aniline

77. Decreasing order of the basic character of three amines and ammonia is:

A. $NH_3>CH_3NH_2>C_2H_5NH_2>C_6H_5NH_2$

B. $C_2H_5NH_2>CH_3NH_2>NH_3>C_6H_5NH_2$

C. $C_6H_5NH_2>C_2H_5NH_2>CH_3NH_2>NH_3$

D. $CH_3NH_2>C_2H_5NH_2>C_6H_5NH_2>NH_3$

78. Which of the following is carbamide?

A. CH_3CONH_2 B. NH_2CONH_2

C. $CH_2(NH_2)CONH_2$ D. $CO(OH)NH_2$

79. Carboxylic acid on reacting with N_3H gives:

A. Amines B. Amides

C. Acids D. Aldehyde

80. Dehydration of an amide gives:

A. Cyanide B. Amine

C. Isocyanide D. Fatty acid

81. Reaction of Primary amine with aldehydes gives:

A. Amide B. Aldimine

B. Nitrile D. None of these

82. Which substance when boiled with NaOH will evolve NH_3?

A. Ethylamine B. Aniline

C. Acetamide D. Acetoxine

83. Hinsberg method to separate amines is based on the use of :

A. Benzene sulphonylchloride

B. Benzene sulphonic acid

C. Ethyl oxalate

D. Acetyl chloride

84. An amine reacts with $C_6H_5SO_2Cl$ and the product is soluble in alkali, amine is:

A. 1° B. 2°

B. 3° C All of these

85. Ethyl amine on acetylation gives:

A. Acetamide

B. Methyl acetamide
C. N-ethyl acetamide
D. None of these

86. When $(NH_4)_2\ SO_4 + KCNO$ are heated, we get:
A. Nitrogen
B. Carbon dioxide
C. Biuret
D. Ammonium carbonate

87. Which of the following will give a primary amine on hydrolysis?
A. Nitroparaffin B. Alkyl cyanide
C. Oxime D. Alkyl isocyanate

88. The type of isomerism shown by C_6H_5CN and C_6H_5NC is:
A. Position B. Functional
C. Enantiomerism D. Tautomerism

89. Primary aliphatic or aromatic amines can be distinguished from secondary and tertiary amines by reacting with:
A. Choloroform and alcoholic KOH
B. Methyl iodide
C. Chloroform alone
D. Zinc dust

90. Which of the following is least basic?
A. $(C_2H_5)N$ B. $C_2H_5NH_2$
C. $(C_2H_5)_2NH$ D. $C_6H_5NH_2$

91. Mark the correct statement:
A. Methyl amine is slightly acidic
B. Methyl amine is less basic than ammonia
C. Methyl amine is a stronger base than ammonia
D. Methyl amine forms salts with alkalies

92. Which of the following is a weakest basic?
A. Ammonia B. Methylamine
C. Dimethylamine D. Trimethylamine

93. Which one of the following amines will not react with HNO_2 acid to give nitrogen?
A. CH_3NH_2 B. $CH_3CH_2NH_2$
C. 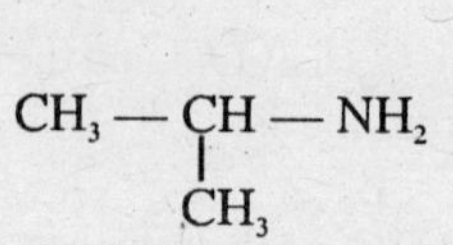 D. 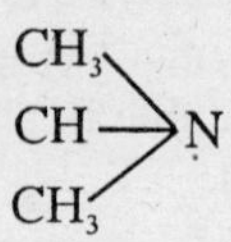

94. What is decreasing order of basicity of PST ethyl amines and NH_3?
A. $NH_3 > C_2H_5NH_2 > (C_2H_5)_2NH > (C_2H_5)_3N$
B. $(C_2H_5)_3N > (C_2H_5)_2NH > C_2H_5NH_2 > NH_3$
C. $(C_2H_5)_2\ NH > C_2H_5NH_2 > NH_3 > (C_2H_5)_3N$
D. $(C_2H_5)_2NH > (C_2H_5)_3N > C_2H_5NH_2 > NH_3$

95. 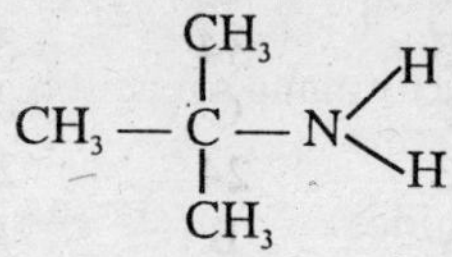 is a :
A. Primary amine B. Secondary amine
C. Tertiary amine D. Ammonium salt

96. Urea on heating with ethanal gives:
A. Urathane B. Urea alcohol
C. Ureides D. None of these

97. Alkyl nitrite on reduction with Sn/HCI gives:
A. Alcohol B. Hydroxylamine
C. Both (A) and (B) D. Hydrazine

98. Primary, Secondary, tertiary nitroalkanes can be identified by the action of:
A. HNO_2 + NaOH aq.
B. $CHCl_3$ + NaOH aq.
C. $CHCl_3$ + KOH alc.
D. None of these

99. Which statement is not true among the following:
A. Amines are bases
B. They turn red litmus blue
C. Trimethyl amine is less basic than dimethyl amine
D. Amines yield alkanals on aqueous hydrolysis.

100. Which of the following compounds is expected to be most basic?
A. Aniline
B. Ethylamine
B. Hydroxylamine
D. Methylamine

ANSWERS

1	2	3	4	5	6	7	8	9	10
A	B	A	B	A	B	B	C	A	B
11	**12**	**13**	**14**	**15**	**16**	**17**	**18**	**19**	**20**
B	C	A	C	C	D	A	A	A	A
21	**22**	**23**	**24**	**25**	**26**	**27**	**28**	**29**	**30**
A	A	A	B	C	B	B	D	A	C
31	**32**	**33**	**34**	**35**	**36**	**37**	**38**	**39**	**40**
C	D	B	C	A	B	B	B	B	B
21	**22**	**23**	**24**	**25**	**26**	**27**	**28**	**29**	**30**
A	A	A	B	C	B	B	D	A	C
31	**32**	**33**	**34**	**35**	**36**	**37**	**38**	**39**	**40**
C	D	B	C	A	B	B	B	B	B
41	**42**	**43**	**44**	**45**	**46**	**47**	**48**	**49**	**50**
A	D	A	A	B	A	A	B	D	D
51	**52**	**53**	**54**	**55**	**56**	**57**	**58**	**59**	**60**
C	C	B	D	D	D	C	C	A	B
61	**62**	**63**	**64**	**65**	**66**	**67**	**68**	**69**	**70**
C	A	A	C	D	C	A	B	B	B
71	**72**	**73**	**74**	**75**	**76**	**77**	**78**	**79**	**80**
C	C	C	C	B	D	B	B	A	A
81	**82**	**83**	**84**	**85**	**86**	**87**	**88**	**89**	**90**
B	C	A	A	C	C	D	B	A	B
91	**92**	**93**	**94**	**95**	**96**	**97**	**98**	**99**	**100**
C	A	D	D	A	A	C	A	D	B

19

POLYMERS

Introduction

In 1833, Jons Berzelius suggested that compounds having same empirical formula but different molecular weight should he called 'polymers' (literally, many parts). The term polymer eventually came to mean compounds with usually large molecular weights, such as natural rubber. In 1920 Hermann Staudeyer proposed the first explanation for why polymer molecules are so heavy. He argued that polymers contain long chains of relatively simple repeating units. Natural rubber, for example is polymer that contains large number of

$$[-CH_2C(CH_3) = CHCH_2—]\text{ units.}$$

Polymers are substances of high molecular mass formed by the combination of large number of simple molecules called *monomers.* Polymerization is the process by which the monomers are converted into polymers. The number of types a monomer unit is repeated in a polymer, is called 'degree of polymerisation'.

Polymers are generally classified into:

(a) **Natural Polymers:** The polymers which are found in nature. Proteins, polysaccharides, natural rubber etc.

(b) **Synthetic Polymer:** The polymers which are synthetic or man made. Polythene, nylon, dacron are some examples.

The term rubber was first used in 1770 by *Joseph Priestley* to describe the gum from a South African tree that could be used to rule out pencil marks. *Nathaniel Hayward* was the first-to note that natural rubber loses some of its stickey properties when treated with sulphur.

Charles Goodyear accidently dropped a mixture of natural rubber and sulphur onto a hot stove and discovered *vulcanized* rubber which is stable over a wide range of temperature and far more durable than natural rubber. In the last hundred years, cellulose has served as a starting material for the synthesis of the first plastics and first synthetic fibre. Viscous solution of cellulose in NaOH and CS_2 when forced through tiny holes in a nozzle into a acid bath the cellulose fibre known as *Rayon* is generated. A similar process is used to make a thin film of regenerated cellulose known as *Cellophane*. In 1869 John Wesley Hyatt found that mixture of cellulose nitrate and camphor disolves in alcohol to produce a plastic substance. He named it celluloid. No plastic has yet been found that has as high bounce as celluloid has.

Straight Chain Polymers: Polyethylene is called a straight chain polymer because it consists of a long string of carbon-carbon bonds. The term is somewhat misleading because the geometry around each carbon is tetrahedral and chain is not quite linear. Furthermore as the chain grows, it folds back on itself in a random manner.

Branched Polymers: Polymers with branches at irregular intervals along the polymer chain are called branched polymers. These branches make it difficult for the molecule to pack in a regular array and, therefore, make the polymer less crystalline.

Cross-linked Polymers : They contain branches which connect-chains. At first, adding cross-links between polymer chains makes the polymer more elastic.

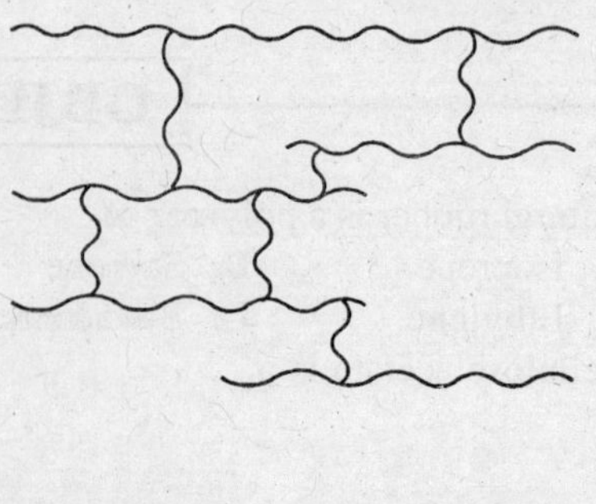

The vulcanization of rubber results from the introduction of short chains of sulphur atom that link the polymer chains in the natural rubber. When the number of cross-links is relatively large; the polymer becomes more rigid.

The linear and branched polymers form a class of materials known as *thermoplastics*. There materials flow when heated and can be molded into a variety of shapes; which they retain when they cool. Heavy cross-linking produces materials known as *thermoselplastics*. Once the cross-links form, these polymers take on a shape that cannot be changed without destroying the plastic. Polymers formed by polymerizing a single *monomer* are known as *homopolymers*. Polyethylene is a homopolymer. When a polymer is formed by polymerizing two or more than two kinds of monomers it is called a copolymer.

Addition Polymers: Polyethylene, polypropylene, and polyvinyl chloride are examples of addition polymers which are formed by adding monomers to growing polymer chain repeating unit in them is always having the same formula as the monomer from which the polymer is formed.

Condensation Polymers: To condense means to make something more dense or compact. Polymers are formed when a small molecule is given out during condensation. $(CH_3)_2$ $Si(OH)_2$ polymerizes to form polymer known as silicon rubber. Repeating unit in a condensation polymer is invariably smaller than the monomer from which it is made.

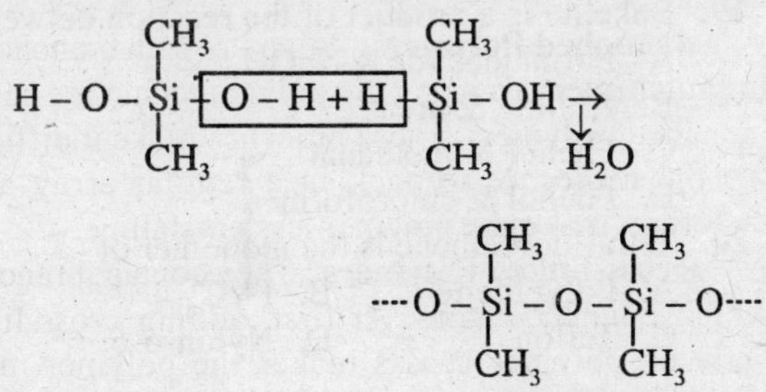

Silicon nucleus

Synthetic Polymers : The fibre is originally referred to naturally occurring materials such as cotton, jute, wool etc. However, it is now used extensively to the man made products which include both semisynthetic and synthetic materials. Cellulose is the main constituent of most of natural fibres. Semisynthetic fibres are obtained from natural polymeric materials such as cellulose. Viscose rayon and acetate fibres are well known examples of semisynthetic fibres.

There are four important kinds of rayon or artificial silk derived from cellulose:

(i) Nitrocellulose (pyroxelin or chordonet silk)

(ii) Cuprammonium rayon.

(iii) Acetate rayon

(iv) Viscose rayon.

Following are important synthetic fibres:

Nylon-66, Nylon 6, 10, Nylon-6, terylene or dacron, orolon, earon, vingon, dynel etc.

Thiokol is a variety of synthetic rubber which is a copolymer of ethylene chloride and sodium tetra sulphide (Na_2S_4). Polymers having ester linkages are called *Polyestar. Valcanization* of rubber was introduced by *Charles Goodyear.* Proteins, nucleic acid and polysaccharides, which control various activities in plants and animals are known as *Biopolymers.* Silicon resin were produced in 1943. They have good thermal and oxidative stability, excellent electrical properties and they are good repellents. They have widely been used as defoamers, propellents rubbers etc. Epoxy resins are thermosetting polymers'. *Carbowx* made by polymersation of ethylene oxide is the first epoxy resins. These resins have excellent chemical resistance, electrical properties, good heat resistance. They are strong and tough and are used in laminates, adhesives, surface coatings and propellents.

OBJECTIVE QUESTIONS

1. Natural rubber is a polymer of

A. Isoprene B. Styrene

C. Ethylene D. Butadiene

2. Cellulose acetate is a

A. Natural polymer B. Semisynthetic rubber

C. Sythetic polymer D. Plasticiser

3. The catalyst used for the polymerization of olefins is

A. Pd-catalyst
B. Ziegler-Natta catalyst
C. Wilkinson's catalyst
D. Zeise's salt complere

4. Which of the following is used in plants?
A. Terylene B. Nylon
C. Glyptal D. Chloroprene

5. A condensation polymer among the following is
A. Dacron B. PVC
C. Polystyrene D. Teflon

6. Buna-S is obtained by the copolymerisation of butadiene and
A. Chloroprene B. Styrene
C. Acrylonitrile D. Adipic acid

7. Natural rubber is
A. Polyisoprene B. Polyvinyl chloride
C. Polychloroprene D. Polyfluoroethylene

8. Plexiglass is a commercial name of
A. Glyptal
B. Polyacrylo-nitrile
C. Polymethyl methacrylate
D. Polyethylacrylate

9. The weakest interparticle forces are present is
A. Thermosetting polymers
B. Thermoplastic polymer
C. Fibres
D. Elastomers

10. Chemical name of *melamine* is
A. 2, 4-Diamino – 1, 3, 5 triazine
B. 2 Amino – 1, 3, 5 traizine
C. 2, 4, 6 Triamino – 1, 3, 5 triazine
D. 1, 3, 5 – Triamino – 2, 4, 6 triazine

11. Which of the following is not a polyamide?
A. Leather B. Natural rubber
C. Wool D. Nylon-66

12. The abbreviation PDI refers to
A. Name of the polymer
B. Poly dispersity index of polymer
C. Application of polymer
D. Poly diagonal index

13. Which of the following is common example of fibres?
A. Bakelite B. Buna-S
C. Nylon-66 D. PVC

14. Synthetic polymer prepared from caprolactum is known as
A. Nylon 6, 10 B. Teflon
C. Terylene D. Nylon-6

15. Synthetic rubber (Neoprene) is
A. Polyester B. Polyamide
C. Polysaccharide D. Poly (halodiene)

16. The turbidity of a polymer solution measures
A. A light absorbed by solution
B. Light transmitted by solution
C. Light scatterred by solution
D. None of the above

17. Peptide bond is a key feature is
A. Proteins B. Aminoacids
C. Nitrogen D. Nucleic acids

18. Synthetic human hair wigs are made from a copolymer of vinyl chloride and acrylonitrile, and is called
A. PVC B. Polyacrylonitrile
C. Cellulose D. Dynel

19. Bakelite is a product of the reaction between
A. Formaldehyde & NaOH
B. Aniline & urea
C. Phenol & methanal
D. Phenol & chloroform

20. Tetrafluoroethene is the monomer of
A. Polyethene B. PVC
C. Teflon D. Nylon-6-6

ANSWERS

1	2	3	4	5	6	7	8	9	10
A	B	B	C	A	B	A	C	D	C
11	12	13	14	15	16	17	18	19	20
B	B	C	D	D	C	A	D	C	C

20

BIOMOLECULES (BIOCHEMISTRY): CARBOHYDRATES, PROTEINS AND NUCLEIC ACIDS

Carbohydrates: Carbohydrates are compounds of carbon, hydrogen and oxygen where hydrogen and oxygen occur in the ratio of 2:1 and the general formula is $C_nH_{2n}O_n$. Carbohydrates are also called saccharides because their basic components are sugars. They are elaborated by autotrophic plants and constitute 80% of their dry weight. Carbohydrates may have an aldehyde (aldoses) or Ketone (ketoses) group. Simple carbohydrates having free aldose or ketose group are called reducing sugars because they can reduce cupric ion to cuprous state (Fehling's or Benedict's solution). Simple carbohydrates are of two types, monosaccharides and oligosaccharides. Monosaccharides are monomer sugars which cannot be hydrolysed further into smaller units, e.g. trioses, tetroses, pentoses, hexoses, heptoses. Fats and amino acids are formed from simple carbohydrates. Glyceraldehyde and dihydroxyacetone are trioses. Erythrose is a tetrose which forms the raw material for synthesis of anthocyanin and lignin. Pentose sugars, ribose and deoxyribose, occur in nucleotides and nucleic acids. Xylose is non-nutritive sweetener. It is available as Xylitol. Hexose sugar are common. Fructose (= levulose) is fruit sugars while glucose (= dextrose) is grape sugar as well as blood sugar. Glucose is main respiratory substrate and hence immediate source of energy. Fructose is the sweetest of all sugars. Galactose is a constituent of Agar-Agar. Mannitol is alcohol of mannose. Ascorbic acid (Vitamin C) is sugar acid. Glucosamine (raw material of chitin and fungal wall) is aminated glucose. Oligosaccharides are formed by condensation of 2-9 monosaccharides. Some of them are attached to membrane proteins and lipids to function in recognition, antigen specificity and attachment. Hexosan disaccharides are more common. Sucrose is commercial sugar (glucose + fructose). It is non-reducing. Maltose or malt sugar is reducing sugar made of two molecules of glucose while lactose is another reducing sugar called milk sugar (glucose + galactose). Raffinose is a trisaccharide made of glucose, fructose and galactose residues. Pentosans arabinose and xylose form polymers arabans and xylans that are constituents of hemicellulose. Insulin is a polymer of fructose, e.g. Dahlia root.

Proteins: Proteins (Berzelius, 1838) are amino acid polymers (C, H, O and S) formed of one or more polypeptides (monomeric proteins and oligomeric proteins). The minimum molecular weight of a protein is 4500 (adrenocorticotrophin hormone with 39 amino acids), 5733 (bovine insulin, two polypeptides, 51 amino acids 51 with 21 + 30 in bovine and 53 with 22 + 31 amino acids in humans) and 6000 (bacterial ferredoxin). Haemoglobin has 4 polypeptides with 574 amino acid residues and molecular weight of 64,500. Glutamate dehydrogenase has a molecular weight of about 1 million with 40 polypeptides and 8300 amino acids. Isocitrate dehydrogenase (mol. wt. 1 million polypeptides), pyruvate dehydrogenase complex (mol. wt. 4,600,000) and haemocyanin (8200 amino acids) are other large sized proteins. A polypeptide is formed of a linear row of amino acids joined by peptide bonds. This constitutes the primary structure. Secondary structure is of two main types, α-helix and β-pleated. In α-helix, a single amino acid chain is coiled spirally by establishing hydrogen bonds between first and fourth amino acids. In β-pleated arrangement a sheet is produced by holding of two or more polypeptide chains in parallel or antiparallel manner by means of hydrogen bonds. The polypeptide chains are folded variously in tertiary structure. The bonds formed during tertiary structure can easily be broken by high temperature, high energy radiations and salts of heavy metals. The process is called denaturation. Quaternary structure is present in case of oligomeric proteins. In shape, proteins can be fibrous (e.g., elastin, collagen, actin, myosin, Keratin) or globular (e.g., histone, haemoglobin, egg albumin, serum globulin). In function, they can be structural (e.g., elastin in ligaments, collagen in tendons and cartilage, tubulin in microtubules, chondrin in cartilage, ossein in bone, fibroin in silk, keratin in hair skin and nails), Contractile (e.g., actin, myosin), carrier/ transport proteins (haemoglobin for oxygen, lipoprotein of plasma for lipids from liver to other organs), visual pigments (e.g., rhodopsin) receptor (e.g., adrenaline receptor); hormones (e.g., insulin, GH, parathormone), blood clotting (viz., fibrinogen, thrombin), protective (antibodies like immunoglobins), enzymatic (e.g., amalyse) and storage (e.g., glutelens, albumins, globulins, prolamines). Proteins can be simple (e.g., most storage proteins like hordein, zeatin, glutenin of wheat, oryzenin) or conjugated (with additional groups). Conjugated proteins include nucleoproteins (with DNA, RNA), chromoproteins (flavoproteins with FMN or FAD), haemoglobin and cytochromes with Fe, rhodopsin with vitamin A, haemocyanin and cytochromes oxidase with Cu, chloroplastis with chlorophyll, biliproteins with phycobilins), metaproteins (Fe in ferritin), lipoprotein (with lipid like lipovitellin of egg yolk), phosphoprotein (phosphate as in casein, ovovitellin of egg yolk), glycoprotein, mucoprotein (e.g., much of saliva) etc. Derived proteins include proteases, peptones and metaproteins. The sweetest chemical is also a protein called monellin. Proteins present in meat, egg and milk are called complete proteins as they contain all the essential amino acids. Amongst plant foods, only soybean protein is nearly complete. The most abundant protein is rubisco (RuBP carboxylase) present in chloroplasts.

Nucleic Acids: They are formed of C, H, O, N and P. Nucleic acids were first discovered by Niescher (1868-69) as nuclein and named nucleic acids by Altman (1889). Nucleic acids are of two types—DNA and RNA.

DNA-Deoxyribose nucleic acid is helically coiled macromolecule which is made up of two antiparallel polydeoxyribonucleotide chains held together by hydrogen bonds. The two chains are plectonemically (interlocked) coiled around a common axis. Maximum amount of DNA occurs in chromatin of nucleus in eucaryotes and nucleoid of procaryotes. A small amount (1-5%) occurs in plastids and mitochondria DNA has a diameter of 20 Å. One turn of spiral has a distance of 34 Å. It contains 10 nucleotides in each chain so that the distance between adjacent nucleotides is 3.4 Å. Each DNA chain has a backbone of alternate deoxyribose sugar ($C_5H_{10}O_4$) and phosphate. Nitrogen bases are attached to sugar molecules at right angles to the main strand. Phosphate is connected to sugar of its nucleotide at 5' carbon, sugar is attached to nitrogen base at 1'·carbon while nitrogen base is attached by N-atom at 3' (pyrimidine) or 9' (purine) position. Phosphate is attached to next sugar by its 3' carbon. The direction is 3'→ 5' in one chain and 5' → 3' in the other. Nitrogen bases are of four types—adenine guanine (purines), cytosine and thymine (pyrimidines). Adenine (purine) of one chain lies opposite to thymine (pyrimidine) of the other. They are held together by two hydrogen bonds. Similarly, cytosine of one chain lies opposite to guanine of the other. They are held together by three hydrogen bonds. Because of this, the two chains of DNA are complementary. Hydrogen bonds are easily broken at high temperature (80°-90°C). The phenomenon is called denaturation or melting. Renaturation or annealing occurs on cooling. Structure of DNA was discovered by Watson and Crick (1953). Prior to them, Chargaff (1950) had discovered certain structural peculiarities called Chargaff's rules—(*i*) Purines and pyrimidines occurs in equal amounts. (*ii*) Phosphate and deoxyribose sugar occur in equal number. (*iii*) Molar amount of adenine is equal to that of thymine and cytosine equal to guanine. (*iv*) Base ratio A + T/C + G is specific for a species. It is rarely one. DNA duplex of Watson and Crick is right handed and is called B-DNA. The plane of base pairs are perpendicular to axis of the helix. Four more models have been proposed. In A-DNA a single turn of right handed helix contains 11 base pairs which are tilted 20° away from perpendicular to helix axis. Right-handed C-DNA has 9 base pairs while D-DNA has 8 base pairs per turn of spiral. Z-DNA is left handed double helix which contains zigzag back and 12 base pairs per turn.

DNA can form its duplicate in the process of replication (autocatalytic function). It is semi-conservative where both the strands function as templates for synthesis of new chains. DNA also produces RNA in the process called transcription (heterocatalytic function). Genetic information is contained in the base sequence of DNA strands with three adjacent nitrogen bases functioning as a codon. Cistron is a linear sequence of codons which determines the synthesis of a polypeptide.

DNA has been synthesised *in vitro* by Kornberg in 1959.

RNA-Ribose nucleic acid is a single stranded chain of ribonucleotides. Four types of ribonucleotides are involved AMP, GMP, CMP and UMP. Backbone of the stand is produced by alternate ribose and phosphate molecules. Nitrogen bases (Uracil, adenine, guanine and cytosine) are attached to ribose sugar molecules ($C_5H_{10}O_5$) (*i*) Ribosomal RNA (rRNA). It constitutes 70-80% of total RNA of the cell which is present inside ribosomes as 28 S, 58 S, 5 S (larger subunit) and 18 S (smaller subunit). Some rRNA (28 S and 23 S) are also the longest of all RNAs. (*ii*) Messenger RNA (mRNA). It is a long RNA which constitutes only 5% of the total. It brings coded information from DNA to cytoplasm for polypeptide synthesis. mRNA has codons for initiation and termination of polypeptides (*iii*) Transfer RNA (tRNA = sRNA) or soluble RNA or adaptor RNA. It constitutes about 15% of the total RNA. tRNA is the smallest. It has an anticodon and amino acid carrying point. It is folded to form clover-leaf or L-shaped structure. tRNA carries amino acids to exposed codons of mRNA. RNA has been synthesised *in vitro* by Ochoa (1967).

OBJECTIVE QUESTIONS

1. Carbohydrates are stored in the body as:
A. Sugars B. Starch
C. Glucose D. Glycogen

2. Monosaccharides containing ketonic group are called:
A. Aldoses B. Ketose
C. Sucrose D. Cellulose

3. Glucose is used in:
A. Manufacture of vitamin C
B. As preservative
C. In the manufacture of alcohol
D. All

4. Glucose reacts with acetic anhydride to form:
A. Monoacetate B. Tetra acetate
C. Penta acetate D. Hexa acetate

5. Carbohydrates containing more than 10 simple units of sugar are called:
A. Monosaccharides B. Disaccharide
C. Trisaccharides D. Polysaccharide

6. Now carbohydrates are regarded as:
A. Aromatic compounds
B. Poly functional compounds
C. Alicylic compounds
D. Polysaccharides

7. Cellulose, starch and glycogen are the polysaccharides having.....monosaccharide unit:
A. Glucose B. Ribose
C. Fructose D. Pentose

8. Colour of osazone of glucose is:
A. Red B. Brown
C. Yellow D. Orange

9. Fehling's solution and Benedict's solution are reduced by glucose to form:
A. CuO B. Cu_2O
C. $Cu(OH)_2$ D. Cu

10. When glucose is heated with nitric acid, the product is:
A. Gluconic acid B. Glucaric acid
C. Glycalic acid D. Oxalic acid

11. Starch is made up of:
A. Glucose and fructase
B. Amylase and amylopectin
C. Amylose and glycogen
D. Amylopectin and glycogen

12. Cane sugar is made of:
A. 5 membered glucose ring and 5 membered fructose ring
B. 6 membered glucose ring and 6 membered fructose ring
C. 6 membered glucose ring and 5 membered fructose ring
D. 6 membered galactose ring and 6 membered fructose ring

13. Proteins mainly contain:
A. C, H, O and N B. Only C and H
C. C, H and O D. N and H

14. Proteins are composed of:
A. Nucleotides B. Nucleasides
C. Dipeptides D. Amino acids

15. In human body enzymes hydrolyse protein into:
A. A ketonic acid like $CH_3COCOOH$
B. A hydroxy acid like $CH_3CHOHCOOH$
C. Dicarboxylic acid like COOHCOOH
D. Amino acid like CH_2NH_2COOH

16. Which statement about protein is wrong?
A. Proteins occur in all living cells
B. Proteins invariably contain N, O, C and H
C. Proteins are synthesised by plant kingdom only
D. Proteins are also synthesised in laboratory

17. Proteins do not respond to:
A. Biuret test B. Lucas test
C. Ninhydrin test D. Xantheproteic test

18. The helical structure or a secondary structure of proteins is stabilized by:
A. Peptide bonds B. Dipeptide bonds
C. H-bond D. None

19. The sequence in the structure of nucleic acid is:
A. Base + Phosphate group + Pentose
B. Phosphate group + Pentose + Base
C. Pentose + Base + Phosphate group
D. All

20. Who pointed out peptide linkage in proteins?
A. Kekule B. Hofmann
C. Fisher D. Cannizzaro

21. Protein can be most easily removed by:
A. Alkanes B. Alkenes
C. Alkynes D. Benzene

22. The proteins are hydrolysed with acids, alkalies or enzymes finally to:
A. Amino acids B. Ethers
C. Esters D. Cycloparaffins

23. The main structural feature of protein is:
A. The ester linkage
B. The ether linkage
C. The peptide linkage
D. All of the above

24. Protein is an important constituent of our diet. It functions mainly as:
A. A source of energy
B. Construction material
C. Shock absorber
D. Reserve food

25. The end product of protein digestion is:
A. Amino acid B. Glucose
C. Glycerol D. Oxalic acid

26. Proteins give:
A. A violet colour with alkaline $CuSO_4$ solution
B. Form a purple colour on boiling with dilute ninhydrin solution
C. Yellow colour on boiling with HNO_3
D. All

27. Keratin, a structural protein is present in:
A. Hair B. Skin
C. Wool D. Horn
E. All

28. The protein responsible for transport of oxygen in the blood stream is:
A. Haemoglobin B. Insulin
C. Collagen D. Albumin

29. Bases common to DNA and RNA are:
A. Adenine, cytosine, uracil
B. Guanine, adenine, cytosine
C. Guanine, uracil, thymine
D. Adenine, thymine, guanine

30. Nucleic acids contain:
A. 4 Purine bases
B. 4 Pyrimidine bases
C. 2 Purine bases and 3 Pyrimidine bases
D. 4 Pyrimidine bases and one purine base

31. Adenosine is an example of:
A. Nucleotide B. Nucleoside
C. Purine base D. Pyrimidine base

32. Which of the following is protein hormones?
A. Insulin B. Oxytocin
C. Both (A) and (B) D. None

33. The chemical messengers produced in ductless glands are:
A. Vitamins B. Lipids
C. Antibiotics D. Hormones

34. The function of DNA is:
A. To synthesise RNA
B. To synthesise
C. To carry the hereditary characteristics from generation to generation
D. All are correct

35. Which of the following base is found only in RNA and not in DNA?
A. Thymine B. Uracil
C. Adenine D. Guanine

36. The base present only in RNA and not in DNA
A. Uracil B. Cytosine
C. Thymine D. Guanine

37. Which of the following is proteolytic enzyme?
A. Insulin B. Diastase
C. Pepsin D. Adenine

ANSWERS

1	2	3	4	5	6	7	8	9	10
D	B	D	D	D	B	A	C	B	B
11	**12**	**13**	**14**	**15**	**16**	**17**	**18**	**19**	**20**
B	C	A	D	D	D	B	C	C	C
21	**22**	**23**	**24**	**25**	**26**	**27**	**28**	**29**	**30**
D	A	C	B	A	D	E	A	B	C
31	**32**	**33**	**34**	**35**	**36**	**37**			
B	A	D	C	B	A	C			

21

CHEMISTRY IN EVERYDAY LIFE: DRUGS AND MEDICINES

Synthetic Drugs : These drugs are classifed in a number of ways:

(i) The drugs which are used in the treatment and care of specific disease like malaria, syphilis, tuberculosis and diseases caused by micro-organisms. These therapeutic agents do not harm or destory the cells of infected host but can attack and destroy the invading organisms. *Ehrlich* in 1910 introduced the first therapeutic agent by using organo arsenic compounds against syphilis.

(ii) Some drugs which although produce characteristic effects upon the animal organisms but cannot be used as a specific treatment. This group includes pain killers (analgesics), anaesthetics, sedatives, hypnotics, antispasmodics etc. Bacterial and viral infections are also cured by these drugs.

Antipyretics : Chemicals used to bring down the temperature in high fever. For example : Aspirin, paracetamol, analgin, phenacetin etc.

Analgesics : Chemical substances used for relieving pain. For example: novalgin, asprin, analgin etc. It should be noted that asprin, novalgin act both as antipyretic and analgesic.

Antiseptics : Chemical substances which prevent the growth of micro-organisms or kill them but are not harmful to human or animal tissues when used in optimum amount. For example, chlorine, organic dyes, Iodine, Bithional etc. They are used to check the septic of wounds.

Disinfectants : The compounds which kill micro-organism or step-down their growth but are harmful to human tissues. It should be noted that phenol acts as both antiseptic (0.2% solution) and disinfectant (1.0% solution).

Tranquilizers : The chemical substances used as hypnotics (sleep inducers) and sedatives (to relieve mental tension) are known as tranquilizers.

Insecticides : Chemical substances used for killing insects, flies, mosquitoes etc. are known as insecticides. e.g. DDT, BHC. etc.

Antibiotics : Chemical substances which are produced by micro-organisms and are capable of destroying other harmful micro-organisms, are known as antibiotics e.g. Penicillin, ampliclin, streptomycin, chloramphenicol etc.

Antipyretics and Analgesics

The drugs used to lower body temperature in feverish conditions are called antipyretics. Analgesics are the drugs used to relieve the pain in various conditions of health without loss of consciousness. The antipyretic and analgeric action, are usually found together in the same drug. Many synthetic antipyretics and analgesics are known today, most common being aspirin, phenacetin, paracetamol, phenyl butazone etc. Some representative antipyretics/analgesics are discussed below:

A. Aspirin : Salicylic acid derivative; most important synthetic analgesic and antipyretic and antinflammatory agent.

Synthesis :

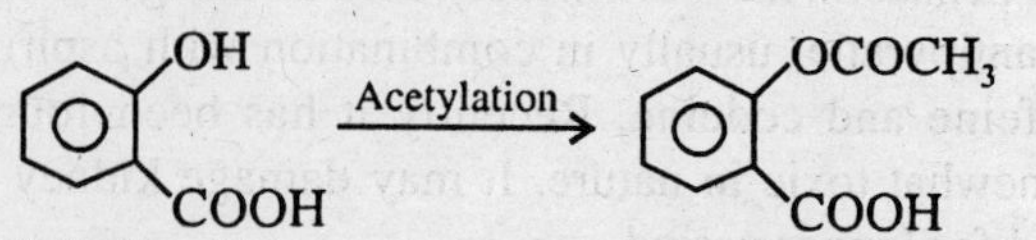

Salicylic acid → Acetyl salicylic acid (Aspirin)

It is common remedy for relieving pain. However, it is not recommended for children. The toxic side-effect is gastric irritation leading to ulcers. Therefore, it should not be taken empty stomach. It is used widely in the treatment of acute state of rheumatism.

The calcium salt of aspirin is better than simple aspirin which is water soluble. It has fewer undesirable side effects and induces analgesia faster than aspirin. A familar preparation of soluble asprin is *Disprin.* Disprin contains calcium carbonate and anhydrous citric acid besides asprin and this reduces pain faster than aspirin.

B. Methyl Salicylate : It is also known as *Oil of winter green.* It occurs in nature and can be made synthetically too. It is applied as such or in linimerts and ointments for the relief of the pain of lumbago, scitica and rheumatic conditions. It is the main constituent of pain reliever, Iodex.

Parcetamol : It is chemically p-acetamidophenol or N-acetyl-p-aminophenol. It also goes by common name *acetaminophen*

Synthesis

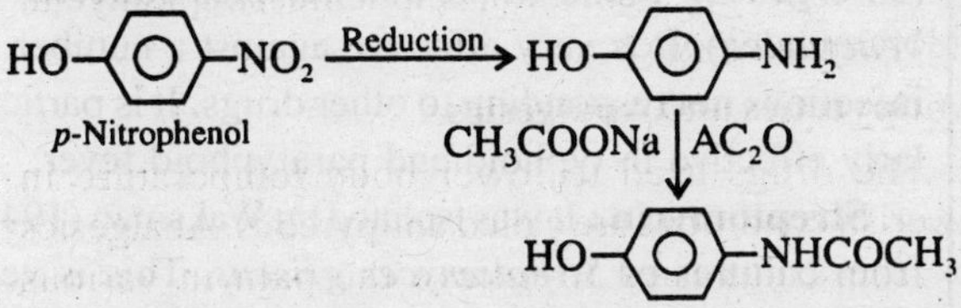

Paracetamol

It has analgesic and antipyretic activities. It is being used as such under various trade names like crocine; metacin etc. It is also marketed in combination with aspirin and caffeine.

D. Phenacetin : It is the ethyl ether of paracetamol and is also known as *acetophenetidine*

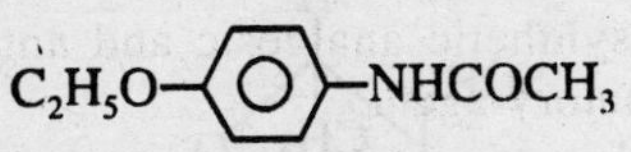

Phenacetin has been widely used as analgesic and an antipyretic; usually in combination with aspirin, caffeine and codeine. Recently it has been found somewhat toxic in nature. It may damage kidney if used for longer period.

E. Analgin : It is sodium 2, 3-dimethyl-1-phenyl-s-pyrazolone-4-yl-N-methylaminomethane sulphonate; commonly known as metamezole. It is made from *ethyl acetoacetate* in a number of steps. It has structural formula as

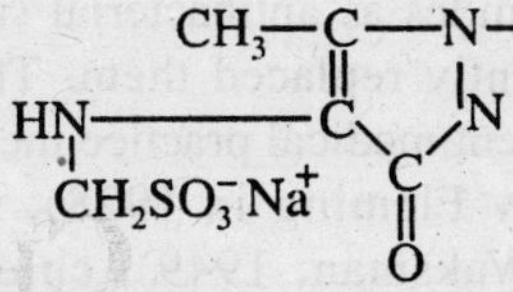

Analgin is widely used for its analgesic and antipyretic properties.

F. Aminopyrine

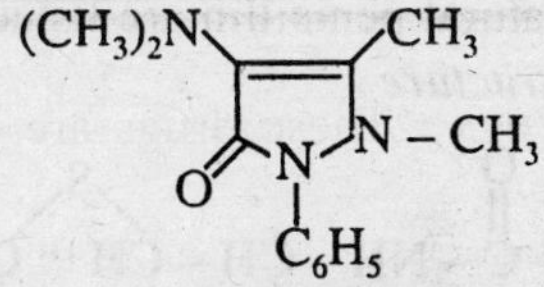

It is used as antipyretic & analgesic, but is slower in action. However, it seems to be much more effective in rheumatic fever.

G. Phenyl Butazone : It is 4-n-Butyl-1, 2 diphenyl-3, 5 – pyrazolidinedione.

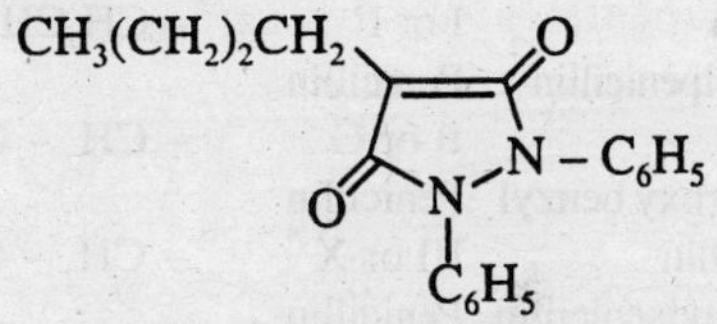

It is commonly used as an antiarthritic and antinflammatory agent. Since it has many undesirable side effect also it should be used under strict supervision of doctor. It can be synthesized from malonic ester.

H. Pethidine : In 1940 Eiselets and Schanmann prepared forty derivatives of piperidine. Among them most important is pethidine. It is known as 1-methyl-4-carboxy ethoxy-4-phenyl piperidine.

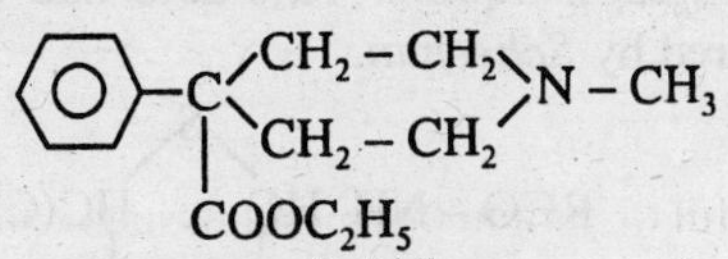
Pethidine

It is used in the form of its hydrochloride. Its analgesic activity is only $\frac{1}{5}$ th of the morphine.

Antibiotics : An antibiotic is a substance produced by micro-organisms which is capable of inhibiting or destroying the growth of other micro-organisms at low concentrations. In the current usage, the term antibiotic includes chemically related and derived substances also. Antibiotics are much more effective than sulphonamides as antibacterial substances and have subsequently replaced them. The antibiotics popular in current medical practice include pencillin (discovered by Fleming in 1928), streptomycin (isolated by Waksman, 1949), chloramphenicol (isolated by Ehrlich in 1947); tetracyclines (introduced in 1948), erythromycine (isolated in 1952) etc.

Some natural penicillin are listed below:

Basic structure

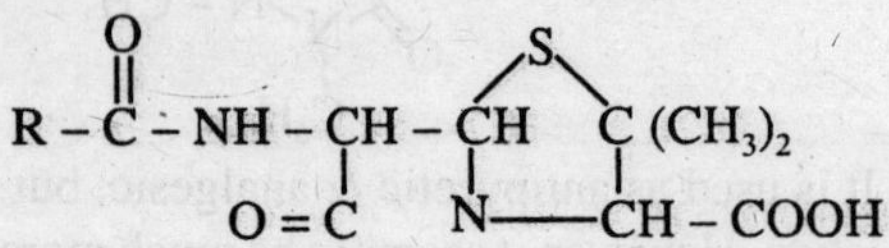

Chemical Name	*Common Name*	*Side-chain R* ...
Pent-2-enylpenicillin	Penicillin I or F	$-CH_2CH = CHCH_2CH_3$
Benzylpenicillin	Penicillin II or G	$-CH_2-C_6H_5$
p-hydroxy benzyl penicillin	Penicillin III or X	$-CH_2-C_6H_4OH$
n-Heptylpenicillin	Penicillin IV or R	$-(CH)_6CH_3$
n-Amylpenicillin	Dihydro-F-penicillin	$-(CH_2)_4CH_3$
Phenoxymethyl penicillin	Penicillin V	$-CH_2OC_6H_5$

Synthetic Penicillins : Of all the natural pencillins, the penicillin G is still the best. Batchelor (1959) isolated pure 6-amino pencillanic acid from fermentation liquors. This acid had already been prepared by *Schechan*.

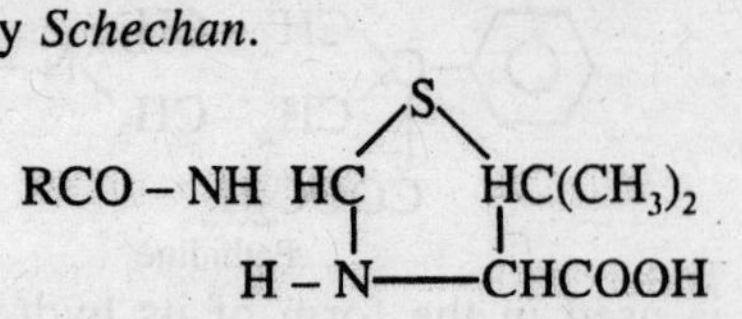

6-amino penicillonic acid

Many synthetic penicillins have now been prepared by adding various compounds to the culture medium. α-Aminobenzyl penicillin ($R = C_6H_5-\underset{\displaystyle NH_2}{\underset{|}{C}H}-$) has been synthesized (Rolinson-1961) and shows considerable activity against many organisms against which benzyl penicillin is not effective. 6-aminopenicillanic acid has also be used as a starting material for synthesising many new penicillins. Penicillins in general are used for infections of respiratory system (e.g. pneumonia, acute bronchitis and bronchopneumonia), urinary track infections, meningitis, gonorrhea and syphilis.

Chloramphenicol (Chloromycetin)

D(–) threo – 2-dichloro acetamido – 1-p-nitro phenyl-propane – 1, 3 diol

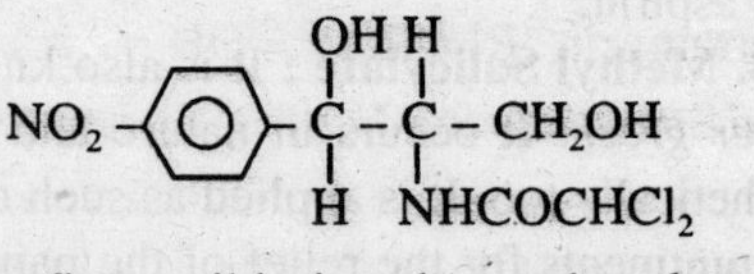

This is the first antibiotic to be produced commercially by a synthetic process rather than by microbiological process. It is also first widely used broad spectrum antibiotic *i.e.* an antibiotic effective against gram negative and gram positive bacteria. It was isolated by Ehrlich in 1947 from *Streptomyces venezuelea* (an organism found in the soil samples collected in *Venezuelea*). It is very effective against a number of infections not responding to other drugs. It is particularly effective in typhoid and paratyphoid fever.

Streptomycin : It was isolated by Waksman (1944) from cultures of *Streptomyces griseus*. This is very effective in treatment of tuberculosis, meningitis and pneumonia. Streptomycin has been shown to be composed of the three units:

(i) Steptose

(ii) N-methyl-L-glucosamine

(iii) Streptidine

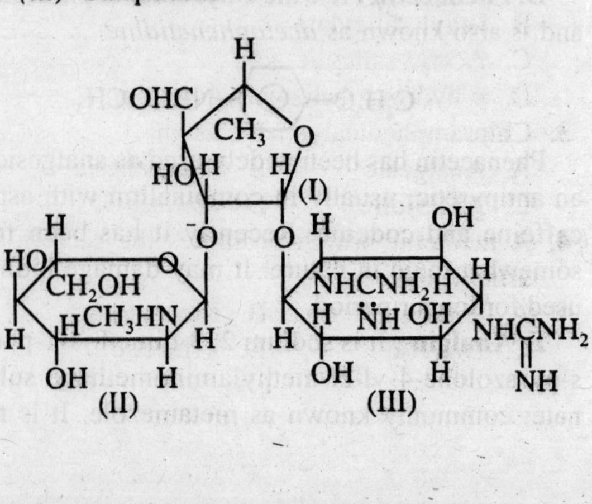

Tetracycline Antibiotics : Aureomycin was isolated from cultures of *Streptomyces aureofaciens,* and is used in the treatment of typhoid fever, etc. Terramycin was isolated from cultures of *Streptomyces rimosus,* and is very effective in the treatment of trachoma. The structure of these antibiotics are:

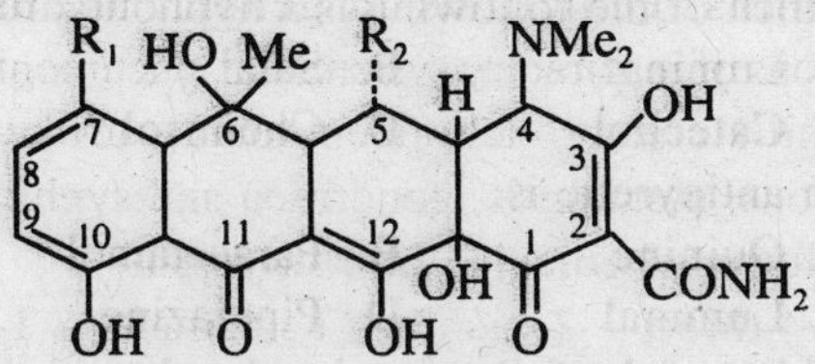

Aureomycin : $R^1 = Cl, R^2 = H$
Terramycin : $R^1 = H, R^2 = OH$

Broad Spectrum and Narrow Spectrum Antibiotics

The first antibiotic penicillin from *Pencillium notatum* is widely used against a large number of infections caused by various *Cocci* (spherical shaped bacteria) and other *gram positive bacteria.* It is an effective drug for pneumonia, bronchitis, sore-throat and abcesses. Other antibiotics like *streptomycin* (produced by *Streptomycetes*)) and tetracyclines are used against diseases caused by gram negative bacteria (e.g., infection of the urinary tract) or infection caused by gram positive bacteria which are penicillin resistant. The full range of *micro-organisms* attacked by antibiotic is called its *spectrum.*

***Broad Spectrum Antibiotics* :** These are medicines effective against a large number of harmful micro-organisms e.g., tetracycline, chloramphenicol etc. On the other hand, penicillin has a narrow spectrum.

Tranquilisers : An example of the many so-called tranquilizing agents used in both human and animals is chlorpromazine (Thorazine) with the structure shown. This drug has effect on the central nervous system, although the exact site of action is not established. It does reduce apprehension and excitement and thus been very useful therapeutically.

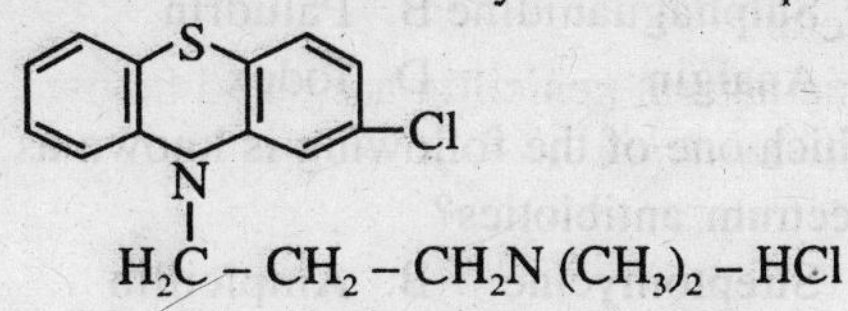

Chlorpromazine hydrochloride

There are two types, the major *tranquilizers* (also called Neuroleptics or antipsychotic agents); such as chloropromazine (Thorazine), and the minor tranquilizer (also called anxiolytics or antianxiety agents): such as diazepam (valium), chlordiazepoxide (Librium); and meprobanate (Equanil).

Valium : It is trade mark for a preparation of diazepam, an anxiolytic and skeletal muscle relaxant.

Chlordiazepoxide : A minor tranquilizer.

Meprobanate : A minor tranquilzer of skeletal muscle relaxant.

OBJECTIVE QUESTIONS

1. Pencillin was first discovered by:
A. A. Fleming B. Tence and Salke
C. S.A.Waksna D. Lewis Pasteur

2. Aspirin is chemically:
A. Methyl salicylate
B. Ethyl salicylate
C. Acetyl salicylic acid
D. *o*-hydroxy benzoic acid

3. Chloramphenical is used as an:
A. Analgesic B. Anaesthetic
C. Antibiotic D. Antiseptic

4. A medicine which promotes the secretion of arine is called:
A. Uretic B. Monouretic
C. Diuretic D. Triuretic

5. An example of a psychodelic agent is:
A. DNA B. LSD
C. DDT D. TNT

6. Veronal a barbiturate drug is used as:
A. Anaesthetic B. Sedative
C. Antiseptic D. None of the above

7. Aspirin is:
A. Antibiotic B. Antipyretic
C. Sedative D. Psychedelic

8. Which of the following is an antipyretic drug?
A. Aspirin B. DDT
C. Salos D. Oil of winter green

9. The name of the organic compound DDT is:
A. Dichloro diphenyl toluene
B. Dichloro diphenyl trichloroethane

C. Diphenyl dichloro trichloroethane
D. Dichloro diphenyl thiosemicarbazide

10. Further growth of cancerous cells in the body is arrested by:
A. Physiotherapy B. Chemotherapy
C. Electrotherapy D. Psychotherapy

11. Which of the following is an insecticide?
A. Bakelite B. TNT
C. BHC D. Aspirin

12. Which of the following drugs is an analgesic?
A. Sulphaguanidine B. Paludrin
C. Analgin D. Iodex

13. Which one of the following is known as broad spectrum antibiotics?
A. Streptomycine B. Ampicillin
C. Chloramphenicol D. Pencillin G

14. Which of the following drugs is a tranquilizer and sedative?
A. Sulphadiazine B. Papaverine
C. Equanil D. Mescaline

15. One of the most widely used drug in medicine iodex is:
A. Methyl salicylate
B. Ethyl salicylate
C. Acetyl salicylate acid
D. *o*-hydroxy benzoic acid

16. Which of the following is a hypnotic drug?
A. Luminal B. Salal
C. Catechol D. Chemisol

17. An antipyretic is:
A. Quinine B. Paracetamol
C. Luminal D. Piperazine

18. Which of the following is a local anaesthetic?
A. Diazepaim B. Procaine
C. Mescaline D. None of the above

19. The drug used as an antidepressant is:
A. Luminol B. Tofranil
C. Mescaline D. Sulphadiazine

20. Chloramine—T is a:
A. Disinfectant B. Antiseptic
C. Analgesic D. Antipyretic

ANSWERS

1	2	3	4	5	6	7	8	9	10
A	C	C	C	B	B	B	A	B	B
11	**12**	**13**	**14**	**15**	**16**	**17**	**18**	**19**	**20**
C	C	C	C	A	A	D	B	B	B